ENCYCLOPEDIA OF
BLACK FOLKLORE AND HUMOR

ENCYCLOPEDIA
of
BLACK FOLKLORE AND HUMOR

Compiled and Edited by

HENRY D. SPALDING

Introduction by
J. MASON BREWER

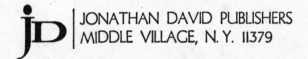
JONATHAN DAVID PUBLISHERS
MIDDLE VILLAGE, N.Y. 11379

ENCYCLOPEDIA OF BLACK FOLKLORE AND HUMOR

JONATHAN DAVID PUBLISHERS, INC.
68-22 Eliot Avenue
Middle Village, New York 11379

1993   1992   1991   1990

10   9   8   7   6   5   4   3   2   1

Library of Congress Cataloging-in-Publication Data

Spalding, Henry D.
    Encyclopedia of black folklore and humor.

    Includes bibliographical references (p.   )
    1. Afro-American wit and humor. I. Title.
PN6231.N5S6   1990   398'.089'96073   90-2906
ISBN 0-8246-0345-1

Printed in the United States of America

Acknowledgements

Grateful acknowledgment is hereby made to:

The Los Angeles Times Syndicate for permission granted to reprint Miss Sandra Haggerty's columns which appeared in the *Los Angeles Times*.

Harvard University Press for permission to use songs from the publication, *On the Trail of Negro Folk-Song*, by Dorothy Scarborough, copyright 1953.

Harold Ober Associates for permission to use a selection from *The Book of Negro Humor* by Langston Hughes, copyright 1958.

Dodd Mead & Co., for "A Note on Humor," by Langston Hughes from *The Book of Negro Folklore*, copyright 1958.

Doubleday & Co. for excerpts from *Lady Sings the Blues* by Billie Holiday, copyright 1956 by Eleanor Fagan and William F. Dufty.

Sunbeam Music Inc. for permission to use the lyrics of "Old Man Cassius," copyright 1963.

Mrs. W. Dubois for permission to use "Darkwater," by W. E. B. Dubois.

The Texas Folklore Society for permission to use anecdotes from *Tone the Bell Easy*, by J. Mason Brewer, copyright 1932.

The Texas Folklore Society for permission to reprint seven stories from J. Mason Brewer's "John Tales," from *Mexican Border Ballads*, copyright 1946.

Quadrangle Books, Chicago, Illinois, for permission to use material from J. Mason Brewer's *Worser Days and Better Times*, copyright 1965.

University of Texas Press for permission to use stories from J. Mason Brewer's *The Word on the Brazos*, copyright 1953.

E. P. Dutton for permission to use material from *Dick Gregory: The Back of the Bus*, edited by Bob Orben, copyright 1962 by Dick Gregory Enterprises, Inc.

South Carolina Negro Folklore Guild for permission to use material from *Humorous Folk Tales of the South Carolina Negro*, by J. Mason Brewer, copyright 1945.

J. Mason Brewer, for permission to use material from "Aunt Dicy Tales," included in *Snuff-Dipping Tales of the Texas Negro*, copyright 1956.

Harcourt, Brace, Inc., for permission to use "John Henry," from *The American Songbag*, copyright 1927.

The Rev. Martin Luther King, Jr.
(1929-1968)

Weep not alone
for the one short moment
in which, stunned and dazed,
he gave his life,
hardly aware of its relinquishment,
but instead
for the years of human destiny
that were denied him.
What blight and ruin
met his anguished eyes,
none can tell;
what brilliant, broken plans;
what baffled, humanitarian visions;
what sundering of warm friendships;
what bitter rending of family ties!
Farewell, dearest Coretta,
wife of my heart.
Goodbye, Yolanda and Martin
and Dexter and Bernice,
my beloved children.
I am going Home!

He stood before the multitude and proclaimed, "I have a dream." And his words were carried on the winds of hope to the far reaches of the planet. But it was not ordained that he should witness the fulfillment of that dream. Without cause, in the very frenzy of wantonness and wickedness, by the red hand of murder, he was thrust from the full tide of earthly existence; from its victories, its aspirations, its tears and laughter, into the visible presence of death—but his soul was not shaken. His people, even in their agony of mourning, were filled with pride and devotion, because in him they found their own example. He trod the wine press alone, yet he was not alone. With unfailing tenderness to his brothers and sisters, the apostle of non-violence ascended to his Glory. Above the whine of the assassin's bullet he heard the voice of God. With complete faith he bowed to the Divine.

Let us believe that his dying eyes beheld a mystic meaning for his long journey which only the rapt and parting soul may know. Let us believe that in the silence of the receding world he heard the gentle waves breaking on a farther shore and felt the breath of the eternal morning.

To Martin Luther King these pages are reverently dedicated.

HENRY D. SPALDING

Contents

Introduction

Humor, a literary ingredient that has been classified as such in English literature since the early eighteenth century, and in American literature since the early nineteenth century, is designed primarily to create laughter and provide amusement; it is one of the major media of writing and is characterized by any number of human practices, among them: to kid, to tease, to make fun of, to laugh at, to gibe, to heckle, to taunt, to jeer at and to mock. I recall, as a child, that one of the most unpleasant feelings that my playmates and I experienced was to be mocked. We would always say "Don't mark me!" or "Stop marking me!" childishly unaware of the correct pronunciation or spelling. It was a long time before I realized that what we were really trying to say was "mock" rather than "mark."

Some of the most outstanding selections of world literature have been written in a humorous vein, extending as far back as Chaucer's *Pardoner's Tale* and Nun's *Priest's Tales*. Shakespeare used it in many of his best plays and Jonathan Swift employed it as a vehicle of satire in his *Gulliver's Travels*. In our own United States of America, the first writer to gain literary fame abroad, Washington Irving, used it as a literary device in his *The Legend of Sleepy Hollow*. Later, other famous American authors—Mark Twain, James Russell Lowell, O'Henry and Joel Chandler Harris employed it in their most enduring works.

The *Encyclopedia of Black Folklore and Humor* is just what was needed, for although numerous anthologies of American humor have been published, Negro humor has rarely been included—this, in spite of the fact that Negro humor is, perhaps, the most original, prolific, diverse and entertaining humor produced by any ethnic group in this country. Fortunately, a work of wide scope and appeal on the subject has now been completed in this volume—a landmark contribution to Black Americana.

The social system of slavery and the black man's role in it created the type of environment that lent itself admirably to the invention of humorous narrative, so the black man became not only the creator of, but the agency through which his humor was channelized. This cultural legacy continued to thrive and expand after the Negro was freed, and still exists for the enrichment of himself and others. The Negro, during his American existence, has had plenty of time and plenty of reason to comment on his American experience, and this he has done in the form of tales, anecdotes, songs, rhymes, superstitions and proverbs, providing a significant array of humorous materials stemming from oral tradition. These productions, born of Negro folklife, have been supplemented by the humorous works of the individual Negro artist and talented author, but both of them—the creations of high art and low art—conform to the basic formulae of humor which are: (1) the feeling of power in the midst of misery; (2) the primary intent of amusement; (3) use as a morale booster. Humor is racial when it becomes impregnated with the convictions, customs and associations of a specific ethnic group. Black humor meets all of these criteria.

Although the bulk of the material contained in this meaningful opus is concerned with the black man in the United States of America, the editor has also included specimens of folklore from blacks in the Old World; nor does he confine his selections to any limited era or area of black history. He presents the old and the new, the upper stratum and the lower stratum, the economic problems of the black man, the social activities of the black man, the political handicaps of the black man, the religious ecstacies of the black man, and his participation in sectional and global wars.

Black humor reveals the soul of the Negro; consequently, in this *Encyclopedia of Black Folklore and Humor,* the black man is presented to American and world literature as a *person* rather than as a type. Here the black man is portrayed in his gay, pathetic, and contagiously humorous moods, investing him with the kind of humanity he justly deserves: genial, likeable—joyous and mellow creature that he is—laughing at what he doesn't have that he knows he ought to have; the propinquity of smiling and weeping—a new kind of humor in American history.

As Kipling said of the British "Tommy," so Mr. Spalding might say of the "Black Man" who is the spokesman in this book:

> *"An' it's Sammy this, an' Sammy that,*
> *An' anything you please,*
> *An' Sammy ain't a bloomin' fool,*
> *You bet that Sammy sees."*

J. MASON BREWER
East Texas State University
Commerce, Texas

Preface

When the first group of captive blacks arrived in the New World they were led down the gangplank and assembled on the wharf. The captain of the frigate noticed one of the slaves muttering angrily to himself. He strode over to the enchained African. "What's the matter with you?" he barked. "You've been in this country for only five minutes and already you're complaining!"

The black man has been complaining ever since, and with good reason. His history in America may well be described as a *comédie humaine* performed on an alien stage before an unresponsive audience. The tableau portrays the struggle of a people to attain their rightful due under the law; all else is rhetoric. For the chronicler of black history, the advances made in the past two decades have been more profound than those which occurred during any other period since Emancipation. But this does not lessen the contributions made by earlier generations of black Americans: Crispus Attucks was as great a hero as Dorie Miller, Frederick Douglass as towering an intellect as Thurgood Marshall, Dr. Mary McLeod Bethune as dedicated a woman as Mrs. Martin Luther King. Yet, the mystic bond of brotherhood is evident in the continuity of their struggle; a symbolic clasping of hands, warm and understanding, bridging the past and the present. It is that handclasp which is the main concern of this volume, for that is the connective link in the socio-historic chain which we term folklore.

The transcendental purpose of this Encyclopedia is to illustrate the interrelationship of folklore and orthodox history. As we know, the former revolves around social, environmental, philosophical and religious factors, while the latter is primarily concerned with the political, military and economic events of the past. A hoped-for goal is to awaken or rekindle a desire in the reader to explore the circumstances in black history to which the folk tales, poems and folk songs allude. The cement which binds classic history and folklore in this work is humor.

For example, the following anecdote was popular during the Spanish-American War and may be used to introduce the heroic role played by black American soldiers in that conflict, or any of the other wars in which this country has been engaged:*

"Isn't my son wonderful?" enthused the proud mother. "He's been in the army only two months, and at eighteen he's been promoted to field-marshal."

"A teenager promoted from private to field-marshal in two months?" protested her brother. "Impossible!"

"Oh, did I say field-marshal?" murmured the lady. "What I meant to say was *court*-martial!"

The above tale illustrates two additional facts: Not all black citizens spoke in dialect at the turn of the century, and the characters are not identified as to race. Some of my white readers who have not heretofore been exposed to black literature may be disconcerted to learn that it is *they* who represent the minority group in this volume. The reason, simply stated, is that this book is about *black* men, women and children and their race is understood. Exceptions occur only when the interplay of personalities between the two races requires such identification for the sake of clarity, and in those cases it is the *white* man who is so identified. However, exceptions will be found in some of the copyrighted works anthologized in these pages.

Here is a brief exchange of dialogue, circa 1868, in which we find that race is implicit and identification not necessary:

Cotton-field Overseer: Sam, what makes your nose so flat?

Sam: I ain't sure, boss, but I figger it's to keep me from stickin' it into other people's business.

As in any other pioneering work, there were few precedents to serve as guidelines. The obstacles which confronted me during the preparation of the original manuscript were many, and required three full revisions before the organization of the material, its content, style and syntax were finally systematized into a comprehensive and cohesive whole. Some of these problems, I must confess, arose from my own approach, rather than from a lack of coordination or advance thought. For example, dialect was modified or entirely eliminated in many instances to avoid offense to the militant young generation of today, and because I realize that dialect has all too often been used to cloak innate prejudice. The first draft was well underway before it became obvious that the characters about whom I was writing had turned to plastic images who were devoid of the fire of life; who, in fact, had never really existed. Slaves, toiling in the fields, were conversing in Harvard accents; the plantation dialect of the Civil War volunteers could not be distinguished from the black English of the men serving in Vietnam. They simply did not speak that way; that is, in the modern idiom. Imagine, if you will, a slave rushing up to the overseer and breathlessly exclaiming,

---

* For a summary of the role played by black soldiers in the military establishment, see *Bayonets, Bullets and Blacks* (introduction), p. 371.

"Sir, I greatly fear that a conflagration has erupted in the abode in which I dwell!" Not likely. He would probably and quite naturally have yelled, "Suh, my cabin's on fiah!"

Plantation dialect, as apart from the perversions of minstrelsy, was the nationally recognized language of the black man of yesteryear. In the main, he bore only a distant linguistic relationship to W. E. B. DuBois, Ralph Bunche or the articulate Dick Gregory. In my original draft, the folk tales, songs and poems had lost their verisimilitude because I had strayed from the fundamental precept which must govern the folklorist—to tell it like it was! As a result, I launched the second revision, this time with the original speech patterns intact. Even this required several rewrites to capture the subtle nuances and pronunciations which varied from region to region. The dialect, and its descendant, black English, are offered here without apology—indeed, with a deep sense of pride.*

Reflect upon the liquid syllables of the 19th-century preacher who saw fit to exhort his converts at the water's edge, awaiting the ceremony of baptism. The music of his plantation dialect rings pleasantly in our ears:

"My brethren an' sistren, hark to my words. 'Tain' 'nuff dat you should have songs of thanksgivin' on yo' lips. 'Tain't ample dat you is shoutin' out hallelujahs an' amens till yo' throats is hoarse an' yo' voices break in de middle. No suh! Onlessen you got de spirit of de Lawd pressin' heavy 'pon you an' de ol'-time 'ligion in yo' souls; onlessen you is filled wid happy hopes of de hereafter an' fear of ol' Satan; onlessen you feels dat de angels is lookin' down on you wid favor from heaven above an' dat de cherubims is singin' sweet praise fo' yo' salvation an' de Pearly Gates is done swung wide open to welcome you ez worthy pilgrims an' de golden harps is tuned fo' you an' yo' wings is waitin' to be fitted onto yo' shoulders; onlessen you has all dese here feelin's, you won't git nothin' when you is immersed 'cept wet!"

What criteria was I to use in the selection of material? What is an authentic black joke? My first reaction to these questions was that the anecdotes and other contributions need only be representative of the black people. Ah, the glee with which I seized upon that restrictive stipulation! But "representative," I soon learned, does not necessarily equate with the kind of authenticity that stems from *personal involvement*; from memories of childhood's day of frolic in a black world; from a lifetime of coping with the problems unique to the black American; yes, and the exuberant joy, the zest for living even under adverse circumstances which he has expressed in song and story. Accordingly, my additional prerequisite was that the selections be confined to those which the folk have exchanged among themselves from the dawn of their arrival in the New World to modern times. This Encyclopedia, as a result, is a compendium of the folk tales, related

---

* For a further study of the evolution of African-American broken English and its progression to plantation dialect and on to today's black terminology, see addenda, *Black English*, p. 564.

anecdotes, folksongs, rhymes and proverbs told by blacks to other blacks, and seldom heard by white Americans.

When is a story meaningful? For the goals which motivated me from the very outset, a story was meaningful when it contained within itself a reference to an historical fact or alluded to one. Relatively few of the folktales and jokes fell into that category, however, but many others were representative of a *region* or an *era* to which historical references could be made in the introductory comments or as footnotes. Let us assume that I wish to interest you in the emergence of the southern black man as a political force in the early days of Reconstruction. For the purpose of opening the subject I might relate the following tale:

A venerable gentleman, himself not long out of slavery, was elected county judge in a rural community of South Carolina, on the strength of the fact that he had a kind and gentle disposition and despite the fact that he knew very little about the law; not an uncommon occurrence shortly after the defeat of the Confederacy.

He had been on the bench only a few weeks when a crime which stirred the entire community was committed. A youth fell out with his aged mother and father. So he took an ax and, while they slept, he chopped both of them into bits. The young man was soon apprehended and brought before the new judge to be held for the grand jury. The attorney for the state described the double murder in all its harrowing, gory detail and then, according to formula, asked that the prisoner be committed to jail.

Throughout the recital, His Honor had been uttering distressed little clucking sounds. But now it dawned upon him that he was expected to say something. He fixed his eyes upon the surly defendant and in a gently reproachful voice said, "Now look heah, son, you know you ain't been actin' right!"

Emotions and attitudes play a vital role in folklore as it does in humor. These feelings and reactions express the humanity—the *soul* of us. Not all are lofty and noble, of course, else we would all be singing hosannahs at the foot of the Almighty throne. In truth, some of our latent desires and overt reactions to those thoughts hardly fit the biblical concept of mankind in the spiritual image of God. Yet, on balance, the positive exceeds by far the negative aspects of man's character. The half-million words, more or less, which comprise this Encyclopedia, reflect Man—irrespective of race—in all his chameleonic moods; from hate to love, from ferocity to gentleness, agnosticism to faith, jealousy to trust, avarice to self-sacrifice, stagnation to ambition, apathy to involvement, timidity to courage and despair to hope.

How are these emotions translated into humorous anecdotes? Let us take one example—that of mounting irritation:

"Honey," said the loving wife, "if I should die before you do, will you promise to keep my grave green?"

"Okay," answered hubby from the depths of the newspaper he was reading.

"It really worries me," she went on. "I want to be sure my last resting-place will not be neglected. You might get married again or something and forget me."

"Don't worry about it, for heaven sake!"

"I just couldn't bear the thought of being forgotten. I suppose it's because I'm so sensitive. Darling, are you sure you'll keep my grave green?"

"Uh-huh."

"You're really certain?"

"Hannah," shouted the pestered man, casting his paper aside, "I'll keep that damn grave of yours green if I have to paint it!"

Sarcasm is well illustrated in the little gem below:

"Why are the passengers looking out of the windows?" a little old lady asked the Pullman porter.

"We ran over a cat, ma'm."

"You mean the cat was on the track?"

The porter's eyes narrowed. "No," he finally replied, "the train done left the track and chased it up an alley!"

The delightful *non sequitur* in the following vignette illustrates the willingness with which small children accept as gospel any explanation offered by an adult, and is representative of the stories included in the *Mini Mod-Squad* section of this volume:

"I is—" began Tommy.

"Oh, Tommy, you must never say 'I is,'" corrected the teacher. "You must always say 'I *am*!'"

Well, teacher knows best, so Tommy began again. "I am the ninth letter of the alphabet."

The reader will note that except for a number of historical references in the various introductory comments and footnotes, there are few stories concerning Africa in these pages. Those which do appear have been selected because they bear some relationship to America or else the activity of the story occurs in the United States. Here is a descriptive anecdote:

The attaché of a newly-created African government which had won its independence only a few months earlier, entered a military tailor shop on Fifth Avenue. His mission was to give contracts for brand new uniforms for all branches of the national defense. It seems that the fancy of the army and navy officers ran to startling contrasts in color and to much use of braid, buttons, rosettes, festoons and plumage.

Undress and full dress had been selected for the navy, for the officers and men of the infantry, and for the artillery. Next, the attaché produced a drawing for a costume more gorgeous than any already shown. There was a cocked hat, rather resembling the kind worn by a Knight Templar in this country, excepting that it was bright red with an adornment of vivid green parrot-feathers floating out behind. There was a double-breasted blue coat heavily embossed with gold lace on the cuffs, sleeves, breast, collar and skirts. There were baggy crimson riding-breeches also, be-laced down the seams There was a pair of shiny black patent leather riding boots with ar adornment of silver spurs and, for final touches, massive bullion epaulets and white crossbelts finished off with huge bright buckles.

"Oh man!" exclaimed the dazzled tailor. "These uniforms must be for your generals."

"No indeed," said the attaché. "They're for our Secret Service!"

I have mentioned the task of organizing the contents of this Encyclopedia. For those with a penchant for statistics, this volume is divided into eight books, each according to its own general category. The books, in turn, represent 47 sub-classifications, or parts, all of which comprise some 1,500 folktales, jokes, folksongs, poems, children's rhymes, proverbs, maxims and such related subjects as "folk talk," superstitions, soul-food recipes and excerpts from letters and diaries.

The two years spent in preparation of the manuscript (aside from the original research, of course), have been among the most soul-satisfying of my life. At the risk of sounding trite, I say, in all sincerity, this has been a labor of love.

HENRY D. SPALDING

July 2, 1971
Hollywood, California

Encyclopedia of
Black Folklore and Humor

1

LONG NIGHT
of
BONDAGE

PART ONE:
   From Aesop to Harris: An Analytical Odyssey
   Uncle Remus

PART TWO:
   Carry Me Back

PART THREE:
   Laughing On the Outside

PART FOUR:
   That Great Gettin' Up Morning

PART FIVE:
   Down On the Farm

PART SIX:
   Old Folks at Home

PART SEVEN:
   Magnolias and Mint Juleps—With Vinegar

BOOK ONE

Long Night of Bondage

PART ONE

FROM AESOP TO HARRIS: AN ANALYTICAL ODYSSEY

Negro history in the Western Hemisphere started with the discovery of the New World by Christopher Columbus in 1492.* The black man's history in "English America" (as opposed to Spanish and French) began on August 20, 1619, in Jamestown, Virginia, with the arrival of twenty slaves aboard a Dutch vessel, preceding the Pilgrims, whose *Mayflower* did not touch the New England shores until 1620.

As with most cultures of the dim past, black civilization knew its time of greatness in which it spread its influence in the then-known world through its military power, its art and its literature.** The ensuing centuries witnessed the gradual decline of this once-mighty people, and as their fortunes waned so too did their ancient culture. Where the written word or graven

---

* Negroes were among the first explorers to come to the New World. Pedro Alonso Niño, identified by many scholars as a Negro, arrived with Columbus. Other blacks accompanied Balboa, Ponce de Leon, Cortes, Pizarro and Menendez on their travels and explorations. Some were commissioned explorers in their own right. For example, Estevanico, a Negro explorer, led an expedition in 1538, from Mexico into the territory of the American Southwest. He is credited with the discovery of what is today Arizona and New Mexico.

** See Introduction to *Bullets, Bayonets and Blacks*, for an account of the black man in the military establishment, from the days of the early Pharaohs to Vietnam.

3

symbol had been the currency with which mental wealth was passed from mind to mind, it was now exchanged by word of mouth.

A rich mythology took root in the fertile minds of these tellers of tales; one shared by the ancient Greeks, Romans and other peoples. A part of this might be properly termed "demonology," an errant cousin to the "man-god" syndrome which is also familiar to students of Greek and Roman myth-folklore, and which was later brought to America as ghost stories or "ha'nts." Another variant of this growing body of folklore revolved around various animal gods, which mythologists will recognize as universal among the older civilizations. It was from this "animal-god" precursor that the black man evolved the fable, applying and modifying the mystique of the supernatural to the more familiar creatures within his own environment. And it was these fables that he brought to the continent of Europe and Asia Minor, and much later to America.

The fable is a brief allegorical narrative, in verse or prose, illustrating a moral thesis or satirizing human beings. The characters are usually animals who talk and act like people while retaining their animal traits. The oldest known fables are those in the *Panchatantra,* a collection written in Sanskrit, and those attributed to the Greek, Aesop, perhaps the most famous of all fabulists.

There is a striking similarity between Aesop's fables and those told by Joel Chandler Harris in his many Uncle Remus stories in which the exploits and antics of Brer Rabbit and other creatures of the swamp, farm and forest are recounted. The parallel becomes even more pronounced when one considers the eons that separated the two: Aesop flourished in the sixth century, B.C., while Harris was a product of the nineteenth century A.D. We may well marvel that these tales survived some 2,600 years, granting the surface changes in language and locale.

Harris, of course, was not the creator of the tales told through the lips of his fictitious narrator, Uncle Remus, any more than Aesop was the inventor of the earlier fables. Indeed, Harris is explicit in his acknowledgments to the slaves and their progeny for all of the anecdotes. "My purpose has been to preserve the legends themselves in their original simplicity," he wrote in his introduction to *Uncle Remus: His Songs and Sayings,* "and to wed them permanently to the quaint dialect . . . and I have endeavored to give to the whole a genuine flavor of the old plantation." In a following paragraph, he states, "I have retained that particular version which seemed to me to be the most characteristic and have given it without embellishment and without exaggeration."

That Harris was not the creator of the tales does not, of course, detract in any measure from his well-deserved fame. Not only did he record the Negro dialect of the day with uncanny accuracy, he also captured the essence of the life and character of the Negro of the Old South as no one else had done before. "The dialect is wholly different from the intolerable misrepresentations of the minstrel stage," he wrote in his candid introduction, "but it is at least phonetically genuine." Another important distinction is that, however humorous in effect, the *intention* of his writing was serious, as Harris himself observed.

In the following paragraphs, this editor will attempt to prove that Aesop was *not* black, despite the assertions by some scholars who maintain that his true name was Ethiop. In any event there seems to be little question that the folklore and mythology for which he is credited actually originated with the people of Africa who, as slaves, brought the stories to Greece and, much later, to Rome. The tales, as might be expected, underwent changes in their new habitats, as they did some 2,000 years later when captive Africans brought them to America. Thus, as Arna Bontemps points out, the African jackal survived as the American fox, the African hare as the American rabbit, and the African tortoise as the American dry-land turtle or terrapin.*

It appears that Aesop was born in Phrygia, about 2,600 years ago, and that he was a Caucasian. The fables attributed to him were preserved principally through Babrius, Phaedrus and Planudes Maximus. It is the latter with whom we are concerned, for it was Planudes, an eastern monk who lived in Constantinople toward the end of the 14th century, who was the great distorter of Aesop's life. He published several *Fables in Greek* under the name of Aesop, and prefixed his personal version of Aesop's life to his editions. For reasons of his own, none of them moral, he attributed to Aesop what may have been true of the Ethiopian fabulist and slave, Lokman.**

Lokman is described as "deformed, of a black complexion, with thick lips and splay feet." He is either slighted by Planudes or ignored entirely, while at the same time he portrays Aesop as a man of handsome face and carriage. Nevertheless, it is important to note that Planudes' insistence that Aesop was the author of his fables and that he was a black man has no authority from the Greek and Roman writers who preceded him. Conversely, we have good reason to believe that Lokman was of African birth, while the weight of evidence shows that Aesop was not. One can only assume that this was done deliberately to erase the identity of the true author of the fables—Lokman. Today's black American knows, from bitter experience, how often the achievements of his people have been twisted so that black becomes white or just as frequently deleted from history books altogether.

We are not yet done with Planudes, who seemingly wrote many of the fables himself, but whose fictions betrayed him. In his *Fables* he makes Aesop quote Euripides, who was not born until almost eighty years after his death; and he speaks of Piraeus as the port of Athens, which did not exist until more than eighty years later. Demades, the rhetorician, is the

---

* *The Book of Negro Folklore,* edited by Langston Hughes and Arna Bontemps. Dodd, Mead and Co., 1958.
** Corroboration is made in a number of old books; among them, *Sales Koran* and *Selected Fables of Aesop,* by R. Dodsley, 1812. While by no means abundant, copies do exist in private collections, libraries and in some stores which specialize in rare books.

subject of one of them. He was a rival of Demosthenes, and therefore lived at least 150 years after Aesop. In the moral of another, he goes so far as to mention the order of monks, which did not exist until nearly a thousand years after his death; and he compounds his falsehood by putting into Aesop's mouth the words and sentiments used in the Scriptures. In the same manner, Planudes has Aesop go to the court of Nectanebus in Egypt, whereas Nectanebus did not reign there until 200 years later. He carries him, likewise, to that of King Licerus at Babylon, who never reigned there at all, and indeed is only a king of his own creation.

From all these fictions, mistakes and absurdities, when considered together, it should be sufficiently evident that Planudes deserves to be rejected as an authority of no credit at all. There is no denying that Aesop was a brilliant story teller who could enunciate a moral viewpoint in an entertaining and novel manner; nor can the long corridors of time diminish his charming and superior talents. But Planudes' final attempt to cast him as a black man can only be seen for what it was—a shoddy device to divert attention from Lokman whose African folk tales were credited to Aesop who, in turn, propagated them for posterity.

Thus we come full circle: from the fables of a black slave, as told to Aesop and popularized by him, to the Americans of African heritage whose fables were refined and polished by Joel Chandler Harris. Each performed the vital function of helping to perpetuate these precious gems of folklore which had a common origin.

UNCLE REMUS

Introduction

It is no coincidence that today's black man refers to others of his race as "Brother" and "Sister," nor was it anomalous that the animal characters, which rolled so tenderly from the lips of Uncle Remus, referred to each other as "Brer"—the dialectal contraction of "brother."

This feeling of kinship is as old as the black race itself, stemming as it does from the family relationships that comprised the individual African tribes, cemented in the horror of the slave ships, and maintained during the agony of the long night of bondage. Emancipation brought with it a soaring, joyous exhilaration; the Day of Jubilee had arrived! But the black intellectuals of the times knew better, and it was not long before the Brothers and Sisters on the farms and in the cities recognized that the battle for true freedom had just begun: It does not require a college education for a man to know that he is being persecuted. The punitive and repressive laws and covenants of the south and the more subtle restrictive measures of the north (which were designed to accomplish the same purpose) tended to make of the American Negroes an even more cohesive community.

It is true that the black man in America, as elsewhere, has his intra-fraternal disputes, dislikes, and even hatreds. But these are marginal. Every race has its family quarrels and disagreements, its internecine conflicts. What *is* important is that the black people have marched hand-in-hand through the anguished centuries, drawn together in their common needs and interests by the silken cords of brotherhood. And so, once again we return to that meaningful word, *brother!*—or "Brer," as recorded by Joel Chandler Harris.*

For all his compassion, technical excellence and perspicuity, Harris apparently did not perceive the full significance of the fables which he garnered among the black people of his day. He failed to recognize, for example, that many of the tales were veiled protests against enslavement. He did not comprehend that the characters of the stories were telling him, "God's eye is on the sparrow, not the hawk." He overlooked the fact that the use of the word "Brer" was a common denominator for *a brotherhood of spiritual and material goals and ideals.* Yet, in isolated flashes of intuition he would grasp a fleeting pinpoint of light. "The story of the rabbit and the fox needs no scientific investigation to show why he (the American Negro) selects as his hero the weakest and most harmless of all animals, and brings him out victorious in contests with the bear, the wolf and the fox. It is not virtue that triumphs, but helplessness."

A minuscule number of freed men did not take kindly to emancipation: real-life prototypes of Harriet Beecher Stowe's Uncle Tom did exist. In the main they were the house servants, whose lot was not as harsh or degrading as that of their fellow slaves who toiled in the fields. But even among this class, the numbers who preferred bondage to freedom was very small—probably less than three percent. For the overwhelming majority, the smattering of education they received, and their closer association with the society in which their masters lived, enabled them to perceive that while their status as house servants conferred on them a few material benefits, the precious right so dear to the hearts and spirits of all men—personal liberty—was denied them. One of the unabashed "Uncle Toms" is represented in the chapter, "Carry Me Back. . . ." Another such, it is suggested by his creator, Harris, was Uncle Remus. If so, however, he does not run true to form.

Harris tells us that Uncle Remus was well satisfied with the moral, spiritual and often physical chains and shackles of bondage. ("He has nothing but pleasant memories of the discipline of slavery.") But if this

---

* Joel Chandler Harris (1848-1905). Creator of *Uncle Remus.* Harris' stories and sketches of the South were originally published in the *Atlanta Constitution,* with which he was associated from 1876 to 1900. His first collection, *Uncle Remus: His Songs and Sayings* (1881), brought him much fame. The demands for similar stories grew so widespread that Harris published nine additional books centering around Uncle Remus and his animal characters. These included *The Tar Baby* (1904) and Uncle Remus' *Brer Rabbit* (1906). See biography by Julia C. Harris (1918). The selections represented in this Encyclopedia have been abridged.

were true, Uncle Remus could not possibly have recited the fable, *The Story of the Deluge,* whose significance he would have grasped. He was too perceptive a man and a narrator to fail to realize that the Crawfishes (note the capitalized "C") represented the smallest and most oppressed of the animals while the others were cast in the roles of oppressors. The reader may judge *The Story of the Deluge* for himself:

One time, way back yander 'fo' enny un us wuz borned, de animils en de creeturs sorter 'lecshuneer roun' 'mong deyselves, twel at las' dey 'greed fer ter have a 'sembly fer ter sorter straighten out matters en hear de complaints. En w'en de day come dey wuz on han'. De Lion, he wuz dar, kaze he wuz de king, en he hatter be dar. De Rhynossyhoss, he wuz dar, en de Elephent, he wuz dar, en de Cammils, en de Cows, en plum down ter de Crawfishes, dey wuz dar. Dey wuz all dar. En w'en de Lion shuck his mane, en tuck his seat in de big cheer, den de sesshun begun fer ter commence.

Dey spoke speeches, en hollered, en cusst, en flung der langwidge 'roun'. Howsumever, dey 'ranged der 'fairs en splained der bizness. Bimeby, w'ile dey wuz 'sputin' 'longer one er nudder, de Elephent trompled on one er de Crawfishes. Co'se w'en dat creetur put his foot down, w'atsumever's under dar wuz boun' fer ter be squshed, en dey wa'nt nuff er dat Crawfish lef' fer ter tell dat he'd bin dar.

Dis make de udder Crawfishes mighty mad, en dey sorter swarmed tergedder en draw'd up a kinder peramble wid some wharfo's in it, en read her out in de 'sembly. But, bless grashus! sech a racket wuz a gwine on dat nobody ain't hear it, 'ceppin maybe de Mud Turkle en de Spring Lizzud, en dere enfloons wuz pow'ful lackin'.

Bimeby, w'iles de Nunicorn wuz 'sputin' wid de Lion, en w'ile de Hyener wuz a laughin' ter hisse'f, de Elephent squshed anudder one er de Crawfishes, en a little mo'n he'd a ruint de Mud Turkle. Den de Crawfishes, w'at dey wuz lef' un um, swarmed tergedder en draw'd up anudder peramble wid sum mo' wharfo's; but dey might ez well sung Ole Dan Tucker ter a harrycane. De udder creeturs wuz too busy wid der fussin' fer ter 'spon' unto de Crawfishes. So dar dey wuz, de Crawfishes, en dey didn't know w'at minute wuz gwineter be de nex'; en dey kep' on gittin madder en madder en skeerder en skeerder, twel bimeby dey gun de wink ter de Mud Turkle en de Spring Lizzud, en dey bo'd little holes in de groun' en went down outer sight.

Dey bo'd inter de groun' en kep' on bo'in twel dey onloost de fountains er de earf; en de waters squirt out, en riz higher en higher twel de hills wuz kivvered, en de creeturs wuz all drownded; en all bekaze dey let on 'mong deyselves dat dey wuz bigger dan de Crawfishes.

As a pioneer in the propagation of the fables of the American Negro, and for the profound insight which this 19th century Caucasian displayed in his presentations, Joel Chandler Harris merits our praise and appreciation; and it is for these reasons that his tales have been selected as the opening stories in this Encyclopedia, rather than those of other early American fabulists. Nevertheless, his name need not be sanctified. He has since been equalled and in many instances surpassed by many black folklorists and other writers. To name a few, we might mention J. Mason Brewer, James Weldon Johnson, Paul Dunbar, Arna Bontemps, Langston Hughes, Philip Sterling and Zora Neale Hurston.

✓ ✓ ✓

The Wonderful Tar-Baby Story

One day Brer Fox went ter wuk en got 'im some tar, en mix it wid some turkentime, en fix up a contrapshun wat he call a Tar-Baby, en he tuck dish yer Tar-Baby en he sot 'er in de big road, en den he lay off in de bushes fer to see what de news wuz gwineter be. En he didn't hatter wait long, nudder, kaze bimeby here come Brer Rabbit pacin' down de road—lippity-clippity, clippity-lippity—dez ez sassy ez a jaybird. Brer Fox, he lay low. Brer Rabbit come prancin' 'long twel he spy de Tar-Baby, en den he fotch up on his behime legs like he wuz 'stonished. De Tar-Baby, she sot dar, she did, en Brer Fox, he lay low.

"Mawnin'!" sez Brer Rabbit, sezee—"nice wedder dis mawnin'," sezee.

Tar-Baby ain't sayin' nothin', en Brer Fox, he lay low.

"How duz yo' sym'tums seem ter segashuate?" sez Brer Rabbit, sezee.

Brer Fox, he wink his eye slow, en lay low, en de Tar-Baby, she ain't sayin' nothin'.

"How you come on, den? Is you deaf?" sez Brer Rabbit, sezee. "Kaze if you is, I kin holler louder," sezee.

Tar-Baby stay still, en Brer Fox, he lay low.

"Youer stuck up, dat's w'at you is," sez Brer Rabbit, sezee, "en I'm gwineter kyore you, dat's w'at I'm a gwineter do," sezee.

Brer Fox, he sorter chuckle in his stummick, he did, but Tar-Baby ain't sayin' nothin'.

"I'm gwineter larn you howter talk ter 'spectubble fokes ef hit's de las' ack," sez Brer Rabbit, sezee. "Ef you don't take off dat hat en tell me howdy, I'm gwineter bus' you wide open," sezee.

Tar-Baby stay still, en Brer Fox he lay low.

Brer Rabbit keep on axin' 'im, en de Tar Baby, she keep on sayin' nothin', twel present'y Brer Rabbit draw back wid his fis', he did, en *blip!* he tuck 'er side er de head. Right dar's whar he broke his merlasses jug. His fis' stuck, en he can't pull loose. De tar hilt 'im. But Tar-Baby, she stay still, en Brer Fox, he lay low.

"Ef you don't lemme loose, I'll knock you agin," sez Brer Rabbit, sezee, en wid dat he fotch 'er a wipe wid de udder han', en dat stuck. Tar-Baby, she ain't sayin' nothin', en Brer Fox, he lay low.

"Tu'n me loose, fo' I kick de natal stuffin' outen you," sez Brer Rabbit, sezee, but de Tar-Baby, she ain't sayin 'nothin'. She des hilt on, en den Brer Rabbit lose de use er his feet in de same way. Brer Fox, he lay low. Den Brer Rabbit squall out dat ef de Tar-Baby don't tu'n 'im loose he butt

COUNTRY STYLE VEAL STEW

A very popular recipe at the close of the nineteenth century. The less expensive margarine may be substituted for butter.

(May also be made with lamb)

2 lbs. breast of veal
   (meat and bone)
2 tsp. salt
2 whole cloves
½ tsp. pepper
1 quart water or stock

3 potatoes
1 tbs. butter
3 small onions
3 carrots
3 turnips

Cut meat into small pieces. Place in saucepan. Add salt, pepper, cloves and cold water or stock. Simmer 2 or 3 hours until tender. Cut vegetables into small pieces, brown them in butter and add to the stew. Allow at least ½ hour for vegetables to cook. When vegetables are done, thicken gravy with 2 tablespoons flour and 2 tablespoons water, mixed into a thin paste. Cook 5 minutes longer. Serves 4.

'er cranksided. En den he butted, en his head got stuck. Den Brer Fox, he sa'ntered fort', lookin' des ez innercent ez one er yo' mammy's mockin'birds.

"Howdy, Brer Rabbit," sez Brer Fox, sezee. "You look sorter stuck up dis mawnin'," sezee, en den he rolled on de groun', en laughed en laughed twel he couldn't laugh no mo'. "I speck you'll take dinner wid me dis time, Brer Rabbit. I done laid in some calamus root, en I ain't gwineter take no skuse," sez Brer Fox, sezee.

Did Brer Fox eat Brer Rabbit? Dat's all de fur de tale goes. He mout, en den again he moutent. Some say Jedge B'ar come 'long en loosed 'im—some say he didn't.

How Mr. Rabbit Was Too Sharp for Mr. Fox

W'en Brer Fox fine Brer Rabbit mixt up wid de Tar-Baby, he feel mighty good, en he roll on de groun' en laugh. Bimeby he up'n say, sezee:

"Well, I speck I got you dis time, Brer Rabbit," sezee; "maybe I ain't, but I speck I is. You been runnin' roun' here sassin atter me a mighty long time, but I speck you done come ter de een' er de row. You bin cuttin' up yo' capers en bouncin' roun' in dis neighborhood ontwel you come ter b'leeve yo'se'f de boss er de whole gang. En den youer allers some'rs whar you got no bizness," sez Brer Fox, sezee. "Who ax you fer ter come en strike up a 'quaintance wid dish yer Tar-Baby? En who stuck you up dar whar you is? Nobody in de roun' worril. You des tuck en jam yo'se'f on dat Tar-Baby widout waitin' fer enny invite," sez Brer Fox, sezee, "en dar you is, en dar you'll stay twel I fixes up a bresh-pile en fires her up, kaze I'm gwineter bobby-cue you dis day, sho'," sez Brer Fox, sezee.

Den Brer Rabbit talk mighty 'umble.

"I don't keer w'at you do wid me, Brer Fox," sezee, "so you don't fling me in dat brier-patch. Roas' me, Brer Fox," sezee, "but don't fling me in dat brier-patch," sezee.

"Hit's so much trouble fer ter kindle a fier," sez Brer Fox, sezee, "dat I speck I'll hatter hang you," sezee.

"Hang me dez ez high ez you please, Brer Fox," sez Brer Rabbit, sezee, "but fer de Lord's sake, don't fling me in dat brier-patch," sezee.

"I ain't got no string," sez Brer Fox, sezee, "en now I speck I'll hatter drown you," sezee.

"Drown me des ez deep ez you please, Brer Fox," sez Brer Rabbit, sezee, "but don't fling me in dat brier-patch," sezee.

"Dey ain't no water nigh," sez Brer Fox, sezee, "en now I speck I'll hatter skin you," sezee.

"Skin me, Brer Fox," sez Brer Rabbit, sezee. "Snatch out my eyeballs, t'ar out my years by de roots, en cut off my legs," sezee, "but please, Brer Fox, don't fling me in dat brier-patch," sezee.

Co'se Brer Fox wanter hurt Brer Rabbit bad ez he kin, so he cotch 'im by de behime legs en slung 'im right in de middle er de brier-patch. Dar wuz a considerbul flutter whar Brer Rabbit struck de bushes, en Brer Fox sorter hang roun' fer ter see w'at wuz gwineter happen. Bimeby he hear somebody call 'im, en way up de hill he see Brer Rabbit settin' cross-legged on a chinkapin log koamin' de pitch outen his har wid a chip. Den Brer Fox know dat he bin swop off mighty bad. Brer Rabbit wuz bleedzed fer ter fling back some er his sass, en he holler out:

"Bred en bawn in a brier-patch, Brer Fox—bred en bawn in a brier-patch!" En wid dat he skip out des ez lively ez a cricket in de embers.

Mr. Terrapin
Appears on the Scene

One day, atter Sis Cow done run pas' 'er own shadder tryin' fer ter ketch Brer Rabbit, he tuck'n 'low dat he wuz gwineter drap in en see Miss Meadows en de gals, en he got out his piece er lookin'-glass en primp up, he did, en sot out. Gwine canterin' 'long de road, who should Brer Rabbit run up wid but ole Brer Tarrypin. Brer Rabbit stop, he did, en rap on de roof er Brer Tarrypin house, en ax wuz he in, en Brer Tarrypin 'low dat he wuz, en den Brer Rabbit, he ax 'im howdy, en den Brer Tarrypin he like-wise 'spon' howdy, en den Brer Rabbit he say whar wuz Brer Tarrypin gwine, en Brer Tarrypin, he say w'ich he warn't gwine nowhar skasely. Den Brer Rabbit 'low he wuz on his way fer ter see Miss Meadows en de gals, en he ax Brer Tarrypin ef he won't jine in en go 'long, en Brer Tarrypin 'spon' he don't keer ef he do, en den dey sot out. Dey had plenty er time fer confabbin' 'long de way, but bimeby dey got dar, en Miss Meadows en de gals dey come ter de do', dey did, en ax um in, en in dey went.

W'en dey got in, Brer Tarrypin wuz so flat-footed dat he wuz too low on de flo', en he warn't high nuff in a cheer, but while dey wuz all scramblin' 'roun' tryin' fer ter git Brer Tarrypin a cheer, Brer Rabbit, he pick 'im up en put 'im on de shelf whar de water-bucket sot, en ole Brer Tarrypin, he lay back up dar, he did, des ez proud ez a cook wid a 'possum.

Co'se de talk fell on Brer Fox, en Miss Meadows en de gals make a great 'miration 'bout w'at a gaily ridin'-hoss Brer Fox wuz, en dey make lots er fun, en laugh en giggle same like gals duz deze days. Brer Rabbit, he sot dar in de cheer smokin' his seegyar, en he sorter kler up his th'oat, en say, sezee:

"I'd er rid 'im over dis mawnin', ladies," sezee, "but I rid 'im so hard yistiddy dat he went lame in de fo' leg, en I speck I'll hatter swop 'im off yit," sezee.

Den Brer Tarrypin, he up'n say, sezee:

"Well, ef you gwineter sell 'im, Brer Rabbit," sezee, "sell 'im some'rs outen dis neighberhood, kase he done bin yer too long now," sezee. "No longer'n day 'fo' yistiddy," sezee, "Brer Fox pass me on de road, en whatter you reckin he say?" sezee.

"Law, Brer Tarrypin," sez Miss Meadows, sez she, "you don't mean ter say he cust?" sez she, en den de gals hilt der fans up 'fo' der faces.

"Oh, no, ma'am," sez Brer Tarrypin, sezee, "he didn't cust, but he holler out—'Heyo, Stinkin' Jim!'" sezee.

"Oh, my! You hear dat, gals?" sez Miss Meadows, sez she: "Brer Fox call Brer Tarrypin Stinkin' Jim," sez she, en den Miss Meadows en de gals make great wonderment how Brer Fox kin talk dat a way 'bout nice man like Brer Tarrypin.

But bless grashus! W'ilst all dis gwine on, Brer Fox wuz stannin' at de back do' wid one year at de cat-hole lissenin'. Eave-drappers don't hear no good er deyse'f, en de way Brer Fox wuz 'bused dat day wuz a caution.

Bimeby Brer Fox stick his head in de do', en holler out:

"Good evenin', fokes, I wish you mighty well," sezee. En wid dat he make a dash fer Brer Rabbit, but Miss Meadows en de gals dey holler en squall, dey did, en Brer Tarrypin he got ter scramblin' roun' up dar on de shelf, en off he come, en blip! he tuck Brer Fox on de back er de head. Dis sorter stunted Brer Fox, en w'en he gedder his 'membunce de mos' he

OPPOSUM AND SWEET POTATOES

When people had no choice, and had to "make do" with what was available, they fell back on this receipe—and made of it a culinary delight.

(Gourmet Style)

1 opossum
1 tsp. pepper
1 tsp. leaf sage
4 or 5 slices bacon

2 tsp. salt
1 tsp. paprika
2 garlic cloves
6 to 8 medium sweet potatoes

Clean, dress and wash opossum well. Place overnight in freezing compartment of refrigerator or on ice. Drain and wipe dry. Rub well with mixture of spices. Lay in a baking pan. Cover with thin slices of bacon and set in a slow oven about 300°. Bake and baste for 1 to 1½ hours. During the last half hour of baking, arrange sweet potatoes that have been parboiled, around meat. Bake until brown, basting with drippings. Serve with country salad, corn bread and buttermilk.

seed wuz a pot er greens turnt over in de fireplace, en a broke cheer. Brer Rabbit wuz gone, en Brer Tarrypin wuz gone, en Miss Meadows en de gals wuz gone.

Brer Rabbit, he skint up de chimbly—dats w'at turnt de pot er greens over. Brer Tarrypin, he crope under de bed, he did, en got behime de cloze-chist, en Miss Meadows en de gals, dey run out in de yard.

Brer Fox, he sorter look roun' en feel er de back er his head, whar Brer Tarrypin lit, but he don't see no sine er Brer Rabbit. But de smoke en de ashes gwine up de chimbly got de best er Brer Rabbit, en bimeby he sneeze—*huckychow!*

"Aha!" sez Brer Fox, sezee; "youer dar, is you?" sezee. "Well, I'm gwineter smoke you out, ef it takes a mont'. Youer mine dis time," sezee. Brer Rabbit ain't sayin' nothin'.

"Ain't you comin' down?" sez Brer Fox, sezee. Brer Rabbit ain't sayin' nothin'. Den Brer Fox, he went out atter some wood, he did, en w'en he come back he hear Brer Rabbit laughin'.

"W'at you laughin' at, Brer Rabbit?" sez Brer Fox, sezee.

"Can't tell you, Brer Fox," sez Brer Rabbit, sezee.

"Better tell, Brer Rabbit," sez Brer Fox, sezee.

" 'Tain't nothin' but a box er money somebody done gone en lef' up yer in de chink er de chimbly," sez Brer Rabbit, sezee.

"Don't b'leeve you," sez Brer Fox, sezee.

"Look up en see," sez Brer Rabbit, sezee. En w'en Brer Fox look up, Brer Rabbit spit his eyes full er terbarker joose, he did, en Brer Fox, he make a break fer de branch, en Brer Rabbit he come down en he tole de ladies good-by.

"How you git 'im off, Brer Rabbit?" sez Miss Meadows, sez she.

"Who? me?" sez Brer Rabbit, sezee; "W'y I des tuck en tole 'im dat ef he didn't go 'long home en stop playin' his pranks on spectubble fokes, dat I'd take 'im out en th'ash 'im," sezee.

Mr. Wolf Makes a Failure

Brer Fox feel so bad, en he git so mad 'bout Brer Rabbit, dat he dunner w'at ter do, en he look mighty downhearted. Bimeby, one day wiles he wuz gwine, 'long de road, ole Brer Wolf come up wid 'im. W'en dey done howdyin' en axin' atter one nudder's fambly connexshun, Brer Wolf, he 'low, he did, dat der wuz sump'n wrong wid Brer Fox, en Brer Fox, he 'low'd der warn't, en he went on en laugh en make great terdo kaze Brer Wolf look like he spishun sump'n. But Brer Wolf, he got mighty long head, en he sorter broach 'bout Brer Rabbit's kyar'ns on, kaze de way dat Brer Rabbit 'ceive Brer Fox done got ter be de talk er de neighberhood. Den Brer Fox en Brer Wolf dey sorter palavered on, dey did, twel bimeby Brer Wolf he up'n say dat he done got a plan fix fer ter trap Brer Rabbit. Den Brer Fox say how. Den Brer Wolf up'n tell 'im dat de way fer ter git de drap on Brer

Rabbit wuz ter git 'im in Brer Fox house. Brer Fox dun know Brer Rabbit uv ole, en he know dat sorter game done wo' ter a frazzle, but Brer Wolf, he talk mighty 'swadin'.

"How you gwine git 'im dar?" sez Brer Fox, sezee.

"Fool 'im dar," sez Brer Wolf, sezee.

"Who gwine do de foolin'?" sez Brer Fox, sezee.

"I'll do de foolin'," sez Brer Wolf, sezee, "ef you'll do de gamin'," sezee.

"How you gwine do it?" sez Brer Fox, sezee.

"You run 'long home, en git on de bed, en make like you dead, en don't you say nothin' twel Brer Rabbit come en put his han's onter you," sez Brer Wolf, sezee, "en ef we don't git 'im fer supper, Joe's dead en Sal's a widder," sezee.

Dis look like a mighty nice game, en Brer Fox 'greed. So den he amble off home, en Brer Wolf he march off ter Brer Rabbit house. W'en he got dar, hit look like nobody at home, but Brer Wolf he walk up en knock on de do'—blam! blam! Nobody come. Den he lam aloose en knock 'gin—blim! blim!

"Who dar?" sez Brer Rabbit, sezee.

"Fr'en'," sez Brer Wolf.

"Too menny fr'en's spiles de dinner," sez Brer Rabbit, sezee; "w'ich un's dis?" sezee.

"I fetch bad news, Brer Rabbit," sez Brer Wolf, sezee.

"Bad news is soon tole," sez Brer Rabbit, sezee.

By dis time Brer Rabbit done come ter de do', wid his head tied up in a red hankcher.

"Brer Fox died dis mornin'," sez Brer Wolf, sezee.

"Whar yo' mo'nin' gown, Brer Wolf?" sez Brer Rabbit, sezee.

"Gwine atter it now," sez Brer Wolf, sezee. "I des call by fer ter bring de news. I went down ter Brer Fox house little bit 'go, en dar I foun' 'im stiff," sezee.

Den Brer Wolf lope off. Rabbit sot down en scratch his head, he did, en bimeby he say ter hisse'f dat he b'leeve he sorter drap 'roun' by Brer Fox house fer ter see how de lan' lay. No sooner said'n done. Up he jump, en out he went. W'en Brer Rabbit got close ter Brer Fox house, all look lonesome. Den he went up nigher. Nobody stirrin'. Den he look in, en dar lay Brer Fox stretch out on de bed des ez big ez life. Den Brer Rabbit make like he talkin' to hisse'f:

"Nobody 'roun' fer ter look atter Brer Fox—not even Brer Tukkey Buzzard ain't come ter de funer'l," sezee. "Even down ter Brer Wolf done gone en lef' 'im. Hit's de busy season wid me, but I'll set up wid 'im. He seem like he dead, yit he mayn't be," sez Brer Rabbit, sezee. "W'en a man go ter see dead fokes, dead fokes allers raises up der behime legs en hollers, *wahoo!*" sezee.

Brer Fox he stay still. Den Brer Rabbit he talk little louder:

"Mighty funny. Brer Fox *look* like he dead, yit he don't *do* like he dead.

Dead fokes h'ists der behime leg en hollers *wahoo!* W'en a man come ter see um," sez Brer Rabbit, sezee.

Sho' nuff, Brer Fox lif' up his fot en holler *wahoo!* en Brer Rabbit he tear out de house like de dogs wuz atter 'im.

Mr. Fox Tackles Old Man Tarrypin

One day Brer Fox strike up wid Brer Tarrypin right in de middle er de road. Brer Tarrypin done heerd 'im comin', en he 'low dat he'd sorter keep one eye open; but Brer Fox wuz monstus perlite, en he open up de confab, he did, like he ain't see Brer Tarrypin sence de las' freshit.

"Heyo, Brer Tarrypin, whar you bin dis long-come-short?" sez Brer Fox, sezee.

"Lounjun 'roun', Brer Fox, lounjun 'roun'," sez Brer Tarrypin.

"You don't look sprucy like you did, Brer Tarrypin," sez Brer Fox, sezee.

"Lounjun 'roun' en suffer'n'," sez Brer Tarrypin, sezee.

Den de talk sorter run on like dis:

"W'at ail you, Brer Tarrypin? Yo' eye look mighty red," sez Brer Fox, sezee.

"Lor', Brer Fox, you dunner w'at trubble is. You ain't bin lounjun 'roun' en suffer'n'," sez Brer Tarrypin, sezee.

"Bofe eyes red, en you look like you mighty weak, Brer Tarrypin," sez Brer Fox, sezee.

"Lor', Brer Fox, you dunner w'at trubble is," sez Brer Tarrypin, sezee.

"W'at ail you now, Brer Tarrypin?" sez Brer Fox, sezee.

"Tuck a walk de udder day, en man come 'long en sot de fiel' a-fier. Lor', Brer Fox, you dunner w'at trubble is," sez Brer Tarrypin, sezee.

"How you git out de fier, Brer Tarrypin?" sez Brer Fox, sezee.

"Sot en tuck it, Brer Fox," sez Brer Tarrypin, sezee. "Sot en tuck it, en de smoke sif' in my eye, en de fier scorch my back," sez Brer Tarrypin, sezee.

"Likewise hit bu'n yo' tail off," sez Brer Fox, sezee.

"Oh, no, dar's de tail, Brer Fox," sez Brer Tarrypin, sezee, en wid dat he oncurl his tail fum under de shell, en no sooner did he do dat dan Brer Fox grab it, en holler out:

"Oh, yes, Brer Tarrypin! Oh, yes! En so youer de man w'at lam me on de head at Miss Meadow's is you? Youer in wid Brer Rabbit, is you? Well, I'm gwineter *out* you!"

Brer Tarrypin beg en beg, but 'twant no use. Brer Fox done bin fool so much dat he look like he 'termin' fer ter 'stroy Brer Tarrypin. Den Brer Tarrypin beg Brer Fox not fer ter drown 'im, but Brer Fox ain't makin' no prommus, en den he beg Brer Fox fer ter bu'n 'im, kase he done useter fier, but Brer Fox don't say nothin'. Bimeby Brer Fox drag Brer Tarrypin off little ways b'low de spring 'ouse, en douze 'im under de water. Den Brer Tarrypin begin fer ter holler:

"Tu'n loose dat stump root en ketch holt er me—tu'n loose dat stump root en ketch holt er me."

Brer Fox he holler back:

"I ain't got holt er no stump root, en I is got holt er *you*."

Brer Tarrypin he keep holler'n':

"Ketch holt er me—I'm a drownin'—I'm a—drownin'—tu'n loose de stump root en ketch holt er me."

Sho nuff, Brer Fox tu'n loose de tail, en Brer Tarrypin, he went down ter de bottom—*kerblunkity-blink!*

Ole man Tarrypin wuz at home. *Kerblinkity-blunk!*

Mr. Fox Goes A-Hunting
But Mr. Rabbit Bags the Game

Brer Fox en Brer Rabbit, dey 'gun ter got kinder familious wid wunner nudder like dey useter, en it got so Brer Fox'd call on Brer Rabbit, en dey'd set up en smoke der pipes, dey would, like no ha'sh feelin's 'd ever rested 'twixt um.

Las', one day Brer Fox come 'long all rig out, en ax Brer Rabbit fer ter go huntin' wid 'im, but Brer Rabbit, he sorter feel lazy, en he tell Brer Fox dat he got some udder fish fer ter fry. Brer Fox feel mighty sorry, he did, but he say he b'leeve he try his han' ennyhow, en off he put. He wuz gone all day, en he had a monstus streak er luck, Brer Fox did, en he bagged a sight er game. Bimeby, to'rds de shank er de evenin', Brer Rabbit sorter stretch hisse'f, he did, en 'low hit's mos' time fer Brer Fox fer ter git 'long home. Den Brer Rabbit, he went'n mounted a stump fer ter see ef he could year Brer Fox comin'. He ain't bin dar long, twel sho' nuff, yer come Brer Fox thoo de woods, singin' like a fiel' han' at a frolic. Brer Rabbit, he lipt down off'n de stump, he did, en lay down in de road en make like he dead. Brer Fox he come 'long, he did, en see Brer Rabbit layin' dar. He tu'n 'im over, he did, en 'zamine 'im, en say, sezee:

"Dish yer rabbit dead. He look like he bin dead long time. He dead, but he mighty fat. He de fattes' rabbit w'at I ever see, but he bin dead too long. I feard ter take 'im home," sezee.

Brer Rabbit ain't sayin' nothin'. Brer Fox, he sorter lick his chops, but he went on en lef' Brer Rabbit layin' in de road. Dreckly he wuz outer sight, Brer Rabbit he jump up, he did, en run roun' thoo de woods en git befo' Brer Fox agin. Brer Fox, he come up, en dar lay Brer Rabbit, periently cole en stiff. Brer Fox, he look at Brer Rabbit, en he sorter study. Atter while he onslung his game-bag, en say ter hisse'f, sezee:

"Deze yer rabbits gwine ter was'e. I'll des 'bout leave my game yer, en I'll go back'n git dat udder rabbit, en I'll make fokes b'leeve dat I'm ole man Hunter fum Huntsville," sezee.

En wid dat he drapt his game en loped back up de road atter de udder rabbit, en w'en he got outer sight, ole Brer Rabbit, he snatch up Brer Fox game en put out fer home. Nex' time he see Brer Fox he holler out:

"W'at you kill de udder day, Brer Fox?" sezee.

Den Brer Fox, he sorter koam his flank wid his tongue, en holler back: "I kotch a han'ful er hard sense, Brer Rabbit," sezee.

Den ole Brer Rabbit, he laugh, he did, en up en 'spon', sezee:

"Ef I'd a know'd you wuz atter dat, Brer Fox, I'd a loant you some er mine," sezee.

Mr. Rabbit Finds His Match At Last

One day w'en Brer Rabbit wuz gwine lippity-clippitin' down de road, he meet up wid ole Brer Tarrypin, en bimeby atter dey pass de time er day wid wunner nudder, dey gotter 'sputin' 'bout w'ich wuz de swif'es'. Brer Rabbit, he say he kin outrun Brer Tarrypin, en Brer Tarrypin, he des vow dat he kin outrun Brer Rabbit. Up en down dey had it, twel fus' news you know Brer Tarrypin say he got a fifty-dollar bill in de chink er de chimbly at

BAKED 'POSSUM

'The succulent opposum was in constant demand in pre-Civil War days, and led to this masterpiece of cookery.

A small, young 'possum is the most tender. Clean and soak the 'possum overnight in a solution of salted, cold water. Season to taste with salt, pepper and a sprinkling of sugar. Place in a roasting pan. Peel sweet potatoes or yams and place them, whole, around the 'possum, so that the juices of the meat will cook the potatoes. Bake in a slow oven (350°) until tender. Cooking time depends upon the size of the 'possum.

Suggested menu:

> Baked 'possum
> Sweet potatoes or yams
> Black-eyed peas (or green peas)
> Tossed green salad
> Rhubarb drink
> Dessert

home, en dat bill done tole 'im dat he could beat Brer Rabbit in a fa'r race. Den Brer Rabbit say he got a fifty-dollar bill w'at say dat he kin leave Brer Tarrypin so fur behime dat he could sow barley ez he went 'long en hit 'ud be ripe nuff fer ter cut by de time Brer Tarrypin pass dat way.

Enny how dey make de bet en put up de money, en ole Brer Tukky Buzzard, he wuz summonzd fer ter be de jedge en de stake-holder; en 'twant long 'fo' all de 'rangements wuz made. De race wuz a five-mile heat, en de groun' wuz medjud off, en at de een' er ev'y mile a pos' wuz stuck up. Brer Rabbit wuz ter run down de big road, en Brer Tarrypin, he say he'd gallup thoo de woods. Fokes tole 'im he could git long faster in de road, but ole Brer Tarrypin, he know w'at he doin'. Miss Meadows en de gals en mos' all de neighbers got win' er de fun, en w'en de day wuz sot dey 'termin' fer ter be on han'. Brer Rabbit he train hisse'f ev'y day, en he skip over de groun' des ez gayly ez a June cricket.

Ole Brer Tarrypin, he law low in de swamp. He had a wife en th'ee chilluns, ole Brer Tarrypin did, en dey wuz all de ve'y spit en image er de ole man. Ennybody w'at know one fum de udder gotter take a spy-glass, en den dey er li'ble fer ter git fooled.

Dat's de way marters stan' twel de day er de race, en on dat day, ole Brer Tarrypin, en his ole 'oman, en his th'ee chilluns, dey got up 'fo' sun-up, en went ter de place. De ole 'oman, she tuck 'er stan' nigh de fus' mile-pos', she did, en de chilluns nigh de udders, up ter de las', en dar ole Brer Tarrypin, he tuck his stan'. Bimeby, here come de fokes; Jedge Buzzard, he come, en Miss Meadows en de gals, dey come, en den yer come Brer Rabbit wid ribbons tied 'roun' his neck en streamin' fum his years. De fokes all went ter de udder een' er de track fer ter see how dey come out. W'en de time come Jedge Buzzard strut 'roun' en pull out his watch, en holler out:

"Gents, is you ready?"

Brer Rabbit, he say "yes," en ole Miss Tarrypin holler "go" fum de aidge er de woods. Brer Rabbit, he lit out on de race, en ole Miss Tarrypin, she put out fer home. Jedge Buzzard, he riz en skimmed 'long fer ter see dat de race wuz runned fa'r. W'en Brer Rabbit got ter de fus' mile-pos' wunner de Tarrypin chilluns crawl out de woods, he did, en make fer de place. Brer Rabbit, he holler out:

"Whar is you, Brer Tarrypin?"

"Yer I come a buljin'," sez de Tarrypin, sezee.

Brer Rabbit so glad he's ahead dat he put out harder dan ever, en de Tarrypin, he make fer home. W'en he come ter de nex' pos', nudder Tarrypin crawl out er de woods.

"Whar is you, Brer Tarrypin?" sez Brer Rabbit, sezee.

"Yer I come a bilin'," sez de Tarrypin, sezee.

Brer Rabbit, he lit out, he did, en come ter de nex' pos', en dar wuz de Tarrypin. Den he come ter de nex', en dar wuz de Tarrypin. Den he had one mo' mile fer ter run, en he feel like he gittin' brefless. Bimeby, ole Brer Tarrypin look way off down de road en he see Jedge Buzzard sailin' 'long en he know hit's time fer 'im fer ter be up. So he scramble outen de woods, en roll 'cross de ditch, en shuffle thoo de crowd er folks en git ter de mile-pos' en crawl behime it. Bimeby, fus' news you know, yer come Brer Rabbit. He look 'roun' en he don't see Brer Tarrypin, en den he squall out:

"Gimme de money, Brer Buzzard! Gimme de money!"

Den Miss Meadows en de gals, dey holler en' laugh fit ter kill deyse'f, en ole Brer Tarrypin, he raise up fum behime de pos' en sez, sezee:

"Ef you'll gimme time fer ter ketch my breff, gents en ladies, one en all, I speck I'll finger dat money myse'f," sezee, en sho nuff, Brer Tarrypin tie de pu's 'roun' his neck en skaddle* off home.

Co'se, dat wuz cheatin'. De creeturs 'gun ter cheat, en den fokes tuck it up, en hit keep on spreadin'.

Hit mighty ketchin'.

Mr. Rabbit Meets His Match Again

Dey ain't no smart man, 'cep' w'at dey's a smarter. Ef ole Brer Rabbit hadn't er got kotch up wid, de neighbors 'ud er took 'im fer a ha'ant, en in dem times dey bu'nt witches 'fo' you could squinch yo' eyeballs. Dey did dat.

One time Brer Rabbit en ole Brer Buzzard 'cluded dey'd sorter go snacks, en crop tergedder. Hit wuz a mighty good year, en de truck tu'n out monstus well, but bimeby, w'en de time come fer dividjun, hit come ter light dat ole Brer Buzzard ain't got nothin'. De crop wuz all gone, en dey wa'nt nothin' dar fer ter show fer it. Brer Rabbit, he make like he in a wuss fix'n Brer Buzzard, en he mope 'roun', he did, like he fear'd dey gwineter sell 'im out.

Brer Buzzard, he ain't sayin' nothin', but he keep up a monstus thinkin', en one day he come 'long en holler en tell Brer Rabbit dat he done fine a rich gole-mine des 'cross de river.

"You come en go 'long wid me, Brer Rabbit," sez Brer Tukky Buzzard, sezee. "I'll scratch en you kin grabble, en 'tween de two un us we'll make short wuk er dat gole-mine," sezee.

Brer Rabbit, he wuz high up fer de job, but he study en study, he did, how he gwineter git 'cross de water, kaze ev'y time he git his foot wet all de fambly kotch cole. Den he up'n ax Brer Buzzard how he gwine do, en Brer Buzzard he up'n say dat he kyar Brer Rabbit 'cross, en wid dat ole Brer Buzzard, he squot down, he did, en spread his wings, en Brer Rabbit, he mounted, en up dey riz. W'en dey lit, dey lit in de top er de highes' sorter pine, en de pine w'at dey lit in wuz growin' on er ilun, en de ilun wuz in de middle er de river, wid de deep water runnin' all 'roun'. Dey ain't mo'n lit 'fo' Brer Rabbit, he know w'ich way de win' 'uz blowin', en by de time ole Brer Buzzard got hisse'f ballunce on a lim', Brer Rabbit, he up'n say, sezee:

"W'iles we er res'n here, Brer Buzzard, en bein's you bin so good, I got

---

* In all probability the word "skedaddle," about which there was some controversy during the Civil War, came from the Virginia Negro's use of "skaddle," which is a corruption of "scatter." (J.C.H.)

sump'n fer ter tell you," sezee. "I got a gole-mine er my own, one w'at I make myse'f, en I speck we better go back ter mine 'fo' we bodder 'longer yone," sezee.

Den ole Brer Buzzard, he laugh, he did, twel he shake, en Brer Rabbit, he sing out:

"Hole on, Brer Buzzard! Don't flop yo' wings w'en you laugh, kaze den if you duz, sump'n'ill drap fum up yer, en my gole-mine won't do you no good, en needer will yone do me no good."

But 'fo' dey got down fum dar, Brer Rabbit done tole all 'bout de crop, en he hatter promus fer ter 'vide fa'r en squar. So Brer Buzzard, he kyar 'im back, en Brer Rabbit he walk weak in de knees a mont' atterwuds.

The End of Mr. Bear

One time when Brer Rabbit wuz gwine lopin' home fum a frolic w'at dey bin havin' up at Miss Meadows's, who should be happin up wid but ole Brer B'ar. Co'se, atter w'at done pass 'twix um dey wa'n't no good feelin's 'tween Brer Rabbit en ole Brer B'ar, but Brer Rabbit, he wanter save his manners, en so he holler out:

"Heyo, Brer B'ar! how you come on? I ain't seed you in a coon's age. How all down at yo' house?" Den Brer Rabbit, he ax him howdy, he did, en Brer B'ar, he 'spon' dat he wuz mighty po'ly, en dey amble 'long, dey did, sorter familious like, but Brer Rabbit, he keep one eye on Brer B'ar, en Brer B'ar, he study how he gwine nab Brer Rabbit. Las' Brer Rabbit, he up'n say, sezee:

"Brer B'ar, I speck I got some bizness cut out fer you," sezee.

"W'at dat, Brer Rabbit?" sez Brer B'ar, sezee.

"W'iles I wuz cleanin' up my new-groun' day 'fo' yistiddy," sez Brer Rabbit, sezee, "I come 'cross wunner deze yer ole-time bee-trees. Hit start holler at de bottom, en stay holler plum ter de top, en de honey's des natally oozin' out, en ef you'll drap yo' 'gagements en go 'longer me," sez Brer Rabbit, sezee, "you'll git a bait dat'll las' you en yo' fambly twel de middle er nex' mont'," sezee.

Brer B'ar say he much oblije en he b'leeve he'll go 'long, en wid dat dey put out fer Brer Rabbit's new-groun', w'ich twa'n't so mighty fur. Leas'ways, dey got dar atter w'ile. Ole Brer B'ar, he 'low dat he kin smell de honey. Brer Rabbit, he 'low dat he kin see de honey-koam. Brer B'ar, he 'low dat he kin hear de bees a zoomin'. Dey stan' 'roun' an talk biggity, dey did, twel bimeby Brer Rabbit, he up'n say, sezee:

"You do de clim'in', Brer B'ar, en I'll do de rushin' 'roun'; you clime up ter de hole, en I'll take dis yer pine pole en shove de honey up whar you kin git 'er," sezee.

Ole Brer B'ar, he spit on his han's en skint up de tree, en jam his head in de hole, en sho nuff, Brer Rabbit, he grab de pine pole, en de way he stir up dem bees wuz sinful—dat's w'at it wuz. Hit wuz sinful. En de bees dey swam'd on Brer B'ar's head, twel 'fo' he could take it out'n de hole, hit wuz done swell up bigger dan a dinner-pot, en dar he swung, en ole Brer Rabbit, he dance 'roun' en sing:

> "Tree stan' high, but honey mighty sweet—
> Watch dem bees wid stingers on der feet."

But dar ole Brer B'ar hung, en ef his head ain't swunk down, I speck he hangin' dar yit—dat w'at I speck.

✓ ✓ ✓

PART TWO

CARRY ME BACK

> *We ain't what we oughtta be;*
> *We ain't what we wanna be;*
> *We ain't what we gonna be;*
> *But thank God,*
> *We ain't what we was!*

Introduction

For the slave, there was little that was humorous about his bondage. The conditions under which he was forced to survive were not calculated to evoke laughter, nor did the knowledge that his very soul was measured in dollars bring forth any waves of merriment. He might hear "My Country, 'Tis of Thee," but the lines, *Sweet land of liberty . . . Let freedom ring,* could hold no other emotion for him than bitterness. They were written and sung by and for the oppressors. The very laws of the land proclaimed him a chattel, equal to the domestic animals which he tended.

Yet—and not as paradoxical as it may at first seem—it was from these very depths of agony that the slave's wit and humor emitted its first faint sparks—sparks struck from the flint-stone of grinding hardship; fanned to glowing embers by the dawning realization that these humorous allegories were a comparatively safe means of protest and intra-communication; and finally the bright flame of overt laughter as the black man's spirit spread its fledgling wings in its maiden flight, to soar on the currents of inchoate hope.

Juneteenth*—that Great Day in the Morning which signified emancipation —brought with it a new horizon to black literature, implementing that of Northern brothers in the "free" states, but far more subjective and revealing of the horrors endured by this unique and indomitable people. The stories, anecdotes and remembrances inevitably included the humorous situations and activities which were employed by the slaves to inch their way along in their snail's-pace advance to ultimate freedom. With the passing years, the lighter as well as the more serious aspects of bondage became embodied in the folklore of the American Negro.

Yet, there were a few who still spoke with affection of their former owners and the very institution of slavery itself. In the main, they constituted the "privileged" house servants who often viewed the field hands with disdain. So completely brainwashed were they that they adopted the mannerisms of their masters, including their prejudices. As a rule, the house servant was in an enviable position as compared to the less fortunate slaves who toiled in the fields. He was generally dressed better because he had first call on cast-off clothing. Occasionally he would be outfitted with new clothes when his master wished to make "a good impression"—a status symbol among the more affluent Southern whites. Withal, he was generally close to the family and strong bonds of affection were not uncommon—as long as he "kept his place."

This chapter concerns one such "Uncle Tom," a prototype of most of the others who believed, as he did, that slavery had its merits. A glimpse of the anger and contempt which the other slaves felt for the house servant is revealed in the romantic interlude when Granddaddy, reminiscing about his courting days, describes his rejection by Dilsey who scorned him as a "house nigger."

However irritating we may find Granddaddy's romanticized recollections of slavery, he merits a place in Negro folklore if for nothing more than his historical significance. He existed. He was a sentient human being, and as we travel down the dim path of memory with him we see him in all his very human foibles and attributes until we realize that we are laughing *with* and not *at* him. Granddaddy, for all his indoctrination, was a gentleman, and if occasionally we want to shake him until his teeth rattle, we must also admire that integrity which, in the period of Reconstruction, led him to the life of an unreconstructed rebel to the end of his days. He was wrong, but lovable in his wrongness.

---

* "Juneteenth" refers to June 19, 1865, when General Granger, in Galveston, proclaimed freedom for all Negroes in Texas. "Juneteenth" has been celebrated by generations of blacks in Texas and throughout the South where former Texas Negroes migrated

Granddaddy Reveals a Poetic Soul*

Granddaddy, de win' is howlin' roun' de house an' de snow is comin' down, but I gwine roas' you some sweet 'taters in dis big fahr, an' bile a strong pot of coffee fur yo' supper; an' while we's eatin' you kin tell me 'bout dem good ole times befo' de war, when ole Marse an' ole Miss wuz livin'.

Yas, Honey, dem wuz times to live in; dese is times fur free niggers to strut 'bout wid a empty stummuck doin' nothin'.

Our white folks wuz quality. We own many a mile on de Jeems Riber, an' fur ez de eye could retch 'twuz ourn. De colonial house sot on a high hill, all by itself, an' de Jeems Riber bend mos' roun' it. 'Twas mighty big an' 'posin'. Ef you look down at de bunyance uv de craps it put you in mine uv dat Sam in de Bible who say, "De valleys stan' so thick wid corn it make de hills laugh an' clap dey han's." We all had de fines' drive, from de gate up to de house, an' we called it Magnolia Abenoo.

When dem trees wuz in bloom de whole place wuz so sweet it make de mockin' birds mos' kill deyself singin'. I heah Marster tell Miss he wouldn' take nothin' in de worl' fur dem trees, caze dey look like dey always got dey arms stretch out ter welcome frien's.

Eatin'-Eggs versus Settin'-Eggs

All of us use ter raise chickens an 'aigs an' things, an' sell 'em to Missy at de highes' market price. I reckerleck wunst Liza Jane's hen went ter settin', but she only sot a week fo' she lef' de nes'. Liza Jane wuz pow'ful 'stressed 'bout dem aigs but she didn' say nothin'. Den, onbeknownst ter us, she tuck 'em fur ter sell ter Missy.

Missy say, "Liza, what make dese aigs look so dark?"

"Law! Miss; ain' nothin' matter wid dem aigs, scusin' de hen wuz black an' she lay 'em on de dark uv de moon."

So Missy bought 'em. De nex' day, de cook broke 'em fur ter make some cake. She see dey warn't fitten ter use, caze dey wuz all spile, so she show 'em ter Miss, an' she sent fur Liza Jane.

She say, "Liza Jane, you ought ter be 'shame uv yo'se'f, to do me sech a trick es dis."

"Why, Miss, 'twar nothin' de matter wid dem aigs eff'n you use 'em right. I never knew you gwine make cake outen 'em—I wuz sartin you want 'em fur nes' aigs."

Heah me; de apple might'a temp' Eve, but chickens an' watermillyuns is been de ruination uv mo' uv our people den anything in dis worl', scusin' freedom!

* Selections from *Dem Good Ole Times*, by Mrs. J. H. Dooley, published by Doubleday, Page and Co., 1906.

Unequal Equality

In dem days, ladies an' gem'en never knew what twuz ter sell nothin'. Ef dey had things ter spyar, an' dey always did, dey give it free ez air. Now dey even sells milk. Dese times, de men mos' gen'ly in sech a hurry ter make money, ef dey seed a lady drap in de mud dey wouldn' stop ter he'p pick her up, like de Bible folks, de Republicums an' de Scarisees. No, dey jes' cross ober ter de other side of de street. De whole worl' done tu'n tocksy-turby.

Dey say now, a black man jes' ez good ez a white one, dat de erf ain' squar' an' de sun don' move. One dem meddlin' white men from de Norf come 'long t'other day when I wuz at wuck, an' ax me somepin, an' I tol' 'im what Marse Charles say. He say, "What you call 'im Marster fur? You jes' ez good ez him." I say, "I knows I jes' ez good ez *you*, but I ain' good ez Marse Charles." He never ax me no mo' queshuns.

That Savory, Satisfying Soul Food

I always did love our ol' time cookin', caze it wuz bes'. De kin' uv high-ferlutin' cookin' dey has now, 'specially white folks, is all name an' nothin' ter eat. Dar's sickafree chicken—what is dat? 'Tain' neither fried nor briled, nor yit stewed—a kin' uv mix uv all an' nothin' much at dat. 'Pears like cullud cookin' soothe my stomach an' settle my min'. It de soul dat does it—dat an' good ol' Virginny middlins. Virginny middlins stan' jes' as high over West'n po'k ez possum meat do over coon.

Days of Romance

I reckerleck when I wuz young an' already de haid gard'ner. I warn't married den, but I been takin' notice uv a gingerbread-color gal name Dilsey who ten' de cows an' milk. Whensomever we meet we pass de compliments uv de mornin'. She ax me, "How is yo' flowers dis mornin'?" "Dey is fine an' sweet," I say, "an' how is you gittin' 'long wid de cows an' de milk?" "Dey is well, an' de milk jes' ez fresh an' sweet ez yo' flowers." Dat sorter pleases me, an' I thinks ter myse'f, "Dat gal smart an' handy ter have aroun'. Ternight I gwine see what she think uv me." 'Cordin' ter dat I put on my good cloze, what I keep in sage an' horsemint, fur ter make 'em smell sweet, an' starts ter her house.

When I gits dar she wuz sottin' under a apple tree. I brung some 'lasses candy wid me ter he'p pass de time an' ter sweeten her up a leetle. Dey ain' nothin draw a woman closer ter you den a leetle candy an' plenty uv praise. 'Tain' de same wid a man; terbacker an' whuskey is what gits him.

While we wuz talkin' an' eatin', I say kin' uv consarned like, "Miss Dilsey, I come fur ter offer my objeckshuns ter you an' ter 'splain dat you is de onlies' gal I be lookin' at, fur you is de simmon uv my eyes an' de possum uv my heart. I gives you my body ter ten' an' my soul ter love an' pray fur, ter be jined tergether in de holy state uv ol' Virginny, an' in de boun's of solem' macrimony, till death us do partin'."

She jump up an' her eyes on fiah. She say, "Who give you de permission ter 'stend yo' 'tenshuns ter me? When I wants a man I ruther tuck one outen de woods den a house niggah sech ez you!"

I say, "I much 'bleeged fur yo' decision, caze only a fiel' niggah suit a onmanner woman like you better'n a gem'un what don' do nothin' 'cep' wuck in flowers an' 'sociate wid de white folks."

Wid dat, she grab a cha'r an' flung it at me, but I dodge an' git away quick ez I could.

Dat gal fin'ly seed de day she sorry she didn' 'cep' me, caze she sech a wil'cat her husban' beat her constant. I warn't noways down in de mouf an' cast away 'caze Dilsey dejeck me. I knowed dar wuz jes' ez good fish lef' in de sea ez ever walk on de sho'. So I tu'n my intenshuns ter a real nice leetle gal name of Ginny who war seamstress fur Missy an' sew fur de big house. She war so chirpy an' quick in her ways she got de name uv Ginny Wren.

'Twarn't long 'fo' I 'ceed in 'suadin' her ter share her life wid me, an' Ginny 'gree ter git married ez soon ez we could.

Orange Blossom Time

Miss say we could be married in her parlor, an' she would git her own preacher—she was Pistical—ef'n we choose. We have real marriages in dem ol' times. But now, ef you got plenty uv money you gits a divo'ce, an' husban's an' wives change each other 'roun' whensomever dey please, same's de birds.*

Ginny wuz like de budderflies; she love de brightes' colors. So she choose red fer her weddin' garmint. She want orange blossoms, but bein' ez how she couldn' git none, it 'peared ter her de oranges would be jes' de same ez de flowers, an' a sight priddier. So she pick out de fines' she could git an' she sew one on each shoulder uv her dress, an' one right in de middle; de bigges' she tie on de tiptop uv her haid. She always wa'r tasty, Ginny wa'r.

Den we march in terguther an' we had ter go mighty slick an' stiddy, 'caze Ginny skyared 'bout dem oranges drappin' off'n her. De room wuz pow'ful full, but I seed nobody ontwel I stop plum 'fo' de preacher.

De preacher say, "Ben, you take dis woman ter be yo' awful wife?"

---

* The house servant's unswerving belief in the advantages of slavery was so unalterably rigid that he could not or would not recognize the simple truth that "marriage" among slaves was "sacred" only until the master decided to sell one or the other, and that the ceremony (often there was none) was little more than an inducement to breed a new generation of slaves for which the owner paid nothing.

I speak up quick, "Ob co'se, Marse Preacher—dat what I ax her fo'."

Ginny never los' a orange ontwel we mos' froo; den she bow her haid an' de bigges' one roll off an' knock de preacher's book clean outen his han'. I try ter cotch it but I couldn', an' seem like dat make de confusion wusser.

Dat wuz long 'fo' I ever hyar tell uv de woman dat writ 'bout Unc' Tom's Cabin. Now dey done sot us free 'pears like dey don' know what ter do wid us no mo'n we know what ter do wid ourse'fs.

Ode to Virginia

Granddaddy, you ever been up Norf?

No, Honey, an' I ain' 'spectin' ter go, nuther! When I's daid an' gone, don' you never 'low nobody ter 'suade you ter go Norf fer ter live. Mebbe you gits mo' wages, but you ain' never know what a day's wuck is ontwel you draw ter Yankee money. It mos' like takin' his blood, an' you has ter be up an' doin' 'fo' de sun shines in de mornin' 'fo' dey think you zarve it. Soon's ever fall come, up dar in de Norf, you shake an' freeze an' you don' thaw out no mo' ontwel mos' summer. Den dey speak so sho't an' look so col' at you, you feels fros'bited in yo' feelin's all de time. You wucks an' eats yo' bread, but it ain' wid de sweat uv de brow 'cordin' ter de Comman'mints. It too col' up dar fur any kin' uv 'ligion whatsomever, an' w'ar you is so sich'ated you has ter go agin Scriptur' you better lef' on de fus' train an' go back home ter Dixie.*

De Yankees is pow'ful fond uv we-all, when dey is dar an' we is hyar, but soons'ever we gits any clos'ter dey ain' got no mo' use fur us den a rabbit got fur a tar pot. De Souf is de place fur quality white folks an' fus'-class cullud folks. Dis is de lan' uv milk an' honey, an' possums an' simmons, an' de bes' uv ev'ything what is appetitin'. Nowhar is dar sech a nuther place dat you walks froo de woods knee-deep in jewberries. An' when you come out in de road, all you got ter do is ter retch out yo' han' an' bring it back full'r blackberries:

> De simmons nowhar grow so sweet,
>   ez in Virginia;
> An' dar's nowhar sech possum meat,
>   ez in Virginia;
> De black man's heart am always light
>   Caze dar is leetle wuck in sight,
>   Down in Virginia.

---

* Illustrative of the warnings told to slaves by their owners, in a scarcely veiled attempt to frighten them from thoughts of fleeing to the North. Needless to say, the slaves rejected the tales of hardship and atrocities awaiting them in the North for the falsehoods they were. The house servant, Granddaddy, running true to form, believed the stories to the end of his days. It is important to note that he was no hypocrite. The tales were as real to him as his own existence.

De folks ain' nowhar else so kine,
    ez in Virginia;
De weather ain' nowhar so fine,
    ez in Virginia;
You never pestered wid much cloze,
    You drap down anywhar an' doze,
        Down in Virginia.

De mellyons nowhar grow so big,
    ez in Virginia;
De s'ile so light we seldom dig,
    down in Virginia;
An' whar yo' home so good an' sweet,
    Dat heaben an' earf bofe seem ter meet,
        Dat's ol' Virginia.

That Old Time Religion

You ever took notice dat 'ligion sots mighty light on de stomach uv de puss'n what never goes ter chu'ch? He so smart he speck ter go ter heaben his own way, jes' like he done made de road up ter dar hisse'f. He so blin' he don' know de debil leadin' him. De mole don' know nuther dat oberhaid is de blessed sunshine.

'Ligion ain' ever de real thing now it use'ter wuz. In de ol' times, folks had ter starve deyse'f an' pray an' seek, sometimes a month er mo', 'fo' dey come froo. You had ter be right good an' ser'us 'fo' you could make up yo' min' ter go under de deep, dark waters what de Baptis's frowed you in. But den when you got it you had it. Now dey go ter chu'ch widout ever rasslin' wid de debil an' gits sprinkled like de white folks, an' comes out ready-made Christians. It don' las' long caze what come easy go easy. It like de seed on de rock; dey come up but don' byar no fruit, caze de root is lackin'. Dat's why de white folks has week-en' 'ligion an' our people has soul-'ligion—it dar ter stay.

Punkins, Taters and Yams

Granddaddy, you say de beatines' things I evah heah tell on.

An' den I ain' tell but half. Us boys use'ter have de bes' fun—an' mos' uv it huntin' rabbits when de groun' wuz kivered wid snow. Sometimes we cotch mo'n we able ter bring home. An' den, sech suppers! It make my mouf water jes' talkin' 'bout 'em. It impossible ter git 'em like dat now caze de cookin' stove an' de white folks done ruint de tas'e uv ev'ything. A coon foot br'iled in a open fire, on red hot coals, is better'n anything dem Monicos up in New Yawk kin do. Ef dey could tas'e we'all's eatin's dey'd quit de business ontwell dey come down here an' larnt what wuz what. De way my Ginny barbecue rabbit would make a daid man riz up outen his grabe an' go hare huntin'.

I reckerleck, when we wuz chillun, Marse put mo' groun' in sweet 'taters den anybody 'roun', caze de slaves an' sarvints eat 'em jes' ez much ez de white folks, an' de chillun bleeged ter have 'em on 'count uv dey keep off de malaria. Arter de harves', de cullud chillun wuz tu'n loose in de fiel' ter he'p deyse'f. Early in de mornin' dey start wid dey baskits an' buckets an' bags ter pick up 'taters. Some uv 'em wuz so leetle dey couldn' tote no more'n dey apron could hol'. From de racket dem chillun make, laughin' an' hollerin', it soun' like de blackbirds done lit in dat fiel' fur ter pick up dey own corn.

Punkins am mighty good squashy things, an' I ain' findin' no fault wid 'em, but dey ain' noways got de stayin' power like de sweet 'tater. Dey fills up mo' wrinkles in de stomach, an' is de mos' satisfyin' sweet thing dat grows. All de craps on de plantation put terguther don' 'sply de same 'mount uv goodness ez de sweet 'tater do. You kin roas' an' bake 'an fry an' b'ile 'em, an' den tu'n 'em inter puddin's an' pies an' custids an' you kin even eat 'em raw, same ez apples.

De real thing don' grow nowhar, 'cep'in ol' Virginny. Dem roots dey call yams ain' no better'n b'iled Orrish 'taters, wid sweeten' water po'd over 'em.

How to Tell the
'Coon from the Possum

Granddaddy, I always git mixed up wid de 'coon an' de possum, an' don' know t'other from which.

Well, you sho' in a bad fix. Dar is jes' ez much diffunce twix' dem ez dar is twix' de foot an' de han'. But if you l'arn dis, it impossible ter make a mistake:

> Raccoon tail am ring aroun',
> Possum tail am b'ar,
> Rabbit got no tail a-tall,
> But stumpy grow de h'ar.

Guinea Peter's Disappearing Possum

Guinea Peter could beat any man er woman on de plantation cookin' a possum. But he wouldn' tell nobody how he done it. Ef you eat it wunst it so good de reckerlecshun stay in yo' mouf an' tu'n yo' stomach agin all t'other vittles mos' a month. But he wuz a monstus se'f-consarned, stingy man, an' never would ax nobody ter eat wid 'im—less'n dey cotch 'im on de sly. He always keep a live possum on han', an' whensomever we ax 'im when he 'speck ter kill it, he shake his haid an' say "I dunno—seem like it impossible ter fatten dis possum."

Dat de truf, in a way. It wa'r impossible ter fatten dat possum any mo' caze his body cain't hol' it.

One day he kilt an' clean it, an' when night come, 'twuz pow'ful dark an' drizzlin', an' wid all dat bad weather he sho' nobody 'bout ter drap in. 'Cordin'ly, he let down de winder an' bolt de do', an' den put de possum on de fahr. His mouf water an' his han' trimble ez de cookin' scent smite de nose, an' he think he gwine have it all ter hisse'f. Mebbe—but you kin 'speck de cherry bird ter fly roun' de tree 'dout eatin' cherries, an' a brother ter sot by a fahr 'doubt drappin' off ter sleep; but you sho' git fooled, caze it plum again natur'.

An' dat jes' what happen ter Giunea Peter. Ez he wuz watchin' an' tendin' dat possum, de fus' thing he know he didn' know nothin' caze when dat brother git ter sleep you kin stan' him on his haid an' he wouldn' know it.

Sam wuz jes' ez cunnin' ez Guinea Peter, an' he 'speck somethin' wuz up, so he walk dataway an' creep up ter de winder. Sho' nuff, dar sot Peter an' de possum—one in de cha'r an' t'other on de fahr. He put his han' froo a hole in de winder an' arter he riz it up he let hisse'f in easy-like. It take mighty leetle time ter eat sech a appetitin' meal ez dat possum, an' when 'twuz all gone he tuck de leavin's an' he grease up Guinea Peter's mouf all 'roun', an' Guinea's fingers too, an' den sot de plate uv bones befo' him. Den he slip out an' listen.

By'm by, Guinea Peter wake up an' rub his eyes an' he look roun' but don' see de possum. Den he smack his lips an' tas'e his fingers, an' he say, "Dis sho' am possum grease, an' dar am de bones, but ef I eat dat possum it set lighter on my stomach an' gib less sat'sfacshun den any possum I ever et."

Of Hogs and Men

De hog am de po' man's bes' frien'; not dat I's much 'quainted wid po' folks. I see 'em sometimes gwine 'long de road, but ef'n I wuz po', an' didn' have but a dolluh, I'd 'vest it in a pig, sho'. It better'n de bank, caze dat do bus' up now an' den, but it diff'unt wid de hog—he always roun' you, an' in dese unsartin times it wuth consid'able ter have yo' ownin's wha'r you kin retch out yo' han' an tetch 'em.

Den, s'posin' he die 'fo' his time, it ain't so much loss caze you kin b'ile 'im up an' make sorf soap outen 'im. He de mos' ekernomical, de mos' increasin'is' an' de mos' yieldin'is' critter dat goes. He 'stroy all de trash an' slops an' weeds roun' de house 'doubt botherin' nobody ter tote 'em off. He always gittin' bigger an' fatter, an' when he's kilt, de yieldin's is so numersome you sca'cely got de room ter sto' 'em. You kin eat 'em from de yurs down ter de foot, an' sprang out ter de tip uv de tail.

We eat 'im hot, we eat 'im col';
We eat 'im young, we eat 'im ol';
We eat 'im tender, we eat 'im tough;
An' yit we never got enough.

De hog live so close ter po' folks he larn a heap uv deir ways. Ef you gin 'im sup'n he grunt; ef you don' gin 'im nothin' he grunt; an' whatsomever you do, he grunt an' complain. Ef'n he got thanks inside dey comes out in grunts—jes' like some people I kin mention.

Of Queens, Pippins
and Virginia Hams

I ain't noways a-braggin', but we sends our Virginny hams an' Albemarle pippins clean acrosst de water ter Queen Victorious. She sot so much sto' by 'em she eats 'em all husse'f, an' she say dey bes' she ever tas'e. Ef she smack her mouf when she eat 'em dar in her own country, what would she do ef she could git 'em cooked like Sary Jane have 'em? I reckon she be mos' ready ter lef' de frone an' come hyar ter live wid us, caze anyhow, oneasy lays de haid dat w'ars de crown, like it say in de Good Book, 'scusin' de cropper crown chicken—she always lay easy—mos' ev'y day!

The Civil War ...
One Man's Profile

You ever notice I don' talk much 'bout dat war what sot us free? Well, it never 'ceeded in sot'n me free caze I wouldn' be sot! Bes' ez I kin make out, freedom ain't nothin' but comin' an' goin' when you please, an' dat priddy much all de po' folks do—come an' go. I don' kyar ter think 'bout de war, les' mo' talk 'bout it.

But I do reckerleck one story. 'Twuz a summer day, way back yander— 'pears like it been mos' a hunnerd y'ars—I wuz talkin' wid Missy 'bout de gardenin', an' all uv a sudden seem like one dem cycloons done struck us. We look up de road but couldn' see nothin' fur de clouds uv dus'. But we know soon 'nuff 'twuz one uv dem Yankee raids, caze we done hyar dar wuz a pow'ful battle at Sas'frus Bridge—priddy nigh kilt Joe Ginnins, de plantation co'n-shuckin' king. When dey bus' loose an' t'ar roun' like dat, you mought-a thought de debil wuz arter 'em, ef'n you didn' know he wuz wid 'em.

Two uv 'em rid up ter de house an' one look at me an' say, "How you do, ol' skyar crow?" I say, "Howdy, buzzard." Den, wid de ins'lence uv ol' Scratch hisse'f, dey tell Missy dey want sup'n ter eat an' drink, an' dey want it quick. She tell 'em she done sen' ev'y drap uv liquors 'an wines ter de horspittle fur de sick an' wounded sojers. Dat buzzard say, "You lie!" I never hear no mo'. Quick ez it lef' his mouf I knock 'im down an' jump on top'n 'im wid my fis's flyin' roun' his haid same's lightnin'. Ain't no tellin' what mought-a happen ef Missy didn' stop me.

T'other one done had too much ter drink a'ready, but time he spy a jimmy-john settin' by de kitchen do' he tuck it up an' drink mos' a pint a kaysene ile 'fo' he know twarn' whuskey. Den he went down hill an' lay down an' die. Soon's Missy know 'bout it she run in de house an' git medicine an' things, an' we bofe go down dar ter see what we kin do ter save his life. She tuck his han' an' pray fur 'im, an' she wuck on 'im two hours, but 'twarn' no use—he die 'fo' de doctor could git dar.

Arter a while I ax Missy hoccum she so 'stressed 'bout dat Union sojer. She say, "Ben, mebbe he wuz a good man at home but he fall inter bad comp'ny an' bad habits when he jined de Yankee army." It so sad I 'gin ter cry, but dey wuz de fus' an' onlies' tears I ever was'e on Yankees.

Ez I wuz sayin' 'bout dat Yankee raid—dey put me in min' uv bees swarmin' ev'ywhar you didn' want 'em, an' leavin' dey sting wharsomever dey light. I been oneasy ev'y since I bounce de buzzard caze I 'speck trouble gwy come outen it. De nex' day, ez I wuz at wuck, sho' nuff I look up an' dar stan' two Yankees, come fur ter 'res' one po' ol' gard'ner. Sech a creepy feelin' ez I had, jes' like when you mos' tread on a big snake an' ain't got nothin' ter kill 'im wid. I feel mighty wobbly 'bout de laigs an' kin' uv chattery in de teef, an' I tu'n sorter sick in my stomach. 'Course, I wouldn' 'low dem ter see it fur nothin' in de worl', so I jes' speak up chirpy de bes' I could an' tell Missy how I be back 'fo' long caze my coluh gwy sho' 'tect me.

'Twarn' no use makin' no fuss, so I start 'long wid 'em, quiet an' 'spectable as I war brung up. By'm by, ez my sperrits riz, I talk so much foolishness dem men think I wuz a ijiot monkey. I say, "Marse Sojer, dis a mighty long hot road you gwine. Eff'n you tu'n to de lef' when we gits ter de forks, de road is cool an' shady, an' two er three miles nigher yo' camp den dis. I wuz bo'n an' raised right hyar, thank Gord, an' I know all de brier patches same's de rabbits, an' ev'y foxhole an' ev'y bee tree, an' whar all de wile varmints live, good ez dey does deyse'fs."

Den dey look at one t'other an' whisper, an' I hyar 'em say, "He sech a fool he ain't got sense 'nuff ter lead a duck ter water."

I say, "Dis road suit me mighty well. I don' never feel extry good less'n de sun so brilin' hot it kink de wool on top'n my haid. De hotter de sun, de louder me an' de jarfly sing." Den I riz my voice an' bus' out a'singin':

> "Brer Rabbit wink at de possum,
>   De possum grin at me;
> I shy a rock a rock at de critter,
>   He clum a hick'ry tree."

Dey holler an' laugh an' say, "Go 'haid, ol' coon, but ef'n you playin' any yo' monkey tricks on us, you never monkey no mo'." I say "Yas suh, you kin 'pend on me 'bout dat, 'caze dis ain't no playin' time wid me."

Den dey tell me fur ter sing some plantation songs, an' I gin um:

"I couldn' live bedout de flowers
Uv dat sweet magnolia tree;
I couldn't sleep whar de mockin' bird
Couldn' sing his song ter me.
I'd soon be nothin' but skin an' bones
Ef de codfish wuz my meat;
I'd pine an' die on Boston beans,
Caze possum is what we eat."

Dey say, "He's a reg'lar jaybird." How you like dat? Fus' I a skyar crow, den a coon, den a flower, den again a bird! An' jes' like I plan, dey laugh again widout thinkin' uv nothin' 'cept my silly talk.

We go 'long like dat a good ways, an' dey never 'spicion nothin' ontwel I lan' 'em plum in de Confed'rate lines, an' 'stead uv dey havin' me—I had dem! I seen many a black cloud in summer time, but de looks an' words uv dem two men wuz wussen any thunder an' lightnin' I ever see. I got outen de reach uv 'em quick ez I could an' ez I start home I makes 'em a bow an' say, "Dis fool black man didn' have 'nuff sense ter lead a duck ter water, but sho's you bo'n, he lead two geese ter sech troubled waters dar won' be no swimmin', nur flyin', nuther."

When I git home, leetle Mary rush up ter me an' put her arms 'roun' my neck an' say, "Daddy Ben, I so 'fraid de Yankees done et you up."

Prisbiteriums, Cat'lics and Pisticals

It go agin me ter say dis but dar's mighty leetle 'ligion in de Pistical Chu'ch, 'cep'n hyar an' dar in spots. De Mephdis's ain't much better, but dem Prisbiteriums is de wuss uv all caze who ever hyur uv a Prisbiterium nigger? Tain't none. An' whar de fole is so narrer dat it can't take in a few black sheep 'long wid de white, you kin be sho' de pickin's mus' be mighty small an' too sca'ce ter go roun'.

Den agin, nex' ter eatin', dar ain't nothin' our folks love like buss'n out in a good laugh. Now nobody ain't never hyur de true blue Prisbiterium laugh. It agin natur', caze dey brags dat dey bo'n in a state uv sin an' mis'ry, an' 'pear like dey bleeged ter stay dar. From de cradle ter de grabe dey spen's dey time buryin' pleasure an' dey is always de natchul pall-byarers uv de same. Eben dat outlan'ish Roman Cat'lic Chu'ch do take in a few cullud folks. It do 'em some good, too. 'Stead uv hangin' roun' doin' nothin' all day de Cat'lics count beads an' de pries' dissolves 'em from all sin. Dis also give 'em de chance ter spen' all dey money right dar, 'steader scatterin' it roun' on foolishness.

But, Granddaddy, ain't ouah white folks Pistical?

"Yas, honey, all de quality white folks is Pistical, but our folks jes' natch'ly bo'n so good de chu'ch cain't hu't 'em. I bleej ter say dis much: de Pistical 'ligion don' do nobody no harm, no mo'n it don' do 'em no good. 'Pears like it lets 'em do priddy much ez dey please."

Prophecy

Leetle Ginny, in de name a sense, what you make all dat mess in hyar fo', wid all dem papers scatter roun'? Ev'y time I talk, lately, you got dat pencil in yo' han' 'steader a broom.

Granddaddy, I know sup'n gwy 'sprise you so 'twill make yo' hyar stan' on een', an' ef'n you promise not ter cut up no shines mebee I mought tell you.

I ain't promise you nothin', caze you is too outdashus an' disrespeckable. Talk 'bout me cuttin' up shines same's I a mule! Whar yo' manners at? But it jes' dat freedom a'creepin' out agin, an' I don' 'speck no better.

Granddaddy, I 'clar ter goodness, I never went fur ter make you mad! I jes' been waitin' ter tell you sup'n. Ev'y time you reckerleck a story I tries ter 'member ev'ything you say an' write it down. Missy say someday it gwy be publick'd in a book.

Gal, what dat you say? Is you clean 'stracted? You ain't gwine do no sech thing! Nobody kin make a book outen me! I's a 'speckable man, an' always hol' myse'f 'bove gittin mix up wid newspapers an' printin' an' all dem scan'lous things. I dunno what make you study 'bout doin' sech a outlan'ish wuck, less'n you done git tetched wid too much uv dis freedom. When dat take hol', seem like it driv all 'sponsibility outen you.

But, Granddaddy, we-all ain't got no notion how things use ter wuz. A hunnerd y'ars from now de cullud folks will l'arn supp'n from yo' reck'leckshuns.

Well, honey, don' 'sgrace me too much, fur it go mighty hyard wid me ter be one dem no-count public chyaracters. Arter I daid an' gone 'twill be time 'nuff ter put me in de print. Ef'n any uv our people read 'bout me a hunnerd y'ars from now, tell 'em dat de bes' I could say fur myse'f was dis: I wuz a faithful husban', father, an' gard'ner, in dat order, in dem good ol' times 'fo' de war, an' dat I loved ev'ything an' ev'ybody in de whole worl'—'scusin' Yankees.

PART THREE

LAUGHING ON THE OUTSIDE

*"If I laugh loud enough,
maybe no one will hear me cry."*

Tired of Livin',
Feared of Dyin'*

Old man Jemmy-John was so aged and useless that even his master did not want him any more. Why feed a slave who could no longer earn his keep? So the oldtimer was ordered off the plantation, to live or die—whichever.

Jemmy-John had heard that black people were better treated in the North so he directed his aching feet in that direction. But he grew so very tired as he trudged along, and so weary of life, that he really didn't care much, one way or the other, whether he reached his goal or not. On the third night he came to a barn, went inside and fell exhausted into the hay.

However, he was seen by the farmer. That worthy grabbed a pitchfork and descended upon the old man like Satan himself, breathing fire and brandishing his weapon.

"I got ya, nigger," he snarled. "I got ya!"

Old Jemmy-John raised his head, and his voice was scarcely above a hoarse whisper as he groaned, "All right, you got me, mister. But a hell of a git you got!"

Grandpa Roasts a Pig*

My father, in his boyhood, heard this tale many times from his grandfather, a slave on the Hammond plantation in Georgia. Here is the way it was told to me:

Grandpa had the best job on the plantation, working in the main house where he served at the dinner table, among his other household duties. Master Hammond and grandpa had two things in common; they both loved roast pig and each had a lively sense of humor. But there all spiritual or moral resemblance stopped. Hammond was also a greedy man. It should also be reported that Hammond's sense of humor only was self-evident when the joke was turned against one of his slaves—or any white man whom he could browbeat.

---

* *Laughter in Chains*, by Velma McCloud, Lenox Press, New York, 1901.

Although he had several pens teeming with fat piglets and grown, healthy sows, Hammond would never give a morsel to the slaves. Indeed, even Grandpa, who served the succulent pork, would never be offered a taste. The leftovers? Hammond saved them for his next meal while his servant stood nearby, his mouth watering.

Grandpa decided to remedy the situation. One moonless night he slipped into one of the pens, selected a choice young piglet and, together with some of the fieldhands who lived in adjacent cabins, they had a feast. For some of them, it was their very first taste of pork. Thereafter, for the next several months, Grandpa would occasionally sneak into the pen, capture a likely-looking candidate for the pot, and bring it to his cabin where he cooked it as only he knew how.

But, despite the large number of pigs which Hammond had never thought necessary to count, he soon noticed the diminishing supply and rightly suspected that Grandpa was the culprit. He took to watching the pens from his upstairs bedroom window until, one night, he saw a shadowy figure enter one of the pens and then, a few minutes later, emerge with a squirming bundle inside a sack. "Now I got him!" he thought. Waiting until he was sure the pig was on the stove and cooking, he went over to Grandpa's cabin and rapped on the bolted door, certain he would catch him with the evidence in plain view.

"Who dar?" called Grandpa.

"You know very well who it is," said Hammond grimly. "Open the door."

" 'Scuse me, Massa. I - I - er - I's comin' right out. You don' hafta come intuh no ole slave cabin."

"You needn't come out. Just open the door."

"But, Massa, this place ain't fittin' fo' a fine genelmun like you. I'll come on out."

"Open the door this instant!" roared Hammond. "I'm coming in."

With a sinking feeling, Grandpa opened the door and Hammond strode inside. There was no question that something mighty good was simmering in the big pot atop the old wood stove. Grandpa knew his spices, and the little cabin was permeated with the aroma of bubbling juices.

"What's that cooking in the pot?" asked Hammond as innocently as he could. "It certainly smells good."

"N-n-nothin' but a li'l ole skinny possum," Grandpa faltered.

"It smells so good I think I'll have some."

"It - it ain't ready fo' eatin' yit."

"Bring a plate and start serving!"

"But you jes' ate yo' suppah. You ain't hongry."

"Bring me a plate or I'll take the hide off your back!"

Grandpa was in no mood for a whipping, but he knew he would be given a real horse-hiding if Hammond learned for certain that he was the pig-stealer. Unfortunately, there remained no other choice. He brought a plate and then went to the stove, his mind working furiously. Slowly, he lifted the lid from the pot and the fragrance was even more savory than before.

"Reckon I wuz wrong, Massa," said Grandpa. "Dis possum am done to a tu'n. Mus' be all dat good spittin' we done."

"The *what!*"

"Spittin'," answered Grandpa sweetly. "Us nigguhs allus spits in possum gravy. Makes de meat mo' tenduh. Aunt Janie done spit in it; Uncle Amos done spit in it; de chilluns done spit in it; an' I spit in it myse'f fo' er five times." He reached into the meat with a fork. "You wants a nice big piece, Massa?"

Hammond, his stomach churning, rose from the table. "That's the most disgusting habit I ever heard of," he rasped. "You're a pack of damned savages." He slammed the door behind him as he left.

"Cain't say ez I blame 'im," said Grandpa to his grinning fellow slaves when they had finished eating and he had told them of his narrow escape. "I wouldn'a et it myse'f."

Deviled Ham

When a human being is owned by another, and is deprived of the very food which he himself has produced, it is axiomatic that he cannot feel he is stealing what should have rightfully been his. The absence of guilt is well illustrated in this plantation tale.

There had been a bumper crop in that year of 1849, and the plantation owners throughout Mississippi fed their livestock exceptionally well—better, in some cases, than they fed their slaves.

In her cabin, toothless, wrinkled Granny heaved a deep sigh: "Oh, how I'd like a tas'e uv ham!"

Isaac, her grandson, thought a moment, and then offered a suggestion: "Ol' Massa's smokehouse is bustin' with hams; I seen 'em myse'f. I kin sneak in dar some evenin' an' take one. He'd nevuh miss one li'l ol' ham."

Granny threw up her hands in dismay. "Now you looka heah, Isaac; dat's de devil hisse'f put dem wu'ds in yo' mouf. Wouldn' nobody but Satan eat stole ham. You stop dat kinda talk, boy!"

But Isaac, who had not eaten a piece of meat in weeks, could not rid himself of the vision of big, juicy hams hanging from the rafters in Massa's well-stocked smokehouse. Granny, too, dreamed of those hams, knowing that she could not hope to have one. Her mouth watered whenever she thought about it.

A few evenings later, as she bent over the fire, preparing a supper of greens and ashcakes, she thought she heard the cautious scraping of feet outside her cabin. She was about to investigate when suddenly a great big ham came hurtling through the window and landed at her feet. Faintly, she could hear the tattoo of rapidly departing footsteps in the darkness beyond her door.

"Praise be de Lawd!" cried Granny. "Thank Gawd fer dis ham—even ef He did sen' de devil ter bring it!"

No Rest for the Weary

"No Rest for the Weary" illustrates, in subtle language, the plight of the enslaved field hand.

General Grant had just taken Richmond, and it looked like the Civil War was nearing its end. A group of Union soldiers were patrolling the outskirts of the city when they came upon a slave toiling in a field. They hailed him and he drew up his mule and acknowledged the greeting with a forefinger to the brim of his wide straw hat.

"Didn't we see you plowing here early this morning?" asked the platoon leader.

"Yassuh," agreed the slave. "I done stahted wuck at five dis mawnin'."

"But here it is four in the afternoon! Don't you ever get tired?"

"Sho' I does," said the weary black man as he mopped his perspiring brow, "but I knows how ter reg'late myse'f. When I gits too tired plowin' I quits an' goes ter hoein', an' it res's me."

All Toh Up

Pompey and Jim, two slaves, were comparing notes about their respective masters.

"I gits 'long tol'ble well wid my massa," said Pompey.

Hoccum you gits 'long tol'ble well wid yo' massa?" demanded Jim. "He meaner'n *my* massa!"

"I jes' cuss 'im out real good when I's a mind ter," said Pompey coolly. Jim was astonished. "An' nothin' happen ter you?"

"Nothin' a'tall. Try it yo'se'f—it sho' make you feel good."

Jim agreed, but when he met Pompey the following afternoon his face was badly bruised and his back a mass of ugly welts from the rawhiding he had received. "I done like you say an' really cuss 'im out," Jim moaned, "but Massa, he toh me up."

"Whar you wuz when you cuss 'im out?"

"Why, I wuz stannin' right befo' his face, dat's whar."

"You oughtta have mo' sense dan dat," reproached Pompey. "Now when I cuss my massa I wait ontwel he up at de big house an' I stannin' down at de othuh en' uv de fiel'."

Such Outrageous Prices

Abraham had never worked in the fields a day in his life, but had been a servant to his master and had his own room in the attic of the main house. He had also managed to educate himself after a fashion and consequently became an added asset, keeping accounts, purchasing supplies and paying bills.

One day, Abraham bought a lottery ticket from his meager savings earned from performing odd jobs for other landowners. To his glee, he won a thousand dollars. He was well aware of his favored status, of course, but he also knew he was a slave. So he decided to buy his freedom.*

"Master," he began, "how much am I worth on today's slave market?"

"Oh, about fifteen hundred, more or less. Why?"

"I won first prize in a lottery. I want to buy my freedom."

"Well, good for you!" responded the owner feelingly. "In that case I'll make it an even thousand.

Abraham's face fell. He nodded and walked away scowling.

"What's the matter?" asked his master. "Don't you have that much money left?"

"Yes, master, I have enough. But the price of slaves right now is too high. I'll wait for the market to ease up a bit and buy when we're cheaper.

How a Sly Slave City-Slickered
Sleepy Slaver Sloane

There is an obscure little street in lower Manhattan called Peck Slip. But it had a glorious though brief moment in the sun. Back in the early 1800's, Peck Slip was a major port of call for ships from the far reaches of the earth, and housed all the docking, loading, unloading, provisioning and storage facilities expected of an important seaport. Peck Slip is little more than a memory today (although the street still exists), but it merits a niche in Negro folklore because it was here that many a rendezvous occurred between abolitionists and runaway slaves from the South who made this a stopover on their way to New England or Canada via the Underground Railroad.

(This story was told to me by my mother-in-law, Margarite Woolsey, herself an escaped slave who arrived in Canada in this year of our Lord, 1859.)**

* The relationship between folklore and orthodox history is evidenced in this tale. Telemarque—also known as Denmark Vesey—bought his freedom by winning a $1,500 lottery. He paid $600 for his own liberty but was refused permission to purchase his children. Telemarque (1767-1822), became a Methodist minister, planned an insurrection to seize the city of Charleston and free his people. After two years of organizing the revolt, and one postponement, zero hour was fixed for June 16, 1822. Hundreds of slaves, free blacks and a few whites were armed and ready when, at the last moment, a renegade Negro revealed the plan to the white authorities. A blood-bath followed in which four whites were imprisoned, thirty blacks hanged, and on July 2, 1822, Telemarque died on the gallows. Thus did a lottery ticket bring freedom, hope, fame and death to an obscure slave.

** *Memoirs of One Wayburne Washington, A Former Slave Who Ventured from Georgia to Massachusetts.* Cleighton, Simpkins & Sons, 1862. 10 Peck Slip, New York.

There was a white man named Kingsbury, of Charleston, South Carolina, whose business it was to buy the ownership titles of runaway slaves for a fraction of the prevailing prices. He would then hunt them down and re-sell them at a goodly profit. It was in this manner that he purchased title to an escaped slave named Billy, and in the course of his pursuit found himself in New York.

Further investigation led him to a warehouse on Peck Slip, a place that was known for harboring refugee slaves. Mr. Kingsbury was well aware that this particular warehouse was a "station" of the Underground Railroad, and he also knew that there were a few greedy souls there who would turn in their own mothers for the right price . . . or at least he hoped so. As he expected, he was soon approached by a black man. "Who are you hunting for?" the stranger asked bluntly.

"Slave named Billy, from the Eastland plantation in Georgia," said the hunter of humans. "I'm paying $25 reward for his capture."

"That's a good business you're in," said the black man. "If you catch him you can re-sell him at a handsome profit. Tell you what I'll do. You sell that title to me and if I catch him that's *my* good luck." He paused a moment and then added, "Without my help you'll *never* catch him and you'll lose your investment altogether."

Kingsbury, far from an angel himself, regarded the Negro with unconcealed contempt. After all, here was this stranger trafficking in the flesh of his own people. But business was business, so he agreed. "You can buy title to Billy's ownership for one hundred dollars," he said. "The slave is worth far more than that—if you catch him."

The other agreed. "I'll be back in an hour with the money."

Good as his word, he returned within the hour, handed over the $100, and accepted the title to Billy's physical being.

Kingsbury stuffed the bills into his pocket, smiling with satisfaction. "By the way," he said conversationally, "we may be able to do some future business. Who are you?—What's your name?"

The black man drew himself up and his own smile outshone that of his new business partner. "Me?" he laughed. "I'm an ex-slave, and my name is Billy!"

At Last—the Truth!

Slave Owner: "Ah, dear, faithful, loyal Uncle Tom! Lincoln has forced you to accept freedom—against my wishes, and, I am sure, against yours. Dear old friend and servant, you need not leave this plantation. Stay here with us; kindly, gentle, self-sacrificing Uncle Tom!"

Uncle Tom: "Thank you, deah, kine, lovin', gen'rous Massa. I reckon I'll leave. But befo' I go I wants you ter know I will allus 'membuh you ez de son uv a bitch you is an' allus wuz!"

Outta My Way, Hoss!

Two young slaves managed to escape from the plantation during the height of the Civil War. Trudging along a dusty side road they came upon a regiment of Union troops. They were received with glad cries of welcome from other former slaves who had made their way to freedom and were now fighting the Confederacy.

"We might ez well jine up too," said the older of the two escapees. "I think I'll jine de calavary."

"Not me!" said the other. "I ain't jinin' no calavary. "I's gwine intuh de infantary."

"You gwine tuh do lots uv walkin'," the older youth reminded his companion. "In de calavary you gits tuh ride a hoss."

"Man, you ain't thinkin' rightly," retorted the other. "When dem bullets start a-flyin', I ain't gwine have time ter pull no dang hoss 'long wid me!"

Position Available

With the help of abolitionist sympathizers, a Mississippi slave undertook the perilous journey to the North via the Underground Railroad.* Upon his arrival in Boston where he finally found freedom, a group of well-wishers gathered at the local minister's house to question the former slave so that they might familiarize themselves with the many hardships he had known ever since his birth.

"You undoubtedly had to endure back-breaking work from dawn to dark," said one of the kind Bostonians.

"Not really," replied the black man, surprising everyone with his precise English. "My master allowed us to sleep a full eight hours, we were permitted an hour for lunch, and we quit work in time for dinner."

"How did you learn to speak so well?" asked another. "Were you in fear of your life when you educated yourself? I understand that a slave can be whipped to death for seeking to improve his lot."

The man smiled. "My master encouraged all of his slaves to learn to

---

* The Underground Railway (or Railroad) was an organized network of way-stations which helped slaves escape from the South to the free states and as far north as Canada. The way-stations were mainly homes whose residents and helpers were both white and free Negro. The metaphor, "Underground Railroad," first appeared in print in the early 1840's and other railroad terminology was soon added. The escaping slaves were called passengers; the homes where they were sheltered, stations; and those who guided them, conductors. While all due credit must be given to the whites who participated in the Underground Railroad, the major part was played by free Negroes of the North and South, and by slaves on plantations along the way. The extent of their participation has been reported in very few books. It should be further noted that the Railroad could not have been so successful had it not been for the resourcefulness and daring of the escaping fugitives themselves.

read and write," he said. "And I have never been whipped in my life. My master did not believe in physical punishment."

"Well," said the minister's wife, breaking into the discussion, "I'm going to fix you a good meal and get you some decent clothes. I'll bet you've been half starved all your life and never had a decent thing to wear—poor man."

"On the contrary," was the response. "My master fed us well and gave us proper clothing."

"Then what in tarnation did you run away for?" demanded the minister, breaking the deadly silence that now pervaded the group.

"Sir," answered the black man respectfully, "I assure you that the position I just vacated is still available, should any of you want the job."

Who's Afraid of the Big Bad Massa?

"Major" Kingsley and "Colonel" Williams, who had conferred their respective titles on each other years earlier, were life-long friends and river gamblers. Now retired, they had purchased adjoining plantations and were agreeably prepared to spend the rest of their days as country gentlemen. But they could not lose their fondness for gambling and were always seeking opportunities to make a wager.

One sunny afternoon they were discussing the relative merits of their slaves.

Said Major Kingsley: "I have a black named Joshua who is the strongest, fightin'est slave in the whole state. Why, I've seen him whip five other husky slaves and never even work up a sweat."

Colonel Williams perked up his ears. "I have a slave called Muscles, and he is so ferocious that we have to keep him in chains so that he doesn't kill all the other slaves at one time. Why, Muscles could easily tear your Joshua to pieces with one hand."

Quickly they made a substantial bet and arranged that Joshua and Muscles would fight that very next Saturday afternoon. Word spread immediately, and more than a hundred people arrived to witness what promised to be a bloody confrontation.

Muscles arrived early with his master, gazed contemptuously at the throng, and flexed his biceps. His face had an ugly sneer as he focused his eyes on Major Kingsley's group, but it turned to an expression of puzzlement when he saw that Joshua was not present.

If the truth be known, Joshua was in no mood to tangle with the savage Muscles. There isn't a slave within fifty miles who had not heard of this giant of a man who could bend horseshoes with his bare hands and who could and would lift a hundred pound rock and use it as a weapon. Joshua knew that brain would have to overcome brawn, and for the past several days he had invented one strategum after another, rejecting them as soon as he realized their weaknesses.

Now the hour had arrived and Joshua was nowhere to be seen. Finally, when all the spectators had decided that Joshua was too terror-stricken to appear, there he came, ambling lazily into the clearing that was to be their arena. He was whistling a carefree tune and was as unconcerned as though he were about to fight a little puppy.

"Where have you been?" roared Major Kingsley. "You were supposed to be here two hours ago."

"Now jes' a damn minute, white boy!" snapped Joshua. "Don' you talk tuh me in dat tone o' voice or I'll knock you on yo' behine!"

A deathly quiet spread over the onlookers. Colonel Williams reached for his pistol. As for Muscles, his face turned to a mask of incredulous horror. In a moment he sprang to his feet and raced into the dense underbrush, putting as much distance as possible between himself and that madman, Joshua.

Major Kingsley's lips were as taut as violin strings. "Joshua, do you know I can have you whipped near to death for talking to me like that?"

"Massa, I didn't mean no onrespeck," explained Joshua. "But effen I had tuh fight Muscles I'd a bin kilt sure. It wuz de onlies' way I knew tuh run 'im off. He done figguh effen I could talk tuh you like dat I'd a toh his head off!"

Travelin' Man

Silas, a powerful young slave, was condemned to be whipped for bad-mouthing his master, but he had no intention of submitting to a beating that might cripple him or perhaps cost him his life.

As the slave-owner advanced with whip in hand, Silas walked forward and before the astonished plantation owner realized what was happening the whip was torn from his hand and thrown to the ground. As the other terrified slaves watched, Silas snarled, "Awright, Massa, put up yo' han's. We see who de bes' man is."

The owner backed off, absolutely horrified, and appealed to the cowering slaves. "Kill this nigger! You hear? A hundred dollars to anyone who kills him."

Silas let fly a punch. His huge fist, hard as concrete from a lifetime of bone-cracking work, exploded on the slave-owner's jaw. Then, with murder in his eyes, Silas raced from the plantation.

A few hours later, he came upon a regiment of Union troops and promptly joined the Yankee army. He explained at length why he had run away.

"So you hit your master—your *former* master?" asked the Union captain.

"I knock 'im cleah offen dis erf," Silas acknowledged.

"That must have been quite a punch," said the captain, smiling. "I don't suppose you know how long it took him to get back."

"Cap'n," answered Silas after giving the matter some thought, "effn it don' take no longuh tuh git back den it did tuh go, he done got back yestiddy!"

Slave Owner's Justice

Little John was not very tall in stature but he had a heart as big as an oak, and just as tough. The Civil War was still raging and he had heard rumors of President Lincoln's Emancipation Proclamation, but, in Mississippi, the glad tidings had done little to lighten the hearts of the blacks: a slave could be put to death for merely talking about it.

Little John, slave though he may have been, was also a *man*, by God! He approached the plantation owner. "Suh, I heah dat Massa Linkum done give de slaves ouah freedom. Kin I please have my 'mission?"*

"Why, you impudent black scoundrel!" roared the owner. He reached for his gun, faltered, and then offered an oily grin. "Tell you what I'll do, considerin' that I'm a gen'rous man. We caught an old wildcat last night and put him in a cage. Now, if you can whup that cat you go free. If not—" he shrugged, still grinning, "you'll have your freedom in the next world."

Little John nodded. "I'll fight 'im," he said.

Word of the coming contest spread like a grass fire on a windy day, and scores of people came to see the fight. At the designated time, five men leaped forward, seized Little John, tied his hands behind his back, bound his ankles together, and then buried him in the ground standing upright, so that only his head and neck were above the earth. Next, they turned the wildcat loose.

Snarling ferociously, the animal sprang at the helpless man's head, but Little John twisted his neck and as the great cat flew by he grabbed its tail in his mouth and bit so hard the beast cried out in pain.

The wildcat, now more cautious, began circling around Little John, and was just about to pounce again, when the slave-owner yelled, "If you want your freedom you better fight fair this time!"

↑   ↑   ↑

The technique of the bare-faced lie, coupled with an assumed look of angelic innocence, was one of the resources employed by many slaves to avoid punishment, gruelling work and other indignities. The black man, of course, is no more addicted to falsehood than members of any other race: the use of the lie arose from his deprivations rather than from any innate compulsion. A man will lie, cheat and steal to feed his family and himself when society refuses him the barest return for his labors. So it was with the slave.

The following stories represent the white man's reaction.

---

* Letters of Manumission were documents which certified that a slave had been released from bondage and was henceforth to be considered a free man or woman.

A Possum Sorter Squar' Like*

I bought from a Negro boy, in the days of slavery, at Jackson, Mississippi, what he said were two possums. Many masters allowed their slaves large liberty, and even encouraged them in such trafficking on their own account. One of the so-called possums was very large, the other quite small. The smaller one had been cut off at both ends—head and tail. I asked the boy why he had shorn it of its fair proportions, and he said:

"Well, boss, I had ter cut off 'is head 'cause I squashed it up mons'us bad when I kill 'im, an' mos' folks don't like possum tail much nohow, an' I cut dat off too so de possum'd look sorter squar' like."

Satisfied with this plausible lie, I paid the price and took the possums. I always knew that an experienced Negro could lie as adroitly as a white man, but I confess I was not expecting to find such originality and ingenuity in a mere child of either race.

By chance, Dr. Mitchell, a local scientist of some note, dined with us on the day we ate the abridged animal. When we had completely demolished the thing, except one piece which still remained on the dish, I discovered some peculiarity about the bones on my plate, of which there were not a few. So I said:

"Doctor, these don't look like possum bones."

He looked attentively at the bones on his own plate for a moment, and then said:

"All of you please pass your bones to me."

He was evidently getting interested. We all watched him in breathless suspense. He placed the bones together, studied them carefully for several minutes, and reluctantly accepted the only conclusion that was consistent with his knowledge of "bonology" and the facts before his eyes. Finally he said:

"Parson, this thing was a cat!"

His conclusion created a panic at the table. Mrs. Caskey beat a hasty retreat, the children laughed, the doctor looked non-plused, and I vowed vengeance upon the little black salesman. After the first shock of surprise and mortification, the practical elements of my nature asserted themselves. It was plain to see that apologies were useless. The cat was all eaten but one piece, and there could be no place found for repentance. Having set my hand to the plow, I was not the man to turn back. It was needless to hesitate or falter at that stage of the case. Procrastination is the thief of time. . . .

I wavered no longer, but boldly stuck my fork into the last remaining piece of the misrepresented animal, and quietly finished my meal.

---

* *Seventy Years in Dixie: Recollections and Sayings of T. W. Caskey*, pp. 114-118. F. D. Srygley, Publishers, 1878.

John Went Running*

Willis, a slave, states about one o'clock on the night the murder was committed, John (the accused) came to the shanty where they both slept, and John called Nathan out to take a drink with him, and Nathan returned, but John went off, and he did not see him any more until about one hour before daybreak next morning; that, on the day the inquest was held over the body, and John asked him, witness, where all these people were going, when he replied that they were going to have a jury and make all the railroad hands go before them and put their hands on the dead body, and that blood would follow the hand of the murderer; that John took off his cap and asked Nathan to take care of it; and then jumped over the fence around the shanty, and went off, running.

Sojourner Squelches a Squawker**

It was a pleasantly warm evening in Cincinnati, in the year 1853, and the lecture hall was thronged with people who had come to hear the famous platform speaker, Sojourner Truth, expound on her favorite subject, the Abolitionist movement.

When she had finished her lecture, a Southerner who was in full accord with the concept of slavery, aproached her and, sneering, commented, "You were wrong in everything you said. Why, without slavery, the Negroes would starve to death. They were *made* to be slaves. As far as I am concerned, you made no more impression than a flea-bite."

"I am sorry to hear that," replied Sojourner sweetly, "but perhaps, with God's help, I can keep you scratching!"

Aw Gee!—Only One "G"!

Not all black humor is created by the brothers, as illustrated in this little gem which dates back to 1861.

Gen. Algernon Winthrop, of the Sovereign State of Georgia, called on President Abraham Lincoln to plead the cause of slavery. "Unless you abandon your plan to free the niggers I will have to resign my command in the Union Army," he announced.

---

* *"John (a slave) v. the State"*—Reports of Cases Argued and Determined in the High Court of Errors and Appeals of the State of Mississippi, published by Charles C. Little and Joseph Brown, 1851, pp. 571-572. (24 *Mississippi*, Annotated Edition, St. Paul (West Publishing Company, 1909.)

** Sojourner Truth was a former slave girl who took her cause to the lecture platform and to the courts, becoming one of the most powerful abolitionist lecturers of the 19th century. Standing over six feet tall, herself illiterate, she nonetheless could captivate an audience and, when necessary, rebuff any hecklers with her sharp and telling rejoinders. Sojourner Truth settled in Battle Creek, Michigan, after the Civil War, but continued her lecture tours until a few years before her death in 1883, at the approximate age of 85.

BAKED 'COON

This recipe was contributed by Mrs. Mabel Washington, 85 years old, of Oakland, California. She conceded that old folks might not approve of her suggestion that 'coon or 'possum be wrapped in foil when roasting.

Prepared similarly to 'possum. Clean and soak in salted water, overnight. Season to taste, with salt, pepper and sprinkling of sugar. Wrap in aluminum foil and bake in a slow oven (350°) until tender. Juices of the 'coon can be used to make a water-and-flour gravy.

Suggested menu:

> Baked 'coon
> Collard greens
> Mashed potatoes and 'coon gravy
> Vegetable salad
> Corn bread

President Lincoln sat perfectly still for several moments and then rose from his chair. Walking across the room, he took down a dictionary from the bookcase and thumbed through it until he reached the *n's*. He then returned to his desk.

"Sir," the President said at length, "I just wanted some corroboration before making a reply, and I have found it. You are no longer a general, *Mister* Winthrop. No man can hold such high rank in the Union Army who spells Negro with two *g's!*"

Frederick Douglass Impresses a Deacon*

Generations of Negroes have enjoyed telling the story of the time Frederick Douglass made his famous speech in Rochester, New York, in the year 1852. Stately, eloquent of speech, forceful of manner, brilliant in his logic, he invariably drew large audiences whenever he used the platform to speak out against slavery.

On this occasion, he delivered his scathing oration, *What to the Slave is the Fourth of July?* His voice rose in passion as he thundered: ". . . your celebration is a sham; your boasted liberty an unholy license; your national greatness, swelling vanity. . . ."

Seated in the audience were the white minister and deacon of the local Rochester Baptist Church.

"That was a mighty fine speech—for a Negro," commented the deacon.

"Not when you consider that he's half white," said the minister.

"You don't say!" exclaimed the deacon. "Just think—if only half a Negro can speak that well, what could a whole one do?"

---

* Abolitionist, statesman, publisher, Frederick Douglass was born in February, 1817, in Talbot County, Maryland. At the age of eight, the young slave was sent to Baltimore where his mistress taught him to read and write. At the death of her husband, Douglass was sent to the country as a field hand, and, in his early teens, he began to teach in a Sunday school which was forcibly closed by hostile Southerners and Douglass severely flogged.

After making one unsuccessful attempt to escape, Douglass managed to make his way to New York disguised as a sailor. There, he soon found his true calling—leader in the anti-slavery crusade. As the years passed, he became an increasingly familiar figure to abolitionists throughout the country. In 1845, after having published his *Narrative* at great personal risk (that of re-enslavement as a fugitive), he went to England where he raised enough money through his lectures on slavery to buy his freedom. Upon his return to the United States he founded the famous newspaper, *The North Star*.

With the outbreak of the Civil War, Douglass met with President Abraham Lincoln and assisted him in recruiting the celebrated 54th and 55th Massachusetts Negro regiments. In 1871 he was appointed to the territorial legislature of the District of Columbia, and in 1877, after a term as police commissioner of Washington, D.C., he was appointed Marshal—a post he held until he was named Recorder of Deeds in 1881. Eight years later, he was appointed Minister Resident and Counsel General to the Republic of Haiti and, after that, Chargé d'Affaires for Santo Domingo. Frederick Douglass died in 1895, at his home in Washington, D.C.

NECK BONES

Another of Mrs. Mabel Washington's recipes of yesteryear. See page 47 for another one of her suggestions.

Neck bones may be of either beef or pork. As Mrs. Haggerty points out, you can boil, roast, barbecue, gravy or navy (bean) them. A selection of Mrs. Washington's favorite recipes follow:

Boiled Neck Bones

Wash thoroughly and season to taste, with salt, pepper and a pinch of sugar. Boil slowly until tender. Serve with:

> Green salad
> Candied sweet potatoes
> Corn bread

PART FOUR

THAT GREAT GETTIN' UP IN THE MORNING

(THE SLAVERY IS ENDED BUT THE MALADY LINGERS ON)

Capitalistic Heaven

The Civil War was over and old Bill was now free. But the attachment between his former owner and himself was so close that he refused to leave, preferring, instead, to remain and work for wages.

The ex-master was so touched he decided to give Bill a small plot of ground with a modest cottage on it, but he knew that the old man was too proud to accept charity, now that he was a free man. So he conceived a plan. He would see to it that Bill got the money to buy the place.

"Bill," he said, "I know you love the old homestead and I want to sell it to you at a reasonable price. You can have the house and lot for only two hundred dollars."

Bill shook his head sadly. "Whar I gonna git two hunnert dolluhs?"

"Trust in the Lord," replied the other, piously. "Just ask Jesus to send you the money, and he'll do it. He always answers prayers."

So Bill went down to the prayer tree in the orchard to ask for the divine gift.

Meanwhile, the kindly white man sacked up all the money he could accumulate on that particular day, a total of $199.90. He raced to the praying tree, arriving there ahead of the old man, and climbed to the highest branches. There he waited until, a few minutes later, old Bill made his appearance, sank to his knees, and prayed fervently.

High up in the tree, the former slave owner smiled and dropped the sack of money. Bill gazed at it as it lay on the ground and his eyes grew round with astonishment and awe. He gasped a "Thank you, Lawd," picked up the sack, and shuffled off to his quarters to count the money.

When he had finished, he rushed over to the main house. "Jesus done give it ter me!—Jesus done give it ter me!" he cried. Now I kin buy de house."

"Fine! Let's count it." Grinning to himself, the white man watched while old Bill counted out the money.

"Looks like you got cheated," said the former master. "You only got $199.90."

"Not cheated a'tall, boss," retorted Bill. "De Lawd give me what I ax fo'. He jes' charged me a dime fo' de sack!"

Quit Gummin' Yo' Food!*

The Union Army had just entered the city of Atlanta and the slaves of the Oglethorpe plantation were set free. All were deliriously happy, but Amos had his reservations. He was scolded by a Northern army officer. "Amos, I don't believe you realize that you are now a free man. You can go where you please, do as you please, eat what you please."

"I awready bin eatin' ez I please," grumbled Amos.

The officer was taken aback. "I wager, Amos, you never even tasted chicken before," he said.

"I eats chicken ev'ry Sund'y," maintained Amos doggedly. "An' whut's mo', Massa allus save me de tenderes' paht."

"What part is that?"

"De gravy, uv co'se!" said Amos.

Near Miss

"Thomas," the Kentucky Colonel said to his newly-freed cook, "I want you to get me a nice fat turkey for Thanksgiving. But make sure it isn't a wild one. I don't like the taste of wild game. Here's the money."

Thomas soon returned with an 18-pound turkey and, in due course, prepared it for the holiday festivities.

At the table, the Colonel took one bite and spat into his plate. "Thomas," he roared, "I told you to get me a domestic turkey. What's the idea of bringing me this wild one?"

"Dat ain't no wild tu'key, boss."

"Don't tell me that! I just spat out a bullet. Look—here's another bullet—and another—and another!"

"Boss," explained Thomas, "I sw'ar dat's a tame tu'key. When I tooken it off de roost dem bullets wuz meant fo' *me!*"

Semi-Divine Punishment**

Dat wuz a bad yeah in 'bama. De craps done fail an' us cullud folks hab mighty leetle ter eat. We's all free, but widout jobs an' money. We cain't go noplace nohow, so we stays an' wucks fo' boss Wilcox whut useter be ouah massa. He ack like we still slaves, but whut kin we do?

* *The Atlanta Constitution*, June 13, 1867. A similar story was included in a Ph.D. thesis by Vincent Quarles, Princeton University, 1899.

** As far as can be determined, this is the only story in Negro folklore in which a black man terrorizes a white man with a hood in the manner of the Ku Klux Klan, and represents a high degree of wishful thinking, considering the harsh codes which existed in the post-Civil War South. The tale dates back to 1869 and was published in a poorly-printed pamphlet by Simon Washburn (undoubtedly an alias), under the title *Stand Up and Shout.*

I say ev'ybody hongry, but hit ain' so. Big Nate an' Li'l Sam nevuh hongry caze dey got a supply uv hams an' coffee an' flouah ter las' de whole yeah froo.

Boss Wilcox, he git 'spicious caze he missin' zackly whut Big Nate an' Li'l Sam got so much uv. He go ter dey cabin an' see fo' hisse'f an' he madder'n a rile-up polecat. He say, "You bettuh 'splain hoccum you got all dese vittles wid my bran' stomp't on 'em er I gwine give you de wuss whippin' uv yo' life."

"You got no cause fer tuh fink we done stoled yo' vittles," say Big Nate. "We's 'ligious folks, boss. When we wants vittles we kneels down onduh de prayin' tree an' de Lawd pervides ouah needs."

Ol' Boss Wilcox he grine 'is teef an' say, "I gwine wid you. Ef'n de Lawd don' drap down de same vittles wid my bran' on 'em, I gwine skin yer alive."

But Big Nate an' Li'l Sam dey 'speckin' dis yere visit all de while an' dey done made dey plans. While Nate an' de boss walkin' ter de prayin' tree, Sam he skootch 'roun' de house an' sneak off ter de tree an' clum' up in de branches wid 'is ahms full uv vittles.

Bimeby Big Nate an' de boss come ter de tree an' de boss say, "Now, staht a-prayin', an 'membuh dat whut come outen dis tree bettuh have my bran' er yo' skin git strip off'n yo' back."

Big Nate he git down on 'is marrer bones an' ax de Lawd ter sen' a sign. Up in de tree, Li'l Sam he shake de branches an' moan *whooo-eee*, an' he drap a ham. De boss he see 'is own bran' stomp't on de meat an' he say, worry-like, "Mebbe we bettuh git outen heah."

But Nate, he say, "We gwine prove we hones', 'ligious folks whut don' go 'roun' stealin' no vittles. An' he pray loud, "Oh Lawd, sen' down a nuthuh sign, an' Sam he drap a bag uv flouah. Boss he git white in de face an' say, "Nate, le's git outen heah. I b'lieve you."

But Nate he don't let up, an' Sam frow down what Nate pray fo'.

Den de boss, he say, "I's leavin'. I ain't gwine whup you fo' whut de Lawd bin pervidin'."

But Nate, he 'sist one mo' time. He say, "Boss, I done prove I ain' bin stealin' yo' vittles—de Lawd done sen' 'em. Now I gwine ax de Lawd ter come down in pusson an' whup yo' tail ontwel you cain't set down fo' a week."

Wid dat, he pray, "Oh Lawd, git down heah an' give dis sinnah whut he 'zarve fo' holdin' back vittles when us folks am hongry."

Up in de branches, Sam he done put a sheet ovah his haid wid two holes fer ter see froo. He drap down, an' de boss fall flat on 'is face an' cry out, "I's a good man. I ain't evuh whup nobody 'ceppin nigguhs, an' dat don' count."

Li'l Sam, he say it *do* count. An' he lay de whip to dat mean ol' boss an' strip de skin off'n his back.

Arter dis, Boss Wilcox riz up off'n de groun' an' skootch all de way home an' he nevuh bothah us'ns no mo'.

Abraham Lincoln Asserts Himself

It was the first Juneteenth celebration in our nation's history, and little Abe, age seven, was all dressed up for the occasion.

"Do you know the meaning of Juneteenth?" asked a visiting preacher.

"Dat's de date we wuz sot free," replied Abe.

"And what is your name, little boy?"

"Abraham Linkum."

The preacher smiled. "Would you like to grow up to be like him?"

"Like who?"

"Abraham Lincoln."

The boy's face expressed his bewilderment. "But dat's who I is. Abraham Linkum—in pusson!"

Long Gone John

Le's see, now—mus' be neah 'bout thutty yeahs since I seed ol' John dat use'ter wuck on de Suwannee plantation. Hit w'ar a big place, 'bout a thousing acres down Geo'gia way neah de Flo'da line, an' 'longside de Okefenokee. I heah dat swamp strotch all de way ter Canady, but howsomevuh, it big 'nuff.

De Suwannee plantation b'long ter Massa Ogletho'pe. He a hahd man wid de slaves but sometime he like ter laugh an' play jokes. Dat hoccum John ter dis'peah inter de big Okefenokee. One Sund'y mawnin', Massa Ogletho'pe he pass by John's cabin an' he heah John prayin', "Sweet Jesus, sot me free so's I kin be a man! O Lawd, give me my freedom!"

Any othuh time, John he git a whippin' fo' sayin' dat. De slaves ain' even 'lowed ter talk ter Gawd dat way. But, 'stead uv de whip, Massa Ogletho'pe 'cide he gwine have some fun. So he sneak up ter John's windah an' he say wid a voice like a ghos', "John, dis is de Lawd. I come ter take you outen dis life an' sot you free in heaben."

John, he want his freedom in dis heah life, not in heaben, an' he shake an shivuh, an' den he moan, "Lawd, I done change my min'. I ain' in dat much a hurry."

But Massa Ogletho'pe havin' too much fun ter stop. He say, "John, ef'n you don' come outen dat cabin right now I's comin' in an' git you." He wait fo' a minute, den he say, "You done pray fo' yo' freedom an' dat's whut you kwine git."

John, he beg an' he cry an' he moan an' he groan, but hit ain' no use. So fin'ly he say, "Lawd, I's coming out, but stan' back jes' a mite when I come froo de do', caze I a sinnuh an' scairt uv gittin' too close ter yo' powah."

Massa Ogletho'pe laughin' fit ter bus', but quiet-like, so his po' scairt slave cain't heah. He open de do' an' he step back.

Zip!—Zap! Out de do' flew John, fas' ez lightnin', headin' fo' de big swamp. He run so fas' he make de dogs whut chasin' 'im look like dey stan'in' still. Massa Ogletho'pe he look at dat empty space whar John jes' bin, an' 'is mouf hang open. He know he done los' a thousing dollah slave.

Nobody evuh seed John ag'in. I heah tell he tu'k up wid de Senimole Injuns. An' sometimes, when de Norf win' am right, an' de night am real quiet, you kin heah a voice comin' fum deep inside de Okefenokee, an' dat voice sing soft an' melluh:

> "I got a spoon, a knife, a Injun wife,
> An' I own ev'y minute uv my free life;
> De gater he free, de mushrat he free,
> An' de coon an' de possum, same ez me.
> You heer'd me, Lawd, an' you come t' my call,
> So I counts my blessin's, an' I thanks Y'all!"
>
> —*Dan Sping*

PART FIVE

DOWN ON THE FARM

Alphie Hatches a Donkey

Grandma, bending over a large tub of laundry, was trying to be patient with her grandson, Alphie, age five, who repeatedly interrupted her labors with his nagging request for a baby donkey. At last she painfully straightened her weary back and faced the little boy. "Alphie," she said with a slight smile, "you go on ovuh to de punkin patch an' hatch yo'se'f out a donkey—jes' lak a chicken hatches out a aig."

A wide grin spread across Alphie's face and he raced to the garden, seated himself on a ripe pumpkin and hummed a little tune as he waited for it to hatch a donkey.

A half hour passed with no signs of life stirring within the pumpkin, and Alphie grew impatient. But as the time lengthened into an hour he finally jumped up, disgusted and disappointed. Aiming a kick at the pumpkin, he sent it careening off to one side where it rolled down an incline, hit a rock and was shattered by the impact. The commotion startled a rabbit. It jumped high in the air and then took off, in great, bounding leaps.

"Hey, git on back heah, li'l donkey!" yelled Alphie, giving chase, "I's yo' mammy!"

Rusting Rooster

Jones: There ain't nothin' lazier in the whole world than a mule.

Brown: Yes there is. I got a rooster that's so lazy he waits for another one to crow—and he nods his head.

Credit Where Credit Is Due

For years, Joseph Harris had dreamed of owning his own farm, but all he could save was just enough to buy a run-down, abandoned piece of scrub land. It had poor soil, was covered with a tangle of weeds and filled with rocks and stumps. But Joseph was a hard worker, and before long he had cleared the place of the debris, fertilized the soil, and was now enjoying a bumper crop of corn, peas, tobacco and cotton.

The local pastor visited him one day. "Brother Harris," he said, "I must say that you and the Lord have sure done wonders with this farm."

The farmer hesitated, smiled, and then nodded. "Yes, the Lord has been good to me, but . . ." he paused and then added, "you should have seen this place when the Lord had it all to Himself."

The Brighter Side

A country boy had just caught a rabbit and was walking down the road with the squirming little creature.

"Mistuh Rabbit," crooned the boy, "pretty li'l rabbit, sweet li'l rabbit, why you wigglin' so? I ain't gonna do nothin' but knock you upside yo' haid, an' skin an' cook you!"

No Profit in Progeny

The town of Delta had a new preacher, and the good man decided to make the rounds and visit members of his flock to get better acquainted.

His first call was at farmer Bill's place where he was ushered in and introduced to Bill's wife. But the preacher could scarcely make himself heard. At least ten youngsters, ranging in age from six months to twelve years, milled about the house.

"My goodness!" exclaimed the visitor, "You suttinly has a lot of good he'p fo' yo' fahm wuck."

Bill shook his head. "No, cain't say ez I do, beggin' yo' pahdon, Rev'n," he answered sadly. "In dese yere moduhn times, seems lak a man cain't raise chillun at a profit no mo'."

Cotton-Pickin' Chicken-Plucker

The unwarranted stereotype of the oldtime chicken thief is well illustrated in this example; circa 1890:

Grandpa arose early one morning, went outside, and noticed a note that had been tacked onto his cabin door. It read: *"If you don't stop stealing my chickens I'm going to skin you alive!"*

The old man grabbed the note and rushed to the sheriff's office. "Whut I gonna do 'bout dis?" he asked.

"You can stop stealing the man's chickens—for a start," suggested the sheriff.

"How I gonna know which man's chickens to stop stealin'?" Grandpa asked plaintively. "He didn't even sign his name."

Little White Lies

When you stop to think about it, white lies from a black man are usually nobler than black lies from a white man. Here is a case in point:

A farmer with a small but fertile piece of blackland acreage was out in the field one day when his old mule up and died. So he went to town and the white man who sold him a new mule said it was the most willing, gentle animal that had ever been born. Well, the farmer found out it was no such thing, but that's the way some white people are with blacks—you can't win for trying.

A couple of days later he took the mule out to start his spring plowing. He shouted, but that old mule wouldn't move. "Git on dar! Gee-Haw!— you mizzuble devil!" he yelled. But the mule refused to budge. "Move, you no-count, lazy, shif'less bag o' bones!"

Rev. Johnson, who had come to discuss some church business, heard all the shouting and walked to where the farmer was cussing out the mule. "Now, now," he said in soothing tones, "dat's no way to talk to one o' Gawd's li'l creechuhs. Let me try."

The preacher put his arm around the mule's neck and murmured lovingly, "Come, sweet chile o' Gawd; yo' innuh beauty am showin' right outen yo' pretty brown eyes. Move 'long now, you lamb o' goodness." In a moment, the mule started forward and pulled the plow willingly.

The preacher turned to the farmer. "See how easy it am widout all dat cussin' you wuz doin'?"

"Yeah, you didn't do no cussin'," agreed the farmer, "but how 'bout all dem lies you done tol'?"

Familiarity Breeds Reprisals

A prosperous farmer was seeking a man to handle livestock, and an aged man with wise old eyes applied for the job.

"Are you familiar with routine chores around a barn?" asked the farmer.

"Yes suh!" said the applicant.

"How about the stable? Are you familiar with horses?"

"I kin han'le hosses blinefolded."

"Good!" said the farmer. "One more question: Are you familiar with mules?"

"Suh," answered the oldtimer, "I know 'nuff 'bout mules t' *nevuh* git too f'milyuh wid 'em!"

Snake-Bite Remedy

The farmer had finished plowing the north section of his cornfield and he pulled up his mule alongside a little brook that ambled at the edge of his property. The mule lowered its head for a drink of cool, clear water, and the farmer withdrew a pint bottle of whiskey from a paper bag.

He took a long drink, pleasantly aware of the warm glow that diffused through his body. Then he took another, equally as large as the first. He was about to take a third drink from the bottle when a huge rattlesnake slithered into view, coiled up right in front of him and sounded its rattles.

Calmly, the farmer took another big swig. "Go 'haid an' strike, Mistuh Rattluh," he said. "I ain't nevuh bin mo' ready."

Who Says Mules Are Dumb?

Ever notice how a mule will sometimes stop and prick up its ears, and then get moving again? That's so he won't miss hearing *"whoa!"*

The Yule Mule

It was Christmas, and as a holiday gift Sam's neighbor gave him an old mule.

A few weeks later they met on the way to church. "Looka heah," complained Sam, "I 'preciates dat mule you gived me fo' Chris'mus, but it's blin' ez a bat. Cain't see nothin'!"

"Why you say dat?"

"Dat mule steps in holes, bangs his haid agin walls, walks intuh rocks an' trees. Blin', I tells yuh—blin'!"

"He ain't blin', Sam," the other said calmly. "I shoulda tol' yuh dis befo', but dat mule jes' don' give a damn!"

All Questions—No Answers

It was a very foggy night in Neckbone Junction, and two farmers were returning home after a day in town stocking up on supplies. Neither was aware that the other had also gone to town and that they were approaching home on different roads.

At the intersection of the two roads, one of the farmers spotted the vague outlines of the other looming darkly out of the foggy night. "Who dat?" he called.

The second farmer halted abruptly. "Who dat say 'who dat' "?

The silence was fearsome for a few moments. Then the reply rang out: "Who dat say 'who dat' when I say 'who dat' "?

Hoss Sense and Boss Sense*

Old Buck Hopkins, during his youth one of the top cowboys in all of Texas, was watching his grandson trying to break a horse. Each time the young fellow got astride the critter he would be tossed off. Old Buck watched in silence until his grandson was thrown for the fourth time. He could no longer remain quiet. It had been twenty years or more since he had attempted to break a horse, but a glimmer of his younger days sparkled in his eyes as he called out, "All right, boy; you watch *me!* I'll show you how to break that hoss!"

He mounted the animal, held on tight, and, exactly as he used to do so many years ago, he began to cuss it out—just to let it know who was boss. "Git goin', you no-'count, spavined animule! Start walkin' easy-like, you flop-eared, small-brain Mistuh Nothin'. You got a *man* on yo' back now, not a li'l boy!"

The horse took two steps forward, hunched its spine, and with one mighty leap threw old Buck from its back and into the dirt. He picked himself up, dusted his britches with his hat, turned to his grandson and said: "Now that's the way to do it! When you see the hoss is gettin' ready tuh th'ow yuh—*jump!*"

The Horse with the Strange Compulsions

In de spring o' 1879, plumb in de middle o' de plowin' season, Gran'pap's ol' hoss drop daid, widout no wahnin'. So Gran'pap he go intuh town tuh git 'im anuther'n.

Mistuh Goobuh, whut own de liv'ry stable, he say, "Gran'pap, I knows yuh ain't got but a few dolluhs, but I goin' sell you de stronges' wuck-hoss yuh evuh seed. He easy wuth a hunnuhd dolluhs but you kin have 'im fo' ten."

---

* The role of the black man in the opening of the Midwest, Southwest, and Far West has been largely ignored in the nation's popular novels, textbooks, motion pictures and television. The above story, *Hoss Sense on a Mule*, is not in the least unusual. According to *Man, Beast, Dust,* Clifford Westermeier's authoritative history of rodeo, Negro Bulldogger Bill Pickett founded the sport of bulldogging when, failing to drive a steer into the corral, he jumped from his horse, twisted the steer's head, clamped his teeth on the animal's lower lip like a bulldog and held on until the animal fell to the ground. Pickett's fame spread and he was hired to appear in rodeos throughout the west. In 1910 bulldogging became a regular rodeo feature.

SMITHFIELD HAM

Bill Pickett (see footnote opposite page) would rather eat ham than beef. "Ham fixed this way is what I call 'the ham what am!'"

Wash thoroughly. Soak in cold water for at least 18 hours, changing water several times during this period. Then boil in fresh water to which the following ingredients have been added:

1 cup brown sugar or molasses	1 cinnamon stick
8 peppercorns	few slivers lemon rind
3 bay leaves	1 whole peach
1 tablespoon Worcestershire sauce	1 cup apple cider
	celery tops

Boil gently, figuring about 25 minutes per pound of ham. Keep ham covered, adding boiling water when necessary. When cool, remove skin, but leave ¼ inch of fat (or more) on the ham. Set aside about a half cup of the liquid to make the crust.

To make the crust:

Add to the half-cup of ham-water, the following ingredients so as to form a paste: 3 egg yolks, ¼ cup brown sugar, 1 tablespoon Worcestershire sauce, 1 teaspoon dry mustard, 1 cup cracker meal. Spread the paste evenly all over the ham. Place in pre-heated oven (450°). Brown quickly until crust is golden. Slice very thin, when serving.

"Whuffo' you so good tuh me?" ax ol' Gran'pap, who don't tek no truck wid whites doin' favuhs fo' black folks.

"I tell yuh why. Dis hoss he got de damnes' habit you evuh heer'd tell. Whenevuh he see a aig he jes' natchly got tuh sot on it. He cain't he'p hisse'f. Dis heah's a aig-sottin' hoss."

Gran'pa, he say, "Effen he a good plow-hoss dat's all I cyah 'bout. Dey ain't no aigs in de fiel's nohow." So he buy de hoss 'caze de price so cheap.

He walkin' dat hoss back tuh de fahm when dey pass a white lady wid a basket o' aigs. Dat hoss went outen he min', he did. He knock de lady down an' she go sprawlin' feet ovuh neckbone, an' den he sot down on dem aigs an' bus' ev'y one. Gran'pap, he he'p de lady up an' pay fo' de aigs an' 'pologize an' den he git de hell outten dat place, fas' ez he kin git.

Soon dey come to de crick whut run 'longside Gran'pap's fahm, but 'stead uv follerin' him ovuh de bridge, dat hoss he jump intuh de watuh an' scrootch his behine down an' jes' sot. Aftuh a houah o' tryin' tuh move dat animule outten de crick, Gran'pap he run all de way back tuh de liv'ry stable an' he yell at Mistuh Goobuh, "What kine o' hoss you done solt me?"

"I tol' you de truf," say Mistuh Goobuh. "Dat hoss he sots on aigs."

"I ain't studyin' 'bout no aigs," say Gran'pap, madder'n a wilecat. "He done sot down in de crick an' I cain't git 'im outten de watuh."

"Oh!" say Mistuh Goobuh, like he jes' 'membuh somethin'—"I fo'got t' tell yuh: Dat hoss he also like tuh set on fish!"

A Rose by Any Other Name . . .

Down in the southern part of Georgia, along the Florida line, there was a little farming community called Yams. That's all, just Yams, a name given to their home town by the 85 people who lived there back in the 1890's.

For years, the farmers had been getting fewer and fewer returns on their crops, and this was the worst of all. Where an acre would produce ten bushels, it was now yielding four. Where it once yielded thirty, it now gave nine or ten.

But there was one farmer who was prospering beyond the wildest dreams of anyone in the entire area. He had actually increased his production so that his piece of land was giving many times more than anyone had a right to expect. Corn, sweet potatoes, peanuts, whatever he planted came forth in abundance, while his neighbor's fields yielded next to nothing. They begged him to tell them his secret, and he agreed. A meeting was arranged for that very night in the church.

"Ladies an' gennelmens," he began, his eyes sweeping over the assembled farmers and their wives, "I ain't really got no secret. The answer tuh bettuh crops is manure! Yuh heah me, my frien's? Manure, manure, an' mo' manure!"

In the audience, the preacher's wife leaned aside and whispered to the speaker's wife, "Chile, ain't you evuh gonna teach yo' husban' tuh say *fertilizuh?*"

"Listen," snapped the wife, "it done tuk me ten yeahs t' teach him t' say *manure!*"

Reciprocity

The city boy had never been outside of his hometown of New Orleans in his life, until one day he accepted an invitation from his country cousin to come for a visit.

A day or two after his arrival, the country cousin suggested that they go 'coon hunting. This was really something new for the city boy, and he gladly agreed. After several hours of tramping through the woods they grew hungry and decided to stop for lunch. "I'll build the fire," said the knowledgeable country cousin. "You take this bucket and get some water from that spring over yonder."

A few minutes later the city boy return, but with the bucket empty and his eyes wide as saucers.

"Why didn't you bring the water?" asked the country cousin.

"Man, you wouldn't either, if you saw what I saw."

"What did you see?"

"A great big alligator. It musta been ten feet long. It looked like it could swallow a man with one bite."

The country cousin laughed. "Don't you go worryin' 'bout no 'gators," he said reassuringly. "He's more afraid of you than you are of him."

"Well, if that's so," replied the city boy, "that water ain't *fit* to drink!"

Aunt Margaret's Surprise

Roy had worked hard all year on the farm and had saved up a tidy sum of money. "I think I'll go surprise Aunt Margaret," he said to himself.

He was walking through town when he passed a livery stable. "I think I'll buy me a horse and wagon, and surprise Aunt Margaret," he repeated.

While driving the wagon he passed a clothing store. "I think I'll buy me a new suit, a new shirt, a new pair of shoes and some new underwear, and surprise Aunt Margaret," he said.

Once again seated atop the wagon, with all the new clothes neatly wrapped in a big box beside him, he headed for the next town, where Aunt Margaret lived. For the first few miles it was hot but fairly pleasant. But soon the heat grew oppressive and the roads increasingly dusty. He was feeling quite uncomfortable when suddenly, as he rounded a bend in the road, he came upon a secluded stream. The water looked so cool and inviting that he stopped the horse. "I think I'll take a bath and put on all my nice new clothes and surprise Aunt Margaret."

Whistling gaily, he gathered up all his dirty old rags and threw them into the stream, playfully waving them goodbye as they floated away. He splashed around in the water for awhile and his feeling of well-being was so intense that he let out a shout of pure joy, laughing loudly with the exuberance of youth.

Unfortunately, however, the shouting and laughter frightened his horse and the animal sped away; wagon, new clothes and all, disappeared into the distant hills.

"Oh well," he said philosophically, crawling back to dry land, his naked body glistening in the sun, "I think I'll go on anyway, and surprise Aunt Margaret."

PART SIX

OLD FOLKS AT HOME

Never Too Old

A delegation from the church approached the aged, work-gnarled man sitting on the top step of his little house in the country.

"Good evenin'," said the leader of the three-man committee, "Brother Brown Sr.?"

"No, I'm Junior," corrected the old man. "You want my father. What's he done?"

"Not a thing. We are honoring him as our oldest member, that's all."

"Well, you can find him down at the crick, takin' a bath."

"Ain't that mighty dangerous for a man his age?" asked the committee spokesman. "He must be ninety-five years old."

"Yeah, that's his age, all right. But he has t' take a bath. Pa's fixin' t' get married."

"Married! Isn't he too old to want to get married?"

"Well," Brown Jr. drawled, "it ain't that he *wants* t' get married—he *got* to."

Speak for Yourself!

Bent and white-haired Uncle Moses was brought before the Rev. Shelby Wyatt of the Hope To Rise Again Baptist Church. A neighbor had complained that the old man was annoying his wife.

"Now looka heah, Moe," scolded Rev. Wyatt, "you mus' be gettin' on tuh eighty—almos' ez ol' ez me. Ain't you got no shame—a man yo' age?"

"I ain't bin botherin' no woman," said Moses in his cracked voice. "You oughtuh know, yo'se'f, Revun. At ouah age, we cain't do nothin' ceppin set on de po'ch an' rock an' sech."

Rev. Wyatt sat bolt upright, his face hardened in indignation. "Speak fo' yo'se'f, Brothuh Moses," he spat. "Speak fo' yo'se'f!"

Hope Springs Eternal...

Old Acey and his two young neighbors had enjoyed a good day of fishing, and now, gathered around the oldtimer's woodstove, their plates heaped with golden fried morsels of perch, trout and catfish that once were abundant in that area of the Mississippi river, they began the usual small talk.

"In all mah fo'ty-nine yeahs, Ah nevuh seed sech good fishin'," said one of the neighbors.

"Is dat how ol' you be?" asked the other. "Ah figg'd you t' be no mo'n thutty-five. Me, Ah'm fifty-eight."

The first neighbor then turned to old Acey and asked his age. Acey scratched his head and pondered the question before answering. "Ez neah ez Ah kin figguh," he said uncertainly, "Ah mus' be goin' on ninety-nine."

They stared at him, their mouths agape and their fish fry momentarily forgotten. "Man, you sho' don't look it. You ma'ied?"

"Sho'! Bin ma'ied six times. Got papuhs on one of 'em."

"How many chilluns yuh got?"

Again there was silence as Acey made a few rapid calculations. "Reckon Ah got right 'roun' nineteen, mo' o' less." He rubbed his chin reflectively, and continued, "Mah oldes' mus' be gittin' on tuh sixty, an' mah younges' is three months ol'."

The two younger men looked at him with increased respect. "Acey," asked one, "you mean tuh say you almos' a hunnuhd yeahs ol' an' you have a baby jes' three months?"

Old Acey gave a slow, shy smile. "Yas, Ah *hopes!*"

Stamp of Approval

We don't believe this one either, but according to the postmaster in Culpepper, Virginia (and he doesn't lie much, except when he's drinking heavy), Grandma Wicks entered the postoffice and asked for a book of stamps.

"What denomination?" asked the clerk.

"Same ez me," replied Grandma. "Baptis'!"

Horns of a Dilemma

Grandma was getting mighty worried about her husband. After all, they were getting along in years. Grandma would never tell her exact age, but her husband was at least eighty.

"Now you listen t' me," she scolded. "It's high time you stahted goin' tuh chu'ch an' mendin' yo' wicked ways. Ain't gonna be long befo' de Lawd calls, an' den whut yuh gonna do?"

But Grandpa would just laugh. "I don't b'lieve in dat stuff."

One day, however, when the old lady was more vehement than usual, he patted her on the shoulder and, repressing a grin, he said, "T' tell de truf, I bin studyin' 'bout Heavun, but dere one thing botherin' me."

"Ain't no botherin' in Heavun," muttered Grandma.

"Sho' dere is. Tell me, how I gonna git my shirt on ovuh my wings?"

Grandma stared at him as though he had lost his senses. Then she sighed. "Dat ain't yo' worry, ol' man. All you got tuh study 'bout is how you gonnat git yo' hat on ovuh yo' ho'ns."

Plessis Confesses How
He Dresses His Tresses

It isn't often that the title is almost as long as the story, but here is a worthwhile example.

Old man Plessis arose early on New Year's Day and took his stance in front of the mirror. "Ah'll nevuh onnuhstan' how in de name of Gawd othuh folks combs dey haiah ev'y day," he muttered. "Ah don't comb mine but wunst a yeah, an' den it mos' kills me!"

Down Memory Lane

These two old guys, both in their nineties, were sunning themselves on the porch. It was a warm, summer day and the two oldtimers were discussing their youthful adventures.

"You reckerleck how we use t' set on dis heah same po'ch when we wuz young, an' whistle at de gals?"

"Yas, Ah sho' does. Dey had sech purty dresses in dem good ol' days. Ah 'membah how we use t' look at deir swingin' bottoms."

"Ah reckerlecks dat too," said the other. "Whut Ah cain't 'membah is *why!*"

It's a Long, Long Time,
From May to December

It was Grandpa Jones' ninetieth birthday and he was indulging in a bit of excusable boasting:

"I can still do all the things I used to do sixty or seventy yeahs ago," he bragged. . . . "I jes' don't feel like it!"

All God's Chillun Got Troubles

Ike and his buddy of fifty years were discussing the problems of old age as they sipped a beer at the corner tavern.

"I dunno whut I gonna do," said Ike. "Nobody wants t' hire a ol' man like me. "I'm broke, no money comin' in, an' the jobs I do git I ain't much good at."

"Ain't you got a trade or somethin'?" asked the friend sympathetically.

"Well, I wuz a preachuh in my younguh days."

"Hey, man—you got it made! Why don't you go back to preachin'?"

Old Ike shook his head. "No, I don't think so," he said, a sad note in his voice. "I wuzn't much good at that, nuthuh."

One-Way Grandma

Grandma was one of the oldest women in the south, having been born soon after the close of the Civil War. Now, her great, great, granddaughter was getting married in New York and the old lady was about to take her very first ride on a train, to attend the ceremony up north.

She was seated in a car, but with her back to the engine. When the train began to move she frantically summoned the conductor.

"Git me offen dis yeah train!" she demanded shrilly. "I ain't ridin' de way I'm goin'!"

PART SEVEN

MAGNOLIAS AND MINT JULEPS— WITH VINEGAR

When Discretion Is the Better Part of Valor

Venerable old John was trudging through the woods, anxious to be home after a hard day's work. It had grown quite dark, and he was thinking of nothing in particular except a hot meal, when suddenly he heard the sound of men cursing, the moaning of a man in pain, and then the sound of heavy blows and more cursing. He stepped behind a tree and watched. In a few moments he saw a group of men dragging a half-unconscious black man. Around the victim's neck was a rope.

Old John recognized the appalling scene for what it was—a lynching party. Terrified, he held his breath and remained stock still. But the sinister group halted just a few yards away and completed their grisly business. Just as they were about to leave, they spied old John and dragged him into their midst.

The leader of the killers fingered the length of rope significantly, as though ready to lynch John right then and there. "You ever say one word about this and we'll give you the same treatment," he rasped.

"Nevuh a wuhd!" said John, choking.

"Anyway, that black bastard deserved getting lynched," added the leader.

"He sholy did," agreed old John, trembling. "I's surprised you let 'im off so easy!"

Native Intelligence

Back around the turn of the century, the governor of Mississippi was driving along a remote country road in a horse-drawn buggy. He was making a rather sharp turn when one of the shafts broke. Completely at a loss as to how to repair it, he waited for help. It was almost three hours later when a young boy came sauntering by.

"Boy," called the governor, "can you fix this shaft?"

"Sho', boss," said the youth, grinning. He set about his task with sure knowledge and dexterity, peeling long strips of hickory bark and cutting two flat pieces of wood. With these he made a crude but perfectly serviceable splint. When finished, the shaft was about as strong as it had been before the break.

"Boy, do you know who I am?" asked the governor.

"No suh."

"I am the highest elected official in the entire state of Mississippi—the Governor! My daily decisions affect the lives of a million people. Yet, you have done something that, with all my power and importance, I could not do. Tell me, boy, how do you account for that?"

"I don't rightly know, suh," replied the boy. "I reckon its 'cause some folks is bo'n wid sense an' some ain't!"

Liberty and Justice for All— Alabama Style

No matter what you say about Birmingham, you can't deny that it is a city which earnestly believes in justice. Take this story, for example.

Judge Witherspoon rounded the corner of Courthouse Square, and there, under the Hanging Tree, was a mob preparing to lynch a young black lad.

"Hold, on there!" shouted the Judge as he hurried over to the group.

"Are you gonna besmirch the name of our fair city with these carryin's-on? Are you gonna do somethin' that will bring down the wrath of the damyankee press on our innocent heads? No, my fella suthanuhs, you must not lynch this man without a proper trial. We gotta do this legal. First give him a fair trial—*then* lynch him!"

Black History in Two Paragraphs

A New Yorker, born and raised in Harlem, went to visit his relatives in a small Mississippi town. But as soon as he arrived, he noticed the complete absence of any other black people. He turned to a white man standing nearby. "Where do all the colored folks hang out in this town?"

The stranger pointed to a big oak tree in front of the court house. "See that limb. . . ?"

Dis Heah Yeah Heah

Miss Rosetta Clark, fifth grade teacher in a Chicago school, volunteered to teach an adult class in Mississippi during her summer vacation.

"I must warn you," said her principal, "the Delta people have a very pronounced and unique dialect. You may not be able to understand them."

"Don't you worry about that, sir," Miss Clark smiled. "I believe I've heard just about every dialect our people use."

Upon her arrival she was presented to the local school board and the minister of the village's only church. At once she was invited to the parsonage where the minister's wife attempted to set the northern schoolteacher's mind at ease.

"Honeychile," said the good woman, "Ah heah dis heah yeah heah am yo' fus' yeah heah!"

Who's On First?

Passenger: Hey, Porter! How come this train is slowing down?
Porter: Suh, de train befo' is behine an' we wuz behine befo' besides.

The Dixie Liberal

A Southern senator retired after some thirty years in Congress. Having long grown accustomed to Washington, D. C., he remained there rather than return to Dixie. This evening, he was reminiscing with a group of cronies in the exclusive, lily-white Cosmos Club.

"Ah want y'all t' know that Ah have always had the hahyest reegard for mah Nigra constitchints," he said between puffs of billowing cigar-smoke.

"And why not? Ah had a black mammy as a small chee-ild. Ah have known Nigras in every walk of life. Among mah intimate frien's, Ah can numbah such famous people as Ralph Bunche, Thurgood Mahshall, Mahtin Luthuh King, Marion Anduhson, Cassius Clay and many othah fine Nigras—all a credit to their race."

"You should write a book about them," suggested a listener.

"Funny you should mention that," said the Dixiecrat grandly. "Ah'm thinkin' of doin' that very thing. Ah'm gonna call it *Nigguhs I Have Known!*"

Caucasian Nightmare

A small-town cracker was raking the leaves on his front lawn when he saw a black man strolling by.

"Hey, boy, you finish this here rakin' mah lawn an' Ah'll give you a quahtuh an' a slice o' watuhmelon."

The stranger regarded him coolly, and then replied, "Sir, the present inflationary trend in our economy precludes any such exchange of my labor for an emolument of only twenty-five cents and the watermelon you gratuitously offered. Should the trend reverse itself, and my own financial condition suffer as a consequence, I shall at that time reconsider your offer. Meanwhile, sir, if you so desire, you may rake the leaves from *my* lawn, but unfortunately our family does not care for watermelon, so I have no alternative but to offer you a curmudgeon."

The cracker, mouth agape and eyes wide in utter astonishment, stumbled back into his house, bawling for his wife. "The sunstroke done got me," he gasped. "I wuz standin' out there rakin' the lawn when I musta fell unconscious, 'cause I had the gawdamnest dream you evuh heard!"

Progress

Just think—It was only yesterday that a black man in the South could call a Dodge a Dodge, a Chevrolet a Chevrolet, a Cadillac a Cadillac. But not a Ford. He had to call it *Mister* Ford. . . .

And God help him if he didn't have a good excuse for singing *White Christmas.*

2

PLANTATION
to
EMANCIPATION

Introduction

PART ONE:
Juneteenth[1]

PART TWO:
Humorous Folk Tales of the
South Carolina Negro[2]

PART THREE:
John Tales[3]

PART FOUR:
Aunt Dicy Tales[4]

PART FIVE:
The Word on the Brazos[5]

PART SIX:
Worser Days and Better Times[6]

---

[1] "Juneteenth," J. Mason Brewer, from *Tone the Bell Easy*, copyright 1932, Texas Folklore Society.

[2] *Humorous Folk Tales of the South Carolina Negro*, copyright 1945 by J. Mason Brewer. Published by the South Carolina Negro Folklore Guild, Claflin College, South Carolina.

[3] "John Tales," by J. Mason Brewer, from *Mexican Border Ballads*, copyright 1946, Texas Folklore Society.

[4] "Aunt Dicy Tales," from *Snuff-Dipping Tales of the Texas Negro*, J. Mason Brewer, copyright 1956.

[5] *The Word on the Brazos*, J. Mason Brewer, copyright 1953, University of Texas Press.

[6] *Worser Days and Better Times*, J. Mason Brewer, copyright 1965, Quadrangle Books, Inc.

BOOK TWO

Plantation to Emancipation

Introduction

J. Mason Brewer, considered the nation's most illustrious black folklorist, comes to this Encyclopedia with impeccable credentials, having published seven highly-acclaimed volumes of folk tales. Additionally, more than 450 of his anecdoes have been published in various periodicals and anthologies, including the 86 stories which appear in the following section, *Plantation to Emancipation*.

Born in Goliad, Texas, in 1896, his grandfathers, both wagoners, hauled farm tools, lumber, groceries and other cargo from Victoria, Texas, to merchants in Goliad and Mission Refugio long before the advent of the railroads. His father, J. H. Brewer, was a cowboy and assistant trail boss who drove cattle from the Santa Rosa, or Media Luna Ranch, in Hidalgo County, owned by Colonel D. R. Fant, to Fort Supply in the Indian Territory during the trail driving days. "It was from the lips of these three that I heard, as a child, fascinating and dramatic stories of early life in Texas," he wrote in his *The Word on the Brazos*. "From them stemmed the resolution that some day I would collect and record some of the Texas Negro's folk tales."

A *Doctor of Letters*, Brewer received his Bachelor's degree from Wiley College and his Master's from Indiana University, where he studied under the renowned folklorist, Stith Thompson. In the vanguard of his people, he has challenged and surmounted obstacles which heretofore prevented black scholars from attaining membership in formerly all-white organizations, thus opening doors of opportunity for younger Negroes to enter. He is the only black member of the Texas Institute of Letters, and the only black to serve

ROAST HAM

This recipe for roast ham calls for Worcestershire sauce. The addition of this condiment, many connoisseurs of soul food agree, makes for a distinct improvement.

1 fresh ham, 5 to 7 pounds
Salt and pepper to taste
2 garlic cloves
2 small onions, chopped
1 tablespoon Worcestershire sauce

⅓ cup lemon juice and water
1 tablespoon sugar
1 teaspoon paprika
½ cup vinegar
¼ cup catsup purée

Mix all the ingredients except the garlic cloves, salt and pepper. Trim off all excess fat and skin from ham. Make small incisions in meat with a sharp knife and insert peeled, thin slices of garlic. Sprinkle with salt and pepper. Place fat side down in open roasting pan and cook in moderate oven for one hour. Remove from oven and drain off fat. Cover with the vinegar, onion, purée mixture and return to the oven. Baste with the drippings every 20 minutes until tender. Allow 40 minutes per pound of ham.

on the Research Committee and Council of the American Folklore Society. (In 1954 he was Second Vice President of that organization.) Currently, Dr. Brewer is associated with the Advisory Council of the National Folk Festival, Washington, D.C., and is First Vice President of the North Carolina Folklore Society. Recently he was elected to life membership in the Louisiana Folklore Society.

Dr. Brewer's use of ethnic dialect and his authentic portrayals of the Negro in his proper setting and circumstance mark him as a man of deep compassion and as a writer of integrity. Folklore is not propaganda to be rewritten at will to meet the psychological and political needs of each generation. The historian must record the experience of each, while maintaining, intact, those of previous eras if there is to be a reliable history embodying continuity and authenticity.

The experiences of the poor and downtrodden are seldom noted in our textbooks, race notwithstanding. We are indebted to J. Mason Brewer for contributing so much to the history of one segment of the inarticulate and oppressed in America.

The 86 anecdotes which comprise *Plantation to Emancipation* are unique in several respects. We are at once struck with the recognition of a recurrent pattern: The comparative well-being of the slave, if not his very survival, often depended upon his ability to think quickly—and in his own interests. Objective thought, for him, was in the exclusive province of the white man who was free to exercise any number of options. The slave and his descendants who fell victim to the Black Codes and subsequent legal and illegal indignities had no alternative but to think *sub*jectively, knowing, as they did, that, for them, *justice* meant "just us."

But glibness of tongue merely to escape punishment could not long satisfy the yearnings of the hapless blacks, and they found themselves using their wits, not alone to maintain the status quo, but to turn unfavorable situations to their own material advantage. J. Mason Brewer presents several examples of "maintaining the status quo," in which the protagonists, although making no tangible gains, emerge victorious by winning on points.

In *How Uncle Steve Interpreted Spanish,* the central character induces his master to take him to Mexico on a horse-trading expedition, on the assumption that the slave is fluent in Spanish—though he speaks not a word of that language. How Uncle Steve overcomes the various challenges in his "Spanish" dialogue with a Mexican whom they meet by chance provides a hilarious episode, but the tale makes its unspoken point: Uncle Steve is permitted to continue on what for him is a vacation from the hard work on the plantation . . . and he has escaped the whipping he would surely have received had his master learned that his slave had outwitted him.

Again, in *Uncle Israel and the Law,* the central character is tricked by the local constable into a near-admission that he has been stealing chickens. Uncle Israel, whose mind and tongue are synchronized to work with lightning speed, talks his way out of a prison term. Thus, the status quo has been maintained.

Material gain, the logical next step or progression from the status quo anecdote, is seen in such tales as *A Laugh That Meant Freedom*, one which has been told and re-told in many versions. In this instance a slave breaks the chains of bondage by making his master laugh against his will. In the very funny story, *Uncle Bob's Voyage to New England*, we find an attempted material gain that boomeranged. Here, the oldest slave on the plantation decides to escape to the North via the water route. Expecting the tides to carry him to freedom, he goes to sleep in a rowboat and is surprised to find that, upon his awakening the next morning, the "Northerners" know his name. The "material gain" inherent in the story lies in its implications. The anecdote presents a perfect wedding of fact and humor as it illustrates a point often overlooked by teachers and students of black history: The longing for freedom that culminated in flight to the North was not necessarily confined to the younger, more hardy slaves, but to the old as well. One can almost visualize the free soul in captivity as a bird without wings. The thought is sweetly conveyed in an old plaintive melody, *Saturday Night and Sunday Too*, full of beauty, expressing the ideas and images that can fill a man's mind when he is permitted a brief respite from work:

> *Saturday night and Sunday too,*
> *True love on my mind;*
> *But Monday mornin' good and soon,*
> *The white man's got me goin'.*
>
> *Redbird sittin' on a sycamore limb,*
> *Singin' out his soul;*
> *A big black snake crawled up that tree*
> *And swallowed that poor boy whole.*
>
> *Bluejay pulled a four-horse plow,*
> *Sparrow, why can't you?*
> *"Because my legs is little and long*
> *And they might get broke in two."*
>
> *Wild geese flyin' through the air,*
> *Through the sky of blue;*
> *They're now a-floatin' where the south wind blows,*
> *So why not me and you?*

Scrupulous attention to local color is invested by Brewer in his stories, notably in his *Humorous Folk Tales of the South Carolina Negro*. Here, we learn of a little known group of people called "Brass Ankles," native to Summerville, and which makes for fascinating as well as amusing reading. In *Little Ernest's Grammar Lesson* we are introduced to the blacks of the Pee Dee River section and their favorite expression, "putting in time." This, we see, alludes to the season when tobacco leaves are gathered and put into the barns to be cured. It is then that the workers make most of their money, and it is a time of joy.

As in so many of his anecdotes, we find in *How Uncle Ezra Freed Himself* a superb fusion of history, local mores, humor, and, once again, the slave's propensity to think on his feet. The story is told against the background of the indigo industry in Marion County when planters would meet slave-trading boats on the Little Pee Dee River and trade indigo for slaves—pound for pound. And we learn of the cotton and pecan industries of Orangeburg County; the "suitcase teachers" in the rural areas of South Carolina who pack their suitcases every Friday so that they can return home for the weekend; the peculiar institution known as the "praise-house," on St. Helena Island; the Reform Methodists of Clarendon County, a group who pulled out of the original African Methodist Church because the mother church was too liberal with what they considered to be the truth.

There is a mass of detail in *Humorous Folk Tales of the South Carolina Negro,* the result of Dr. Brewer's painstaking attention to background data. As president and founder of the South Carolina Negro Folklore Guild, he delegated the Jeanes teachers (as deputy collectors of the Guild) to interview "informants" throughout the state, in quest of suitable, authentic lore. The collectors and informants are identified as annotations to each of their respective stories. Jeanes teachers, it should be noted, are those employed as supervising teachers of rural teachers. Some of their duties are: to introduce simple home industries; to promote improvement of school houses and grounds; and to organize clubs for the betterment of the school and neighborhood. Participating in this program were all 36 of the Jeanes teachers, presiding over 36 of the 46 counties and touching 2,000 or more of the rural Negro schools in the state. Farmers, teachers, preachers and rural pupils alike, as collectors or informants, contributed to this collection. The carefully preserved simplicity of the stories will be understood when it is remembered that they were gathered and edited by Dr. Brewer with a view to launching an intercultural reading program, to inform as well as entertain school children, and to preserve local lore. The delightful *Question and Answer Tall Tales of Negro School Children* are presented in the exact words of the children themselves, while the other tales have been rewritten by Brewer and localized for the sake of verisimilitude as well as for the reader's amusement.

Part Four, *Aunt Dicy Tales,* provides an insight to the newly freed slave, but we are also introduced to an endearing (and we believe enduring) woman who emerges as one of the most dominant characters in Negro folklore. A former slave, Dicy Johnson, refused to chop cotton for her former master so, together with her husband and three small children, she struck out on her own. The strong-willed, snuff-dipping young Dicy made a home for her family and managed to earn and save enough to buy a farm; later, to send her daughters to college. The six stories anthologized here represent progressive eras in her life—a life full of joy and pathos, told with a rare depth of feeling and empathy by her creator, J. Mason Brewer.

The reader will not soon forget Dicy's retort when her pastor warns of the consequences of dipping snuff: ". . . you've done stopped preaching and gone to meddling," or that the town of Dime Box derived its name from Aunt Dicy's fondness for a certain "dime box" of snuff. Indeed, she is a composite of all the courageous black women who walked hand-in-hand with their menfolk and who soared on eagle's wings to that high plateau called Emancipation. One identifies with her because her one vice as well as her many virtues are noted with such compassion as well as humor. It is very easy to love Dicy Johnson.

"Hit tecks lots of patience to deal wid a sinnuh at de mounah's bench. Dey hab a haa'd time comin' thoo 'caze dey ain't yit ready to jar loose from dey sinful acks." So begins *The Word on the Brazos*. Here are the trials and tribulations of the dedicated preachers who spread the Word throughout the Brazos River Bottoms, in Texas. We meet preacher Whirlwind Johnson, Elder Cyclone Williams and other colorful champions of the Lord as they struggle to maintain their churches and to guide the footsteps of their flocks along the narrow path that leads to the Pearly Gates. Most of the stories in this collection stem from the half-century immediately following Emancipation, and have found favor among historians and folklorists as well as those who simply enjoy charming, humorous, stories skillfully told. First published in 1953, and now in its fourth printing, *The Word on the Brazos* was acclaimed by *The New York Times* as one of the finest collections of Negro folk tales since *Uncle Remus*."

The religious tale, Brewer reminds us, antedates the coming of Christ. In medieval Europe, short narratives employed to illustrate or confirm a moral were called "exempla." In the 14th century, the use of the exemplum in the pulpit grew so widespread that serious opposition was registered against it by Chaucer, Dante, John Wycliffe and other writers. Protest against the use of this form of narrative by churchmen caused it to suffer rapid decline in the 16th century, although it remained in use both in England and on the European continent until a much later date.

The sending of Francis Asbury to America in the year 1771 to propagate the faith of John Wesley was indirectly responsible for creating a situation that stimulated the use of exempla in this country, explains Brewer in his introduction. Through early experimentation, Asbury and the frontier preachers associated with him learned that the best way to hold their audiences was by the frequent use of anecdote. Lorenzo Dow, who was delegated to expand the cause of Methodism in the South, was also aware of the practicality of the comic tale, and used it to impress his scattered congregations. Dow's contemporaries of the Baptist and other creeds likewise adopted the anecdote as a device for clinching a sermonly point.

Brewer concedes that Negro religious tales fail, in many instances, to conform to the pattern of the traditional exempla and fall short of the requirements that would qualify them to be classed with the moralizing or illustrative tale of antiquity. Nevertheless, he writes, they have one character in common with this particular genre of folk-narrative—the attribute of entertainment.

Brazos Bottom Negro preacher tales, although humorous in nature, are not meant to convey the idea that the Brazos Bottom Negro preacher and his followers did not take their religion seriously. They were devout and sincere Christians even though their religious tales were often satirical. These tales followed the pattern of a popular folk tale type found in the oral literatures of other ethnic groups—a device invented by the masses to lampoon their leaders and others in authority. The preacher has always been the acknowledged leader in the Negro community, and as such he has been the target of many witty stories told by his followers. The tales concerning "the Word" on the Brazos are indigenous examples of this type of folk expression.

The stories in this collection were culled in the bottom lands along the banks of the Brazos River in Central and South Texas. Because of the fertility of the soil in this section, pioneers were early attracted to settle here and establish extensive plantations. Stephen F. Austin, the colonizer of Texas, planted his first families around old Washington, on the Brazos River. Other settlements soon followed, and almost simultaneously slave labor was introduced to plant, cultivate and harvest the crops. Thus, the Negro became a part of the land, worked it, and drew life from it. Some of the largest plantations in this district were located in Falls, Robertson, McLennan, and Washington Counties.

Today, in the Brazos Bottoms, few vestiges of the old plantation life remain, Dr. Brewer concludes. The times that these tales tell about have almost passed into oblivion. But the original Brazos Bottom Negro has left his tracks in the soil, enriched it with his dust, and flavored it with what we call, in a broad sense, his culture.

The 22 anecdotes selected from *Worser Days and Better Times* considers the Negro folk materials of post-bellum North Carolina. The author did not cull these tales from the writings of other folklorists but created a distinctive literature of his own by traveling more than six thousand miles within the state, visiting practically every county and township, and talking with Negroes of every class and age group, with both the inter- and intra-cultural aspects of their lives revealed and recorded. Many indigenous characteristics consistently manifested themselves in the wealth of material he gathered in his extensive, statewide journeys.

A number of these characteristics constitute the focal points of Brewer's stories, around which he wraps the raiment of humor; for it must always be remembered that some social, political, economic or "protest" factor lies at the heart and core of the anecdotes. Occasionally, a tale will be simply informative, describing a pattern of life—a way of existence, a means of survival in a hostile environment; a story that instructs as it entertains. It is within the walls of his own fortress—the bailiwick of the educator—that Brewer evokes a pang to the soul, a smile to the lips, and a visual, compelling picture to the brain.

The "preacher tale" syndrome, for example, is the antithesis of the tales which appear in *Parables in Black*, Book Three of this volume. Brewer introduces a gentle type of humor which may be directed at the congregants or the various programs and beliefs of the church, but seldom at the preachers themselves. This is especially true of such folk tales as *How the Preacher Broke Up the Church*, *The Preachers and the Cab Driver* and *Both Were Proud*.

The latter story employs a once-popular, but now fast-disappearing literary methodology: the use of the dramatic story in tandem with the animal tale. The mirth-provoking account is designed to deflect the pardonable pride of the parents in their two sons who have been ordained in the ministry, and to transfer that pride to the rooster and hen who are the parents of the young fryers which were served to the ministers for dinner. Thus, the barnyard fowls are prideful of the fact that their offspring, too, have "entered the ministry."

Nevertheless, the cold realities of life are always with us, as illustrated in *The Preacher and the Runaway Lion*. In this instance we meet a Durham preacher whose faith in the Word is boundless and who, on meeting a hungry lion, equates himself with the biblical Daniel and his experience in the lion's den. The inference is clear: Defend yourself and *then* ask for divine intercession.

The "protest" tale is exemplified in *The North Carolina Negro and the Alabama Sheriff*, wherein an outraged black man asserts himself with the authority of a blue-steel revolver. Those readers who have experienced the contemptuous disregard of their basic civil rights at the hands of certain police officers (and the victims are legion) will react with a smile of approval at the forceful ending of the anecdote. But there will also be a reaction of sad remembrances and perhaps a rekindling of indignation at the harassment implicit in this story.

The humorous conclusion detracts not a whit from the problem that remains with us today. Many of our "law" enforcement officers, with the tacit approval or overt participation of their departmental superiors, flout the most fundamental tenets of the Constitution in their treatment of blacks, Latin Americans and poor whites. The Negro, being black and, in most cases, poor, has fallen heir to a double whammy, and has borne the brunt of discriminatory practices for generations. The evidence is all too abundant to merit further exposition here. Suffice it to say that many of the nation's police departments remain anachronisms in this day of burgeoning civil and social enlightenment.

The same type of protest is vividly portrayed in *The Arrest of the Two-year-old*, in which a sick infant is arrested for drunkenness and his parents are charged with aiding and abetting. The grin quickly evaporates, however, when the implication hits home.

The Intelligent Slave is one of the funniest stories in this volume, and at first reading appears to have no other function than to entertain. "Massa, Massa," yells the slave Tom, "you better get up out of yo' flowery bed of ease, an' put on yo' tramp-tramps, 'cause yo' high-ball-a-sooner done run through yo' flame of evaporation an' set yo' high-tower on fire." When Tom ultimately translates this into understandable English he is, in effect, heaping satire on the pretensions of those whites who enjoy using the black man as a foil for their condescending humor . . . "tryin' to be somethin' they ain't."

Another type of anecdote, which Brewer calls the "migrant tale," comments on the plight of North Carolina Negroes who leave the state and go to New York City ("up the road" or "up the country") to live. Not all are successful, and those who do forge ahead are not necessarily worldly wise. The premise that material gain is not always equated with mental achievement is evidenced in *The Cabarrus County Boy Who Told the Church What to Do* (when confronted with the problem of whether to purchase a chandelier or a piano). The choice was fine, but his homespun reasoning provides a jolly conclusion to the story.

Like Hercules, folklore has always found its strength in its contact with the earth; that is, with the lore that its workers have turned up. J. Mason Brewer knows the people of the regions about which he writes, and he speaks their language, whether they be field hands or members of the intellectual community. His phenomenal repertoire of anecdotes stems from countless interviews with the "folk," and he has faithfully recorded their responses with an abiding belief in their destiny as well as love for their heritage.

It is evident that Brewer views folklore as part of the larger culture and history of the Western Hemisphere; that it is not independent of broader movements. He wisely sets folklore in its proper context, imparting a rare quality of interrelationship between the factually historical and the folk-traditional.

This Encyclopedia is the richer for his generous contributions.

PART ONE

JUNETEENTH

A Laugh That Meant Freedom

There were some slaves who had a reputation for avoiding work through their wit and humor. These slaves kept their masters laughing most of the time, and were able, if not to keep from working altogether, at least to draw the lighter tasks.

Nehemiah was a clever slave, and no master who had owned him had ever been able to keep him at work, or succeeded in getting him to do heavy work. He would always have some funny story to tell or some humorous remark to make in response to the master's question or scolding. Because of this faculty for avoiding work, Nehemiah was constantly being transferred from one master to another. As soon as an owner found out that Nehemiah was outwitting him, he sold him to some other slaveholder. One day David Wharton, known as the most cruel slave master in Southwest Texas, heard about him.

"I bet I can make that darkey work," said Wharton, and he went to Nehemiah's master and bargained to buy him.

The morning of the first day after his purchase, he walked over to where Nehemiah was standing and said, "Now you are going to work, you understand? You are going to pick four hundred pounds of cotton today."

"Awright, Massa," answered Nehemiah, "but eff Ah makes yuh laff, won' yuh lemme off fo' terday?"

"Well," said the new owner, who had never been known to laugh, "if you make me laugh, I won't only let you off for today, but I'll give you your freedom."

"Ah decla', Boss," said Nehemiah, "yuh sho' is uh good-lookin' man."

"I am sorry I can't say the same thing about you," retorted David Wharton.

"Oh, yes, Boss, yuh could," Nehemiah grinned, "ef yuh tole ez big uh lie ez Ah did."

David Wharton laughed before he thought. Nehemiah got his freedom.

How Uncle Steve Interpreted Spanish

During slavery times it was the custom among some of the owners of land and slaves to go every year or two on a horse-trading expedition into old Mexico across the border. If the owner could not speak Spanish, he usually carried along as interpreter some Mexican living in the vicinity.

Master Phil Potts had his plans all made to leave for the border on a horse-trading expedition the following Monday morning. On Sunday he received word that the Mexican he had engaged to go along as interpreter was sick and could not go. Without an interpreter the trip would be useless. An interpreter had to be found.

Now Steve, a sharp slave, had for a long time wanted to make a trip into Mexico. On more than one occasion he had maneuvered to be taken along as a hand, but had never succeeded in his purpose. Here, he thought, was his opportunity. He hunted up Master Phil and told him he could interpret Spanish. Master Phil was rather surprised to learn of Steve's linguistic accomplishments, but as there was no choice, he agreed to take him.

The expedition, everybody in it in high spirits excepting Steve who was wondering what he was going to say when the test came, traveled all day and did not see a soul until close to sundown. Then, as they approached a water hole, they saw some Mexicans camped. One of them had a very fine-looking bay horse that at once caught the eye of Master Phil.

"Steve," he said, "ask that Mexican how much he will take for that horse."

HAM HOCKS AND COLLARD GREENS

With the "best parts" of the hog reserved for their white masters, the slave put his unique talents to work and evolved this epicurean delight. It was soon borrowed by the "po' whites," and later by everyone.

Time was, in the not too distant past, when ham hocks were considered as "poor folks' eatin'." At today's prices, however, 'tain't necessarily so. Ham hocks can be prepared in a number of ways that are economical and tasty, as well as eye-appealing. They may be boiled, cut from the bone after boiling, and used in ham salad or for creamed ham; or ground and made into patties, croquettes or hash. The juice in which the meat is cooked should be saved and stored in the refrigerator for later use as stock for soups and gravies.

The collard, for the benefit of our white readers, is a variety of kale native to the southeastern part of the United States.

Slice the leaves off stalks of 9 lbs. of collard greens. Wash the leaves thoroughly in salted cold water to remove the sand. (Usually, two or three such washings are required.) Rinse in unsalted water. Cut leaves across into three slices and soak for at least one hour.

Rinse 6 medium-sized smoked ham hocks. Place in three quarts of water. Sprinkle with crushed red pepper, or two fresh hot peppers.

Cover and cook for 2½ hours. Mix lightly once or twice to turn greens so that all cooks evenly.

"Boss," said Steve, "dat Mescan don't wanna sell dat hoss. Mescans don't trade on Monday, no-how."

"That's all right," answered his master; "go on and ask him what he wants for the horse."

"Sho', Boss," agreed Steve, "but Ah jes' knows he ain' gonna sell 'im terday."

"Oh, hombre," Steve called out, "fo' how muchee you sellee de hossy?"

The Mexican, disgusted at Steve's attempt to speak Spanish, replied, *"Usted no bueno"* ("You are no good").

"What did he say, Steve?" asked his master.

"He sez," answered Steve, "that he don't want ter sell 'im till Wednesday."

"Ah, go on," said the master. "Tell him we'll give him a good price; that we really want that horse."

"Aw right, boss," answered Steve. "Ah'll tell 'im, but Ah done tol' yuh dat Mescans don't trade on Mondays."

"Oh, hombre," said Steve. "No sellee de hossy sho' nuffee?"

"No sabe" ("I do not understand"), answered the Mexican.

"Well," asked the boss, "what did he say this time, Steve?"

"He sez he don't wanna sell 'im till Sat-day now, boss. Ah done tol' yuh dese Mescans don't trade on Monday."

"Now see here," replied the master, "we've just got to have that horse. He is a wonderful animal. Go on and tell him that we will pay him a big price for it."

"Aw right, boss. Yuh sho' is wastin' time though, 'case Ah knows dat Mescan ain' gwine trade on Monday."

"Oh, hombre," said Steve, "no sellee de hossy fo' biggee de mon?"

The Mexican, who had some wood piled up beside the road, now thought that Steve, who was pointing in its direction, was asking him the price of it, and replied, *"Cinco pesos"* (five dollars).

"What did he say this time, Steve?" asked his master.

"Boss, he sho' gone an' talk foolish dis time. He sez sometime dat hoss is trottin' an' he thinks he's pacin'."

"All right," said his master, "let's go on to Mexico."

Swapping Dreams

Jim Turner, an unusually good-natured master, had a fondness for telling long stories woven out of what he claimed to be his dreams, and especially did he like to "swap" dreams with Ike, a witty slave who was a house servant. Every morning he would set Ike to telling about what he had dreamed the night before. It always seemed, however, that the master could tell the best dream tale, and Ike had to admit that he was beaten most of the time.

One morning, when Ike entered the master's room to clean it, he found him just preparing to get out of bed. "Ike," he said, "I certainly did have a strange dream last night."

"Sez yuh did, Massa, sez yuh did?" answered Ike. "Lemme hyeah it."

"All right," replied Mr. Turner. "It was like this: I dreamed I went to Nigger Heaven last night, and saw there a lot of garbage, some old torn-down houses, a few old broken-down, rotten fences, the muddiest, sloppiest streets I ever saw, and a big bunch of ragged, dirty niggers walking around."

"Umph, umph, Massa," said Ike, "yuh sho' musta et de same t'ing Ah did las' night, 'case Ah dreamed Ah went up ter de white man's paradise, an' de streets wuz all ob gol' an' silvah, an' dey wuz lots o' milk an' honey dere, an' putty pearly gates, but dey wuzn't uh soul in de whole place."

Uncle Israel and the Law

Every week on the Hunter plantation five or six chickens would be missing, and the master couldn't find out what had become of them. At length he started a thorough investigation. After a good deal of questioning among the slaves, he found that Uncle Israel's wife had recently made some feather pillows and that chicken feathers had been seen under Uncle Israel's cabin a few days before.

With this information, the master laid his trap. One evening a strange white man driving a wobbly old buggy with a chicken coop tied on the back end of it halted at Uncle Israel's cabin. He was a chicken buyer, he said, and was paying fancy prices. Uncle Israel was not long in suggesting that he might have a few very fat chickens to sell.

"All right," said the stranger, "bring them out."

"No, sah, no sah," said Uncle Israel, "Ah cain't ketch 'em till da'k."

The stranger went on to say that he didn't much want to hang around the plantation and be seen by Mr. Hunter and finally asked Uncle Israel point-blank where he was going to get his chickens.

"Wal, Ah tell yuh," chuckled Uncle Israel. "Ah's got uh hoodoo on dem chickens up dar in Massa's hen-house. Dey comes into mah sack after da'k lak crows flyin' to de roost-tree in de ebenin'."

"Aw," sneered the stranger, "you know you are afraid to go into your master's hen-house."

"Yuh jes' wait an' see," answered Uncle Israel. He was all eagerness. "Why, two of dem pullets flewed right into mah ol' 'oman's stew las' night."

"You don't say!" exclaimed the stranger in a changed tone. "Do you know who I am?"

"No, sah, Boss, 'ceptin' yuh's a chicken buyah. Who else is yuh?"

"I'm the biggest constable in this county," answered the stranger.

"Sez yuh is, Boss?" said Uncle Israel. "Wal, Ah'll decla'. An' don' yuh know who Ah is? Ain't Massa an' de oberseeah tol' yuh who Ah is? Wal, Ah's de bigges' liah in dis county."

Dey's Auganized

One day Ananias, tall, black coachman of the Kaufman estate, was driving his master down a long lane on the way to a neighboring plantation when a horse-fly alighted on the mane of one of the horses. "Massa," said Ananias, "you see dat hoss-fly on dat hoss's mane? Watch me git 'im." Ananiah had the reputation of being the most exact wielder of the coach-whip in the county, and his master always enjoyed watching him wield it. Ananias raised his whip and split the horse-fly into two neat parts.

A little farther down the lane Ananias looked over and spied a bumble-bee on a sunflower. "Massa," said Ananias, "yuh see dat bumblebee on dat sunflowah? Watch me git 'im." Ananias raised his whip again and the bum-blebee was torn to shreds by the snapper on the end of it.

After a little while the master noticed a hornets' nest hanging from the limb of a tree by the side of the road. "Look, Ananias," said he. "You see that hornets' nest? You are such an expert with the coachwhip, let me see you cut that nest off the limb."

"No, sah, Massa," said Ananias, "Ah ain't gwine bothah dem hornets. Dey's auganized!"

The Prophet Vindicated

Uncle Phimon was the most useful slave on the Pettus plantation. Master Tom Pettus did not have to worry about dissatisfaction among his slaves or their plans for rebelling; he had a way of knowing what was going on in the dark and of anticipating future events. Uncle Phimon prophesied for him, and he had for so long a time been so accurate in his predictions that Master Tom had actually come to take the old fellow for a fortune-teller endowed with some sort of supernatural power or foresight, though in fact Uncle Phimon gathered his information from eavesdropping.

One day while Master Tom was talking with some of the other planta-tion owners in the settlement, they expressed a great deal of concern over a vague kind of unrest working among their slaves. Master Tom, after lis-tening awhile, informed his neighbors that he owned a remarkable slave who always warned him of any trouble brewing, and that, consequently, he could manage to head off trouble and keep his slaves pacified. The other men were in doubt about the prophetic powers of Uncle Phimon, but Master Tom was so confident that he invited them all to come over to his plantation the fol-lowing Saturday morning to witness a demonstration of Uncle Phimon's powers of divination. They accepted the invitation.

Saturday came; it was summertime; and not long after sunup not only the owners of neighboring plantations, but most of their slaves were gath-ered together to see Uncle Phimon demonstrate his magic powers of looking into the hidden world. A wooden box was provided for him to stand on. In front of this box was an old-fashioned wash-pot turned over. Under the pot one of the planters had placed something, the nature of which was unknown even to Master Tom Pettus. When all was ready, Master Tom led Uncle Phimon forth to the box blind-folded and helped him mount the box. "Now neighbors," Master Tom announced, "Uncle Phimon will tell us what is hidden under the pot."

For a long time Uncle Phimon stood on the box, working his hands through the air and over his face. He seemed to be in a kind of trance. He thought and thought, and the longer he stood there blindfolded, the more uncertain he became as to what to say was under the pot. He was to have only one guess. Finally Uncle Phimon decided that it was no use for him to guess anything. He might as well give up and acknowledge that he was not a fortune-teller.

"Wal, Massa," he finally began, speaking very slowly, "de ol' coon run uh long time, but dey cotch 'im at las'." Of course, what he meant was that his claim to being a prophet had been exposed and now he was "'fessing up."

At Uncle Phimon's announcement, two planters turned the pot up, and there under it was an *old coon!* Master Tom Pettus was more thoroughly convinced than ever that his prize slave was a prophet, and so was everybody else.

Abraham Explains His Master's Shot

Deer hunting was a favorite sport of many planters in Texas during the days of slavery. Frequently, the hunters made up a party, at which time each planter took along a slave to bag the game, tend the horses, and help with the work in the camp. The merriest part of the day was at meal time, when jokes and anecdotes were rife. Among the plantation hunters of Goliad County, Jim Fant was the king of story-tellers. He was a magnificent liar and always had his slave Abraham bear him out in his lies. The day came for the big hunt and, after a morning filled with good luck, the planters sat down to dinner and the story-telling began. Jim Fant, as usual, was the last to tell his story.

"Well, fellers," he began, "Abraham and I just couldn't wait for our regular hunt. We couldn't keep from going out last week and hunting some deer. After we had hunted all day until it was almost sundown and not shot a thing and were just about ready to go home, a big buck rushed out of the woods and headed straight for Abraham and me. I drew down my old rifle and fired. He fell dead and, well, sir, when we got to him we found that the bullet had shot him first through the ear, then through the hind foot, and then through the head."

"How did you do all that with one bullet?" the other plantation owners chimed in.

"Abraham," said Master Jim Fant, turning to his slave, "tell 'em how I did it."

Abraham scratched his head and thought for a moment, and then said slowly, "Wal, yuh see, hit wuz lak dis. When Massa shot 'im, he wuz scratchin' 'is ear wid 'is hin' foot."

On the way home that evening Abraham said to his master, "Looka hyeah, Massa, yuh tell yo' lies a li'l closer tergedder fo'm now on. Dat lie yuh tol' terday wuz uh li'l too fur uh-paht."*

Uncle Pleas's Prayer

Prayer was one of the essential factors in the life of nearly all slaves. They prayed in public, and they also prayed in private. The woods near their cabins seemed to lure them after the day's work, and many stole away to some tree after nightfall to make their petitions to God. The Negroes on the Fant plantation were especially religious. They were especially prayerful; and they were especially prayerful in secret.

Among those who visited a favorite prayer spot each night was Uncle Pleas Brown. Pleas would leave his cabin each evening about dusk and make his way to a large live oak tree where he could be "alone with his Gawd," as he put it, and "talk to his Jesus." Pleas would always pray the same prayer: "Oh, Lawd, kill all de wha' fo'ks, an' save all de niggahs. Oh, Lawd, kill all de wha' fo'ks, an' save all de niggahs."

One night Master George Fant, who had become suspicious of Pleas's nocturnal trips away from the cabin, followed him and found out where he went and what he was doing. The next night the master decided he would get to the tree first and hide in its branches so that he might hear exactly what Pleas said. Incidentally, the master carried four or five rocks up the tree with him.

Shortly after the master had hidden himself in the branches of the tree, Pleas appeared and, kneeling down beneath the tree, started to praying, "Oh, mah Gawd, kill all de wha' fo'ks, an' save all de niggahs. Oh, mah Gawd, kill all de wha' fo'ks, an' save all de niggahs."

Just as Pleas started to repeat this prayer the third time, the master let two or three rocks fall on his head. Pleas, frightened and thinking God was throwing the rocks, called out, "Look out dere, Gawd! Stop dat th'owin' dem rocks. Don' yuh know uh wha' man f'om uh niggah?"**

---

* The universality of this folk tale is evidenced in the lore of other races and nationalities. The Russian version mentions a hare; a British anecdote employs a boar. A similar story uses a bird, as recounted in the *Encyclopedia of Jewish Humor*, by H. D. Spalding, Jonathan David Publishers, 1969.

** A slave who was overheard to beseech God for his master's death, would himself be whipped to death or hanged. The offense was considered even more serious than running away, considering the climate of fear among white planters of a general slave uprising. The humor of this story, handed down from slavery times, owes its longevity not so much to its humor but to the sheer audacity implicit in Uncle Pleas's entreaty—one which many other slaves felt but dared not utter.

Lias's Revelation

Lias Jones was a praying slave. Lias would pray any time, but no matter what he was doing, at twelve o'clock noon he would stop short, kneel and pray to God. The prayer Lias prayed at this hour was a special one: "Oh, Lawd," he would pray, "won't Yuh please gib us ouah freedom?" Lias had been praying this prayer a long time and nothing had happened yet.

But, Lias was not discouraged. Without variation he continued at high noon every day to pray that God would give him and his slave brothers freedom. Finally, one day, the master sent for Lias to help clean the big house. Lias at twelve o'clock was starting in on the parlor, but had not been in the room long enough to examine the furnishings. Just then the big gong that called the Negroes to dinner started sounding. Lias stopped, as was his custom, to pray for freedom. So he knelt down in the parlor and began to pray: "Oh, Lawd, cum an' gib us all ouah freedom." When Lias got up, it happened that he was standing just opposite a life-size mirror in the parlor, which reflected his image in it.

Since the slaves had no looking-glasses, Lias had never seen one before, and now he was amazed to see a black man gazing at him from the glass. The one thing he could think of in connection with the image was that God had come down in answer to his prayers; so he said, looking at the image in the mirror, "Ah decla', Gawd, Ah didn't know Yuh wuz uh niggah. Ah thought Yuh wuz a wha' man. Ef Yuh is uh niggah, Ah's gwine *make* Yuh gib us ouah freedom."*

Bringing Home the Bear

All of Jeremiah's five sons liked to hunt. Their master, Henry Jones, had the best hunting grounds in the country; and when on a Saturday afternoon or night they went to hunt, meat-in-the-pot for Sunday was almost a certainty. The five brothers usually hunted together, but one Saturday night while the older boys were gone to a plantation dance and only Rufus, the youngest son, and his father and mother remained at home, the lad decided that he would take the dogs and go hunting alone. Jeremiah wished him good luck, and with the eager dogs he disappeared into the woods.

After Rufus had been away from the cabin about two hours, Jeremiah

---

* Arab folklore contains a similar "mirror" story. In a remote village in Yemen, a husband brings home a mirror. The wife gazes into it and thinks he has taken another wife—a young, beautiful girl. But her mother looks into the mirror and consoles her daughter: "You have nothing to worry about. He could never love such an ugly old crone." (*Encyclopedia of Jewish Humor*, Jonathan David Publishers, N. Y.). Mexican and Chinese versions also exist, all steeped in antiquity. This Negro telling differs from all others, however, because of its social significance. All other versions are told for innocuous entertainment only.

heard the dogs barking loudly and someone running toward the cabin as fast as his feet could carry him. He went quickly to the door and, looking out into the moonlight, saw a big black bear chasing Rufus, who was now almost to the cabin.

"What yuh runnin' f'om dat beah fo'?" yelled Jeremiah.

"Ah ain't runnin' f'om no beah," yelled Rufus, rushing into the open door of the cabin. "Ah's jes' bringin' 'im home."

Voices in the Graveyard*

One night two slaves on the Byars plantation entered the potato house of the master and stole a sack of sweet potatoes. They decided that the best place to divide them would be down in the graveyard, where they would not be disturbed. So they went down there and started dividing the potatoes.

Another slave, Isom, who had been visiting a neighboring plantation, happened to be passing that way on the road home, and hearing voices in the graveyard, he decided to stop and overhear what was being said. It was too dark for him to see, but when he stopped he heard one of the thieves saying in a sing-song voice, "Ah'll take dis un, an' yuh take dat un. Ah'll take dis un, an' yuh take dat un."

"Lawd, ha' mercy," said Isom to himself, "Ah b'lieve dat Gawd an' de debbil am down hyeah dividin' up souls. Ah's gwine an' tell ol' Massa."

Isom ran as fast as he could up to the master's house and said, "Massa, Massa, Ah's passin' th'oo de graveya'd jes' now an' what yuh reckon ah heerd? Gawd an' de debbil's down dar dividin' up souls. Ah sho' b'lieves de Day ob Judgment am come."

"You don't know what you are talking about," said the master. "That's foolish talk. You know you are not telling the truth."

"Yas sah, Massa; yas sah, Ah is. Ef yuh don' b'lieve hit, cum go down dar yo'se'f."

"Very well," said the master, "let's find out."

"Aw right, Massa," said Isom, "'case Gawd an' de debbil sho' am down dere."

Sure enough, when Isom and the master got near the graveyard they heard the sing-song voice saying, "Yuh take dis un, an' Ah'll take dat un."

"See dar, didn't Ah tell yuh, Massa?" said Isom.

In the meantime the two thieves had almost finished the division of the potatoes, but remembered they had dropped two over by the fence—where Isom and the master were standing out of sight. Finally, when they had

---

* A similar story tells of the running of a frightened Negro, rather than a white man: "He Heard the Bullet Twice," from *Brazos Bottom Philosophy*, by A. W. Eddins, *Southwestern Lore*, published by the Texas Folklore Society, No. IX, for 1931.

only two potatoes left, the one who was counting said, "Ah'll take dese two an' yuh take them two over dere by de fence."

Upon hearing this, Isom and the master ran home as fast as they could go. After this the master never doubted Isom's word about what he saw or heard.

Uncle Bob's Voyage to New England

To Negro slaves the words *New England* meant escape from bondage. Many of them looked forward to some day getting to this promised land and obtaining their freedom.

In Matagorda County, near the Gulf of Mexico, was a large plantation owned by Master George Kearnes. The oldest slave on this plantation was Uncle Bob Kennedy. Uncle Bob did not talk much, but was always a very attentive listener, and he usually remembered what he heard. One time he overheard white people talking about how slaves had run away to the New England states and gained their freedom. Some of them, it seems, had made their escape in boats.

Since the Kearnes plantation was on the edge of the Gulf, and since he had a small boat, Uncle Bob decided to take the water route to New England. One evening, about dark, he got a sack of meal and a jug of molasses and made his way down to the little cove where the master's boat was tied. He got in it with his meal and molasses. Uncle Bob had heard about low tide and high tide, and so he thought that some time during the night the high tide would take him and the boat out to sea, and eventually land him somewhere in New England. Confidently, he lay down in the boat and soon was asleep.

Early next morning another slave on the plantation, Ezekiel, passed close to the boat and, seeing Uncle Bob in it, shouted to wake him up. "Uncle Bob, Uncle Bob," he called, "wake up, wake up!"

On hearing his name called, Uncle Bob woke up, rubbing his eyes in a confused manner. Yes, the boat had carried him far away from the plantation to New England, but, still, there was something not just right about this foreign shore.

"Who is dat knowin' me up hyeah so early in New England?'" he called out.

Elijah's Leaving Time

Master Dan Waller was a very sympathetic master. He visited all the cabins on his plantation every night to see how the slaves were getting along, and to find out whether anyone was sick. The slaves all liked Master Dan, and generally left his chickens and hogs alone.

One Saturday evening, however, Elijah, one of the slaves who had a family, decided he would like to have some pork chops for Sunday. About nine o'clock that night Elijah went down to the master's hog pen and stole a pig. Just about the time he got back inside his cabin, the master, on his customary round of evening visits, knocked at the door. Elijah, the pig still under his arm, hurriedly put it in the baby cradle and covered it over with a quilt. He was rocking the cradle backwards and forwards when the master entered.

"What's the matter?" asked the master.

"Mah po' baby's sick," answered Elijah, "an' Ah's tryin' to rock 'im to sleep."

"Well, I'm sorry," said the master, starting over to the cradle. "Let me see him. He may need some medicine."

"No, sah; no, sah." Ef you pulls de kivver offen 'im he gwine ter die, Massa."

"Well," answered the master, "I am not going to let him suffer. I am going to pull the cover off him and see what the trouble is."

"Aw right, Massa, aw right," answered Elijah, sidling to the door. "You kin pull de kivver offen 'im ef yuh wants ter, but Ah ain't gwin stay hyeah an' see 'im die!"

Bubber's 'Rithmetic

On the Rogers plantation in Refugio County there was a mulatto boy named Bubber. Bubber was considered by the other slaves as having the easiest job on the plantation. He never had been given any work to do in the fields, but had also worked up at the big house for "Ol' Massa" and "Ol' Missus." Bubber was well liked by the master and his family, and they treated him better than any of the other slaves. One of the master's boys, who was about the same age, liked Bubber so well that he undertook to teach him how to count. Bubber finally learned to count up to forty.

One day, soon after Bubber's mathematical education, he found an old watch that had been thrown away by the master. Attaching it to a piece of wire, which he called a chain, he put it in his shirt pocket so that it would be conspicuous. As he strutted around among the other slaves, he was not disappointed in his plan to draw questions about the time. Every prayer meeting night after the slaves had been praying and shouting for awhile, some of them would ask the time. These meetings were supposed to last only until nine o'clock. Bubber always replied that it was "gettin' close to nine o'clock."

One night, however, the slaves got to shouting and remained so long down in the grove that Bubber, when asked the time, replied, "Hit's thirty-nine now; hit'll be forty in uh few minutes. Yuh bettah skee-daddle."

PART TWO

HUMOROUS FOLK TALES
of the
SOUTH CAROLINA NEGRO

No water in de well
Ah'm ketchin' hell
An' mama's in de kitchen
Havin' a spell

Master and Slave

Jes' tryin' to live lowly an' humble;
Take what dey put on me an' never grumble.

The Faithful Slave*

During slavery times, some of the South Carolina slaves were very devoted to their masters and wished to follow them everywhere they went.
This was especially true of the slaves who served as coachmen and who
drove their masters from place to place in fine carriages drawn by beautiful,
stately horses.

Among these coachmen who enjoyed driving their masters from countryside to countryside was Uncle Josh, whose master owned a large plantation
on Beaufort Island. Uncle Josh was so accustomed to being in his master's
company each day that he always became very sad when his master found
it necessary to leave the plantation and go to New York on business for a
week or two. So, one day, he decided that the next time his master planned
a trip to New York he would think of some way to accompany him.

It wasn't long afterwards that he learned that his master was going to
New York on the following Saturday, so he put some of his clothing in a
cotton sack and followed him to Beaufort, where the ship on which he was
to leave was anchored. The master did not know that Uncle Josh had followed him until he started up the gangplank to board the ship. When he
looked back and saw Uncle Josh, he scolded him and ordered him to go
back to the plantation, but the slave did not go home as he was ordered.
He went only a short distance, and as soon as his master disappeared from
view he went back to the ship and persuaded the fireman to let him work

* *Source*: Folklore files of Penn School, Beaufort County, February 6,
1945. *Collector*: Catherine G. Boyd.

his way to New York. He remained in the hatchway, out of sight, until they reached the New York pier, but the moment he saw his master on the gangplank he jumped overboard hollering, "Master! Master! save me! Ah swim all de way f'om Beaufort!"

The master called to the ship's crew to rescue him, and after they had gotten Josh out of the water the slave was taken uptown and advertised as a champion swimmer who would challenge all swimmers in the city of New York. The contest was scheduled for the next day at two o'clock.

On the following day the crowd gathered at the appointed place to witness the great swimming contest and see the prize swimmer. As time passed and the minute hand almost reached two, the crowd became quite anxious as the "champion" had not yet put in his appearance. But, at the last second, the crowd looked up and saw Uncle Josh coming towards them with a cook stove on his back and a frying pan in his hand. As he drew near he announced, "Ah'm gonna swim an' cook on de water."

Overawed, the other swimmers backed away and refused to swim against the remarkable Uncle Josh.

How Uncle Ezra Freed Himself*

One of the chief industries in South Carolina during the slavery period revolved around indigo. The planting and cultivation of the indigo plant and dye-making proved very profitable to the planters in Marion County and slave labor was in great demand. The planters would meet slave-trading boats on the Little Pee Dee River and trade indigo for slaves, pound for pound. A Negro weighing 200 pounds could be bought for 200 pounds of indigo.

One of the best workers on an indigo plantation near Bethel was an old slave by the name of Uncle Ezra, but he was getting old now, and tired of working sixteen hours a day. As he would say, "Ah goes tuh de fiel' at four in de mawnin' an' don' knock off till eight at night." But long hours and hard work were not his only worries; his wife, "Aunt" Susan, fussed at him and nagged him during the entire time he was at home. The only time she did not nag him was when he was asleep. So Uncle Ezra grew tired of his work and tired of her nagging and decided that he would try to think of some way to get rid of the work—and Aunt Susan.

Uncle Ezra knew that his master, Mr. Pinckney, hid outside the slaves' cabins at night and listened to their conversations in an effort to keep them frightened. So he devised a plan: He would tell Aunt Susan that he was going to ask the good Lord to come and take him away if she didn't stop nagging him. She didn't pay him any mind at all, but Master Pinckney, who had been listening outside as usual, put a white sheet over his head one night

---

Informant: Edward Elliott, Cherokee County, Jan. 18, 1945. *Collector*: Miss H. C. Foster.

CHITTERLINGS

As an aftermath of Emancipation, former slaves could select better fare, but many preferred such old favorites as "chitlins"—and still do.

(The small intestine of the swine, usually pronounced "chitlins")

(1) Chitterlings—Mississippi Style

10 lbs. chitterlings	2 tsp. salt
2 med. size onions	2 garlic cloves
½ cup vinegar	½ tsp. black pepper
2 tsp. crushed red pepper (or 5 red pepper pods)	celery stalk with tops or 1 tsp. dried parsley

Clean thoroughly in warm water, turning the chitterlings inside out to remove all lining, but leaving a small bit of fat for seasoning. Wash thoroughly in 4 or 5 waters. Place in pot and add onions, vinegar, red pepper or pepper pods, salt, garlic cloves, black pepper, celery or parsley. Cover with water and boil over low heat for five to six hours or until tender. A small potato may be added to the mixture to absorb the odor, but not to eat.

(2) Chitterlings—Louisiana Style

Prepare as in recipe No. 1, but add 1 bay leaf, 2 garlic cloves, ½ to 1 tsp. black pepper (to taste). Cut chitterlings into pieces. During last 30 minutes of cooking, add 1 cup tomato sauce.

(3) Chitterlings—Georgia Style

Prepare as in recipe No. 1. Drain off liquid. Remove the cooked chitterlings from the pot and cut into small pieces. Add ¼ tsp. black pepper. Sauté gently with 1 tbs. vinegar in bacon drippings until most of the liquid is cooked away.

(4) Fried Chitterlings—Country Style

Prepare as in recipe No. 1. Drain and cut into 2-inch squares. Dip pieces in beaten egg and flour. Fry in deep fat to golden brown. (Many prefer cracker crumbs to flour, and moderns prefer a good fritter batter.)

and waited until the slave had finished his prayer. Then he knocked on the cabin door.

"Who is dat?" shouted Uncle Ezra, still on his knees.

"It's me, the good Lord," replied the master. "I come to take Uncle Ezra away."

Uncle Ezra got up off his knees, turned to Aunt Susan, and said, "Yuh see, Ah tol' yuh if yuh didn' stop fussin' de good Lawd wuz gonna come an' take me away." He then got a flour sack and stuffed all his clothes down into it, stepped up to the door where his master stood with his arms spread out, and said, "Good Lord, step aside so Ah kin come out."

Master Pinckney stepped back out of the doorway, and Uncle Ezra, the flour sack of clothing tightly clutched in his hand, ran past him as fast as he could. And that was one slave they never did see in South Carolina anymore.

The Negro Congressman's Answer To Ben Tillman*

Beginning immediately after Emancipation and lasting in most Southern states until 1895 was a time in United States history known as the Reconstruction Period. During this era the slaves who had been freed and given the rights of citizenship, including the right to vote and hold public office, became members of the state and national law-making bodies; the state legislatures and national Congress, and the constitutional conventions of the various Southern states. Many of these blacks who served as senators and representatives were well educated and extraordinary students of law. They were also very courageous and fluent speakers.

Among them was a fearless political leader from Charleston who served in both the state and national legislatures. He was a member of Congress, but the story concerns an important incident in his legislative career in South Carolina. The occasion was the session of the Constitutional Convention of 1890, at which time Ben Tillman, a white member of the convention who did not like blacks and who wanted to disenfranchise them, made some slighting remarks about the Negro representative during his absence. The other, in turn, made some uncomplimentary remarks during Tillman's absence.

Someone told Tillman what the black legislator had said. The next morning when the convention opened, Tillman arose, got the floor, and proceeded to denounce the Negro in vile terms. He became so angry that he was shaking with fury. Losing his temper entirely, he pointed his finger at the Negro and shouted, "Why, you dirty black rascal, I'll swallow you alive."

* *Informant*: Murray Holliday, Orangeburg County, Oct. 7, 1944. *Collector*: J. Mason Brewer.

"If you do," replied the black congressman, pointing *his* finger in Ben Tillman's face, "you'll have more brains in your belly than you've got in your head!"

On The Farm

Sift de meal—save de bran;
You can't raise 'taters on sandy lan'.

Too Many Ups*

Cotton is raised to some extent in a large number of South Carolina counties, but Aiken is one of the leading cotton-producing counties in the entire state. Quite a few white farm owners in this section have Negro share-croppers working their land. They have found this to be a profitable system of farming because they clear a large sum of money without doing a lot of work themselves. Therefore, they always make an effort to keep the share-croppers on their farms. The Negroes, however, get wise occasionally and leave. They move into the city of Aiken and find that they can make a better living in town for their families than they can on a white man's farm. Sometimes the white farmers look them up in Aiken and try to get them to leave the city and return to the farms. But rarely, if ever, do they go back.

One time there was a Negro share-cropper by the name of George Davis who left the farm he was working on and went into Aiken to work. While he was downtown at a grocery store one Saturday, he met his former boss.

"George," said the farmer, "how about gittin' you to farm for me again this year?"

"Naw, suh, Cap," replied George. "Ah wouldn't mind it, but dere's too many *ups* in dat thing."

"What do you mean by too many *ups?*" asked the farmer.

"Well," explained George, "when Ah goes to bed at night de first thing in the mawnin' Ah got to *wake* up; then Ah got to *git* up; then Ah got to *dress* up—go to de mule lot an' *feed* up. When Ah gits back to de house Ah got to *eat* up. Time as Ah finish Ah got to *gear* up—then *hitch* up. Ah can't let the mule stan' dere so Ah hafta say *git* up! Time Ah done work all de summer an' *gather* up mah crop an' sell it, Ah come to you to *settle* up; you gits yo' pencil out an' *figger* up an say to me, 'Ah'm sorry but yo' profit is done *et* up. . . .'

"Naw, suh, Ah don't think Ah'll try it!"

---

* *Informant*: Edna Mae McCants, Florence County, Dec. 9, 1944. *Collector*: Ida E. Greene.

The Selfish Farmer*

Orangeburg County is one of the richest in the state of South Carolina. It is not only the leading cotton-growing county in the state, but is also noted for its pecan orchards which net some individual owners as much as $2,250 per year. He owned eight head of mules, six milk cows, four buggy their own farms. They do not depend on their pecan orchards alone to bring in revenue; they are successful cotton farmers, too, and in many cases poultry and stock producers as well.

One of the wealthiest black farmers in this county was Tom Hampton. Tom owned 400 acres of choice land and timber and had one of the largest pecan orchards in the area. At times his orchard netted him as much as $2,250 per year. He owned eight head of mules, six milk cows, four buggy horses and kept about forty good fat hogs in his pen all the time. His house was very modern. It had eight rooms including a library and was lighted and heated with electricity. It was equipped with modern plumbing devices and was constructed of the best brick. The furniture in all of the rooms was modern and up-to-date.

He and his wife Laura had worked hard to acquire the farm which was now paid for, but Tom had a bad habit of wanting to take all the credit for what had been done. This was the only thing that Laura disliked about him. Every time some friend or acquaintance or relative came to visit, he would take them around the farm and say, "How do you like *my* pecan orchard? How do you like *my* cotton patch? How do you like *my* milk cows? How do you like *my* pigs?"

Not once did he include Laura in the ownership of their belongings, and she often reminded him that he should say, "How do you like *our* pecan orchard, *our* milk cow, *our* pigs, *our* house?" Tom paid no attention to Laura's requests, until one day when Tom's brother from New York came out to the farm and Tom proceeded as usual to ask him how he liked the place.

That night after the brother left, Laura grabbed up a broom and started beating on Tom saying, "Didn't I tell you to stop saying *my* this and *my* that and to start saying *our* this and *our* that?"

Tom, frightened, ran into the bedroom and hid under the bed, but every time he would start to come out Laura would hit him with the broom. Finally, he went to sleep. The next morning, when he woke up, he knocked on the underside of the bed and called out, "Honey, will you please, ma'm, hand me *our* pants!"

Cured!

Informant: Paul R. Webber, Jr. Orangeburg County, Dec. 22, 1944. *Collector*: J. Mason Brewer.

Tales Out of School

Hickory leaves an' calico sleeves;
All dese teachers be's hard tuh please.

Tim and Bill from Summerville*

Summerville, South Carolina, is one of the beauty spots of the state. It has long been famed as a winter-resort, but it is also interesting for another reason. It is the home of a strange group of people of Indian descent who vary greatly in their physical characteristics, from pale white with blue eyes, to dark brown with hair of negroid texture. These people are called "Brass Ankles." No one knows their origin, but they consider themselves the equals of whites in the communities in which they live.

In Summerville and vicinity they are accorded all the rights and privileges granted the whites, except in a few instances. Some of these exceptions are as follows: White barbers will not cut their hair in their shops, and the city operates a separate school for the Brass Ankles that goes as high as the seventh grade. This school is taught by white teachers and very seldom, if ever, do the Brass Ankles go to high school. All of the Brass Ankle children, regardless of the color of their skin, attend this elementary school that the city has provided for them. After they finish the sixth grade at this school they are permitted to enroll in the white or the Negro school—either one that they might choose to attend. Usually those who can pass for white attend the white school, and those of darker complexion attend the Negro high school.

Once there were two Brass Ankle brothers by the name of Tim and Bill. Both were in the same grade and both finished the Brass Ankle elementary school the same year. One was white and the other was brown.

When the school term opened the next September, the boys were sent by their parents to enroll in high school. The light boy who had blue eyes (Tim) enrolled in the white high school, and his brother with copper-colored skin (Bill) enrolled in the Negro high school.

The teachers at the Negro high school did not know that Bill had a brother attending a white school until the day he came to enroll his second year. It happened that Bill struck a boy that day and was told by the principal to remain after school.

"But I can't," Bill replied. "Ah got to go uptown and meet my brother. He gits his books up to de white school."

Informant: Mr. C. S. McIver, Dorchester County, March 12, 1945. *Collector*: Miss Mattie E. Mouzon.

Little Harry's Reply*

Although it is generally conceded that race relations are strained in southern communities, there are some notable exceptions. One of the places where whites and Negroes have had cordial and friendly relations for a long time is in the little town of Orangeburg, South Carolina. The reputation of this township as a peaceful haven for both races is national in scope and is due largely to the fine influence the two Negro colleges of the town have exerted on the citizens of both races over a long period of years. Paralleling this influence is the fact that the city government of the town has remained under the control of the wealthier and more cultured class of whites.

It is not too common an occurrence to find whites and Negroes living next door to each other in northern and eastern cities, and it is almost an unheard of condition in the south. Nevertheless, that is exactly what one finds in Orangeburg. In the western section of the city near the Edisto river, on Seaboard and Bull Streets, one finds many instances where white families live next door to Negro families, and from all reports they live in this manner without having trouble of any kind. Little white and colored boys often play ball together and each team or side is composed of boys from both racial groups.

Two of these small boys were great friends. The little colored boy was named Harry, and the little white boy was named Lloyd. Harry and Lloyd were such good friends that they walked to school together each morning and Lloyd waited for Harry's school to turn out every afternoon so they could walk home together.** There were many things that the little boys talked about, but neither of them ever said anything that would hurt the other's feelings.

One afternoon, however, when they were on the way home from school, Harry was surprised to hear Lloyd say, "Harry, God loved us better'n He did y'all 'cause He made us white."

"Naw, that ain't right," replied little Harry. "He love us better 'cause he taken time to color us."

Little Ernest's Grammar Lesson***

The Negroes who work on the tobacco farms in the Pee Dee River section of South Carolina around Darlington, Lake City, and Timmonsville do not send their children to school as regularly or as often as they should. The harvest season on the tobacco farms, which is usually during the months of July and August, is the time when Negroes in this section, both old and

---

Informant: William L. Davis, Orangeburg County, February 19, 1945. *Collector*: J. Mason Brewer.

** The spirit of "equality" did not include the educational system.

***Informant*: Henry Pearson, Orangeburg County, February 5, 1945. *Collector*: Cora V. Green.

young, help in the sorting of tobacco leaves. Everyone works together. Even the smallest children hand the tobacco—that is, pass it on, several leaves at a time—to some older person who strings the leaves on long sticks. The larger boys and their fathers hang the sticks full of tobacco in the tobacco-curing barns.

"Putting in time," as they called the season in which the tobacco leaves are gathered and put into the barns to be cured, is one of the most exciting times of the year for the Pee Dee Negroes. It is then that they make most of their money, so they look forward to its coming each year with great joy. The children earn enough money by their own labor to buy their fall and winter clothing, so their parents are relieved of this responsibility. The bad feature about this, however, is the fact that most of the children wish to continue to make money and lose interest in going to school. If they can find other jobs they sometimes quit school altogether, and regular attendance in the schools in this district is almost a thing of the past. Money making, to the children in this area, is more important than book learning.

One year they had a very good teacher out at the Lake City school. She was especially interested in teaching the children how to conjugate verbs, but her efforts were not especially successful. The children did not try to learn. She was very patient with them, however, and continued to make an effort to teach them conjugation. Ernest, one of the little boys in the sixth grade, was the only one who would try to learn anything at all, so the teacher always took great delight in helping him. There was one time, though, that she became discouraged with little Ernest, and that was when she was attempting to teach him to conjugate the verb "to go" in the negative. She had him repeat over and over again, "I'm not going, we're not going, you're not going, they're not going." She went over the conjugation about ten times, and still he could not understand it. Finally, becoming disgusted, she yelled, "Ernest, don't you understand it yet?"

"Yassum," replied little Ernest to the great relief of the teacher, "Ah unnerstan's it now—dey ain't nobody gwine!"

Aunt Hannah's Arithmetic*

Immediately after the Negroes were freed in Oconee County, they began to establish themselves as tenant farmers on the various plantations where they were formerly slaves. Since they had not had time to earn enough money to purchase land and build homes for themselves, a large number lived in the same little houses that were used as slave quarters on the premises of their former masters. Often the grandparents, parents and children in the same family dwelt together under the same roof.

Among those living under these conditions was the Jones family which was composed of Andrew Jones, the grandfather; Hannah Jones, the grand-

*Informant: H. E. Frederick, Orangeburg County, March 7, 1945. Collector: J. Mason Brewer.

mother; Mariah Jones, the daughter, and Paul Thomas, the husband of Mariah. There were also two grandchildren, Andrew Thomas, age 11, and Maria Thomas, age 9.

The Jones family lived on a farm near Seneca, and all were very ambitious. Consequently, they were happy to learn that there would be a night school started at the little Methodist church down in the woods. The children went every night, and so did Grandmother Jones. She went right along with the children and studied her reading, writing and arithmetic just as they did. Aunt Hannah was interested in all these subjects, but she liked arithmetic best and spent most of her time studying this subject.

One cold, winter night when Aunt Hannah and the children returned from night school, they found a warm fire in the fireplace with just the back logs burning. After warming their hands and feet, the children sat down and began to study their lessons, but Aunt Hannah looked at the red hot coals falling off the back logs and the ashes underneath them and thought about how good some sweet potatoes would be if they were roasted in those glowing coals and ashes. She went into the kitchen and got five large sweet potatoes and covered them over with the hot coals and ashes. As she sat there in her rocking chair watching the fire, she became drowsy and fell asleep.

While Aunt Hannah slept, her daughter, Mariah, went into the kitchen and got five more sweet potatoes and put them in the fire to roast. When they were done, Mariah took out three of the five potatoes she had put in the fire and ate them, leaving the remaining two with Hannah's five.

When Aunt Hannah woke up, Mariah and the children had gone to bed, so she took the sweet potatoes out of the ashes one by one and counted them.

"Some daw-gone body been stealin' mah pertaters," she cried after she finished counting them. "Ah put five uv 'em in de fiah; now Ah ain't got but seben!"

Question and Answer Tall Tales Of Negro School Children*

THE DARKEST NIGHT

Question: What de darkest night you ever done see?

Answer: De darkest night Ah ever done see, a raindrop knock on my doorstep an' ast fer a light to see how to hit de groun'.

---

* *Informants*: The Eighth Grade pupils of the Wilkinson High School, Orangeburg County, January 11, 1945. *Collector*: Alfred Isaac.

THE BLACKEST BABY

Question: What de blackest baby you ever done see?
Answer: De blackest baby Ah ever done see, his mama was carryin' 'im up de street an' de policeman arrest her fer carryin' a blackjack.

THE KICKINGEST MULE

Question: What de kickin'est mule you ever seen?
Answer: De kickin'est mule Ah ever seen kick de trumpet out o' Gabul' han' an' disappoint judgment.

THE CROOKEDEST ROAD

Question: What de crookedest road you ever see?
Answer: Ah seen a road so crooked till a gnat broke his neck goin' aroun' de curve.

THE TALLEST MAN

Question: What de tallest man you ever see?
Answer: De tallest man Ah ever see was gittin' a haircut in Heaven an' a shoeshine in Hell.

THE SHORTEST MAN

Question: What de shortest man you done see?
Answer: De shortest man Ah done see took a ladder to climb a grain o' sand.

THE HIGHEST HILL

Question: What de highest hill you ever seen?
Answer: Once upon a time Ah seen a hill so high till de lightnin' have to take low gear to git over de top.

THE RUNNINGEST CAR

Question: What is de runningest car you ever see?
Answer: De runningest car Ah ever see was my uncle's ol' car: It run over Monday, kill Tuesday, sen' Wednesday to de hospital, cripple Thursday, an' tol' Friday to tell Saddy to be at de fun'al Sunday at 4 o'clock p.m.

THE FATTEST WOMAN

Question: What de fattest woman you done see?
Answer: De fattest woman Ah done see, her husban' have to hug her on de installment plan.

THE LONGEST DOG

Question: What de longest dog you done seen?
Answer: De longest dog Ah ever done seen, his head was in New Jersey an' his tail was in Orangeburg. When his head died dey had to telephone de news to his tail.

THE LOWEST PERSON

Question: What de lowest person you ever seen?
Answer: De lowest person Ah done ever seen kin sit on a dime wid his feet hangin' down.

THE TALLEST STALK OF CORN

Question: What de tallest stalk o' corn you done ever seen?
Answer: Ah seen a stalk o' corn so tall till de angels in heaven was pickin' roastin' ears off o' it.

THE BIGGEST FOOL

Question: What de biggest fool you ever did see?
Answer: De biggest fool Ah ever did see,
Run all de way from Tennessee.
His eyes was red an' his lips was blue,
God A'mighty shook 'im till his shirt-tail flew.

THE POOREST LAND

Question: What de poorest lan' you ever done see?
Answer: De lan' in de graveyard whar my uncle buried. De lan' so po' till dey hafter put bakin' powder in de coffin so he kin rise in de jedgment day.

Church Folks

Rabbit in de springtime, rabbit in de fall;
Some o' dese ole folks can't shout at all.

How Uncle Jonas Interpreted
The Scriptures*

Immediately after the slaves were freed in Georgetown County, they began to establish churches. Since there were no preachers among the Negro ex-slaves, and Protestant churches had not yet begun to send ministers into the Southland to organize conferences and establish churches, the Negro freedmen in Georgetown found it very difficult to get someone to preach for them.

Among the churches in the county that were successful in obtaining the services of a pastor, however, was the little church at Plantersville. Uncle Jonas, a devout old man who had led the prayer services on one of the plantations in the county during slavery, was appointed as their minister, but he accepted the job only under the condition that he be given two weeks before he would be required to preach his first sermon. Uncle Jonas had a reason for making a request of this nature. He could not read and write, and the only way that he could get the subjects for his texts was to stand outside one of the white churches in Plantersville and listen to some white preacher deliver his sermon. In this manner he could memorize the text, and deliver the same sermon to his congregation on the following Sunday.

The first white preacher to whom he listened took for the subject of his text, "Oh Ye Generation of Vipers." So when the next Sunday came, Uncle Jonas took his place in the pulpit and said, "Brothers and Sisters, de subject fer mah text dis mawnin' be: 'Oh Ye Jimmie, don't you bite me.'" The next Sunday when he rose to give his text which was taken from the white preacher's text entitled, "There was a man of the Pharisees named Nicodemus who came to Jesus by night and said, Rabbi—" he said, "Mah text fer de mawnin' be: 'There was a man name Nick who caught a musk an' come to brudder Jays's an' sister Sue's house one night an' say rabbit.'"

Uncle Jonas had gotten along all right for two Sundays now, and the members of the little church were well pleased with his sermons. But he took sick after he left the church and did not get a chance to stand outside a white church that Sunday night and listen to the preacher's sermon. So the next Sunday morning he was at a loss to know what to talk about. He remembered, however, having heard a white minister preach a good sermon, during the time he had been a slave, on the subject of "Samson the Great."

When the time came for him to deliver the message for the morning, he arose and said, "Mah text fer de mawnin' be: 'Samson de Great,' who carried off de gates uv Gazer in de days uv Budarack, who tuck de jawbone uv a gray mule, killed fifteen hundred people out uv a thousan', an' de rest uv 'em got away."

---

* *Informant*: H. E. Frederick. *Collector*: J. Mason Brewer.

Sister Rosie Changes Her Mind*

The new preacher had just come to the little Baptist church at Bishop-ville and was having a meeting with the sisters of the church to see if they couldn't think of some plan to get rid of the large church debt that the preacher who preceded him had left on the building.

Among the faithful sisters who were present at the meeting was Sister Rosie Wright. She had always been known as a great church worker. Sister Rosie's husband died about a year before the new preacher arrived, and she was not able to give nearly as much money as when her husband was living. He had not left her any insurance money, and she was forced to pay off a large funeral bill after his death. It took all the money she could rake and scrape to buy food and clothing for herself. She had to keep up the payments on the little four-room house she was buying, too.

So it was a little embarrassing to Sister Rosie to sit there at the meeting and hear the other sisters get up and say what they would give in order to pay off the church debt, when she was unable to do anything herself. When all of them had finished stating how much they would give to relieve the church's indebtedness, Sister Rosie arose and said slowly, "Ah don't have nothin' to give, Revun, but if I had a thousand dollars Ah sho' would give it to the church."

About two weeks later Sister Rosie's house caught fire and burned down. The house was insured, and in less than a week the fire insurance company paid her a thousand dollars. The preacher heard about it and went to see her.

"Sister Rosie," he said, "Ah hears you got a thousand dollars insurance on yo' house. Now you can gimme dat thousand dollars you said you gonna give to de church."

"Well, Revun, it's like dis," replied Sister Rosie. "When Ah was tellin' yuh 'bout it Ah had de will but Ah didn't have de money; an' now Ah's got de money, but Ah ain't got de will!"

Uncle John and the Upcountry Girl**

There are numerous churches on St. Helena Island, but by far the most important religious institution to the church folks of the island is the praise-house, located on each plantation.

The praise-house plays a very important part in the religious life of the island people, for it is at these places that the church folks meet on Tuesday and Thursday nights of each week for their prayer services. They usually remain at the praise-house until daybreak, singing and praying. The praise-

---

* *Informant*: Emma Lloyd, Marlboro County, November 2, 1944. *Collector*: Mattie E. Fisher.

** *Informant*: Lurline James, Dorchester County, February 9, 1941. *Collector*: Mattie E. Mouzon.

house is not a denominational institution; it is used by Baptists and Methodists alike. Any number of churches may use the same praise-house.

It is a very interesting religious institution in many ways, for new members of the church must first enter through the praise-house. If anyone in the community desires to become a member of the church, he must first make his wishes known to the praise-house group and ask them to pray for him. He is then given detailed instructions as to what he must do if he wants to be recommended for acceptance into church membership. The first requirement is that he pick out some person in the praise-house group as his teacher, to train him in such a way that he will qualify for church membership.

The manner in which he selects his teacher is the "dream method." The candidate for church membership must see his teacher in a dream. The person that he sees in a dream is then placed in charge of his training, and his training period begins. It has been said that people often wander around through the snake-infested swamps of the island, praying to God, and asking Him to show them their teacher in a dream. Strange to say, no one has ever been bitten by a snake while on this kind of mission. Once the candidate's teacher is shown him in a dream, he is under the supervision of this person, and then his period of probation and training which involves, among other things, the sacrifice of something worldly, begins. If the candidate is an unmarried person, he or she is usually required to give up courtship during the training period. If the candidate is a young person attending school, he must stop going to school during his probationary period.

Finally, when the candidate is found worthy of membership in the church, he is recommended by the president or leader of the praise-house to the pastor and to the official board of the church. Most of the candidates meet the requirements and are admitted to the church of their choice. Only now and then does one fail.

One occasion of failure was the time when a young woman from the "upcountry" section of the state met a praise-house group and expressed a desire to join the church. The "presider" of this particular praise-house, an old man by the name of Uncle John, was the one she saw in her dream as her teacher. This was very unfortunate for the young lady because Uncle John required all the candidates that he taught to see him somewhere in their travels on the day they were admitted to the church. The girl, however, being a newcomer to the island community and the low country, did not know this, so when the day came for her to be accepted into the church, and was called upon to make her statement, she arose and said, "An' Ah went way up to Heaben an' Ah seent a lot o' angels flyin' aroun' up dere wid dey putty white wings, an' Ah seent Paul an' Silas an' Peter an' all de 'sciples sittin' roun' a shiny gol' th'one eatin' milk an' honey."

After the girl had finished giving her experience, the chairman of the Deacon Board rose and asked if there were any objections to the girl's becoming a member of the church. Uncle John did not give him time to finish his statement, but jumped to his feet, stomped them on the floor, and said,

"Ah objec's! She sure didn't see me nowhars in her travels." Whereupon the girl was told by the chairman that she would have to go back and give her experience over again and see Uncle John somewhere in her dream. So the poor frightened girl stood up and started to give her experience again. She said: "An' Ah went down in Hell an' Ah seent de Devil an' all his imps wid dey long forky tails a-stannin' 'roun' a great big fiery furnace wid dey pitchforks, an' in de middle o' de red hot coals in de furnace Ah seent Unker John wid his long forky tail, jes' a-burnin'."

On hearing this, Uncle John leaped to his feet, pointed his finger in the girl's face, and yelled, "You's a liar, madam—you ain't see me nowhars!"

The Wise Preacher*

The old time African Methodist preachers were very careful about whom they took into the church and about saying things during the preaching of funerals that were not true. This was especially so in the South Carolina county of Clarendon located in the upcountry section of the state. The African Methodists were strict enough about this, but a group of them who had pulled out of the original African Methodist Church and who called themselves Reform Methodists were more particular about matters of this sort than the mother church.

Once upon a time there was a woman named Sadie White who belonged to the New Hope Reform Methodist Church at Pinewood. She herself was a good Christian woman but her husband, Jack, was a gambler and a drunkard and would not support her. Neither would he attend the church services at New Hope. His wife had entreated him to go to church with her, but he would just laugh and go somewhere to gamble instead.

One Sunday, while his wife was at church, Jack got into an argument about some money at a dice game and a man shot and killed him. Sadie made arrangements for the funeral and asked Reverend Wright, the pastor of the Reform Methodist Church, to preach at the funeral. Reverend Wright refused to have anything at all to do with the affair, and so the A.M.E. preacher was asked to preach Jack's funeral. He too, however, turned down the request. So Sadie had to go out in the country near Pinewood and get an A.M.E. preacher off the Lewisville Circuit to preach at her husband's funeral.

The preacher that Sadie engaged agreed to preach the funeral, but he was very careful about what he said. He had heard some bad things said about Jack as he entered the church house, so he decided to be very cautious in his remarks about the dead man. After delivering a very short funeral sermon, he ended up by saying, "Some o' you brethren seems to be in doubt 'bout whar dis brudder b'longs, in Heaven or Hell, so Ah jes' gwine put 'im on de Jordan an' let whosoever want 'im, God or de Devil, come an' git 'im."

---

* *Informant*: Henry Pearson, Orangeburg County, January 5, 1945. *Collector*: J. Mason Brewer.

Mose Johnson at the Heavenly Gates*†

Mose Johnson was the outshoutin'es' member of the St. James Baptist Church up at Pinewood. He was the only man in the church who could outshout the sisters and was known far and wide for his unique ability. Mose often said that he knew he was going to walk the golden streets when he got to heaven because he had been such a loyal Christian down here on earth. The members of the church and the people in the community thought the same thing, but when Mose died and went to heaven, the gates did not fly open to welcome him as he thought they would.

Mose was very surprised that no one paid attention to him. So, after sitting down in front of the Heavenly Gates for a long time, he walked up and tapped on the wall. The guardian angel who was on watch at the time said, "What do you want?"

"Ah wants in," replied Mose. "Ah's Mose Johnson, an' Ah wants to git in de gate."

"What have you done to deserve entering the High Gates of Heaven?" inquired the angel.

"St. Peter knows all 'bout me," replied Mose. "Ast him 'bout what Ah's done."

So the angel called St. Peter and asked him if he knew Mose Johnson. "Seems like to me I remember a little something about him," replied St. Peter, "but I don't recall what it is just now. Let me call St. James and have him look up his record." He then called St. James and told him to look it up. In a few minutes St. James came back with the record book and St. Peter asked him what the record said Mose had done for the Lord.

"He didn't do much o' nothin'," replied St. James, "but I see here where he did give a dime one time."

"A dime!" yelled St. Peter. "That ain't enough for him to get into Heaven. Just give the dime back to him and let him go to Hell!"

On the Railroad

If you's black, git back!

---

* *Informant:* Rev. P. H. Carmichael, Clarendon County, February 10, 1945. *Collector:* J. Mason Brewer.

† This anecdote is another universally known parable familiar to many cultures. More or less similar versions will be found in *Moslem Laughter,* by Habeeb Khalif, privately published in New York, 1906; *Wit and Humor of Ireland,* by Marshall Brown, S. G. Griggs and Co., Chicago, 1884; *Encyclopedia of Jewish Humor,* by Henry D. Spalding, Jonathan David Publishers, New York, 1969, and in other volumes. Of the Negro versions, J. Mason Brewer's is the most anthologized.

The Atlantic Coast Line 10:51*

People in Orangeburg, South Carolina, who wish to catch the Atlantic Coast Line night train to Atlanta, Georgia, do not have to bother about getting to the railroad station on time. The night train is scheduled to arrive at 10:51, but is always from one to three hours late when it pulls into the station. For this reason people who wish to leave on this train never begin to pack their belongings until shortly before eleven o'clock. They know that the 10:51 will be arriving late and that there is no need of hurrying.

There is only one time in the history of Orangeburg that the 10:51 came in on time, and what an exciting event that was for the good people of the town!

It was a Saturday night and quite a few people were down to the station to meet relatives and friends who were coming in on the 10:51. One old man who had just moved to Orangeburg walked up to the ticket window and asked the agent if the train was on time. The agent told him "yes." At this, a longtime resident of the town, who did not know that the old man was a newcomer and unacquainted with the truth about the 10:51, became excited and said to the other folks in the station, "Did you hear that? The 10:51 is coming in on time. Let's take up a collection, and if it comes in on schedule we'll give it to the engineer." The others all agreed so he passed his hat around and pretty soon he had a hundred dollars collected and all ready to hand over to the engineer.

Everybody was as excited as could be. They all lined up beside the track and looked up towards the bridge where the train first made its appearance; and sure enough, about 10:45, they heard the 10:51 blow and saw its headlight shining brightly around the curve. It raced into the station at exactly 10:51.

As soon as it came to a stop the man who collected the one hundred dollars reward jumped up into the engineer's cab, shook hands with him, and said, "Here's a hundred dollars for you."

"What's this for?" asked the engineer.

"That's for bringing the train in on time," replied the man.

"Well, I thank you for the money all right," said the engineer, "but this is *yesterday's* train!"

The Sleepy-Headed Ellenton Boy**

Once upon a time there was a boy in Ellenton, South Carolina, by the name of Ed. He used to work at the hotel in Ellenton and wait on the

---

* *Informant:* Murray Holliday, Orangeburg County, September 23, 1944. *Collector:* Cora V. Green.

** *Informant*: Beulah Steadman, Jasper County, March 2, 1945. *Collector*: Bertha Meyers.

drummers who came from New York to sell goods to the merchants in the little town. He liked to hear them talk about New York City and was always asking questions about it. Finally, he became so interested that he decided to quit his job in Ellenton and go to New York to work.

After living in New York for two or three years he got homesick and decided to visit his parents in Ellenton and let them see how well he was getting along in the great city of New York. He bought himself a new style suit, a new hat, a new pair of shoes and a new traveling bag. He dressed up in his new clothes and went down to Pennsylvania Station. He purchased a ticket for Ellenton and boarded the train.

As it happened, he left New York on the night train, and so he didn't get a chance to sleep much. There were a lot of people who were going to Washington and other places who kept up a lot of laughter and boisterous activities all night long, preventing everybody from going to sleep. So Ed slept nearly all the next day. He slept so long that he passed Ellenton. When he woke up the train had reached Mansfield, a little town in the central part of Georgia.

Ed grabbed up his suitcase and got off the train, intending to catch the next train back to Ellenton, but he did not know what kind of town he was in. He found out quickly enough, however, for as soon as he alighted from the train some white men grabbed him by the collar, shook him and said, "Boy, don't you know we don't allow no blacks in this town? We gonna whip you good."

"Naw, suh, boss," pleaded Ed, "please don't whip me. Ah didn't know whar Ah was."

"Well," replied one of the men, "if we don't whip you, will you catch the next train out of here?"

"Yas suh, yas suh," said Ed, trembling with fear. "Ah'll go you one better'n dat; if you gimme two minutes Ah'll ketch dat un what done jes' went!"

Little Joe and the Bald-Headed Money*

One time up in Abbeville County a little boy named Joe was being carried by his mother to Spartansburg in order to buy him some Easter clothes. It was the first time that he had ever ridden on a train, so he talked constantly. He kept looking out of the window, pointing out everything that he saw to his mother. He was a regular chatterbox, and everybody on the train was looking at him as if they were becoming quite annoyed.

He slept for a long time, to the delight of the other passengers, but was finally aroused from his slumber by the train coming to a sudden halt. The noise of the engine and the jolt of the coach woke him, and he started looking out of the window and talking again. Several new passengers boarded

---

* *Informant:* Henry Pearson, Orangeburg County, February 3, 1945. *Collector:* J. Mason Brewer.

the train, among them a bald-headed man. Little Joe saw him at once and yelled, "Oh, mama! Look at dat bald-headed man, bald-headed man!"

"Madam," said the man angrily, "why didn't you leave that brat at home? Children who don't know how to act ought not to be brought on trips." Then, turning to the little boy, he handed him two quarters and said, "Here, sonny, take this money and see if you can't keep your mouth shut and quit talking so much."

The little boy, holding the money up high in the air, turned to his mother and yelled, "Dis is mah bald-headed money, bald-headed money, bald-headed money! . . ."

Taking No Chances

Don't crow till you git out o' de woods;
Dey mought be a bear behin' de las' tree!

Uncle Jasper and the Watermelon Bet*

Quite a few watermelons are raised in the state of South Carolina, but one of the counties where they thrive best is Barnwell County. During the season, a large number of people in the small towns make a business of selling watermelons. Most of them usually buy a large melon on Saturday and carry it home to use as part of their Sunday dinner. The watermelon business is so prosperous that many of the vendors buy an entire wagonload at a time.

One of the best watermelon peddlers in the county was a white man at Allendale by the name of Dillon. Most of the Negroes in Allendale bought their melons from him because he had special ways of attracting their attention and getting them interested in buying.

There was only one time that he made a mistake in his advertising methods, and that was one Saturday when he picked up a big forty-pound watermelon from his wagon and said, "I'll give anybody who can eat this whole melon to the rind a ten dollar bill, but under one condition only: if he fails to eat it to the rind he will have to pay me a dollar for the melon."

No one said anything at first, but finally an old man by the name of Uncle Jasper got up off the box he was sitting on and said, "Will you gimme ten minutes to decide?"

"Sure," replied Dillon. So Uncle Jasper left. In exactly ten minutes he came back and announced that he was ready to eat the forty-pound melon. Dillon handed it to him and he ate it to the rind in about four minutes.

Dillon, who was very much surprised that Uncle Jasper was able to eat the large watermelon, and who hated to pay him the ten dollars that

Informant: Mrs. L. T. Rivers, Clarendon County, February 12, 1945.
Collector: Mrs. L. J. Samuel.

he had promised, said, "Uncle Jasper, I'm gonna pay you the ten dollars all right, but before I pay you I'd like to know why you wanted ten minutes to decide."

"Well," replied Uncle Jasper, "Ah knowed dat Ah had one at home dat weighed forty pounds, so Ah went home an' et dat un, an' Ah knowed ef Ah et dat un, Ah c'd eat dis un, too."

The St. Matthews Boy and the Rainstorm*

The weather in South Carolina is unpredictable. It is very difficult to forecast, to any extent, just what the weather will be like on any certain day. There are times when you have winter, spring, summer and autumn all on the same day. In the short span of twenty-four hours one may use his overcoat, his raincoat and his umbrella, his electric fan, and go about in his shirt sleeves. For this reason, people are often caught away from home in rainstorms and are forced to remain where they are until the downpour is over.

One night, out in the country near St. Matthews, a young man went to call on his best girl. When he left home the moon was shining and the stars were twinkling. There wasn't a cloud in the sky, nor a breeze blowing from any direction. Since it was a summer night and very warm, the young man did not even wear his coat, but it wasn't long before he wished that he had worn it, and had taken along his raincoat too.

All of a sudden the raindrops began to beat heavily on the roof of the house, and a strong wind blew the rain against the window panes with such strong force that it made them shake and rattle. It was ten o'clock when the rainstorm started, and at twelve o'clock it was still raining hard.

Seeing that the young man did not have the proper clothing to go out into the rain, the girl's mother invited him to spend the night. The boy accepted the invitation and then asked the girl and her mother to excuse him for a minute. When he came back into the house he was out of breath from running so fast. The old lady noticed this and asked him where he had been.

The boy hesitated for a moment, "Ah's been home fer mah sleepin' clothes."

Joshua and the Moonshine**

Greenville County is in one of the leading peach-growing sections of South Carolina. Hundreds of bushels of peaches are shipped from this county to various regions of the country each year. Many of them are also canned

---

Informant: Helen Spears, Marlboro County, March 12, 1945. *Collector:* Mrs. Willie E. Windom.

**Informant*: Genora Gray, Greenville County, October 2, 1944. *Collector*: Bessie A. Goldsmith.

and preserved by the local residents, but there is also another use to which they are put by some of the folks who live in the mountains of Upper Greenville County.

One of the mountaineers who used the peaches for purposes other than canning and preserving was a Negro named Joshua Jones. He was an expert maker of moonshine liquor. For years he had made his whiskey and brandy without interference from the Greenville County Sheriff or revenue officers. This was because the other Negroes living in the little mountain community kept his secret.

Joshua got along all right with his neighbors until he built himself a two-story brick house and purchased a Cadillac. This made some of the women in the community jealous and they persuaded their husbands to tell the county sheriff about Joshua making moonshine liquor. Since the men could not give their wives what Joshua was giving his, they agreed to report him to the sheriff.

The very next Saturday several of the men went into Greenville and told the sheriff what Joshua was doing.

One day, while Joshua was busy making moonshine, the sheriff and some of his deputies came up and arrested him. They carried him into Greenville and ushered him into the courthouse. The judge, after finding out what the charge against him was, said, "So you're the Joshua who made the sun stand still, I guess."

"Naw, suh, Boss," replied Joshua, "you's got me sorta mixed up. I's de Joshua dat made de moonshine!"

PART THREE

JOHN TALES

John and His Boss-Man's Watermelon Patch

Some of the plantation owners in the neighborhood gave their hands an acre of land on which to raise vegetables, corn, and watermelons, but Colonel Clemons was so mean that he would not let John and the other hands raise any food at all for themselves. He wanted them to buy everything at his commissary.

So it was hard for Colonel Clemons' hands to get a watermelon even in watermelon season. He wouldn't let them have any from his own patch, and he wouldn't give them any money to buy them from other plantations. So John secretly visited the Colonel's patch once or twice a week and took several melons home. David and Joseph, his little boys, always went with him and helped him bring them down to the cabin.

This had been going on for three years now and the Colonel hadn't caught up with them. But one Saturday evening when he was returning from town, he saw John and the little boys leaving his watermelon patch. All had a melon on each shoulder. The Colonel rode up to them and stopped his horse.

"I've been missing a lot of watermelons out of my patch lately," he said to John. "Lots of tracks lead up this way, and it seems like those watermelons you have may be mine, you thievin' rascals."

"Things ain't always what dey seems, Boss," replied John.

"Well," said the Colonel, "you are coming from the direction of my patch."

"What direction got to do wid a hones' man?" answered John.

The Colonel was so outdone with John's reply that he headed his horse toward the Big House and went on home.

John as a Coachman
and the Rats

Occasionally, on Sunday afternoons, John drove the Boss-man and his family over to the Boss-man's brother's plantation. Since these visits usually lasted three or four hours, John always grew tired of waiting, but the Colonel gave him orders not to get down off the coach and to stay in the driver's seat for fear the horses would run away. Sometimes he would get so sleepy that he could hardly keep his eyes open.

One summer the Colonel got to visiting his brother twice a week, and each time John would get sleepier and sleepier. He finally decided to disobey the Colonel and find himself a place to lie down. Fortunately, his little boys, David and Joseph, always went with him and played with the ducks and guineas in the barnyard. So John found him a place to rest and got the little boys to watch for the Colonel's return. He told them to wake him up when they saw the Colonel start out of the house.

John went to a large haystack not far from the place where he stopped the coach and lay down and went to sleep.

Now the Colonel usually stayed three or four hours, but on this day David and Joseph were fooled, because he stayed only one hour. The Colonel had come out of the house and had almost reached the coach before they saw him. In a big hurry, they shook John, woke him up, and told him the Colonel was coming. John got up, half asleep and half awake, and started running toward the coach at full speed.

"What are you doing off that seat, John?" said the Colonel.

"Catchin' rats, Boss, catchin' rats," replied John.

"How many you caught?" asked the Colonel.

"Well, when Ah ketch dis one Ah'm after an' then one more," replied John, "Ah'll have two!"

John, McGruder, and the Boss-man's Wife

Of all the hands on the Clemons Plantation, John liked McGruder best. He and John were the only hands who had been kept on by the Colonel when the slaves were freed, and for this reason they were the best of friends. Another reason why John was fond of McGruder was that he could always play some prank on him. John had learned to read and write and count since freedom, while McGruder could neither read nor write and could count only to ten. So John had a great deal of fun out of knowing things his friend didn't know.

McGruder was a good marksman, however, and owned an old double-barrel shotgun that the Colonel had laid aside as unfit for use. John was a poor shot and did not have a gun, but sometimes McGruder invited him to go with him down into the woods to hunt. When they returned home McGruder would always divide whatever game he had killed with John.

One winter day, when the cotton had all been picked and bacon was scarce at the Colonel's commissary, McGruder decided that he would go down into the woods and kill some rabbits and squirrels for dinner. He asked John to go along with him because he knew that if Colonel Clemons caught him with any game beside possum John would be clever enough to get them out of it.

They had not gone far into the woods before a rabbit jumped up in the weeds and McGruder killed it.

"We killed a rabbit, didn't we?" said John.

"Yeah, we killed a rabbit," replied McGruder.

In a few minutes McGruder sighted some squirrels playing high up among the branches of a tall tree. He took aim with his gun and killed two of them.

"We killed some squirrels, didn't we?" said John.

"Yeah, we killed some squirrels," replied McGruder.

And then, since it was almost twelve o'clock, McGruder decided that he would take the rabbit and the squirrels on home so his wife could cook them for dinner.

As they came in sight of the Big House, McGruder saw a covey of quails flying low and took a shot at them. But instead of the shots striking the birds, they went past them into the Colonel's lot and killed one of his mules.

The Colonel heard the shot and saw the mule fall. He ran up to where John and McGruder stood trembling with fear.

"Who killed my mule?" he shouted.

"We did," answered McGruder.

"We *nothin'!*" replied John. "You killed dat mule yo'self. Ah ain't got no gun."

How John Got McGruder's Chickens

Every year when the chickens got to be plentiful on the large plantations, John and McGruder would take some large sacks and make trips two or three nights each week to the chicken houses. They always went together. One of them would watch while the other took the chickens off the roost. In this way they were never caught stealing. They always came back with five or six fat hens or frying-size chickens.

One night, however, when John went down to McGruder's cabin to look for him, he was not at home. John searched the entire plantation but couldn't find him anywhere. But early the next morning, when John was on his way to the mule lot to feed the mules and horses, who should come towards him with his chicken sack slung across his shoulder but McGruder!

"Where you been?" said John. "Ah been lookin' fer you all night long."

"Ah been out hustlin'," replied McGruder.

"What did you git?" asked John.

"Chickens," replied McGruder. "Guess how many Ah's got in dis sack an' Ah'll give you both of 'em."

"Two," said John.

"Humph," said McGruder, "somebody musta tol' you."

John, McGruder, and the Barrel of Apples

Once each month Colonel Clemons took John and McGruder down to his commissary on the river to get the month's supply of groceries for himself and his hands, and feed for the stock. John drove the grocery wagon and McGruder drove the feed wagon.

One year on the second Saturday in December, when John and McGruder went with the Colonel down to the commissary to get the supplies for Christmas, they saw a large shipment of apples being unloaded from a freight train. Because they were so busy, the clerks didn't have time to carry the barrels inside as they were unloaded from the freight cars, but left them out behind the store.

While John and McGruder were carrying the groceries and the feed to the wagons, they started thinking how nice it would be to take one of the barrels of apples home with them. They could bury it in the ground until Christmas, and then dig it up and fill the children's stockings with apples on Christmas eve.

So that night they stole a barrel of apples. Since it was moonlight, they decided to divide the apples that same night. So, John started counting them out. "One for you, and one for me," he said, placing one apple on the right hand side of the barrel for himself, and one on the left hand side for McGruder.

"Two for you," continued John, putting one apple in McGruder's pile, "and two for me," he said, dropping two apples in his pile. "Three for you," he went on while throwing one more apple in McGruder's pile, "and one, two, three for me," this time letting three apples fall in his pile.

John continued in this manner, never giving McGruder more than one apple at a time, but always giving himself the exact number mentioned. When he had taken all of the apples out of the barrel, McGruder, who could not count, but who had been watching his pile and John's pile and comparing the size of them, said, "John, is yuh countin' dem apples right?"

"Sho' Ah is, fool!" said John. "Didn' yuh hear me countin' 'em? Evuh time Ah took one Ah give you one; when Ah took two Ah give you two."

"Well, is dey as many apples in yo' pile as dey is in mine?"

"Sho' dey is," replied John.

"Well den," said McGruder, "Ah'll jes take yo' pile!"

John and the Two White Men in Court

One year the boll-weevils got into the cotton crop on Colonel Clemons' plantation and destroyed most of it. This made times very hard for the Colonel, and since he did not make any money, he did not provide sufficient food and clothing for the hands. So naturally they stole anything they could get away with.

Never did a week pass that some of the hands were not arrested and carried to jail.

One day the sheriff came out to Colonel Clemons' farm and arrested John. With him were two white hands he had arrested on a neighboring plantation. John and the two white hands were all charged with stealing and they were to be tried on the same day, at the same hour.

When John and the two white men were brought into the court room and arraigned for trial, John was very nervous and was trembling. This was the first time in his life that he had not been able to think of an excuse. He knew, however, that they were going to try the white men first, so he decided to listen to their answers and imitate them when his turn came.

The first case called was that of one of the white hands who was accused of stealing a horse.

"Guilty or not guilty?" demanded the judge.

"Not guilty," replied the man. "I've owned that horse ever since he was a colt." The case was dismissed.

Then the judge called the second white man to the stand. He was accused of stealing a cow. "Guilty or not guilty?" asked the judge.

"Not guilty," replied the defendant. "I've owned that cow ever since she was a calf." The case was dismissed.

Then John was called to the stand. He was accused of stealing a wagon.
"Guilty or not guilty?" asked the judge.

"Not guilty," replied John. "Ah's owned dat wagon ever since it was a
wheelbarrow."

PART FOUR

AUNT DICY TALES

Snuff and tobacco you'd better quit,
'Cause when you get to heaven
There'll be no place to spit.

Aunt Dicy and the Mailman

When General Granger landed in Galveston, Texas, on June 19, 1865, and
issued a proclamation declaring all Negro slaves in the state of Texas free,
the plantation owners in Burleson County were greatly disturbed. It was the
cotton-chopping season and they needed the slaves they had formerly owned
to thin out the hundreds of acres of cotton they had planted. They would
need the slave labor again in August, and in September, too, because the
cotton bolls would be open at that time, and the cotton would be ready for
picking.

Many of the plantation owners bargained with their former slaves and
made contracts with them to pay a certain sum of money for every acre of
cotton they chopped. But there were a few among the freed Negroes who
refused to work for the prices offered. Among them were Uncle June and
Aunt Dicy Johnson. Both had been married previously. They had three
children born to them as a result of their second marriage: Pomp, a boy
aged 16, and two girls, Serelia and Samantha, aged 14 and 12.

Uncle June and Aunt Dicy had heard that there was a German community just across the Burleson County line in Lee County where the farm
owners wanted to hire Negro families to help them work their farms. So, one
Saturday morning about two months after freedom had been declared,
Uncle June, Aunt Dicy and their children bundled up their clothes and put
them in an old wheelbarrow they had bought from their former slave master.
They walked all day, each taking turns at pushing the wheelbarrow until
they finally reached Lee County. Soon after they had crossed the county
line, they met a man on horseback, and he told them that there was a
German by the name of Schultze who lived about four miles farther down
the road who wanted to hire a Negro family to work on his farm.

So the Johnson family continued to trudge along until they came to a

ROAST SUCKLING PIG

This old "Dime Box" recipe may well have been Aunt Dicy Johnson's
own (see page 119).
Deceptively simple, the preparation has lasted for more than a century,
pleasing palates everywhere, from its original Texas home to the Cana-
dian border.

1 young piglet	2 tsp. salt
1 tsp. pepper	1 tsp. paprika
1 tbs. lemon juice	1 tbs. vinegar
1 tbs. dry mustard	

To be sufficiently tender for roasting whole, the piglet should be five or
six weeks old—no older! Clean piglet thoroughly and then scald. Salt and
pepper inside and out as you would a fowl. Fill with your favorite dressing.
Sew up.

Rub outside of piglet with a paste made from salt, pepper, paprika,
lemon juice, vinegar and mustard.

Place piglet in roasting pan and bake 3½ to 4 hours, basting from time
to time. When ready to serve, remove from oven and place a red apple in
piglet's mouth. Garnish with water cress or parsley. Serves 10 to 12.

gate beside the road that had William Schultze's name painted on it. About five hundred yards back on a hill, nestled along a clump of trees, could be seen a large white house. The Johnson family entered the gate and started walking towards the house. Before they arrived, however, a man came forward to meet them. The man was Mr. Schultze, and he asked Uncle June and Aunt Dicy what they wanted. They told him they were looking for a job on a farm and that they had been told he was looking for help. He replied that he certainly was, and right then and there he hired Uncle June and Aunt Dicy to work for him.

Mr. Schultze had a little three-room shack that he let the Johnson family live in. There was a well of fresh water in the back yard, and an old woodshed where they could keep their cordwood dry when it rained. Mr. Schultze also allowed them one acre of land free on which they could raise as many vegetables as they liked to help provide them with food. There was a big stretch of woods too, and he told Uncle June that he could hunt rabbits, squirrels and doves there any time he pleased. He gave Aunt Dicy permission to gather several buckets full of plums and peaches from the orchard to make preserves, and he told the Johnson children they could go down into the pecan grove any time they felt like it and get a flour-sack full of pecans.

So the Johnson family was very happy; that is, all except Aunt Dicy, who was a snuff-dipper, and who was worried because there was no general store near the Schultze farm where she could buy a box of snuff. She was accustomed to receiving a free box of snuff every Saturday from her former master, and now that she had used up the supply she had brought with her from Burleson County she was very irritable.

This kept up for almost a month until, one Saturday when Aunt Dicy was out in her front yard, she looked down the lane and saw the mailman from Lexington loping his horse towards Mr. Schultze's mail box. She ran as fast as she could and reached the mailman before he could get back into his buggy and drive off.

"Mister, mister," said Aunt Dicy handing him a dime, and almost out of breath from running so fast, "would you mind bringing me a dime box of snuff from Lexington the next time you come to bring the mail?"

"I'd be glad to," replied the mailman. So the next Monday morning when he came by, Aunt Dicy met him at the mailbox and he gave her the box of snuff she had sent for.

Every Saturday, from that time on, for as long as she lived on the Schultze farm, she would meet the mailman and gave him a dime to bring her a dime box of snuff. Everybody in the little community knew about Aunt Dicy's practice of sending for snuff by the mailman, so they called a meeting one night and they decided to call the little community *Dime Box of Snuff*, in honor of Aunt Dicy.

They shortened the name later, and to this day the little community still goes by the name of Dime Box.

According to Where the Drop Falls

One Sunday morning about eight months after Aunt Dicy and Uncle June had been living on Mr. Schultze's farm, Aunt Dicy's nephew, Hezekiah, who lived in Caldwell, rode up to their little house and knocked on the front door. Aunt Dicy was busy cooking Sunday dinner in the kitchen, so Uncle June, who was sitting in an old rickety straw-bottomed rocking chair in the front bedroom, opened the door and let Hezekiah in.

They shook hands, and then Hezekiah asked where Aunt Dicy was.

"She's in the kitchen cooking dinner, son," replied Uncle June. "You know how Dicy is about always fixing something extra for me and the children to eat on Sunday."

"I certainly do," said Hezekiah as he made his way to the kitchen where Aunt Dicy was busy making biscuits.

Aunt Dicy stopped what she was doing as soon as she saw Hezekiah. She ran to him and gave him a big hug, at the same time asking about his mother, her sister Liza. After the greeting, she invited him to sit down in the old rawhide chair next to the kitchen stove where she went to work finishing the biscuits she was making. Her head was directly above the biscuit dough, and every now and then, as she kneaded it, she would take a thumbful of snuff out of her snuff-box and put it underneath her lip. She was bending over the biscuit dough and some of the snuff juice had begun to trickle down to the end of the hickory toothpick she had in her mouth, forming a little round ball at the end.

As Aunt Dicy continued to make the biscuit dough ready for baking she turned to Hezekiah and said, "Son, how long are you going to be with us?"

"I don't know, Aunt Dicy," replied Hezekiah, watching the small drop of snuff on the end of her toothpick as it threatened to jar loose and fall into the biscuit dough. "It's according to where the drop falls."

Aunt Dicy in the Courtroom

After Aunt Dicy's son, Pomp, got his diploma from the Giddings High School, he went to Caldwell and got a job working at a cotton gin. But instead of saving the money he earned each week he would shoot dice every Saturday night with a bunch of the men he worked with, and invariably he would lose nearly all of the money he had earned during the week.

One Saturday night Pomp came to Giddings and started a dice game with some of the men who worked at the Giddings cotton gin. Somebody told the county sheriff where the gambling was going on, so he went down to the place where Pomp and the other men were shooting dice and arrested them.

When the day came for the trial Aunt Dicy went to the court house in order to pay Pomp's fine. As a general rule, when Aunt Dicy went to public places she always carried a paper bag with her to dispose of the snuff-juice after she had dipped it, but she was so worried about Pomp that particular morning that she forgot to bring a bag with her.

After taking a big dip of snuff, she spat the snuff-juice on the floor. One of her neighbors, Bill Wilson, went over to where she was seated and said, "Aunt Dicy, don't you know there's a five dollar fine for spitting on the courtroom floor?"

"No, I didn't know that, son," replied Aunt Dicy taking three five-dollar bills out of an old-handkerchief in which she carried her money, "so I tell you what you do: take this fifteen dollars and give it to the judge for me right now, 'cause I'm going to spit two more times before I leave."

Aunt Dicy and Rev. Jackson's Sermon

Aunt Dicy had gotten to the point where she did not like Reverend Jackson because he was always butting into her business—especially her snuff-dipping, and this was the one thing that she wouldn't stand for: anyone to interfere in any manner with her habit.

She had not liked it the time Reverend Jackson had caught her dipping snuff when she was feeding the hogs, and she had to pretend she was eating chocolate and spitting it out because it had such a bad taste. And now he had gotten to the place where he included snuff-dipping along with the other sins he listed in his sermons every Sunday. Aunt Dicy was not pleased with this at all, so she swore that the very next time the Reverend said anything against snuff-dipping in his sermons she was going to stop him and tell him exactly what she thought about him.

The very next Sunday morning after Aunt Dicy had made her statement, when Reverend Jackson got up to preach, he started out as usual listing the kind of people who were going to Hell.

"All you drunkards," he said, "you're going to lift your eyes in Hell one of these mornings; all you liars, you're going to lift your eyes in Hell one of these mornings; all you gamblers, you're going to lift your eyes in Hell one of these mornings; and all of you snuff-dippers, too," he continued, "you're going to lift your eyes in Hell one of these mornings."

Aunt Dicy jumped up from the bench she was sitting on and yelled, "Look ahere, Reverend, you've done stopped preaching and gone to meddling!"

Aunt Dicy and
Booker T. Washington's Speech

After remaining on Mr. Schultze's farm for sixteen years, Uncle June and Aunt Dicy had saved enough money to buy them a small 50-acre farm of their own, two miles south of Mr. Schultze's place.

Aunt Dicy had learned to love the community in which her employer's farm was located, and she wanted to live in that same neighborhood for the rest of her life. Uncle June, being a good husband, did not object.

Several of Aunt Dicy and Uncle June's Negro neighbors, who had worked on nearby plantations, had also saved enough money to buy farms, so they all purchased small parcels of land in the same section of Lee County as had Aunt Dicy and Uncle June. Now they could still be together.

There were quite a few farms owned by white people that separated the new community of Negroes from Old Dime Box, but Aunt Dicy's friends, remembering that Old Dime Box had been named in her honor, decided to call the new community Dime Box too.

Serelia and Samantha were away attending school at Prairie View College, and Pomp had long since moved to Houston, so Aunt Dicy and Uncle June, being lonesome, traveled quite a bit to public lectures, camp meetings and revivals in nearby towns.

One Sunday, about five years after they had moved to their new home, Aunt Dicy read an article in an Austin newspaper announcing that the great Negro leader, Booker T. Washington, principal and founder of Tuskegee Institute, Tuskegee, Alabama, was scheduled to speak at Wooldridge Park, in Austin, on the next Friday night.

Aunt Dicy and Uncle June had heard about Booker T. Washington and his great work, so they decided to go to Austin and hear him speak. When they reached the park the crowd was already seated and nearly all the seats were occupied. But Uncle June finally found two seats vacant near the back of the audience, and he and Aunt Dicey sat down. Shortly after they had taken their seats, Mr. Washington, his secretary, Emmett J. Scott, the mayor of Austin, the members of the City Council and a few Negro preachers mounted the platform that had been built for the renowned educator's appearance.

The subject of Mr. Washington's address was "Great Americans and Their Contributions." He mentioned George Washington and his contributions to the country; Benjamin Franklin and his contributions to the country; Sam Houston and his contributions to the country; Thomas Edison and his contributions to the country; Frederick Douglass and his contributions, and many others.

After he had finished his speech, the crowd, Uncle June among them, applauded so much that the eminent Booker T. Washington had to take several bows. But Aunt Dicy did not join in the hand-clapping.

"Dicy," asked Uncle June, turning to her, "how come you are not clapping for Mr. Washington like everybody else? Didn't you enjoy his speech?"

"Humph! No, I didn't," replied Aunt Dicy. "He ain't said nothing about Levi Garret—and he wasn't nobody's fool!"*

---

* Levi Garret, trade name for Aunt Dicy's favorite brand of snuff.

Aunt Dicy and the Family Will

As soon as Uncle June died and was buried, Serelia and Samantha began to find fault with everything that Aunt Dicy did. She could not cook to suit them; they complained about the way she arranged the furniture in the house; they scolded her for waking them up at five o'clock every morning, and even made fun of the kind of clothing she wore.

Serelia and Samantha had both graduated from Prairie View Normal College, the state college for Texas Negroes, and they did not feel that Dime Box and the neat little five-room cottage that belonged to their parents were good enough for them—since they were now educated.

Aunt Dicy was very patient with her two daughters at first, even though she remembered the fact that Serelia and Samantha had asked her and Uncle June not to come to Prairie View College to see them graduate. She also recalled that on the last "Nineteenth of June,"* Serelia and Samantha had gone to Brenham for the day in order to meet their sweethearts instead of inviting them to come to Dime Box for the day's celebration. The girls felt that Aunt Dicy did not measure up to the standards of their sweethearts' parents and they were ashamed to let the boys see their father and mother.

The thing that finally caused Aunt Dicy to lose patience with Serelia and Samantha, however, was the fact that they began to fuss at her all day and night about dipping snuff. The girls even went so far as to tell her that they thought her habit the dirtiest and filthiest they had ever seen, and they wished she would stop.

The more Serelia and Samantha scolded Aunt Dicy about dipping snuff, the angrier she became, so she tried to think of some way to get revenge on them for the way they were treating her. Finally, one day a thought struck her. Shortly after Uncle June died, she had bought out her son Pomp's share in the Johnson farm, which meant that everything would now be left to Serelia and Samantha.

The climax came one day when the girls were told by Aunt Dicy that she could not give them the money to go spend the Christmas holidays with their sweethearts in Waco and Fort Worth. Both of the daughters told Aunt Dicy in very strong language that she would have had enough money to give them for the trip if she hadn't spent so much money for snuff. This made the old lady angry and she proceeded, in turn, to tell them that if they didn't stop fussing at her about dipping snuff, she was going to destroy the deeds to the property and make a will leaving the farm to her sister Liza's children. But Serelia and Samantha did not stop.

As the Christmas holidays approached they scolded her more than ever about dipping snuff. So one cold day, about a week before Christmas, when the girls' fussing had become almost unbearable, Aunt Dicy rushed into her bedroom, took the deeds to the farm out of her trunk, and threw them into the blazing fire in the fireplace. Then, looking defiantly at Serelia and Samantha, she placed her hands akimbo on her hips and said triumphantly:

"Now I'll spit where I please!"

* Emancipation Day in Texas.

PART FIVE

THE WORD ON THE BRAZOS

God Throws a Tree Limb

Hit tecks lots of patience to deal wid a sinnuh at de mounah's bench. Dey hab a haa'd time comin' thoo 'caze dey ain't yit ready to jar loose from dey sinful acks. Hit don't matter how pulpit-wise a preachuh be, he hab a job on his han's gittin' de haa'd-haa'ted sinnuh man to settle on de chu'ch. Ah calls to min' a han' offen de ole Cole plannuhtation by de name of Pink Jackson. He de bigges' cotton pickuh on de plannuhtation, but he de rankes' sinnuh, lackwise, an' 'sides dat he kinda simple-minded, too.

His wife an' chilluns b'long to de Bethesda Baptis' Chu'ch down to Reagan, an' dey ve'y upset 'bout Pink. He know how to git de cotton togethuh for de boss-man, but he cain't hitch hosses wid de Lawd. He know hit bes' to teck one row o' cotton at a time an' to ca'ie a light drag so's to pick de mos' poun's o' cotton, but he don' know you got to hab a clear conscience to git rail converted an' be save. De preachuh work wid Pink evuh way he know how, but Pink don' chance to come thoo.

Fin'ly, one night though, Revun Randle, de pastuh, pray to de Lawd speshly for Pink. He say, "Gawd, please come down heah an' he'p me wid dis heah sinnuh man what go by de name of Pink. Dis job Ah got for you is too haa'd for a man an' too tedious for de angels." But wid all dis prayin', Pink ain't nevuh chanced to come thoo yit. So fin'ly Revun Randle say, "Pink, Ah tells you what to do, if'n you railly wants to be a true chile of Gawd: Go down in de pasture attuh sundown an' pick yo'se'f out a pos'-oak tree an' light out down dere evuh night. Git down on yo' knees unnuhneaf de tree an' ast de Lawd to convert you."

So Pink goes down to de pasture dat ver' same night, picks him out a pos'-oak tree, gits down on his knees an' say, "Lawd, please convert me! Oh, Lawd, please convert me!"

Dis heah goes on awright for three nights, but while Pink is prayin' on de fo'th night, a dead limb falls offen de tree an' almos' hits 'im, so he lights out to runnin'. Hit's 'bout a week attuh dis 'fo' Pink gits up 'nuff courage to go back out to de tree again, but on de Friday night 'fo' de nex' Sunday, Pink goes out to de tree, kinda sidles up to hit an' say, "Gawd, Ah come out heah to hab a close-up talk wid you 'bout dat tree limb you th'owed at me t'othuh night. You know if'n you had of hit me, dese nigguhs nevuh would of had no mo' confidence in you."

White and Black Theology

Ah calls to min' a Mefdis' preachuh what fill de pulpit at St. James in Waco. He de bigges' preachuh on de Upper Brazos. He been teachin' de

RIBS

See recipes for homemade barbecue and red rib sauce on page 144.

Barbecued Ribs—Chicago Gourmet Style

5 lbs. fresh spareribs
   salt, pepper, paprika to taste
2 onions, quartered
5 garlic cloves, crushed
   juice of 1 lemon and grated
   rind
2 tbs. brown sugar
2 tbs. Worcestershire sauce
1 cup tomato catsup
2 tbs. pepper sauce
2 tbs. chili powder

1 tsp. leaf thyme
1 tsp. cumin seed
1 tsp. paprika
2 tbs. hickory salt
1 cup water
¼ cup prepared mustard
2 tbs. butter or bacon fat
1 can tomato sauce
1 tsp. sweet basil
1 tsp. celery seed

Wipe ribs with damp cloth and cut into individual servings. Sprinkle as above, with salt, pepper and paprika. Then place all the other ingredients in a large frying pan and simmer for about a half hour at the most. When the sauce has cooled, place ribs in large shallow flat dish and marinate with the sauce on both sides. (If the ribs are barbecued on a pit, do not cut them into individual serving pieces but barbecue them in slab form.)

preachuhs in Waco for many a yeah, but hit happen oncet dat he 'lected to go to de genul conf'unce in Philadelphia an' he gone mo'n a mont'. Dat's a long time for de teachuh to stay way somewhar, so while he's gone a white preachuh comed 'long an' de preachuhs 'gage his servuses to teach 'em. De white preachuh meck a charge of ten dolluhs an' he gib all de preachuhs a D.D.

When Revun Dawson come home from de genul conf'unce de preachuhs don' relish 'im teachin' 'em no mo'. Dey 'low dey's smaa'tuh 'n he be'caze dey got a D.D. an' he ain't got nare one. Revun Dawson so outdone he don' know what to do wid hisse'f, so de nex' Sunday attuh he come back he ast his membuhship to gib 'im ten dolluhs to git 'im a D.D. But de membuhship done gib 'im a suit of clothes for de genul conf'unce and fifty dolluhs for spendin' change; so dey don' raise but five dolluhs for 'im in de collection for de D.D. De Revun tell 'em he don' relish dat way of doin', but de trustee boa'd tell 'im dey don' relish gibin' 'im no mo' money lackwise, so dey don' gib 'im anothuh red copper cent. Dey say, "Elduh, you jes' hab to be 'Doctuh D.' stid of Doctuh D.D.'"

Not long attuh dis de same white preachuh comed back to de Bottoms an' Revun Dawson, 'caze he outdone on de D.D. bizness, ast 'im to teach de collud preachuhs theology. So de white preachuh, he say he think dey oughta staa't off de course in theology by studyin' readin', writin' an' 'rithmuhtic, but dey say, "No brothuh, we knows what we wanna study; we wanna study theology, an' if'n we cain't git dat we don' wan' nuffin'."

So fin'ly de white preachuh git off to hisse'f an' he study haa'd, 'caze he don' wanna lose dat good ole Brazos Bottoms money. So a plan come to 'im an' he trace his footsteps back to de cullud preachuhs an' he say, "Brothuhs, Ah tells you what Ah done 'cided to do. Ah'm gonna teach y'all Biblical recordin', heabenly articulation, an' ecclesiastical calculation." Den dey all squall at de same time, "Brothuh, dat's jes' what we wants."

Dey ain't hab de wisdom to know dat's de same thing ez readin', writin', an' 'rifmuhtic.

Halley's Comet
and Judgment Day

You know, de Word tells us dat de man ain't been bawn what kin live 'bove sin; de Lawd an' Savior Jesus Chris' de onlies' one what done rech dis stage on dis putty green-carpeted soil what we calls de erf. De preachuhs stray off from de fold jes' lack de membuhship an' haf to be fetch back to hit, jes' lack Hezekiah one time haf to fetch de peoples back in de Bible from dey sinful acks. Many a preachuh rat heah in de Bottoms c'mit 'dult'ry, drunk his lickuh, an' ebun done swo' in de pulpit; an' some of 'em ebun toted a pistol when dey comed to preach.

You know, de Mefdis's an' de Baptis's 'spised one anothuh in de Bottoms so much 'reckly attuh freedom when de chu'ch fuss staa't up dat dey hab fis' fights, cuttin' scrapes, an' shootin' sprees all de time. 'Fo' dey builded de chu'ch houses, de Baptis's an' de Mefdis's used to sometime use de same buildin' when dey hol' chu'ch servus. Dey call dis "pulpit 'filiation." De Mefdis's used de house de secon' an' fo'th Sundays in evuh mont', an' when de fifth Sunday roll 'roun', sometime dey bofe hol' servus togethuh.

One time dey was a Baptis' preachuh by de name of Whirlwin' Johnson. So he say dat when de fifth Sunday come he gonna preach a baptismal sermon down to de house what dey rentin' for de chu'ch to a mix conguhgation. De Mefdis' preachuh, Elduh Cyclone Williams, tell 'em he dare 'im to preach hit, but Whirlwin' preach hit jes' de same on de fifth Sunday. De nex' day Cyclone Williams meet 'im on de court house steps rat heah in Marlin, an' walk up to 'im, an' say, "Didn Ah tole you dat if'n you preach dat sermon Ah's gonna whip de hell outen you?" An' he lam Whirlwin' rat smack dab on de jawbone wid his fis'. Whirlwin' den tuck his cap an' ball an' shot Cyclone in de laig, an' de country shurf put 'im in de jug, an' de Baptis' 'nomination tuck up money ovuh de whole state to git Whirlwin' outen de jail house.

Yas suh, de ole time preachuh man cuss, fight, haa'k an' spit an' do lots of things what ain't laid down in Holy Writ. 'Spechly dem what go 'bout all ovuh de country preachin' heah an' dere, 'way somewhar. You know de Word say, "Go ye into all de worl' an' preach de Gospel." De ole time preachuh didn' git into all de worl' but he git into as much as he kin. Dey was 'vangelis's an' runned 'tractive meetin's. Dem's de kin' what got out 'mongst de sistuhs de mos' too.

Ah calls to min' a Baptis' preachuh, Elduh Joshua Dennis, what come to be ordained to preach by his boss-man on de ole Watkins plannuhtation at Pitts' Bridge, 'bout eight mile down de main highway from heah. You know wuhk comed fus' on de Brazos, an' de Word come secon'. De way Joshua comed to be a preachuh was by bein' de bestes' cotton-pickuh on de Watkins fawm. He pick 'bout a thousan' poun's a day, evuh day. So ole man Amos Watkins say dis de kinda man he want preachin' to his han's; a man dat gonna preach "wuhk haa'd an' 'bey yo' boss-man," an' tell 'em dat all a nigguh needs is "a bad row, a sharp hoe, an' a mean boss."

Fin'ly, Joshua tuck up wid dis preachin' bizniss for keeps an' he come to be one of de bestes' preachuhs up an' down de Brazos. He turnt to be a great 'vangelis'. His wife, Mary Ann, is a good farm manager, so he leave her an' de chilluns on de plannuhtation, an' he go roamin' all ovuh de Bottoms a-preachin', an' jes' stop by home of occasion. De yeah dat Halley's Comet was s'pose to 'stroy de worl', Joshua comed home de night 'fo' de day dat was set for de worl' to be 'stroyed an' he say to Mary Ann, "Wife, set down! Ah wants to tell you sump'n 'fo' Halley's Comet 'stroy de worl' tomorruh; Ah wants to 'fess to you an' die wid a clear conscience. You know Sistuh Janie Jones up to Mudville? Ah been goin' wid her fo' yeahs."

"Well," say Mary Ann, dryin' her han's whar she been washin' de suppuh dishes, "Ah sho' is proud you done cleared yo' conscience. Ah don' wanna die widdout clearin mah conscience, lackwise. You see dat boy Jim ovuh

dere on de pallet? Dat ain't yo' boy; dat's Deacon Abe Solomon's boy.
An' you see dat gal Mirandy settin' on de flo' playin' wid dat cat? Well,
dat's Elduh Henry Sim's gal. Fact of hit is, dey ain't none of dese chilluns
yourn."

"What?" yell Joshua, jumpin' up outen de rockin' chair he settin' in.
"Hit mought be Judgment Day tomorruh, but hit's gonna be hell heah
tonight!"

Brother Gregg
Identifies Himself

Ah calls to min' de fam'ly what was croppers down on de ole Davis
plannuhtation, what runned jam up to de Li'l Brazos an' stretch hitse'f out
ez far ez you could peel yo' eye 'long de banks.

Dey hab a li'l ole chu'ch house down dere what dey done builded rat
attuh freedom done come in a bulge an' hit yit stannin' cep'n dey cain't in no
wise hol' servuses in hit when hit comes a big pour-down, or a northuh. De
roof needs shinglin' pow'ful bad, an' some of de planks in de sides of de
li'l ole chu'ch done jarred loose, an' some no-count triflin' Brazos Bottom
nigguhs done toted 'em off home for kindlin' wood. Dey calls dis heah
chu'ch Li'l Mount Zion, an' de Gregg fam'ly was one of de fus' fam'lies to
jine hit. Dey was four Gregg boys, an' evuh one of 'em hab a whole passel
of younguns, what of occasion brung salty tears to dey mammies an' pappies'
sorrowful eyes, 'caze mos' of 'em growed up to be Saddy night gamblers,
sloppy drunkards, fas' womens, an' de Lawd in heabun knows what else
dese yaps didn't tuhn out to be.

All de bruthuhs cep'n Bud Gregg, de ol'es' brothuh, gits so fed up an'
disgusted wid de sinful acks of dey younguns till dey done stop tryin' to
square accounts wid de Lawd. An' de why dat Bud ain't gone got on de don'-
keer ban' wagon lack his brothuhs am dat he hab a good Christun wife,
Carrie, an' a tol'able fair set of younguns. His gals was all married off to
hard-workin' croppers an' his boys was all lucky 'nuff to git gals for wives
dat could do ez much work on de fawm ez dey could. 'Sides dat, Bud's wife,
Carrie, was de stan'by of de fam'ly when it comed to de chu'ch an' de why
an' wharfo' of all de chillun bein' chu'ch membuhs. Carrie hab a good influence on Bud lackwise, an' keep a bee line on 'im cep'n Bud don' in no
wise 'ten' chu'ch servuses on Sundays. Sistuh Carrie go to chu'ch an' plank
herse'f rat down in de amen cawnuh evuh Sunday de Lawd sen', but ole
Bud, what was quick ez greased lightnin' wid a shotgun, spen' all his Sundays a huntin' an' a shootin' doves an' plovers an' rabbits evuh time he
heah a flip-flappin' in de bushes an' weeds. Ole Bud was jes' a number in de
chu'ch book, dat's all. Sistuh Carrie go pieceways wid 'im on de huntin' side
of de fence, but she 'low dat de week-a-days am time 'nuff for carryin' on in
dis wise. Bud don' give a whoop how much Sistuh Carrie try to 'suade 'im
to go to chu'ch on a Sunday wid her, he jes' keep his tatuh trap shet an'

don' say a mumblin' word when Sistuh Carrie talk to 'im 'bout chu'ch. But dis don' in no wise disencourage Sistuh Carrie; she 'low she b'lieve de Lawd kin still turn a miracle wid His pow'ful awmighty han', so she don't gib up de cross.

Sistuh Carrie ain't in nowise gonna be disap'inted neithuh, 'caze 'tain't long 'fo' a nachul bawn preachuh by de name of Hotwind Johnson comed to de Bottoms to 'duct a 'vivul an' tole de Brazos Bottom folks dat de Lawd was gonna lay a heavy han' on 'em if'n dey didn' git shed of dey sinful ways. Dis heah kind of th'owed a scare into Ole Bud, so de nex' comin' Sunday night attuh Hotwind done comed to de Bottoms, Bud goes down to de chu'ch house wid Sistuh Carrie an' tecks a seat rat in de amen cawnuh whar Sistuh Carrie drops herse'f all de time. Dis de fus' time Bud done set foot in de chu'ch house in ten yeahs so evuhbody in de chu'ch turnt 'roun' an' look at 'im. Dis meck Ole Bud feel kind of out of place too, but he try haa'd to brace hisse'f an' ack lack he used to bein' in a chu'ch house. He hol' hisse'f togethuh putty good too, till Hotwind comed in de pulpit an' raised a song an' attuh de song done been finish turnt to whar Sistuh Carrie an' Bud was settin' an' say, p'intin' his finguh at Bud, "Brothuh Gregg, lead us in a word of prayer."

Bud ain't prayed in his whole life befo', so he tremblin' lack a leaf an' he don' feel lack doin' a jumpin' thing 'bout prayin'. But Sistuh Carrie nudge 'im in de side wid her elbow an' tell 'im to go ahaid an' do lack Hotwind done tole 'im to do, so Ole Bud pays heed to her an' kneels down on de chu'ch house floor. Den he puts his han's ovuh his eyes an' says "Lawd, Ah reckon Ah bettuh tell you who Ah is befo' Ah staa'ts dis prayer. Ah ain't John Gregg, de one what kin pick eight hunnud poun's of cotton when he teckin' one row at a time; Ah ain't Jim Gregg, de one what plays de fiddle an' de banjo evuh Saddy night for de platform dances, an' Ah ain't Tom Gregg, de one what stealed his boss-man's bes' pair of mules one Sunday night an' runned off way somewhars. Ah'm Ole Man Gregg; de one what shoots de gun so good."

Uncle Ebun and the Sign of the Shooting Star

Evuh time dey hab a big camp-meetin' down to de Ebunezuh Baptis' Chu'ch at Hearne all de han's on de plannuhtations in dem paa'ts come to de meetin' evuh night 'caze dey allus hab de bigges' preachuhs of de Baptis' 'nomination to run dese meetin's.

Oncet dey was a fam'ly livin' on de ole Steele plannuhtation by de name of Hunt what was a good Christun fam'ly, but dey ain't yit got dey pappy, Unkuh Eben, to jine de chu'ch. He gittin' putty ole now an' his wife, Aunt Eerie, worryin' rat smaa't 'bout his soul goin' to torment.

So one summuh, dey was habin' sich a rousin' meetin' down to de Ebunezuh Chu'ch down to Hearne till Unkuh Ebun for de fus' time in yeahs an' yeahs goes down to de meetin' on a Sunday night. Dey hab a pow'ful preachuh runnin' de meetin' by de name of Elduh Sanford. He preach a sermon dat Sunday night 'bout "Evuhthing dat is, was; an' evuhthing dat ain't, ain't nevuh gonna be." Unkuh Ebun lissen good to evuhthing de preachuh say an' he 'low dat he gonna meck de preachuh out a lie 'caze he ain't nevuh b'long to de chu'ch, but he gonna jine when dey calls for 'em to come to de mounah's bench. So sho' 'nuff when dey calls for 'em to come up to de mounah's bench, Unkuh Ebun gits up wid de res' an' tecks a seat on de front row. Evuhbody glad to see Unkuh Eben teck a stan' for de Lawd, but he don't chance to come thoo. Seem lack he cain't meck up his min' whether or not he rail converted; so dat night on de way back to de plannuh-tation, his wife, Sistuh Eerie say, "Ebun, if'n you's in doubt ast de Lawd to show you a sign if'n you's rail converted."

Hit was a putty moonlight night an' Aunt Eerie calls to min' de sign of de shootin' star, an' she say: "If'n you's done gone up to de mounah's bench an' don' chance to come thoo an's in doubt, ast de Lawd to shoot you a star, an' if'n you sees a star shoot crost de heabuns reckly attuh dis, you's rail converted, but if'n you don't see no star shoot dat's a sho' sign you ain't gone thoo de change."

Unkuh Ebun's ol'es' boy was drivin' de mules along at a slow pace an' Unkuh Ebun was settin' on de front plank wid him whar he could see de stars good, so he looked up to de skies an' he say, "Lawd, shoot me a star." In a few minutes he seed a star shoot crost de sky, but Unkuh Eben ain't satisfied yit; so he say, "Lawd, shoot me anothuh star." In 'bout five minutes mo' Unkuh Ebun seent anothuh star shoot crost de heabuns rat 'fo' his gaze, but dis ain't satisfy him yit; so when dey staa't into de lane offen de dirt road what lead to de plannuhtation, Unkuh Ebun look up at de sky ag'in an' say, "Lawd, looks lack hits kinda haa'd for me to git up mah faith tonight; so Ah tells you what you do: Shoot me de moon."

"De moon!" yell Gawd. "Ah wouldn' shoot you de moon for all de nigguhs in de Brazos Bottoms!"

The Preacher Who Walked on Water

De preachuhs in de Bottoms allus lack to meck a bettuh show dan de othuh one. All de new preachuhs what follow de ole ones what leave de Bottoms an' go way somewhar to preach wanna show de membuhship dey knows mo' an' kin do mo'n de pastuh what done gone way somewhar. Dey wanna show how dey stan' in wid de Lawd. Oncet dere was a new preachuh what been 'lected to pastuh de Bethesda Baptis' Chu'ch down to Cedar Springs. He 'pend on Gawd an' b'lieve Gawd ain't gonna fuhgit 'im, don' keer what he tell de membuhship he gonna do. Dis preachuh, Elduh Wash-in'ton, hab a big 'vival de fus' week he come to de Bottoms an' a heap o' sinnuhs 'fess an' jine de chu'ch.

De nex' Sunday he 'nounce dat he gonna hab a baptizin' down de rivuh where dey's lots o' wattuh. He 'low dat John de Baptis' didn't pick no shallow wattuh to baptize in, an' dat he ain't gonna pick no slough hisse'f, 'caze he gonna walk on de wattuh too, lack Christ done did. So he tuck de haid deacon down to de deepes' spot of de rivuh whar he gonna walk on de wattuh an baptize de nex' Sunday an' hab 'im he'p 'im buil' a suppo't fo' a plank out in de rivuh 'bout two feet wide, so hit won't fall down.

Elduh Washin'ton got evuhthing set, he think, but he don' know dat some li'l ole boys what was fishin' on de rivuh done seed 'im an' de haid deacon teck de big plank an' put hit in de rivuh an buil' a suppo't fo' hit. He don' know lackwise dat de minnit him an' de haid deacon gits out of sight dese li'l ole boys goes down to de place whar dey done buil' de platfawm in de wattuh an' tecks de plank an hits suppo'ts outen de wattuh an' th'ows 'em out in de rivuh an' watch 'em float on down de Brazos.

De nex' Sunday evenin' when de time come fo' Elduh Washin'ton to walk on de wattuh an' do his baptizin' in de middle of de rivuh de whole eas' side of de rivuh was lined wid han's from all de plannuhtations from fo' counties 'roun'. Dey done heerd 'bout de great miracle Elduh Washin'ton gonna puhfawm, so dey ain't aimin' to miss de 'casion. Putty soon heah come Elduh Washin'ton, de haid deacon, an' de converts, comin' down de paff dat lead to dat paa't de rivuh whar de plank done been put. Elduh Washin'ton was leadin' out, so when he gits to de edge of de wattuh whar de plank done s'pose to be, he walk rat off into de wattuh lack he know he safe, an' *kerflop!* he fall smack dab in de rivuh an' staa't yellin'.

De haid deacon, seein' 'im fall in de rivuh, holler, "Look out dere, Elduh!"

"Look out, hell!" squall Elduh Washin'ton. "Who moved dat plank?"

The Old Moderator's Farewell Message

'Reckly attuh de Yankee soldiers done come in a bulge from way some-whars down de Gulf an' brung freedom to dem what was raised unduh de whip an' lash, de po' slave 'tempt to git hisse'f togethuh an' staa't up chu'ch servus in de Bottoms. De Mefdis', hit staa't off kinda slow lack, but de Baptis' 'nomination 'tempt to git hitse'f on foot rat now; hit don't hab de wisdom to know dat hit got to crawl 'fo' hit kin walk; dat hit got to folluh de style of de li'l ole boby when hit fus' try'n pull hitse'f up on a straight chair an' stan' lonely; dey ain't peek far 'nuff back into de Word to know dat you cain't stan' on yo' feet solid lack 'fo' de nachul time come less'n you stumbles an' falls.

De Mefdis', he don't gib no nevuhmin' who de leaduh be, but in de Baptis' 'nomination, evuh dawg an' his brothuh wanna be de big dawg in de chu'ch. Dis 'speshly true when hit come to de big chu'ch gath'rin' what go by de name of de 'sociation. Dey staa't sich fussin' an' fumin' an' a goin'-on 'bout who gonna be de leaduh till dey 'cides de bes' way outen de mess is to 'leck what you calls a moderatuh to 'zide ovuh de 'sociation what meet evuh yeah durin' of de cotton pickin' season while de han's in de Bottoms is got a li'l money dey kin call dey own. 'Count of hit bein' so haa'd to keep down trouble, dey allus 'leck a big black six-foot preachuh to be de moderatuh of de 'sociation, 'caze he de onlies' style o' preachuh kin hol' his groun' an' keep de preachuhs from tacklin' one anothuh an' habin' fis' fights rat in de pulpit. Dese moderatuhs was ez strong ez oxens, toted pistols, an' was ez quick on de trigguh ez greased lightnin'. Ah tells you, de ole-time moderatuh was a pow'ful man in de 'nomination; but lack ez allus, dis heah style cain't las' fo'evuh, so putty soon de young membuhs staa't leanin' to'a'ds de min'stry an' gittin' on boa'd de Gospel Train. De membership, lackwise, staa't teckin' up wid de young preachuh's style.

Ah calls to min' down to Yeawah Creek one time when de Missionary Baptis' 'Sociation meet dere, dey hab a 'leckshun of de moderatuh an' stid of 'lectin' de rail tall black preachuh what been de moderatuh of de 'Socia-tion for twenty-fo' yeahs, dey 'lects a tall han'some brownskin preachuh 'bout thirty-five yeah ole to be de moderatuh. Dis meck Revun Holoway, de ole moderatuh, pow'ful mad, an' he eye de young moderatuh lack he wanna tar 'im in two. So when de preachuh what was 'zidin' ovuh de leckshun call on de ole moderatuh to hab a farewell say, de ole ole moderatuh riz up outen his seat, scowled at de brothuhs an' sistuhs an' preachuhs what done tuck his job 'way from 'im, tuck a face towel what he use for a hankershuf outen his pocket, wipe de sweat offen his face an' say:

"You know sumpin', y'all is jes' lack fishes. Now you teck de suckuh fish; you don't ebun haf to th'ow no bait in de wattuh to ketch 'im; jes' th'ow de hook in de wattuh an' he'll bite at hit. Dat's de way some of you chu'ch membuhs is; de fuss thing de preachuh say, you bites at hit an' dey ketches you nappin'.

"Den you teck de catfish; he's a ver' popluh fish—evuhbody lacks 'im. You kin th'ow any kin' o' bait in de wattuh an' he'll bite at hit; tain't much trouble to ketch 'im, but if'n you don't watch 'im close, he'll git 'way from you. Dat's de way 'tis wid some of you membuhs; you jines de chu'ch on mos' any kin' of sermon—don't keer who preach hit an' dey ketches you nappin'.

"Den, dere's de flyin' fish; he's so fas' you cain't ketch 'im in de wattuh or outen de wattuh; paa't de time he's in de wattuh an' de nex' minnut he's in de air. He don't stay nowhars. He jes' lack some o' you no-'count triflin' membuhs; dis week you b'longs to St. John Chu'ch, nex' week you jines up wid Mount Moriah; week attuh nex' yo' name's on de books of St. James; nex' month you done move yo' membership to Mt. Pisgah; you don' stay nowhars.

"Den you teck de blowfish; he look lack a fish, he acks lack a fish, an' you thinks deys a lots to 'im, but dey ain't. As soon as de win's blowed outen 'im dey ain't nothin' to 'im; he ain't no use to hisse'f an' nobody else. Dat's de way 'tis wid some of you preachuhs; you acks lack a preachuh, you gits up 'fo' de chu'ch an' you brags an' you puffs yo'se'f out, but dey ain't nothin' to you. You's jes full o' win' lack de blowfish.

"Den dere's de gol'fish; evuhbody lacks 'im; he's putty, he's allus whar you kin see 'im, but you ain't s'pose to tech 'im. He's 'tractive, he's easy to look at, dey keep 'im in de house in a putty bowl. Folks don't try to ketch 'im—dey tecks food to 'im, but if'n you tech 'im he'll die. Dat's de way 'tis wid dese young preachuhs; he's dressy, he's cute, he's got his hair all slicked back, he ca'ies a powduh puff wid 'im in de pulpit, he tecks his hankershuf an' brushes hisse'f off durin' of de sermon, he tecks a fan an' fans hisse'f in de pulpit; he's easy to look at; de sistuhs feeds 'im an' tecks on ovuh 'im, but he's easy kilt lack de gol'fish.

"An' las', but in no wise de leastes', Ah wants evuh livin' soul heah tonight to keep dis in yo' 'membrance—dat Ah mought gib out, but Ah ain't in no wise evuh gonna gib up. Amen!"

Sister Sadie Washington's Littlest Boy

Sistuh Sadie Washin'ton was a widow woman, but one of de trues' chillun of Gawd dat you gonna evuh run 'cross durin' of a lifetime. Sistuh Sadie hab de record thoo de whole Bottoms of bein' one o' de good uns when hit come to dem what hab pahlance wid de Lawd, an' she done got dat thing lack de Word say git hit.

But Sistuh Sadie hab one pow'ful regret—she hab a boy, her littles' boy, what go by de name of Pete, what ain't yit jine de chu'ch an' come to be a Christun. Pete out of his thutteen crowdin' his fo'teen, an' done growed to de shape of a man, so Sistuh Sadie don' feel lack she 'sponsible to Gawd for 'im no mo'.

Don' keer how haa'd Sistuh Sadie an' de membuhship of de Mt. Zion Chu'ch try, dey cain't in no wise toll Pete off to de Christun faith. Sistuh Sadie de mammy of fifteen yaps, an' Pete de onlies' one what ain't come thoo an' be converted; he done rech his own 'sponsibility to de Lawd, an' he ain't 'fessed 'ligion yit. So Sistuh Sadie heah 'bout a rousin' 'vival dey was habin' up to Bryan 'mongst de Town folks an' de Pos'-Oak folks, an' she tuck li'l ole Pete an' dragged 'im out to de meetin' one night. She set 'im down rat by her so de triflin' rascal cain't slip outen de chu'ch house an' cut buddy short back home.

Putty soon de preachuh, what come from way somewhars to 'duct de 'vivul, line a hymn for to staa't de servus an' den staa't blowin' Gawd's word outen his system lack ole Numbuh Three blow steam outen hits smokestack when hit git to de railroad crossin' on de ole Cartuh plannuhtation. Dat's de plannuhtation whar Sistuh Sadie an' her chilluns all mecks de day an' gits dey pay from Ole Man Cartuh what own de plannuhtation. Pete, he de wattuh boy for de han's on de plannuhtation, an' he lackwise beats de sweep for de han's to knock off from work an' come to dinnuh.

De preachuh hab a great big voice, an' weigh 'bout three hunnud poun's. When he walk 'cross de flo', de whole chu'ch house rock an' shake lack a cyclone done hit it. Dis kinda scare li'l ole Pete; dis de fus' time in his life he done evuh seed a preachuh dis big what kin shake de flo', so he thinks hit's de Lawd shakin' de flo', an' he goes up to de mounah's bench an' meck out he converted. Dat was de secon' Saddy night in de mont' an' de pastuh of de chu'ch set de fo'th Sunday ez de day for de baptizin' of de new converts.

Sistuh Sadie so proud dat Pete done come thoo she don' know what to do, so she go all up an' down de whole Bottoms tellin' evuhbody she sees to be at de big baptizin' on de fo'th Sunday, down on de Big Brazos, 'caze Pete gonna be baptized. So de fo'th Sunday comed an' 'bout sebun hunnud Town folk, Pos'-Oak folk, an' Bottom folk congugates on bofe sides of de Big Brazos, jes' 'fo' hit gits to de fork of de rivuh on de ole Washin'ton plannuhtation, to see de baptizin'. De pastuh an' de 'vangelis' lines up de cannuhdates on de banks of de rivuh. Li'l Pete was numbuh sebun in de line, an' evuhthing gittin' 'long fine till dey gits to Pete. De converts what baptized 'fo' Pete 'ud all holler, "Ah b'lieves de Lawd done saved mah soul," when de preachuh'd duck 'em unduh de wattuh; but when dey duck li'l ole Pete, he don' say narry word, jus' stan' dere in de wattuh an' look.

So de preachuh push Pete to one side in de wattuh, an' go on an' duck anothuh convert, an' dis convert lack all de res' 'cep'n Pete yell, "Ah b'lieves de Lawd done saved mah soul." Den de preachuh turn 'roun' to Pete, grab 'im an' duck 'im again, but Pete don' say nothin' yit; he jes' stan' dere lack he in a transom or sumpin'. So de preachuh shove 'im to one side ag'in an' go on an' duck anothuh convert, an' dis heah convert squall out jes' lack de res', "Ah b'lieves de Lawd done saved mah soul." Den de preachuh turn 'roun' an' grab li'l ole Pete an' duck 'im again, an' dis time, when Pete come outen de wattuh, he yell, "Ah b'lieves; Oh! Ah b'lieves!"

Sistuh Sadie was stan'in' on t'othuh side of de rivuh, an' she so happy dat Pete done come thoo an' confess till she yell back at 'im, "What you b'lieve, Son? Oh! what you b'lieve?"

"Ah b'lieve," yell Pete, "dat dis damn preachuh tryin' to drown me—dat's what Ah b'lieve!"

Scott Mission Methodist Church
Gets a Full-time Pastor

Used to be a li'l bitty ole chu'ch house rat ovuh yonduh on dat slew whar mah finguh's p'intin' at, dat de Mefdis's builded reckly attuh de circuit-ridin' preachuhs done staa'ted rovin' 'roun' de country. Dey don' hab no preachin' in de li'l ole chu'ch but one Sunday durin' of de mont', 'caze dey ain't no more'n a han'ful of Mefdis's on de ole Burleson Plannuhtation. Dat's de why de membuhship cain't in no wise pay a full-time preachuh, an' dat's de why de bishop allus sen' 'em a circuit-ridin' preachuh to preach de Word to 'em evuh fo'th Sunday.

But dis heah li'l ole membuhship am rail hones' to goodness Christuns an' dey don' relish de idea of holdin' servuses jes' one time de whole mont' long, so one yeah dey hol's a boa'd meetin' an' sen's in a petition to de bishop astin' him to sen' 'em a full-time preachuh, 'caze de Mefdis chu'ch am suff'rin' in dem paa'ts of de Bottoms.

An' well, suh, if'n hit didn' come to pass sho' 'nuff dat same yeah dat a ole-timey preachuh by de name of Revun Wheeler, what done rech de pension age, was pleadin' wid de bishop to gib him a charge someplace or nothuh to he'p 'im keep body an' soul togethuh, so de bishop pays heed to 'im an' sen's 'im down to dis heah li'l ole chu'ch on de Burleson plannuhta-tion, what go by de name of Scott Mission. De membuhship so happy dey don' know what to do wid deyse'f, but dey done brung double-trouble on deyse'f, 'caze dey ain't ebun dun got no house for de preachuh to live in. So dey hol's a meetin' an' dey say, "What in de worl' we gonna do 'bout gittin' de preachuh a house?"

Dey studies an' dey studies till hit comes to 'em dey's a li'l ole woodshed rat in de chu'chyaa'd dey mought kin whup into shape for de preachuh to live in. So some of de brothuhs gits some hammers an' nails an' saws, an some ole pieces of tin what's layin' 'roun' on de ground in de mule lot what was lef' ovuh from de time when Ole Man Burleson done put a roof on his cottonseed house, an' dey fixes de li'l ole woodshed so hit fitten to live in by de time Revun Wheeler done rech de Bottoms.

But dey don't hab de wisdom to knew dat Revun Wheeler's wife done gone to Glory an' he too feeble to cook for hisse'f. De membuhship say when dey done foun' hit out, "We sho' done got us se'fs in a jam now, 'caze we's fo'ced to figguh out a way for Elduh Wheeler to git his grub." But dey don't hab de wisdom to know dat dey don't in no wise hab to lose no sleep 'bout Elduh Wheeler's grub, 'caze he got de sumpin'-to-eat question all figguhed out 'fo' he hits de Bottoms good.

Yas, suh, he got hit all cut an' dried. De ver' fus' mawnin' he done lit on de Bottoms, he hangs his ole frock-tail coat an' preachin' breeches on a nail in de wall an' th'ows his ol' croaker-sack full of bed clothes in one of de room cawners, an' den he tecks some ole tin knives an' forks an' spoons an' plates an' cups an' saucers outen a ole straw basket he done brung wid him, an' he lays 'em on de ole rawhide chair what's settin' by de do' of de li'l ole room. Den he puts his ole hick'ry walkin' cane in his rat han', grabs up his basket, chucks hit unnuh his lef' arm, an' haids straight for Brothuh Turner's house, what was catuhcawnuhed crost de road from de chu'ch house. When he done rech Brothuh Turner's house he walks up an' raps on de do' an' when Brothuh Turner opens hit he say, "Good mawnin', Brothuh Turner, yo' honorey, Ah'm de new pastuh, Revun Wheeler. Jes' look in dis heah ole empty basket Ah'm totin' 'roun'; wouldn't some good ole thick slices of bacon an' some fresh fried eggs look good in hit?"

"Sho' would," say Brothuh Turner, so he calls his wife, Mandy' an' tells her to go an' cook Elduh Wheeler some good ole home-cured bacon an' half a dozen fresh yahd eggs. Elduh Wheeler thanks 'em for de bacon an' eggs, puts 'em in his basket, an' den tuhns to Brothuh Turner an' asts him wharbouts do de nex' closetest chu'ch membuh live.

Brothuh Turner p'ints out Brothuh Tim Jordan's li'l ole shack to 'im, what's 'bout a qua'tuh of a mile up de lane on t'othuh side of a stretch of pos'-oaks, an' Elduh Wheeler staa'ts on his roun's again. When he gits to Brothuh Jordan's house Brothuh Jordan an' Sistuh Jordan am settin' on de steps of dey gall'ry in front of de house mendin' cotton sacks what done got holes in 'em from bein' drug ovuh rocky lan'. Revun Wheeler ain't a bit shy; he walks rat up to whar Sistuh Jordan an' Brothuh Jordan doin' dey mendin' an' say, "Good mawnin', Sistuh an' Brothuh Jordan, yo' honoreys, Ah'm de new preachuh, Revun Wheeler, an' Ah wants y'all to come heah an' look in dis heah basket at dis good ole home-cured fried bacon an' fresh yahd eggs Brothuh Turner done gimme for mah breakfas'; wouldn't some good ole fat hot biscuits go good wid 'em?"

Dey bofe say "Sho' would," so Sistuh Jordan go rat in de house an' bakes a steamin' pan of great big thick hot biscuits an' gibs 'em to Elduh Wheeler. Elduh Wheeler puts de biscuits in his basket, thanks Brothuh an' Sistuh Jordan for 'em, an' den asts 'em wharbouts do de nex' closetest membuh of de chu'ch live?

So Brothuh Jordan p'ints out Sistuh Fanny Brown's li'l cabin to him, what's about half a mile crost a big sugah cane patch. Smoke was comin' outen de chimney of de li'l ole shack, so Revun Wheeler ain't gonna hab no trouble findin' hit an' he staa't goin' his roun's ag'in. He wobbles 'long till he fin'ly gits to Sistuh Brown's yahd whar he spy her hangin' out her washin' on de clothesline, so he walks rat up to whar she takin' her clothes outen a wash pot an' hangin' 'em on de line an' say, "Good mawnin', Sistuh Brown, yo' honorey, Ah'm de new preachuh, Revun Wheeler, an' Ah wants you to come heah rail quick an' teck a peek in dis heah basket at dis good ole fried bacon an' eggs, an' dese good ole steamin' hot biscuits Ah's got. Wouldn't some good ole home-made 'lasses an' fresh buttuh go good wid 'em?"

"Sho' would," say Sistuh Fanny, so she go out to her smokehouse an' fetch Revun Wheeler a whole gallon jug of good ole thick home-made sorghums an' a putty poun' of buttah she done jes' churned an' gibs 'em to him. Elduh Wheeler got evuhthing he need now for his breakfas', so he thanks Sistuh Brown, puts his 'lasses an' buttah in de basket, wheels 'roun' rail quick an' lights out for home.

Soon as he lights in de house he tecks his victuals outen de basket an' puts 'em on de table, gits him a plate an' knife an' fork offen de chair whar he done lef' 'em, an' say his blessin's:

> "De Lawd am good, an' life am sweet;
> Thank you for dis sumpin' to eat."

Elduh Wheeler sho' done put his bes' foot fo'wuhd, 'caze he ca'ie on in dis same wise for his dinnuh an' suppuh dat same day, an' evuh day de Lawd sen' de whole year thoo, goin' 'roun' from membuh to membuh's house astin' for de kind of grub he wants, an' dey pays heed to him, an' gives hit to him, an' comes to be thankful to de bishop for sennin' 'em a full-time pastuh.

The Pole That Led to Heaven

Sometime de road git moughty rocky for de fawm han's in de Bottoms in de ole days, an' lots of 'em sing dat ole slav'ry-time song:

> *Oh Freedom, Oh Freedom!*
> *Befo' Ah'd be a slave*
> *Ah'd be buried in mah grave*
> *An' go home to mah Jesus an' be save.*

Dey 'speshly sing dis heah song jes' 'fo' cotton choppin' an' cotton pickin' time evuh yeah, 'caze dey knows dey got to put in some long days an' some haa'd work, an' dey ain't gonna git nothin' much outen hit.

One yeah, jes' 'fo' cotton choppin' time roll 'roun', de membuhs of de Mt. Moriah Baptis' Chu'ch, what hab a rail chile of Gawd pastuh, go to 'im an' say, "Elduh Johnson, de work on de plannuhtations is so haa'd on us dis heah time of yeah we wants you to pray for sumpin' to happen to git us outen de fix we's in." So Elduh Johnson say, "Awright," he gonna ast Gawd to show 'im a sign to help de membuhship out.

So sho' 'nuff, he ca'ie out his promus he done meck 'em, an' Gawd tells 'im in a dream dat He gonna put a pole on de wes' side of de Brazos rat whar de chu'ch hab its baptizin' de ver' nex' Sunday at three o'clock, an' dat all de membuhs what tiahed of livin' an' workin' so haa'd kin climb dis pole to heabun if'n dey brings a box of chalk an' mecks a mark for evuh lie dey done tole in dey life. But dey haf to be dere on time, 'case de pole jes' gonna stay for fifteen minnits. Elduh Johnson 'nounce dis to de membuhship at de prayer servus on a Wednesday night. So all dem what rathuh go on to heabun now gits 'em a box of chalk an' comes down to de wes' side of de rivuh at de baptizin' hole long 'fo' three o'clock dat Sunday, an' was stan'in' dere waitin' wid dey boxes of chalk. Zackly at three o'clock de membuhs heah a loud noise lack a erfquake or sumpin' 'nothah, an' jes' lack de pastuh say, a great big pole what rech so far to'a'ds de sky 'till you cain't see de top, comed up outen de groun', an' all de membuhs what got dey chalk gits on de pole what habs a rope ladder on hit an' staa'ts to climbin' an' a markin'. When de las' one done clum up on de ladder, de pole vanish jes' lack dat into thin air an' you don't see hit no mo'.

Dat ver' same night de Lawd come to de preachuh ag'in in a dream an' tell 'im dat dis same time anothuh yeah he gonna meck a pole appear to de membuhship ag'in at de baptizin' place. De preachuh 'nounce dis dream to de membuhship at de Monday night class meetin' an' when de time rolle 'roun' de nex' yeah for de pole to show up, dey was a bigguh bunch of han's on de rivuh banks dan dey was de yeah befo'.

When de pole pop up outen de groun' ez befo', de fus' membuh of de chu'ch to staa't up de pole was Elduh Roberts, what was de fus' pastuh of de Mt. Moriah Chu'ch. His whole fam'ly done die out, an' he say dey ain't no need of 'im stayin' heah no longuh. So, soon as de pole comed outen de groun', he hobbles ovuh to hit, gits on de ladduh an' staa'ts to climbin'. But 'fo' narry othuh han' kin git staa'ted to climbin', dey looks up an' sees Elduh Roberts almos' to de groun' ag'in comin' down de pole, so dey all wonduhs what de mattuh wid de pole dis yeah. But 'tain't de pole, hit's Elduh Roberts.

When Revun Johnson, de pastuh, spy Elduh Roberts comin' down de pole, he yell, "What's de mattuh, Elduh, ain't evuhthing awright up dere?"

"Sho', sho'," say Elduh Roberts, jumping down offen de pole, "Ah'm jes' comin' back attuh some mo' chalk!"

Who Can Go to Heaven

Hit's some sistuhs in de Chu'ch what meck de preachuh rail pow'ful in de pulpit by doin' what dey calls "talkin' back to 'im." Ah mean by dat, when a preachuh put ovuh a good lick agin de devil, dey say, "Preach de Word, son!" or "You sho' is tellin' de truf now." Dis he'p de preachuh to git right wid his preachin', so he lack for de sistuhs to talk back to 'im. Dis meck 'im git in de sperrit hisse'f.

Ah calls to min' a sistuh down to Mudville by de name of Sistuh Flora Hanks, what talked back to de preachuh all de time. Oncet de pastuh, Elduh Waller, was preachin' a sermon 'bout de good-for-nothin' young generation. He say, "Yeah, dey's goin' to hell in Cad'laks; dey's goin' to hell in Pack-'uds; dey's goin' to hell in Buicks; dey's goin' to hell in Dodges." He kep' on talkin' in dis fashion, namin' de diffunt kinds of cars de young genera-tion goin' to hell in, till fin'ly Sistuh Flora jumps up an' say, "Well, mah boy'll be back, 'caze he's goin' in a T-model Fo'd."

Well, dis heah wasn't so bad, but when Sistuh Flora cap de climax was de Sunday Elduh Waller preach his sermon on "Who Kin Go to Heavun." He say, "None of you liahs, you cain't git in."

"Tell de truf!" shout Sistuh Flora.

"None of you gamblers, you cain't git in," say Elduh Waller.

"Speak outen yo' soul," squall Sistuh Flora.

"None of you whiskey drinkers, you cain't git in," say Elduh Waller.

"Tell de truf!" shout Sistuh Flora.

"None of you snuff-dippers," say Elduh Waller, "you cain't git in."

Sister Flora, what got her mouf full of snuff rat den, jump up an p'int her finguh in Elduh Waller's face an' say, "Wait a minnit, Bub; you bettuh say 'ez you *knows* of!'"

Why So Many Negroes Are in Heaven

Ah calls to min' durin' de fus' Worl' War when de flu gits on a rampage in de Bottoms an' staa'ts killin' folks goin' an' comin'. Hit done lay so many low till de doctuhs an' de nusses calls a meetin' down to Calvert so dey kin tell de peoples how to teck keer.

De doctuhs an' de nusses has dey say. Den dey calls on a ole-time cullud preachuh what go by de name of Rev. Aaron to hab a say. Rev. Aaron a stan'-pat man wid de white folks, so when dey calls 'im up to de platform, he climbs up de steps, leans ovuh on his ole hick'ry walkin' stick an' say, "Ah done lissen to all yo' logics, an' all yo' isms an' de lack, 'bout de flu. But de Lawd's teckin' you white folks outen de worl' 'caze He ain't pleased at de way y'alls treatin' de black folks. Dat's de why He teckin' so many y'all outen de worl'."

"But, Rev. Aaron," say one of de doctuhs, "de stisticks shows dat dey's mo' blacks dyin' wid de flu dan dey is white folks."

"Dat's awright," low Rev. Aaron; "Ah still hol's mah p'int. Don' you know huccome de Lawd's teckin' all dem black people up to heabun? He's teckin' 'em up dere to testify 'ginst you white folks!"

Good Friday in Hell

De fawm han's seed sich a turble time on de ole Timmons plannuhtation down to Big Creek till dey hab a lots of 'em to run off. One of de fam'lies what b'long to dis fawm was name Johnson. Ole man Johnson was de pappy of twenty-fo' chilluns by de same 'oman. De boss-man 'vide Jonas Johnson wid a three-room shotgun house, two bedrooms an' a kitchen, an' a grocery 'lowance at de commissary. But dis heah ain't mean much wid twenty-fo' chilluns to feed, 'caze Jonah's chilluns work pow'ful haad. Fin'ly, one de ol'es' boys gits tiahed of workin' 'dout gittin' Sunday clothes. He was gittin' to de courtin' age an' didn't wanna w'ar brogan shoes on a Sunday. He 'low dey gits by in a week-a-days, but dat dey ain't fittin' for dance an' chu'ch servus. Jes' de same ol' Jonas don' pay 'im no heed, 'caze he a cropper on one of dem ride-off fawms—dats a fawm where de obuhseer rides hoss-back all ovuh de plannuhtation to keep de han's at work, an' if'n he evuh run 'cross a han' dat's shirkin' he jumps offen de hoss's back on to de nigguh's back and gibs 'im a good floggin'.

Anyways, dis boy, Dick, run off 'bout cotton choppin' time one yeah an' dey couldn' fin' 'im nowhars, but wasn't long attuh dis dat dey was lots of stealin' goin' on 'roun' Marlin. De reports was out dat dem dat was doin' de plunderin' was a Jew, a Nigguh an' a Meskin. Dey 'lowed de Nigguh in de bunch was Dick, dat de Jew was de triflin' no-good son of a sto'-keepuh in Marlin, an' dat de Meskin was a hoss thief what comed into Marlin from Wharton.

Dese hoodlums don' ebun skip de chu'ch in dey stealin'; dey tuck de oil lamps outen de Mefdis chu'ch down to Mudville, an' when de St. Paul Mefdis' Chu'ch was puttin' up a new chu'ch house rat heah in Marlin dey stealed de chu'ch bell 'fo' dey c'd put hit in de bell tower. Wasn't nothin' unduh Gawd's sun dey wouldn' teck if'n dey tuck a notion.

Fin'ly, dey all gits kilt one Saddy night in a dice game down to Eloise, an' dey dies an' goes to hell. But dey ain't in hell no time 'fo' dey ast to talk to de Devul, but de Haid Imp tells 'em dat de Devul don' talk but oncet a yeah an' dey cain't hab no conf'unce wid 'im till dat time roll 'roun'.

Hit was de fall of de yeah when dey was kilt an' come to hell, an' when hit come to be almos' Eastuh, dey was in a deep study as to when de Devul gonna talk, 'caze dey don' relish stayin' down dere in hell. Fin'ly, Good Friday roll 'roun', de day de Devul talk evuh yeah, so de Haid Imp call all de imps to de 'sembly room an' say de Devul gonna talk. So sho' 'nuff, putty soon de Devul walk down de aisle an' tuck his seat on de platfo'm. De fus' ones he speak to is dese three gambluhs from de Brazos Bottoms, Levi, de Jew; José, de Meskin; and Dick, de Nigguh. He 'vites 'em to come up on de platfo'm an' he say, "Felluhs, dis am Good Friday an' evuh yeah when hit comes to be Good Friday Ah lets de imps what kin do what Ah say go back up to de erf an' dey don' nevuh haf to come back to hell no mo'. Now, Ah tells you what," he say to Levi, "has you got ten dolluhs? If'n you's got ten dolluhs, Ah'll let you go back to de Bottoms an' you won' nevuh haf to come back to hell no mo'."

"Naw," say Levi, "Ah's got nine dollars."

"Dat ain't 'nuff," 'low de Devul. "You gonna haf to stay heah."

Den he turnt to de Meskin an' say, "José, is you got ten dollahs? If'n you's got ten dollahs you kin go on back to de Bottoms an' won' haf to nevuh come back heah no mo'."

"Me no got nothin'," say José.

Den you haf to stay heah too," say de Devul.

Den de Devul p'int his finguh at Dick an' he say, "Nigguh, is you got ten dollahs? We treats evuhbody alack down heah; so if'n you's got ten dollahs Ah'll let you go back to de Bottoms an' you won' nevuh haf to come back to hell no mo'."

"Naw, suh," say Dick, "Ah ain't got no ten dollahs, but Ah tell you what Ah'll do; if'n you lemme out, Ah'll gib you lebun dollahs Saddy!"

Uncle Si, His Boss-man and Hell

De han's in de Bottoms mos' allus drawed envelopes wid a li'l' green-back in 'em or a dollah or two in change when de time roll 'roun' for dey share of de crops evuh yeah. Dem what drawed envelopes or a li'l' cash was de han's dat hab a wife an' no chilluns. Dem what hab lots of chilluns was de ones what didn' draw no envelopes an' didn' git no cash. Unkuh Si

Moore was one of dem who didn' draw no envelope an' didn' draw no cash. He hab a big bunch of chilluns when he comed to de ole Wilson plannuhtation down to Jerusalem an', evuh yeah since he lit dere, his wife Sadie hab a baby. But hit don' meck no diffunce how big Unkuh Si's fam'ly come to be. When Unkuh Si go up to Colonel Wilson's house evuh yeah at settlement time de Colonel 'ud say, "Well, Unkuh Si, lemme see: you got fawty gallons of sorghums; 'bout eighty yaa'ds of calico, gingham an' percale; fifty-eight pair of brogan shoes; twelve pair of duckins, thutty-six jars of snuff, six barrels of sugah, fifteen barrels of flouah, a hunnud plugs of chewin' tobackuh, fo' dozen pair of black cotton stockin's, five dozen pair of socks, ten bottles of castuh oil, lebun boxes of Black Draf', seventy poun's of dry salt bacon, ten sacks of navy beans, an' 'bout twenty-five work hats."

When de Colonel git thoo readin' off dis list, he'd say, "Unkuh Si, yo' bill am settled; you don' owe me nothin'."

Unkuh Si moughty tickled evuh yeah, 'caze his bill am settled. So things run on in dis fashion for quite a spell. Ebun down when Unkuh Si hab fo' gran'chilluns to come an' live wid 'im, de Colonel still 'low dat Unkuh Si don' owe 'im nothin' evuh yeah when settlin' time come. Unkuh Si lackun de Colonel to David dat de Word tell 'bout, who hab a good haa't an' was allus bein' good to somebody. But he don't pay heed to how many han's he furnishin' for de Colonel's fawm; he furnishin' de plannuhtation wid twenty-fo' good han's evuh yeah. He jes' call to min' what de Colonel do for 'im an' he allus goin' 'roun' talkin' 'bout de Colonel boun' to hab lub in his haa't for Jesus, 'caze he don' meck 'im pay nothin' for stayin' on de plannuhtation.

Putty soon, though, de Colonel staa't to losin' lots of han's an' he meck Unkuh Si's fam'ly do mo'n dey share of de work on de plannuhtation. He ebun down meck 'em work on a Sunday. Unkuh Si don' lack dis heah Sunday work 'caze he say dat de Word say de Sabbath ain't no work-day. So he sets down an' begins to keep comp'ny wid de Lawd to fin' out if'n he ain't done error 'bout de Colonel bein' a good man. So he talks dis thing ovuh in secret wid de Lawd an' switch his min' 'roun' 'bout de Colonel.

So de nex' yeah when de time roll 'roun' for de crop settlement, de Colonel reads off Unkuh Si's list lack ez usual an' when he gits thoo readin' hit off, he say lack ez allus, "Well, Unkuh Si, yo' bill am settled; you don' owe me nothin'."

"Dat's awright, Boss," say Unkuh Si, "but gimme a receipt dat mah bill am settled in full."

"A receipt?" yell de Colonel. "Cain't you teck mah word for hit? Ain't I been dealin' fair wid you all dese yeahs?"

"Yas, suh, dat's awright," 'low Unkuh Si. "But Ah'm gittin' ole now, an' you's gittin ole too, an' we mought die fo' de next yeah dis time, when hit comes to be time for de settlement, an when Ah gits up to heabun an' St. Petuh asts me is mah bills all paid 'fo' he lets me in de heabunly gates, Ah wants a receipt to show 'im; Ah don' wanna be runnin' all ovuh hell lookin' for you!"

The Sinner-Man's Son
and the Preacher

Lack as evuhwhar, heaps of han's on de plannuhtations in de Bottoms didn't b'long to de Christun fam'ly. Lots of 'em was rank sinnuhs an' raise dey chilluns lackwise. Mos'ly dey ain't nevuh trace dey steps outen de Bottoms. All dey knowed was haa'd work, mean obuhseers, chu'ch oncet a mont', big dinnuhs on a Sunday, Saddy night chu'ch suppuhs, an' string ban' flang-dangs. In dat time comin' up, dey didn' keep tune wid de pace of de worl'. Dey come up in what you calls "Beck-time"—dat's de mule, you know, an' de time was when ole Beck, an' cotton, an' de black folks was de stan'bys of de country. Dey lived mos'ly in de settlements far off from de train track. When dey travel, dey do hit in fawm wagons a-settin' in chairs wid dey bottoms kivvered wid de hides of cows dey done kilt for market meat to peddle all roun' de Brazos Bottoms. Lots of 'em nevuh seed a train till dey come to be growed up. Dey's li'l yaps in de Bottoms to dis day what ain't nebuh seed a engine pullin' coaches on a track.

Oncet a li'l' boy what live wid his mammy an' pappy on de ole Wallace plannuhtation 'bout eighteen miles from town comed to Calvert to ketch de train an' go to see his cousins what live in Dallas. He de son of Jim Perkins, a sinnuh man, an' he ain't nevuh chanced to see no train since he been bawn. He fifteen yeah ole now, an' he so fidgety at de depot he don' know what to do wid hisse'f. Zack (dat's what his name) ain't ebun been far as Calvert offen de plannuhtation in his whole life, let alone seein' a train.

Putty soon heah comes de Houston Texas Central jes' a comin' 'roun' de curve an' a blowin' loud ez hit kin. Zack so scairt he try to pull loose from his mammy an' pappy an' run, but his pappy hol' 'im fas' an' he cain't git loose. He jes' shakin' lack he got de chills an' fever an' when de engine comed to a stop dey gits 'im on de train somehow 'fo' it pulls out from de depot. He cain't read an' write so his mammy hab his name an' whar he goin' writ on a piece of paper an' pinned to his duckins. Dey tell Zack whar he's haided for, but he's so scairt of de train till he done clear forgot whar he's s'pose' to go.

Fin'ly, de train staa'ts to pickin' up speed an' go to makin' 'bout thuhty miles a houah. Zack ain't nevuh seed nothin' in his life run dis fas'. De fastes' thing he done seed 'fo' today was one of de boss-man's ole mares name Nellie; she de fastes' hoss on de plannuhtation. So when de train staa't to makin' thuhty miles a houah, Zack poke his haid outen de window an' say, "Dawg gone!" Dey was a preachuh settin' nex' to 'im in de train, so when he say dis de preachuh stop readin' de papuh he hab in his han' an' eye Zack rail haa'd, but he don' say nothin'.

Putty soon de train staa't to makin' fo'ty miles a houah. Zack stick his haid outen de window again an' say, "Gawd dawg!" De preachuh stop readin' de papuh an' eye Zack again, an' dis time he say, "Li'l' boy, don't you know hit's wrong to use bad language?"

Zack eye de preachuh, but he don' gib 'im no ansuh.

Fin'ly de train staa't to meckin' fifty miles a houah, an' dis time Zack poke his head outen de window so he kin see de engine goin' 'roun' de curve, an' he yell, "Gawd damn!"

"Li'l' boy," say de preachuh, "you's goin' straight to hell."

"Ah don' gib a damn," say Zack. "Ah's got a roun' trip ticket."

PART SIX

WORSER DAYS AND BETTER TIMES

*That's all the girl lives next door to me does
is tell tales; she talks real loud, too.*

The Cabarrus County Boy Who
Told the Church What to Do*

Sittin' 'roun' listenin' to old folks you can learn a lots, but you can learn a lots by goin' up de road to New York, likewise.

One time dere was a boy what left home in Cabarrus County, went up to New York, an' comed to be in good shape. When he done comed to be in good shape, an' have him a little money on de side, he makes his way back to see his mama an' papa what done been his standbys 'fo' he lef' home. Dey is real proud of de boy, 'cause he got a lots of fancy clothes, a bran' new car, an' some money in his pocket. So dat next comin' Sunday dey all gets ready an' goes on down to de church.

Dey gets dere a little 'fo' de services starts, so de boy shuck an' reshuck de hands of most of de members what know him from a little chap, an' den goes on into de church house wid his mama and papa.

After de sermon am over de preacher gets up an' say, "Now brothers an' sisters, I has sumpin' dat got to be 'cided on right here dis mornin'. It's 'bout de money we done raised; an' de question am, what must us get wid de money, a piano or a chandelier?"

---

* A parallel to this anecdote apparently made its first printed appearance in *The Book of Negro Wit and Humor*, London Publishers, 1875, wherein a cuspidor rather than a chandelier was employed. Other versions are cited in *Listen for a Lonesome Drum*, Carl Carmer, Garden City Publishers, 1940; Richard M. Dorson's *Bloodstoppers and Bearwalkers*, Cambridge Press, 1940, and in the Louisville *Courier-Journal*, November 1, 1964, Sec. 4, p. 5.

SWEET AND HOT MEAT SAUCES

The above sauces may be used for neckbones (page 49) and red ribs or barbecued ribs (page 125). Favorites before and after the Civil War, these sauce preparations represent the basic recipes from which most later refinements were developed.

Sweet Barbecue Sauce

1 cup catsup or tomato sauce
¼ cup vinegar
2 tsp. olive oil
1 tbs. brown sugar or molasses
1 tsp. salt
1 tsp. dry mustard

¼ tsp. tobasco sauce
dash cayenne pepper
¼ tsp. garlic powder
1 clove garlic minced
1 onion, medium, chopped
2 tsp. sweet pickle relish (optional)

Simmer slowly until hot, stir thoroughly.

Red Rib Sauce

Prepare as for sweet barbecue sauce, adding 2 teaspoons red peppers or increasing the tobasco to taste (hot).

Den one of de members what been knowin' de boy from time he was knee-high to a duck riz up an' say, "Brother pastor, we has a visitor 'mongst us dis mornin' what done been up de country an' done come to be a knowledge man. S'posin' we asks him what we ought to buy wid de money?"

De pastor say dat's awright wid him; just whatsomever de membership want to do wid de money, an' whosomever dey wants to pass judgment, 'cause dey raised it.

So de boy gets up, pokes his chest way out, rams his han's way down in his pockets an' say, "Well now, I tells you. If'n I was y'all I believe I'd buy a piano wid de money, 'cause as far back as y'all in de woods I don't believe you gonna find nobody out here can play no chandelier."

How the Parrot Broke Up
the Church Meeting

A preacher was running a revival, and every night he would tell the people that they were going to hell by the wagon-loads. Old boss had a parrot, so he told the parrot to go down to the church and ask who was going to bring the wagon back. The next night as the preacher made the statement the parrot said, "Who'll bring the wagon back?" Everybody ran out of the church but one old lady, so the parrot lit on her shoulder and said, "Who'll bring the wagon back?" The old lady said, "I don't know, Mr. Jesus. I ain't a member here; I'm just a visitor."

The Preachers and the Cab Driver
at the Heavenly Gates

One time there were two preachers and a cab driver who died and went to Heaven at the same time. They all went up to the pearly gates to be judged by St. Peter. One of the preachers was the first to approach St. Peter and make his confession. He said, "I have been preaching for fifty years." But Peter did not let him in the pearly gates; he told him to step aside. Then the next preacher came forward and made his confession. "I have been preaching for twenty-five years," he said. But Peter told him to step aside, like he did the first preacher. Then the cab driver came up to where Peter was seated, and he confessed that he had been driving a cab for fifteen years. So Peter told him to enter.

When the preachers saw this they asked Peter why he let the cab driver enter the pearly gates and would not allow them inside, considering that the two of them together had preached a total of seventy-five years while the cab driver had only been driving a cab for fifteen years.

"I let him in," replied Peter, "because he's scared the hell out of more people in that fifteen years than both of you have in seventy-five."

The Divided Church

Some churches is sho' hard to pastor. One of 'em dat I knows 'bout is right here in Kinston—dat is, it's 'bout ten miles out on dat ol' dirt road what runs into de main highway. Dey calls de church Mount Zion, an' as far back as I can remember ain't no preacher stayed dere more'n a month o' two. My mind reaches back forty years o' more, too, an' I ain't never seed dat church hol' a preacher ver' long at a time.

But las' year sumpin' 'nother happened dat make me switch my mind 'roun' 'bout dis church can't hol' no preacher. It was long 'bout watermelon time las' summer when a new preacher come to Mount Zion to try hisse'f out. De first Sunday he preaches he gets along jus' fine, but de secon' Sunday he take notice dat de ver' same members what set on de right han' side o' de church sets on de right han' side o' de church de secon' Sunday likewise, an' dat de ver' same members what set on de lef' han' side o' de church de first Sunday sets on de lef' han' side o' de church on de secon' Sunday.

On de third Sunday, de fourth Sunday, an' de fifth Sunday he take notice dat dis here same thing happen, so after de services was over on de fifth Sunday he calls de head deacon an' say, "Listen here, Brother Deacon, I wants to ask you a question 'bout sumpin' I sees dat I doesn't like."

De deacon say, "What dat you don't like, Brother Pastor?"

"I don't like it 'bout de church bein' divided," say de pastor. "De same members settin' on de same side o' de church ever' Sunday, so I wants you to tell me why dey carryin' on in dis wise.

"Well now, Elder," say de deacon, "I ain't gonna tell you nothin', 'cause dey ain't nothin' dat you o' me o' nobody else can do 'bout it."

So de pastor turnt on his heels 'thout sayin' another mumblin' word, an' got in his car an' drive off.

But dat nex' comin' Sunday he gets up in de pulpit to preach 'bout brotherhood an' 'bout how church folks ought to be together 'stead of bein' separated. His sermon ain't hit bed-rock nowheres though, 'cause dat nex' Sunday all dem what been settin' on de right han' side o' de church-house comes right back an' sets on de right han' side like dey always do, an' dem what been settin' on de lef' han' side o' de church comes in an' takes dey seats on de lef' han' side, like as always.

De preacher be outdone; he don't know what to do, so after de services he tell de head deacon dat he want to have confab wid him again. He done stayed dere longer'n any preacher dey done ever have, so he know dey won't get rid of him if'n dey can help it. So he say, "Now look-a-here, Brother Deacon, I means business; if you don't tell me why de same members o' dis here church sets on de right han' side ever' Sunday, an' de same members sets on de lef' han' side o' de church ever' Sunday, I's gonna pack up my clothes an' find me another church."

De head deacon don't want de church to lose dis preacher, so he finally give in an' say, "Well den, Brother Pastor, I tell you. Ever since I was a little fella runnin' 'roun' in pigtails an' my mammy an' pappy brung me to church, dis here been goin' on. You see, it's like dis: dem what sets on de right han' side o' de church house ever' Sunday says, 'Dey ain't no Hell,' an' dem what sets on de lef' han' side says, 'De hell dey ain't!' "

The Angel Who Wanted to Go to Hell

One time dere was a ol' boy 'roun' China Grove what come to be de bes' gospel singer in dem parts. 'Nother thing, he lib a good Christian life, too. His name ain't nevuh been up on de signboard lack mos' all de res' o' de younguns 'roun' China Grove. Dis ol' boy, what go by de name o' Jasper, hab a good name wid de ol' peoples an' de young. All he do was go to choir practice durin' o' de week, an' to chu'ch services all day on Sunday. He ain't never yet been to no flang-dang* dat dey hab ever' Saddy night, an' he ain't never been in no pool hall neither. He just stay in de house all de time an' practice singin' chu'ch songs.

One Sunday night, how-be-evuh, when he was drivin' his ol' car home from chu'ch, de brakes gib out an' de car leaves de highway an' falls ovuh in a ditch 'side de road an' kill 'im.

Nachully, he was 'mitted to de pearly gates o' Hebun, an' was one o' de choice angels. De first Saddy night he was dere, all de choice angels was settin' roun' God's throne lookin' at de TV program an' it happen dat ever' Saddy night dey looked at a special broadcas' from Hell. Dis ol' boy, Jasper, seed a jazz ban' playin' de blues, an' some putty gals shakin' deyse'f an' doin' de "twis' " an' de "jerk" down in Hell, so he touch God on de shoulder an' he say, "God, how 'bout lettin' me go down to Hell?" So God say dat's awright wid Him, but if'n he go down to Hell he gonna hab to stay down dere an' he can't nevuh come back to Hebun no mo'. Jasper say dat be awright wid him, so he leaves Hebun an' goes on down to Hell.

It was 'bout nine o'clock dat night when he lef', but 'long 'bout midnight God hears somebody knockin' on de Hebunly gates, an' when He peeks ovuh de wall to see who it is knockin' on de gates dat time o' night, He sees dis ol' boy Jasper, an' say, "Look a-heah, what's de matter wid you comin' back up heah to Hebun? Ain't I done tol' you dat if you went down to Hell you's gonna hab to stay down dere?"

"Oh, yassuh," say Jasper, "I unnerstood dat in de first place. I jus' come back aftuh my clothes!"

---

* A dance.

Both Were Proud

One time dere was a mainstay of a church down in Davie County what have twin boys. He such a good church-member till de boys 'cides dey wants to be preachers when dey grows up. So after dey done end up wid high school dey papa sends 'em off to 'nother school where dey can learn to know how to preach.

After dey done wind up dey lessons at de preacher-school dey come back home to 'liver dey first sermon. De mainstay o' de church an' his wife was proud as dey can be o' dere sons, so whilst dey was preachin' dey was sayin' "Amen" all de way through de sermons.

De way dey have it set up—one o' de boys would preach ten minutes, den de other'n would preach ten minutes. Dey preached a whole hour long off an' on, an' de whole congregation liked de way dey carried out.

After de service was over de mainstay o' de church an' his wife carries de boys on home where dey have a big dinner for 'em to smack on. 'Mongst de food was two young fryin'-size roosters what dey catched off dey yard an' kilt.

When dey done et, dey all goes out into de yard to get a li'l whiff o' cool air, 'cause hit was in de month o' August, an' a turble hot day. De mainstay an' his wife was settin' on a old bench under a tree, an' dey two sons was settin' in some old rickety chairs underneath 'nother tree fannin' deyse'fs wid some newspapers. De mainstay o' de church say to his wife, "Ain't you proud o' our two sons what just entered de ministry?" An' when he talk in dis wise, de ol' rooster what was de pappy o' de two fryin'-size chickens de young ministers done et for dey dinner, and what was listenin' to what de mainstay say to his wife, turn to de hen what was de mammy o' de fryin'-size roosters, an' say, "Ain't you proud o' our two sons what just entered de ministry?"

The Preacher and the Runaway Lion

One Sunday in Durham an old preacher was telling his congregation about belief and faith in prayer before the eleven o'clock services began. He had been informed just a few minutes earlier that a lion had broken loose from a nearby zoo, so he was telling his audience to have faith in God and not be afraid of the lion if they should run across him on the way home after services.

"If you pray hard enough," he said, "fear not, for the lion outside will not bother you." He shouted very loudly, "Fear not, for thou art with me; watch and I will show you a way to get out. I have the faith in God that y'all should have."

But after the services were over, before the preacher had gone more than a few yards from the church-house steps, he was met by the lion. The preacher got down on his knees and said, "Oh Lord, please hear my prayer! You saved Daniel from a lion, and I know you gonna save me from this here lion." His prayer was loud and sincere, but, all the same, he raised his head after awhile to see what the lion was doing. To his surprise, he saw that the lion was also kneeling, with his paws clasped over his eyes. So he said, "Brother lion, are you praying wid me?"

The lion looked up at him and replied, "No, brother, I's sayin' my grace befo' I eat!"

The Preacher and the Board Meeting

A country minister around Mocksville ended his sermon and then announced that he would like to have all the Board to remain for a few minutes. A stranger in the village who had worshipped at the church that morning made his way to the front pew and seated himself with the deacons and elders.

The minister approached him and said, "My dear sir, perhaps you misunderstood. I asked that only the Board remain."

"Well, that included me too," replied the stranger, "cause I was never mo' bored in my life."

The North Carolina Negro and the Alabama Deputy Sheriff

One time a young fellow who lived in Durham bought him a new Oldsmobile. Since he had a girlfriend who lived in Mobile, Alabama, he decided to drive the car down to Mobile so she could see it.

Everything went along all right until he ran into a curb near a little town in northern Alabama, and punctured one of his front tires. He got out of the car and was jacking up the wheel when a deputy sheriff drove up in his car, jumped out of it, and ran over to where the colored fellow was changing his tire. He said, "Hey, nigger, what you doin'?"

"Fixin' my automobile."

"What kind is it?"

"Oldsmobile."

"Where you goin', nigger?"

"Mobile."

"What's your name?"

"Henry Keel."

"What's your girl's name?"

"Lucille."

"What's that I'm gonna make you run across?"

"A cornfiel'."

About that time the sheriff heard a *click-click*, and said, "What's that, nigger?"

"Forty-five blue steel," said the young fellow, pointing the gun in the sheriff's face. "Now let me see you start runnin' through that cornfiel'."

The Mother's Last Words
to Her Son in the Country

One time there was an old Negro lady who had a son that she tried to rear to be a respectable young man.

When the son became twenty-one years old he left her and went to live in town. While there, he got in trouble and had to go to court. The judge sentenced him to death in the electric chair.

The son was carried home to see his mother for the last time. When they got there, the guards asked her to say her final words to him.

She looked at her son and said, "Now, John, you know I tried to raise you like good people. So you just go on down there and get 'lectrocuted, and then come on back home and act like you got some sense."

The Intelligent Slave*

Durin' slavery time dere was a rich old massa in Brunswick County what owned mo'n three hundred slaves. Among dem was one very smart slave named Tom. What I mean by smart is dat he was a smooth operator —he knew what was happenin'. De way he come to be smart was by crawlin' under de massa's house ever' night and listenin' to de massa tell his wife what kind o' work he was gonna have dey slaves do de next day. When de massa would come out o' de house ever' mornin' an' get ready to tell de slaves what kind o' work he wanted dem to do dat day, Old Tom would say, "Wait just a minute, Massa. I knows zactly what you's gonna have us do."

So de massa would stop talkin' an' let Old Tom tell de slaves what he had in mind for 'em to do dat day. Old Tom could always tell de slaves zactly what de massa wanted 'em to do, too; an' de old massa was very much surprised, 'cause he didn't know how Old Tom was gettin' his information.

De reason Old Tom would go under de house ever' night an' find out what de massa was gonna do de next day was 'cause he wanted to prove to his massa dat he was de smartest slave on de plantation. De smartest slave always got de easiest work, and Old Tom was tired o' workin' hard. Sometimes de massas let dere smart slaves sleep in a bed in de Big House,

---

* European and especially British versions of this internationally known tale have been published as *The Barn Is Burning*, as well as under other titles.

too; so Old Tom had been dreamin' about one day, maybe, he would get to sleep in a real bed instead of on a old quilt on his cabin floor. And it wasn't long before his dream come to be true, 'cause dat next comin' week after Old Tom done started prophesyin' de work for de slaves ever' day, de old massa tell his wife dat he think he gonna bring Old Tom to live in de house wid dem, an' give him a room to sleep in. So dat next comin' mornin' he moved Old Tom in de house wid him an' his wife. Old Tom was so tickled he didn' know what to do wid hisse'f—just think, livin' in de same house wid his old massa!

One winter night when de massa an' his wife were seated around de fire de massa called Old Tom in to test his smartness. He pointed to de fire an' said, "Tom, what is dat?"

"Dat's a fire, massa," said Tom.

"No, it ain't either," replied his old massa. "Dat's a flame of evaporation." Just den a cat passed in front o' de fire, and de old massa say, "Tom, do you know what dat was dat just passed by de fireplace?"

"Dat's a cat, sir," replied Tom.

Then his old massa said, "No, it ain't either. Dat's a high-ball-a-sooner."

Old Tom was gettin' tired o' answerin' questions by dis time, so he goes over to de window an' starts lookin' out. De old massa walk over to de window where Tom was an' say, "Tom, what is dat you's lookin' at out de window?"

"I's lookin' at a haystack," say Tom.

Den old massa say, "Dat ain't no haystack. Dat's a high-tower."

Den Old Tom set down in a chair an' started gettin' ready to go to his room up in de attic and go to bed for de night. He didn' wanna get de carpet all spotted up wid dirt in de livin' room, so he started to unbucklin' his shoes and takin' 'em off. When de old man looked an' seen Tom takin' off his shoes, he say, "What's dem, Tom?" An' Tom say, "Dem's my shoes."

"No, dey ain't either," say his old massa. "Dem dere's yo' tramp-tramps." Den de old massa pointed through the archway to where a bed could be seed in his bedroom, and said, "What's dat dere I's pointin' to in dere, Tom?" "Dat's a bed," say Old Tom.

"No, it ain't either," said his old massa. "Dat's a flowery bed of ease, an' I's goin' right now an' get in it 'cause we's all got a hard day's work comin' up tomorrow." So de old massa an' de old missus goes on in dey bedroom an' goes to bed. Den Old Tom goes on up to de li'l attic room where dey lets him sleep an' gets in bed.

But just as Tom started to get in his bed de cat runned through de fire in de fireplace and caught on fire, and run out to de haystack and set it on fire. Old Tom run to de window an looked out and seed de cat on fire an' de haystack on fire, so he started yellin' as loud as he could, "Massa, Massa, you better get up out yo' flowery bed of ease an' put on yo' tramp-tramps 'cause yo' high-ball-a-sooner done run through yo' flame of evaporation an' set yo' high-tower on fire."

His old massa didn't move a peg—he just hunched his wife an' said, "Lissen at dat high-class slave up dere usin' all dat Latin."

Den once mo' Old Tom yell out, "Massa, Massa, I say dat you better get up out yo' flowery bed of ease, an' put on yo' tramp-tramps, 'cause yo' high-ball-a-sooner done run through yo' flame of evaporation an' set yo' high-tower on fire."

But Tom's old massa just hunched his wife again, an' say, "Dat's sho' a smart slave, dat Tom, ain't he? Just lissen at him talkin' all dat Latin up dere again."

Old Tom went on yellin' like dis 'bout five mo' times, but when he seed dat his old massa wasn't gettin' out of bed he yelled, "Massa, you better git up out of dat bed an' put yo' shoes on, an' go out dere an' put dat haystack fire out dat yo' cat done started, or else yo' whole damn farm's gonna burn up!"

The Tobacco Stacker's Mistake

One year, during tobacco-stacking time, a tobacco grower near Winston-Salem brought some Negroes up from Georgia to stack his tobacco for him. The reason he did this was that he could hire them cheaper.

The Georgia men had heard about how bad the Winston-Salem Negroes were, so every Saturday when they got their week's pay they would slip off, two or three at a time, and go into town and buy guns, knives and wine. The reason they could not stay in town long at a time was that they worked all day Saturday—they just got paid at ten o'clock in the morning and had two hours off for the day, from ten to twelve.

There was one in the bunch who never went into town but who'd always send by some of the others for a quart of "Eleven Star" wine every Saturday. He kept up this practice for about four weeks, but finally, on the fifth Saturday after they had started to work on the tobacco farm, he decided that he'd go into town himself and get his "Eleven Star" wine. When he got there he went into the first store he saw, which was a hardware store, and told the owner that he wanted a bottle of "Eleven Star" wine.

Said the owner, "We don't have nothin' but hardware here."

"Well," said the Georgia man, "gimme a bottle of that."

The Spelling Bee and the County Superintendent

My gran'ma said when she was a little bitty girl jes' startin' to school out to Tobaccoville, dat dey jes' hab a one-room school wid one teacher, and dat mos' o' de little school scholars was boys. Some o' de little boys names was Tom Miller, Jimmy Brown, Bob Thomas, Chuck Connor, Raymond Moore and Bill Johnson. But dey was one little fellow dat was named **Damn-it Jones.**

Gran'ma say dat little Damn-it was a top scholar in rifmetic—dat he could work wid figgers real good, but dat he was at de bottom o' de class when it come to spellin' day. Gran'ma say dey'd have a "spellin' bee" ever' Friday jes' 'fo' school turned out, and dat little Damn-it was always at de bottom o' de row.

One Friday, how-be-ever, gran'ma say, de County Sup'inten't comed by de school an' tuck him a seat whilst dey was havin' de spellin' match. Gran'ma say dat her an' de other li'l girls an' all de boys spelled all de words de teacher give out till finally de teacher ask 'em to spell de word Nebuchadnezzar an' dey all missed out, cep'n she ain't got to Damn-it Jones yet, so li'l Damn-it riz up his han' real high in de air an' say, "Teacher, let me spell it."

"Damn-it Jones, you can't spell it," say de teacher, an' when she say dis de sup'inten't stan' up real quick an' say, "Hell, teacher, let him try!"

Love I See, Love I Stand,
Love I Holds in my Right Hand*

Long time ago, 'fo' de blue coats what dey call Yankees come roamin' 'roun', things was rockin' 'long putty good here betwixt de slaves an' dey old massas. Lots of de massas lack to carry on foolishness wid dey slaves, speshly when it rain, an' it get too wet to work in de 'bacco fields.

One time up 'roun' New Bern dey was a good old massa what have a slave name Joe, what he like to joke wid all de time. Him an' Joe was always swappin' jokes an' riddles, so one day he say, "Massa, you gimme a riddle to figger out today, so spose'n I brings you one in de mornin', an' if'n you can't guess what de answer be you give me my freedom."

"Awright Joe," say de old massa, "if'n you can bring me a riddle what I can't figger out I'll sho give you yo' freedom."

So dat nex' comin' mornin' 'fo' daybreak Old Joe knocks on de old massa's door, an' de massa, what already done got out of bed an' put on his clothes, say, "Come on in, Joe. Has you got dat riddle you was tellin' me you gonna bring wid you dis mornin'?"

"I sho has," say Joe, who done killed his old dog what named Love de night befo', an' what done take an' cut him up an' take a piece o' his skin

---

* This riddle tale is one of the best known of the so-called "neck-saving" riddles. In a useful comparative article, "The Prisoner Who Saved His Neck with a Riddle," *Folklore*, LIII (1942), F. J. Norton gives examples of the "Love" riddle from England, Bermuda, Germany, Denmark and other European countries (pp. 35-41). American Negro references will be found in (North Carolina) Parsons, "Guildford County," p. 203 (two versions); (South Carolina) *Journal of American Folklore*, XXXIV (1921), pp. 26-27; Parsons, *Sea Islands*, pp. 157-158; (Louisiana) *Journal of American Folklore*, XXXVII (1925), p. 281; (Nova Scotia) Fauset, p. 142.

an' wrap 'roun' his right hand. So he say, "Yassuh, I's got de riddle all set to go."

"Well awright den," say de old massa. "Let's have it."

"Well den, here she go," say Joe:

> *"Love I see; Love I stan'*
> *Love I holds in my right han'.*

"Now, what dat be, massa?" say Joe.

Joe's old massa try hard as he can to guess de riddle, but he don't never come up wid de rat answer. So after 'while he say, "Joe, I gives up, so I's gonna give you yo' freedom, but 'fo' I gives it to you I wants you to do me one favor: Tell me what de answer to de riddle be."

"Sho, Massa, sho," say Joe. "You see dis here brown piece of old dog's skin I's got in my right han'? Dat's a piece of my old dog's skin name of Love.

"All de time I was talkin' to you I was stannin' dere wid it, an' I was holdin' it in my han' lookin' at it. So dat's why I says:

> *"Love I see; Love I stan';*
> *Love I holds in my right han'."*

The Deputy Sheriff and the Negro Bootlegger

Negro bootleggers from Wilkes County were very hard to catch. Most of 'em always went down to Winston-Salem or Greensboro or Raleigh to sell their mash. One of the smartest of these bootleggers did most of his sellin' in Winston-Salem, but as is always the case, some member of his own race told a deputy sheriff about this man and pointed him out one day when the bootlegger had finished disposing of his liquor.

The deputy sheriff found out what part of town the Wilkesboro man operated in, however, and the days that he came into town to sell his merchandise. So the very next day that the bootlegger was scheduled to come to Wilkesboro to sell liquor the sheriff disguised himself, walked up to him, and asked if he knew where he could get some good home-made whiskey.

"How much do you want?" asked the black man.

"About five dollars worth," replied the sheriff.

"Well, gimme the five dollars," said the Negro, "and I'll go and see what I can do." He then handed the deputy sheriff a shoe box. "Here," he added, "hold these shoes for me till I get back."

The sheriff took the shoe box and waited for three hours, but the Negro never returned. So he decided to look in the box and see what was in it.

When he opened it up, there was a fifth of bootleg liquor.

Jesse James and the Buried Money*

It is said that Jesse James, the famous robber, robbed a bank one time in North Carolina, right after slavery time, and wanted to hide the money, but he did not know where to hide it. His brother Frank told him to hide it in the colored graveyard because all the ex-slaves were afraid of dead folks and the money would be safe there.

What Jesse did not know was that a Negro runaway from justice was hiding out in the graveyard, and that when he saw Jesse and Frank coming he went and climbed up in a tree and hid.

Jesse buried the money and put a sign over it which read: *Dead and Buried.* After Jesse and Frank left, the Negro dug up the money, took it, and made his escape.

When Jesse returned for the money several months later, the sign read: *Risen and Gone!*

Jim Johnson and His
New Suit of Clothes

One Saddy long 'bout dusk dark, Jim Johnson what lived out to Five Row, 'cided dat he wanna buy him a new suit o' clothes to go to de ball game what gonna be played at Mocksville dat next comin' Sunday.

All de big sto's on Main Street was closed—wasn't but one sto' open an' dat was a sto' runned by a white man name of Rubenstein. So Jim walks into de sto' and looks 'roun', an' a putty blue serge suit finally catch his eye. He try on de suit an' it fit him jes' right. He pay fo' it, and Mr. Rubenstein wrap it up an' Jim carry it on home an' hangs it on a nail on de wall. Sunday evenin' he take de suit down an' put it on, an' jumps in his ol' "T" model Fo'd what ain't got no top on it, an' drives up to Mocksville to see de Carolina Quick Steppers play de Mocksville Black Hornets.

De game ain't got started good 'fo' it come up a big cloudburst an' Jim's suit o' clothes got soak an' wet from de rain. When he gits home he takes de suit off an' puts it on a ol' rockin' chair by de wood stove to dry. After de suit done dried off, Jim puts it on an' de breeches comes way up twix his knees an' his ankles—when he put on de coat he couldn't button de buttons on it. So when Monday morning comes Jim puts on de suit an' goes down to Mr. Rubenstein's sto' to show him how de suit done drawed up.

"Sho, I remembers you," say Mr. Rubenstein, pattin' Jim on de back an' de suit of clothes all at de same time, "but my! how you has growed!"

_____

* In a Negro tale from Philadelphia, a Negro buries money in a graveyard and puts a gravestone above it reading "Dead and Buried." A white man has watched him. He digs it up and changes the message to "Rose and Gone to Glory." A. H. Fauset, "Tales and Riddles Collected in Philadelphia," *Journal of American Folklore,* XLI (1928), p. 551.

The Mountain Man and the Mirror*

One time a mountain man found a small mirror—the first one he'd ever seen. He looked in it and said with surprise, "By cracky, it's a pitcher of my old pappy!"

Sentimentally, he hid the mirror under the bed. His wife saw him hiding it. When he went to work the next morning she went under the bed, took the mirror out, looked into it, and snorted, "So that's the old bag he's been chasin'!"

Big Mountain and Little Mountain

In a mountain town of North Carolina there lived a man about eight feet tall. One day a little fellow about five feet four walked up to him and said, "Man, if I was as big as you I would go up the mountain and grab a big bear and whup him to death."

The big man looked down on him and said, "There's some little bears up there too!"

The Mountain Man and the Motorcycle**

Right over there to the left, on the side of the road lookin' over yo' right shoulder, in that li'l cabin up on the mountain-side, was where my gran'ma's half-brother used to live. He was real handy with a shotgun and took a shot at everything he saw.

One evenin' just before sunset when it was just beginnin' to get dark, gran'ma's brother an' his wife was settin' out on a bench in front of the cabin when they looked up an' saw a man ridin' down the road on a motorcycle. They had never laid eyes on a motorcycle before, so they thought it was some kind of animal from the noise it made and the way it looked. As soon as gran'ma's brother saw it, he grabbed up his shotgun that he had layin' on the ground next to the cabin steps, and fired. The buckshot hit

---

* This anecdote has been collected in England, the United States and in the Middle East. See F. M. Wilson, "Some Humorous English Folk-Tales, Part Two," *Folklore*, XLIX (1938), pp. 277-278; N. H. Thorp and N. M. Clark, *Pardner of the Wind* (Caldwell, Idaho, 1945, p. 209; Spalding's *Encyclopedia of Jewish Humor* (1969) which cites a similar version from the Arab state of Yemen.

** Another story in which a motorcycle is thought to be an animal is given in H. Halpert's "Folktales and Jests from Delaware, Ohio," *Hoosier Folklore*, VII (1948) p. 72.

the motorcycle and made it turn 'round and 'round, causing the man to fall off.

When the motorcycle fell to the ground, gran'ma's brother's wife said, "Did you kill it?"

"No, I didn't kill it," he replied, "but I sho' made it turn that man loose!"

The Revenue Agents and the Mountain Boy

One time some Government revenue agents went up in the mountains near North Wilkesboro to try and locate some stills they heard two brothers were operating. They reached the cabin of one of the brothers, but there was nobody at home except the mountain man's twelve-year-old son.

The revenue agents asked the boy where his father and uncle were, and he replied, "They're just over the hill."

"Well," said the revenue agents, "take us over the hill to where they are, and we'll give you fifteen dollars when we come back."

"Naw," replied the boy. "You gimme the fifteen dollars now, 'cause if you go over the hill you ain't *comin'* back!"

The Arrest of the Two-Year-Old

De Mocksville Picnic is big doin's ever' year. Look like policemens just hangin' 'roun' waitin' for de time to come when de Mocksville Picnic roll 'roun' so dey can 'rest lots o' colored people an' put 'em to jail an' make 'em some money.

Dey makes a whole lots of 'rests ever' year, but de worse one I done ever seen was las' year. A man's little two-year-old baby boy what been eatin' too many hamburgers an' drinkin' too many Coco-Colas took sick an' was vomitin' all over de groun', an' wobblin' from side to side. A policeman seed de li'l fellow an' come up an' 'rested him for bein' drunk. But dat ain't all; he 'rested his papa for aidin' an' abettin'.

3

PARABLES
in
BLACK

BOOK THREE

Parables in Black

Introduction

Probably no other group of people in the United States is as devoutly Christian as the black American. A walk through any predominantly Negro section, anywhere, will reveal an astonishing number of churches; far more, per capita, than in any other area. These places of worship may range from the imposing Roman Catholic cathedrals to the far less pretentious store-front churches which not only serve as spiritual sanctuaries but are often the only community centers in which the brothers and sisters may communicate freely. Despite the militancy of the younger, more widely educated blacks and their discontent with what they sincerely believe to be the apathy of their elders in the field of civil rights, the church continues to serve as a focal point in the community; the minister is still respected as a leader of his people, although there is no gainsaying that the more politically aware youths of today may well provide the leadership of tomorrow.

From his earliest arrival in the New World, the black slave was exposed to and accepted Christianity as a spiritual and moral force. The concepts inherent in the Sermon on the Mount and the Ten Commandments, the espousal of the brotherhood of man and the soul-felt *need* for a faith that promised deliverance from bondage, all tended to make him receptive and responsive to the exhortations of the church.

It is difficult for 20th-century Americans to understand the slave's acceptance of Christianity in the face of what we today can only regard as the sheerest hypocrisy. The new faith constituted a dichotomy of ideal and practice. It preached the noble and inspiring concept that all men are brothers in the eyes of God; and yet, with the exception of the Quakers, it not only supported but encouraged slavery, holding out little hope for the sev-

159

erance of their chains. Indeed, Christianity would not have been presented to the black man in the first place if the white missionaries had dared to express as much concern for his earthly servitude as with his glorification in the hereafter. One can only conclude that the basic dilemma of being a "Christian slave" was resolved in the knowledge that it was not Christianity but its perversion by many of its white followers which remained at fault.

It should be borne in mind, however, that *all* agencies which attempted to alleviate the plight of the slave were subject to close scrutiny by the authorities of the day. The various white religious groups were particularly suspect; yet a few did strive to bring the fundamentals of their beliefs to the blacks. Nearly always, their texts, teachings and philosophies were carefully censored by the slaveowners. The ideal of fraternity—that all men are children of God and equal in His eyes—became a prohibited subject. "Do unto others as you would have them do unto you" was prostituted to mean that it applied only between whites and whites or blacks and blacks, but never interracially. "Render unto Caesar that which is Caesar's" was interpreted to mean that Jesus had condoned slavery as an institution answerable only to Caesar (the nation), but not to God. Under such conditions, for example, the Society for the Propagation of the Gospel in Foreign Parts, and other similar agencies, aimed at the conversion of black children, but always under the supervision of the pro-slavery segment of the population, which, in the South, meant nearly all of it. Outstanding among those who took a firm stand against slavery and who brought the Word to the slaves without distortion were the Quakers (Society of Friends). They not only took a moral position on slavery, but condemned it as anti-Christian and forbade their members to own slaves or to participate in any manner in the traffic of human beings.

The Negro denominations have a long and respected history. In 1796, a group of black men and women, led by James Varick, withdrew from the John Street Methodist Church in New York City because of its policy of segregating black and white congregants. They formed their own denomination, and four years later they built their first church which they called the African Methodist Episcopal Zion (AMEZ). In 1801, several other churches with similar views, held a joint conference and Varick was elected first president.

The African Methodist Episcopal (AME) Church was founded by Richard Allen in 1816. Allen, a deacon in the Bethel Church, called together the representatives of separate Negro churches in Delaware, Maryland and New Jersey to lay the foundation for the denomination—one of the earliest Negro Methodist denominations in the United States. Today the AME Church is divided into 18 Episcopal districts and flourishes throughout the country as well as in Africa, Canada and the Caribbean Islands.

Before the establishment of the AME church, large numbers of Negroes joined the Methodist Church in colonial and pre-Revolutionary times. In some areas they were organized into separate congregations presided over by white preachers, while in others, they participated in services on a segregated basis, taking communion after their white counterparts had done so. Dissatisfaction with the latter system grew so pronounced that by 1785, several influential members of Methodist churches in the North had voted to establish their own places of worship. The leader in this movement, Richard Allen, a freedman, was the same Allen who later organized the AME Church and became its bishop. By 1787, he and his followers were convinced that Negroes would best be served by breaking away from the white Methodist church altogether, and accordingly severed their affiliation. The Negro Methodist movement experienced its first real flowering after the Civil War, due, in part, to the greater mobility enjoyed by the black man—both preacher and convert—as a result of emancipation. Despite its growth, however, the Methodist gospel never succeeded in matching the appeal generated by the Baptist movement. Nevertheless, the Methodists of today, although split into three main denominations, lay claim to more than two million members.

The Baptist Church became a major force in Negro religious life in the years immediately following the Civil War. By 1870 (four years after the movement had been launched in North Carolina), Baptist state conventions were organized throughout the South. The Consolidated American Baptist Convention, organized in 1867 and lasting until 1880, represented the Negro's first attempt to create a national body independent of, and separate from, white-dominated groups. With the dissolution of this convention, three smaller ones sprang up in its place: the Foreign Mission Baptist Convention of the U.S.A. (1880); the American National Baptist Convention (1880), and the American National Educational Baptist Convention (1893). These organizations were then united as the National Baptist Convention of the U.S.A. At the time of its formation in 1895, this convention had three million members and was the largest single denomination of Negro Christians in the world. Since then it has itself undergone a number of splits, the largest of which resulted in the creation of the National Baptist Convention of America.

As in the case of the Methodists, the Baptist worship has tended to reflect the religious thinking and spiritual expectations of the Negro masses. As such, it is usually evangelistic in tone and relies heavily on the dynamism and personality of the preacher, rather than on any strict adherence to the articles of faith he espouses. Because of this very factor, the preacher is not only regarded as a spiritual leader in his community but as a judicious arbiter and counselor as well.

It is in this context of his authoritative role that he also becomes the target of the humor and witticisms of his people; for the black man in America has usually been able to see through pretense and bombast, whether his own or anyone else's. As a result, he not only views his pastor as a gifted leader or advisor, but also as a human being who is subject to all the frailties of mortal flesh. It is a practical and quite affectionate outlook, but tolerant only to a point, and it is within that range that a body of humorous folklore—the preacher tale—has evolved.

The stories which comprise *Parables in Black* differ from the preacher tales told by J. Mason Brewer in that the former aim their slings and arrows at preacher, church and doctrine alike, while Dr. Brewer, in the main, seldom employs the preacher as the object of ridicule. This is especially apparent in his collection of North Carolina tales wherein it is clearly indicated that the Negroes of that state are quite conservative in religious matters.

Poketown may be regarded as "Anywhere, U.S.A." It has been variously located in New Jersey, the southern part of Pennsylvania, the Eastern Shore region of Maryland, and as far south as Mississippi. In any case, it describes an all-black community in the late 19th century, probably during the closing years of the Reconstruction era (1885-1890). The reader will note that the female inhabitants of Poketown are referred to as "Aunt" and the males as "Uncle." It was this editor's initial intention to substitute *Mr.* and *Mrs.* for the unfavorable and inappropriate "Aunt" and "Uncle" but, after serious reflection, he decided to let them stand as originally written, for the same reason that he faithfully recorded their dialect: To make such changes for the sake of modern attitudes would destroy the very authenticity which earned the tales their place in this Encyclopedia.

Aside from their high humor, the stories selected for *Poketown People* offer a glimpse into the past. They describe a way of life which has all but disappeared—they tell of *people* rather than events. There are no "protest" elements in this grouping, but the reader will find here an entertaining and instructive insight into the daily activities of a village in which black people lived, loved, worshipped and—yes—fought among themselves. Poketown of almost a hundred years ago was not unlike that of many other sleepy little rural communities, black or white; the exception being, of course, that the inhabitants were spared many of the insults and humiliations suffered by their contemporaries elsewhere. In the modern sense, Poketown might be termed a "ghetto," but its citizens would have undoubtedly greeted such a description with derisive jeers and quite probably with chauvinistic outrage.

That these stories are wildly ludicrous (one of their charming assets) is hereby acknowledged, nor is there any need to stipulate the obvious: that Poketown's attitude towards its preachers was not representative of the times. Nevertheless, the sociologist, the historian, and the interested general reader will find a wealth of background information and "important minutae" which will help illustrate small-town family life of days long since past.

PART ONE

POKETOWN PEOPLE

Brother Johnsing's Sperience

"An' now, all true b'lievahs o' de wuhd o' de Lawd am axed tuh be in dey places on nex' Chuesday night at de watch-meetin'. We's gwine tuh watch de Ole Yeah out an' de New Yeah in, an' I hopes dat many will be moved by de Sperrit tuh give in dey sperience on dat solemn 'casion.

"Befo' we jines in singin' de las' hymn we'll pass 'roun' de hat wunst mo', an' 'tain't no mannah o' use fuh de young men on de back benches tuh be aidgin' to'ds de do', 'caze it am locked!"

So saying, Brother Eli Wiggins, pastor of Little Bethel, Poketown's principal church, wiped his brow with his red bandanna and sat down. The congregation slowly dispersed, discussing the watch-meeting as they walked down the one long, straggling street which composed the settlement known as Poketown and inhabited solely by black people.

"I wondah now," remarked Aunt Martha Young, as she paused at her front gate, "ef Brothah Sam'l Johnsing's gwine tuh come to de watch-meetin'."

"Don' call 'im 'brothah,' Aun' Ma'thy," replied Uncle William Stafford. "Sam'l Johnsing am backslidin' too fas' tuh evah git redimption. 'Peahs like ole Satan done got hol' him ag'in good an' tight, an' I reckon he's gwine tuh keep him dis time."

"I done heah tell," said Aunt Janty Gibbs, who shared with the first two speakers the right of seniority in Poketown, "dat he kin splain it all ef he gits a chance."

"Splain it all, kin he?" Aunt Martha snorted. "I'd like tuh heah him splain leavin' his wife wid dat passel o' chillun tuh suppo't an' settin' up tuh co't de yallah gal f'om de Crossroads right undah huh nose."

When the night of the watch-meeting arrived, Poketown turned out handsomely; among others appeared Mr. Samuel Johnson boldly escorting the yellow girl from the Crossroads and apparently oblivious of the indignant glances cast upon him from all directions. Brother Wiggins rose to address the meeting.

"It is mah painful duty," he said, after the opening hymn had been sung, "tuh look ovah de faces befo' me an' separate de wheat f'om de chaff; de sheep f'om de goats."

An uneasy rustle pervaded the congregation, as though many were in doubt regarding the class to which they belonged.

"De true an' faithful," resumed the pastor, "will set on de right han'. Dem as has nevah got 'ligion will set in de middle row of benches an' we'll labah wid 'em an' hope de sperrit o' de Lawd will move dey hahts tonight. But dem dat has wunst got 'ligion an' backslid, dem as is walkin' ahm-in-ahm wid Satan, an' dem as is indulgin' in scan'lous conduc', will set in de benches on de lef'-han' side. Dat dey shan't be no mistake, an' no chance o' de sheep gettin' messed up wid de goats, I'll call de names o' de faithful fust; den de onreginrit. Dem as is lef' uncalled knows whut dey is 'thout no mo' wuhds f'om me, an' will go whah dey b'longs."

This classification filled the benches on the right to overflowing; it also crowded the middle row somewhat uncomfortably with the youth of the congregation, among them the yellow girl from the Crossroads; while quite alone in the left-hand benches, calm and undisturbed, sat Mr. Samuel Johnson—a solitary goat. And the meeting proceeded as usual.

The first hour or two were devoted to alternate prayers and hymns, instigated by one or the other of the congregation, but as ten o'clock approached, Brother Wiggins again rose for a few remarks. "De houah am come," he announced in solemn accents, "fuh me tuh ax y'all tuh 'membah whut you's heah fo'; de time am rollin' 'roun'. . . ."

"*Roll, Jordan, roll!*" shouted an excitable sister.

The refrain was taken up by all present and sung through from beginning to end.

"De ol' yeah am mighty nigh gone," continued the preacher when he could make himself heard, "an' we ain't got but two houahs lef' befo' de New Yeah am gwine tuh be 'mongst us. An' wid it comes de moon. Bewah o' de moon, mah brothahs; tuhn yo' backs tuh it, mah sistahs, specially de spring an' summah moon. Dat's de time tuh watch an' pray. It am pow'ful easy tuh do right wintah nights when de kitchen stove am buhnin' hot, an' yo' feet gits fros'bit ef yuh goes outside; but when de spring comes creepin' in, wid de frogs a-croakin' in he ditches, an' de breezes blowin' sof' ovah you, how 'bout dat? Kin you 'membah de Comman'ments when de harves' moon am hangin' in de sky, big an' raid? When de smell o' de wile grape fills yo' nose an' de katydids am callin' tuh you—how 'bout dat? When de cawn am standin' in de shocks an' de watahmillions am a-layin' on de vines, fit tuh bus' wid ripeness an' glistenin' wid de dew—how 'bout dat? Does yo 'member de Comman'ments den? When yo' heels am lightah den yo' haid, an' somethin' sends de blood a-chasin' thu yo' veins—I ax you once mo'—how 'bout dat?"

He paused for breath and closely scanned the faces before him. "De time am passin'," he continued, "de ole yeah am 'mos' gone. Ain't you got nothin' tuh say, mah frien's? Is you gwine tuh shake han's wid de New Yeah 'thout givin' in no sperience tuh he'p you git thu it? Uncle William Staffo'd, you's de oldes' membah heah; ain't you got nothin' tuh say? Aun' Janty Gibbs, huccum de sperrit not tuh move you dis las' night?"

Uncle William Stafford rose slowly to his feet. "Brothah Wiggins," he began, his voice determined, "I feels it mah juty tuh tell you dat dey won't be no speriences guv in dis evenin'. When I done heah tell dat Mistuh Sam'l Johnsing wuh gwine tuh be heah tuhnight, bol' ez brass wid all his backslidin' onrepented, I wuz 'stonished; dat's whut I wuz—'stonished! I axed Aun' Janty Gibbs an' we done come tuh de seclusion dat ef you 'lowed de snake in de pusson o' Mistuh Sam'l Johnsing tuh entah de meetin' dis evenin', dah shouldn't be no speriences guv in by dem as tries tuh keep dey feet f'om slippin' f'om de paff dat Abraham, Isaac, an' Jacob done set fuh us tuh walk in. Dat's all, Brothah Wiggins."

Uncle William sat down with much dignity and Aunt Janty Gibbs took the floor.

"Whut Uncle William done say am gospel truf," she began. "Dey won' be no movin' o' de sperrit ez long ez Mistah Johnsing sets up dah so biggity an' brazen. Ef he kin splain 'bout leavin' his wife an' fambly tuh shif' fuh deyse'fs an' 'bout de way he's bin gwine on lately, now's de time fuh him to speak up an' do it; ef he cain't splain dis nohow, now's de time fuh him

PORK CHOPS

"Poketown people," those living in small, all-Black villages on the Eastern seaboard and on down into Mississippi (see page 162), prepared pork chops in what might seem extravagant styles for poor folks.

Baked Pork Chops

6 to 8 pork chops
¼ cup flour
2 large onions
1 tbs. prepared mustard

1 green pepper
2 tsp. grated lemon rind
salt, pepper, paprika, celery
and garlic salts to taste

Cover chops with mustard. Sprinkle with pepper, seasoned salts, paprika and flour. Brown in a heavy skillet, in a small amount of fat. Place in flat baking dish. Cover with onion and green pepper rings, water, and lemon rind. Bake in a slow oven (325°) for about 45 minutes. Potatoes may be baked at the same time.

Stuffed Pork Chops—Tennessee Style

6 double pork chops
1½ cups bread crumbs
1 tsp. salt
½ tsp. pepper
1 tbs. grated onion
1 tsp. sage

½ tsp. leaf thyme
¼ cup chopped celery leaves
3 tbs. bacon fat
1 tbs. parsley
3 tbs. water
1 tsp. paprika

Cut a pocket on bone sides of each chop. Sprinkle with salt and pepper inside and out. Sauté onions, celery and parsley. Add bread crumbs and seasonings. Stuff each chop with dressing. Brown on both sides in skillet with a bit of fat. Add water and bake in oven about 50 minutes or until tender.

tuh git outen de sight o' speckable folks. Dat's de seclusion we's all come tuh, Brothah Wiggins, an' dey won' be no movin' o' de sperrit ez long ez dat low-life niggah sets up in dat bench 'thout sayin' nothin'.''

Aunt Janty resumed her seat amid a low murmur of approval. Brother Wiggins was somewhat embarrassed as to the proper course to pursue. "Mistah Johnsing," he said at last, "you done heah whut Brothah William Staffo'd an' Sistah Janty Gibbs has said. Whut you got tuh say fuh yo'se'f, Mistuh Johnsing; whut you got tuh say?"

Mr. Johnson remained silent, smiling inscrutably, while the yellow girl from the Crossroads fidgeted uneasily in her seat. Brother Wiggins made a last pathetic appeal. "Does you 'membah whut night it am, Mistah Johnsing? Don' you wantuh entah de New Yeah wid clean han's an' feet an' yo' backslidin' confessed an' washed away? 'Membah, po' sinnah, dat even ef yo' sins be scahlet dey kin be made whitah dan snow."

> *"Whitah dan snow; yes, whitah dan snow,*
> *Wash me, an' I shall be whitah dan snow . . ."*

sang Aunt Martha Young, rocking herself back and forth, while the hymn was taken up by one after another until the roof rang with the refrain: *Wash me, an' I shall be whitah dan snow."*

As the last notes died away Mr. Samuel Johnson arose. "Brothah Wiggins," he announced, "de sperrit o' de Lawd am wuckin' inside me tuhnight, an' I'd like tuh give in mah sperience befo' de New Yeah am 'mongst us."

"Precede, Mistuh Johnsing, precede," said the preacher.

"Brothah Wiggins, you done made reffunce tuh de moon in yo' speechifyin' tuhnight. Whut you done say am gospel truf. It am de harves' moon 'specially dat am 'sponsible fuh many things. Ez ev'ybody know, it am full three nights."

"Reckon 'twant no fullah dan you wuh," said a voice from the rear. It was the injured Mrs. Johnson, who occupied a seat near the door, surrounded by her offspring.

"On de firs' o' dese nights las' summah," he continued without regarding the interruption, "ez I wuz comin' home f'om huskin' cawn an' walkin' 'long by de canal, I seen somethin' on de towpath befo' me. It wuh a gal dancin' tuh de music o' de cordeen dat somebody in de bushes wuh playin'. 'Who dat?' sez I. 'Come dance,' sez she, holdin' out huh skirt wid one han' an' feet twinklin' in de moonlight. Brothah Wiggins, I ain' tryin' tuh 'scuse mah conduc'; no suh—I's tellin' you de truf. De light o' de moon wuh in mah haid, de music o' de cordeen got intuh mah feet, an' befo' I knowed it I wuh on de towpath wid mah ahm 'roun' de wais' o' dat yallah gal I nevah seen befo'."

"'Twant so much de light o' de moon in yo' haid ez de feel o' de applejack you done tuck intuh yo' stomach," proclaimed Mrs. Johnson from the rear.

"Sistuh Johnsing, hol' yo' peace," said the pastor. "Let him precede."

"De nex' night," Mr. Johnson went on, "I come home by way o' de towpath ag'in an' I tuck mah fiddle wid me so's I could play fuh huh tuh dance. An' de thuhd night, ez I wuh fiddlin' away an' she wuh a-dancin' in de light o' de moon, sho's yuh bawn, Brothah Wiggins, I seen de wuhd SIN in lettahs o' fiah 'cross mah fiddle!"

A sudden thrill ran through the congregation as they bent eagerly forward, intent on hearing every word. Mr. Johnson, after a suspenseful pause, continued.

"I done flung de fiddle intuh de canal an' stahted fuh home, but I wuh dat skeert mah knees trimbled undah me, 'caze I knowed 'twuz de han' o' de Lawd done writ dat wuhd on mah fiddle, an' I 'spected it wuh gwine tuh be laid on me pow'ful heavy in jedgmint."

"Dat am a mighty movin' sperience," said Brother Wiggins, "but you fuhgot tuh tell us huccum you tuh leave a lady like Sistah Johnsing heah fuh a no-'count gal f'om de Crossroads. Splain yo'se'f, Mistah Johnsing. Huccum you tuh do dat?"

"Dat's whut I's tryin' tuh do, Brothah Wiggins," said Mr. Johnson plaintively. "Fuh some time I done keep away f'om de canal an' come home 'cross de ma'sh, but I wa'nt happy 'caze I kep' thinkin' o' de gal I done lef' by huhse'f on de towpath 'thout no wuhds tuh tell huh 'bout de sin o' whut she wuh doin'. She done cas' a spell ovah me, Brothah Wiggins, dat's whut she done, an' I couldn' git away f'om it nohow."

"Watch an' pray, Mistah Johnsing, watch an' pray. Dat's whut you mus' do," suggested Brother Wiggins.

"Dat's jes' whut I done," returned Mr. Johnson. "An' den one day ez I wuh walkin' 'long de Dutch Neck road I done heah a Voice callin' tuh me f'om de empty aiah. 'Sam Johnsing,' it say, 'Sam'l Johnsing!' 'Dat's me,' sez I wid de sweat breakin' out all ovah me. 'Sam'l Johnsing,' it say ag'in, 'huccum you leave dat gal on de towpath 'thout p'intin' out tuh huh whuh she gwine when she die ef she don' leave off dancin'? Huccum you do dat, Sam'l Johnsing?' "

"Lies, all lies!" Mrs. Johnson was heard to mutter.

"I done flop down on mah knees," continued Samuel Johnson, "an ax de Pusson speakin' tuh me whut I mus' do. Sho's yuh bawn, Brothah Wiggins, de Voice ansuh back: 'Sam'l Johnsing, go back tuh de canal an' walk down de towpath till you fin' dat yallah gal. Take huh by de han' an' zort wid huh; labah wid huh ev'y evenin' till she leave off huh scan'lous conduc'.'

"An' dat's whut I done, Brothah Wiggins. But did she repent an' tuhn huh back on de music o' de cordeen an' de fiddle? No, suh! De mo' I zorted de mo' she laugh an' dance, till I done feel obligated tuh spen' mo' an' mo' time wid huh.

"At las', jes' ez I wuh makin' up mah min' tuh let huh go huh own way, I done heah de Voice ag'in. It say: 'De Lawd am angry wid you, Sam'l Johnsing. Whuh dat stray lamb He done sont you out fuh tuh bring intuh de fol'?' I make ansuh dat I couldn' do no mo'. Den de Voice say, pow'ful loud an' strong, 'Yes, you kin, Sam'l Johnsing; yes, you kin. Leave yo' happy home fuh awhile; leave de wife o' yo' buzzom—de lady o' yo' 'fections—tuh suppo't de fambly. She kin do it 'caze she am so pow'ful smaht an' hus'lin'. You's got tuh live at de Crossroads an' snatch de bran' f'om de buhnin'.' Den I axes kind o' weak like, whut mo' I got tuh do, an' de Voice done make ansuh, 'Spen' yo' money on huh, Sam'l Johnsing,' spen' yo money on huh. Dat's de way tuh tech huh haht.' "

The yellow girl from the Crossroads simpered and touched some glittering ornaments pinned to her dress as Mr. Johnson continued.

"De Voice say tuh spen' mah money on huh; I done so. It say, 'Go live at de Crossroads; I done so. 'Twa'nt easy fuh me, Brothah Wiggins, tuh leave mah wife an' chillun. I done heah whut's bin said 'bout me in Poketown, but I fuhgive it all. I wuh wuckin' ovah a strayin' sistuh, same ez I I wuh tol' tuh do. I labah'd 'roun' de clock an' spent mah money lib'ral— she come high, Brothah Wiggins. But now mah duty am done. I's gwine back tuh mah home tuhnight, an' ef anybody heah have got any mo' tuh say on de mattah we'll ahgufy outen de back yahd. Is you satisfied wid de wuck I's done fuh yo' chu'ch, Broth Wiggins? Does you think de New Yeah am gwine tuh fin' me wid clean han's an' a righteous sperrit?"

"*Brothah* Johnsing," said the pastor, emphasizing the title, "I is. You's done noble: you's lived yo' 'ligion in yo' life, not talked it wid yo' mouf. I's proud tuh know you, Brothah Johnsing."

"Dat am mah sperience fuh de Ol' Yeah, Brothah Wiggins," said Mr. Johnson modestly. "I done fotched de lamb intuh de fol', but it am yo' place tuh look aftah huh an' keep huh feet f'om strayin'. I 'vise you, Brothah Wiggins, tuh zort huh tuh stay in de house on moonlight nights, dat's all."

"It am now twelve o'clock," said Brother Wiggins as the bells pealed forth their greeting. "De New Yeah am wid us, an' I hopes dat when it am ovah you's gwine tuh have ez much tuh yo' credit ez Brothah Johnsing have tuh his'n dis las' yeah. Me an' Brothah Johnsing's gwine tuh stan' side by side befo' de pulpit, an' de congregation am invited tuh shake han's wid us an' wish us a happy New Yeah."

"Brothah Johnsing," said Aunt Martha Young, "you's got de gif' o' gab pow'ful slick, an' when I heahs you talkin' I's obleeged to b'lieve you, spite o' mahse'f. But when I tuhns mah back I ain' so sho'."

Last of all came Mrs. Johnson and family. As she laid a proprietary hand on her husband's arm, a worried expression might have been observed in Mr. Johnson's eyes.

"Come home wid me, Sam'l Johnsing, an' heah *mah* sperience! I's gwine tuh tell it tuh you good an' strong. Den you kin splain yo' conduc' ovah ag'in tuh me. I ain' got it intuh mah haid yit huccum de Lawd tuh give you sech pow'ful ordahs. Come home an' splain."

"Go home wid yo' fambly, Brothah Johnsing," said the pastor, with the air of one who pronounces a benediction. "You's airned de right tuh live peaceful an' happy. Go home rejoicin' wid de wife o' yo' buzzom."

Mrs. Johnson turned suddenly upon her husband as he followed her to the door. "Tote de baby," she commanded, thrusting the heavy child into his reluctant arms; "I's tah'd mahse'f. I ain' gwine tuh do no mo' wuck till you splains so's I kin onnerstan' yo' meanin'. You ain' done yit, Sam'l Johnsing—not yit!"

The Offending Eye

Brother Noah Hyatt, one of the chief pillars of the church, a member of the Sessions, a leader of class-meetings, and one especially gifted in exhortation, had a certain peculiarity which was a matter of comment in Poketown.

This was his apparent ability to fix one eye sternly upon a given point while the other rolled independently about, seeking new worlds to conquer. The stationary eye was light blue while its roving companion was brown.

Brother Jacob Sutton was pondering upon this eccentricity as the two men walked home from class-meeting one Friday night.

"It jes' entah mah mine, Brothah Hyatt," he began somewhat tentatively, "tuh wondah huccum yo' haid suppo't a blue eye on de lef' an' a brown eye on de right. Huccum de Lawd tuh favah you dat a-way?"

Brother Hyatt's brown eye flashed angrily, in direct opposition to the pleasant smile of the blue one. "Reckon He done it fuh de same reason He tuck an' favah you wid one straight laig an' one bow laig."

Brother Sutton felt impelled to change the subject. "De case o' James Pollahd gwine tuh be laid befo' de chu'ch nex' class night," he said hastily. "You 'membahs dat he done tuck a pai'h pants f'om de sto' on Main Street an' dey 'rested him 'caze dey seen him gwine tuh chu'ch in 'em."

"Dem plaid pants done lay him low fuh sho'."

"'Peahs like, bein' ez how de done wuck out he time in jail, de sin am spashiated," hinted Brother Sutton, who was inclined to be lenient.

"Ef plaid pants am de undoin' o' James Pollahd," said Brother Hyatt unctiously, "den he got tuh stick tuh plain goods. Sich am de konsekinses o' vanity."

"Po' James! 'Peahs like I kin see him now, standin' up in dem pants an' givin' he sperience fuh de ol' yeah when dey tuck an' 'rested him."

"De chu'ch," said Brother Hyatt severely as he paused at his gate, "am obligated tuh sterminate sech acks. Dem what 'dulges in cuss wuhds had oughtta slit dey tongues; dem what takes de goods o' othahs had oughtta chop dey han's offen dey body."

They exchanged goodnights and Mr. Hyatt entered his house. Once inside he removed his left eye and placed it carefully in his vest pocket. The existence of this glass eye was the skeleton in his closet, and he guarded the secret jealously. When bargaining for its purchase it had been suggested to him that perhaps brown would be a better choice than blue, owing to the prevailing custom of having eyes to match when possible. But he had repudiated the suggestion with scorn. "Whut yuh reckon I wants tuh git a brown eye fo'?" he demanded. "Ain' I jes' done wo' one clean out? I's gwine tuh git a blue eye, nuffin' else!"

And blue it was.

Going to his back door, Brother Hyatt surveyed the landscape. The quiet of an August night reigned supreme, and overhead the moon shone with enticing brilliance. Beyond two adjoining fields an irregular dark outline was plainly visible. It was the watermelon patch of a neighboring truck farm.

✔ ✔ ✔

Meanwhile, Brother Jacob Sutton, after leaving his companion, paused at his own residence and secured an empty grain-sack. "De speckled pullet ovah tuh de fahm mus' be 'bout fryin' age now," he reflected as he climbed the fence. Soon the young fryer and several companions fluttered uneasily in the grain-bag. " 'Mought ez well come home thoo de watahmellion patch," he thought.

The dew lay thick upon the vines, glistening brightly in the light of the moon. Scattered closely about the field were the melons themselves, large and luscious and tempting. But someone had arrived before him. Brother Sutton hesitated an instant, then approached boldly. "James Pollahd!" he exclaimed sternly. "Whut you doin' heah?"

James Pollard, he of the plaid trousers, turned apprehensively around, then chuckled with relief. "Clah tuh goodness," he said, "I done thunk it wuh ol' man Noahy Hyatt."

"James," said Brother Sutton solemnly, "you done lef' de jail yestiddy; is you gwine zume evil actions dis soon?"

The unhappy James entered into a rambling explanation when he was interrupted by Sutton. "James," he said, his eyes fixed on the open melon at his feet, *"am she ripe?"*

✔ ✔ ✔

Over the brow of the hill now appeared a third figure, walking slowly and stooping now and then to tap a melon, testing with thumb and forefinger. Suddenly he paused and listened intently. He heard a murmur of voices which gradually grew more distinct. Hastily his hand sought his vest pocket and fumbled there, *but his eye was gone!* He had lost it, apparently while bending over to test the fruit.

A famous general has said that the best mode of defense is by attack, and it is evidently true that great minds run in the same channels, for Brother Noah Hyatt promptly advanced to meet the enemy, with one hand held over the empty eyesocket and the other raised in stern denunciation. "Brothah Sutton!" he exclaimed, "whut you doin' heah? Whut you aftuh? I ax you, Brothah Sutton, whuh yo' 'ligion?"

Mr. Sutton pointed dumbly towards James Pollard at his side. James was clad in the identical plaid trousers which had occasioned his downfall, given him by the kindly shopowner upon his release from jail. "I come heah, Brothah Hyatt," Sutton began loftily, "tuh snatch de bran' f'om de buhnin'. I done come to rassle wid de Son o' Sin an' Wickedness, an' tuh keep he feet f'om strayin' whuh dey done strayed befo'."

"I ain' done nothin'—hope tuh die," stammered the wretched James. "He tuck an' et ez much ez me."

"James," said Brother Hyatt, his powers of exhortation aroused, "I zorts you not tuh add lyin' tuh yo' crap o' sins. You's got 'nuff tuh spashiate an' tuh sterminate 'thout dat."

"Ax him whut he got in he bag," muttered James, his knees knocking together as he encountered Brother Hyatt's brown eye fixed upon him— "ax him whut he got in he bag."

Brother Sutton shifted the bag to his other shoulder, the captive chickens stirring as he did so. "I got mus'rats in mah bag," he said. "I done bin down to de crick."

Mr. Hyatt reached forward and squeezed the bag with his right hand. A muffled squawk resounded. "'Peahs like de lanwidge o' mus'rats done changed since yestiddy," he remarked drily, his other hand still covering his eye.

"Whut you doin' heah yo'se'f, Brothah Hyatt?" demanded Brother Sutton, rallying sufficiently to return the attack. "Kin you splain yo' own actions?"

"Brothah Sutton, I done come heah 'caze ol' Satan he beckon me; dat's huccom me tuh be heah. He done drug me ovah de fence an' tuck an' p'inted out de ripes' mellion in de patch. I sets mah eye on it an' I wants it—yaaas, I wants it pow'ful bad. I couldn't git mah eye f'om offen it nohow; de zire growed an' swelled in mah buzzom twell I feel fit tuh bus'. Whut you think I done, Brothah Sutton; whut you think I done?"

Reckon you tuck an' cut de mellion," said Brother Sutton, speaking from long experience.

"No, sah!" said Brother Hyatt piously. "I 'membahs de wuhds o' de Book: "If yo' eye offen' you, pluck it out an' cas' it f'om you—an' dat's whut I done, Brothah Sutton; dat's whut I done." He dramatically removed his hand and the eyelid collapsed into the cavernous socket. The two men gaped with astonishment and Brother Hyatt resumed:

"She come out pow'ful hahd," he said pathetically. "Dem roots wuh sho'ly in good an' tight. But I kep' a-pullin'—yaaas, I kep' a pullin', 'caze I ain' gwine tuh suppo't no onruly membahs tuh mah body. No sah! I'se gwine tuh cas' 'em f'om me. An' aftah I done fling that sinful blue eye into de crick de Lawd come down in a cha'iot o' fiah an' stanched de bleedin' an' tuck away de huht. He sez tuh me, sez He: "Well done, Noahy Hyatt— well done!"

"I nevah heah no sperience de equal o' dat," said Brother Sutton, awe-struck.

"Does you still hone fuh de mellions, Brothah Hyatt," inquired James Pollard.

"James," said Brother Hyatt severely, "I tells you mighty solemn dat ef you reaches out yo' han' tuh tech dem mellions whut don' b'long tuh you, you's gwine tuh see a Eye lookin' at you. Dat Eye am watchin' you cyahful, an' you cain't hide f'om it nohow. An' you, Brothah Sutton, has you disremembahd 'bout de All-Pervadin' Eye? Huccum you do dat? It done bin spyin' aftah you dis night. De Session am gwine tuh heah 'bout dem mus'rats, sho's you bo'n. Dey's somebody 'sides James Pollahd fo' de chu'ch tuh deal wid, Brothah Sutton."

Mr. Hyatt turned and walked majestically away, complete master of the situation.

✓   ✓   ✓

Brother Sutton started for home, his soul awed with the spartan resistance of Brother Hyatt to the promptings of the devil. James Pollard, now alone beside the creek, pondered thoughtfully upon the events, sadly puzzled. "Ol' man Noahy Hyatt nevah done pull out dat eye hisse'f nohow," he muttered. "Yit, huccum dat hole in he haid?"

James scratched his own head as he strolled homeward. Observing what seemed to be an especially fine melon, he paused and bent over to examine it. *What was that looking up at him from among the dark leaves?* James' heart was in his mouth for several moments. Gathering courage, he put forth a cautious finger and touched the object, with fear and trembling at first, and then with curiosity, contempt, and finally hilarity. "De eye," he laughed. *"Noah Hyatt's eye!"* James Pollard thrust the accusing orb in the pocket of his plaid trousers and proceeded on his way, rejoicing.

As for Brother Hyatt, he deeply regretted the loss of his eye but felt that its absence would give him added prestige in class-meetings. Therefore, he bore it with fortitude. At the moment he was sitting in the shadow of an oak tree, refreshing himself with the produce of the field after the exhausting events of the night.

Suddenly, James Pollard emerged from behind the tree like an avenging ghost. "I done pick up whut you drap a-ways back," said the intruder. There was no mistaking the craftiness, the pure cunning in every word. James, it was clear, was about to make someone dance to his own tune— for a change. Although quite at ease, his manner was somehow distantly menacing.

Mr. Hyatt's lower jam dropped in astonishment and he was speechless. He pointed at the blue eye in the other's open hand and gasped, "Huccum— huccum! . . ."

"Brothah Hyatt," said James, "I knows all 'bout you an' I's pow'ful glad I does. I ain' gwine tuh 'spose yo' lyin' 'bout de eye 'caze I wants tuh git back intuh de bes' s'ciety of Poketown. Ef you he'ps me, I he'ps you."

He paused and looked searchingly at his companion. "Ef de chu'ch take an' hold out huh ahms tuh me, Brothah Hyatt, an' fuhgit de plaid pants an' de jail; ef de bes' s'ciety in Poketown am zorted tuh open de do' tuh me, I reckon de Lawd mought up an' wuck a merrycle an' a eye mought up an' spring out same ez Jonah's gourd tuck an' growed in a night. 'Peahs like tuh me," added James enticingly, "I kin see it sproutin' now."

"James," said Brothah Hyatt, rising, "come home wid me an' go intuh mah back do'. De Lawd done favah you wid secon' sight."

✓   ✓   ✓

There was a full attendance the next class-night, rumors of an unusual and interesting nature having excited the curiosity of Poketown to its highest point. Brother Hyatt rose to address the meeting, and a stifled moan of despair came from Brother Sutton, who half rose to his feet and then sat down again.

"Brothah Sutton," began Brother Hyatt impressively, "I calls on you fo' yo' sperience las' Friday night, jes' aftah I done pull out mah lef' eye an' cas' it f'om me 'caze it res' too long on de goods o' othahs—las' Friday night, Brothah Sutton, when you done went aftah *mus'rats!* Tell de chu'ch I's speechifyin' de truf 'bout dat eye."

And Brother Sutton, in faltering accents, testified that he had met and conversed with Brother Hyatt when the eye was lacking. A thrill ran through the congregation as the story progressed with graphic description.

"James Pollahd," said Brother Hyatt, as Brother Sutton resumed his seat, "you done seen dat eye resto'd tuh mah haid. Speak up now an' give in yo' sperience."

"Me an' Brothah Hyatt," said Mr. Pollard, "wuh settin' on he do'step an' he wuh p'intin' out de way tuh heaven tuh a po' sinnah like me, when dey come a light, same ez de light when de mule stables on de towpath tuck fiah.

"*Yaaas!* Dey come a light!" interrupted Brother Hyatt. "Praise Gawd!"

"An' I done heah a Voice outen de middle o' de night," James resumed. "It say, 'Brothah Hyatt, de Lawd am pleased wid you. Heah am yo' eye back ag'in, good ez new.'"

"An' den I done feel a ticklin' way back in de roots," said Brother Hyatt, taking up the thread of the discourse, "an' somethin' came a-bulgin' an' a-scrouchin' outen mah haid—glory! glory! hallelujah!—outen mah haid intuh de hole. *Glory!*"

James took his turn again. "De light done fade, an' I up an' sez, 'You got yo' same ol' eye back ag'in,' I sez."

"But 'twa'nt de same ol' eye," Brother Hyatt once more interrupted, 'caze I done see diff'unt wid it. Dis heah eye done bin in glory, an' de way it see now am de right way fo' sho'. It done tell me plain whut am de juty o' de chu'ch to'ds its wanderin' lambs. I axes you, mah brothahs an' sistahs, tuh welcome back James Pollahd tuh yo' midst; I zorts you tuh open yo' do's wide tuh him."

Brother Hyatt reached for James Pollard's hand and led him forward before the pulpit.

"Brothah Sutton," he said, fixing that trembling gentleman with his brown eye, "I knows dat you's gwine tuh be 'mongst de fust tuh welcome Brothah Pollahd back tuh de ahms o' de chu'ch.

"Brothah Sutton," admonished Brother Hyatt, "'tain't no time tuh speechify 'bout mus'rats; I sho'ly would hate tuh be obligated tuh tell all I knows 'bout 'em dis night. Step up, Brothah Sutton, an' welcome de lamb back tuh de fol'. Step up lively now, an' set de zample tuh de res' o' de Session."

Brother Sutton stepped.

An Unwilling Delilah

"I's knowed de day when de benches wouldn' hol' de folks whut wanted tuh come tuh Little Bethel, no mattah how close we sot," mourned Aunt Martha.

"Room tuh spaiah now," said Aunt Janty gloomily.

There was trouble in Poketown directly traceable to the arrival of the new pastor at Zion Church. Hitherto, Little Bethel had been the tabernacle of the elite of the village, and had tolerated with haughty indifference the existence of a humble edifice across the bridge known as Zion and patronized by a few faithful spirits, chiefly from the surrounding country.

Little Bethel had a gracefully tapering steeple, and the ladies of the congregation were particular about wearing straw hats in summer and felt ones in winter: Zion had no steeple whatever, and the ladies who worshipped within its unplastered walls were fortunate if they had any hats at all. The benches of Little Bethel were provided with backs, and the gentlemen of the congregation usually wore brightly polished, loudly creaking boots, and displayed the corner of a handkerchief artistically drooping from the pockets of their waistcoats. The benches of Zion were backless, and the gentlemen who sat thereon used grease instead of blacking on their boots—when they had any—and were ignorant of the advantages of pocket-handkerchiefs. In a word, Little Bethel did not associate with Zion: it was the invidious distinction of class.

It was therefore not surprising that Aunt Martha Young and Aunt Janty Gibbs, pillars of Little Bethel, viewed with consternation the expansion of Zion after the arrival of Brother Tyndal. "Tyndal, Son of Thunder," he preferred to be called. It was the title bestowed upon him him because of his eloquence, and he felt he had earned it.

"Look at 'em," said Aunt Janty resentfully, indicating the stream of people crossing the bridge and meandering down the street, "dey come from Zion!" Judging from her tone, coming from Zion was equivalent to going to perdition.

Brother Tyndal passed, surrounded by an admiring coterie. He was a tall, slender young man whose most remarkable attribute appeared to be the thick black hair which reached well below his shoulders, and which he kept brushed until it stood out like a glistening but bushy aureole.

Close behind, but alone and unworshipped, followed Brother Wiggins, the once popular pastor of Little Bethel. He paused to exchange a few words with his faithful adherents at Aunt Martha Young's gate.

"Come in," said that lady hospitably, opening her front door. "Brothah Wiggins, now's de time fo' you an' me an' Aun' Janty tuh discuss dis mattah o' Zion. Dey ain' gwine tuh be no Little Bethel lef' 'cep'n us ef we don' up an' ack rapid-like."

Brother Wiggins sank wearily into a chair and thrust his hands deep in his pockets. Walking home alone from his deserted church behind the triumphant Zionites had been to him a journey through the Valley of Humiliation.

"I dunno huccum Brothah Tyndal tuh git sich a hol' ovah de lambs of Little Bethel," he commented sadly.

"I knows," said Aunt Janty in the sepulchral tones of one who feels that the time has come to speak out. "It am he haiah!"

"Splain yo'se'f, Aun' Janty," suggested Brother Wiggins, clearly puzzled.

"Brothah Tyndal ain' de fus' man whut am beholden tuh de haiah o' he haid fuh stren'th an' pussonal 'traction," said Aunt Janty. "'Membah Sampson."

"Dat's so, Aun' Janty, dat's so!"

"Well, sho's yo' bo'n, hit am de haiah whut am 'sponsible. Kin you grow haiah like his'n, Brothah Wiggins?"

He shook his head. It was manifestly impossible for him to compete with his rival, nature having endowed him with hair which kinked tightly from the roots and covered his head like a skullcap. "I knowed f'om de fus' dat he done got outside 'sistance," he remarked vindictively. "Reckon he tongue ain' quite ez slick ez he haiah, aftah all."

Aunt Martha had been recalling to the best of her ability the history of Sampson, and had arrived at a definite conclusion. "It got tuh be cut off," she said abruptly. "Who gwine tuh do it?"

"Not me!" said Brother Wiggins at once, and with evident relief. "Hit wuh a lady whut done cut de haiah offen he haid. She done 'ticed him tuh go tuh sleep an' up an' tuck huh scissuhs outen huh pocket an' snipped it off. Dem am de wuhds in de Book; 'tain' gwine tuh do no good fuh a man tuh go messin' whuh he ain' no use. Ef sich mattahs ain' done reg'lah, whut's de good o' doin' 'em at all? Kin a man 'tice a man? Tell me dat!" He paused a moment and then asked, "Whut kin you do, Aun' Ma'thy? You's got a way wid you dat am pow'ful takin'."

Aunt Martha settled her ample form more comfortably in her chair. "Reckon mah days fuh 'ticemints an' sich am ovah."

Nor was Aunt Janty more encouraging. "Me too," she muttered. As they considered the question, a shadow fell upon the window.

"*Melindy!*" exclaimed Aunt Janty.

Brother Wiggins nodded, greatly relieved. "Ev'body know dat when Melindy 'swade no man kin deny."

"Dey ain' a man in Poketown whut wouldn' shave hisse'f bald ef Melindy spressed a zire fuh he haiah," Aunt Janty chimed in. "'Tain' no reason Brothah Tyndal gwine tuh be diff'unt."

Aunt Martha smiled with conscious pride. It was no small matter to be grandmother to the belle of Poketown. "Me an' Melindy will do whut we kin," she promised.

The next evening the three pillars of Little Bethel met again in Aunt Martha Young's parlor. This time they were reinforced by the presence of Melinda, who sat sulkily aloof.

"Aun' Ma'thy," said Brother Wiggins, "has you done splained tuh Melindy whut she got tuh do?"

"I done make huh read out loud twice't ovah 'bout Mistah Sampson an' he lady-frien'," she replied delicately.

"Whut you got tuh say fo' yo'se'f, Melindy?" asked Aunt Janty.

Melinda answered with a question of her own. "Does you sho' nuff b'lieve Brothah Tyndal am like Sampson?"

"I does."

"An' kin he do whut Sampson done?"

"Ez long ez he haiah float out behin' he haid dey ain' nothin' he cain't do."

The girl cast a rebellious glance at her grandmother. "Den do yo' own clippin'," she muttered sullenly. "'Tain' faiah tuh ax me tuh do whut you's feahed tuh do yo'se'f."

"Melindy!" snapped Aunt Martha.

"Don' keer: I ain' gwine tuh be kilt wid no jawbone of a ass," said Melinda, on the verge of tears. "Ol' Samson kilt folks wid a jawbone an' I reckon Brothah Tyndal done got he jawbone 'roun' handy. I ain' gwine tuh die yit; I's too young."

"Lemme zort wid huh," offered Brother Wiggins as Aunt Martha was about to make an angry retort. He laid his hand on Melinda's shoulder as he spoke. "Honey, you's wrong in yo' notions. Samson didn' kill nobody; he slew his enemies, dat's all."

"Dat's all," exclaimed Aunt Janty, herself reassured.

"Dey's a heap o' diff'unce 'twixt killin' an' slewin'," he explained. "It am only wicked men whut kills, but it am de righteous an' dem whut is sanctified whut knows how tuh slew."

Melinda was now listening intently. "I dunno ez it makes any mattah tuh dem whut gits hit wid de jawbone whethah dey wuh kilt or slewed," she remarked.

Brother Wiggins resorted to another expedient. "Melindy," he said, "does you know why you done been s'lected tuh do dis pious ack fuh yo' chu'ch?"

"'Caze you's feahed tuh up an' do it fuh yo'se'f."

"No, 'caze dey ain' no lady in Poketown ez kin 'swade like you kin. An' if dat long-haiahed zorter up in Zion kin hol' out 'gin you, Melindy honey, den he am mo'n morshial man."

Melindy smiled. The right string had at last been pulled. Brother Wiggins, seizing his chance, extorted a promise from her to waylay his rival at the first opportunity.

"You mought begin by axin' de straightes' way tuh heaven," suggested Aunt Janty after some thought, "an' say you done feel you's bin stahted wrong 'caze you's bin trabellin' in de way Brothah Wiggins p'inted out."

"An' keep yo' scissuhs handy in yo' pocket," added the preacher; "dey ain' no tellin' when yo' chance gwine tuh come."

Melinda's fears returned. "I's skeert tuh tech Brothah Tyndal's haiah," she said nervously. "Dey ain' no tellin' whut bones he done keep 'round' tuh slew wid. Ef he go tuh grapplin' down in he pocket I's gwine tuh up an' run away. I's skeert, dat's whut I is," finished the reluctant Delilah.

✓   ✓   ✓

Brother Tyndal passed his hand caressingly over his sleek and shining hair, and smiled encouragement at the girl beside him. "Is you mo' easy-like in yo' min', li'l sistah?" he inquired with a gentle pressure of his hand, and moving closer to her.

The little sister said that her mind was quite at rest but that she needed just one thing to make her happiness complete. "I feels, Brothah Tyndal, dat ef I kep' a lock o' yo' haiah in mah buzzom, ol' Satan couldn' git in nohow."

Brother Tyndal responded vaguely that he would think about it. Melinda sighed: her lot in life appeared most undesirable. Then, too, the long-haired preacher's fascinations had not been exerted in vain, and Melinda felt she could not deprive him of his great strength without acute regret on her part. Her thoughts also dwelt upon the concealed weapon with which his enemies were presumably destroyed.

"Brothah Tyndal," she asked timidly, "does you keep yo' jawbone wid you constan'?"

He was evidently surprised. "I couldn' git 'long widout it nohow," he said with a curious, sidelong glance.

They paused at Melinda's front gate and he refused her invitation to enter, saying he must go home and rest before the evening service.

"Is you gwine tuh be dah, li'l sistah?" he inquired, his voice full of masculine tenderness.

"Is you keerin' 'bout li'l ol' me?" she asked coyly, returning his appealing look with ten percent interest. Brother Tyndal convinced her that he cared very much.

Melinda reluctantly entered the house, and Brother Wiggins and Aunt Martha greeted her with cold disapproval; they felt that the girl must be spurred on towards her duty.

"How much longah," demanded the grandmother, "is you gwine tuh higgle an' haggle ovah dis business?"

"Dem ez puts dey han' tuh de plough an' looks back mus' take de konsikinses," admonished Brother Wiggins, his manner severe. He had ample reason for his severity: the paucity of dimes and nickels in the offeratory of Little Bethel had become appalling. As for Melinda, she seated herself by the window and waited until time to go to church. Evening service begins late in Poketown; therefore twilight deepened and the moon rose slowly over the towering steeple of Little Bethel and the flat roof of Zion. Hurried footsteps approached the house and Aunt Janty Gibbs burst into the room, breathless.

"Now am de time!" she gasped. "He am done gone tuh sleep in he back gyahdin! I done seen him f'om mah kitchen windah."

"Come on, Melindy," said Brother Wiggins, rising. "De houah am at han'. Come fo'wahd, Chile o' Little Bethel."

The Child of Little Bethel hung back, protesting vainly against her fate.

"Dis ain' no time tuh stop fuh trifles," said Aunt Janty. "Take huh by de han', Brothah Wiggins, an' pull hahd; me an' Aun' Ma'thy gwine tuh push."

In this manner they proceeded by a circuitous route to Brother Tyndal's back yard. There, indeed, lay the Son of Thunder stretched upon a bench, sleeping soundly but audibly, his wealth of hair gently stirred by the evening breeze. The sight of his flowing locks exasperated Brother Wiggins beyond endurance. "Do yo' juty," he commanded, pushing the shrinking girl forward.

"I's skeert," quavered Melinda, drawing her scissors slowly from her pocket.

"Whut you's gwine tuh do am gwine tuh make you fuhevah blessid," the preacher assured her.

Thus encouraged, Melinda walked ahead. "Oh Lawd," she prayed, "keep he han' offen de jawbone!" Now she had reached the sleeping figure. Desperately, she thrust her scissors into the black hair. The blades were very sharp and cut clean and quickly, but years of growth had formed a felt-like covering on his head which resisted the cutting edges. Again and again she thrust the shears, listening to them crunch their way through the soft, resisting mass with a strange thrill of pleasure. A demon of destruction seized the girl, and she slashed away in every direction, across and around Brother Tyndal's head. The victim stirred uneasily.

"Come away," whispered Brother Wiggins, pulling at her skirt. "Come away: you's done noble, but he am gwine tuh wake up."

With a parting slash of her shears Melinda obeyed and the conspirators stole swiftly homeward.

✓   ✓   ✓

Tyndal, Son of Thunder, yawned and sat upright. Such was the thickness and tenacity of his hair that, in spite of the recent attack, most of it still clung together upon his head, though ready to fall apart at the touch of a finger. He realized that he had been asleep and feared he was late for church. Therefore, he hurried off without the usual caress to his head. Brother Tyndal's route was marked by stray locks of black hair which fell here and there by the wayside unnoticed.

And he was very late. The congregation, taxing Zion's limited capacity to the utmost, had been impatiently waiting for the best part of an hour. Brother Tyndal hurried, perspiring, into the pulpit.

"We will jine in singing' de fus' hymn," he announced, wiping his glistening forehead. A thick lock of black hair remained in his fingers when he withdrew his hand from his brow. Brother Tyndal laid it on the pulpit before him and stared long and earnestly. Then, cautiously, he felt the crown of his head; a second ringlet lay upon the pulpit beside the first. A few youthful spirits giggled outright, and the preacher shook his head at them in reproof. Quite a shower of black locks fell upon the floor around him. He sank upon his sofa, dazed and mortified, until at last he struggled to his feet and addressed his flock.

"Mah brothahs an' sistahs," he began, "I dunno whut have done happen tuh me. I tuck some needful res' in mah back gyahdin in de quietude of de buhds an' de flowahs. . . ."

A ripple of laughter stirred the congregation. Indeed, the pastor did present a ludicrous spectacle, for here and there a long lock had escaped Melinda's vigilance and stood boldly erect, or hung at right angles to the various almost bald spots scattered over his cranium. No wonder the congregation laughed!

Verily, the strength of Samson had departed.

✓ ✓ ✓

Brother Wiggins sat in the pulpit of Little Bethel the following Sunday and viewed with satisfaction the return of his straying lambs to the fold.

"I rises tuh 'nounce dat de shanty ovah de bridge dat some folks called de Chu'ch o' Zion am done shet up fo' good. De swo'd o' Jedgmint have done fell heavy on de haid o' dat zumptious niggah whut zumed tuh call hisse'f de Son o' Thundah. Sich am de fate o' de sinful. I didn't say nuffin' when you done tuck yo'se'fs ovah tuh Zion 'caze I knowed de Lawd gwine tuh stan' by me an' Little Bethel. An' He done so; *yaaas*, he done so!"

"Hallelujah, praise de Lawd!" shouted Aunt Janty Gibbs.

"He done cleave de haid o' de upstaht," continued the preacher when he could make himself heard—"yaaas, dat's whut He done. De Swo'd o' Vengince done com down f'om heaven while he slep' an' pull de haiahs o' 'ception outen he haid. An' whut's mo', mah frien's, de Lawd up an' done dis pious ack 'thout no wuhds f'om me. He done lay de upstaht low an' 'prive him of de wicked haiah dat he done kunjah wid. Sich am de konsekinses o' sinfulness; sich am de fate o' de biggity! May de Flamin' Swo'd keep on fallin' on dem whut seek tuh hahm Little Bethel; may de han'. . . ."

"A-a-a-men!" called Aunt Martha Young, unable to keep silent any longer. "Glory! Glory! Hallelujah!"

The foundation of Little Bethel rocked with the fervent hosannahs of its returned flock.

✓ ✓ ✓

In the shadow of the deserted Zion stood Samson, shorn indeed of his strength and bitter in his denunciation of the unknown shearer. Brother Tyndal had been obliged to visit the barber, and the result was not pleasing to him. By his side was Melinda. She had cast her lot with him and had promised to comfort him by becoming Mrs. Tyndal, and seeking other fields than Poketown. But her guilty secret worried her.

"I likes you lots bettah 'thout all dat haiah," she remarked tentatively. She slipped her hand within his arm, her voice low and caressing.

A loud burst of thanksgiving arose from brilliantly lighted Little Bethel which was plainly visible from where they stood. Brother Tyndal turned towards Zion, dark and silent, the scene of his triumphs and also of his humiliation. "Jes' lemme git hol' o' de pusson whut done it," he said grimly. "Jes' wunst, dat's all I ax, O Lawd! Jes' wunst!"

Melinda, with a show of affection, laid her head on his shoulder. "Honey," she said, "I's gwine tuh he'p you look fuh dat sinful pusson. Me an' you, we gwine tuh look fuh him all de time. Jes' wait till *I* gits holt on him. I's gwine tuh show him whut I thinks o' sich acks. I has mah own 'pinions 'bout 'em. You ain' gwine tuh fin' him 'thout me, honey; we'll jes' lay holt on de wicked pusson whenevah we ketches him."

"Dat's so," answered the unsuspicious Brother Tyndal, gathering her into his arms. "You's pow'ful sweet an' hones' as de day am long—dat's whut I like mos' 'bout you—yo' honesty."

Melinda smiled quietly as she changed the subject.

The Feast of Locusts

"You ain' gwine tuh git thoo de Golden Gate nohow, Aun' Hestah, ef you ain' baptized," said Brother Brice, his manner solemn.

"Laws, ain' I jes' told you dat I's done bin sprinkled by de Methodis', an' de 'Piscopals, an' de Chillun o' Zion; an' I come mighty nigh j'inin' de Lambs o' Jerusalum las' wintah?"

"De road o' de Baptis' am de sho' an' safe way fuh you tuh trabbel, Aun' Hestah. I's 'stonished dat a lady o' yo' refinery kin even study 'bout 'sociatin' wid de Lambs o' Jerusalum."

Aunt Hester Johnson grew indignant. "I's got ez good a chanst o' glory ez you has. I's done bin sprinkled by de Chillun o' Zion an' de. . . ."

Mr. Brice rose and extended a hand majestically, as though from the pulpit. "Ef you thinks dem few draps o' watah am gwine tuh float you intuh glory, I's sorry fo' you, Aun' Hestah, 'caze it ain' gwine tuh do it nohow."

"Whut I got tuh do tuh git dah?"

"You's got tuh put on yo' white robes an' come down tuh de watah, dat's whut you's got tuh do, same ez othah sinnahs does."

"An' aftah I gits tuh de watuh, whut den?"

"Den," said Brother Brice, "I takes holt o' you an' I dips you up an' down in de watah twell yo' sins am washed away."

"How 'bout mah haid?" Aunt Hester asked nervously. "'Tain' noways right tuh drown de haid 'caze o' de sins o' de body."

"You goes clean undah—three times, haid an' all."

"It am puffeckly scan'lous," she snapped. "Whuh you git sech notions?"

"Read de Book, Sistah, read de Book. 'Membah John de Baptis'."

"Heap o' diffunce twix' you an' John de Baptis'."

"'Membah de watahs o' Jo'dan," Brother Brice persisted.

"Heap o' diffunce twix' de watahs o' Jo'dan an' de watahs o' de Appo-quinimink Crick," said Aunt Hester under her breath.

Mr. Brice made ready to depart. "I leave you to yo' 'flections, Aunt' Hestah," he said. "I done come heah 'caze de Session tuck an' p'inted you out ez a foolish virgin an' a riotous livah. You's a pow'ful short bref, I sees —reckon yo' days am glidin' swif'ly by. Make yo' peace, Aun' Hestah, make yo' peace. Git yo' sins washed away an' be ready tuh ansuh up when yo' name am called."

He left Aunt Hester a victim of conflicting emotions, the scorn with which she had received his first remarks having been gradually replaced by a vague feeling of apprehension. Brother Brice was indeed a powerful ex-horter. She did not like his reference to her custom of puffing heavily after even a trifling exertion, a tendency due entirely to her two hundred pounds of avoirdupois. She laid her hand on that portion of her well-padded anatomy under which her heart was supposed to lie. "We's heah tuhday an' gone tuhmorrow," she sighed as she sank into a rocking-chair and swayed luxuri-ously to and fro.

Outside, the August sun shone brightly and a little brown wren sang cheerfully as he balanced on the slender twig of a lilac bush which grew close to the house. A sudden breeze, however, twisted the twig almost double; the bird ceased singing and flew straight before him through the open win-dow and into the kitchen. Bewildered by his strange surroundings, he flut-tered aimlessly about for a moment and finally lighted upon the ample figure in the rocking-chair, his small breast palpitating with fright.

An ashen hue slowly spread over Aunt Hester's chocolate countenance. She threw back her head, almost choking, and her bosom heaved as con-vulsively as that of the bird upon her lap.

"De Sign!" she gasped. "De Sign o' Death!"

The wren, seeing his opportunity, flew out of the window, but there was no escape for Aunt Hester from the pall of terror that enveloped her in its gloomy folds. A bird had flown through the window and lighted upon her; therefore she must die within a year.

Meanwhile, the Reverend Kinnard Brice sat upon his doorstep, some-what discouraged with the result of his visit. Aunt Hester was an important personage, known to have two hundred dollars in the bank, and without in-cumbrances in the way of family. The coffers of the Baptist Church sadly needed replenishing, and Brother Brice felt chagrined at his failure to entice a sheep so well worth shearing into his fold.

All at once, something loomed before him which at first appeared to be a dark mountain of flesh, but resolved into the figure of Aunt Hester Johnson.

"Brothah Brice," said the lady, "I's come tuh tell you dat I don' reckon dat baptizin' gwine tuh huht me none. I bin studyin' yo' wuhds, Brothah. You's a pow'ful fine zortah, dat's whut you is."

"De Lawd put de wuhds intuh mah mouf," Mr. Brice replied modestly.

"An' I's come tuh ax you when you spec's tuh 'merse de nex' batch o' sinnahs."

He concealed his exultation with great effort. "Two weeks f'om yestiddy, Aun' Hestah. Is you gwine tuh be dah?"

Mrs. Johnson affirmed that she would be present, and having thus made her first praperation to meet her fate, waddled homeward, reflecting on the uncertainty of human life.

✓ ✓ ✓

The baptism was scheduled for Sunday immediately following morning service. The preceding Saturday, Aunt Hester, wandering dejectedly upon the banks of the creek, chanced to encounter Mr. Brice issuing from the little patch of adjoining woodland.

"Whuh you gwine, Aun' Hestah?" he inquired, concealing a fishing-line in his pocket. "You had ought tuh be home on yo' knees 'stid o' traipsin' 'roun' on yo' feets. 'Membah de pack o' sins you's got tuh shed on Sunday."

"Reckon I kin manage mah knees an' mah feets mos' ez well ez you kin," retorted Aunt Hester. She fixed her eye upon the pastor's pocket from which a fish-hook could be seen hanging to a bit of string. "Whut you doin' heah yo'se'f?" she demanded. "Huccum you ain' home on yo' own knees? Tell me dat!"

"I's gwine tuh tell you whut I's doin' heah," answered the quick-thinking Brother Brice. "I's done gone out intah de wildahness, same ez John de Baptis'. Yaaas, Aun' Hestah, I girds up mah loins an' fasts an' prays in de wildahness tuh take an' git ready fuh de 'mersion on Sunday."

"Am dat a wildahness?" demanded Aunt Hester, indicating the shallow strip of woodland beside them.

He ignored the interruption. "I fasts an' prays. Yaaas, dat's whut I does. All dis heah week I takes an' lives on locusses an' wile honey; dat's all I gits tuh eat de long week thoo."

"Whut does you do wid dat fish-hook an' line?" she asked, pointing to the bulging pocket.

"Dat's whut I ketches de locusses wid," he said, looking her squarely in the face. "I's gwine tuh be a saint someday, ef I eats 'nuff of dem."

"Brothah Brice, I's pow'ful slack 'bout dis heah 'mersion. Ef you don' stay by me all de time I ain' so sho' I's gwine tuh be dah Sunday."

"Keep a-prayin', Aun' Hestah; keep a-prayin'."

"Come home wid me, Brothah," she implored, her voice pathetic. "Come suppo't me thoo dis heah tryin' time. You kin eat yo' locusses tuh mah house ez well ez in de wildahness. I kin git you plenty of 'em."

"I couldn' do it noways, Aun' Hestah." He fingered the pocket holding the fishing-line and wished she were a thousand miles away.

"Well," she sighed, turning to leave, "I reckon I mought ez well tuhn dat white robe intuh sheets. I ain' gwine tuh need it nohow tuh go intah de watah."

"Won't nothin' else do?" he asked, thinking of her bank account.

"Ef you wants me," said Aunt Hester loftily, "you's got tuh wuck fuh me. I don' come cheap."

Casting a regretful eye at the creek, Mr. Brice followed her to her house.

"Aun' Hestah," he commented as they drew near her door, "you needn' trouble 'bout dem locusses. I's gwine tuh pray double dis time an' hol' up on de insec's."

"You ain' gwine tuh lose yo' saintship 'caze o' me," she said tartly. "I's got mah niece, Junie, an' huh chillun in de house sence de buhd—sence you —done come tuh see me. Dem boys kin pick up all de locusses you wants in de yahd. Does you like 'em fried er stewed?"

"You's pow'ful thoughtful," he replied with a sinking heart.

"I ain' got no wile honey," she continued with some regret, "but I reckon good black 'lasses gwine tuh do mos' ez well."

Mr. Brice's digestive organs recoiled involuntarily at the prospect of the coming ordeal.

⸎⸎⸎ ⸎⸎⸎ ⸎⸎⸎

"June," said Aunt Hester to her niece on the eventful Sunday morning, "has you done tuck Brothah Brice he breakfus'?"

"He say he don' cyah 'bout none," she answered from the depths of the kitchen. "He ain' et a mossel sence he bin heah."

"He jes' got tuh have it," said Aunt Hester, determination in every word. "Ef dey's any 'ligion in locusses dis heah am de time he need it mos'. Dish 'em up good an' hot. I's gwine tuh tote 'em in an' make him eat ev'ry one."

"Sho' glad I ain' makin' no tracks to'ds bein' a saint," murmured June, shuddering, as she placed Mr. Brice's breakfast on a plate.

Aunt Hester approached her house guest where he sat mournfully beside the window. "Brothah Brice, heah am yo' locusses."

He glanced at the plate and immediately turned away. "I don' evah eat nothin' on de mo'nin' o' de Great Day."

"Ef you wants tuh baptize me you's got tuh take an' eat dese bugs."

"I dunno ez I keer whethah you's baptized er not," he spat, goaded to desperation.

"Brothah Brice," said Aunt Hester, coming closer, "when you's standin' on de aidge o' de watah in yo' sacrificial robes, would you like me tuh up an' tell de company 'bout dat raid roostah an' de tukkey hen I seen on yo' shouldah las' wintah when you jes' pass by Mistah Tuhnah's henhouse?"

Brother Brice jerked to sudden attention.

"I mought tell 'em 'bout dat flat bottle dat drap outen yo' pocket yestiddy when you wuh comin' out de wildahness," she continued relentlessly, "an' 'bout de widdy woman on de towpath."

Aunt Hester paused, confident that she had the upper hand. "Reckon you mought ez well eat yo' locusses," she went on.

Brother Brice, his innards churning, began his breakfast.

⸎⸎⸎ ⸎⸎⸎ ⸎⸎⸎

A large assemblage had gathered upon the banks of the Appoquinimink from all around the neighborhood to witness the immersion. Brother Brice, full of the sense of his own importance, was arrayed in his gown of dark chintz ornamented with large colored figures, and his black silk hat.

"Let dem in de white robes 'semble togethah on mah lef'-han' side," he commanded. "Aftah dey's done bin undah de watah dey ain' goats no longah an' kin stan' on mah right-han' side 'mongst de sheep. When de hymn am bein' sung I's gwine tuh wade out ez fah ez I thinks propah. Now, will Sistah Roxy Bristow kin'ly staht de hymn?"

Mrs. Bristow raised her high, sweet soprano in *Swing Low, Sweet Chariot*, which was taken up by one after another of the entire company and sung to a finish.

Mr. Brice, meanwhile, had waded out to the desired location, his un-buttoned gown floating out on the water behind him. "Let Sistah Johnsing come fo'wahd," he shouted, now thoroughly imbued with the spirit of his occupation.

"Sistah Hestah Johnsing come fo'wahd," repeated Brother Noah Hyatt. "Why ain' Sistah Johnsing heah tuh ansuh de call?"

A dozen officious hands assisted Aunt Hester to the edge of the water. There she stopped, her confidence all but gone.

"Roll, Jo'dan, roll," sang Sister Roxy Bristow, hoping to encourage the unwilling Aunt Hester.

"Sistah Johnsing," admonished Brother Brice, "I's waitin'! Don' hol' back no longah. Even de li'l buhds o' de aiah do huvvah ovah you tuh he'p you on yo' way."

Aunt Hester cast a terrified glance upward at the flock of wild ducks making their way towards the marsh, and again recalled the evil omen of the bird.

> *"Will you be dah?*
> *When de gin'ral roll am called,*
> *Will you be dah? . . ."*

sang Sister Roxy Bristow.

"I's comin'!" cried Aunt Hester, shutting her eyes and advancing blindly. "Lawd ha' mussy, I's comin'! Amen!"

The current of the Appoquinimink is swift and strong, and because of this the immersions had heretofore been made in the waters near the shore. Now, however, Brother Brice advanced towards the center of the stream, towing the reluctant lady rapidly behind him. Brother Brice was tall and thin; Sister Johnson was short and fat. So it was that when she was im-mersed almost to her neck, the head and shoulders of the gentleman were well above the water and his arms were free for action.

"Sistah Johnsing," said Brother Brice, "does you repent yo' sins an' evil actions?"

Aunt Hestter nodded vigorously, anxious to get the ordeal over and done with and return to terra firma.

"Let yo'se'f loose, Sistah Johnsing," Mr. Brice entreated as she clung in desperation to his arm; "let yo'se'f loose. Is you ready? *Wid dese heah watahs I renounces yo' sins washed away!*"

Repeating the formula, he thrust Aunt Hester's head and shoulders under the water and held her there a second or two. She emerged puffing like a porpoise, her eyeballs protruding with fright and anger.

"Don' you do dat ag'in," she gasped, regardless of the consequences in the hereafter.

A peculiar expression crossed Mr. Brice's face. "Aun' Hestah," he snarled through clenched teeth, "dem locusses you done cook fuh me dis mo'nin' make me see mah juty pow'ful plain." He tightened his grip upon the back of her neck. "You's goin' undah, Aun' Hestah, ez many times ez I chooses. *Wid dese heah watahs I renounces yo' sins washed away,*" and under she went.

Now it was difficult for Mr. Brice to maintain an upright position under the circumstances, and a violent kick in the abdomen from one of Mrs. Johnson's wandering legs completely doubled him up. For a moment they struggled together on the bottom of the Appoquinimink, then rose to the surface and were promptly whirled away with the power of the current. Some distance down the creek they were picked up by a passing boat, faint and exhausted, but still very much alive, and were escorted to their respective homes.

✓   ✓   ✓

Late that evening Brother Brice arose from the couch where he had been deposited under many blankets and with fervent expressions of thanksgiving by some of his faithful sheep. Casting a furtive glance about to make sure that his attendants were asleep, he stole quietly to the pantry and proceeded to devour everything within reach. Suddenly he remembered his breakfast of grasshoppers. He paused, a loaf of bread in one hand and a slice of cold bacon in the other.

"Wisht I'd tuck an' hel' huh undah fuh good an' all when I had de chance," he muttered vindictively as he attacked the bacon.

✓   ✓   ✓

Junie, seated in Aunt Hester's kitchen before the fire, heard a peculiar sound in the next room. It seemed to originate in the huge mountain of feather bed upon which reposed the exhausted lady.

"Whut you say, Aun' Hestah?" asked Junie.

"Laws, chile, I didn' say nothin'."

"Pow'ful bad sign tuh heah noises f'om de empty aiah."

"I don' b'lieve in signs no mo'."

Again the mysterious sound.

"Aun' Hestah," cried Junie, "I b'lieve you's laughin'!"

Aunt Hester was no longer able to suppress her mirth and she let her laughter ring in long, rollicking bursts of merriment. When she could finally speak, she gasped, "I jes' done 'membah de way Brothah Brice puckah he mouf when he swallah dem locusses!"

The Return of Sister Juliana

Sister Juliana Jackson, lying motionless upon the one highly prized feather-bed of the house, was about to enter the Valley of the Shadow.

On her right sat her husband, somewhat self-conscious in the dignity of his position as chief mourner. On her left was Brother Reese, her pastor, ready at any moment with an appropriate text or a few words of prayer. At the foot of the bed crouched faithful old Aunt Judy, and at the head stood Sister Roxy Bristow, waving a large turkey-feather fan to and fro with a slow, rhythmic movement.

"Sistah Juliana," said the pastor anxiously, "how does you feel in yo' sperrit?"

Not even the quiver of an eyelid betrayed that the still figure understood him. Her husband leaned forward and took her hand in his, but it fell limp and nerveless from his grasp. Mrs. Bristow immediately restored it to its former position.

"It am mo' fittin', Brothah Jackson," she observed, "fo' a soul tuh go tuh glory wid de ahms crossed pious-like on de breas' den tuh let 'em meandah all ovah de baid."

Brother Jackson groaned heavily. "Take me wid you, Juliana, I wants tuh git in too."

"'Tain' noways likely you's gwine tuh evah see de New Jerus'lum ef you don' go wid huh," muttered Aunt Judy maliciously. "You'll nevah git dar by yo'se'f."

"Brothah Reese," interposed Mrs. Bristow, "cain't you light de way fuh Sistah Juliana wid de lamp o' prayah?"

"I done set huh gropin' soul on de straight an' narrah way twice't in de las' houah, Sistah Roxy," the pastor reminded her. "An' mah mouf do feel pow'ful dry and pa'ched."

"Dey's cookin' de fun'ral ham in de kitchen," suggested Mr. Jackson in properly subdued accents. "Reckon you mought step out an' see whut you kin find, Brothah Reese."

"Brothah Jackson," said Mrs. Bristow when the preacher had left for the kitchen, "I feels fuh you." Her voice was tender.

He permitted himself a small, grateful smile. "I knows dat," he replied, his voice equally tender.

An almost imperceptible movement stirred the surface of the patchwork quilt, and both watchers concentrated their attention upon it. "De rustle o' de Daith Angel," whispered Mrs. Bristow with a long sweep of her fan. "He done huvvah ovah Sistah Juliana dat time."

Aunt Judy raised her head and gazed intently at the bed.

Mr. Jackson sighed. "I's gwine tuh be pow'ful lonely."

"Dat's so, Brothah Jackson," agreed Mrs. Bristow, full of sympathy, "but it am de will o' Gawd. I done been lonely mahse'f dis long time, since Jake got hisse'f drownded." She paused in reverie, and then changed the subject. "I kin fry yo' bacon fuh you ev'y mo'nin'. You kin git it ovah de fence."

"You's mighty thoughtful, Sistah Roxy. It am lucky ouah gyahdens jine at de back."

"You mought take down some o' de fence so' I kin run in an' out an' keep yo' house clean," she suggested further.

"You sho' am gwine tuh be a comfo't tuh a lonely widdah-man, Sistah Roxy."

Again there was a slight movement of the quilt, and again they watched breathlessly for the flight of Sister Jackson's spirit which, however, clung tenaciously to its house of clay.

Brother Jackson wiped the beads of perspiration from his forehead and glanced over his shoulder at the door that led to the kitchen—and from which came appetizing odors and the subdued hum of many voices. "I done been settin' on dis heah stool sence airly mo'nin'," he complained. "It's dat ham whut's gittin' tuh me. Juliana set sich stock on 'em dat de grunt o' de pig am like tuh bus' mah haht, Sister Roxy."

She waved her fan mechanically and glanced about the room in a proprietary manner. "Dem wax flowahs hadn' ought tuh set so close tuh de window," she remarked irrelevantly, "de sun done melt de watah-lily scan'lous."

"You kin change de place, Sistah Roxy," replied Mr. Jackson. "Ack ez ef de house wuh yourn, an' den do jes' whut you 'zires." Mrs. Bristow smiled as though satisfied as she moved the glass vase of waxen blossoms to the other side of the room.

"I feels faint-like an' hollah inside," said Mr. Jackson after a long silence. "Dis am a mighty sad 'casion fo' me, Sistah Roxy, an' mah haht am soon gwine tuh be ez empty ez mah stomach, but it am de will o' Gawd, ez you done said, Sistah."

"De stomach kin git filled up ag'in, easy-like," she said, choosing her words with care, "but how 'bout de haht, Brothah Jackson, how 'bout de haht?"

"Sistah Roxy, will you walk home wid me f'om de grave when we lays Sistah Juliana away? I's gwine tuh need de suppo't o' frien's ez well ez 'ligion tuh keep me up, Sistah."

"Brothah Jackson, you kin lean on me ef you so 'zires. I's gwine tuh he'p you beah up undah yo' 'fliction."

"Sistah Roxy," he answered gallantly, "come wid me tuh de kitchen. You an' me has done sot heah dis long time watchin' fo' de Daith Angel tuh light on Juliana. You mus' be tiahd an' hongry, 'caze you done fan huh long an' faithful. Lemme conduc' you tuh de kitchen, Sistah Roxy. Aun' Judy kin watch out fuh de flies."

Had they looked behind them as they offered the fan to Aunt Judy and made their way to the kitchen, they might have noticed that Sister Juliana's eyes had opened and were fixed upon them with the expression of one who contemplates earthly rather than heavenly transactions.

"Juliana," whispered Aunt Judy, bending close over the bed, "does you see him, Juliana? He makin' eyes at de widdah Bristow an' yo' body not yit even col'."

But the heavy eyelids dropped wearily as though to shut out forever all unwelcome sights.

"She done move yo' flowahs, honey," continued the old woman. "She tuck an' move yo' flowahs f'om de place you done s'lected. You heah me, Juliana?"

Juliana did not stir.

"Dey done kilt yo' raid roostah," she went on grimly, "an' de ol' speckle hen too, tuh bile fuh de fun'ral dinnah. Dey done got you mos' buried, honey. You heah me, Juliana? Yo' husban' am up tuh his ol' tricks. Dey ain' a mo' fluhtatious man in Poketown dan Jeremiah Jackson."

Encouraged by a slight quiver of the eyelid, Aunt Judy went on breathlessly: "Am it yo' 'tention fuh Roxy Bristow tuh set up in yo' house an' fry yo' bacon? Am you gwine tuh 'low huh tuh move yo' flowahs an' pass de time o' day wid yo' husban' ovah yo' haid? Come back an' spite 'em, Juliana. Come back, honey! I knows you kin, 'caze yo' time ain' come yit. I knows it by de almanac. Come back, you heah me? Juliana!"

The door suddenly opened to admit Brother Reese who entered with the sleek and unctious manner of one who has dined well. He was followed by a mixed assembly of neighbors who had been assisting in the preparation of the funeral meats, and finally by Brother Jackson and Sister Roxy, who at once resumed their former positions.

"Sistah Juliana, has you gone home yit?" inquired Brother Reese.

"Take me wid you, Juliana," intoned Mr. Jackson automatically, with the air of one who knows the proper thing to say under the circumstances.

Mrs. Bristow resumed fanning the quiet figure on the feather-bed.

"Dat's right, Sistah Roxy," said Brother Reese. "Keep de flies offen de co'pse."

Sister Juliana's eyes slowly opened. "I ain' daid yit," she said quietly but distinctly.

The effect upon the assembled company was paralyzing, but Brother Reese immediately recovered his composure. "Repent, Sistah Juliana," he cried. "De Lawd done give you dis li'l time longah tuh spashiate yo' sins. Now's yo' chance, Sistah Juliana, repent!"

"Juliana!" cried Aunt Judy on the verge of hysterics. "You done heah me. Praise de Lawd!"

Sister Juliana caught weakly at the feathers of the fan as it passed annoyingly close to her nose. "Stop dat!" she commanded, and Mrs. Bristow paused in asttonishment.

"Lawd," entreated Brother Reese as he dropped to his knees, "reach out yo' ahms tuh dis po', flutterin' li'l soul. It am on'y a po' weak female woman, good Lawd. She done fell by de wayside maybe, but she am on'y. . . ."

"Say 'Amen,'" interrupted Sister Juliana irreverently, sitting upright in her bed and glaring at the uninvited guests. "Say 'Amen' quick now, an' git offen yo' knees."

"Huh min' do wandah," said Brother Reese as he rose to his feet. "Prepaiah fuh de wuss, Brothah Jackson. De houah am come. Lawd, open de Golden Gate an' let dis sinnah in."

Sister Juliana pointed with trembling finger to the outer door. "You mought ez well go home," she said to her stunned neighbors. "Dey ain' gwine be no fun'ral in dis heah house yit awhiles."

Aunt Judy was ecstatic. "Juliana!" she exclaimed, almost weeping, "you's back ag'in fuh sho', honey."

One by one the guests departed in silence, omitting the customary farewell to the hostess.

"Reckon you mought ez well light out wid 'em," suggested the revived lady of the house to her pastor. He shook his head, clearly unhappy about this unseemly interruption to the planned funeral services, and he too departed.

Sister Jackson then turned to her husband, resolution in her whole attitude. "Put back dem flowahs," she commanded quietly.

"Jes' ez you 'zires, Juliana," he said, hastening to obey. "I don' know how dey come tuh be moved in de fus' place."

Juliana now addressed Mrs. Bristow who seemed reluctant to leave with the others. "Goodbye, Sistah Roxy," she murmured, sinking wearily down in her feather-bed. "Aun' Judy kin show you de way outen de *front* do'. Sistah Roxy, you needn' trouble yo'se'f 'bout no back fence; we's gwine tuh move 'cross de bridge nex' month anyhow. Aun' Judy, open de do' fuh Sistah Roxy."

"Fol' up de patchwuck quilt," continued Mrs. Jackson, speaking to her husband, "an' tote in de co'n-shuck mattress—cain't was'e dis heah good feathah baid tuh git well in."

"Juliana," he ventured, "honey, is yuh sho'?"

"Git tuh wuck," she interrupted, her manner quite ruthless. "You ain' gwine tuh walk home f'om *my* grave on yo' tip-toes wid Roxy Bristow nohow, 'caze dey ain' gwine tuh be no grave. You done thunk de noise o' de cherrybims pickin' dey banjos make me so deef I didn't heah you speechifyin' wid huh? I done see de sheep's-eyes you cas' at huh ovah my dyin' baid. Git de co'n-shuck mattress"—Sister Juliana paused and looked long and earnestly at her lord and master—"you ornery, lazy, triflin', big-mouf niggah!"

She then ordered him to wield the fan, as had Mrs. Bristow just a short time earlier. Throughout the long summer day Brother Jackson sat alone beside the wife so unexpectedly returned from the brink of the grave, and he waved that fan.

Occasionally she would awaken from her slumbers and remind him: "I ain' dead yit, Jeremiah Jackson. I's come back, I has. Keep on fannin', I's still heah."

And he kept fanning, disappointment fairly oozing from his eyes.

A Very Wise Virgin

"Dey wuz ten o' dem virgins," said Mrs. Simmons to her daughter Lavinia. "Five of 'em wise an' five wuz fullish." She brought her iron down upon the garment spread before her with considerable force. "Dem ez wus wise lighted dey lamps an' cotched dey man all safe; dem ez wuz fullish stayed ol' maids."

"Whut you speechifyin' tuh me dis a-way fuh?" demanded Lavinia with an aggrieved air.

"'Caze it am shameful fuh a gal tuh be a ol' maid, an' ef you don' up an' hustle fuh a bridegroom you's gwine tuh be one sho'. Des you s'pose dem virgins set on de sofy an' waited tuh be co'ted? No *sah!* Dem gals up an' hunted fuh deyse'fs, dat's whut dey done."

Lavinia muttered that she did not care.

"An' whut's mo', it don' seem tuh me ez ef ol' maids gits tuh heaven," continued the mother after a moment of reflection. "Leas'-ways I don' 'membah no mention of 'em gettin' pas' ol' Petah at de Gate."

"Dey ain' nothin' wicked 'bout ol' maids," said Lavinia in faint protest against such a wholesale exclusion.

"It am dis a-way," explained Mrs. Simmons. "Ef a gal ain' got gumption 'nuff tuh hook a man o' some soht, den dey ain' got no use fuh huh Up Above. Ef she cain't do dat, she cain't do nothin' nohow."

Lavinia took on the manner of a martyr. "Whut mus' I do fus'?"

"Dat am 'co'din' tuh who you has yo' eye on. Dey's a heap o' diffunce in men. Some of 'em 'zembles flies—ef you wants tuh cotch 'em, all you got tuh do am tuh set wid yo' mouf open an' in dey draps."

Mrs. Simmons took a fresh iron and held it near her cheek to ascertain its temperature. "But den ag'in, dey's men whut you has tuh ack mighty cautious-like wid," she added as an afterthought. "Wid dat kin', a gal mus' sashay 'roun' on huh tip'toes an' make huhse'f faskinatin'. It 'zembles huntin' aftah possums; de mo' you has tuh chase, de mo' tickled you am in yo' insides when you gits him up a tree. 'Tain' de same feelin' you has fuh de runts you gits 'thout no wuck tuh ketch 'em."

"Heap mo' trouble," said Lavinia, yawning.

"Heap sweetah possum," retorted her mother as she put away her ironing-board and prepared to carry home the clothes.

On her way she mentally reviewed all the eligibles of Poketown, not omitting Brother Noah Hyatt, notorious for his aversion to the fair sex. Mrs. Simmons surveyed his neat little cottage as she passed by, and regarded it with evident approval. "Dey'd be some credit tuh de gal whut could tree Brothah Hyatt," she thought.

A knot of chatting women were gathered at Aunt Martha Young's door as she approached, all engaged in excited discussion.

"He done got a house wid a gyahdin," exclaimed Aunt Martha.

"An a yallah mule an' a no-top buggy wid blue wheels," added Aunt Janty Gibbs.

"A melojian in he bes' room, pictuhs on he walls, an' two pigs, fat tuh bustin' in he pen," added Sister Rebecca Brown, who had a taste for the material as well as the ornamental.

"An' he done guv out at de sperience meetin' ovah in Sin Go'ges* dat he on de lookout fuh a wife," finished Mrs. Mary Jane Finney, bringing the conversation to its grand climax.

Mrs. Simmons, with her daughter Lavinia ever uppermost in her mind, deposited her basket of clothes on the ground and paused. "Whut he name?" she demanded.

"William Smif," answered Aunt Janty, "an' he live on de Dutch Neck Road. He got 'nuff hawg meat salted down tuh las' all wintah, an' fifty dollahs in de bank."

Mrs. Simmons was quite overcome by the last statement. "Laws!" she gasped.

"I reckon Vinny gwine tuh walk in de cakewalk down tuh Po't Penn nex' week," continued Aunt Janty. "Mistah Smif done 'low dat he gwine tuh be dah tuh look de gals ovah an' take he pick. All de Poketown gals will walk dey prettiest 'caze dey ain' no tellin' whuh de lightnin' mought strike. I's got a new frock fuh Liza. . . ."

"Aun' Janty," interrupted the severe voice of Brother Hyatt who had approached unseen from the rear, "whut dat I heah? I's 'stonished at you, Aun' Janty, dat's whut I is—'stonished. You bettah set Liza tuh makin' huh shroud so's huh wicked min' kin study 'bout hell an' damnation. Cakewalks am 'ticements o' ol' Satan. Keep de gal home, Aun' Janty, keep de gal home."

"Dat whut I say, Brothah Hyatt," interrupted Mrs. Simmons eagerly, glad for any chance to reduce the competition for Mr. Smith's attentions. "My Vinny ain' gwine nohow ef I kin keep huh back."

"Brothah Hyatt," said Mrs. Simmons timidly as they walked down the street, "kin you drap in tuh my house an' zort wid Vinny? She done got so wor'ly-minded dat I trimbles fuh huh lattuh end."

"Watch an' pray, Sistah Simmons, watch an' pray," he counseled. "An' ef dat don' wuck, bring de gal befo' de Session. Dey knows how tuh han'le obstropolous sinnahs." His voice was as grim as the look on his face.

These measures, however, formed no part of Mrs. Simmons' plans, and before she parted from him she exacted his promise to interview Lavinia privately and point out the error of her ways, particularly with reference to cakewalking. Yes indeed, Mr. Hyatt would make a fine son-in-law should the unknown William Smith fail to succumb to her daughter's manifest charms.

Home at last, Mrs. Simmons immediately launched into her morsels of news. She told Lavinia of the prospective cakewalk, and of Mr. William Smith in search of a wife. The prospects of the future Mrs. Smith were painted in glowing colors and his bank account multiplied by three. But

---

* Saint George's

she carefully omitted all reference to Mr. Hyatt as her ace-in-the-hole runner-up, should her daughter fail to snare Mr. Smith's matrimonial interest.

"An' now," finished Mrs. Simmons, "who you gwine tuh walk de cake-walk wid?"

"William Smif, I reckon," said Lavinia uneasily. "Laws! I 'membahs him, wid he bow laigs an' he fat stomach."

"You didn' cotch dem virgins talkin' dat a-way 'bout de bridegroom."

"James Pollahd done 'low he gwine tuh ax me when de nex' cakewalk wuh called."

"He mighty no-'count, but he do walk pow'ful spry an' he know jes' how tuh shake an' bend he laigs, fuh sho'," said Mrs. Simmons. She hesitated for the barest fraction of a second and then added, "Brothah Hyatt am gwine tuh drap in some night an' rassle wid you 'bout cakewalkin' an' sich."

"Whut I gwine tuh do 'bout it?" asked Lavinia. She was well acquainted with his dislike of frivolities such as dancing, and could hardly be blamed for growing nervous.

"Vinnie, ain' yuh got no sense?" snapped her mother. "You's gwine tuh snuffle an' wipe yo' eyes frequent when Brothah Hyatt zorts, an' up an' tell 'im dat you's ready tuh give up all sich wicked ackshuns 'caze he axed yuh to. An' you's got tuh say, kine o' low-voice an' teary, 'Pray fuh me, Brothah Hyatt, pray fuh me,' or some sich wuhds."

"Whut den?" asked Lavinia, very much interested.

"Well," said her mother, grinning, "when Brothah Hyatt am down on he knees prayin' fuh yo' soul, you kin be on yo' own two feet treadin' de cakewalk fuh Mistah Smif."

Lavinia laughed aloud.

"But ef Mistah Smif don' s'lect you," warned Mrs. Simmons, "you's got to light out tuh Brothah Hyatt's house nex' day an' up an' tell 'im dat you cain't 'zist ol' Satan nohow 'thout he be by yo' side tuh suppo't yuh. Dat's de way tuh cotch a man like him."

Mrs. Simmons now produced a lantern and trimmed the wick. Lavinia watched her closely.

"Git de coal-ile, an' fill it chuck full," commanded the mother.

Lavinia obeyed, her eyes wide with curiosity.

"On de night o' de cakewalk," explained Mrs. Simmons, "you's gwine tuh light de lamp an' staht fo' Po't Penn; you's gwine tuh lingah on de road twell you sees Mistah Smif's yallah mule an' he no-top buggy comin' to'ds yuh."

"Whut den?" asked Lavinia breathlessly.

"Den, ef you's got any sense you's gwine tuh ride de res' o' de way side o' Mistah Smif in he no-top buggy wid de blue wheels."

Lantern oil was in great demand in Poketown on the morning of the cakewalk. Lavinia had imparted her mother's plan to her closest friend, Wilhelmina Stafford, and it had accordingly been transmitted from one to another until all the chaperones of Pokestown were in the market for oil, feeling it best to leave no stone unturned to insure success; and many a reluctant virgin was therefore started off on foot, accompanied only by her lantern, in the direction of Port Penn.

✓ ✓ ✓

Mr. William Smith stood before his mirror and put the finishing touches to his attire, a paste solitaire about the size of a marble. He fastened it carefully to his red necktie and retreated a few paces. Then, satisfied with the effect, he withdrew from his pocket a ring with a setting as big as a grape. He looked at it with genuine affection. "It do seem like a pity tuh was'e it on some triflin' gal," he soliloquized, returning it to its resting place. Evidently, Mr. Smith was not a cheerful giver.

"Reckon I's gwine tuh be mighty sorry fuh dis heah night's wuck," he muttered as he unhitched his yellow mule, "but de scriptuh say 'tain' good fuh a man tuh live alone, an' I done calc'late dat it gwine tuh be cheapah tuh suppo't a wife den tuh put mah washin' out."

Now ready for the big cakewalk, Mr. Smith drove off in the direction of Port Penn.

✓ ✓ ✓

Brother Noah Hyatt had been to see Lavinia, according to promise. He had admonished sternly, warned gravely, pleaded ardently, and finally persuaded gently. Brother Hyatt was naturally as unsociable as Diogenes, but he was human. Lavinia was soft of voice and slight of form, with eyes not unlike that of a young gazelle. She was open to conviction and overcome with remorse at her sins of omission and commission. She had wept copiously and promised to amend her sinful ways; and finally had confessed that she doubted her ability to keep to the straight and narrow way without the assistance of Brother Hyatt to guide her wandering footsteps. Verily, Lavinia had lights trimmed and burning in several directions, and was a very wise virgin indeed.

Brother Hyatt became deeply interested. Here, it seemed, was a brand worth snatching from the burning. It would not be unpleasant, he reflected as he washed his supper dishes, to have such duties performed by a swiftly-moving, trim-waisted young wife. He thought of the brand smouldering in the cinders of worldliness, sighed, shook his head and his dish-cloth simultaneously, and decided to snatch.

His evening chores completed, Mr. Hyatt repaired to the Simmons residence and knocked as one having authority. There was no response. Again he knocked, and the window of the adjoining house was cautiously raised. "Dey ain' nobody home," said a voice from within. "Dey's all done gone tuh de cakewalk."

Brother Hyatt set his teeth and squared his shoulders. "I's gwine tuh bring de lamb safe tuh de fol'."

With this pious declaration on his lips and bitter resentment in his heart at the duplicity of the lamb, Brother Hyatt started forth in the direction of Port Penn.

✦   ✦   ✦

The first notes of the band, imported from New Castle for the occasion, were wafted upon the night air as Lavinia drove into Port Penn seated beside Mr. William Smith in his blue-wheeled buggy. It had happened as planned:

Mr. Smith, driving slowly along, found his progress impeded by a female figure which stood in the road and waved a lantern under the very nose of the yellow mule.

"Who dat?" called the gentleman.

"Ef you please, suh," crooned a soft voice, "I's done los' my way. Kin you tell me how tuh git tuh Po't Penn?"

After a little more conversation, during which the lady several times mentioned how tired she was, Mr. Smith proffered the half of his buggy and, incidentally, enjoyed the remainder of the drive very much.

"Whut all dem gals streakin' 'long by deyse'fs fuh, wid lantuhns tuhned up so high dey jes' p'intedly smokin'?" inquired Mr. Smith as they passed one virgin after another, weary and footsore, but persevering.

"Dunno," replied Lavinia innocently as she passed her friends with no sign of recognition.

✦   ✦   ✦

The cakewalk was a success. Never were the girls so light of foot and coquettish of manner. One couple after another pirouetted down the long room, posturing, bowing and executing intricate and difficult steps to the strains of *Georgia Camp Meeting*. There is something in this tune which affects the feet and makes them dance, willy-nilly; even the spectators, and Mr. William Smith, with his overly-long heels, shuffled his feet noisily upon the judges' platform.

At the end of the front row of spectators sat Mrs. Simmons, her fat face shining with excitement and pleasure. Owing to an excess of avoirdupois, it had been many a year since she had participated actively in a cakewalk, but she beat time vigorously and yearned most ardently to be up and doing.

Just within the open door, unnoticed and alone, stood Brother Hyatt, like a skeleton at a feast. He pushed his rusty silk hat well down on his head and glowered at the company as he waited for the appearance of his particular lamb. He meant to rescue her before her feet executed any sinful tripping, and after that to address the assemblage generally. Brother Hyatt thought he could make some remarks which would be long remembered, and he took a gloomy pleasure in his opportunity to note the faces of professing church members, now apparently given over to the world, the flesh, and the devil.

The room grew very hot and the band played on with redoubled energy. Brother Hyatt mopped his brow and shuffled his feet uneasily. He wished

Lavinia would appear. So too did Mr. Smith who held on to the large, iced cake—to be awarded to the winning "walkers." The airs and graces of the other girls were lost upon him and their coy advances wasted.

At last James Pollard and Lavinia stepped into position and saluted each other. She was dressed in the very best clothes her mother could collect from the washes of various surrounding families, while James was resplendent with the inevitable silk hat and walking-stick adorned with ribbons. Lavinia swayed her supple figure to and fro in time to the music and took a few steps forward, her head held coquettishly on one side. She looked extremely well, and Mrs. Simmons beamed with maternal satisfaction.

The music grew yet more rollicking and the room became hotter. A filmy haze crossed Brother Hyatt's eyes and he could no longer distinguish faces. His body swayed with the rhythm of the tune and his feet moved involuntarily. Brother Hyatt had once been young.

Mrs. Simmons, dizzy and excited, had risen to her feet to watch her daughter's progress. As Lavinia's slight young form swayed from side to side or bent far backward, the corpulent figure of her mother did the same, and she took as many and as dainty steps as did her daughter.

Faster and faster played the band; swiftly and yet more swiftly moved the respectable feet of Brother Hyatt. He shut his eyes and let those dancing feet carry him where they would: he had no longer any will or volition of his own. Reaching the center of the room, he became aware that he had no partner and sought to remedy the lack. All at once he realized that a stout female form was posturing opposite him. Brother Hyatt felt no surprise. He held out his hand and together they executed the figure which required very high stepping, with the body bent backward as far as it will go. The spectators no longer looked at Lavinia and James Pollard. Mrs. Simmons knew how to cakewalk. She reached forward and removed Mr. Hyatt's silk hat, placing it upon her own head, and with arms akimbo danced lightly around him. He took several rapid steps, and whirling around in front of her, fell upon one knee. Promptly the lady responded to the challenge by placing her foot upon his lap and gazing loftily towards the ceiling as he tied her shoe. Then they again went forward, hand in hand, in perfect time. Verily, the Georgia Camp Meeting was responsible for much.

The band broke into the grand march, and Mrs. Simmons and Mr. Hyatt took their places to parade past the judges' stand, utterly oblivious of each other's identity. They followed closely behind Lavinia and James Pollard, but the tune was changed and the spell was broken. Before they crossed the room Mrs. Simmons, with a gasp of astonishment, had recognized her partner, and Mr. Hyatt with a throb of mortification, realized what he had done. He made a great effort to rally his departing courage.

Mr. William Smith arose, cake in hand, as Lavinia approached. The hour of triumph was at hand.

"I pernounces Miss Lavinia Simmons de spryes' walkah in de room," he said, bestowing the prize upon her with a bow.

Smiling in her victory, Lavinia received it and was about to retire when Mr. Hyatt's voice fell harshly upon her ear.

"Drap it!" commanded that gentleman in his most authoritative manner. "Drap it, I say!"

Taken by surprise, Lavinia dropped the cake and her lower jaw at the same moment, much to the detriment of the former. She had been so much occupied by her own performance that she had failed to look behind and behold her mother and Mr. Hyatt in their triumphal course down the room, and therefore believed that the sword of justice was indeed about to descend upon her guilty head.

"I—I ain' done nothin'," she faltered.

"Chile o' Sin an' Wickedness," denounced Brother Hyatt sternly, "huccum you in dis heah place tuh-night?"

"Don' you ahgify wid de lady, an' wipe dat tone o' voice fum yo' face," said Mr. Smith, feeling he already had a proprietary right in that direction.

"Dawtah o' Eve, sistah o' Jezebel," continued Brothter Hyatt, as Lavinia trembled; "cousin o' Delilah, frien' o' Jael, come wid me. Huccum you heah?"

"Huccum you heah yo'se'f?" interrupted Mrs. Simmons. "You done drug me intuh de dance, dat's whut you done. De sin be on yo' haid. You up an' make me dance, you done did. You's a double-faced ol' sinnah, Brothah Hyatt, dat's whut you is, an' I's gwine tuh tell de Session."

"Peace, woman," said Mr. Hyatt majestically. He turned to Mr. Smith who appeared deeply interested.

"Young man," he warned, "let de ladies be. Don' you have nothin' tuh do wid 'em. Dey 'ceives you an' dey timpts you an' dey 'tices you. You see how dis ol' woman cas' a spell ovah me wid huh wicked ways. I done come heah tuh save huh dawtuh f'om hell an' damnation. She ain' wuth savin'. Let huh go."

Mr. Smith began to weaken in his allegiance. "I ain' anxious tuh git ma'ied nohow," he said slowly.

"De fall o' man am due tuh woman," continued Mr. Hyatt. "She hel' out de apple an' he tuck it an' bit it. It tuhn tuh ashes in he mouf. I's a membah o' de Session, an' 'caze o' a woman an' de spell she cas', I up an' backslid like you seen dis night. Dey ain' no tellin' whut dat gal gwine tuh do tuh you."

The crowd pressed closer around them, not wishing to lose a word of the discourse.

"Ef you takes huh to yo' house," Brother Hyatt went on, with hand raised as though in exhortation, "whut she gwine tuh do? She gwine tuh set in yo' pahlah an' fade yo' cahpet; she gwine tuh eat de bes' paht o' yo' hawg meat an' leave de chitlins fuh you; she gwine tuh spen' yo' money— yaaas, dat whut she gwine tuh do—spen' yo' money."

That final comment touched Mr. Smith's most sensitive chord. "Ef you's ready tuh go back tuh Poketown, Mistah Hyatt," he said, "I kin take you ovah in mah buggy."

The two gentlemen departed without a glance at Lavinia, who occupied herself with gathering together the fragments of the cake.

✓ ✓ ✓

Mrs. Simmons and her daughter trailed along the road in silence; there seemed to be nothing to say. At last the older woman looked behind her and broke the silence: "Whut you done fotch dat cake fuh?" she inquired bitterly.

To her mother's amazement, the girl actually laughed.

"You ain' got nothin' tuh laugh at," Mrs. Simmons fumed. "You's a likely virgin tuh be sho'. Whut you gwine tuh do now?"

"Do? I reckon I's done gone an' done it," said Lavinia with another giggle.

"Whut yuh mean?"

"Well, James Pollahd, he up an' ax me tuh ma'y him las' night, an' I done did."

Mrs. Simmons gasped. "Is you ma'ied now?"

Lavinia nodded. "Brothah Wiggins, he tuck an' tied de knot," she explained. "I war'nt noways sho' how dis heah night's wuck gwine tuh tuhn out, so I tol' James ef he wants me he got tuh take me quick. He want me!"

"Well," said her mother after a moment's thought, "he a moughty po' runt fuh sho', but I reckon dem virgins would o' took him ef dey had de chanst."

The Blast of the Trumpet

"Yes, de daid do walk, fuh sartin," claimed Aunt Janty.

"Does dey walk all tuh wunst?" asked her grandson, Gabriel Gibbs, an imaginative boy with an unquenchable thirst for information on all subjects.

"No, chile, dey walks sometimes in two's an' sometimes in threes, but mos'ly dey walks alone in de nighttime."

"Dey's a time comin'," remarked Brother Eli Wiggins with conviction, "when dey's all gwine tuh walk tuh wunst." Aunt Janty handed him a cup of tea and he poured some into his saucer. Unnoticed, Gabriel slipped from the room.

"Whut yuh 'ludin' tuh, Brothah Wiggins?" asked the old lady.

"I's 'ludin' tuh when ol' Gabriel soun's de note on he hawn good an' loud. Den de graves am gwine tuh bus' open an' de daid come fo'th tuh walk up an' down in de worl'." He paused and added solemnly, "Dat time ain' so fuh off ez mos' folks b'lieves."

Aunt Janty froze, teapot uplifted, and looked at her visitor. "Whut yuh mean, Brothah Wiggins?" she whispered, glancing apprehensively about her.

"One night I up an' dream a dream; yaaas, Aun' Janty, dat whut I done; an' I seen de daid come tumblin' outen dey graves."

"Laws!" exclaimed Aunt Janty.

"An' den I heah a Voice," continued Brother Wiggins, enjoying the effect, "an' it done tell me de time am come fuh de end o' de worl'. Dat dream done significate de night ol' Gabriel gwine tuh blow he hawn." He paused, and in a dramatic, sepulchural whisper, added, "Aun' Janty, *dis am de night!*"

Aunt Janty was unquestionably shocked. "Is you sho'?"

He nodded. "I's gwine tuh tell de Faithful 'bout it at de sperience meetin' tuhnight. I's gwine tuh tell de sinnahs 'tain' no use to lay low nohow 'caze ol' Satan he know whuh tuh look. But you ain' got no call tuh be skeert, Aun' Janty. Jes' keep close tuh me when de time draws nigh an' you kin slip in undah de tails o' my coat. I'll perteck you, sho'. I's sanctified."

Aunt Janty looked much worried as her visitor departed, and made ready to follow him to the church of Little Bethel. So troubled in mind was she that she entirely forgot her grandson, and also overlooked the fact that her ancient father remained dozing in his armchair with only the shelter of a patchwork quilt to screen him from the eye of the Recording Angel.

"Wisht I knowed whethah tuh b'lieve him er not," she muttered, her hand on the latch of Little Bethel.

✔   ✔   ✔

Outside his house, in back of the woodpile, Gabriel Gibbs surveyed a group of his friends. "You cain't play Injun in dem clo's," he told them with deep sarcasm. "Git sheets an' wrop 'em 'roun' yo' bodies, an' take hatchets er somethin' in yo' han's."

"Whut you gwine tuh wrop roun' yo'se'f?" demanded one Alonzo Burris.

"Go git yo' sheets," Gabriel repeated with lofty condescension, "an' watch fuh me tuh come outen de back do'. I's de chief, I is, an' I knows how Injuns does."

Gabriel stole back to the house, having observed his grandmother depart for church. Quietly, he approached his slumbering ancestor and removed the patchwork quilt from his aged legs. It was an easy matter to pluck the longest feathers from Aunt Janty's turkey-tail fan and place them in his hair; also to take possession of the tin dinner-horn which hung behind the kitchen door. A can of red paint stood in the wash shed, and he liberally daubed it upon his round, ebony countenance. Then he rejoined his followers, enveloped in the old patchwork quilt.

"Now," said Gabriel to his ghostly band of white-draped *Indians,* "we's gwine tuh lay down in de hayfiel' behine de graveyahd an' wait twell de time come tuh set de brush-heap on fiah. Lonzy Burris, whut you doin' wid dat laddah?"

Alonzo shifted his burden to the other shoulder but declined to answer. Isaiah Bristow appeared on the scene with a pitchfork, and the band of warriors proceeded to the hayfield to camp there until it should be time to set fire to the brush heap.

✔   ✔   ✔

Brother Wiggins concluded his impassioned discourse and resumed his seat. He had spoken for fully two hours and, with hymns and prayers introduced by various members of the congregation, the service had lasted until almost eleven o'clock. An air of excitement pervaded the assembled company and they lingered in the building, unwilling to venture from beneath the sheltering roof of Little Bethel. Brother Noah Hyatt rose to make a few remarks:

"Brothahs an' sistahs, you done heah whut Brothah Wiggins say. De en' o' de worl' am comin' dis heah night; de good folks am gwine tuh flap dey wings in glory, an' de bad folks tuh roas' on de gridiron o' ol' Satan."

"Whuh, oh whuh, am de good ol' Moses?"

sang Sister Roxy Bristow in her soprano voice.

"Safe now in de Promised Lan',"

immediately responded the deep, sweet contralto of Sister Rebecca Brown, and Little Bethel rocked on its foundations as the entire congregation sang the refrain:

> *"By an' by we's gwine tuh jine him,*
> *By an' by we's gwine tuh jine him,*
> *By an' by we's gwine tuh jine him,*
> *Safe now in de Promised Lan'."*

"Ez de Day o' Jedgmint am so nigh," resumed Brother Hyatt when he could make himself heard, "I b'lieve we bettah wait de soun' o' de trumpet right heah in Li'l Bethel, wid song an' prayah."

"Whuh, oh whuh, am Wres'lin' Jacob?"

struck up Sister Bristow in reply, and again the night air resounded with the refrain—

"Safe now in de Promised Lan'."

"Come wid me," said Brother Wiggins, leading the way to the door and beckoning his flock to follow. "Out in de graveyahd am de place tuh watch an' wait. Come wid me."

With faltering steps and apprehensive murmurs his congregation obeyed him.

Brother Wiggins and his flock grew quiet as they assembled in the churchyard and cast stealthy glances at the dark shadows and patches of pale moonlight.

"Glory Hallelujah!" shouted Sister Roxy Bristow, breaking the silence. "Gwine tuh see Fathah Abraham dis heah night. Glory!"

"Gwine tuh jine de cherrybims an' pick de golden hahps," chanted Aunt Martha Young.

"Oh, I's a sinnah!" cried Mary Jane Finney. "I's a sinnah! Git me in, Brothah Wiggins, git me in!"

"Me too, Brothah Wiggins, me too!" shouted an excitable sister from the rear, pushing her way closer to the front. Brother Wiggins narrowly escaped suffocation as his anxious followers crowded around him.

"You done promised me yo' coattail," asserted Aunt Janty Gibbs, taking possession as she spoke. "Ef you gits in, I gits in too."

"De othah tail b'longs tuh me," announced Aunt Martha Young. "Me an' Aunt Janty done stay by you when all de res' tuck an' flop ovah tuh de chu'ch o' Zion, 'membah dat!"

As the hour of midnight approached, Brother Wiggins' knees shook in spite of his efforts at self-control. He huddled in the shadow of Little Bethel with his trembling followers and waited for the blast of the last trumpet.

The moon shed its soft light impartially upon slumbering Poketown, unconscious of its impending doom.

✦ ✦ ✦

The moon also shone upon the amateur Indians reposing comfortably upon fragrant haycocks, utterly indifferent to the day of reckoning so close at hand.

Gabriel awoke from his nap and jumped to his feet. It was quite time to arouse his tribe and begin operations, for he yearned to see the pile of brush afire and to perform the much-practiced war dance around the flames. He patted the feathers fastened in his hair and draped the patchwork quilt around his shoulders. Then, standing erect upon his haycock, his whole energy concentrated upon his task, Gabriel blew three blasts upon his horn.

✦ ✦ ✦

"De las' trump!" gasped Brother Noah Hyatt.

"Lawd ha' mussy!" shrieked Sister Rebecca Brown.

Shadowy white figures appeared in the distance and silently advanced.

"De daid am riz!" shouted Brother Wiggins, falling face downward upon the ground. Aunt Janty Gibbs and Aunt Martha Young likewise prostrated themselves, the one on his right hand, the other on his left.

The ominous figures became rather more distinct, and the light of the moon fell directly upon the many brilliant colors in the patchwork quilt which enveloped Gabriel Gibbs.

"De angels f'om heaven am come down," whispered Sister Roxy Bristow. "Yondah's Joseph; I knows him by he coat. Glory! Glory!"

Aunt Janty cautiously raised her head, but her grandson had passed and was replaced by Alonzo Burris who still clung to his ladder.

"Praise Gawd f'om who all blessin's flows!" she exclaimed. "Mistah Jacob done fotch he laddah tuh he'p us climb up."

Gabriel and his band of warriors marched silently in single file across the back of the churchyard to the brush-heap in the adjoining field, where they produced matches and set fire to it in various places. The wood was old, rotten, and very dry; it therefore burned quickly and fiercely, much to the delight of the counterfeit Apaches. A row of tall pine trees formed a dark background against which the flames shone with a lurid and startling effect.

"De gates o' hell am open wide!" shrieked Mary Jane Finney, drawing back from the blazing pile.

Brother Wiggins raised himself to his knees; and Aunt Janty Gibbs and Aunt Martha Young did likewise, firm in their determination to follow his slightest movement, thus insuring salvation.

"Pray, Brothah, pray," entreated Sister Rebecca Brown, her voice frantic.

Casting aside the restraining sheets, the Indians started to perform the amazing and intricate dance invented by their chief, giving vent to their war whoop at frequent intervals.

"De howls o' dem in tormint," said the awe-stricken Brother Hyatt.

"Pray, Brother, pray," urged Sister Brown again.

Brother Wiggins raised a shaking hand towards the sky, and immediately the hands of Aunt Janty and Aunt Martha flew upwards also, as though moved by invisible springs.

"Git tuh prayin'!" commanded Brother Hyatt sternly. "Whut we bin payin' yo' sellery fuh dis long time ef you ain' no use tuh us now? Git tuh prayin'!"

Brother Wiggins tried to comply but his tongue clove to the roof of his parched mouth and speech was impossible. Great drops of perspiration stood out upon his brow and he mechanically drew his arm across it. The foreheads of the ladies between whom he knelt were straightway mopped also.

The terrified sheep of Little Bethel shrank closer together as the fire blazed yet more brilliantly. In its red light they beheld small black imps skipping excitedly back and forth while the air was continually rent with shricks, presumably of souls in anguish.

"I's done bin sanctified, O good Lawd!—don' You make no mistake 'bout dat," implored Sister Roxy Bristow in an agony of supplication. "I's done got 'ligion in all de chu'ches in Poketown."

"*Baptis', Baptis' I wuh bawn, an' Baptis' will I die,*" chanted Mary Jane Finney.

Meanwhile, Gabriel was enjoying himself immensely. The feathers in his hair had dropped out one by one until only two remained, both standing erect, one over each ear. In his hand he carried the pitchfork he had snatched from Isaiah Bristow that he might poke the fire. At last he mounted the fence and, standing on the top rail, waved the fork about his head in the exuberance of his delight.

"Yondah's ol' Satan hisse'f," moaned Aunt Martha. "I know him by he hawns."

"Brothah Wiggins," said Mary Jane Finney, close to tears, "whut you got tuh say?"

But Brother Wiggins had nothing at all to say. He could only lift his other trembling hand upward. Aunt Martha and Aunt Janty did not imitate this motion; to do so they would have been obliged to relinquish the tails of his coat.

At this point Gabriel on the fence dropped his pitchfork into the grave-yard and sprang after it. A general stampede ensued, and the congregation of Little Bethel scattered to the four winds of heaven. Gabriel recognizing several familiar figures gave a shrill whistle of warning and the Indians dispersed swiftly and in consternation

Aunt Janty stumbled in her flight and fell headlong upon something warm and soft. She grasped it convulsively to her bosom. In a few moments, surprised by the silence which followed the thud of departing feet, Aunt Janty raised her head and, with the utmost of caution, she looked about her. Mechanically she glanced at the soft substance upon which she lay. She looked long and earnestly.

"Nevah thunk I'd take my patchwuck quilt tuh heaven," she muttered, examining it carefully by the light of the moon. Something lay on the ground beside her and she touched it gingerly. It proved to be a tin horn, crushed flat from being stepped upon, and it looked strangely like the one she used to call the family to dinner. "Jerusalem Jehosaphat!" she exclaimed as she removed a turkey feather from its mouthpiece.

Aunt Janty sat motionless for some minutes, absorbed in thought. Then she arose and folded her horn and muddy quilt across her arm and, gathering her damaged horn and as many feathers as she could find, she started for home. On her way she encountered the brush-heap smouldering in its ashes. She stopped and looked at it. "So dat's de fiahs o' hell," she muttered. "Ain' nothin' but Mistah Clayton's ol' bresh-pile."

She walked on. "Ol' Satan, eh? Seems like *young* Satan am mo' tuh de p'int."

Reaching her house, she went at once to her grandson's cot. It was empty. She then re-covered her father who complained of the cold, and replaced the can of red paint on its shelf in the wash shed; it had been overturned and its contents had stained a pile of clothes waiting to be washed. Aunt Janty ground her teeth and then picked up the wreck of her turkey-feather fan and looked at it also. Her eyes were hard as stone.

Extinguishing the lamp, she opened the front door a crack and sat down just behind it.

"Janty," called the querulous old man, "come tuh baid."

"I's gwine tuh wait fuh Gabriel," Aunt Janty answered, her voice cold and grim.

The Intervention of Gran'pap

"Gwine tuh Buck Camp, Sistah Simmons?"

"Well, I dunno hahdly, Uncle Ben. I 'lowed I'd be dah sho', but Vinny she's hopin' tuh go 'long wid Ike Lewis in a buggy, so dah's nobody tuh leave wid de baby."

"You bettah go, Sistah. It gwine tuh be a great day at de Buck; de new preachah f'om de State's comin', an' dey say he's a pow'ful zorter. I spec' he'll bring de sins of many home tuh 'em. We needs you, Sistah Simmons; we needs you bad tuh labah wid po' souls aftah we gits 'em to de mo'nahs bench."

Uncle Ben turned to leave. "See you at de camp meetin'. Try tuh be dah, Sistah."

Mrs. Simmons went on hanging out the family wash. Through the open window she could see her daughter, Lavinia, busily engaged in ironing a white frock to be worn at the big event. Asleep on the lounge lay the baby, Violet Clare, on whose account Mrs. Simmons must forego the camp meeting. Near the woodpile, digging for angleworms for bait, was her son, Isaiah, a youth of thirteen. She looked around on her assembled family and shook her head.

"I sho'ly ought tuh be dah," she said to herself.

✓   ✓   ✓

"I's got mah frock all ironed, mama," chirped Lavinia as they sat at supper that evening, "an' it do look mighty nice. I nevah seen a real big camp meetin' befo'. Spec' maybe I'll git 'ligion."

"Ligion? Hah!" snorted Isaiah as he accomplished the difficult feat of putting a whole corncake into his mouth. "All you wants is tuh go wid Ike Lewis an' w'ar yo' bes' clo's."

Mrs. Simmons gave an audible sigh. "Vinny, po' ol' gran'pap's failin' rapid. I wuz tol' down tuh de sto' dat he cain' las' many days mo'. Po' ol' gran'pap! I's all de chile he's got.'

"Laws, mama," cried Isaiah, "I seen gran'pap—"

"Shet yo' big mouf, yuh limb o' Satan," snapped his mother, turning hastily upon him. "Ain' yuh got no mannahs? Settin' dah stuffin' yo'se'f till you's fit tuh bus', an' interruptin' yo' eldahs wid yo' mouf full o' vittles. Keep quiet twell you's spoke tuh."

"But, mama—"

Mrs. Simmons glanced at the mantel shelf on which she kept a stout hickory switch. Isaiah had a personal acquaintance with that punishing switch and judged it best to be silent, but he relieved his feelings by sticking his tongue out at his mother whenever she looked the other way.

"Vinny, honey," resumed Mrs. Simmons in tones of liquid sweetness, "I does mos' mightily hate tuh disapp'int you, chile, but I mus' go tuh gran'pap tuhmorrah. I's de onlies' chile he got, Vinny, an' dah's nobody else tuh he'p him pass ovah Jo'dan. O' co'se, darlin', you mus' take keer o' de baby fuh mama while she gone."

Lavinia, completely surprised at this unexpected disruption of her plans, could only remain silent, while Mrs. Simmons resorted to her apron to wipe the tears from her eyes. At least, they looked like tears.

"It's a mighty sad 'casion fuh me," she continued in broken accents. "Mah onlies' daddy passin' away so fas'. Ain' you got nothin' tuh say, you onnat'ral gal? Yo' own gran'pap! An' you not willin' tuh stay home jes' wunst an' let 'im die! But you got tuh stay, Miss, whuthah yuh likes it er not. So min' whut I say."

Experience had taught Lavinia the futility of argument with her mother. She doubted her grandfather's illness but was afraid to say so, and merely lapsed into sullen silence.

Bright and early the next morning Mrs. Simmons prepared to set out on her errand of mercy. "Goodbye, honey," she said to Lavinia. "Don' you let nothin' happen tuh de baby. An' as fuh you, Isaiah, don' you leave dis yahd today, an' min' whut yo' sistah tells yuh. I hopes I'll git tuh po' ol' gran'pap in time, but I dunno. I spec' he's gittin' weakah ev'y minute."

Lavinia watched her mother's broad back disappear down the road, then went up to her room, the light of a mighty resolution shining in her eyes. "I's gwine," she muttered. "I's gwine wid Ike when he comes fuh me. I don' keer whut happens, I's gwine tuh de Buck tuhday."

She arrayed herself in her best clothes, sought out her brother who sat on the doorstep whittling, and deposited the baby in his unwilling arms, charging him to take good care of it until her return. Turning a deaf ear to his inquiries as to where she was going, she started off in the direction her mother had gone, and was shortly overtaken by a young mtn with a fine new buggy. Smiling, she climbed aboard and they drove off.

Isaiah sat on the doorstep and held little Violet Clare. He had no love for babies at any time, but today they seemed especially unnecessary. The Jones family passed on their way to camp; they were all going, even the little children. As Isaiah pondered the unequal division of the good things of this world, Aunt Sarah Dixon inquired if she might leave her basket, to be called for later. Isaiah had no objection so she put it in the kitchen. Two cronies of his own appeared. Evidently they were not going to camp, for they carried fishing rods and lovely tin cans full of earthworms. Isaiah had a tin can of his own out by the gate. He placed the baby on the ground and ran down to speak to them.

"Whuh yuh gwine?"

"Feeshin'. Come along."

"Don' wan' tuh go feeshin'."

"Ho! 'Fraid o' yo' mammy! 'Fraid-cat, 'fraid-cat! Got tuh min' de baby. Yaaaah!"

There was murder in Isaiah's eyes as he threw stones at his retreating friends. Violet Clare on the ground wailed dismally, and he regarded her with an unfraternal expression. "Well, cry den. Hollah! Who keers ef yuh does? Wisht dah wahnt no babies in de worl'. Wisht dah hadn' nevah bin none."

Isaiah passed a miserable morning, but about noon his baby sister fell asleep. He laid her on the lounge and went into the yard. The sun had disappeared behind a cloud, but between the trees he could see the glimmer of the canal.

"Spec' de feesh is bitin' fine," he thought.

His fishing rod stood suggestively near at hand; the wriggling worms in the tin can seemed to be begging for the hook. Isaiah dug his bare toes in the earth and quivered. Then he went and looked at the sleeping baby. He knew she was safe for awhile, so why not enjoy himself?

Suddenly an inspiration occurred to him. On the shelf was the paregoric bottle, known as "draps." Many a time he had seen the child quieted by a judicious dose; perhaps if he gave her some now she might sleep for another hour or two. He knew the proper amount, but wishing to be doubly sure he largely increased the quantity and poured it down the sleeping child's throat. Then he looked for a safe place to put her. She might roll off the lounge; the same objection held good with regard to the bed. In doubt, he scratched his head, but at that moment his eye fell on the basket left by Aunt Sarah Dixon. It was a straw hamper with lids opening on each side of the handle, and quite large enough to hold the baby. Isaiah thought she might sleep very comfortably there. Somebody's laundry was on its way to the wash, but he had no scruples about removing it and placing a pillow on the bottom. He then laid the sleeping infant inside, on the improvised mattress, replaced the mosquito netting which had covered the clothes, and closed one lid, leaving the one at her feet open for ventilation.

"Nobody won' know," he reflected. "I'll be home fus' an' nobody won' know." He closed the door, but when he got outside he leaned through the window and looked once more at the basket. Then he applied his thumb to his nose, wriggled his fingers derisively at the slumbering infant, and, with a wild whoop, started for the canal.

✦ ✦ ✦

Down at the Buck, Lavinia was finding the camp not quite all her fancy had painted it. She had quarreled with her escort and he had not come near her since their arrival. It now seemed as though she would have to walk home. She was not altogether surprised to see her mother, and much of the day had been spent in dodging her. Consequently, she was not happy. Night approached, and as darkness gathered, the woods filled with people from all over the surrounding country. She thought she would go and hear the preaching.

The speaker stood on a log in a cleared place near the center of the woods. Behind him in a semicircle stood men with lighted torches which flickered strangely, casting lurid flames against the black background of trees. In front of him were gathered the faithful who had long ago got religion and were close at hand to start the singing and to comfort and exhort those whose sins had suddenly become oppressive to them. Prominent in this group was Mrs. Simmons.

Lavinia sat on a tree stump and listened to the preacher:

"Breddern an' sistern, ez I done tol' yuh befo', I takes mah tex' f'om de Bible. Not f'om de New Tessamint nuh de Ol' Tessamint, but f'om de good ol' *Bible!* Anywhus betwix its kivvahs, scusin' maybe de Song o' Solomon, you kin fin' it. An' whut do it say? It say 'be good,' an' it say it loud an'

strong. Does you want tuh go tuh heaven? Ef yuh does, yuh got tuh min'
yo' mannahs. Whut yuh come heah fo' tuhday? Did yuh come tuh walk ahm-
in-ahm wid Laz'rus? Did yuh come tuh climb de laddah wid Jacob, an'
fight de lions wid Daniel? Or did yuh come tuh show yo' clo's an' meet yo'
frien's?"

"A-a-a-a-men! Praise de Lawd!" arose from the faithful.

Here an old man raised his voice in song: "*When de roll is called up
yondah I'll be dah.*" The refrain was taken up by one after the other until
the woods rang with the chorus.

"Sistah, will *you* be dah? Dat's whut I wants tuh know. When ol' Jo'dan
am a-rollin' an' a-ragin', will *you* be dah, in yo' white robes an' wid yo'
crown o' glory? I's feared you ain' all gwine tuh be gettin' in de Kingdom
tuh heah sweet Jo'dan roll when ol' Gabriel am a-blowin' of de las' ho'n."

With a loud cry of "Lawd, ha' mussy on mah soul," Lavinia rushed forward and cast herself on the mourner's bench.

"Heah's a po' li'l lamb strayed f'om de fol'," said the speaker, vastly
pleased with his powers of exhortation. "Sistah Simmons, will you pray
wid huh, an' show huh de way Home?"

Mrs. Simmons, whose attention had been wandering, did not recognize
her daughter in the prostrate figure, so she bent over her and half carried
her to a secluded spot nearby. "Po' soul," she said, "don' take on so, honey.
Yo' po' sinful haht's strivin' fo' peace, an' de good Lawd's gwine tuh give
it t' yuh. Look up now an' be thankful yo' sin has foun' you out.'

She forcibly removed the girls hands from before her face. For a moment
the two sat on the ground and stared at each other, speechless. Mrs. Simmons was the first to recover herself. "Vinny! Sakes alive!" she exclaimed,
punctuating her words with vigorous shakes. "Whuh mah baby! Whuh
Vi'let Cla'r?"

Lavinia rallied, her mind functioning at top speed. "Mama," she said,
"how's po' ol' gran'pap? Wuz you in time tuh he'p 'im pass ovah Jo'dan?"

"Lavinia Simmons," said her mother after some quick deliberation, "we's
all sinnahs, mo' er less. Me an' you'll staht fuh home dis instan' an' see ef
any hahm's come tuh mah baby—an' ef it have. . . ."

✐   ✐   ✐

Isaiah was in a cheerful mood as he started home from the canal when
it suited him to do so, untroubled by any remembrance of neglected duty.
He was surprised not to hear the lamentations of Violet Clare as he approached the house, so he went in and looked around.

There was no basket; there was no baby. Frantically he searched both
house and woodshed. The child was gone. Suddenly a horrible idea occurred
to him. He had often heard his mother discuss medical students generally,
and the various ways by which they got children and hid them in the dissect-
ing rooms for future use. Isaiah knew all about these dark practices and
trembled with fear.

"It's stujints," he thought. "Stujints has got huh an' dey'll git me too."

Night came on and he cast apprehensive glances at the gathering darkness. The lost baby and the retribution awaiting him when his mother returned were both forgotten, and he thought only of the dreadful fate in store for him when the students decided they would carve him up as they undoubtedly had his little sister. At last footsteps were heard on the path and he made a wild dash for the woodshed, from which he was presently dragged by ruthless hands.

"Lemme go," he gasped, expecting a surgeon's knife to pierce his hide at any moment. "Lemme go, I ain' done nothin'."

"Ain' done nothin', ain' yuh?" rasped his mother's voice. "Whut yuh hidin' fo' ef yuh ain' done nothin'? Whuh mah baby? Has yuh bin an' los' mah chile? Tell me, quick; whut yuh done wid mah baby?"

"I nevah done it. Hope tuh die I nevah done lef' de house. Stujints come an' stole huh while I wuz gittin' huh bottle fixed. I seen 'em hidin' huh in de kerridge an' I hollahd tuh dem tuh drap huh, but dey kep' right on, an' dey's comin' back fuh me, too. Oh mama, don' let 'em git me! Don' let 'em git me!"

"Oh, mah baby!" wailed Mrs. Simmons, wringing her hands. "Oh mah li'l chile! Stole by de stujints! I knowed dah wuz trouble comin' tuh dis house when I seen de cha'r a-rockin' an' dah wahn't nobody in it. I knowed I's gwine tuh see trouble when de buhd flew in de windah. Whuh mah baby? Whut dey done tuh mah chile?" Mrs. Simmons wept aloud in an agony of grief; Lavinia joined her in a tumult of regret at having deserted her charge; and Isaiah, his imagination conjuring up visions of his body floating in a pickling vat in front of a class of medical students, howled loudest of all.

"De stujints!" gasped Isaiah, his blood turning to ice in his veins.

Suddenly, loud, determined knocking was heard on the front door.

"Vinny," whispered Mrs. Simmons, seizing the poker, "fill de dippah wid b'ilin' watah, an' when I h'ists de pokah fling it in dey faces. Dey done got mah baby, but dey ain' gwine tuh git no mo'."

The knocking was repeated.

"W-h-h-h-o dah?" asked Mrs. Simmons, her teeth chattering.

"Fo' de Lawd's sake," answered Aunt Sarah Dixon as she opened the door and walked in, bearing in her arms the missing baby. "Whut de mattah wid y'all? Heah's yo' chile, Mis' Simmons. Rube, he done tuck huh home wid him in de clo's basket whuh she wuz a-sleepin', an' nevah knowed it. He done fotch huh back twice't, but dah wuz nobody 'roun', 'ceptin' Isaiah—he seen him kitin' off to'ds de canal—so he tuck huh home an' kep' huh safe all day. Rube done stop heah like I ax him to, fuh Miss Molly's wash dat I lef' in de hampah, an' he foun' de baby 'stid o' de clo's when he unkivvahed de basket. But she ain' a mite wuss, an' so no hahm's done. So long, Mis' Simmons."

Dead silence prevailed after Mrs. Dixon's departure. The eye of his mother was on Isaiah and he quailed before it. Presently she said in a dangerously polite tone: "Huccum mah baby in dat basket?"

No answer.

Mrs. Simmons reached for the switch on the mantel. "Whuh yo' spec' tuh go when yuh dies?" she demanded. "You done went off an' lef' de baby, an' tol' me you seen de stujints hidin' huh in de kerridge. Maybe I could ha' 'scused yo' runnin' off feeshin'; maybe I could. But whut I cain' 'scuse nohow is de lies yuh done tol' me. Don' yuh know whut comes tuh boys dat tell lies? It's a wondah de good Lawd don' strike you daid. You done make me b'lieve mah baby wuz stole by stujints, an' now I's gwine tuh make yuh wish de stujints had a-got you sho' 'nuff. I's gwine tuh l'arn you tuh tell lies tuh yo' mama."

Isaiah watched his mother and breathed quickly. He saw that he must act, and at once. "Mama," he cried, "I seen gran'pap down at de canal, an' de done tol' me. . . ."

The hand stretched forth to seize Isaiah's collar dropped heavily as Mrs. Simmons gazed from one to the other of her offspring. Her expression underwent several changes, and it was difficult to determine whether she was going to laugh or cry. Her frown slowly gave way to a smile, and then to one of lovely tenderness. Suddenly she threw an arm around each, drawing both into her capacious embrace.

"We's all po', mizzable sinnahs," she crooned, "but mah baby am back all safe an' soun', an' gran'pap am snatched f'om de jaws o' death by de han' o' de Lawd. So we won' say no mo' 'bout it, but jine in singin an' den take off ouah bes' clo's an' go tuh baid."

In a moment the little cottage rang with music as Mrs. Simmons, Lavinia and Isaiah sang, *"Praise Gawd, f'om who all blessin's flows."*

PART TWO

PREACHER, PRAYER AND PULPIT

Heavenly Visitation

Back in the 1880's, before the airplane was invented, the gas or hot air balloon was the master of the big-city skies, although rarely ever seen in remote country areas.

One sunny June day a balloon was blown far off course by a strong, persistent wind and it landed in a cotton patch in rural Georgia. The balloonist stepped out and was confronted by a milling throng of wide-eyed, awe-struck field hands. One of them, a raven-hued woman well past her allotted three-score-and-ten, remembered the Scriptures closely enough to step forward and greet the strange visitor from Above:

"Good mawnin', Massa Jesus," she said. "How's yo' Pa?"

The Gospill Truth*

"Breth'n an' sist'n, this mawnin' I'm gonna preach on the dividin' of the loaves an' the fishes, an' the subjec' of my tex' is Pills.

"Pills is one thing all poo' people kin affo'd. Pills come in ev'y color; green pills, orange pills, red pills, yallah pills, white pills an' all kines of colah pills.

"An' there's all shapes an' sizes of pills; an' all flavahs of pills; good-tastin', bad tastin', sweet, sour, peppahmint an' lic'rice.

"But heah this, friends; in that Great Day of Jedgmint, you am done lost an' cast into the outah darkness if you ain't got the onliest pill that can save you—the *Gos*pill!"

Jail Is Too Good

The entire congregation of Rose of Sharon Baptist Church, in the little town of Delta, was bursting with the news of Rev. Hosiah Henshaw's return. Just a year ago he had disappeared with $200 of the church's "roof money." Now he was back, minus the missing funds, and as big and brazen as you please.

The deacons held an emergency meeting to determine what to do about the dishonest preacher.

"I say, put 'im in jail, whuh he belongs," demanded the irate treasurer.

There was a murmur of approval, and the motion was about to be carried when one of the other deacons spoke up.

"Frien's an' fella chu'ch membahs," he began, "jail am too good fuh him. 'Sides, he cain't earn nothin' fuh us locked up in a jailhouse. So we got tuh make him pay back the money ouah way."

The speaker was greeted with deafening applause as he concluded, "He got tuh *preach* it out!"

Law of Compensation

A Baptist and a Methodist preacher were discussing their hard lot in terms of economics. They both loved their calling, but you know how it is when rent time rolls around.

"Calvary Methodis' don' pay much," admitted the first minister, "but at leas' I git chickens an' a free parsonage to help out."

"You's lucky," said the second preacher. "Ovah at Ebeneezah Baptis' Chu'ch, all I kin expec' is some neckbones an' jes' 'nuff money tuh keep me an' mah family alive."

The Methodist preacher clucked in sympathy. "That's mighty po' money," he said.

"Well," the other confessed, "they gits mighty po' preachin'."

---

* *The New York World*, April 9, 1881.

Practical Preacher

They used to baptize people by immersion in the river, and in some rural areas they still do. In one of those backwoods communities a preacher put a sister under. When she came up, instead of praising the Lord she shouted, "I seen Jesus! I seen Jesus!"

"No you didn't," said the preacher. "Jus' say 'Blessed be the Lawd, I'm saved.' "

"But I seen Jesus!" she yelled hoarsely.

"Oh, hesh up, Sistah," he snapped impatiently, "I seen that too. It warn't nothin' but a turtle!"

Celestial Competition*

You nevah seen de beat, how Baptis's an' Mefdis's always bad-moufin' each othah.

Brings tuh min' this heah Baptis' preachah an' a Mefdis preachah, an' dey on a train goin' to a con'funce o' one kin' o' 'nuthah, when de enjine sploded. De cullahd coach, bein' right in back o' de enjine, it blowed up too, an' de preachahs dey blowed up wid it.

When dem two riz sky-high, de Baptis' preachah hollah out to de Mefdis' preachah, "How much you bet I goes highah den you?"

But Do It Gently, Please!

Reverend Stokes needed just a few more contributions to buy some needed hymnals. He knew that his congregation was poor, so he stated his request for the contributions as modestly as possible:

"An' now, ev'ybody kinely come up front an' put yo' li'l constitutions on de table."

Down-Home Wisdom

The country preacher glared balefully at the Brother who had a habit of correcting his grammar and even his choice of texts for the Sunday sermons.

During this particular sermon he noticed that the know-it-all Brother had written down some notes and that he would soon be offering his gratuitous advice. Fixing a baleful eye on the culprit, the preacher ended his sermon by shaking his finger at the offender.

"An' don' you evah fuhgit one thing," he warned. "It ain't the things whut you know dat gits you intuh trouble; it's the things you know fuh sho' whut ain't so!"

---

* *Treasury of Folk Humor*, J. Robeson, Applegate and Co., N. Y. 1901.

A Dynamic Prayer*

How many of the good citizens of Charleston who have passed by the Cotton Wharf, where Negroes are employed by vessel owners, have ever noticed the neatly painted little church called the House of Jesus? The preacher, one Rev. Orrin Stone, is an exhorter of fine mettle. His flair for rhetoric, self-taught, is flamboyantly funny, but a glance at his merry eyes and a minute's conversation with this man, convinces one that he knows precisely what he is saying; that he could, if he wished, deliver a sermon in impeccable English; that he understands the difference between conscious wit and unconscious humor.

Rev. Stone is pulling our leg, but innate artistry must be applauded, no matter what the reason. Here is his prayer, as closely followed as we can recall it:

"O Lawd, gib dy sarvint, dis Sunday mawnin', de eye of an eagle dat he may see sin f'om afar. Put his han's to de gospel pulpit; glue his ears to de gospel telefoam an' conneck him wid de Glory in de skies. 'Luminate his brow wid a holy light dat will make de fiahs of hell look like a tallah candle. Bow his head down in humility, in dat lonesome valley wheah de pearl of truth is much needed to be said. Grease his lips wid possum 'ile to make it easy fo' love to slip outen his mouth. . . .

"Turpentime his 'magination; 'lectrify his brain wid de powah of de Word. Put 'petual motion in his arms. Fill him full of de dynamite of Dy awful powah; 'noint him all ovah wid de kerosene of Dy salvation, an' den, O Lawd, sot him on fiah wid de sperrit of de Holy Ghos'."

'Coon in the Treetop

It was a lovely summer's day in Leesville, Louisiana. The birds were chirping merrily, bees hovered and buzzed among the blooming flowers, and a gentle breeze wafted the fragrance of many blossoms through the door and windows of the Church of the Lily of the Valley.

The Rev. Robert Thompson thought it too nice a day to preach indoors. "Let us move outside, under the trees in the arbor where I can speak the Word—under the Lord's own skies," he announced to the perspiring congregation. Pleased with the suggestion, they arose as one and trailed him outside the church and into the grove of trees. Among them was little Willie, desperately trying to hide his pet baby 'coon. Somehow, it escaped, climbed one of the trees in front of the table which the preacher was using as a pulpit, and hid itself in the leafy foliage.

---

* While the origin of *A Dynamic Prayer* is unknown, it may have first appeared in a crudely printed pamphlet titled *The Good Shepherd*, published privately in Charleston, South Carolina, June, 1889. Many other versions have since been published in American anthologies, but the above version is based on the "Good Shepherd" story, the original of which is anonymous.

Rev. Thompson began his sermon. "God Almighty created this land of milk and honey," he began. "God Almighty created the blue sky which gives us rain for our crops. God created the sun which gives us warmth and light. God created all the green things that grow upon this earth. God. . . ."

At this precise moment the preacher lifted his head to the heavens as though seeking Divine inspiration for the closing of his sermon, and there, peering intently at him from among the leaves in the tree was Willie's pet raccoon. He froze amid-sentence in an attitude of stunned silence and then, "God—DAMN! *What a rat!*"

Addled Addition

Preacher: Our finances are mighty low. Maybe we should ask for a tenth of every member's income.

Deacon: A tenth ain't enough. Better make it a twentieth.

That's the Hat, Cat!*

Reverend Scofield emitted a deep sigh. "The chu'ch roof needed fixin' so I passed the hat aroun' this Sunday mawnin'."

"How much did you git?"

"Nawthin'," answered the good preacher. "In fack, I wuz lucky tuh git my hat back."

Really Hot Down There!

The minister had dwelt on the rewards awaiting the born-again Christians. Now, as a firm believer in the law of compensation, he launched into a discussion of punishment as opposed to reward. .

"When I tell you that Hell ain't no place for messin' aroun' an' havin' a good time, you better believe me! You have seen molten iron bubblin' an' boilin' in them big furnaces. Well, let me remin' you, down where I'm talkin' about, they use that stuff for ice cream!"

Greetings, You Backsliders!

It was Easter morning and the pastor gazed out at the congregation that packed the little church. He noted the flower-bedecked hats worn by the ladies, the new dresses and suits worn by the children, and the brand new suits sported by the men. He frowned.

"Brothers an' sisters," he began, his voice low but rising with every

---

* *Bishop's Book of Humor*, Lawrence Bishop, Bruckner Press, 1909.

syllable, "I know an' you know that many of you here this Easter mornin' will not be back to church until nex' Easter. So I take this opportunity to wish all sech trash a merry Chris'mas!"

Fundamentalist Reasoning

The Baptist preacher was in fine form and his voice resounded throughout the little country church. "The Meth'dis's tell you that the onlies' diffunce 'tween their chu'ch an' ours is in the baptizin' service. They b'lieve in sprinklin' an' we b'lieve in 'mersion."

Now the preacher's voice rose as he shook his fist and continued. "But that ain't all a-tall! It all started with Moses. Us Baptis's b'lieve that the daughter of Pharioh foun' Moses in the bullrushes. But the Meth'dis's b'lieve she jes' *say* she foun' him in the bullrushes!"

Piling It On

Parson: De Lawd always de Lawd fo'evuh mo'! De Lawd wuz de Lawd f'om de fus' day He wuz bo'n. De Lawd wuz de Lawd *befo'* He wuz bo'n. De Lawd wuz de Lawd even befo' His pappy an' mammy wuz bo'n!"

Deacon: Pahson, ain't you stretchin' things jes' a mite?"

Reasonable Objections

A Methodist preacher suggested to his flock that they could beautify the surroundings by erecting a picket fence around the burial plot in back of the church.

"I protes'!" declared one of the stewards.

"State yo' objections, ef yuh got any."

"I got two objections, not jes' one," retorted the steward. "In the fus' place, nobody in that cemetary kin git out nohow. In the secon' place, nobody on the outside is even studyin' 'bout gittin' in!"

Can't Win for Losing

A brother died and found himself at the gates of Heaven.

"Write yo' name down in dis heah book," ordered St. Peter.

The brother did so, and St. Peter looked around and asked, "Wheah's yo' hoss?"

"I ain't ridin'," said the man.

"Dat's too bad, 'caze we ain't takin' walkin' people in dis week. You gotta be ridin'."

Dejectedly, the brother walked on down the road to the crossroad where the bus stops for those going the Other Way. He was almost there when he came upon a white man. "Wheah you goin'?" asked the brother.

"To Heaven," said whitey.

The brother shook his head. "You ain't gonna git in," he said. "I jes' came f'om theah an' St. Petah ain't takin' walkahs—only ridahs."

They sat down on a rock to think about it when suddenly the brother got an idea. "Hey, I know how we both kin git in," he said excitedly. "You git up on my back an' I'll be the hoss." The white man's face lit up in a smile of approval and, mounting the black man's shoulder's, they headed for the celestial entrance and knocked loudly.

"Who dat?" called St. Peter.

"It's me, a good and honest man," replied whitey.

"You walkin'?" asked St. Peter.

"No, I'm riding."

"All right, you kin come in," said St. Peter, "but you'll have tuh leave yo' hoss outside."

Homesick Ghost

Pop, he mighty prideful 'bout his twin boys, Bowie an' Billy. Bimeby, Bowie got kilt in a fight an' Pop tuck tuh grievin' somethin' fierce. Ev'y day he go to de cemet'ry an' cry an' carry on. It wuz turble, de way he miss dat boy, an' he done dis fo' a whole yeah.

Billy, he miss Bowie too, but he don' cry 'bout it fuh no whole yeah, an' he gittin' fed up wid Pop's moanin' an' weepin'. One day he seed Pop goin' to de cemet'ry so he 'low he gonna stop de ol' man f'om spendin' his days cryin' like dat. He dress hisse'f up in a white sheet an' he run aroun' de othah way an' hide back of Bowie's gravestone. Soon Pop come to de bur'l groun' an' he begin' weepin' like he allus do. "Oh, mah po' daid li'l Bowie! Please come back an' show me yo' smilin' face wunst ag'in."

Billy riz up f'om back of de gravestone an' he moan, "Heah Ah is, Pop."

Pop, he back off, an' he staht a-chokin'. "Go on back!" he yell. " 'Tain't fittin' fuh no ghos' tuh talk back tuh live folks's."

Billy, he stan' in de dahk an' he voice soun' jes' like de daid brothah. "No, I ain't goin' back no mo'! I's goin' home wid you!"

Pop, he staht runnin', an' he yell ovah he shouldah, "Dat's jes' whut's wrong wid you, Bowie. Ef you hadn' bin so hahd-haided you wouldn' be in dis mess in de fus' place!"

De Sun Do Move*

by
John J. Jasper
(1812-1893)

'Low me to say dat when I was a young man and a slave, I knowed nothin' worth talkin' 'bout concernin' books. Dey was sealed mysteries to me, but I tell you I longed to break de seal. I thirsted for de bread of learnin'. When I seen books I ached to git in to 'em for I knowed dat dey had de stuff for me and I wanted to taste dere contents, but most of de time dey was barred against me.

By de mercy of de Lord a thing happened. I got a roomfeller—he was a slave, too, and he had learned to read. In de dead of de night he give me lessons outen de New York Spellin' Book. It was hard pullin', I tell you; harder on him, for he know'd just a little and it made him sweat to try to beat somethin' into my hard head. It was worse with me. Up de hill every step, but when I got de light of de lesson into my noodle I fairly shouted, but I know'd I was not a scholar. De consequence was I crept 'long mighty tedious, gittin' a crumb here and dere, until I could read de Bible by skippin' de long words, tolerable well. Dat was de start of my education—dat is what little I got. I make mention of dat young man. De years have fled away since den but I ain't forgot my teacher and never shall. I thank my Lord for him and I carries his memory in my heart.

'Bout seven months after my gittin' to readin', God converted my soul and I reckon 'bout de first and main thing dat I begged de Lord to give me was de power to understand His Word. I ain't braggin' and I hates self-praise, but I bound to speak de thankful word. I believes in my heart dat my prayer to understand de Scriptur was heard. Since dat time I ain't cared 'bout nothin' 'cept to study and preach de Word of God.

Not, my brothren, dat I's de fool to think I knows it all. Oh, my Father, no! Far from it. I don't hardly understand myself nor half of the things 'round me and dere is millions of things in de Bible too deep for Jasper and some of 'em too deep for everybody. I don't carry de keys to de Lord's closet and He ain't tell me to peep in and if I did I'm so stupid I wouldn't know it when I see it. No, friends, I knows my place at de feet of my Master and dere I stays.

But I can read de Bible and get de things what lay on de top of de

---

* *De Sun Do Move* expressed the fundamentalist belief in its most orthodox sense. The sermon was first delivered by the Rev. John J. Jasper in the mid-1870's, and subsequently repeated and refined through the years as thousands of people, black and white, flocked to Rev. Jasper's church in Richmond to hear the famous text. While many other sermons in this genre have been produced, *De Sun Do Move* remains the classic expression of folk art in the Negro fundamentalist Baptist tradition, its humor notwithstanding.

soil. Outen de Bible I know nothin' extry 'bout de sun. I seen its course as he rides up dere so gran' and mighty in de sky, but dere is heaps 'bout dat flamin' orb dat is too much for me. I know dat de sun shines powerfully and pours down its light in floods and yet dat is nothin' compared with de light dat flashes in my mind from de pages of God's book. But you knows all dat. I knows dat de sun burns—oh, how it did burn in dem July days! I tell you he cooked de skin on my back many a day when I was hoein' in de corn field. But you knows all dat—and yet dat is nothing to de divine fire dat burns in de souls of God's chillun. Can't you feel it, brothren?

But 'bout de course of de sun, I have got dat. I have done ranged through de whole blessed Book and scoured down de last thing de Bible has to say 'bout de movement of de sun. I got all dat pat and safe. And lemme say dat if I don't give it to you straight, if I gits one word crooked or wrong, you just holler out, 'Hold on dere, Jasper, you ain't got dat straight!', and I'll beg pardon. If I don't tell de truth, march up dese steps here and tell me I's a liar and I'll take it. I fears I do lie sometimes—I's so sinful, I find it hard to do right; but my God don't lie and He ain't put no lie in de Book of eternal truth and if I give you what de Bible say, den I bound to tell de truth.

I goin' to take you all dis afternoon on an excursion to a great battle-field. Most folks like to see fights—some is mighty fond of gittin' into fights and some is mighty quick to run down de back alley when dere is a battle goin' on for de right. Dis time I'll 'scort you to a scene where you shall witness a curious battle. It took place soon after Israel got de Promise Land. You 'member de people of Gideon make friends with God's people when dey first entered Canaan and dey was monstrous smart to do it. But, just de same, it got 'em in to an awful fuss. De cities 'round 'bout dere flared up at dat and dey all joined dere forces and say dey gwine to mop de Hebrew people off the ground, and dey bunched all dere armies together and went up for to do it. When dey come up so bold and brace, de Gideonites was scared outen dere senses and dey sent word to Joshua dat dey was in trouble and he must run up dere and git 'em out. Joshua had de heart of a lion and he was up dere directly. Dey had an awful fight, sharp and bitter, but you might know dat General Joshua was not dere to get whipped. He prayed and he fought and de hours got away too fast for him, and so he asked de Lord to issue a special order dat de sun hold up awhile and dat de moon furnish plenty of moonshine down on de lowest part of the fightin' grounds. As a fact, Joshua was so drunk with de battle, so thirsty for de blood of de enemies of de Lord, and so wild with de victory dat he tell de sun to stand still till he could finish his job.

What did de sun do? Did he glare down in fiery wrath and say, 'What you talkin' 'bout my stoppin' for, Joshua? I ain't never started yet. Been here all de time and it would smash up everything if I was to start.' No, he ain't say dat. But what de Bible say? Dat's what I ask to know. It say dat it was at de voice of Joshua dat it stopped. *I* don't say it stopped; 'tain't for Jasper to say dat, but de Bible, *de Book of God,* say so. But I say dis:

nothin' can stop until it has first started. So I knows what I'm talkin' 'bout. De sun was travellin' 'long dere through de sky when de order come. He hitched his red ponies and made quite a call on de land of Gideon. He perch up dere in de skies just as friendly as a neighbor what comes to borrow somethin', and he stand up dere and he look like he enjoyed de way Joshua waxes dem wicked armies. And de moon, she wait down in de low grounds dere and pours out her light and look just as calm and happy as if she was waitin' for her escort. Dey never budged, neither of 'em, long as de Lord's army needed a light to carry on de battle.

I don't read when it was dat Joshua hitch up and drove on, but I suppose it was when de Lord told him to go. Anybody knows dat de sun didn't stay dere all de time. It stopped for business and went on when it got through. Dis is 'bout all dat I has to do with dis particular case. I done showed you dat dis part of de Lord's Word teaches you dat de sun stopped, which show dat he was movin' before dat and dat he went on afterwards. I told you dat I would prove dis and I's done it and I defies anybody to say dat my point ain't made.

I told you in de first part of dis discourse dat de Lord God is a man of war. I expect by now you begin to see it is so. Don't you admit it? When de Lord come to see Joshua in de day of his fears and warfare and actually make de sun stop stone still in de heavens so de fight can rage on till all de foes is slain, you're obliged to understand dat de God of peace is also de man of war. He can use both peace and war to heap de riches and to scatter de host of de aliens. A man talked to me last week 'bout de laws of nature and he say dey can't possibly be upset and I had to laugh right in his face. As if de laws of *anything* was greater dan my God who is de lawgiver for everything. My Lord is great! He rules in de heavens, in de earth and down under de ground. He is great and greatly to be praised. Let all de people bow down and worship before Him! Dere you are! Ain't dat de movement of de sun? Bless my soul! Hezekiah's case beat Joshua. Joshua stop de sun, but here de Lord make de sun walk back ten degrees; and yet dey say dat de sun stand stone still and never move a peg. It look to me he move 'round mighty brisk and is ready to go any way dat de Lord orders him to go. I wonder if any of dem philosophers is 'round here dis afternoon? I'd like to take a square look at one of dem and ask him to explain dis matter. He can't do it, my brothren. He knows a heap 'bout books, maps, figgers and long distances, but I defy him to take up Hezekiah's case and explain it off. He can't do it, my brothren. De Word of de Lord is my defense and bulwark and I fears not what men say or do—my God give me my victory.

'Low me, my friends, to put myself square 'bout dis movement of de sun. It ain't no business of mine whether de sun move or stan' still, or whether it stop or go back or rise or set. All dat is out of my hand entirely and I got nothin' to say. I got no the-o-ry on de subject. All I ask is dat we will take what de Lord say 'bout it and let His will be done 'bout everything. What dat will is I can't know except He whisper into my soul or write it in a book. Here's de Book. Dis is enough for me, and with it to pilot me I can't get far astray.

But I ain't done with you yet. As de song says, dere's more to follow. I invite you to hear de first verse in de seventh chapter of de Book of Revelations. What do John under de powers of de Spirit say? He says he saw four angels standin' on de four corners of de earth, holdin' de four winds of de earth and so forth. 'Low me to ask, if de earth is round, where do it keep its corners? A flat square thing has corners, but tell me, where is de corner of an apple or a marble or a cannon ball or a silver dollar? If dere is anyone of dem philosophers what's been takin' so many cracks at my old head 'bout here, he is cordially invited to step forward and square up dis vexin' business. I hear tell dat you can't square a circle but it looks like dese great scholars done learned how to circle a square. If dey can do it, let 'em step to de front and do de trick. But, my brothren, in my poor judgment, dey can't do it; 'tain't in 'em to do it. Dey is on de wrong side of de Bible—dat's on de out-side of de Bible, and dere's where de trouble comes in with 'em. Dey done got out of de breastworks of de truth and as long as dey stay dere de light of de Lord will not shine on dere path. I ain't care so much 'bout de sun, though it's mighty convenient to have it, but my trust is in de Word of de Lord. Long as my feet is flat on de solid rock, no man can move me. I's gittin' my orders from de God of my salvation.

The other day a man with a high collar and side whiskers come to my house. He was one nice Northern gentleman what thunk a heap of us colored people in de South. Dey are lovely folks and I honors 'em very much. He seem from de start kinder strict and cross with me and after awhile he broke out furious and fretted and he says: 'Allow me, Mister Jasper, to give you some plain advice. Dis nonsense 'bout de sun movin' is disgracin' your race all over de country, and as a friend of your people I come to say it's got to stop.' . . . Ha! Ha! Ha! . . . Mars Sam Hargroven ever hardly smash me dat way. It was equal to one of dem old overseers way back yonder. I tell him dat if he'll show me I's wrong, I'll give it all up . . . My! My! . . . Ha! Ha! . . . He sail in on me and such a storm 'bout science, new discoveries, and de Lord only knows what all, I never hear before; and den he tell me my race is urgin' me, and poor old Jasper must shut up his fool mouth.

When he got through—it look like he never would—I tell him John Jasper ain't set up to be no scholar and don't know de philosophies and ain't tryin' to hurt his people, but is workin' day and night to lift 'em up, and his foot is on de rock of eternal truth. Dere he stand and dere he goin' to stand till Gabriel sounds de judgment note. So I say to de gentleman what scolded me, I hear him make his remarks but I ain't hear where he get his Scriptur from, and that between him and de Word of de Lord, I take my stand by de Word of God every time. Jasper ain't mad; he ain't fighting nobody; he ain't been appointed janitor to run de sun; he nothin' but de servant of God and a lover of the Everlastin' Word. What I care 'bout de sun? De day comes on when de sun will be called from his race track and his light squinched out forever; de moon shall turn to blood and this earth be consumed with fire. Let 'em go; dat won't scare me nor trouble God's elected people, for de Word of de Lord shall endure forever and on dat Solid Rock we stand and shall not be moved!

Has I got you satisfied yet? Has I proven my point? Oh, ye whose hearts is full of unbelief! Is you still holding out? I reckon de reason you say de sun don't move is 'cause you are so hard to move yourself. You is a real trial to me, but never mind, I ain't given you up yet and never will. Truth is mighty; it can break de heart of stone, and I must fire another arrow of truth out of de quiver of de Lord. If you has a copy of God's Word 'bout your person, please turn to dat minor prophet, Malachi, what write de last book in de whole Bible, and look at chapter one, verse eleven. What do it say? I better read it for I got a notion you critics don't carry any Bible in your pockets every day in de week. Here is what it says: 'For from de rising of de sun even unto de goin' down of the same, My name shall be great among de heathen, say de Lord of hosts!' How do dat suit you? It looks like dat ought to fix it! Dis time it is de Lord of Hosts hisself dat is doin' de talkin' and He is talkin' on a wonderful and glorious subject. He is tellin' of de spreadin' of His Gospel, of the comin' of His last victory over de Gentiles, and de worldwide glories dat at de last He is to get. Oh, my brothren, what a time dat will be! My soul takes wing as I anticipate with joy dat millenium day! De glories as dey shine before my eyes blinds me and I forget de sun and moon and stars. I just remember dat 'long 'bout dose last days dat de sun and moon will go out of business for dey won't be needed no more. Den will King Jesus come back to see His people and He will be de sufficient light of de world. Joshua's battles will be over. Hezekiah won't need no sun dial, and de sun and moon will fade out before de glorious splendors of de New Jerusalem.

But what de matter with Jasper? I most forgot my business and most gone to shoutin' over de faraway glories of de secon' comin' of my Lord. I beg pardon and will try to get back to my subject. I have to do as de sun in Hezekiah's case—fall back a few degrees. In dat part of de Word dat I'm givin' you from Malachi—dat de Lord hisself spoke—he declares dat His glory is gwine to spread. Spread? Where? From de risin' of de sun to de goin' down of de same. What? It don't say dat, does it? Dat's exactly what it says. Ain't dat clear enough for you? De Lord pity dese doubtin' Thomases. Here is enough to settle it all and cure de worse cases. Wake up here, wise folks, and get your medicine. Where is dem high-collared philosophers now? What dey skulkin' 'round in de brush for? Why don't you get out in de broad afternoon light and fight for your collars? Ah, I understand it; you got no answer. De Bible is against you and in your consciences you are convicted.

But I hears you back dere. What you whisperin' 'bout? I know! You say you sent me some papers and I never answer dem . . . Ha, ha, ha! . . . I got 'em. De difficulty 'bout dem papers you sent me is dat dey did not answer *me*. Dey never mention de Bible one time. You think so much of yourself and so little of de Lord God, and thinks what you say is so smart, dat you can't even speak of de Word of de Lord. When you ask me to stop believing in de Lord's Word and to pin my faith on your words, I ain't goin' to do it. I take my stand by de Bible and rest my case on what it says. I take what de Lord says 'bout my sins, 'bout my Saviour, 'bout life, 'bout death, 'bout de world to come, and I take what de Lord say 'bout de sun and moon and I cares little what de haters of my God chooses to say. Think dat I will forsake de Bible? It is my only Book, my hope, de arsenal of my soul's supplies, and I want nothin' else.

But I got another word for you yet. I done work over dem papers dat you sent me without date and without name. You deals in figures and thinks you are bigger dan de archangels. Lemme see what you done say. You set yourself up to tell me how far it is from here to de sun. You think you got it down to a nice point. You say it is 3,339,002 miles from de earth to de sun. Dat's what you say. Another one say dat de distance is 12,000,000; another got it up to 27,000,000. I hears dat de great Isaac Newton worked it up to 28,000,000, and later on de philosophers gone another rippin' rise to 50,000,000. De last one gets it bigger dan all de others—up to 90,000,000.

Heaps of railroads has been built since I saw de first one when I was fifteen years old but I ain't hear tell of a railroad built yet to de sun. I don't see why if dey can measure de distance to de sun, dey might not get up a railroad or a telegraph and enable us to find something else 'bout it dan merely how far de sun is. Dey tell me dat a cannon ball could make de trip to de sun in twelve years. Why don't dey send it? It might be rigged up with quarters for a few philosophers on de inside and fixed up for a comfortable ride. Dey would need twelve years rations and a heap of changes of raiment— mighty thick clothes when dey start and mighty thin ones when dey git dere.

Oh, my brothren, dese things make you laugh and I don't blame you for laughing 'cept it's always sad to laugh at de follies of fools. If we could laugh 'em out of countenance we might well laugh day and night. What cuts into my soul is dat all dese men seem to me dat dey is hitting at the Bible. Dat's what stirs my soul and fills me with righteous wrath. Little cares I what dey says 'bout de sun, provided dey let de Word of de Lord alone. But never mind. Let de heathen rage and de people imagine a vain thing. Our King shall break 'em in pieces and dash 'em down. But blessed be de name of our God, de Word of de Lord endureth forever! Stars may fall, moons may turn to blood, and de sun set to rise no more, but Thy kingdom, oh Lord, is from everlastin' to everlastin'!

But I has a word dis afternoon for my own brothren. Dey is de people for whose souls I got to watch—for dem I got to stan' and report at de last— dey is my sheep and I's dere shepherd and my soul is knit to dem forever. Ain't for me to be troublin' you with dese questions 'bout dem heavenly bodies. Our eyes goes far beyond de smaller stars. Our home is clean out of sight of dem twinklin' orbs. De chariot dat will come to take us to our Father's mansion will sweep out by dem flickerin' lights and never halt till it brings us in clear view of de throne of de Lamb. Don't hitch your hopes to no sun nor stars. Your home is got Jesus for its light and your hopes must travel up dat way. I preach dis sermon just for to settle the minds of my few brothren, and I repeats it 'cause some kind friends wish to hear it, and I hopes it will do honor to de Lord's Word.

But nothin' short of de Pearly Gates can satisfy me and I charge my people, fix your feet on de Solid Rock, your hearts on Calvary, and your eyes on de throne of de Lamb. Dese strifes and griefs will soon get over; we shall see de King in His glory and be at ease. Go on, go on, ye ransomed of de Lord! Shout His praises as you go! And I shall meet you in de city of de New Jerusalem where ye shan't need de light of de sun—for de Lamb of de Lord is de light of de saints!

Sartin, de Sun Do Move!

by
M. Quad
July, 1878

SCENE: Paradise Hall, Detroit
EVENT: Regular meeting of the Lime-Kiln Club

The meeting was called to order by Giveadam Jones.
Brother Gardner, club president, is now speaking:

I hold here in my hand a letter from Philadelphia axin' me if I believe wid de Rev. Jasper, of Richmond, dat de sun do move. Sartin I do. I know de white folks claim dat it am de airth which am movin' while de sun stands still, but right dar we split. Joshua was about as nigh bein' an angel as any white man will ever git, an' when he ordered de sun to stand still he knew what he was talkin' about. It would have been just as easy fur him to hev commanded de airth to stand still, but he didn't do it. If Joshua didn't know his business de rest of us might as well hang up.

An' now, you mind what I's gwine to say. Don' let de 'stronomy business keep you awake nights. De sun am up dar by day, an' de moon an' stars am up dar by night. De Lord put de sun dar to thaw de ice off de back doah-step, make cucumbers grow, an' fotch up de grass an' de corn. It didn't do any wuss when 'stronomy was unknown, an' it wouldn't do any better if every family in de kentry had a telescope four hundred feet long. De moon was hung up dar dat folks might see to move by night when de rent got too high; dat lost cows could see to find dar way home; dat folks could see to chop wood and empty bar'ls of ashes on de street; dat women comin' home from prayer meetin' could avoid de nail heads stickin' up in de planks, an' fur varus other reasons. You jist take de sun as he runs, an' de moon as you find it, an' de less you worry 'bout 'em de more meat an' taters you'll have in de winter. De poorest man I ever knowed was an ole black man down in Virginny who was always wonderin' if dey had a reg'lar lock on de gates of Heaven, or only a latch string. While his neighbors war plantin' he was theorizin'; while dey war hoein' he was wonderin'; while dey war reapin' he was ragged an' hungry.

Let de sun move or stand still, let de moon be made of old silver or green cheese, let de stars be ten miles or 10,000,000 miles away—keep de whitewash brush goin' an' de buck-saw in good order an' you'll be all right.

4
A
PEOPLE
SING

Introduction

PART ONE:
Epic Ballads and Other Folk Songs

PART TWO:
Dance Songs or Reels

PART THREE:
Songs About Animals

BOOK FOUR

A People Sing

Introduction

The mark of scholarship in a work such as this, is (or should be) its verisimilitude; that is, its probability or likelihood, its appearance or semblance of truth. All statements are expected to be fully annotated and well documented, with precise dates and proper designation of the authors or composers. At the outset, however, this editor was confronted with the unyielding knowledge that a certain degree of imprecision would have to be tolerated if, indeed, there was to be a music section at all.

Generally speaking, the folk song may be described as music (with or without lyrics) of anonymous composition, transmitted orally. Until recently it was thought that folk songs were composed by the people as a communal effort, but comprehensive studies now indicate that the germ of a folk melody is produced by an individual and subsequently altered in transmission into a group-fashioned expression. National and ethnic individuality can be observed in folk music that has even been transplanted from one country to another, and from one race to another. There is scarcely any people whose folk song is wholly indigenous. Notable among such cases of transplanting are the English, Scottish and Irish ballads found in various parts of the United States.

As in the case of the white, brown and yellow races, the black man, too, has borrowed from early European sources, as well as from his own African heritage. But the result has been a folk expression distinctively unique among American ethnic groups—and, it may be said, distinct from white America as a whole. The Negro has carried the message of his social, economic, political and spiritual life down through the years, almost intact. The songs reenact the futility of the slaves (and also their daring), the laughter of children, the sobs of parting sweethearts, the agony of repression and the joys of the black man's all-too-few victories. For the American Negro, his folk songs tell a story that springs from the very source of his being, touching at the core of all human emotion in a way that few white men can truly comprehend.

In the main, the songs represented here are those of the *old* South; not today's South with its bustling airports, its juke boxes and Jax beer, its flashy cars and super-highways reaching all the way to the Florida Keys. The folk expressions contained in these pages conjure up visions of dusty roads dappled with shade from trees whose branches hang limp in the summer heat; a shimmering river flowing sluggishly to the sea, its calm surface broken only by a paddle-wheeler or a raft; a warm and easy-going land where music seemed to grow as easily as cotton. Yes, there was also the other side—the South of the colonial mansion that no black man dared approach without his hat in his hand; the lovely and fragrant magnolia tree under whose leafy foliage the slave was often shackled for some minor offense, or on whose lower limb he was hanged. Yet, from the depths of his sorrows and the ecstacies of his loves, the fulfillment of his labors and the nobility of his religious life, he evolved a spectrum of folk music that gripped the soil even as it aspired to the stars. And he was able to do so because the ember of hope glowed within his breast.

It is difficult to establish a definite period in which Negro songs first assumed their own character because there were few successful attempts to collect them before 1840. The very small number that were contained in letters and articles prior to that date were either discarded or poorly preserved.

Dr. John W. Work, of Fisk University, home of the famous Fisk Jubilee Singers who first presented Negro spirituals to the world, tells us in his *American Negro Songs and Spirituals,* that music was an inherent part of the African's life and it was to be expected that he would continue his singing upon reaching these shores. No doubt, the agony of his enslavement stirred him to sing more than he did in his native land, for music is an expression of all emotions and is not necessarily confined to joy or love. It is reasonable to suppose, however, that although they sang, the slaves had no uniformity of song. A point to be remembered is that the blacks were taken from a vast area of the African continent—East, West and South Africa and the interior—and it was only natural that their customs, languages and music expressions differed widely from each other. After their arrival in the American colonies they gradually evolved a homogenous type of song, fostered by the general interchange of slaves and, to no small degree, by the effect of Christianity and their acceptance of the new faith. Unfortunately, we cannot estimate how much of the original African idiom has been retained in the evolution of American Negro music. The traumatic experience of forced removal from their native land, the loss of all loved ones as well as the psychological shock of separation from friends and other members of their tribes, and their sudden introduction into an alien culture on the other side of the world, inevitably resulted in an interruption of African culture in America—a culture that has only lately been re-introduced.

Does the African culture still exist in American Negro folk music? Here again we can only rely on imprecise data. Some authorities, such as Edward King, in his book, *The Great South*, offer fragments of evidence which support the theory of African influence; others of equal stature believe it to be negligible. In the final analysis it would seem that the black man in this country has retained some of the African characteristics, although the end product, today, is genuinely American.

Yet, when we turn to the *Blues*, we find a type of song that has a distinctly Afro-American character. The three-phase form is unique, the plaintiveness of the melody and its scale are different from that of "white" music. One is immediately struck with the wide disparity between the blues and spirituals. The latter are intensely religious and the former just as intensely worldly. The exalted verse of many spirituals could be read appropriately from the most dignified pulpit, while much of the verse of the blues is unprintable.* The spirituals were created as chorals, to be performed without instrumental accompaniment. On the other hand, the guitar, piano or orchestral accompaniment is an integral part of the performance of the blues. Again, the spiritual creators thought of every happening as epic—some dispensation from God or a message from Him. The blues singer translated every happening into his own intimate inconvenience. To the spiritual creators, the great Mississippi floods of a few decades ago would have been considered as visitations of a wrathful God upon a sinful community. To a blues singer they simply raised the question, "Where can a po' girl go?"

The man most closely associated with the blues was W. C. Handy.** With remarkable insight and uncanny creative skill he captured the essence of this new musical form and first presented it successfully to America in dance halls and in concerts. The precise origin of the blues may never be known, but this much may be said with certainty: the first of the great blues singers, and the one who gave this type of song its very name was Ma Rainey.*** In

---

* The exceptions, of course, are the "commercial" blues specifically written for radio, television and recordings.

** W. C. Handy, born in 1875, first won national acclaim as a composer with his *Memphis Blues*, published in 1912. His most famous song, *St. Louis Woman*, was published in 1914, and in that year he also wrote *Yellow Dog Blues*. Among his other compositions that have become perennial favorites are *Joe Turner Blues* (1915), *Beale Street Blues* (1916), and *Aunt Hagar's Blues* (1922). Handy, who died in 1958, lived to see his songs extended beyond the world of jazz and into the general field of pop music in innumerable forms. His influence is indelibly stamped on the music of today.

*** Ma Rainey, a woman with a picturesque stage appearance, a deep contralto voice and an authentic manner of singing the blues, is widely regarded as the most famous blues singer of all. In addition to her own great talent, she also "discovered" Bessie Smith who was only 13, but who already showed promise. In 1923 Miss Smith recorded *Downhearted Blues* which sold more

the year 1902, in a small town in Missouri, she was appearing in a tent show when a girl came to the tent one morning and began to sing for her—a strange and poignant song about the man who had left her. Miss Rainey was instantly intrigued. She learned the song from the visitor and thereafter used it in her act as an encore, until the audience response grew so insistent for more that she incorporated it into her act. In 1903, Handy first heard this "soul music" of the day and fashioned it into a genre that expressed the mood, temperament and heartfelt emotion of the black people as had no other music, separated as it was from the classic spirituals, the popular gospel songs, and traditional ballads and dance tunes. Ma Rainey was often asked what kind of song it was that she was now singing, and one day, in a moment of inspiration, she replied, "The *blues*."

We have touched on the African influence embodied in the folk music of the American Negro, but what of the other origins whose contributions have helped to shape his songs? Among the most fascinating discoveries to be made in a study of such lore—at least for those not familiar with the genre—is that Negroes have preserved orally, and for generations, independent of the whites, many of the familiar English and Scottish ballads, and have their own distinct versions of them.

To understand this phenomenon we have to recall the history of our colonization and remember that the new land, particularly the South, was settled largely by Cavaliers and Scots, both of whom loved song. Folk songs required no room in the ships that crossed the oceans, but they were among the most precious cargo that came to our shores, and they have survived through the years; through the poverty, the hardships and all the struggles of pioneer life—better than the material goods that accompanied them. While the hearts that cherished them and the lips that sang them are now indistinguishable dust, these songs live on. Students of balladry know that America is still rich in the traditional songs of Europe, that in remote areas, even today, there is perhaps a rarer heritage of English and Scottish folksongs actually being sung from oral tradition than in any part of Great Britain. The old songs and ballads have been lovingly remembered, transmitted from mouth-to-ear-to-mouth, from generation to generation, with variations such as inevitably result in a change of surroundings and social conditions.

In the early days of the South, when books and newspapers were far less plentiful than they are now, songs formed a large part of plantation social life. At the "big house"—the master's residence—the old ballads would be sung over and over again, until the house servants, being quick of memory

---

than two million copies, and for the next four years she earned better than $2000 a week, working with such musicians as Louis Armstrong and James P. Johnson. In 1933, now in abject poverty because of personal reasons and the mismanagement of her funds, Miss Smith was about to enjoy a change in her fortunes. She started an auto trip from Mississippi to New York, but met with an automobile accident and bled to death after being refused admission to a segregated hospital.

PIGS' FEET

The "Man" got the ham, and the slave got the "chitlins" and feet. Spiced or baked, the house "servant" introduced the delicacy to the white folks who quickly adopted it. Except for the Worcestershire sauce, these are the oldtime recipes.

Spiced Pigs' Feet

6 pigs' feet
1 tsp. cloves
1 red pepper pod
1 tbs. paprika
2 cups vinegar or wine
salt and pepper to taste

2 bay leaves
1 tsp. dry mustard
1 tsp. celery seed
2 onions
pinch marjoram

Select young, tender pigs' feet. Have them split. Wash well, cover with cold, salted water, and soak. Drain. Place in a stew pot. Cover with cold water and cook about 1 hour. Add spices, vinegar, and onions. Simmer slowly until tender. Serve with red and green cabbage slaw.

Pigs' Feet in Tomato Sauce

6 med. size pigs' feet
3 large chopped onions
1 garlic clove
1 chopped green pepper
3 bay leaves

½ cup vinegar
salt, pepper and paprika to taste
3 stalks chopped celery and tops
2 red pepper pods
1 can tomato purée

Split pigs' feet in half; wash, rub with lemon juice; place in water to cover. Cook ½ hour. Add pepper, onions, garlic, celery and tops, vinegar and seasonings. When the water boils add tomato purée. Cook slowly until well done. Serve with hot potato salad.

and apt of ear, would learn them and then pass them on to their fellow
slaves in the fields. This process would be altogether oral, since the slaves
were not taught to read or write (save in exceptional cases) and their com-
munication with each other and with the outside world would of necessity
be the spoken word.

At cabin firesides, as before the great hearths in the big houses, the old
songs would be learned by the youngsters as part of their natural heritage—
along with the spirituals—to be handed down in the course of time to their
children and their children's children. Such a survival among the blacks
was remarkable—far more so than song-preservation among the whites who,
in many instances, kept the old ballads by writing them down in notebooks
and learning them from old broadsides or keepsake volumes, while the
Negroes had none of these visual aids but had to sing each song as they
learned it from hearing others sing the tunes and, to the best of their remembrance, repeat the lyrics. One would think that this would lead to a
degeneration of the songs, but strangely enough there are some instances
where the interpretations or new versions equalled and sometimes surpassed
the originals.

The adaptation of European traditional folk songs is perhaps best exemplified in the black variant of what has often been called the most familiar
and beloved of all ballads, *Barbara Allan*, also called *Barb'ry Allen*, and in
this version, *Barb-ree Allin*.* In one form or another, *Barbara Allan* is sung
wherever the English language is spoken. As far as this editor has been
able to ascertain, it was first published in *Pepys' Diary*, circa 1665, where it
was called "A Scottish Ballad," but how many decades or centuries it had
already been in existence at that time is not known. The variants occurring
in Europe today, from Italy to the Scandinavian countries, and those in
the United States, are many; and of all these it cannot be denied that the
Negro version is exquisite in its own right:

> In London town whar I was raised,
>   Dar war a youth a-dwellin';
> He fell in love wid a putty fair maid,
>   Her name war Barb-ree Allin.
>
> He co'ted her fo' seben long years;
>   She say she would not marry;
> Po' Willie went home an' war takin' sick,
>   His heart a-bleedin' heavy.

---

* *Barb-ree Allin*, by C. Alphonso Smith, in an article, "Ballads Surviving
in the United States," in the *Musical Quarterly*, January, 1916. Dr. Smith was
Professor of English at the United States Naval Academy at Annapolis,
Maryland.

He den sen' out a waitin' boy,
 Wid a note fo' Barb-ree Allin.
So close, ah, she read; so close, ah, she walk;
 "Go tell him I'm a-comin'."

She den step up into his room
 An' stood dar lookin' at him;
He stretch to her his tremblin' han's:
 "Oh, won't you say you lub me?"

"Seems you fo'got de odder day,
 When we was in de pahlor;
You drank a toas' to de odder gals,
 But none fo' Barb-ree Allin."

"Oh no I didn', my darlin' sweet,
 You know you are mistakin';
Ef I drank a toas' to de odder gals,
 'T war love fo' Barb-ree Allin.

"An' now I'm sick—so ve'y ve'y sick,
 An' on my deathbed lyin';
One kiss or two f'om yo' sweet lips,
 Would take away dis dyin'."

"Now dat's one kiss you will not git,
 Not ef yo' heart am breakin';
I cannot keep you f'om yo' death,
 So goodbye," said Barb-ree Allin.

He tu'n his po' face to de wall
 An' den begin a-cryin';
An' ev'y tear was fo' his love,
 Col'-hearted Barb-ree Allin.

She walked across de fiel's nex' day
 An' heerd de birds a-singin',
An' ev'y note dey seemed to say
 Was "Hard-hearted Barb-ree Allin."

"Oh fahdder, fahdder, dig-a-my grave,
 An' dig it long an' narrer;
My true love he done died today
 An' I mus' die tomorrer.

"Oh mudder, mudder, make-a-my shroud
An' make it long an' narrer;
Sweet Willie died of love fo' me
An' I mus' die tomorrer."

Sweet Willie war buried in de new chu'chyard,
An' Barb-ree Allin beside him.
Outen his grave sprang a putty red rose,
An' Barb-ree Allin's a brier.

Dey grew as high as de steeple top,
An' couldn't grow no higher;
An' den dey tied a true-love knot,
De sweet rose 'roun' de brier.

Barb-ree Allin is no isolated exception. Throughout the fabric of black folk songs is interwoven a skein of lovely sentiment expressed in vibrant beauty; a kind of soul-appeal that shuns pretention and evokes that which is noble and meaningful in our hearts. The element of Greek tragedy implicit in many of the love songs, despite their surface simplicity, is often quite complex. So, too, are the subtleties inherent in the spirituals in which the slaves prayed for the betterment of their brethren in the hereafter, although what they often meant was their betterment right here on earth.

While most of the folk songs institutionalized by American Negroes are in a serious vein, there remains an important body of humorous musical expression which has become classic in its field. Unfortunately, and to the detriment of scholarship, these songs have been ignored or have received inadequate attention from researchers who termed them "frivolous detractions from the agonies of the past"—as though it were possibly to deny the clear evidence that the blacks have a history rich in humor. Even then, it must be obvious to anyone making something more than a cursory study of the subject, that the Negro has long employed humor as a cloak to hide a serious motif. Some, of course, were sung "just for fun"—as in the dance and party songs. But whatever their category, many humorous songs must be considered as an adjunct to orthodox history in that they portray the social customs of a particular era as well as shed light on actual historical events and personalities.

The folk songs which follow have been classified into three sections: *Epic Ballads and Other Traditional Folk Songs, Dance Songs or Reels,* and *Songs About Animals.* The selections encompass a period from slave days to the advent of jazz. This Encyclopedia, as has been stated elsewhere in this volume, is necessarily confined to folk *humor,* and consequently other categories have been omitted. The omissions include spirituals, gospels, work and love songs, "hollers" and the blues, to name but a few.

The ballad of John Henry can hardly be termed humorous, but it is an example of the work-song—perhaps the finest example. It has been included in this anthology only because it illustrates the *epic* ballad and to serve as sort of a model for the humorous ballads which follow. *Mr. Froggie Went A-Courtin'* may also be termed an epic ballad, and *The Escape of Gabriel Prosser* is most certainly in that category.

The very act of collecting and preparing these songs which stemmed from the emotional depths of a people who had precious little to laugh about, but which helped make their darker hours a little more bearable, has been a gladsome adventure for this editor. Perhaps the reader will react in the same joyful manner and, in turn, be stimulated to embark on a pleasant and rewarding journey into the broader spectrum of Negro folk music, of which this collection is a small but significant part.

PART ONE

EPIC BALLADS AND OTHER FOLK SONGS

John Henry*

The Negro's work songs covered many subjects, but apparently he was most fond of singing about men who were heroes in his eyes; and the hero who gripped his imagination more than any other was the bigger-than-life John Henry.

Folklorists are mainly agreed that John Henry was a tall, muscular, and handsome black man employed as a steel-driver on the Chesapeake and Ohio railroad. At the time of his epic demise he was engaged in the construction of the Big Ten tunnel in West Virginia, according to one of the famous stories about him. He was the most renowned steel driver and driller of all the workers there, and the hammer he used was reportedly much larger and heavier than that used by the other "drivers." The "steel driver" was the highest class of workman on the project and, justly, he was a very proud person.

This narrative ballad, which relates John Henry's exploits and untimely fate, is essentially the story of a proud and stubborn man pitted against the onslaught of mechanization—a condition that is relative to the plight of many today. John Henry was a "steel-drivin' man"—that is, he worked with sledge-hammer and hand-drill. Resenting the intrusion of machines to compete with his demonstrated prowess, the steam drill especially aroused his

* *John Henry,* from *The American Songbag,* copyright 1927 by Harcourt, Brace, Inc.

ire and contempt. He challenged the manufacturer's agent to an all-day drilling contest between himself and the steam-driller.

The contest was a grim and heroic one, and out of it John Henry and his hammer emerged immortal. At the close of the contest it was found that John Henry had drilled eighteen inches deeper than the steam drill—but he fell dead as he laid down his triumphant hammer.

Unlike the legendary Paul Bunyan of lumberjack fame, John Henry is an actual, if bigger-than-life, historical figure. True enough, Professor Guy B. Johnson, of the University of North Carolina, undertook to trace the origins of the story surrounding the folk hero, the results of which were published in his book, *John Henry,* and which expressed doubts as to his existence. But Professor John Harrington Cox, in his *Folk Songs of the South,* published by the Harvard University Press in 1924, yielded valuable evidence that John Henry had indeed lived, and Professor Cox was fortunate enough to find a photograph of the folk hero to support his contention.

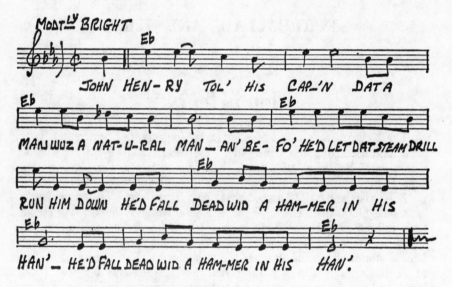

John Henry tol' his cap'n,
Dat a man wuz a natural man,
An' befo' he'd let dat steam drill run him down,
He'd fall dead wi da hammer in his han',
He'd fall dead wid a hammer in his han'.

Cap'n he sez to John Henry:
"Gonna bring me a steam drill 'roun';
Take that steam drill out on the job,
Gonna whop that steel on down,
Gonna whop that steel on down."

John Henry sez to his cap'n:
"Send me a twelve-poun' hammer aroun',
A twelve poun' hammer wid a fo'-foot handle,
An' I beat yo' steam drill down,
An' I beat yo' steam drill down."

John Henry sez to his shaker:
"Niggah, why don' you sing?
I'm throwin' twelve poun' from my hips on down,
Jes' lissen to de col' steel ring,
Jes' lissen to de col' steel ring!"

John Henry went down de railroad
Wid a twelve-poun' hammer by his side,
He walked down the track but he didn' come back,
'Cause he laid down his hammer an' he died,
'Cause he laid down his hammer an' he died.

John Henry hammered in de mountains,
De mountains wuz so high,
De las' words I heard de po' boy say:
"Gimme a cool drink o' watah fo' I die,
Gimme a cool drink o' watah fo' I die!"

John Henry had a little baby,
Hel' him in de palm of his han'.
De las' words I heard de po' boy say:
"Son' yo're gonna be a steel-drivin' man;
Son, yo're gonna be a steel-drivin' man!"

John Henry had a 'ooman,
De dress she wo' wuz blue.
De las' words I heard de po' gal say:
"John Henry, I bin true to you."

John Henry had a li'l 'ooman,
De dress she wo' wuz brown.
De las' words I heard de po' gal say:
"I'm goin' wheah mah man went down!"

John Henry had anothah 'ooman,
De dress she wo' wuz red.
De las' words I heard de po' gal say:
"I'm goin' wheah mah man drapt daid;
I'm goin' wheah mah man drapt daid!"

John Henry had a li'l 'ooman,
Her name wuz Polly Ann.
On de day John Henry he drapt daid
Polly Ann hammered steel like a man;
Polly Ann hammered steel like a man.

Wheah did you git dat dress?
Wheah did you git dose shoes so fine?
Got dat dress f'm off a railroad man,
An' shoes f'm a driver in a mine,
An' shoes f'm a driver in a mine.

The Escape of Gabriel Prosser

Gabriel Prosser lives in the memory of black Americans as a true-to-life folk hero who, had he succeeded, may well have changed the tide of history for his enslaved brothers and sisters, as well as for white America itself. Born around 1775, he was a coachman belonging to Thomas Prosser of Henrico County, Virginia. The revolt which Gabriel Prosser organized was remarkable not only for its organization, but also for the large numbers of people who were to have taken part in it. The environs of Richmond, Virginia, chosen as the site of the rebellion, had some 32,000 slaves, but only 8,000 whites, including a number of Frenchmen and Quaker groups whom Prosser felt would be sympathetic to his cause. Eventually, he hoped that Virginia's remaining 300,000 slaves would follow his lead and take over the entire state. A severe rainstorm made it impossible for most of his followers to assemble at the appointed rendezvous at the Old Brook Swamp outside of Richmond, and before they could reassemble Prosser was betrayed by two slaves. Most of those implicated, some one thousand slaves, were rounded up and hanged. Prosser himself was captured in the hold of a schooner when it docked at Norfolk after a trip from Richmond. Brought back in chains, he refused to divulge any information on the nature of his plans or on the identities of his compatriots, and on October 7, 1800, at the age of 24, he was hanged.

As with so many folk heroes, legends about Gabriel Prosser found their way into the people's musical lore. In the narrative ballad, *The Escape of Gabriel Prosser*, it is claimed that Prosser was not hanged at all but was rescued by a teenaged slave, known only as Billy. The melody and lyrics closely resemble *Old John Webb*, another "escape" ballad popular about 1730.

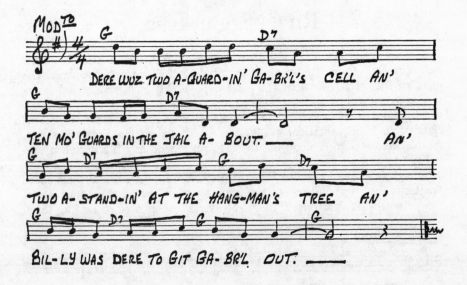

Dere wuz two a-guardin' Gabr'l's cell
An' ten mo' guards in the jail about;
An' two a-standin' at the hangman's tree,
An' Billy wuz dere to git Gabr'l out.

Chorus

Billy bus' chains an' Billy bus' bolts
An' Billy bus' all dat's in his way;
Ontwell he come to Gabr'l's do'
An' he bus' dat too, right silently.

Dere wuz musket shot an' musket balls
Betwix' his neckbone an' his knee;
But Billy took Gabr'l up in his arms,
An' he carried him away right manfully.

Dey mounted a hoss an' away dey went,
Ten miles off f'om dat hangin' tree;
Ontwell dey stop whar de river bent,
An' dar dey rested happily.

An' den dey called fo' a vic'try dance,
An' de crowd dey all danced merrily;
An' de bes' dancer 'mongst dem all
Wuz Gabr'l Prosser who wuz jes' sot free!

Run, Nigger, Run

Among the oldest of the slave songs, *Run, Nigger, Run* is also one of the most authentic to be handed down from pre-Civil War plantation days. The gnawing fear of Southern whites was the possibility of a widespread insurrection—a fear not without foundation, considering the bloody uprisings which began as early as 1663 in Gloucester, Virginia.* In order to prevent clandestine inter-plantation meetings, and also to capture runaway slaves, patrols were stationed along the roads to apprehend any black person who did not have a pass which permitted him to leave the plantation, especially after nightfall. The "patrollers," many of whom were quite brutal, were called "patter-rollers" by the slaves. The amusing songs which were sung about the patter-rollers dealt mostly with the slaves' experiences in eluding them.

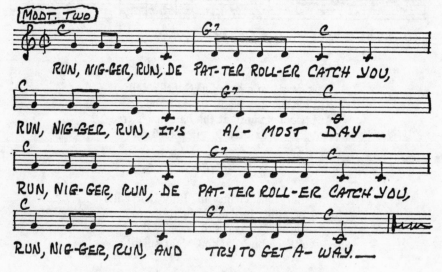

Run, nigger, run; de patter-roller catch you;
Run, nigger, run; it's almost day.
Run, nigger, run; de patter-roller catch you;
Run, nigger, run, and try to get away.

---

* The greatest slave revolt in U.S. history occurred in Southampton County, Virginia, in 1831, when Nat Turner led a rebellion in which 60 whites were killed and the entire South was thrown into a panic. This precipitated the enactment of the Black Codes in several states which denied the slaves whatever few advantages they may have had. The abortive Turner rebellion resulted in the prohibition of all educational facilities involving slaves, the suspension of the practice of manumission by nearly all plantation owners, the prohibition against reading anything not previously censored by the whites, and the stringent observance of all other codes designed to keep the black man "in his place." Nat Turner was captured on October 30, 1831, and hanged in Jerusalem, Virginia, twelve days later.

Dis nigger run, he run his best,
Stuck his head in a hornet's nest,
Jumped de fence and run fru de paster,
White man run, but nigger run faster.

From Louisiana we have these stanzas:

Run, nigger, run; de patter-roller'll catch you;
Run, nigger, run; it's almost day.
Dat nigger run, dat nigger flew,
Dat nigger lost his Sunday shoe.

Run, nigger, run; de patter-roller'll catch you;
Run, nigger, run, and try to get away.
Dat nigger run, dat nigger flew,
Dat nigger tore his shirt in two.

Massa Had a Yaller Gal

From Kentucky, South Carolina and Louisiana come these variants of a slavery-time song still current in some parts of the South. The first version comes from the Shelbyville area of Kentucky.

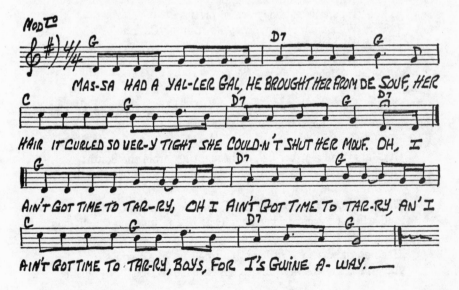

MAS-SA HAD A YAL-LER GAL, HE BROUGHT HER FROM DE SOUF, HER HAIR IT CURLED SO VER-Y TIGHT SHE COULD-N'T SHUT HER MOUF. OH, I AIN'T GOT TIME TO TAR-RY, OH I AIN'T GOT TIME TO TAR-RY, AN' I AIN'T GOT TIME TO TAR-RY, BOYS, FOR I'S GWINE A-WAY.

Massa had a yaller gal, he brought her from de Souf;
Her hair it curled so very tight she couldn't shut her mouf.

Chorus

Oh I ain't got time to tarry, Oh I ain't got time to tarry,
An' I ain't got time to tarry, boys, for I's gwine away.

He took her to de tailor, to have her mouf made small;
She swallowed up de tailor, tailorshop an' all.

Chorus

Massa had no hooks or nails, or anything like that;
So on this darkey's nose he used to hang his hat.

Chorus

The variant emanating from the Charleston area of South Carolina was
often sung as a serenade to the accompaniment of the banjo and guitar.

Ol' Mars'er had a pretty yaller gal, he bought her fum de Souf;
Her hair it curled so berry tight she couldn't shet her mouf.

Chorus

Way down in Mississippi
Where de gals dey are so pretty,
W'at a happy time, way down in ol' Car'line!
Dis darkey fell in love
Wid a han'some yaller Dinah.
Higho—higho—higho!

The following lyrics are probably most popular. There is no chorus in
this version which stems from New Orleans.

Ol' Mars'r had a yaller gal, he brought her from the South;
Her hair it curled so very tight she couldn't shut her mouth.

Her eyes they were so very small, they both ran into one,
And when a fly got in her eye, 'twas like a June-bug in the sun.

Her nose it was so very long, it turned up like a squash,
And when she got her dander up, it made me laugh, by gosh!

Ol' Mars'r had no hooks or nails, nor anything like that;
So on this darling's nose he used to hang his coat and hat.

He took her to the tailor shop to have her mouth made small;
The lady took in one big breath and swallowed tailor and all.

Old Jesse

This pre-Civil War slave song was a plantation favorite in the area of
Evergreen, Alabama.

One cold an' frosty mornin', just as de sun did riz,
De possum roared, de raccoon howled, 'cause he begun to friz.
He drew hisse'f up in a knot, wid his knees up to his chin,
An' ev'ything had to cl'ar de track when he stretched out agin.

Chorus

Old Jesse was a gemman,
Among de olden times.

Nigger neber went to free school, nor any odder college,
An' all de white folks wonder whar dat nigger got his knowledge.
He chawed up all de Bible an' den spat out de Scripter,
An' when he 'gin to arger strong, he were a snortin' ripter!

Chorus

Nigger used to pick de banjo, he play so berry well (strong?);
He allus play dat good ol' tune, "So Go It While You're Young."
He play so clear, he play so loud, he skeered de pigs an' goats;
He allus tuck a pint ob yeast to raise his highest notes.

Chorus

Hesh, Little Baby

This very sweet lullabye has no single author, as is true of many other folk songs. It was improvised and crooned by generations of young black mothers to their children during slavery times and in the period following emancipation. Its maternal tenderness and the playful approach of its gentle concept account for its acceptance in all parts of the English speaking world. *Hesh, Little Baby* is distinctive in that it was the product of a matriarchal society, yet we see that the mother tells her baby that it is *Papa* who will provide the gifts.

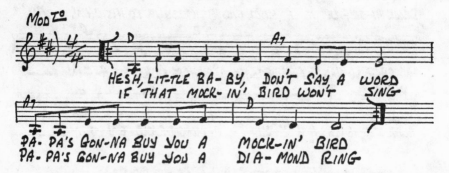

Hesh, little baby, don't say a word,
Papa's gonna buy you a mockin'bird.

If that mockin'bird won't sing,
Papa's gonna buy you a diamond ring.

If that diamond ring turns brass,
Papa's gonna buy you a lookin' glass.

If that lookin' glass gits broke,
Papa's gonna buy you a horse and yoke.

If that horse and yoke fall over,
Papa's gonna buy you a dog named Rover.

And if that dog named Rover won't bark,
Papa's gonna buy you a horse and cart.

If that horse and cart don't pull,
Papa's gonna buy you a baby bull.

And if that baby bull falls down,
You're still the cutest little baby in town.

Careless Love

Careless Love, originally sung by the Negro workers on the Ohio River packet boats, offers the earliest suggestion of the blues tradition that was to follow almost a century later.

Chorus

Love, o love, o careless love,
Love, o love, o careless love,
Love, o love, o careless love,
Cain't ya see whut love hez done to me?

I love my mammy an' my pappy too.
I love my mammy an' my pappy too.
I love my mammy an' my pappy too;
Gonna leave 'em both an' go wid you.

Chorus

It's on dis railroad track I stan'.
It's on dis railroad track I stan'.
It's on dis railroad track I stan';
An' I know I'm gonna kill a railroad man.

He stole my darlin' Mary Ann,
He stole my darlin' Mary Ann,
He stole my darlin' Mary Ann;
An' I'm gonna kill dat railroad man.

Chorus

Railroad Bill

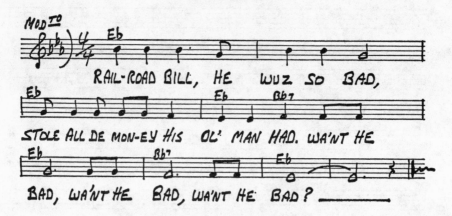

Railroad Bill, he wuz so bad,
Stole all de money his ol' man had.
Wa'nt he bad, wa'nt he bad, wa'nt he bad?

Railroad Bill, he went down Souf,
Shot all de teef outen a constable's mouf.
Wa'nt he bad, wa'nt he bad, wa'nt he bad?

Railroad Bill, he sot on a fence,
Called his gal a brownskin wench,
Wa'nt he bad, wa'nt he bad, wa'nt he bad?

Railroad Bill run his train so fas',
Couldn't see de postes as dey passed.
Wa'nt he fas', wa'nt he fas', wa'nt he fas'?

Lay Ten Dollahs Down

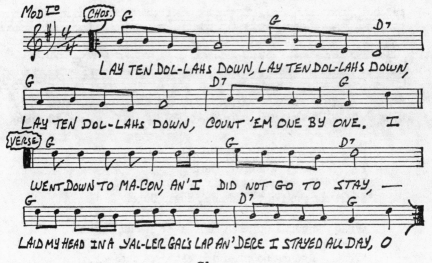

Chorus

Lay ten dollahs down, lay ten dollahs down,
Lay ten dollahs down, count 'em one by one.

I went down to Macon, an' I did not go to stay;
Laid my head in a yaller gal's lap an' dere I stayed all day, O

Chorus

I went down to Clinton, an' I did not go to stay;
Laid my head in a black gal's lap an' dere I stayed all day, O

Chorus

June Bug has a golden wing, lightning bug has a flame;
Bedbug has no wings at all, but he gits dere jes' de same, O

Chorus

I Got a House in Baltimo'

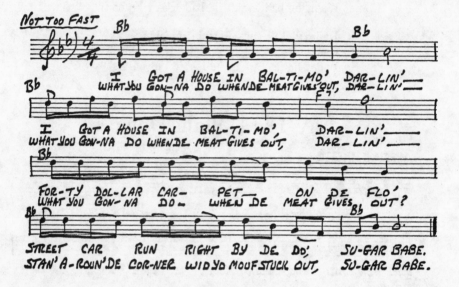

I got a house in Baltimo', Darlin',
I got a house in Baltimo', Darlin',
Forty dollar carpet on de flo',
Street car run right by de do', Sugar Babe.

What you gonna do when de meat gives out, Darlin'?
What you gonna do when de meat gives out, Darlin'?
What you gonna do when de meat gives out?
Stan' aroun' de corner wid yo' mouf stuck out, Sugar Babe.

What you gonna do when de love's all gone, Darlin'?
What you gonna do when de love's all gone, Darlin'?
What you gonna do when de love's all gone?
Stan' aroun' de corner wid a great big stone, Sugar Babe.

Wake Me

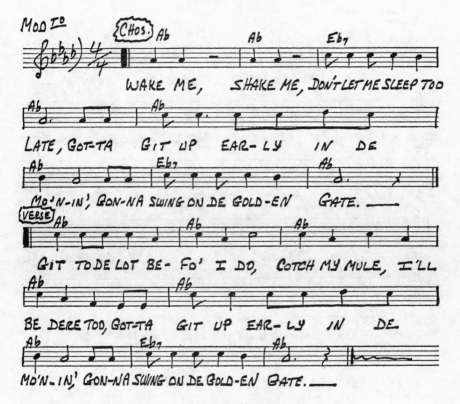

Wake me, shake me, don't let me sleep too late;
Gotta git up early in de mo'nin',
Gonna swing on de Golden Gate.

Git to de lot befo' I do,
Cotch my mule, I'll be dere too;
Dis ol' 'gittin' up jes' 'fo' day,
Nevuh did like dat t'ing no way.

Chorus

Gotta git up early in de mo'nin',
Gonna swing on de Golden Gate.

Got No Money

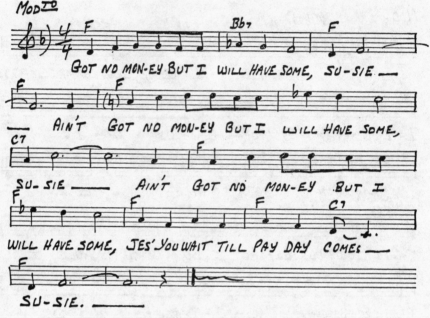

Got no money, but I will have some, Susie;
Ain't got no money but I will have some, Susie;
Ain't got no money but I will have some,
Jes' you wait till pay day comes, Susie.

Daddy sent me to plant a little cotton, Susie;
O Daddy sent me to plant a little cotton, Susie;
O Daddy sent me to plant a little cotton,
Sowed the seed but the seed was rotten, Susie.

PART TWO

DANCE SONGS OR REELS

Juba

The melody of *Juba* is so elemental it is composed of only two notes, yet it was one of the best known of the oldtime "jigs" or short-step dance tunes. It is believed to be based on an old African melody and, according to the slaves, Juba was an old African ghost.

Ole Aunt Kate, which follows, seems to be an elaboration of *Juba,* with its similar tune, although comprising more than two notes. Both are wholly Negro in conception and expression.

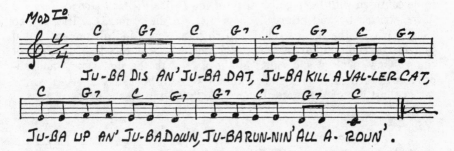

Juba dis an' Juba dat,
Juba kill a yaller cat;
Juba up an' Juba down,
Juba runnin' all aroun'.
       Jump Juba! (optional)

Ole Aunt Kate

Ole Aunt Kate she bake de cake,
She bake hit 'hine de garden gate;
She sif' de meal, she gimme de dus',
She bake de bread, she gimme de crus',
She eat de meat, she gimme de skin,
An' dat's de way she tuck me in.

'Tain't Gwine Rain No Mo'

'Tain't Gwine Rain No Mo' is yet another famous old dance-song not to be confused with the popular ditty of the 1920's, *It Ain't Gonna Rain No More,* written by and primarily for whites. In the former, the leader, who usually played the fiddle, would also sing the song, and all present would join in. In addition to the communal singing, there was also dancing, of course. One couple would enter on the floor with the first stanza and another with each succeeding stanza, till all were in the dance.

The last line of the chorus is for all to "steal up" in the dance.

Ole cow died at the mouth of the branch,
  'Tain't gwine rain no mo'.
The buzzards had a public dance,
  'Tain't gwine rain no mo'.

Chorus

'Tain't gwine rain,
'Tain't gwine snow,
'Tain't gwine rain no mo';
Steal up, ev'ybody,
'Tain't gwine rain no mo'.

What did the blackbird say to the crow?
  'Tain't gwine rain no mo'.
'Tain't gwine hail an' 'tain't gwine snow,
  'Tain't gwine rain no mo'.

Chorus

Gather corn in a beegum hat,
  'Tain't gwine rain no mo';
Ole massa grumble ef you eat much of that,
  'Tain't gwine rain no mo'.

Chorus

Two, two, and round up four,
  'Tain't gwine rain no mo';
Two, two, and round up four,
  'Tain't gwine rain no mo'.

                                        Chorus

Six, two, and round up four,
  'Tain't gwine rain no mo';
Six, two, an' round up four,
  'Tain't gwine rain no mo'.

                                        Chorus

A Texas version contains these verses:

Rabbit skipped de garden gate,
  'Tain't gwine rain no mo';
Picked a pea and pulled his freight,
  'Tain't gwine rain no mo'.

                    Chorus

Oh, ladies, swing yo' heel an' toe,
  'Tain't gwine rain no mo';
'Tain't gwine sleet, 'tain't gwine snow,
  'Tain't gwine rain no mo'.

Rabbit et a turnip top,
  'Tain't gwine rain no mo';
He went of a-hippity-hop,
  'Tain't gwine rain no mo'.

                                        Chorus

Rabbit hidin' 'hine a pine,
  'Tain't gwine rain no mo';
Had one eye shut an' t'other eye bline,
  'Tain't gwine rain no mo'.

                                        Chorus

Bake them biscuits good an' brown,
  'Tain't gwine rain no mo';
Swing yo' ladies roun' an' roun',
  'Tain't gwine rain no mo'.

Buffalo Gals

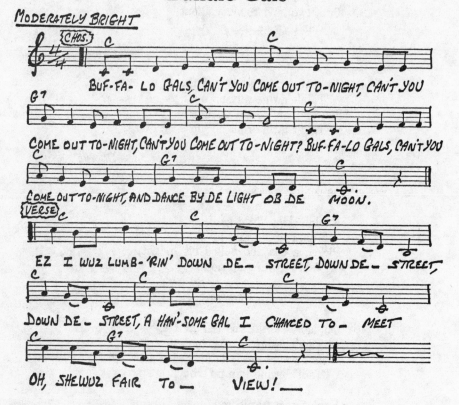

Ez I wuz lumbrin' down de street,
Down de street, down de street,
A han'some gal I chanced to meet,
Oh, she wuz fair to view!

Chorus

Buffalo gals, can't you come out tonight,
Can't you come out tonight,
Can't you come out tonight?
Buffalo gals, can't you come out tonight,
And dance by de light ob de moon?

I axed her would she hab some talk,
Hab some talk, hab some talk.
Her feet covered up de whole sidewalk,
As she stood close by me.

Chorus

I axed her would she hab a dance,
Hab a dance, hab a dance.
I thought dat I might get a chance,
To shake a foot wid her.

Chorus

I'd like to make dat gal my wife,
Gal my wife, gal my wife.
I'd be happy all my life
If I had her by me.

Chorus

Variations of *Buffalo Gal* exist in different parts of the country, usually adapted to local references. Among them is the lilting *Louisiana Gal*. The melody has been slightly altered so that the tune has a merrier air, and the lyrics are not as dialectal as *Buffalo Gal*, but the amusing connotations and romantic imagery remain intact.

Oh, Louisiana gal, won't you come out tonight,
Won't you come out tonight,
Won't you come out tonight?
Louisiana Gal, won't you come out tonight,
And dance by the light of the moon?

Oh, yaller gal, won't you come out tonight,
Won't you come out tonight,
Won't you come out tonight?
Oh, yaller gal, won't you come out tonight,
And dance by the light of the moon?

I'll give you a dollar if you'll come out tonight,
If you'll come out tonight,
If you'll come out tonight;
I'll give you a dollar if you'll come out tonight,
And dance by the light of the moon.

A Texas variant adds this final stanza:

I danced with a gal with a hole in her stockin',
An' her heel kep' a-rockin',
An' her heel kep' a-rockin';
I danced with a gal with a hole in her stockin',
We danced by the light of the moon.

PART THREE

SONGS ABOUT ANIMALS

Mr. Froggie Went A-Courtin'

Mr. Froggie Went A-Courtin' is an ancient and one of the most popular narrative animal tales for children in the English language. It was first published in a Scottish broadside in 1549 as *The Frog Came to the Myl Dur*, and in 1580 it was registered as *A Moste Strange Weddinge of the Frogge and the Mouse.**

Prior to emancipation, the black versions were popular among the slaves and freedmen of Texas, Georgia, South Carolina, Kentucky and, to a somewhat lesser degree, in Mississippi and Alabama (although, of course, it was sung elsewhere). In Louisiana, however, it did not gain wide acceptance because of the French heritage of that state. The song was brought to this country by the English and Scots, and it was from them that the house servant (a transparent euphemism for the household slave) learned the words and melody. In turn, he taught them to the field hands who comprised most of the slave population of the South. Today nearly all folk singers, white and black alike, sing the versions popularized by the slaves who gave it a distinctive flavor that was at once black and uniquely American.

The Kentucky version, which seems to have most captured the imagination of the black children (and their parents) as far back as 150 years ago, and which has endured through time, is presented first.

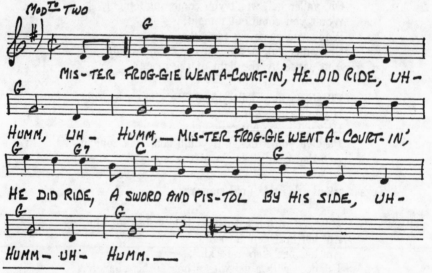

MIS-TER FROG-GIE WENT A-COURT-IN', HE DID RIDE, UH-
HUMM, UH- HUMM, — MIS-TER FROG-GIE WENT A-COURT-IN',
HE DID RIDE, A SWORD AND PIS-TOL BY HIS SIDE, UH-
HUMM- UH- HUMM.

---

* *Journal of American Folklore*, XXV, p. 394.

ROAST TURKEY

The Indians may have introduced turkey to the Pilgrims, but it was the Blacks who developed the fine art of its preparation. This 19th century recipe seems to have originated in Virginia, spreading into the more southerly states before it was adopted by northerners.

Roast Turkey—Old-Fashioned Country Style

Turkey, 12 to 15 lbs.
1 tablespoon salt
1 tablespoon paprika

2 tablespoons bacon fat
1 teaspoon garlic salt
½ teaspoon pepper

Rinse turkey with cold water, and pat dry. Rub inside and out with salt and pepper. Fill with your favorite dressing. Neck cavity may be filled with stuffing, if desired. (Never stuff turkey tightly—allow for expansion.) Sew or close with skewers. Fold wing tips under back.

Rub turkey well with bacon fat, salt, pepper, paprika, and garlic salt. Cover well with a clean white cloth which has been dipped in melted fat or milk. Roast slowly, uncovered, making sure cloth stays damp at oven temperature, 300°. Allow 20 minutes per pound. Baste from time to time with drippings, turning turkey completely to brown on all sides. Cloth may be removed during the last half hour, so the turkey skin will be brown and crisp.

Boil giblets and neck with celery tips, onions and seasonings to make gravy. Allow ½ to ¾ lb. per person.

Mister Froggie went a-courtin', he did ride, uh-humm, uh-humm!
Mister Froggie went a-courtin', he did ride,
A sword and pistol by his side, uh-humm, uh-humm!

He rode up to Miss Mouse's hall, uh-humm, uh-humm!
He rode up to Miss Mouse's hall,
Long and loudly did he call, uh-humm, uh-humm!

Said he, "Miss Mouse, are you within?" uh-humm, uh-humm!
Said he, "Miss Mouse are you within?"
"Oh, yes, kind sir, I sit and spin," uh-humm, uh-humm!

He took Miss Mousie on his knee, uh-humm, uh-humm!
He took Miss Mousie on his knee,
Said he, "Miss Mouse, will you marry me?" uh-humm, uh-humm!

Miss Mousie blushed and she hung down her head, uh-humm, uh-humm!
Miss Mousie blushed and she hung down her head.
"You'll have to ask Uncle Rat," she said, uh-humm, uh-humm!

Uncle Rat laughed and shook his fat sides, uh-humm, uh-humm!
Uncle Rat laughed and shook his fat sides,
To think his niece would be a bride, uh-humm, uh-humm!

Where shall the wedding supper be? uh-humm, uh-humm!
Where shall the wedding supper be?
Way down yonder in a hollow tree, uh-humm, uh-humm!

What shall the wedding supper be? uh-humm, uh-humm!
What shall the wedding supper be?
Two green beans and a black-eyed pea, uh-humm, uh-humm!

The first that came was a possum frail, uh-humm, uh-humm!
The first that came was a possum frail,
A-totin' his house upon his tail, uh-humm, uh-humm.

The next that came was a bumberly bee, uh-humm, uh-humm!
The next that came was a bumberly bee,
Bringing his fiddle upon his knee, uh-humm, uh-humm!

The next that came was a broken-backed flea, uh-humm, uh-humm!
The next that came was a broken-backed flea
To dance a jog with the bumberly bee, uh-humm, uh-humm!

The next that came was an old grey cat, uh-humm, uh-humm!
The next that came was an old grey cat,
She swallowed the mouse and ate up the rat, uh-humm, uh-humm!

Mister Frog went a-hopping over the brook, uh-humm, uh-humm!
Mr. Frog went a-hopping over the brook,
A lily-white duck came and gobbled him up, uh-humm, uh-humm!

The tragic fate that befell Mister Frog is not lessened in the Texas version, a favorite of the 19th-century blacks in the Waco area:

Frog went a-courtin', he did ride, uh-humm!
Frog went a-courtin', he did ride,
Sword and pistol by his side, uh-humm!

Rode up to Lady Mouse's hall, uh-humm!
Rode up to Lady Mouse's hall,
Gave a loud knock and gave a loud call, uh-humm.

Lady Mouse come a-tripping down, uh-humm!
Lady Mouse come a tripping down,
Green glass slippers an' a silver gown, uh-humm!

Froggie knelt at Mousie's knee, uh-humm!
Froggie knelt at Mousie's knee,
Said, "Pray, Miss Mouse, will you marry me?" uh-humm!

"Not without Uncle Rat's consent," uh-humm!
"Not without Uncle Rat's consent
Would I marry the pres-eye-dent," uh-humm!

Uncle Rat he went downtown, uh-humm!
Uncle Rat he went downtown
To buy his niece a wedding gown, uh-humm!

Where shall the wedding supper be? uh-humm!
Where shall the wedding supper be?
Way down yonder in a hollow tree, uh-humm!

First come in was little seed tick, uh-humm!
First come in was little seed tick,
Walkin' wid a hick'ry stick, uh-humm!

Next come in was a bumberly bee, uh-humm!
Next come in was a bumberly bee,
To help Miss Mouse po' out the tea, uh-humm!

Next come in was a big black snake, uh-humm!
Next come in was a big black snake,
In his mouth was a wedding cake, uh-humm!

Next come in was Uncle Rat, uh-humm!
Next come in was Uncle Rat,
With some apples in his hat, uh-humm!

What shall the wedding supper be? uh-humm!
What shall the wedding supper be?
Catnip broth and dogwood tree, uh-humm!

Then Frog come a-swimmin' over the lake, uh-humm!
Then Frog come a-swimmin' over the lake,
He got swallowed by a big black snake, uh-humm!

Mistuh Boll Weevil

While it has been said that this song, also known as *The Boll Weevil* (without the "Mistuh") and *The Ballad of the Boll Weevil*, was first composed in Merivale, Mississippi, it is more likely that it was a product of communal authorship.* The age and general origin of this song can be estimated by its subject matter. Obviously, it originated in a cotton-growing state at or near to the Mexican border, and it could not have been composed, communally or otherwise, before the insect crossed the Rio Grande in 1895 and began its depradations in Texas.

The boll weevil has assumed the legendary status of a sort of Robin Hood of the cotton patch. He is an outlaw, hunted in every field, apparently possessing superhuman powers of resistance to hardship, exposure and attack. Like Brer Rabbit, he is credited with extraordinary cunning which he uses to outwit and flout man despite all human attacks upon him. Thus, despite the damage properly attributed to him, he has been surrounded by so many romantic motifs that he has become one of the heroes of American balladry.

Literally hundreds of verses have been composed which describe the boll weevil's exploits. The following are a composite of those associated with the early black sharecroppers of Texas.

---

* John A. Lomax, in the *Journal of American Folklore*, Vol. XXVIII: "*The Ballad of the Boll Weevil* is absolutely known to have been composed by groups of people whose community life made their thinking similar."

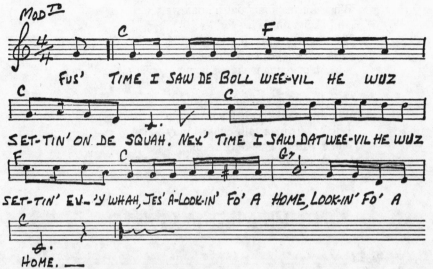

FUS' TIME I SAW DE BOLL WEE-VIL HE WUZ SET-TIN' ON DE SQUAH. NEX' TIME I SAW DAT WEE-VIL HE WUZ SET-TIN' EV-'Y WHAH, JES' A-LOOK-IN' FO' A HOME, LOOK-IN' FO' A HOME. ——

Recitation (Not usually sung)

Oh, have you heerd de lates',
De lates' all yo' own?
All about de boll weevil
Whut made me lose mah home?

Fus' time Ah saw de boll weevil,
He wuz settin' on de squah.
Nex' time Ah saw dat weevil
He wuz settin' ev'ywhah,
    Jes' a-lookin' fo' a home—lookin' fo' a home!

Fahmah say to de weevil,
"Ah'm gonna th'ow you in de red hot sand."
Weevil say to de fahmah,
"Ah'll stan' it like a man.
    Ah'll have a home, Ah'll have a home!"

Fiel' han' say to de weevil,
"Whut makes yo' haid so raid?"
Weevil say to de fiel' han',
"It's a wondah Ah ain't daid,
    Lookin' fo' a home—lookin' fo' a home!"

Says de Cap'n to de Mistis,
"Whut you think ob dat?
Dis boll weevil done made a nes'
Inside mah Sunday hat;
    He made a home—he made a home!"

When Ah fus' foun' dat li'l boll weevil,
Ah put 'im on de ice-col' ice.
But dat weevil, he jes' laugh an' say,
"Dis am mighty cool an' nice,
    Ah'm gonna make dis home—gonna make dis home!"

Now if anybody should ax you
Who it wuz dat writ dis song,
Tell 'em 'twuz a tall, dahk skinny fellah
Wid a pair o' blue-duckins on,
    A-lookin' fo' a home—jes' lookin' fo' a home!

Charleston Gals*

* *Charleston Gals* was published in *Slave Songs of the United States*, in 1867. The song was already so old at the time that it had no tradition of authorship. It may be a combination of fragments from various Negro folksongs of early origin.

As I walked down the new-cut road,
I met the tap and then the toad,*
The toad commenced to whistle and sing,
And the possum cut the pigeon's wing.†

Along came an old man riding by;
"Old man, if you don't mind, your horse will die."
"If he dies, I'll tan his skin,
And if he lives, I'll ride agin."

Hi-ho, for Charleston gals,
Charleston gals are the gals for me.

A related song is *Turkey in the Straw*, itself a parody of *Old Zip Coon*, introduced at the Bowery Theatre in New York in 1834. This is a classic example of a popular tune as the source of a true folk song.

As I come down the new-cut road,
I met Mr. Frog and I met Miss Toad,
And every time Miss Toad would sing,
The old bullfrog cut a pigeon wing.

Chorus

Turkey in the hay pile,
Turkey in the straw,
Turkey in the hay pile,
Turkey in the straw;
Rake 'em up, shake 'em up
Anyway at all;
Turkey in the hay stack,
Turkey in the straw.

I went to milk, and I didn't know how;
I milked a goat instead of a cow.
A monkey settin' on a pile of straw,
Kep' winkin' his eye at his mother-in-law.

Chorus

---

* A distortion by the white recorders who misunderstood "terrapin and the toad" to mean "tap and the toad." It was corrected in later versions.

† Another error due to misunderstanding of the slave's dialect by white folklorists. It should read "pigeon wing," not "pigeon's wing." No actual bird is referred to here, but a characteristic dance movement unique to the slaves.

Well, I met a catfish comin' down the stream;
Says Mister Catfish, "What do you mean?"
I caught Mister Catfish by the snout,
And turned Mister Catfish wrong side out.

Chorus

Well, I come to a river and I couldn't get across,
And I paid five dollars for an old blind hoss;
He wouldn't go ahead and he wouldn't stand still,
He went up and down like an old sawmill.

Chorus

As I was a-goin' down the road,
A tired team and a heavy load,
I cracked my whip and the leader sprung,
The old mare broke the wagon tongue.

Chorus

More authentic is *Picayune Butler*, sung by the slaves on the old plantations of Virginia, particularly in the Richmond area.* In all probability, however, the song originated in Mississippi, where the town of Picayune is located.

As I wuz walkin' 'long de new-cut road,
I met a tarapin an' a toad;
Ebery time de toad would spring,
De tarapin cut de pigeon-wing.

Refrain

Picayune Butler,
Picayune Butler,
Is she comin' in town?

My ole mistis promised me,
When she died she'd set me free.
She lived so long, she died so po',
She lef' ol' Sambo pullin' at de hoe.

---

* *On the Trail of Negro Folk Songs*, Dorothy Scarborough, Harvard University Press, 1925.

Ole Marse John

(Oh Mou'nah, You Shall Be Free)

Ole Marse John come ridin' by;
"Say, Marse John, dat mule's gwine tuh die!
Ef he do I'll tan his skin,
And ef he don't I'll ride him again."

Chorus

Oh, Mou'nah, you shall be free;
Yes, Mou'nah, you shall be free,
When de good Lawd sets you free.

Standin' on de co'nah, wa'n't doin' no hahm;
Up come a p'liceman, grab me by de ahm;
Rang a little whistle, blew a little bell;
Heah come de p'trol wagon, runnin' like hell.

Chorus

> Standin' in de chicken-house on my knees,
> Thought I heerd a chicken sneeze.
> Sneezed so hahd wid de whoopin' cough,
> Sneezed his head an' tail right off.

Chorus

> My old mistis promised me
> When she died she'd set me free.
> She lived so long, she died so po',
> She lef' Ol' Sambo pullin' at de hoe.

The reader will note that the last verse corresponds to that of *Picayune Butler*.

Bile Dem Cabbage Down

Bile Dem Cabbage Down expresses the Gullah dialect, a highly specialized and now rapidly disappearing dialect common to the Sea Islands of South Carolina. A perusal of the lyrics, however, reveals that the song has evolved into the mainland black vernacular, inasmuch as true Gullah is almost incomprehensible to those hearing or reading it for the first time. Here is an example:*

Gullah	*Translation*
Joe: "Me yent hab no massah. Uh free es uh buzzut."	*Joe*: "I have no master. I'm free as a buzzard."
John: "Yaas, bubuh. Buzzut ent free nuf fuh light 'puntop nutt'n 'cep'ne ded, en' nigguh ent free nuf fuh mek buckra fuh bex."	*John*: "Yes, brother. A buzzard isn't free enough to light on anything unless it's dead, and a black man isn't free enough to offend the white man."

The first two verses and the first two lines of the chorus may be said to be a modified Gullah. The remainder has taken on the flavor and folk traditions native to the localities in which the song gained favor. Thus, verses one and two are native to South Carolina; verses three, four and five stem from Virginia; verse six is from Florida, and seven from Texas.

---

* *Laughing on the Outside*, Philip Sterling, Grosset & Dunlap, © 1965.

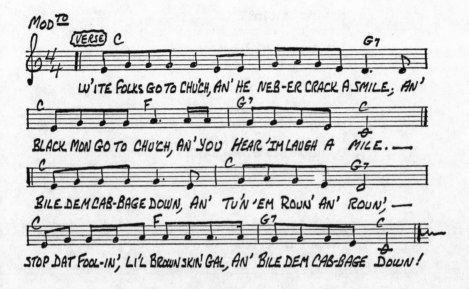

W'ite folks go to chu'ch,
An' he neber crack a smile;
An' black mon go to chu'ch,
An' you hear 'im laugh a mile.

Chorus

Bile dem cabbage down,
An' tu'n 'em roun' an' roun';
Stop dat foolin', li'l brownskin gal,
An' bile dem cabbage down!

Raccoon 'e am bushy-tail',
An' possum 'e am bare;
Raccoon 'e am bushy-tail',
But 'e ain't got none to spare.

Chorus

Fox he got a bushy tail,
Raccoon tail am bare;
Rabbit got no tail at all,
Jes' a leetle bit a bunch er hair.

Chorus

Rat he got a leetle tail,
Mouse it ain't much bigger;
White folks got no tail at all,
Neither has the nigger.

Chorus

De fox he hab a bushy tail,
De possum's tail am bare;
De rabbit hab no tail a-tall,
'Cep' a little bitty bunch o' hair.*

Chorus

Raccoon has a ring aroun' his tail,
Possum's tail is bare,
Rabbit has no tail at all,
Nothing but a patch o' hair.

Chorus

Raccoon carries a bushy tail,
Possum don' care 'bout no hair;
Mister Rabbit he come skippin' by
An' he ain't got none to spare.

Chorus

Mistuh Rabbit

Here, the young Brer Rabbit has grown old—a venerable patriarch. During the 1920's the dialect and whatever buffoonery was originally associated with this song was gradually lost, and it remains, today, a haunting, simple religious affirmation. Following are the verses and melody as sung by the plantation slaves:

---

* It is not often that two or three regional dialects are retained in one song, even though its components may stem from different areas of the United States. The sixth verse is vocalized in the same manner as the others, but its written tradition—the *literature* of the song—contains this dialectal variant. (Note the change in verbs.)

Mistuh Rabbit, Mistuh Rabbit, yo' ears mighty long.
"Yes, my Lawd, dey put on wrong."

Chorus

Ev'y little soul mus' shine, shine, shi-ine,
Ev'y little soul mus' shi-ine, shine, shine.

Mistuh Rabbit, Mistuh Rabbit, yo' coat mighty grey.
"Yes, my Lawd, it made dat way."

Chorus

Mistuh Rabbit, Mistuh Rabbit, yo' tail mighty white.
"Yes, my Lawd, I'm a-gittin' out o' sight."

Chorus

Mistuh Rabbit, Mistuh Rabbit, yo' eyes mighty red.
"Yes, my Lawd, I'm a-almos' dead."

Chorus

Bra' Rabbit—(Oyscha')

This fragment, from South Carolina, is in the Gullah dialect. The translation: "Brother Rabbit, what are you doing there?" "I have been picking oysters for a young girl. That oyster bit my finger and made the young girl laugh."

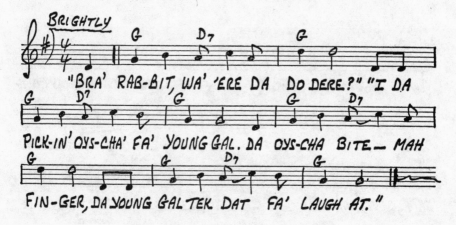

"Bra' Rabbit, wa' 'ere da do dere?"
"I da pickin' oyscha' fa' young gal.
Da oyscha' bite mah finger,
De young gal tek dat fa' laugh at."

Settin' on a Rail

As I went out by the light of the moon,
So merrily singin' this here old tune,
Thar I spies a fat raccoon
A-settin' on a rail,
Settin' on a rail,
Settin' on a rail;
Ha-ha! Ha-ha, Ha-ha, Ha-ha!
Sleepin' mighty sound.

And up to him I slowly creeped,
And up to him I slowly creeped,
And up to him I slowly creeped;
And I cotch him by de tail,
And I cotch him by de tail,
And I cotch him by de tail;
Ha-ha! Ha-ha, Ha-ha, Ha-ha!
And I yank him off dat rail.

Dorothy Scarborough, in *On the Trail of Negro Folk Songs*, has found an old version of this song with no ascription of authorship and no copyright, a fact that indicates its age; at least, whether it be an old ministrel song or a genuine folk expression:

As I walked out by de light ob de moon,
So merrily singin' dis same tune,
I cum across a big raccoon,
    A-sittin' on a rail, sittin' on a rail,
    Sittin' on a rail, sittin' on a rail,
    Sleepin' wery sound.

At de raccoon I tuck a peep,
An' den so sof'ly to him creep,
I found de raccoon fas' asleep,
    An' pull him off de rail, pull him off de rail,
    Pull him off de rail, pull him off de rail,
    An' fling him on de ground.

De raccoon 'gan to scratch and bite,
I hit him once wid all my might,
I bung he eye an' spile he sight,
    Oh, I'm dat chile to fight, I'm dat chile to fight,
    I'm dat chile to fight, I'm dat chile to fight,
    An' beat de banjo too.

I tell de raccoon 'gin to pray,
While on de ground de raccoon lay,
But he jump up an' run away,
    An' soon he out ob sight, soon he out ob sight,
    Soon he out ob sight, soon he out ob sight,
    Sittin' on a rail.

My ole massa dead an' gone,
A dose o' poison help him on,
De debil say he funeral song,
    Oh, bress him, let him go! bress him, let him go!
    Bress him, let him go! bress him, let him go!
    An' joy go wid him, too.

De raccoon hunt so very quare,
Am no touch to kill de deer,
Beca'se you cotch him widout fear,
    Sittin' on a rail, sittin' on a rail,
    Sittin' on a rail, sittin' on a rail,
    Sleepin' wery sound.

Ob all de songs I eber sung,
De raccoon hunt's de greatest one,
It always pleases old an' young,
    An' den dey cry encore, den dey cry encore,
    An' den dey cry encore, den dey cry encore,
    An' den I cum again.

Story of Creation

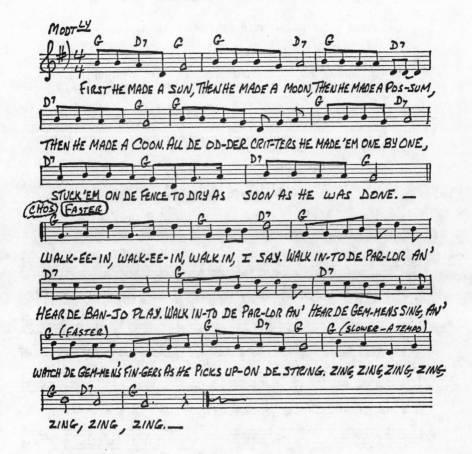

First He made a sun, then He made a moon,
Then He made a possum, then He made a 'coon.

All de odder critters, He made 'em one by one;
Stuck 'em on de fence to dry, as soon as dey was done.

Refrain

Walk-ee-in, walk-ee-in, walk in, I say.
Walk into de parlor an' hear de banjo play.
Walk into de parlor an' hear de gemmens sing,
An' watch de gemmen's fingers as he picks upon de string,
Zing, zing, zing, zing — zing, zing, zing!

Old Mudder Eve couldn't sleep widout a pilluh,
An' de greatest man dat ever lived was Jack de Giant-killuh.

Old Noah was a mighty man an' built a mighty ark,
An' got all de critters in jes' before dark.

'Long come de elephant, Noah, says he, "You're drunk!"
"Oh, no sir," said de elephant, "I stopped to pack my trunk."

Whoa, Mule!

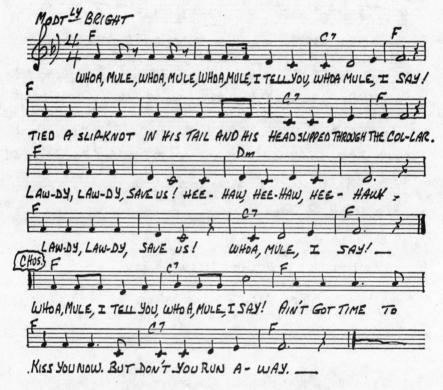

Whoa, mule! whoa, mule! whoa, mule, I tell you!
Whoa, mule, I say!
Tied a slip-knot in his tail,
And his head slipped through the collar.

Lawdy, Lawdy, save us; hee-haw, hee-haw, hee-haw!
Lawdy, Lawdy save us! Whoa, mule, I say!

Chorus

Whoa, mule, I tell you!
Whoa, mule, I say!
Ain't got time to kiss you now,
But don't you run away.

Bullfrog

The bullfrog is recalled with affection in a number of Negro folk songs. In this Texas account, various basso stanzas announce his personality and actions.

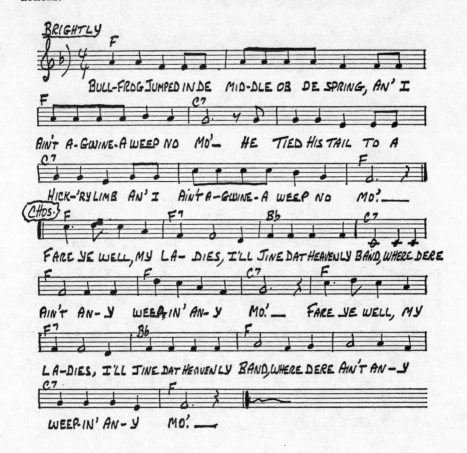

Bullfrog jumped in de middle ob de spring,
  An' I ain't a-gwine-a weep no mo';
He tied his tail to a hick'ry limb,
  An' I ain't a-gwine-a weep no mo'.

Chorus

Fare ye well, my ladies,
I'll jine dat heavenly band,
Where dere ain't any weepin' any mo'.
Fare ye well, my ladies,
I'll jine dat heavenly band,
Where dere ain't any weepin' any mo'.

He kicked an' he ra'red an' he couldn't make a jump,
  An' I ain't a-gwine-a weep no mo';
He kicked an' he ra'red an' he couldn't make a jump,
  An I ain't a-gwine-a-weep no mo'.

Chorus

De Blue-Tail Fly

Although the composer of *De Blue-Tail Fly*, Dan Decatur Emmet, was a white man, born in southern Ohio, his songs have long since become an integral part of Negro music lore. In addition to *Blue-Tail Fly*, which, legend has it, was a favorite of Abraham Lincoln, Emmet also wrote such popular minstrel songs as *Old Dan Tucker* and *Dixie*, neither of which have been able to rise above their minstrel stage origins. The song, *Dixie*, revives so many unpleasant memories of past indignities in the minds and hearts of the black people that understandably most of the younger generation are militantly opposed to its use at school and public functions. Nevertheless, it is relevant to note that Emmett avoided the cruel caricatures of the Negro so common to the ministrel stage.

These are the lyrics sung by post-bellum ex-slaves and their descendants, somewhat modified through the many years of repetition:

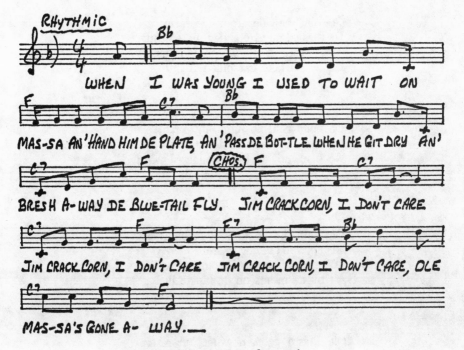

When I was young I used to wait
On Massa an' han' him de plate,
An' pass him de bottle when he git dry
An' bresh away de blue-tail fly.

Chorus

Jim crack corn, I don't care,
Jim crack corn, I don't care,
Jim crack corn, I don't care,
Ole Massa's gone away.

Den arter dinner Massa sleep,
He bid dis sarvint vigil keep;
An' when he gwine to shut his eye,
He tell me watch dat blue-tail fly.

Chorus

An' when he ride in de arternoon,
I foller wid a hickory broom;
De pony being berry shy,
When bitten by de blue-tail fly.

Chorus

One day he ride aroun' de farm;
De flies so numerous dey did swarm;
One chance to bite 'im on de thigh,
De debbil take dat blue-tail fly!

Chorus

De pony run, he jump an' pitch,
An' tumble Massa in de ditch.
He died, an' de jury wondered why;
De verdic' was de blue-tail fly.

Chorus

Dey laid 'im under a 'simmon tree;
His epitaph am dar to see;
"B'neath dis stone I'm forced to lie,
All by de means ob de blue-tail fly."

Chorus

Ole Massa gone, now let 'im rest;
Dey say all things am for de best.
I nebber forget till de day I die,
Ole Massa an' dat blue-tail fly.

Chorus

De Sow Took de Measles

The origin of this song is lost in antiquity. In 1818, William Cobbett, returning to London after a visit to young America, wrote: "Besides the great quantity of work performed by the American farmer, his skill, the versatility of his talent, is a great thing. Every man can use an axe, a saw, a hammer. There are very few, indeed, who cannot kill and dress pigs and sheep, and many of them oxen and calves. Every farmer is a neat butcher, a butcher for market; and, of course, the boys must learn. In short, a good laborer here can do anything that is to be done on a farm."

The pioneer farmers of the 18th and early 19th centuries needed all the resourcefulness they could muster, especially those of African descent whose lot was particularly hard. They could afford to waste nothing, as this humorous old song well illustrates.

Chorus

How do ya think I begin in de worl'?
I got me a sow an' num'rous othuh things.
De sow took de measles an' she died in de spring.

Whut do ya think I made of huh hide?
De very bes' saddle dat you evuh did ride.
Saddle er bridle er any sech thing,
De sow took de measles an' she died in de spring.

Whut do ya think I made of huh nose?
De very bes' thimble dat evuh sewed clo'se.
Thimble er thread er any sech thing,
De sow took de measles an' she died in de spring.

Whut do ya think I made of huh tail?
De very bes' whup dat evuh broke jail.
Whup 'er whup-socket, any sech thing,
De sow took de measles an' she died in de spring.

Whut do ya think I made of huh feet?
De very bes' pickles dat you evuh did eat.
Pickles er glue er any sech thing,
De sow took de measles an' she died in de spring.

Old Blue

Dogs of every description were no novelty to the rural black people of the 19th century, nor are they today. A few of the canines were thoroughbreds, given or sold to the freedmen by their former masters. Most, however, were "Heinz" dogs—57 varieties. These mongrels were as well trained for hunting rabbit, 'coon, and 'possum as any of the aristocratic blooded hounds owned by the wealthy whites, and frequently better. Bonds of devotion were often formed between dog and master in the many hours they spent together in the woods and later before a crackling blaze in the fireplace. This song of an old man and his old dog, Blue, with whom he had obviously done much hunting, is one of the great lyric expressions of such a relationship.

I had an ol' dog, an' his name wuz Blue,
An' I betcha fo' dollahs he's a good un too;
   Singin' "Come on, Blue,
   Ol' Blue!"

Blue chase a 'possum up a 'simmon tree,
Blue look at de 'possum, 'possum look at me;
   Singin' "Go on, Blue,
   You kin have some too."

Baked dat possum good an' brown,
I laid dem sweet 'taters, 'roun' an' roun';
   Sayin' "Come on, Blue,
   You kin have some too."

Ol' Blue died, an' he died so hahd,
Dat he jarred de groun' in my back yahd;
   Sayin' "Go on, Blue,
   I'm comin' too."

I dug his grave wid a silvah spade,
An' I let him down wid a golden chain;
   Sayin' "Go on, Blue,
   I'm comin' too."

When I git to heaven, fus' thing I'll do,
Grab my ho'n an' I'll blow fuh ol' Blue;
   Sayin' "Come on, Blue,
   Fin'ly got heah too!"

Dey All Got a Mate But Me

The musical lore of the American Negro is a vast reservoir from which the songs represented here are but a brief sampling. Those which concern animals, birds, reptiles and insects, from the ubiquitous boll weevil to the slow-witted possum and on to the lumbering elephant, have an earthy appeal seldom found in the literature of other peoples. The black man addressed the live creatures around him with affectionate understanding of their good points, but not blinded as to their shortcomings. He liked them. They interested him, and his lyrics were of the things that honestly appealed to him, not of what he thought a conventional public or white-collared editor expected him to praise. At times he dealt with his subjects impersonally, as figures in a universal comedy in which he was an observer. At others, he treated them subjectively, comparing his lot with theirs, as in the following stanza:

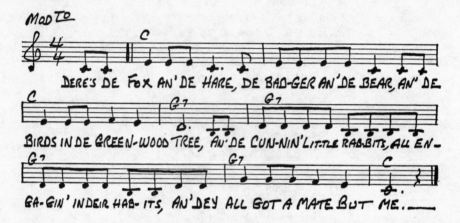

Dere's de fox an' de hare,
De badger an' de bear,
An' de birds in de greenwood tree,
An' de cunnin' little rabbits
All engagin' in deir habits,
An' dey all got a mate but me.

5
POET'S
CORNER

BOOK FIVE

The Poet's Corner

Introduction

The Old South, as represented in Part One, *Yazoo Valley Verse*,* has all but passed into the yesterday. With the advent of concrete roads; consolidated and integrated school systems; the absorption of new ideas from tourists and northern civil-rights workers; the widespread use of the automobile, radio and television; access to metropolitan newspapers and the broadening of general knowledge, the Old South of the log cabins, wretched thoroughfares, vast areas of uncultivated land and plantations maintaining large retinues of black helpers, has been, for the most part, relegated to the musty tomes of history. But here, in these pages, they live again!

At first, the question of supply and demand was responsible, to a degree, for the transformation. Population increased at a rapid rate and cities grew to enormous proportions. There were more people to feed and fewer food producers to meet the demand. The great, fertile south was destined to become the food basket of the nation and vast tracts lay fallow. As a result, and with the advance of agricultural mechanization, many of the farmers and share-croppers turned to more productive enterprises in the towns and cities on both sides of the Mason-Dixon line.

Log cabins and ramshackle hovels gave way to modern dwellings and well-kept premises, although far too many of the former are still in existence.

---

* Several of these verses appeared under the by-line of "Pop" in the famous "Line-O-Type" column and in the Sunday editions of the *Chicago Tribune*, at various intervals prior to 1924. *Yazoo Valley Verse*, Edward F. Younger. The Lakeside Press, Chicago. 1924.

Ox-carts surrendered the road to swift automobiles, the cars eventually pushing into the rural dirt roads and cow-paths. The picturesque "darkey" (he was seldom considered as an impoverished human being held down by a grinding system of injustice), with his solitary, flea-bitten mule and dilapidated vehicle, designated as a wagon by severe strain on courtesy, became a rarity as progress crowded him off the highways.

Among the traits of yesteryear's black man was his implicit faith in his Maker. To him, God was a neighbor, an intimate personality who walked and talked with him; who punished him with barren fields when he was derelict in duty; who laid the rod upon him when he abused birds, animals or flowers. God was the Father of men and all lower creatures, and all His creations must be accorded proper respect and treated as brothers. To him, everything had a personality: trees, flowers, mules, cattle, birds and inanimate objects. It may well be said that, for all their adherence to Christianity, they were America's first Pantheists.

The optimism and undying faith that some day, somehow, things that seemed out of joint would be adjusted, was a psychological mainstay for the oldtime Negro. Ragged, poorly fed, miserably housed, relegated to the lowest menial tasks, he derived much joy out of trifles. Although he might go hungry and half-clad, hope buoyed him up. Inherent faith that his Creator would, here or hereafter, smooth his thorny path and heal his bruises, burned steadily within him and no amount of oppression could stamp it out. It was inconceivable to him that someday he would clench his fists and fight his own way up—that through his own organizations such as the NAACP, the Urban League and others composed largely of younger people, these children who sprang from his own loins would claim their rightful heritage.

Yet, for all its bleak memories of privation and deprivation, the South is *home* for millions of black Americans who have joined the widespread migration to the north, the mid-west and the far west. It is the *land* which is loved, not its past societal structure. Nostalgia tends to turn cold to warmth, salt to sugar, indifference to affection. Minds turn once again to those almost forgotten days when a lover's kisses were like honey to young lips. The fragrance of wild honeysuckle after a spring shower lingers in the nostrils. A hound dog barks at the garden gate. Smoke curls languidly from the chimney, spiraling toward a blue sky dappled with russets and bronze; and we know that mother's airy biscuits, golden fried chicken, billowing mashed potatoes and giblet gravy will soon be on the table.

Persecution? Yes—but at the moment our thoughts dwell ever so tenderly on *home*. What lovely visions that beautiful word conveys. Home! . . . Remember?

> Vagrant roads that scorn surveyor's lines,
> Like brick-red ribbons under lofty pines;
> Garrulous streamlets, dashing to the sea,
> Lashing themselves to frothy ecstasy.

Magnolia, dogwood, laurel, jessamin',
    Tossing rare fragrance to the passing wind.
Palm fronds waving in the listless breeze,
    Festoons of muscadine lacing mighty trees.
Paradise of birds—the soft sweet note
    Bubbling from the mocker's golden throat.
Raucous gibbering of the hoodlum jay
    Tormenting the timid songsters all the day.
Scarlet tanagers on the loftiest tree;
    Mourning doves crooning a weird threnody.
Deepest valleys, bathed in purple haze,
    Stenciled and etched in red japonicas.
Rioting honeysuckle, flinging free and wide
    Its dainty perfume o'er the countryside.
Realm of King Cotton, fluffy potentate,
    Whipped-cream monarch of a vast estate.
Dingy cabins, lacking paint or care—
    Yet Life and Love find lodgement there.
Plenty and Penury, walking side by side,
    Clinging to Tradition, holding fast to Pride.
Nostalgic Dixie, land where roses blow—
    Old South, why tug at our heartstrings so?

There is a widespread belief among white people that most Negro poetry is marked by literary inferiority—a belief shared by some black scholars who should know better. It is true, certainly, that many black poets expressed their heart's longings in feeble verse, but so, too, have poets of all other races. One need only to read the works of James Weldon Johnson, Phillis Wheatley, Paul Dunbar, Langston Hughes, and many of today's young black poets, to feel the magic of grand and beautiful thought embodied in noble, flexible and richly expressive prose.

For the black man, southern chivalry was lace on leg-irons; the lovely magnolia a lynching tree; mint juleps a few gulps of cool water to soothe his parched throat. Much of black folk-poetry tells of the people's struggle to attain equality, the pain of living in humiliation and despair, the hope of better days to come. The verses which appear in this collection, however, express the black man's playful nature; his humor—those things which made him laugh in years gone by as they do today.

The white reader who is introduced to these verses for the first time will note that here are no stereotypes which owe their origins to the caricatures of the minstrel stage, but authentic folk-poetry expressed in jest, irony and satire. Some are hyperbolic, as in the two-line *Tall Tale* which tells of a chicken that was so tall "it tooken a month fo' de aig tuh fall." Others are somewhat pugnacious, as in *Introduce Yourself, Sir!* wherein a feisty little caterpillar identifies himself and then snaps, "Now who de hell am you?" *The Squirrel Game,* considered to be of African origin, is accompanied by

So We Hunted and We Hollered, another game enjoyed by black youngsters which is traced back to the year 1668. The verses in this section span an era from pre-Revolutionary times in the American colonies (*Raccoon Up In De 'Simmon Tree*), to the parody, *Battle of Little Rock,* in 1958. For those readers who wish to explore the origins and backgrounds of black folk-poetry, detailed footnotes have been appended, with additional sources in the extensive bibliography beginning on page 569 of this volume.

As a proper closing, let it again be said that this discussion of the serious as well as the humorous nature of folk-poetry was not meant to dismay the reader, but to illuminate a wide-ranging subject. Hopefully, these verses will evoke an appreciative smile and, perhaps, some earthy laughter.

H. D. S.

PART ONE

YAZOO VALLEY VERSE

The "Lifted" Goose

Dey wuz holdin' a drawed-out meetin' up Yazoo way
    An' Jeff Duncan entuhtain de pahson one day.
Table jes' loaded wid gran' things tuh eat,
    Pones an' baked taters an' fresh hawg meat.
In de centuh, all kivvered wid gravy juice,
    Sot de gran'es' big ol' fat baked goose.

Pahson smack his chops ez he see dat feas'
    An' p'intedly say: "I sho' fon' ob geese.
"Dat sho' a noble fowl," de Revun exclaim,
    An' he pass up his plate fuh some mo' ob de same.
"Didn' know yuh raised geese," he mek out tuh say.

"Well, Revun," splains Jeff, "hit's disyer way,
    "I didn' zackly *raise* dat ol' fat goose—
"I jes' *lifted* hit fum offen de roos'.
    "Reckon ain't much diff'nce in dem dar wuhds,
"Mo' specially when us is speakin' ob buhds."

Pahson smile as he lick off his plate—
    "Dis sho' a gran' meal—an' I craves tuh state
"Dat us po' folks who infestes' de Souf,
    "We don' look a gif' hoss too close in de mouf!"

FRIED CHICKEN

Fried chicken, almost *any* style, will make the gastric juices flow, but these soul recipes, originally from Virginia and Maryland, can't be beat —with one possible exception: Georgia style (see page 289).

Fried Chicken—Virginia Style

1 chicken (2 to 3 lbs.) cut, washed and dried	salt, pepper, paprika to taste
1 tsp. garlic salt	½ cup flour
	1 cup fat

Place salt, pepper, paprika and flour in a paper bag. Shake well. Sprinkle cut chicken with garlic salt and nutmeg. Place 2 or 3 pieces of chicken in bag at one time and shake so that each piece will be well coated. Drop into hot fat and cook 15 to 20 minutes on each side. Avoid sticking fork into meat because juices will escape and pop in hot fat! When brown and crisp on both sides, remove from pan and drain on paper. Serves 4.

If gravy is desired, drain all fat except about 2 tablespoons, add 2 tablespoons of remaining flour. Brown and add 2 cups hot water, salt and pepper. Simmer. Chicken may be added to gravy, if desired.

Fried Chicken—Maryland Style

1 young fryer (3 to 3½ lbs.)	½ cup flour
1 tsp. salt	½ tsp. pepper
½ tsp. paprika	⅔ cup fat
1 cup water	

Quarter chicken, wash and singe. Dry well. Dip in a mixture of flour, salt, pepper and paprika. Place in hot fat in a heavy skillet. Brown on all sides. Allow about 15 minutes to each side. Reduce heat. Cover and simmer 15 to 20 minutes. Remove from pan. Add 2 to 3 tablespoons flour and brown. Add 1 cup water. Mix well. Place chicken in gravy. Simmer another 15 minutes. Serve with rice or potatoes, hot biscuits and honey. Serves 6.

Sad Revolt of Eph'm Snow

Cap'n, is y'all heard bouten Eph'm Snow
    Mekkin' dat big talk down at de sto'?
Shif'less ol' nigguh fum Breshy Crick
    Sez Melissy, his wife, she mek him sick

Wid her jawin' at him all night an' day,
    Ontwell Eph'm jes' bleege t' run away.
Sez she gibs him a mis'ry in de haid;
    Does he bide any longuh, he sho'ly be daid.
"No woman gwine boss me!" Eph'm say,
    "I gwine up Nawf disyer ve'y day;
"I gwine up Nawf all by mahse'f
    "'Fo' dat woman pestuh me t' def!"

Eph'm wuz a-bellerin' cleah an' strong
    'Bout how dat ol' gal treat him wrong—
An' jes' den Melissy bus' in thoo de do'
    An' fling po' Eph'm flat on de flo'.
"Yuh ain't gwine nowhah but home," she said
    An' shebus' ol' Eph'm side ob de head.

"Hol' on dar, Sugahfoot!" Eph'm say,
    "I sho' is comin' home, right away."
Eph'm rale spry ez he run todes he shack,
    Wid Melissy a-snortin' right at he back.
Sto'keepuh say, as he watches 'em go:
    "Guess de Nawf hatter do widout Eph'm Snow!"

Crosswuhd Puzzles

Wuz down tuh de sto' attuh co'n meal t'day.
    "Don' pestuh me now," sto'keepuh say,
"He'p yo'se'f tuh meal an' leave me a note,
    "Dis crosswuhd puzzle sho' got mah goat!"
An' he jes' sot dar, playin' checkers lak,
    Rubbin' out wuhds an' puttin' 'em back.

"Is you evah tried cross wuhds?" sto'keepuh say;
    "Sho' has," I tells 'im—"dat is t'say—
"Melissy, mah wife, who 'low she de boss,
    "She sez all de wuhds, an' dey sho' am cross!"

CHICKEN IN A BLANKET

The Yazoo Valley folks of the Reconstruction era were justly proud of their cooking ability, but they never came up with anything like Georgia's chicken-in-a-blanket, as it was called a hundred years ago. As the great Jack Johnson once remarked, "If you ain't et it, don't bad-mouth it!"

Fried Chicken in Batter—Georgia Style

1 young fryer (about 3 lbs.)	½ tsp. pepper
1½ cups flour	½ cup milk
1 egg, beaten	1 tsp. baking powder
1 tsp. salt	½ tsp. paprika

Cut chicken into small pieces. Wash and dry. Sprinkle with salt and pepper. Mix flour, baking powder and salt. Add egg and milk. Let stand ½ hour. Dip chicken in batter. Be sure it is well coated. Fry in deep hot fat, turning to brown on all sides. Be sure chicken is well done—as batter prevents chicken from cooking thoroughly. Serves 4.

Raw chicken may be steamed in a small amount of water, dried and cooled, dipped in the same batter to fry.

Li'l Splotch Ob Columbine

Li'l ol' splotch ob columbine
  'Longside ob de dusty lane,
Smilin' when de sun shine,
  Laughin' when hit rain.

"Whuffo' y'all so happy dere?"
  I ast dat li'l flowuh.
"You ain't no good tuh eat 'r wear,
  "Yet you joyful ev'y houah."

"Well, suh," dat posy say t'me:
  "I'm bleege t'tell you dat
"I aims t'brighten, faithfully,
  "Dis co'nuh whah I is at."

Vengeance Is Mine

Reckon Mose Brant is de stingies' man
  You gwine fin' anywhah in disyer lan'.
Nevuh gibs a kin' wuhd t'man or beas',
  Jes' downright ornery, t'say de leas'.
His churry trees wuz jes' a-bendin' down,
  Dem loaded limbs mos' tech de groun'.
Some robins wuz dah a-he'pin' deyse'f,
  Tuk a few offen de top; dey wuz plenty lef',
But Mose toh loose wid 'is two-ba'hl gun
  An' shot 'em plumb t' kingdom come.
Po' buhds didn't know dey wuz stealin' f'm Mose,
  Good Lawd put dem churries right unduh dey nose.
Dey wuz 'nuff fo' all an' plenty tuh spa'h,
  But Mose couldn't 'bide tuh gib 'em a sha'h.

Now I isn't sayin' de Lawd punishin' Mose—
  But a mule done flung 'im an' bruk 'is nose.
An' a fiah burnt mos' ob 'is fences down,
  An' de win' th'owed 'is cotton flat on de groun'.
Mose is a-tarin' 'roun' an' sayin' wuhds,
  But I bet he sorry he kilt dem buhds!
In de Good Book, ouah Lawd mos' p'intedly say:
  "Vengeance is Mine: I gwine mek 'em pay!"

Sis Callie's Wris' Watch

Sis Callie (daughter ob Ol' Dunk Smif),
   Got a wris' watch fo' a Chrismus gif';
Wuz p'sented t'her by a yaller boy
   Who wucked fo' weeks t'buy dat toy.
Callie 'lows world bleege staht an' stop
   By dat li'l ol' clock on a leather strop.
Looks at it fo'ty times a day—
   Ask her whut time it is, she cain't say.
Onliest way she evuh knows
   Is when ol' sawmill whistle blows!

Largess and Progressive Titles

Boss, is you got ary ol' clo's
   You bleeged tuh th'ow away?
I kin hab dis coat? Cap'n, now I knows
   Dis sho' my lucky day.

'Co'se dese ovuhalls—dey's all right—
   Is dat ar ves' fo' me?
Kunnel, dis shirt sho' a lubly sight,
   Mos' scrumptious I evuh did see.

Effen I jes' had a paiah ob pants
   T' match disyer coat an' ves'—
Thanky, Guvn'r, I sees at a glance
   Ob all gran' men you's de bes'.

Means t' say you gibs me dem shoes?
   An' dat hat? Lan' sakes an' hot dam!
Pres'dent-Ginral, I jes' cain't refuse,
   You is sho'ly de 'bligenest man!

Crazy—Lak a Fox!

White man rid by mah cabin one day;
   Mus' bin f'm de Nawth, f'm whut he say.
"Huccum you laughin' an' prankin' aroun'?
"You don' own ary foot ob groun'.
"Yo' clo's all tattuhs," dat white man say,
   "Yet yuh 'lows tuh be happy all de day.
"Mebbe you's got 'ligion dat meks yuh ack
   "Jes' happy an' crazy an' foolish-lak?"

"Well, Suh," I 'sponds tuh dat ar man,
  "I meks de bes' ob whut comes tuh han'.
"Mah clo's is rags, but I has good health
  "An' dat's mo' bettuh dan all yo' wealth.
"Effen all banks fail, don' fret me none,
  "Mah worries all sink wid de settin' sun;
"I lives wid de posies an' birds an' trees,
  "Mah conscience clah an' mas soul at ease."

White man, he studied fo' quite awhile,
  Gib me a seegah an' a frien'ly smile.
"Ah reckon," he 'lowed, "you has de right slant,
  "I'd lak tuh trade places—only I can't.
"Don' fret yo' haid bouten bonds an' stocks;
  "You sho 'is crazy—jes' lak a fox!"

Bre'r Robin Redbreas'

Mo'nin', suh, Ol' Mistuh Robin Redbreas',
  Struttin' 'roun' jes' lak yuh owns dis place.
Mekkin' big 'miration wid yo' scahlet ves',
  Stuffin' bugs an' sich intuh yo' ol' fat face.
Bleege t' say you has a cheerful way,
  Nevuh heah yuh cryin' times is hahd.
Reckon dat's 'caze you busy all de day,
  So mek yo'se'f at home right in dis yahd.
Gits us a lesson f'm de bird whut sings;
  Whinin' an' loafin' don' git us anywhah.
Mus' wuhk an' hope an' mek de bes' ob things,
  Jes' lak Ol' Mistuh Robin, obuh dah.

Jeff Duncan Gits a Wahnin'

H'it's bin moughty dry up Yazoo way,
  'Peared lak dey wa'nt no mo' rain in de sky.
Ol' sun jes' a-blazin' down ev'y day,
  Ontwell men an' beas's lak t' die.

Jeff Duncan fretted 'bout his cotton crop;
  Said de Lawd wuzn't givin' him a squah deal,
'Lowed his faith in pra'hr done tuk a drop
  Sence de Lawd too busy tuh heed his 'peal.

Well, suh, things wuz a-lookin' moughty black,
   An' den, one day, kim a turble rain.
Ol' Jeff run f'm de fiel' tuh he shack
   An' 'low he gwine mek up wid de Lawd agin!

Sez he only a-foolin' 'bout whut he said,
   But de lightnin' kim wid a skeerful ro'
An' bus' Ol' Jeff right squah on de haid
   An' lef' him all spraddled out on de flo'.

Attuh Jeff kim to, he jump outen dat shack
   An' lep' nigh a mile afoh he lit.
Neighbuhs ketch 'im an' fotch 'im back,
   Else dat fool sinnuh be a-runnin' yit.

Jeff bin pow'ful meek ev' sence dat day;
   'Lows dat de hint kim f'm de golden sho'.
So he a-walkin' de straight an' narrer way;
   Sez he nev' gwine qua'l wid de Lawd no mo'!

Looking Forward

White men wuz 'sputin' down at de sto'
   Bouten who wuz de stingies' man.
Cap'n Anders 'low, dat as fur ez he know,
   Dat de tightes' in all de lan'
Is Kunnel Fohman, whose fahm adjines
   De plantation ob Jeff Boswick—
Dey prop'ty divided by natch'l lines—
   Jes' a li'l ol' spindlin' crick.

Well, suh, dem men at de sto' dey say,
   All dem white men 'sputified
Dat Kunnel Fohman goes atter a drink ev'y day,
   But he drink f'm de Boswick side!
Kunnel 'low mebbe dat stream, hit gwine run dry,
   So he savin' his share ontwell
De Boswick watuh all done run by—
   Den de Kunnel hab watuh tuh sell!

Bre'r Crow, Sneak Thief

   Ol' black crow struttin' ovuh de groun'
      He fixin' tuh rob mah fiel';
   P'tendin' lak he jes' miratin' aroun',
      But he watchin' a chance tuh steal.

Mekkin' dat "caw-caw" thoo he nose
Evuh sence arly dis mo'n;
Ol' debbil, dressed in he fun'l clo's,
He atter mah sproutin' co'n!

Hoe-Cake an' Hominy

Hoe'cake an' hominy,
  Pass dem collahd greens.
Spill dat gravy ovuh me—
  Lak fo' tas'e dem beans.
Stomach 'low mah th'oat done cut,
  Bin so long 'tween meals,
Jes' could eat dat whole ham butt,
  Dat's de way I feels.
Co'n pones, I lubs yuh so,
  Yams, you is mah frien's,
Bacon rin's, come on, le's go!
  Hope dis nevuh ends.

Las' Call Fo' Mistuh Watuhmilyun

Ah see you, hidin' in dat ar patch ob co'n,
  Yo' ol' green coat a-glistenin' in de sun.
Me an' you gwine 'filiate befo' anothuh mo'n;
  Come t' yo' Pappy, chile—yo' race is run.
Ah's bin a-watchin' you all dis summuh thoo,
  Preenin' yo'se'f an' gettin' fattuh ev'y day;
Bathin' 'in de moonlight, drinkin' in de dew,
  Bin lettin' you hab yo' own sweet way.
Now, honey, you an' me, us gwine hab a feas';
  You gwine be de hos', an' me, Ah is yo' gues'.
Attuh us thoo, you gwine be deceased,
  Yo' red remains reposin' unduhneath mah ves'.

Ol' Mistuh Bluejay, Hoodlum

Ol' Mistuh Bluejay, gibs y'all faiah wahnin',
  Gwine t' smack you silly, onless you 'haves yo'se'f;
Bin watchin' you ruckusin' ev' blessed mo'nin',
  Pesterin' li'l songbuhds ontwell dey outen bref.

Bleege t' say you is a hoodlum, sorter lak a bum,
    Wid yo' ol' blue unifo'm an' yo' snaky eye;
Gwine swat you plum intuh kingdom come,
    Onless you quits mekkin' li'l songbuhds cry.

Huccum you mek sech a pes' outen yo'se'f?
    Jes' let dem buhds go on dey peaceful way,
Gibs you faiah wahnin', gwine bus' you plumb t' def;
    Nex' time you raids a nes'—you thoo, ol' jay!

Lines T' De Yalluh Catfish

Yallah catfish, sizzlin' in de pan;
    Man! Ah sho'ly lubs dat mess.
Ol' catfish, bouten size ob mah han';
    Kin eat a dozen, mo' 'r less.
Yalluh catfish, all wropped up in meal,
    Fried in buttuh ontwell dey's brown;
Nothin' bettuh, dat's de way Ah feel;
    Suits me, plumb t' de groun'.
Dozen baked sweet taters on de side;
    Plenty ob black coffee at my han'.
Me an' ol' catfish a-steppin' high an' wide;
    Ain't no finuh eatments in dis lan'.

New Way T' Glory

I's gwine t' Glory in a airyplane.
        (Hallelujah—hallelujah!)
Po' common trash be a-ridin' on a train.
        (Hallelujah—hallelujah!)
White folks kin hab dey autymobiles;
    Ox-cahts good enough fo' cheap tarheels.
But when Ah stahts fo' de Promis' Lan',
    Gwine step on de gas an' wave mah han'.
Ro'h thoo de skies t' de Golden Gate,
    Ain't even gwine fo' t' hes-i-tate.
Nothin' gwine block me on dat road,
    Track all clah t' mah las' abode.
Pahk mah plane in a fleecy cloud,
    Call fo' mah hahp an' a white silk shroud.
St. Petuh gwine say: "Well, sho's Ah live,
    Halelujah, Boy, you is done arriv!"

OYSTERS

Oysters (or "oshters," as some oldtimers called them), have been part of soul food cookery since colonial times. See "Mine Oyster" on page 307.

Fried Oysters

12 large selected oysters	1 egg
salt and pepper to taste	1 tbs. water
1½ cups bread or cracker crumbs	parsley

Dry oysters thoroughly. Season with salt and pepper. Dip into bread crumbs, then into egg diluted with a little water (1 tablespoon to each egg), and again into bread crumbs. Fry in deep fat. Drain on brown paper, garnish with parsley, and serve on folded napkin. Allow 3 to 4 oysters per serving.

If sauce is desired, serve in individual cups.

Oven Baked Oysters

Roll 1 dozen oysters in flour and salt, dip in beaten egg and roll in bread crumbs. Sprinkle with oil and bake in a hot oven until brown.

Oyster Stew—New England Style

1 quart oysters	1 tbs. butter
2 cups scalded milk	½ tsp. salt
2 cups evaporated milk, or cream	⅛ tsp. pepper

Remove oysters carefully from shells. Add ¾ cup water and cook until oysters are plump and edges curl. Remove oysters and add to milk. Add salt and pepper, then strained oyster juice. Add butter, heat and serve. Serves 6.

The Green-Eyed Monster

Listen, Mistuh Cap'n, is yuh seen Melissy Ann?
 Cooks on de Corby place—Joe Bailey, dat's her man.
Bought herse'f a new blue jacket f'm a catalog,
 Hat wid posies, yaller shoes—sho' puttin' on de dawg.
She say I jes' jealous ob her swell impo'ted clo's;
 Gits plumb uppity wid her talk, but ev'ybody knows
She spendin' ev'y dolluh dat her po' husban' earns.
 Sets in de meetin' house an' grins an' twis's an' turns,
Mekkin' out she de leaduh ob de uppuh cullud class;
 Totin' all dat joolry made outen brass an' glass!
Bet her big ol' splay feet a-achin' in dem shoes,
 P'tending lak she happy, when she got de mis'ry blues.
Folks say she look lak a big ol' fat plush hoss.
 Huh! Co'se I isn't jealous—but listen, Mistuh Boss,
Reckon kin you gib me mah money whut is due,
 An' borry me yo' catalog? Ah craves t' look it thoo.
Effen dat black hussy think she gwine set de style,
 She sho'ly bus' wid envy when I tromps up de aisle.
Gwine hab a hat wid white plumes a-settin' on mah head,
 Blue shoes wid silvuh buckles—an' a jacket dat is red!
An' dem long yaller gloves, lak no'thun ladies weah,
 An' a mess ob silvuh trinkets a-danglin' f'm mah haiah.
Huh! dat ol' Melissy Ann, she jes' po' common trash;
 Atter I gits thoo wid her, she ain't gwine be so brash!
Co'se, Cap'n, I isn't jealous, nossuh, not a-tall;
 Bleege set dat woman in her place, y'onderstan'?
  Dat's all.

Contentment

Has fo' bales ob cotton,
 Don' owe ary dime;
Ten acres co'n in ol' rivuh bottom,
 Ev'y grain ob dat is mine.

Bacon slabs hangin' in mah attic,
 Smellin' mighty fine an' sweet;
Tells yuh, suh, mos' emphatic,
 Knows wha'h I gwine t' eat.

So'ghum 'lasses—bah'l full,
 Big pit full ob yams,
Patch ob peanuts ready t' pull,
 Plenty ob smoky hams.

Six jugs filled wid p'simmon jam,
Colluhds awaitin' mah han';
Wham, bam! allegezam!
I sho' is a happy man!

An' Dey Pays Folks T' Sing!

A frien' dat's bin up No'th wuz a-tellin' me
Bouten mos' wonduhful sights dey's t' see;
Buildin's rarin' clah up t' de sky—
He 'low some of 'em mos' a mile high.
Monst's chu'ch whah *dey pays folks t' sing*
An' dey dance in de chu'ch, an' ev'ything!
Streets full ob people runnin' 'roun' lak dey mad,
So het up dey ain't got time t' be glad.
Sez is yuh hongry or dyin' ob thirs'
Yuh gottuh fling down yo' money firs'!
Shucks! I'll stay right heah in Dixie lan'
Wha'h dey's eatments an' sich right at my han',
Wha'h, in de dim fores', f'm ev'y tree
Birds jes' a-bustin' dey th'oats wid glee.
Craves t' stay wha'h I kin see de sun,
Dem ol' tall buildin's don' fret me none.
Huh! Keep yo' ol' city; I'll live an' die
Wha'h I kin heah de birds an' see de sky;
Wha'h I knows my neighbuhs an' dey knows me;
Wha'h aiah an' sunlight an' singin' is free!

Sid Cox Foun' a Dolluh

Ol' Sid Cox he sho' de squares' man;
He allus a-lookin' down at de groun',
Pokin' de dus' wid he cane an' he han',
All becuz ob a dolluh he foun'.

Yes *suh!* he pick up a dolluh one day,
Right in de road on he way to de sto'.
Mo' dan twenty yeahs ago, dey say,
An' ev' sence he bin a-lookin' fo' mo'.

Now Ol' Sid gittin' feeble an' bent,
Still he sarch de road atter folks go by;
But he nevuh foun' nary othuh cent—
An' fo' twenty yeahs he ain't seen de sky!

Plantation Blues

Nine cents fo' cotton, thutty cents fo' co'n;
  Ol' worl' sho' gone crazy.
Hustlin' t' de hot fiel's ev'y blessed mo'n,
  Mought ez well be lazy!

Ev'thing a-goin' out, nothin' comin' in;
  Wuhk hahd jes' de same.
Ain't dat a downright blisterin' sin?
  Ain't dat a beas'ly shame?

Dunk Kills His Luck

Dunk Jeff'son, wid 'is mail order gun,
  Shot a li'l bluebird jes' fo' fun.
Sho' kilt 'is luck when he kilt dat bird,
  Worses' things happent y'evuh heard.
Well, suh, mus' bin de ve'y nex' day
  Dat 'is mules dey ups an' runs away;
Smeared 'is wagon all ovuh de lot
  An' busted de gear befo' dey wuz caught.
Dunk couldn't pay 'is note come due,
  An' fo' ob he chilluns tuk wid de flu.
High win' toh down 'is ol' cow shed
  An' a flyin' bo'd lit on po' Dunk's head.
Cattle kim home wid a mess ob ticks;
  Ol' Dunk wuz sho' in a awful fix!
De fevuh hits 'im; den de chills;
  So he traded dat gun fo' a mess ob pills
An' a rabbit's foot (lef' hin' one);
  'Lows he ain't got no use fo' a gun.

PART TWO

SHIRTSLEEVE
PHILOSOPHY

We raise de wheat
But we gits de co'n.

We bake de bread
But we gits de crus'.

We sif' de meal
But we gits de hus'.

We peels de meat
But we gits de skin.

An' dat's de way
It's allus bin!

Nigger-Twis'

This poem provides an example in which the use of the word "nigger" has no pejorative connotation, but rather one of affection and, indeed, esteem. "Nigger-twist" referred to a home-cured pipe tobacco used by the Negroes of post and ante bellum Civil War days. It was often copied by poor whites, though under various different names. Very few whites have ever heard the term, although it was a byword among Southern blacks for almost a hundred years, illustrating once again the white man's superficial knowledge of the 19th-century Negro.

Right hard work while it lasts—dat's so—
   Worruming 'backer all day long;
Miz'ry gits in yo' back, yer know,
   Speshly dem what ain't so strong.
Dat's my fix. But it seems ter me
   I's paid fer it all when it comes ter dis:
My long-stem pipe, little Jake on my knee,
   An' my pocket chock full o' nigger-twis'.

FRIED CRABS AND CRAB CAKES

The original recipe for the fried soft-shell crabs came from the Gullah-speaking people of the islands off the coast of South Carolina (see "Bile Dem Cabbage Down," on page 264). The Season-All condiments were, of course, added later.

Fried Soft Shell Crabs

8 soft shell crabs	½ tsp. pepper
1 pint water	½ cup corn meal
1 tsp. Season-All (or similar)	¼ cup flour
2 tbs. salt	

Crabs may be killed and cleaned at the fish market, by the proprietor, on request.

Wash and clean thoroughly. Lay crabs in a pan. Mix 1 pint water, 2 tablespoons salt and pour over crabs. Soak for 30 minutes. Remove and drain. Dip in corn meal, flour and seasoning. Fry in deep fat, turning until brown and crisp on both sides.

Allow 2 small crabs or 1 large crab per person. Serve with tartar sauce, French fried potatoes and cole slaw.

Crab Cakes—Gourmet Style

1 tbs. butter	1 egg, slightly beaten
¼ cup finely chopped onion	2 tbs. mayonnaise
2 tbs. finely chopped celery	1 lb. crab meat
⅓ cup finely chopped green pepper	½ tsp. salt
	½ tsp. thyme
1½ cups soft bread crumbs	½ tsp. ground red pepper

Melt butter in heavy frying pan. Add onion, celery and pepper; stir over low heat until vegetables are tender. Remove from heat. Add bread crumbs and mix well. In large bowl, combine beaten egg and mayonnaise. Add vegetables and bread crumbs, crab meat and seasonings; mix thoroughly. Form into 12 cakes and place on waxed paper. Fry in hot deep fat at 375° for 5 to 7 minutes or until golden brown. Drain on paper toweling. Serve with lemon sauce or tartar sauce.

"Corn cob?" Yes *sir!* It ain't so fine
    As dat 'hagony-colored one o' yourn;
But I gits as much out o' dis o' mine
    As de fines' one you ever did own.
De juice all dries in de cob, you see—
    Dat's de philos'phy o' pipes like dis;
An' a reed-root stem is de stem fer me,
    An' de sweetes' 'backer is nigger-twis'.

Dem matches, dey's cur'us things, sho' 'nuff—
    Dem little splinters what lights jes' so;
Hit dey heads whar de box are rough
    A sort o' hard—an' away dey go!
I never liked 'em. It seems ter me
    De devil's in 'em some way. An' dis
Is jes' as good an' true, you see—
    A red-hot coal on de nigger-twis'.

"Wouldn't I like a cigar?" you say.
    No, sir, I thank you. I's tried dem dar—
Diff'rent, sir, as de night from day,
    Fur apart as a cuss an' a pra'r;
Ain't got no stren'th, it seems ter me,
    Can't begin ter compar' wid dis;
Nothin' onder de sun can be
    Sweet as a cob an' some nigger-twis'.

No—dat nuther! Well, I'll declar'!
    Dat is de beatenes' I's seed yet!
What is de name dat you call dat 'ar?
    Say it again, please? "Cigarette?"
Little Jake, what sets on my knee,
    'Ud turn up his nose at a thing like dis;
I's gwine ter teach him ter do like me,
    An' suck de comfort from a nigger-twis'.

Yes, dat's a fac'! 'Tis a lux'ry, sho',
    'Backer is, whatever you say.
Seems like I never wants nothin' mo',
    'Ceptin' ter set down here dis way,
Take little Jake up on my knee,
    Have me a corn-cob pipe like dis,
Wid a stem as long as from you ter me,
    An' a pocket chock full o' nigger-twis'.

                         (*A. C. Gordon,* 1906)

Ebo

All o' dese here doin's
    Don' suit me;
I's an ole-time nigger—
    Don' you see?

Dis here eddication's
    Humbug, sho'!
It's done played de devil
    Wid Ebo.

Somewhar 'bout lars' summer,
    Dicey she
Tuk 'n struck a notion—
    Don' you see?

Says she: "I's been thinkin'."
    An' I says:
"What you done thunk, honey?"
    Says she: "Yes,

"Is been thinkin' mons'ous
    'Bout Ebo;
He's fo'teen year ole now—
    Don' you know?"

Says I: "Ole 'oman, you is
    Right, I spec';
Dar's fo'teen—he kim fus'—
    Dat's kerrec'!"

Says she: "He's a-growin'
    Up a fool;
An' I's gwine ter sen' him
    Ter de school."

Bein's how it looked like
    She was bent
On de projick, Ebo
    Tuk 'n went.

An' sence dat lars' summer—
    Don' you see?
Dat 'ar boy have p'in'tly
    Outdone me!

Whe-ew! de norrations,
    Dem o' his'n!
Umph! I busses out laughin'
    Jes' ter listen!

What you think dat Ebo
    Come tell me?
Dat all dis here y'arth here—
    Flat—you see—

Dat it's roun', an' rolls jes'
    Like a ball!
"Ebo, dat's a lie," I
    Says, "dat's all!

"Don' you see yer Mammy
    Every night
Set de 'lasses glasses
    Out o' sight

"Ob you chillun, up dar
    On de shelf?—
Now, Mister Spellin'booker,
    'Splain yerself—

"Sunrise, dat 'ar 'lasses
    In dar still;
Ef de y'arth turned over
    It 'ud spill!"

But he keeps resistin'
    It are so—
Eddication's done gone
    Sp'ilt Ebo.

He's forever tellin'
    Some sich lie;
He's gwi' fine out better
    By-um-by.

Ef Ebo keeps l'arnin'
    At dat school,
Nex' thing, he'll be provin'
    I's a fool!

I are p'int'ly gwine ter
Take Ebo
Way from dat ar school-'ouse,
Sartin sho'!

(*A. C. Gordon*)

De Ole 'oman An' Me

We doesn't live as wunst we did—
De grub's done struck a change;
An' when I mentions ash-cake now,
My wife she thinks it strange.

She's got sot-up dese las' few years,
An' wheat-bread's all de go;
But, somehow, seems I'd like ter tas'e
Some ash-cake pone wunst mo'.

De buttermilk has done give way
Ter tea an' coffee now;
"An' 'possum-fat," she always says,
"Ain't fit to eat nohow."

She doesn't ever foot it now,
Like how she used ter do;
But drives my yaller mule ter town,
An' wushes he was two!

She hasn't had a homespun coat
For many a long day,
But w'ars de fines' sort o' clo'es,
Made jes' de white folks way.

She doesn't call me "Ichabod,"
Or "Ich," or "Ole Fool" now;
An' ef I mention "my old crowd,"
'T'ud sartin raise a row.

'Tis "Mister Brown" an' "Mistis Brown,"
Ontwel it seems ter me
We's done gone changed our nat'rel selves
F'om what we used ter be.

I know, beca'se as how I's tried
  An' never seed it gee;
It's awful hard ter teach new tricks
  Ter ole dogs sich as me.

Dat broad-clof coat she made me buy,
  It don't feel half so good
As dat ole jeans I used ter w'ar
  A-cuttin' Marster's wood.

An' beefsteak ain't fer sich as me,
  Instid o' 'possum-fat;
An' "Mister Brown" ain't "Ichabod"—
  I can't git over dat!

So Mistis Brown may go ter town
  A-drivin' o' dat mule
Jes' when she likes; but, sartin sho'
  I ain't gwi' play de fool!

An' as fer her insistin' how
  Dat I should try ter learn
Dem A B C's de chillun reads—
  'Tis no consarn o' her'n.

I doesn't keer what grub she eats,
  Or what she calls herself,
Or ef she has a bo'fy now
  'Stid o' a cubbud-shelf.

I doesn't keer how fine her clo'es
  May be, or what's de style—
I'm able fur ter pay fer dat,
  An' has been so some while.

Dar's only one o' all her ways
  Gits over me fer sho'—
I p'int'ly hones fer possum-fat
  An' ash-cake-pone wunst mo'!

(A. C. Gordon)

Mine Oyster

No, it never did agree wid de likes o' dis here nigger,
    For de a'r is sort o' stiflin' twix' dese mountains Eas' an' Wes';
Ev'y blessed year I lives here, seems dese hills is growin' bigger
    Ter de miz'ry in my knee-j'ints an' de trouble in my ches'.

I's a Tuckahoe V'ginyan f'om Tidewater, V'ginyer
    Whar de oshters am delishus an' de fish is hard ter beat;
Lord, I hain't seed an oshter, in de time dat I has been here,
    Dat dis nigger have cornsidered fittin' any ways ter eat.

Dey fetches 'em in cans up, dese here railroad sojer-fellows,
    An' it takes a good day's workin' ter perkure an oshter stew.
Dese ain't nothin' but runt-oshters; yet de resteranters tell us
    Dat dey come f'om Mobjack Bay, sir. Pshaw! I *know* dat can't be true!

I lived down dar myself wunst, an' I think I l'arnt de fashion
    O' dem oshters in dat water—shape an' size an' tas'e an' all;
Dis here darkey may be ign'ant, an' widout no eddication,
    But a Mobjack oshter p'int'ly *is* beknownst ter Uncle Saul.

You may brag o' roasted possum an' de glories o' hog-killin',
    You can 'numerate de hom'ny, you can shout de ole ash-cake;
But one dish o' Mobjack oshters, an' ole Saul is p'int'ly willin'
    Ter denounce de other eatin's fur de Mobjack oshter's sake!

Umph! Dis mouf o' mine jes' waters at de thought o' dem dar critters—
    Fried, an' baked, an' stewed, an' raw ones—how we 'stroyed 'em
        down dar;
Soft as mush an' fa'rly better dan merlasses on yer fritters—
    But de glory am departed, an' dem oshters ain't nowhar!

I have trabbled through V'ginyer sence Mars' Linkum sont de freedom;
    I have cotch 'em an' I've eat 'em, Norf an' Souf an' Eas an' Wes'.
Oh, dey' prime at Glorster P'int; dar it's mighty hard ter beat 'em;
    But de oshters f'om ole Mobjack am de sugares' an' bes'.

It is seben year, an' ober, sence I 'zided in dat section,
    An' I'm feared dis hilly valley 'ull lay on me when I die;
But I holds de ole Tidewater in my warmes' ree-collection,
    An' I'd like ter slip down dar wunst mo' an' make dem oshters fly.

I would like ter eat dem oshters 'twel I perish jes' f'om eatin';
    Dat's de kind o' death dat seems like it 'ud suit yer Uncle Saul.
Yes, I'd rather go dat way, sir, dan ter drap down dead in meetin';
    Fur ter die f'om eating oshters is de sweetes' death o' all.

                                (A. C. Gordon)

Disappointment

Hol' de light yar! De dogs done treed!
I knowed dey'd almos' co't him,
De way dey barked. What's dat you seed?
    Out on which limb?
    Yes sir! dat's him—
We sartin sho' is got him!

Shet up dat howlin'! Kick him, Joe!
    Dese dogs is p'int'ly eager;
Wait 'twel he gits down here below,
    Onter de groun',
    Den, I'll be boun',
He'll whup 'em like a nigger!

Joseph, my son, gimme de light,
    An' you kin do de cuttin';
I wudden git dat 'coon ter-night.
    Take holt de axe;
    Six or eight cracks
'Ull fix de critter's mutton!

Jes' look-a-dar! I nuver see
    'Coon's eyes so much like fire.
De way he's starin' down at me—
    Hol' on dar, Joe,
    He's 'bout ter go!
No—he jes' crep' up higher.

Here, Caesar—Nero—sic him! Sic!
    Stan' back! de tree's a-fallin'!
Now let de dogs git in dar, quick!
    Ugh! Shoo dar! Scat!
    Ol' Toby's cat!
Jes' lissen at dat squallin'!

I never see de beat o' dat
    In all my times o' seein'!
Folks what can't 'stinguish 'coon f'om cat
    Better be sleep
    In bed, a heap,
Dan up o' nights 'coon-treein'.

                                    (*A. C. Gordon*)

Festina Lente—or—
On Trapping a Christmas Hare

I wush you hadn' gone an' did
　Jes' what I tole ye not ter!
De Chris'mus dinner's tuk an' slid
　Long o' yo' foolin', drot yer!

I axed you, fus', ter be mo' slow;
　But you mus' go a-skeetin',
An' let de hyar out in de snow—
　Our onlies' Chris'mus eatin'.

You needn' stan' up dar an' grin,
　Jes' like 'twar sumpin' funny!
Ef dat 'ar hyar ain't tuk *you* in,
　I are mistaken, honey.

I's 'vized you' time an' time ag'in,
　'Bout rushin' 'roun' an' t'arin';
De way you does, Joe, are a sin
　Ter set a preacher sw'arin'!

Dar ain't no sense in starin' 'roun'
　Ter see ef he's in sight, sir;
He's five miles off, I'll jes' be boun',
　An' sarves you zackly right, sir!

Not fer ter know no mo' dan dat
　'Bout handlin' o' gun triggers,
An' let him go, slick as my hat—
　It's jes' like you young niggers.

Now, lemme tell you wunst ag'in:
　Don't do things in a skurry;
Ixcess o' zeal are boun' ter win,
　But not ixcess o' hurry.

So, Joe, ef ever you lets go
　Another Chris'mus dinner,
I'll lay a hick'ry on you, Joe,
　As sho' as I'm a sinner!

PART THREE

ACCORDING TO DUNBAR*

A Negro Love Song

Heard de wind blow through de pine,
    Jump back, honey, jump back.
Held her hand and squeezed it tight,
    Jump back, honey, jump back.
Heard her sigh a little sigh,
Seen a light gleam from her eye
And a smile go flitting by—
    Jump back, honey, jump back.

Heard de wind blow through de pine,
    Jump back, honey, jump back.
Mockingbird was singing fine,
    Jump back, honey, jump back.
And my heart was beating so
When I reached my lady's do'
Dat I couldn't bear to go—
    Jump back, honey, jump back.

Put my arm around her waist,
    Jump back, honey, jump back.
Raised her lips and took a taste,
    Jump back, honey, jump back.
"Love me, honey, love me true?
"Love me well as I love you?"
And she answered, "Course I do"—
    Jump back, honey, jump back.

---

* The verses which appear under the general heading, "According to Dunbar," were written by Paul Laurence Dunbar, 1872-1906. Dunbar was the first Negro poet (after Phillis Wheatley) to gain a national reputation in the United States, and the first to concentrate on the use of Negro dialect within the formal structure of his work. Born of former slaves in Dayton, Ohio, his first collection of poetry, *Oak and Ivory*, was published before he was 20. Two years later, his book, *Majors and Minors*, won critical favor in a review in *Harper's*. In 1896, he completed *Lyrics of a Lowly Life*, the work which established his reputation. Before his death at age 34, from tuberculosis, Dunbar had become the dominant presence in the world of American Negro poetry. The selections published in this Encyclopedia, of course, represent only his humorous work.

CANDIED YAMS

The ex-slave, Granddaddy, tells us, on page 29, that yams can't compare to sweet potatoes. "Dem roots dey call yams ain' no better'n b'iled Orrish 'taters, wid sweeten' water po'd over 'em," he adds.

6 medium-sized yams	1½ tsp. cinnamon
6 cups water	½ tsp. cloves
3 cups sugar	½ tsp. nutmeg
4 tbs. butter	

Wash yams, cover with water and bring to a fast boil. Cook 5 minutes longer. Drain and cool. Place in 4-quart saucepan. Add sugar, spices, butter and water. Cook uncovered for 1½ hours until thick syrup has almost cooked away. Serves 8.

In the Morning

'Lias! 'Lias! Bless de Lawd!
Don't you know de day's abroad?
If you don' get up, you scamp,
Dey'll be trouble in dis camp.
Think I gwine to let you sleep
While I makes your board and keep?
Dat's a pretty howdy-do—
Don't you hear me, 'Lias, you?

Bet if I come 'cross dis floor
You won't find no time to snore.
Daylight all a-shining in
While you sleep—why, it's a sin!
Ain't de candlelight enough
To burn out without a snuff
But you go de morning through
Burning up de daylight, too?

'Lias, don't you hear me call?
No use turning toward de wall;
I can hear dat mattress squeak;
Don't you hear me when I speak?
Dis here clock done struck off six—
Caroline, bring me dem there stick!
Oh, you down, sir; huh! you down—
Look here, don't you dare to frown.

March yourself and wash your face,
Don't you splatter all de place;
I got something else to do
'Sides just cleaning after you.
Take dat comb and fix your head—
Looks just like a feather bed.
Look here, boy, I let you see
You can't roll your eyes at me.

Come here, bring me dat there strap.
Boy, I'll whip you till you drap;
You done felt yourself too strong,
And you surely got me wrong.
Set down at dat table there;
Just you whimper if you dare!
Every morning on dis place,
Seems like I must lose my grace.

Fold your hands and bow your head—
Wait until de blessing's said;
"Lawd, have mercy on our souls—"
(Don't you dare to touch dem rolls.)
"Bless de food we gwine to eat—"
(You set still—I see your feet;
You just try dat trick again!)
"Give us peace and joy. Amen!"

Accountability

Folks ain't got no right to censah othah
    folks about dey habits;
Him dat giv' de squir'ls de bushtails
    made de bobtails fu' de rabbits.

When Malindy Sings

You cain't sta't no notes a-flyin'
    Lak de ones dat rants and rings
From de kitchen to de big woods
    When Malindy sings.

Theology

There is a heaven, for ever, day by day,
The upward longing of my soul doth tell me so.
There is a hell, I'm quite as sure; for pray,
If there were not, where would my neighbors go?

Encouragement

Speak up, Ike, an' 'spress yo'se'f.

Howdy, Honey, Howdy!

Sweetah den de music of a lovesick mockin'bird,
Comin' f'om de gal you loves better den yo' kin:
"Howdy, honey, howdy, won't you step right in?"

Philosophy

It's easy 'nough to titter w'en de stew
    is smokin' hot,
But hit's mighty ha'd to giggle w'en
    dey's nuffin' in de pot.

PART FOUR

THE LOSER'S CLUB

Peek-a-Boo

I saw Esau kissin' Kate,
An' the truth is that we all three saw.
For I saw Esau, he saw me,
An' she saw I saw Esau.

O Fly—OH, MY!

Po' li'l fly—
Ain't got no mama,
Ain't got no papa,
Ain't got no sister,
Ain't got no brother.

No mama to love you,
No papa to love you,
No sister to love you,
No brother to love you.

Fly, I know who loves you—
God loves you.
Go to God!
BAM!

Eight Cents Cotton

Eight cents cotton an' thutty cents meat,
How in de worl' kin a po' man eat?

Kin Folks

Melindy fell deep in love
With a colored boy she knew;
But it was quite the proper thing,
For she was colored too.

She hastened home and told her Pop
That shortly she would wed
One likely Rufus Brown,
When Pop looked up and said:

"No, honey chile, you cain't do dat,
You'll have tuh fin' another;
Don't tell yo' Ma, but Rufus Brown
Am sho'ly yo' half brother."

Melindy shed a few soft tears,
Then slowly went her way,
And soon she met another boy
And hastened home to say:

"Now Pop, I's gwine tuh marry
Dat Smith boy down de street.
He ain't got no bad habits
An' he sho' do dress up neat."

But Pop, he slowly shook his head
And looked across at Mother;
Then whispered, "No, chile, yuh cain't do dat;
"Dat Smif boy am yo' half brother."

Melindy, she forgot her oath,
And blurted out to mother,
"Pop say I cain't marry Rufus Brown,
"For he be my half brother.

"An' den I tuhns to Sonny Smif,
"Although it seem like treason;
"Pop, he say I cain't marry him
"On account ob de same reason."

Ma said, "Now honey chile, don't you cry.
"Put on yo' weddin' cap
"An' marry either one you likes,
"'Cause you ain't no kin to Pap!"

You Can't Win, Gentlemen!

The black-skin gal craves a house an' lot,
The brown-skin gal wants a car;
The yaller-skin gal wants all a man's got—
An' there y' are!

Say It Again, Man!

I's loved black gals in Arkansas town,
An' brownskin dolls f'om Texas;
But it don't mean nothin' whar dey are—
Dey's all a bunch o' hexes!

Like Man, Like Mule

I knowed a mean ol' kickin' man,
His name wuz Simon Slick;
He had a mule wid ice-col' eyes,
An' how dat mule could kick!

Whenever you got near him,
Dat mule 'ud natch'ly smile,
Den aim a flyin' kick at you
An' sen' you half a mile.

De White Folks Git De Money

De ole bee make de honey-comb,
De young bee make de honey,
De black mens make de cotton en co'n,
En de w'ite folks git de money.

(*Joel Chandler Harris*)

Cruel Justice*

Dere be justice in de co'ts ob dis ol' lan';
Jes' got a divo'ce f'om my ol' man.
Couldn't he'p laughin' at de jedge's decision;
Give *him* all eight chilluns—
An' not a one o' dem his'n.

Duncan and Brady

Duncan and Brady had a talk;
Said Duncan to Brady, "Let's take a walk,
"On down to the nigger saloon
"And whip us a big, ol' uppity coon."

---

* *New York World*, April 6, 1886 (Anon).

They went on down to the colored bar;
First a drink and then a cigar.
Duncan told Brady he was only a bluff,
But Brady showed Duncan he was really the stuff.

Next mornin', Duncan heard a helluva sound;
Wagons and hearses were parked all around,
Takin' ol' Brady to the buryin' ground.

Running Wild*

I went down to de back o' de fiel';
A black snake cotch me by de heel.
I cut my dus', I run my bes',
I run right intuh a horney's nes'.

Miss Dinah**

I wish I wuz a apple
An' Miss Dinah wuz another;
Oh, whut a happy pair we'd be,
On de tree together;

One day, while on de bank of de river,
De wind blowed more'n it ought ter;
An' it made Miss Dinah shake an' shiver,
So in my arms I caught 'er;
But when de wind blowed up ag'in,
It blewed us in de water.

Dat wind it blowed, dat wind it roared,
De people thought us drownded;
Miss Dinah she wuz pulled ashore,
But I wuz never founded.

Doctor in the Well***

Dere wuz a cullud doctah, his name wuz Doctah Peck;
He fell in de well an' done broke his skinny neck.
De cause ob de fall wuz sho'ly his own,
'Case he s'pose tuh look attuh sick folks
An' let de well alone!

---

* From *Johnny Booker*, pre-Civil War plantation song.
** Fragments, excerpted from the pre-Civil War dance song, *Miss Dinah.*
Edited and revised by Dan Sping for Jonathan David, Publishers, New York.
*** Parody of stanza from *Ol' Massa John.* Revised by Dan Sping, for Jonathan David, Publishers, New York.

It's Col' Down Dar!

Li'l Willie f'om a mirror
　　Licked de merc'ry almos' off,
Thinkin', in his chile'ish error,
　　It gwine cure his whoopin' cough.
At de fune-ral his mama
　　She say to Missus Brown:
"'Twar a chilly day fo' Willie
When de merc'ry done went down."

Epitaphs

Beneaf dis stone ouah baby lies,
It neithah cries er hollahs,
It lived fo' on'y 'leben days,
An' cost us fo'ty dollahs.

❦

The way he died was thus:
He got druv over by a bus.

❦

Here lies my wife,
　　　　Here lies she;
Hallelujah!
　　　　Hallelujee!

❦

Since I bin so soon done in fo',
What the hell wuz I begun fo'?

O I C

I'm in a 10der mood 2day
　　& feel poetic, 2;
4 fun I'll just — off a line
　　& send it off 2 u.

I'm sorry you've been 6 o long;
　　Don't b disconsol8;
But bear your ills with 42'd,
　　& they won't seem so gr8.

Ef I Had the Gov'ner

Ef'n I had the gov'ner
Where the gov'ner has me,
Before daylight
I'd set the gov'ner free.

PART FIVE

HAPPY RHYMES OF HAPPY TIMES

Celestial Fish Fry

Dey had a fish fry up in Heaven once,
An' fried some flyin' angel fish dey cotch
Along de Crystal Stream. Bro' Jonah lan'
De bigges' cat. Sis Widders Mite de leedles' one.

Bro' John de Baptis' head an' clean 'em good,
An' Sistah Lot she ten' tuh saltin' 'em.
De cherrybims an' serrybims dey kep'
De kitten angels f'om de piles o' fish,
An' Sistah Martha tuhn de fryin' meat.
Bro' Paul an' Silas done de passin' out,
An' me? I j'ined de folks whut come tuh eat.

Ole Man Dan

Ole Man Dan was a tough ole man,
Washed his face in the fryin' pan;
Combed his hair with a wagon wheel,
Died with a toothache in his heel.

Line From a Louisiana
Gospel Song

Dey ain't no flies on Jesus!

Divine Assistance*

Paul an' Silas layin' in jail,
 An' de ark kep' a-moverin' on;
Lawd come down an' went deir bail,
 An' de ark kep' a-moverin' on.

Ef My Wife Dies**

Ef my wife dies I'll git me another one,
Git me another one,
Git me another one;
Ef my wife dies I'll git me another one,
Down in Alabam.

Great big fat one, jes' like de other one,
Jes' like de other one,
Jes' like de other one;
Great big fat one, jes' like de other one,
Down in Alabam.

Riddle***

I done run out ter happy Wiggy-waggy,
An' I seed ol' Tom Tiggy-taggy.
I holler ter brown Wiggy-waggy
Ter drive Tom Tiggy-taggy.
Thar he go, happy Wiggy-waggy!

'Twas On De Bluff†

'Twas down on de bluff, in de state ob Indiana,
Dat's whar I use-ter lib, (heist de 'federate banner),
Eb'ry mornin' 'bout eight, my marster gib me liquor,
An' I'd take a li'l boat an' push out all de quicker.

---

* Popular in Albemarle County, Virginia, circa 1850, but may have originated elsewhere. See *From a Southern Porch*, Dorothy Scarborough, Harvard
University Press, 1919.
** *Ef My Wife Dies*, from "The Old Gray Horse (or 'Mare') Is Dead,"
widely sung in the Mississippi, Alabama and southern Arkansas areas in the
1880's-'90's.
*** This riddle, a favorite of slave children, refers to a dog (Wiggy-waggie)
and a hog (Tiggy-taggie). The dog was sent to drive the hog out of the field.
† The uniqueness of this poem lies in its stark allusions to seldom-men-
tioned facets of slave life; i.e., the daily ration of liquor given to the slaves
by some masters. The allotment was neither a humanitarian nor social gift,

O, 'twas up de river drif' an' 'twas in er li'l skiff,
An' I cotch es many catfish es any man kin lif'.

I turns aroun' my skiff—think I seed a alligator,
I picks up my rod an' I chunked a sweet pertater.
I picks up my pole an' I tried fer ter vex him,
But I couldn't fool him bad, noways could I fix him.

So I up wid a brick an' fotched him sech a lick
Ontwell I seed 'twas jes' a pine-knot on a big stick.

Den I turn aroun' my skiff, think I see a white man comin';
"Lord," says I ter m'self, "here's no time fer runnin'!"
So I jumped on my horse, threw my cloak aroun' my shoulder,
An' I stood jes' es still as a ol' militia soldier.

An' he pass all aroun', like a houn' upon de soun';
He took me fer a mile-post, stuck inter de groun'.

An' my ol' marster died on de 'lebenteenth of April,
An' I dug de hole at de root of de sugar maple.
I dug a big hole, way down below de level,
An' I ain't got no doubt but he went to de devil!

Jawbone*

I went to ole Napper's house,
Ole Napper warn't t' home;
I took my seat by a pretty yaller gal
An' picked on de ole jawbone.

De jawbone walk an' de jawbone talk,
An' de jawbone eat wid a knife an' fork.
I lef' my jawbone on de fence,
An' I ain't seed dat jawbone sence.

---

but a means of increasing and sustaining the slave's dependence and pacification. The poem also portrays the slave's fear of being apprehended as a runaway by any passing white man. *'Twas On De Bluff* is one of the few examples to illustrate that the slave's lot outside the deep South was frequently comparable to that of the "cotton states."

* Among the crude instruments which the slaves fashioned for their musical accompaniments were the banjo and the jawbone. The banjo was made from a large gourd with a long straight neck or handle. The bowl would be cut level with the handle, the seeds scraped out and a cover of tanned coonskin stretched tightly over it like a drumhead. The strings were passed over a bridge near the center of the drumhead and attached to the keys on the neck. In this poem, the jawbone refers to a musical instrument which was actually the jawbone of a horse, mule or ox, with the teeth intact. It was played by scraping a piece of metal across the teeth for rhythm.

In Old Kentuck'

In old Kentuck in de arternoon
We sweeps de floor wid a hick'ry broom,
An' arter dat we form a ring
An' dis de song dat we do sing:

Chorus

Oh, cla'r de kitchen, young folks, old folks,
Cl'ar de kitchen, all you slowpokes,
We gwine have some hoe-cake now.

I hab a sweetheart in dis town,
She w'ars a yaller stripe'd gown,
An' when she walks de streets aroun'
De holler of her foot make a hole in de groun'.

Chorus

Dis love it am a ticklish fing, you know,
It make a body feel all over so
I put de queshion ter darlin' Rose,
She cuss me out an' turned up her nose.

Chorus

"Go 'way," say she, "wid yo' cowcumber shin,
"Ef you come here ag'in I stick you wid a pin."
So I turn on my heel an' I bid her goodbye,
An' arter I was gone she begin fer ter cry.

Chorus

So now I's up an' off, you see,
Ter take a julep sangeree;
I gwine ter sit upon a 'tater hill
An' eat a li'l ol' whippoorwill.

Chorus

I wish I was back in ol' Kentuck,
'Cause since I left it I had no luck;
De gals so proud dey won't eat mush,
An' when you go ter court 'em dey say, 'Oh hush!"

Chorus

Jes' a-Thinkin'

Massa had a crowin' roostah,
Use-tah crow all day;
Dere came along a harricane
An' blowed dat chicken away.

Wish I had a tin box
To keep my baby in;
I'd take huh out an' kiss huh
An' put huh back ag'in.

Wish I had a needle an' fred
Es fine es I could sew;
I'd sew my baby to my side
An' down de road I'd go.

Some folks say de debbil's dead
An' buried in a shoe;
But I seed de debbil t'othah day
An' he looks es good es you.

If I had a fussin' wife
I'd whup huh sho's you bo'n;
Hitch huh to a double plow
An' make huh plow my co'n.

Sweet Revenge

Sy an' I went to de circus;
Sy git hit wid a rollin' pin.
Sy git even wid dat white man's circus—
Sy buy tickets but he didn' go in.

Dat's Livin'!*

Dere ain't no use in my workin' so hard,
'Cause I got a gal in de white folks' yard;
She brings me meat an' she brings me lard,
So dere ain't no use in my workin' so hard.

---

* Circa 1900, popular in the South Carolina-Georgia areas. These stanzas
are sung to the tune of "Ol' Marse John."

I got a gal an' her name is Maude,
Lives over yonder in de white folks' yard;
Brings me turkey wid all de stuffin',
I ain't ever gwine to want for nothin'!

I got a baby an' a honey, too;
Honey don't love me but my baby do;
An' every night 'bout half-pas' eight
I steps inside de white man's gate;
An' she brings me butter, an' de bread an' de lard,
Dat's de reason why I don't work so hard.

Spring Am Almost Here*

De gentle spring am almost here,
  De sun am gettin' high;
De snow am gently slidin' out,
  De ice begins to fly.

In thirty days, or dar abouts,
  De grass will take its green;
An' all of us kin slosh aroun'
  In April mud an' rain.

De robin will begin to rob,
  De bluebird will feel blue;
De crow will crow-bar on his way,
  De buzzards buzz anew.

Now let us all feel proper glad,
  An' lose no time indeed;
In castin' 'roun' among our friends
  To borry onion seed.

On De Neglected Grave

By de co'ner ob de melon patch,
  Among de bloomin' clover,
I sot me on a grassy mound
  To look de melons ober.
De bee was buzzin' in de sun,
  A-makin' ob de honey—
De skeeter borin' at my shin
  As if he worked for money.

---

* From *The Lime-Kiln Club*, M. Quad, 1883. Belford, Clarke & Co.

A stirrin' ob de melon vine—
　De win' blew from de souf;
An' powerful de melons pumped
　De water in my mouf.
An' den I think, "how soon—how soon,
　No melons I shall see—
How soon—how soon I shall not hear
　De buzzin' ob de bee."

Dis darkey's fleetin' bref done gone!
　(For life am neber long),
De melon-longin' hushed—an' hushed
　De banjo an' de song.
Den lay me in de groun' right heah,
　An' let de skeeter rave!
De melon sho' will ripen on
　De po' neglected grave.

(M. Quad)

White-washing Season

De robin am chirpin',
　De bluebird am singin',
De voice ob de bluejay am heard in de lan'.
　De wild ducks am flyin',
De ganders am sighin',
　An' de big bunko man he am showin' his han'.

De mud's growin' deeper,
　An' thunder's a-comin',
An' de possum comes out of his log fur to see;
　De warm rain's a-fallin',
De spring calf am bawlin',
　An' de white-washin' season has opened fur me.

(M. Quad)

Ode to de Watermellyon

Oblong an' luscious—
　Black seeds or white;
Lemme devour you
　Outer my sight.

Mottled or speckled,
　　Thick rind or thin;
Devoid of all cramps,
　　Colic an' sin.

Georgia or Jarsey,
　　Speckled or spotted;
Dose who doan' like 'em
　　Orter be shotted.

(*M. Quad*)

The Happy Workingman

Blow de horn! Beat de drum!
　　H'ar de bugle blowin'!
Fifty million Yankees here,
　　An' still de kentry's growin'!

Soun' de bones! Shake de hoofs!
　　See de people smilin';
Everybody's on de rush,
　　An' bizness am a-b'ilin'.

(*M. Quad*)

Ol' Dan'l

Outen his cabin to de sun,
Bented ovah comes ol' Dan'l,
His ches' kivvered wid white wool,
His back all ovah flannel.

"Wintah gwine finish 'im," dey say
Ev'y wintah now fo' ten;
But come de fus' warm day ob spring
Ol' Dan'l's out ag'in.

Warm Babies

Shadrach, Meshach, Abednego,
Walked in the furnace to an' fro,
Hay foot, straw foot, fro an' to,
An' the flame an' the smoke flared up the flue.
Nebuchadnezzar he listen some,
An' he hear 'em talk, an' he say "How so?
Dem babies was hawg tied a hour ago!"

Then Shadrach call, in an uppity way,
"A little mo' heat or we ain' gwine stay!"
An' Shadrach bawl so dat de furnace shake:
"Lan'lawd, heat! fo' de good Lawd's sake!"
Abednego yell, wid a loud "Kerchoo!"
"Is you out to freeze us, an' kill us, too?"

Nebuchadnezzar, he rare an' ramp,
An' call to his janitor, "You big black scamp!
Shake dem clinkers an' spend dat coal!
I'll bake dem birds, ef I goes in de hole!"
So he puts on de draf' an' he shuts de door
Till de furnace glow an' de chimbly roar.

Ol' Nebuchadnezzar, he smole a smile.
"Guess dat'll hold 'em," says he, "fer awhile."
Then Shadrach, Meshach, Abednego
Walk on de hot coals to an' fro,
Gulp dem cinders like chicken meat
An' holler out fo' a mite mo' heat.

Ol' Nebuchadnezzar gives up de fight;
He open dat door an' he bow perlite.
He shade his eyes from the glare infernal
An' say to Abednego, "Step out, Colonel."
An' he add, "Massa Shadrach, I hopes you all
Won' be huffy at me at all."

Then Shadrach, Meshach, Abednego,
Hay foot, straw foot, three in a row,
Stepped right smart from dat oven door
Jes' as good as they wuz before,
An' far as Nebuchadnezzar could find,
Jes' as good as they wuz behind.

(*Keith Preston*—1884-1927)

Battle of Little Rock*

'Twas the first of September
And all through the South
Not a word could be heard
From nobody's mouth.
The kiddies were ready
For school the next day,

---

* This parody of *The Night Before Christmas* appeared in an anonymous handbill during the Little Rock school crisis of 1958 and gained popularity on black campuses and youth centers in many areas of the south.

When all hell broke loose
Down Arkansas way.
Ol' Ike had give orders
To mix up the schools,
But ol' Faubus said "Hold it!
We ain't no fools.
If you know what's good
You will stand back and listen,
'Cause we ain't gonna stand
For no nigger mixin'."
He hollered an order
Heard around the nation;
He called on the Guard
To halt integration.
The Guard came runnin'
And took up their stand,
To uphold the right
Of the good ol' Southland.
Ike didn't like this
So he ran to the phone
And called up ol' Faubus
At his Arkansas home.
He said, "Meet me in Newport
Tomorrow night,
'Cause the niggers and white
Folks are fixin' to fight."
Faubus agreed
And he hopped on his plane
And left in a hurry
In a drizzling rain.
Faubus returned home,
But stuck to his rule:
"Ain't no nigger comin'
To this here school."
So on came the troops
In numbers yet bigger,
To make the white folks
Go to school with a nigger.
Ol' Faubus was brave
And made a gallant stand,
But he had to abide
By the law of the land.
Old Ike won the battle
For the time being;
But God help the niggers
When the troops start leaving.

PART SIX

BIRDS AND BEASTS AND INSECTS SMALL

Plantation Serenade

De raccoon he's a cu'us man,
  He never walk twel dark,
En nuthin' never 'sturbs his mine,
  Twel he hear ole Bringer bark.

De raccoon totes a bushy tail,
  De 'possum totes no ha'r,
Mr. Rabbit, he come skippin' by,
  He ain't got none ter spar'.

Monday mornin' break er day,
  W'ite folks got me gwine,
But Sat'dy night, w'en de sun goes down,
  Dat yaller gal's in my mine.

Fifteen poun' er meat a week,
  W'iskey fer ter sell,
Oh, how kin a young man stay at home?
  Dem gals dey look so well.

Met a 'possum in de road—
  "Brer 'Possum, whar you gwine?"
I thank my stars, I bless my life,
  "I'm huntin' fer de muscadine."*

                          (*Joel Chandler Harris*)

Rabbit Hash

Dere wuz a big ole rabbit dat had a mighty habit
Uv settin' in mah gyahdin an' eatin all mah cabbage.
I whack 'im wid a mallet an' I smack 'im wid a maul—
Sech anodder rabbit hash you neber tas'e a-tall.

---

* A grape of the southeastern part of the United States, and a favorite
of the opposum.

Bat! Bat!

Bat! Bat! Fly undah mah hat
   An' Ah'll give you a slice uv bacon;
But don' bring none yo' ol' bedbugs,
   Ef you don' wanna git fersaken.

Teeny Fishes

Teeny fishes in de brook,
Sonny cotch 'em wid a hook;
Mama fry 'em in a pan,
Papa eat 'em like a man.

The Rooster and the Chicken

De rooster an' de chicken had a fight,
De chicken kick de rooster outer sight;
De rooster tol' de chicken, "Dat's all right—
I'll see yer in de gumbo termorrer night!"

I Had a Leedle Rooster

I had a leedle rooster, an' he crowed befo' de day;
   'Long come a big ole owl an' toted him away.
But dat rooster he fight hard, an' de owl let 'im go;
   Now all de dominickuh hens wants dat rooster fo' dey beau.

Rabbit Soup

Rabbit soup! Rabbit sop!
Rabbit et mah tuhnip top!
Rabbit hop, rabbit jump,
Rabbit hide behine dat stump.
Rabbit stop, twelve o'clock;
Kilt dat rabbit wid a rock.
Rabbit's mine; Rabbit's skint;
Clean 'im off an' take 'im in.
Rabbit's on—dance an' whoop!
We gonna have some rabbit soup!

Silly Billy

I had a li'l billy goat,
    I put 'im in de stable.
"R'ar back, you silly goat,
    An' lemme see yo' navel."

Serves Him Right

There was a little river frog
    That was always on the jump,
And 'cause he never look in front
    He always got a bump.

Cackle-Cackle

I had a hen what cackled
From de day dat she was bo'n;
She git es fat es cracklin'
F'om eatin' up de co'n.

Dat dominickuh cackled
An' strut huh yalluh laigs,
She stuff husse'f wid vittles
But don' give any aigs.

Dat dominickuh hen she cackled
When she col' an' when she hot;
So de nex' time dat she cackled
She cackled in de pot.

The Flea

I got to thinkin' 'bout the flea,
An' how you can't figger he from she.
The boys an' girls look the same to me,
But she can tell, an' so can he.

Great Fleas

Great fleas have little fleas upon their back to bite 'em,
And little fleas have lesser fleas, and so *ad infinitum*.
The great fleas themselves in turn have greater fleas to go on,
While these again have greater still, and greater still, and so on.

The Ape

The hairy ape, now, chillun see,
He's lookin' fo' a li'l ole flea.
If he should tuhn aroun' we'd fine
He has no hair on his behine.

The Frog

What a wonderful bird the frog are—
When he stand he sit almost;
When he hop, he fly almost.
He ain't got no sense hardly;
He ain't got no tail hardly either.
When he sit, he sit on what he ain't got almost.

Gettin' Born

When once a chick busts through a egg
　He gives three little squeals,
Then works out backwards through a hole
　By kickin' with his heels.

Or maybe he'll keep peckin' 'round,
　With now and then some cursin',
Until his head pokes through and then
　Comes all his little person.

Or like as not he'll puff his chest,
　A grunt and then some kickin'—
He's standin' there out in the air,
　A promissory chicken.

So We Hunted and We Hollered*

So we hunted an' we hollered an' de fus' thing dat we fin'
　Wuz a barn in de meadow, an' dat we lef' behin'.
One say it war a barn, an' de odder say "Nay!"
　Dey all say a chu'ch wid de steeple washed away.

---

* This version of a child's song was published in various journals and broadsides in 1818-1820. References are made to these lyrics in the *Journal of American Folklore*, XXXV, 349. Similar versions are given by the late Prof. George Lyman Kittredge, of Harvard, in an article published in the book, *Folk Songs of the South*, by Prof. John Harrington Cox. It was also alluded to in the year 1668, during the third act of Davenant's comedy, *The Rivals*.

So we hunted an' we hollered an' de nex' thing dat we fin'
  Wuz a cow in de meadow, an' dat we lef' behin'.
One say it war a cow, an' de odder say "Nay!"
  One say it be a elephant wid a snout washed away.

So we hunted an' we hollered an' de nex' thing dat we fin'
  Wuz a owl in de ivy bush, an' dat we lef' behin'.
One say it wuz a owl, an' de odder say "Nay!"
  One say it wuz de devil, an' we all run away.

Brothuh Ephrum Got de Coon*

I went down to my pea-patch
To see if my ole hen had hatch.
Ole hen hatch an' tellin' of huh dream,
An' de leedle chickens pickin' on de tambo'ine.

Brothuh Eph'um got de coon an' gone on an' gone on an' gone on,
Brothuh Eph'um got de coon an' gone on
An' lef' me here behine.

I see a rabbit a-runnin' down de fiel';
I say, "Mistuh Rabbit, wha' you gwine?"
He say, "I ain't got no time to fool wid you,
Dah's a white man comin' on behine.

The Squirrel Game**

Peep, Squirrel, peep!
  Peep at yo' brothah.
Why shouldn' one fool
  Peep at anothah?

---

* The origin of this old song-poem cannot be ascertained, but an indication of its age is the reference to the primitive banjo, here called a "tambourine." "Pickin' a tambourine" was a well-known expression in the 1850's.
** From *Carols and Child-lore at the Capitol*, W. H. Babcock, *Lippincott's* Magazine, September, 1886. Considered to be of African origin, the Squirrel Game calls for two players, standing face-to-face, to represent trees. A third player, taking the part of a squirrel, peeps around the trunk of one "tree," at another "squirrel" not visible, but apparently off-stage. As the verses progress, the "squirrel" trots faster, the excitement of beating time and singing increases, and the chorus, clapping and patting, becomes more animated as the "squirrel" attempts to elude the "fox" by leaping behind the "trees." The game finally becomes a whirl of dodging and leaping and furious pursuit until the "squirrel" is inevitably caught. It is interesting to note that, while the Squirrel Game was a favorite among black children in the South, it has no history north of the Potomac River.

Jump, Squirrel, jump!
Jump, Squirrel, jump!
Jump, or de fox will cotch you;
Jump, jump, jump!

Trot, Squirrel, trot!
Trot, Squirrel, trot!
Trot, or de fox will cotch you;
Trot, trot, trot!

The Bee

The bee he am a insec' small,
An' cunnin' like a weasel;
An' when he lan's upon you-all,
He leaves a leedle measle.

Chickamy, Chickamy, Crany Crow*

Chickamy, chickamy, crany crow,
I went to the well to wash my toe.
When I came back one of my black-eyed chickens was gone.

Raccoon Up in de 'Simmon Tree

Raccoon up in de 'simmon tree,
Possum on de groun';
Possum say to de raccoon,
"Shake dem 'simmons down."

Ol' Massa had a little mule,
He wuz colored like a mouse;
I went to bridle dat mule one day
An' he kicked me in de mouf.

* Another child's game of antiquity. A witch sits at one side while a leader representing a mother hen enters with a string of "chicks" behind her, each clinging to the garments of the one in front. The line circles fearfully around the witch, chanting the refrain. The leader pauses near the witch and asks, "What time is it?" If the old witch answers with any numeral less than twelve, the mother and chicks are safe, but if the witch replies "Twelve o'clock!" then she springs at them and they flee shrieking in terror. If the witch captures a chick—as she surely does—the prisoner is put into a pen and the game begins with those that are left free. Folklorists will recognize this as a variant of some very old British games enjoyed by children prior to the American Revolutionary War.

Miss Sallie likes a po'm like dis,
  I wish dat we were wed;
Miss Sallie give me one sweet kiss
  An' it almos' killed me dead.

Possum up a 'simmon tree,
  Raccoon on de groun';
Raccoon say, "You cunnin' thing,
  Shake dem 'simmons down."

Quatrains to a Possum

Met a possum on de road.
"Bre'r Possum, whar you gwine?"
"Bress my soul an' thank my stars,
To hunt some muscadine."

Possum up de gum-stump,
Coony up de hollow;
Li'l ole gal at our house
Fat as she kin wallow.

Met a possum on de road,
An' shamed he looked to be;
Stuck his tail between his legs
An' gave the road to me.

Norah Built a Ark*

Didn' ol' Norah build him a ark,
Build it outen hick'ry bark;
Animals come in one by one,
Cow a-chewin' a toas'ed bun.

Chorus

Hallelu, Hallelu,
Hallelujah to de Lamb;
Hallelu, Hallelu,
Hallelujah to de Lamb;
Hallelu, Hallelu.

---

* There are countless variations on the theme of Noah (or "Norah") and his Ark. In this version, however, the emphasis is on the animals rather than on Noah, his household, or his labors in constructing the famous vessel.

Animals come in two by two,
Rhinoc'rous an' de kangaroo;
Animals come in three by three,
Bear a-huggin' a bumble-y bee.

(*Chorus*)

Animals come in four by four,
Norah go wild an' shout for more;
Animals come in five by five,
That's how the animals did arrive.

(*Chorus*)

Animals come in six by six,
Hyena laughed at the monkey's tricks;
Animals come in seben by seben,
Yell the ant to the elephant:
"Who's you shovin'?"

(*Chorus*)

Animals come in eight by eight,
Norah holler, "Go shet de gate!"
Animals come in nine by nine,
Norah holler, "Go cut dat line!"

My Pony, Jack

I had a little pony,
    His name was Jack;
I rid his tail
    To save his back;
The lightnin' roll,
    The thunder flash
An' split my coattail clear to smash.

A Fine Crap Yeah

Las' yeah wuz a fine crap yeah
    On co'n an' peas an matuhs;
My pa didn' raise no cotton an' co'n,
But, I declah, *dose tatuhs!*

Chorus

Haw, Buck! haw Buck, haw!*
Stop ack'in so damfoolie!
Soon's I git de crap laid in
I's gwine back home tuh Julie.

Las' yeah I plowed de horney ox,
Dis yeah I plows de mulie.
Nex' yeah gwine plow wid a ol' grey fox
An' den go home tuh Julie.

Quit Kickin' My Dawg Aroun'

You gotta quit kickin' my dawg aroun',
I don't care if he *is* a houn'.

Ginny's Two Cats**

Ginny she slep' an' had a dream
Dat she wuz floatin' down a stream;
When she wake up she gib a sigh,
De grey cat scratch out de black cat's eye.

Bad, Bad Birds***

Jaybird settin' on a hick'ry limb;
He wink at me, I wink at him.
I pick up a rock an' hit him on de chin;
Jaybird yell, "Dammit, nigguh! Don't you do dat ag'in!

Hawkie is a schemin' bird,
He schemes all 'roun' de sky;
He schemes into my chicken house
An' makes my chickens fly.

---

* "Buck" refers to a mule.
** The cat appears infrequently in black folklore. Of the several thousand songs and poems from which these selections were made, a mere twelve were found in which the cat receives more than a cursory mention.
*** An old myth among yesteryear's Negroes explained that jaybirds were never seen on Friday because, on that day, they spent their time in torment carrying sand for the devil. There was little mawkish admiration for the jaybird's beauty, nor any misconception of his nature.

Ol' King Buzzahd floatin' high,
Say "Sho do wish dat cow would die."
Ol' cow died an' li'l calf cried,
"Oh mou'nah, you shall be free."

The Woodpecker

Peckerwood, peckerwood,
Whut make yo' head so red
You peck out in de sun all day,
It's a wonder you ain't dead.

Bachelor's Lament*

Monkey settin' on de end uv a rail,
Pickin' 'is teef wid de end uv 'is tail.
Mulb'y leaves an' calico sleeves,
All school teachuhs is ha'd to please.

De hen dip de snuff,
De roostuh chew t'backuh,
De guinea don' chew
But strut huh stuff.

Pigs unduh de table,
Rats on de she'f.
I'm so tiahd uv sleepin'
All by myse'f.

The Praying Rooster

Creepin' in de hen house on mah knees,
Thought Ah heerd a chicken sneeze;
'Twarn't nothin' but a rooster sayin' his pra'rs,
Makin' a speech to de hens upsta'rs.

Tall Tale

Had a Shanghai chicken whut grew so tall,
Tooken a month fo' de aig tuh fall.

---

* It appears that *Bachelor's Lament* was composed by a young slave on the Howard Snyder plantation in Mississippi, who daydreamed as he yearned for a wife.

To the White Folks' House

Beef an' veal bofe six weeks ol',
Mice and skippers gittin' mighty bol';
Long-tail mouse wid a bucket o' souse,
Skippin' f'om de kitchen to de white folks' house.

'Tain't Fair!

Looka dat ol' woodpeckuh,
    Learnin' how tuh figguh;
All fo' de white man,
    An' none fo' de nigguh.

Little bee sucks de blossom,
    Big bee eats de honey;
Nigguh makes de cotton an' co'n,
    White man gits de money.

Introduce Yourself, Sir!

I's a li'l catuhpilluh, feelin' mighty blue;
Now it's yo' tuhn, suh—who de hell am you?

(*Dan Sping*)

6

TURN
of the
CENTURY

BOOK SIX

Turn of the Century

Introduction

Folklorists, especially those who employ humor to illustrate a point, are semantically unpretentious; they speak the language of the people. This simplicity of narration, it should be noted, is the result of scholarly discipline; it is never meant to imply simplicity of subject, for the folklorist always writes with an appreciation of ancestral merit. Regrettably, much of black humor, including that which is properly a part of traditional folklore, became the stock in trade for a long succession of literary mountebanks and second-rate performers. At the turn of the century, the caricatures they created were carried over and presented on the legitimate stage, somewhat modified from the crude forms of minstrelsy.

In all fairness, however, some of the earlier representations were not maliciously conceived, but reflected the mores and attitudes of the day. A few, despite their manifest shortcomings, even aspired to nobility. For example, Harriet Beecher Stowe's *Uncle Tom's Cabin* was among the first social documents dealing with the moral issues of slavery to attain wide popularity. Most certainly, it bolstered the Abolitionist cause and helped to recruit new sympathizers. Today, Uncle Tom has become synonymous with the sycophant, fawning Negro, a characterization not intended by the author, nor was he seen as a figure of contempt by the black population of that era. True enough, Uncle Tom's role is comparable to Joe Chandler Harris' creation, Uncle Remus, who had nothing but "pleasant memories of the discipline of slavery," but even this analogy is tenuous; Uncle Tom was well aware of its tragedies. It is clear, whatever else he may have been, that the fictitious

341

Uncle Tom was not the servile, comic buffoon as later metamorphosed by the hacks who forever lurk on the outer fringes of literary respectability. Nor can anything, other than disdain, be expressed for the entertainers, black and white, whose intentionally planned grotesqueries helped perpetuate the stereotypical 19th-century Negro who remains an embarrassment to sensitive people in our own times.

The first musical comedy version of *Topsy and Eva,* based on *Uncle Tom's Cabin,* was performed at the Curran Theatre in San Francisco, in 1920. Starring in this inaugural production were Thelma and Marjorie White, billed as "The White Sisters" (no pun intended), with ten-year-old Thelma in blackface, playing Topsy, and her older sister portraying Eva. The songs were composed by Vivian and Rosetta Duncan, themselves actresses of note. A glimpse of the painfully slow transition from primitive minstrelsy to the legitimate stage is provided in the following excerpts:

SCENE

Slave mart. Topsy, grimacing, stands on auction block

Auctioneer: What am I bid? . . . Not even fifty cents? A quarter? . . . I'll *give* her away!
Eva: I'll take her, sir. I'll pay!

✓   ✓   ✓

Eva: Oh, Papa! Papa, look what I bought—and all with my own money!

✓   ✓   ✓

Eva: Who were your mama and papa?
Topsy: Ah don' know.
Eva: Well, where were you born?
Topsy: Ah don' know dat eithuh. Guess Ah jes' growed.
Eva: You know, if you tell stories you'll turn into a pillar of salt, like Mrs. Lot.
Topsy: No, Ah's gwine tuhn me intuh red peppuh an' make it hot fo' evuhbody.

For the black man, musical comedy and drama evolved slowly, but steadily, from his 19th-century role as an object of ridicule to one of self-assertiveness and human dignity. The ensuing years witnessed such productions as *Carmen Jones;* Leroi Jones' biting plays: *The Dutchman* and *The Toilet;* the daring *For Love of Ivy,* co-starring Sidney Poitier and the exquisitely talented Abby Lincoln; and *The Great White Hope,* in which James Earl Jones gave a visceral performance as the former heavyweight boxing champion, Jack Johnson. The ultimate antithesis of *Topsy and Eva* was reached in April, 1971, with James Damico's play, *The Trial of A. Lincoln,* staged at the Huntington Hartford Theater in Hollywood. Featured was a black militant as the defendant, I. A. T. (for I Am The) Best, who calls Lincoln (the plaintiff) not the Great Emancipator of the white history books, but a "honky bastard" and "the number one racist in American history." I. A. T. Best displayed some high humor as a ditty-bopping, juju-zapping radical, as did his defense lawyer, Lincoln and the judge, but they also reached shattering levels of emotion as they stripped the decaying meat of hypocrisy and myth from the bare bones of reality. It requires only a moment of reflection to realize that a play such as this could not have been conceived, let alone produced, in the days of *Topsy and Eva*.

Someone once said, "Humor is God's aspirin to soothe the headache of reality." Perhaps that is why the black man has learned to laugh in the teeth of oppression—to find mirth in his peccadillos as well as his virtues. Many of the old canards, especially those depicting him as a chicken-stealing, indolent, morally-loose, ghost-fearing, shuffling simpleton, originated during the dark days of bondage when the plantation owners engaged in a calculated effort to demean the slaves. This villification—the greatest mass "put-down" in American history—was not initially motivated by racial prejudice, but rather by what the owners believed were the exigencies attending slavery. The idea of blacks as inferior beings was deliberately inculcated among the slaves to inhibit and prevent wholesale uprisings against the institution of servitude. The nonsensical idea remains with us today, in some quarters, despite the fact that many slave-owners themselves did not believe their own propaganda, as evidenced by the proportionately large number of slaves and freed men who not only learned to read and write under the most adverse conditions but who won national and international distinction for their intellectual achievements.*

Nevertheless, the old stereotypes were continued as the curtain was lowered on the past century. We are reminded, for example, of the exasperated white farmer who erected this large sign on his property: *Warning! Anyone found near my chicken house at night will be found there the next morning!* Today, the old-time chicken thief has surrendered to the technological revolution. He has become sophisticated: "Oh, what a perfectly lovely moon," murmured the girl. "There's romance in the air. Look at all those parked cars here in Lover's Lane. Doesn't that give you any ideas?" The boy nodded. "Yeah, baby," he replied. "Let's go steal some hubcaps!"

The "lazy" motif is another durable theme: "I declare," sighed the weary mother, "that son of mine is the laziest boy ever stood on two feet. Only today I asked him, 'Joe, ain't there nothin' in this world you can do fast?' And he answered, 'Sure, ma, I get tired fast.' "

Yesteryear's Negro was also characterized as an intemperate drinker: "My uncle takes a drink now and then to steady himself. Sometimes he gets so steady he can't move!" He was also pictured as having something less than normal intelligence: "Dumb? If anyone said hello to him he'd be stuck for an answer!" Some whites were convinced that blacks were born

---

* For a condensed directory of 19th century black scientists and inventors, see introduction to *The New Breed*, Book Seven.

liars; to which one Brother wittily replied, "A lie may be a poor substitute for the truth, but it's the only one discovered to date."

Anecdotes involving the stereotypical Negro of a bygone day are well represented in this section. Their saving grace lies in their authenticity; that is, they are the jokes and stories told by generations of blacks to other blacks —told with tongue-in-cheek, perhaps, but with the high humor that stems from a point of view seldom shared with the white populace. In that context, it is easy to enjoy the bubbling vivacity of the lollygaggin' lady who romps through the following chapter; the gallivantin' Lochinvar whose roving eyes keep apace with his roaming hands; the imbiber, the gambler, and that unheralded heroine, the "domestic," whose arduous "day's work" at coolie wages paid for the college education of many contemporary national personalities. Her day-to-day struggles as she tried to cope with an imperious employer, poverty and lack of education are recounted in the chapter, *The Workaday World*, a blend of humor and pathos that evokes both a sigh and a chuckle.

Not all of the stories in *The Workaday World* are concerned with the domestic worker; others include the daily problems of the black male in his occupational rounds. An oblique reference to the physical demands made upon him is contained in the following dialogue:

> *Doctor*: The examination shows that you are in perfect health. All you need is a little hard work.
> *Patient*: Hard work? Man, you gotta be jivin' me! I'm a piano mover!
> *Doctor*: Well, hereafter move two at a time.

It has been said that the traditional clock-watcher has one virtue; at least he always knows what time it is. Sociological studies indicate that the man who is less than capable at his place of work is usually no paragon at home either. The chapter, *Marriages and Mortgages*, seems to bear out the thesis. There is the story of the boastful husband, a tale popular in the 1920's, who bragged, "I always help my wife with the housework. When she washes the dishes, I wash the dishes with her; when she mops up the floor, I mop up the floor with her." In another exchange of dialogue, we find that the black husband is no different than the white man when his peak of exasperation has been reached: "Willie, wake up!" hissed the wife at 2:00 a.m. "There's a mouse under our bed. I can hear it squeaking." Willie opened one eye. "Well, what am I supposed to do," he complained sleepily, "get up and oil it?" In any event it is not always the male who provides the kernels of marital humor, as witness this caustic comment: "My husband would never chase another woman. He's too fine, too loyal, too decent—too old!" The chapter, *Marriages and Mortgages*, tends to support one inescapable conclusion: the battle of the sexes will never be won by either side; there's too much fraternizing with the enemy.

The section dealing with *The Thompson Street Poker Club* resurrects a group of delightful New Yorkers, all devotees of the estimable game of draw poker, whose antics are as funny today as they were almost a hundred years ago. The characterizations are strongly drawn, the high jinks so outrageously hilarious that their vices assume the complexion of virtues and we find ourselves rooting for such unabashed card sharks as the belligerent Gus Johnson, the unscrupulous Tooter Williams, the crafty Rev. Thankful Smith, the timid Cyrus Whiffles and other club members who were convinced that the end (winning the pot) justified the means. With the advent of the 20th-century these stories were adapted for the stage by many entertainers, including the celebrated vaudeville star, Bert Williams.

It will be seen that the folk tales and humorous anecdotes still retained much of the plantation dialect and slapstick situations current in the past century, but to a far lesser degree as the carousel of time turned into the 1900's. Nearly gone was the once-frequent use of the word "nigger"—an epithet, incidentally, that almost disappeared from the black American's lexicon, until the late 1960's when it gained currency as a curse-word among younger militants to describe so-called "Uncle Toms."

Now let us journey back to that period beginning some ten decades ago shortly after World War I. With the exception of the Great Depression, those were the halcyon days for the nation's white population. For the blacks, civil rights had yet to attain practical meaning; atrocities and continued subjugation were the rule rather than the exception. This was the era when Ku Klux Klansmen crawled across the face of the land on all fours. But there was a stirring of the black spirit, too; a mounting awareness of the implications of concerted political action, fostered and nurtured by Negro writers, preachers and educators, but notably through the collective efforts of such organizations as the NAACP, the Urban League and the numerous local neighborhood groups whose inchoate strivings for fundamental justice were to blossom in the years to come.

Somehow, as they fought their way along the hard road to equality, they found time to laugh, these indomitable social pioneers, at themselves and at those very institutions and practices that shackled and confined them. Like the laughter of oppressed minorities everywhere, theirs expressed the longings and yearnings which they were unable or unwilling to articulate openly; so they voiced their emotions in parable, quip and story, sometimes revealing their deeper anxieties and, at others, the passing thoughts and minor problems that are the essence of folklore. Here, then, are the best of the anecdotes told by a gallant if largely untutored generation, recounted in all their original humor and as titillating today as they were before many of us were born.

PART ONE

THOSE LOLLYGAGGIN' LADIES

How Dare You?

The census taker was asking one of his innumerable and highly personal questions.

"You're married, of course," he said, noting a two-year-old child playing on the floor.

"No, I ain't," said the lady. "I've never been married."

"But that's your baby, isn't it?"

"I should say not!" snapped the lady, indignantly. "That's my *gran*'baby!"

O the Shame of It All!

The tiny town of Neckbone Junction was far removed from any big city but the people didn't mind at all. Grace Church provided all the spiritual guidance the traffic would bear, and there was plenty of work.

Not so happy, however, was Dianne who sang in the choir. Dianne had a pretty face, but she was so skinny, dressed so poorly, and was so very shy that none of the local boys would give her a second glance, let alone court her.

Sadly, Dianne decided to leave Neckbone Junction and try her luck elsewhere.

Three long years passed, and then one day the pastor of Grace Church found it necessary to go to Memphis. He was walking along Beale Street when his eyes fell on Dianne. For a moment or two he was speechless. Gone was the shabby, ill-fitting dress. Indeed, she was dolled up fit to kill, with a black satin dress, a glossy wig hat, spike heels and a spangled purse. And she had filled out, too. Her ample curves were very much in evidence.

"'Scuse me, Miss," he began uncertainly, "but ain't you Dianne from Neckbone Junction?"

"Sho' am," she replied, smiling.

"Well, I mus' say, chile, you sho' look fancy. How all dis happen?"

"Luck, I guess," she said. "I bin ruint!"

None of Your Business

The black people of the south enjoyed a brief period of political freedom shortly after emancipation. This very old dialogue still evokes a chuckle.

CORN PUDDING

In the ante-Bellum days when the above recipes were created, people creamed their own corn. Today, it comes in cans. Here are two famous old recipes, one of them updated by Harlem chefs.

Corn Pudding—Country Style

2 cups creamed corn   3 tbs. butter
1 egg, slightly beaten   salt and pepper to taste
3 tbs. flour

Combine ingredients and mix thoroughly. Place mixture in baking dish. Bake in moderate oven (350°) 45 minutes, or until knife inserted in center comes out clean. Serve with sliced tomatoes.

Corn Pudding—Harlem Gourmet Style

2 cups grated corn cut from cob, or   4 eggs
    1 No. 2 can creamed corn   3 tbs. melted butter
1 quart milk   2 tbs. sugar
1 tsp. salt   1 tsp. celery salt
    dash mace or nutmeg

Beat egg yolks. Add sugar, butter and milk. Beat well again. Mix with corn and spices. Beat egg whites until stiff and fold into egg yolk mixture. Place in a greased casserole. Set in oven to bake at 350° for about 1 hour. If pudding browns too fast, place a piece of heavy brown paper on top. Serves 6.

Hannah went to the county court house and approached the registration clerk. "I wants tuh vote," she said.

"What party do you affiliate with," he asked.

"You mean I *got* tuh tell dat?"

"Certainly."

"Den fuhgit it! I ain't gonna vote ef I gotta tell secrets. De pahty I 'filiates wid ain't even divo'ced!"

Old Maid's Complaint

Bob gave his older sister a critical examination. She was dressed in a too-long, old-fashioned skirt, low-heeled oxfords, and a shapeless black blouse.

"Look, Sis," he scolded, "you're pushing thirty and still not married. If you expect to get a man of your own you'll have to dress a lot better. Try to make yourself attractive to men."

"What do you suggest?" she asked wearily. "I've tried everything."

"How about a tight-fitting sweater?"

"I tried that too," she answered, "but it only made me itch."

Fundamental Biology

Dr. Robinson was not only a good physician but a public-spirited man who hated to see his people conduct themselves in a manner that would reflect unfavorably on all blacks. So, when he delivered another baby he spoke to the mother in stern tones.

"Lucille, you just can't go on like this," he scolded. "Here you've had six children in five years. And I wouldn't be surprised if each baby had a different father."

"That ain't so," Lucille protested. "I'm sure the twins has the same pa!"

Miss Melissy Now a Missus

"Melissy," said Parson Biggs, frowning, "you now have three illegitimate children. When are you ever going to marry?"

"I got married las' night," replied Melissy proudly. "I didn't think it looked right for a single girl to have so many kids."

Never Even Left Town

Ollie Mae was in a family way—again! The doctor completed his examination and shrugged. "Ollie Mae," he sighed, "I'll deliver your baby just as I did the others, but you simply must stop all this running around."

"Runnin' around?" echoed Ollie Mae, staring at him in surprise. "Doctah, b'lieve me, I ain't been nowhere!"

Equality Can Go Too Far

White Chick: (Coyly)—Do you believe in interracial marriage?
Black Brother: Baby, I don't believe in marriage *period!"*

Flimsy Excuse

Bertha, a devout Catholic, stood before the bar of justice.

"Young lady," said the judge, "I understand that you told the arresting officer that you are a Protestant. Is that correct?"

"Protestant!" Bertha exploded in utter outrage. "That's a damn lie! "I thought he said *prostitute!"*

Well, as Long as You Asked

Col. Griffin and his wife, like the other officers stationed at Fort Dix, lived on the base in a rented home. On this particular morning Mrs. Griffin was rather irritated because Angela, her household maid, was a few minutes late for work.

"Angela, this is the third time you've been late this week," she scolded.

"I didn't get home until morning," Angela explained, though not as apologetically as Mrs. Griffin would have preferred.

"Perhaps," snapped the colonel's wife, "you'll be on time in the future, now that all the Negro soldiers have been sent overseas."

"I ain't so sure," Angela replied. "The white soldiers are still here."

Let No Man Put Asunder

There is a semblance of truth to this story. It was widely disseminated on television in the mid-1960's, but we shall mercifully allow the central character to remain anonymous.

The mayor of an Alabama town arrived in Washington, D. C., to testify before a Congressional committee regarding his obvious repression of the black people in his city. A strict segregationist and unreconstructed racist, he made front page news throughout the nation with his virulent statements.

When the hearings were over, he decided to have a real fling before returning home, so he taxied up to Q Street which, at that time, was the heart of the black business district. Like so many others of his stripe, he went into a bar to see if he could find a black chick to keep him company for the evening. Nor was he disappointed. Before long he was really swinging.

He awoke the next morning in a strange hotel room, his mind a complete blank. He heard a soft murmur and when he turned his head, there beside him was the blackest girl he had ever seen. He leaped out of bed and reached for his wallet. "Here, I'll give you twenty dollars if you'll just forget the whole thing," he said. But when he opened his wallet it was empty. He didn't have a dollar left.

"What happened to all my money?" he asked the girl accusingly.

"Oh, don't you remember?" she replied brightly. "You gave it all away last night—to our bridesmaids!"

Mistaken Identity

"Sistuh, I heah you gwine have a baby," said the outraged, old-fashioned preacher. "How kin dat be? Yo' husban' he bin daid fo' mo'n a yeah."

"You fuhgittin' somethin', Revun'," answered the good sister. "*He's* the one whut's daid—not *me!*"

Age-Old Quandary

Grandma appeared before the justice of the peace to obtain a marriage license for her granddaughter.

"How old is this girl?" asked the J.P. suspiciously.

"Fifteen, yo' honuh."

"I'm sorry," the man said, "but a girl of fifteen is too young to marry."

"Lawd a-mussy, Jedge, whut we gwine do?" wailed Grandma. "She ol' 'nuff tuh do whut she done did!"

No Day of Jubilee

Despite the warnings of her minister, eighteen-year-old Gracie decided to go ahead and marry a man in his late fifties. "These May-December marriages are never successful," the minister warned her once more as they left the church.

A few weeks later, Gracie returned to the parsonage and asked her minister's help in obtaining a divorce.

"Remember, I told you," he said, "December cannot be married to May."

"It warn't that," corrected Gracie. "It was mo' like Labuh Day married to the Day of Res'."

Honest Anna

Anna may not have been endowed with an oversupply of brains but she more than made up for it in ambition and integrity. Indeed, she had never been known to tell a lie in her life.

Now she was seated at a desk, filling out an application for a job as airline stewardess.

Anna came to the line reading: "Present position." She filled in the blank space with the words "Sitting down."

The next line said, "Sex." Anna bit her lip, hesitated, and then, with firm and quite laudible determination, she wrote, "Just once, after a Black Panther picnic."

Virginity and Relativity

"You gonna marry me or not?" she demanded.

"I been plannin' it for a long time," he acknowledged, "but there's somethin' botherin' me."

He hesitated in embarrassment, but she encouraged him to continue the rather involuntary proposal.

"I hear you been with other guys," he finished lamely.

"Now jes' a cotton-pickin' minute!" she stormed. "I ain't gonna stan' fo' no sech talk. Why, I can count on the fingers of one han' the men what I lived with!"

The Long and Short of It

Mary didn't believe in long engagements. "The shorter the engagement," she explained, "the less chance you have to find out what a louse you're marrying."

Marriage Vows

The couple stood before the altar as the preacher intoned, "Do you, Virginia, promise to love, honor and obey, in sickness and in health, for better or worse, till death do you part?"

Virginia's eyes widened at these awesome demands. "Sir," she faltered, pushing aside her white veil, "maybe I better go home an' study on it for awhile."

Oh, What a Wrong Number!

The telephone rang and Ramona picked up the receiver. "Hello?"

"Darling," responded an excited though cultured voice, "will you marry me?" I've just been appointed Ambassador to the Court of St. James. Now I can present you to the Queen of England as my wife. Oh, sweetheart, please say you will marry me and share my castles, my wealth, and all my earthly goods."

"Suttinly I'll marry you, baby," crooned Ramona, just as enthralled as the caller. "Whut's yo' name an' address?"

Complexion Sexion

Arthur was understandably indignant to learn that his best girl had refused to marry him because of his very dark complexion. To make matters worse, she had referred to him as "Captain Midnight."

"She got no business callin' me Midnight," he protested. "That gal is pretty close to eleven thirty herself."

Pre-Marital Marriage

(A THREE-ACT ACT IN ONE ACT)

Scene: One of those drive-in marriage offices in Las Vegas
where instant weddings are performed.

Justice of the Peace: Do you Joe Cannon take this woman Alice Morgan for your lawful wedded wife do you Alice Morgan take this man Joe Cannon for your lawful wedded husband I now pronounce you man and wife that'll be five dollars please kindly pay on the way out.

Joe: We ain't got but two dollars.

J. of P.: Sorry, but in that case I'll have to unmarry you.

Joe: I protest!

Alice: That's all right, honey. Let him unmarry us. We can always come back and get married after our honeymoon.

No Family Secrets

A young college couple were in love but felt that marriage might hurt their careers.

"Why can't we get married without telling anyone?" asked the girl.

"No, that won't do," he said. "Suppose we have a baby?"

"Oh, we'd tell the *baby!*" she gushed.

PART TWO

MARRIAGES AND MORTGAGES

First Things First

Mae and Bill were the proud parents of seven sturdy children: twins at her breasts, two on the floor, one at her knee, and two yard babies. They loved each other devotedly but, despite Mae's frequent pleas that they marry and give the children a legal name, Bill stubbornly refused. "A marriage certificate ain't nothin' but a piece of paper," he would argue.

One day, however, Bill announced that he had five dollars extra in his pay envelope. "I reckon we might as well get married as long as I have the money," he said grandly.

Mae quieted the squalling children while she gave the matter some serious thought.

"Well, what are you waitin' for?" he demanded. "You finally got your wish."

"I shore do want to get married," she answered, "but let's wait till next week. This week, let's take the five dollars and buys us a nice fat hen."

Ask the Man Who Owns One

"The trouble with wives," grumbled grandpa, "is that they're always trying to find out something they don't want to know."

Rattle Those Chains

Mary was visiting her sister and enjoying a cup of tea.

"By the way, Ella, where's yo' husban'?" asked Mary.

"Upstairs, dressin'," said Ella. "He's goin to a lodge meetin'. They got Hy-wyan dancin' there tonight. A stag meetin', they calls it."

"Lemme tell you somethin', Ella," said Mary as she placed her cup back in the saucer. "Time them gals in their grass skirts git through wigglin' their behines an' twitchin' their bazooms, you ain't gonna have no more husban'."

"But what can I do?"

"I'll tell you what you can do. Go with yo' property an' keep rattlin' yo' chains!"

Kidnapped

Richard arrived home from work at the customary hour, expecting dinner as usual, and a long tirade of complaints—also as usual. But the house was quiet, his wife was nowhere to be found.

"Ah, peace, it's wonderful" he sighed.

His mellow reverie was interrupted by the ringing of the telephone. He answered it and a voice at the other end said: "We have your wife. If you ever expect to get her back it will cost you $5,000. We'll call you back later for your decision."

"Hol' on," said Richard quickly. "I can give you my answer right now. . . . Finder's keepers."

Community Property

Cynthia was suing for child support, and she was now seated in the witness chair while the opposing attorney questioned her.

"You say your husband doesn't support you or your child?" asked the lawyer.

"He ain't zackly my husban'," Cynthia answered.

The lawyer suppressed a smile. "Well, your common-law husband."

"He ain't zackly that, nuther."

"For heaven's sake, what is he then?"

"He's my mo'-right man."

The attorney gaped. "What does that mean?"

"It means," explained Cynthia dourly, "I got mo' right to him than any other woman in town."

Whatever Happened to Washington Butts?

Washington Butts, known everywhere as just plain Wash, had been married for only a few months when his wife realized that her husband had a predilection for stopping off at the local tavern every payday. He didn't spend too much, however, so she let Wash continue his customary visits without argument.

But all that changed, one payday, when Wash did not get home at all. Mrs. Butts waited until dark, and then went in search of her errant husband. First she visited the tavern, but he was not there. Next she tried the poker club, then the pool hall. He was nowhere to be found. Really worried by now, she was returning home when she passed his favorite barbershop. She poked her head through the partially opened door and called out, "Wash Butts here?"

"No, we don't," answered the barber. "Just shaves and haircuts."

A Fishy Story*

Mus' be fifteen mile er so outside Chat'noogah wha'r I wuz bawn—a little bittie place call Mill Pon', on 'count that wha'r the sawmill wuz.

Caleb run the saw. The job don' pay much but him an' his missus allus have 'nough ter eat 'cause that ole pon' got plenty of fish in it.

Caleb an' his missus they git 'long tol'ble, but they wants one thing they ain' got—chilluns. So one day the missus go ter a doctah in Chat'noogah an' he tell huh effen she gits a baby it gonna be a merricle, 'cause she ovah fifty y'ar ole.

The missus cain' h'ar so good an' when she gits back ter Mill Pon' an' Caleb axes huh effen they gonna have a baby, she say yes, an' 'gin ter cry.

He give huh a piece o' fish he cotched in de pon' ter calm huh down, an' he say, "Then whuffo' you cryin'?"

She say, "The doctah tole me effen I do have a baby it gonna be a mack'rel."

Hot to Cold

Preacher: You askin' for a divorce? I'm surprised. I thought you were madly in love with your wife.

Husband: I *was* madly in love with her. When we first got married I could've et her up. Now, I'm sorry I didn't.

She Do, Do She?

Harry had been married for only a week and talked of nothing but his new bride.

"That wife of mine sure knows how to make love," boasted Harry.

"I'll say she do," agreed the friend.

"Wh-wh-what you say?"

"I say, do she?" amended the friend hastily.

Detour

The not-so-loving couple were in the throes of a heated argument.

"You might as well quit yellin'," he said. "Everything you say goes in one ear and out the other."

"No it don't," she barked. "It goes in one ear an' out yo' big fat mouth!"

---

* *Georgia Enterprise*, April 3, 1871.

Not-So-Even Stephen

Steve, who had been living in Los Angeles for several years, returned to his parents' home in Mobile, a picture of dejection.

"What you lookin' so sad for?" asked his father.

"My wife divorced me," explained the son.

"Don't you worry. You'll git a better one nex' time."

"It ain't her I'm grievin' for. It's the house I bought an' paid for that makes me feel so low."

"You didn't give it to her, did you?"

"No, it don't work that way," said Steve. "California has a community property law that says a husban' an' wife gotta divide up everything fifty-fifty when they gits divorced. She got herself a smart lawyer an' divided the house—half fer me an' half fer her."

"That don't soun' so bad," observed the father.

"Bad enough," moaned Steve. "She got the inside an' I got the outside."

Mini-Mini-Mini Skirt

Two brothers were discussing the merits of their respective wives.

"My wife is so smart she made me a tie outta her old dress," bragged the first brother.

"That's nothin'," said the other. "My wife made her a dress outta one of my old ties."

Crash!

Vernon had just fulfilled his life's dream by purchasing a brand new Lincoln Continental. He and his wife decided to test the luxurious automobile by taking a short drive.

They were on 135th Street, approaching Lenox Avenue, when he cautiously slowed down at the corner. "Any cars coming?" he asked his wife.

"No, honey. . . ."

He stepped on the gas and pulled into the busy intersection.

". . . only a big truck," she finished.

Wishful Thinking

My wife sure is a hard-working woman. Wish I had a few more like her!

How to Drive Your Wife Crazy

"I don't know what's happening to this world," grumbled the wife. "Sex —sex—sex! Everywhere you look—sex! In the movies, in magazines, even in the newspapers."

The husband lifted a can of beer to his lips, took a long draught, burped, and then nodded agreeably. "Yeah, you right, baby. But the trouble with sex in the newspapers is that they have it everyplace but where it's most needed—in the Help Wanted columns."

These Modern Couples

Then there's the fellow who has been arguing with his wife about having one night a week out with the boys. . . . He refuses to let her.

Birthday Gift

Now that her husband had obtained a good job at the Post Office, the wife insisted that he give her something important. So he did . . . the Asian flu.

Too Complicated

"Seems to me that mothers don't train their daughters for marriage anymore," grumbled the new bridegroom. "Our first morning together, my wife said she couldn't fix my toast because she lost the recipe."

Through Other Eyes

SCENE: A private investigator's office

She: I want you to follow my husband and his girlfriend.

Private Eye: You want a complete report?

She: I certainly do! I want to find out what she sees in him!

PART THREE

MAMAS AND PAPAS

The Great Water Mystery

Alice left her tiny town in Arkansas and headed for California, promising her aged mother that she would send for her as soon as she was well situated. It wasn't long before Alice found a high-salaried position and bought a home near the Pacific shore. Settled at last, she sent for her mother.

On her first day in California the mother had her initial sight of the Pacific (or any other) Ocean. "Did somebody bulldoze that out?" she asked, awed.

"It's high tide now," daughter Alice explained, laughing. "It won't look so big tomorrow."

On the following day they again viewed the shore line. "Gosh, the tide is really low today!" exclaimed Alice. "Look how far out the water is."

"I jes' don't understand," the old woman said, after some thought. "How come the water so low when it rained so hard las' night?"

That'll Hold Her!

Daughter: I want a man who will support me the rest of my life.
Wise Mama: You don't want a husband—you want a girdle!

Mama's Little Gem

"My, what three lovely daughters you have!" gushed the pastor's wife. "What are their names?"

"De oldes' is Pearl, de secon' is Ruby," exclaimed the proud mama.

"How about the baby?"

"Her name is Onyx."

"What a lovely name! But whatever made you call her Onyx?"

" 'Cause," answered mama, "she was so *onyx*pected."

Divine Transportation

Bob returned home during his summer vacation from college and, stepping off the bus, found his little town a veritable shambles. Houses were splintered, trees uprooted, and many vacant lots appeared where cottages once stood. Deeply concerned for the safety of his parents, he rushed to the family dwelling. Fortunately, his parents' house suffered only minor damage, and neither his mother nor father had suffered a scratch.

"What happened here?" he asked his mother.

"A cyclone done struck. It toh up the town consid'able."

"Is everyone else in the family all right?"

"Sho'," interjected his father, " 'ceptin' yo' Uncle Rafer. His house done lifted right off'n the groun' an' got blowed across town an' sot down on the steps o' the Meth'dis' meetin' hall."

"Why, that's terrible!" cried the young student. "Poor Uncle Rafer!"

"Oh, it warn't so bad," said the youth's father. "Uncle Rafer said he been thinkin' some of goin' to church anyway."

That Maternal Instinct

"Do you always kiss your children goodnight?"
"Of course!—if I happen to be awake when they get home."

Dad Wrestles New Math

The Mabley family were gathered around their television set, silently watching Governor Lester Maddox bad-mouthing their people.

"Dat's it! I got enough o' de state o' Jawja," snarled the outraged head of the family. "We's gittin' de hell outen heah an' go tuh Califo'nia."

In Los Angeles, they enrolled their son in an integrated school. The very next day the boy came home with an armload of homework."

"Whut you got dah?" asked the father.

"New math, Dad," answered the boy. "It's something like the old-style arithmetic you used to learn in school."

"Well, I use-tuh be right smaht wid 'rit'matick," said the older man. "Lemme see yo' papahs when you gits through."

When the boy finally completed the assignment, he brought the finished work to his father. "Hmm," the oldtimer muttered, staring blankly at the alien computations, "so dis heah's new math?"

"Sure is, Dad," the boy said proudly. "And I got all the examples right, too."

The father studied the maze of figures for a few moments and then sighed: "Damn ef you ain't!"

Hoecakes and Bellyaches

Dad Simpson was a victim of that syndrome known to all-too-many brothers—"Last to be hired, first to be fired." Without a job, Dad's meagre funds were running mighty low. Finally came the day when his wife and children had nothing in the house to eat but a pot of beans.

"You know somethin'," said the wife, "I was just thinkin' how nice it would be to give the children some hoecakes for breakfas'. Trouble is, I don't have the flour, the eggs, the milk or the sugar."

"Hmmm, I think I can handle that," said Dad. "I can try to borrow the flour from Mrs. Jones; perhaps the eggs from Mrs. Jackson; possibly the milk from Sam Williams, an' maybe I can borrow the sugar an' other things, too."

"Oh, that would be wonderful!" exclaimed the wife.

The children were ecstatic. "I'm gonna eat five of 'em!" yelled Tommy.

"I'm gonna eat twelve," sang out Betty.

"I'm gonna eat twenny," shouted little Lulu.

Dad glared at the youngsters. "What's the matter with you kids?" he growled. "You wanna ruin your stomachs?"

Getting to the Seat of the Problem

Mrs. Jones: My, your children are so well-behaved! You must have a secret for proper child-raising.

Mrs. Smith: Not really. I simply follow my own parents' advice: A pat on the back develops character if administered young enough, often enough, and low enough.

Conflicting Dates

The United States military forces had just invaded the European continent and Hitler's armies were being mauled everywhere. It was pleasant news to all Americans, especially Sister Mamie Wiggins, who had just returned from church.

"Our boy gonna be back by Chris'mus," she announced to her husband. "In fact, the preacher say the war gonna be over long befo' the duration."

Slight Misunderstanding

A census taker stopped by at a small shack in a remote rural area. It was the baby's feeding time, but the young mother was too embarrassed to nurse the infant in the white man's presence. So she dutifully answered his questions while the infant howled for its dinner.

The baby's crying finally got on the census taker's nerves. "Why is your child crying like that?" he asked irritably. "Is he spoiled?"

"Why, 'course not!" snapped the mother, her voice indignant. "He ain't spoiled a-tall. That's his natch'l color!"

Fragrant Compromise

Ferdinand and Liza had been married for three years and had never had an argument. They got along beautifully—the envy of all who knew them. But the tranquility of their marriage was broken when Liza became pregnant with her first child.

Ferdinand wanted to name the expected baby after himself. Liza was just as adamant about giving it her own name. Finally, after much contention, they compromised by giving the future baby a part of each of their names . . .

Ferdiliza!

Poppy's Boy

An angry preacher burst into the little cottage where a church member lived. A brand new mother, she was nursing her baby.

"Sistuh Grace, I nevuh bin so shocked in all my life," he ranted. "Whut's the big ideah namin' yo' sweet li'l chile Opium? Don't you know opium comes f'om a wile poppy?"

"Sho'," answered Sister Grace placidly. "An' the baby named rightly, too. It got the wil'es' poppy this side o' Jo'dan."

Integrated Spelling

"I ain't much for this here school integration," complained the disappointed father. "My li'l girl got sent to a white school an' the teacher is tryin' to git her to spell 'tater with a 'p'."

Marriage Counselor

"Daddy, in school today we learned that the Mormons had lots of wives."

"That's right, honey. But they don't do that no more on accounta it ain't legal. The law say, if a man has sev'ral wives, that's polygamy; if he has two wives, that's bigamy; an' if he has one wife, believe me, honey, that's monotony!"

Chocolate, Walnut, Vanilla

A mother of three small children was explaining to a friend why her youngsters had such different complexions.

"My first husband was blacker than me," she said. "My second husband was a light brownskin, and my third was a member of the fair sex."

Mama Knows Best

Tom was the only boy in Punkin Junction who ever left the tiny village to attend college. His mother, quite naturally, was extremely proud of her son's achievement.

When he returned home for his first vacation she prepared a sumptuous country dinner for him and then plied the youth with questions while he ate.

"Whut dey teachin' you in college?"

"Algebra," he answered.

"Nevah heerd of it," said the mother. "Lemme heah you say some."

The son shrugged and, smiling indulgently, he intoned "Pi R Square."

"Now dat's jes' plain foolishness," snorted the mother. "Pie are roun'. *Co'nbread* are squar!"

Why Mothers Get Grey

An old-fashioned Christian woman was glad and somewhat relieved to have her only daughter home from college—even if only for the weekend. Mother opened the conversation with a simple question: "Tell me, does your new room-mate smoke?"

"Smoke what?"

This Mod, Mod World

A young fellow—he could not have been more than sixteen or so—was trying on a new suit. He seemed to like it but was hesitant about making a final decision.

The salesman grew somewhat impatient. "It's the exact style you wanted, isn't it?"

"Yeah, man. Groovy!"

"And it fits just right, doesn't it?"

"Right on!"

"Then why don't you take it?"

The youth turned the matter over in his mind and, after a pause, said, "Here's what I'd like to do. Let me take the suit home. If my mother and father dig it—I'll bring it right back."

PART FOUR

THOSE GALLIVANTIN' MENFOLK

Ah Truth—How Lovely Art Thou!

The pastor was visiting at the home of a new parishioner. "I do hope, Mr. Jones, that you are leading a Christian life," he said.

Mr. Jones nodded, though somewhat uncertainly. "The way I sees it," he observed, "a man cain't live a *real* Christian life as long as they's women in the worl'."

Keep the Faith

"There's no middle ground for a married woman," remarked one observant wife. "You got to trust a husband or let him go, 'cause you sure can't watch him *all* the time!"

Gil Pickle

Margaret and Gilbert Haines were happy in their New York apartment, until one day Gil's boss sent him to Chicago on company business. Margaret, alone for the first time since their marriage, paced the floor restlessly, tried to sleep, but could not. Finally she arose and went to the telephone. 'I know my darling misses me just as much as I miss him,' she thought. 'At least we can talk to each other.' So she called him at the Chicago hotel he had mentioned.

"May I speak to Mr. Gil Haines?" she said to the switchboard operator.

Margaret waited a full two minutes before the operator's voice was heard again. "I'm sorry," said the telephone girl, "but Mr. Haines doesn't answer ... and neither does Mrs. Haines!"

Army of Generals

Vernon moved from New Rochelle, New York, to Washington, D.C. Immediately upon his arrival he went to the local lodge to transfer his membership. The secretary opened his admittance book. "What was your title in the New Rochelle lodge?" he asked.

Vernon drew himself up. "I'll have you know I was an Exalted Prince of Perfection," he said haughtily.

The secretary gave him a long, cool stare. "For your information," he said just as haughtily, "Exalted Prince of Perfection is the lowest title in our whole lodge."

Cementing a Friendship

The minute Bill saw his brother Harry approaching his front gate on foot, instead of driving into the parking area, he knew something was wrong. "Harry," he asked when his brother was inside the house, "where's your bran' new Plymouth?"

"I done tol' the finance company they can come pick it up."

"But you make good money," said Bill, puzzled, "an' you really loved that car. What happened?"

Harry's face was a portrait in misery and suppressed rage. "It's a long story."

"Shoot! I got time."

"It all started two weeks ago, when I heerd that Sam Robinson was goin' fishin' with Jimmy, the barber. Well, Bill, you know I been keepin' a eye on Sam's wife, Viola. So I figgered this is my chance."

"Man, you playin' a dangerous game."

"Yeah, I know it now. Anyway, ol' Sam ain't got a s'picion in his head, so jus' aroun' first dark I snuk aroun' to the back of his house an' sure 'nuff, there's Viola settin' in the kitchen fixin' flapjack batter for two."

Bill shook his head in disapproval. "You oughtta be 'shamed of yourself, carryin' on like that," he told his brother. "But what's all this got to do with losin' your car?"

"I ain't said I lost it," Harry retorted. "I jus' said the finance company can pick it up for all I care. But don't rush me. I'm gittin' to it."

"Okay, I'll keep quiet," Bill promised.

"Well, me an' Viola we're makin' out real good until 'bout eleven o'clock, when who should come bustin' into the house but Sam. Seems like Jimmy took sick so they called off the fishin' trip, an' that's how Sam foun' me in his house—with Viola a-settin' in my lap. Now this gonna s'prise you, Bill. 'Stid o' whuppin' me or shootin' or cuttin' or somethin', you know whut he done?"

"Can't imagine."

"He jus' grab me by the front of my shirt an' jerk me up on my feet an' hol' his face close to mine. Then he commence to slow-grin like he done los' his senses. It was scary, Bill, the way he jus' stan' there with that funny half-smile on his face. Then he opened the door an' invited me out— 'thout sayin' a mumblin' word."

"But the Plymouth! You . . ."

"I'm gittin' to that right now. The other day, Jimmy got over his sickness—the flu, I think—an' he's ready to go on that fishin' trip, but Sam can't go on accounta he gotta work, but I sure was itchin' to go, so me an' Jimmy went out to Sun Lake an' we had good luck, too. But Emma, that peanut-brain wife of mine, she parked my shiny new Plymouth nex' to a fire hydrant down at the end of the street while she went off gallahoppin' someplace. I tol' you Sam was workin' that day. He drives one of them cement-mix trucks. You seen the kind what have a couple tons of soft concrete turnin' an' rollin' aroun' while they drivin' to a buildin' site. Bill, you ain't gonna b'lieve this."

"Try me."

"That Sam, he been meetin' me all week an' doin' nothin' but slow-grinnin' at me, an' never sayin' a damn word. I oughtta knowed he didn't mean me no good, but it was sorta spooky an' we all laughed about it. Well, I ain't laughin' now. Come the day I'm up at Sun Lake, fishin' with Jimmy, that Sam went down our street an' stopped his mix-truck 'longside my car an' he let down the spout an' he poured concrete-mix in the back seat till it run over on the front. Then he move the spout over to the front seat an' he poured in more mix till the whole inside of the car is plumb full to the roof. Then he bus' open the trunk an' fill it. An' still he ain't happy. He opened up the hood an' cover the engine till you cain't see it. The rest of the mix he poured out on the tires.

"Man, that sure was one car full of mix. Ain't nobody ever seen nothin' like it before—a solid concrete car. There's always a crowd there, laughin' an' pokin' aroun'—an' you can guess who they're laughin' at—me!

"An' so, Bill, that's why I done tol' the finance company they welcome to come down an' 'tach it whenever it suit 'em. An' when the police phoned me 'bout parkin' nex' to a fire hydrant I tol' 'em they welcome to haul it away any time—if they can move it!"

Harry's eyes flashed with anger. "Bill, I swear to the Lawd Almighty, I'm gonna knock a slow grin offen somebody's face if it's the las' thing I ever do in this here life!"

Setting the Record Straight

Charlie Sykes, the oldest man in his group of friends, arrived in Central Park at noon, as usual, for his daily game of checkers. This time, however, he sported a freshly-pressed suit, his shoes were shined to a luster, and he had just been barbered and shaved.

"You goin' to a party or somethin'?" asked one of his checker-playing cronies.

"Naw, nothin' like that," said Charlie. "This is my golden annivers'ry."

"How come you're wife ain't celebratin' it with you?"

"Suh," retorted Charlie Sykes with quiet dignity, "my present wife ain't got nothin' to do with it."

One-Shirt Sherman

"Sherman Abernathy," demanded the girl indignantly, "how come you didn't answer when I knocked on your door last night?"

"Guess I was out when you called," Sherman replied, almost too casually.

"Oh, no, you wasn't," she snapped. "I seen your shirt on the washline."

... and a Gownless Evening Strap

"I sure miss those old-fashioned girls. The chick I have now is like the rest of these lollygaggin' women: miniskirt, maxicoat and mighty mouth!"

(*Dan Sping*)

Helpful Henry

Wally and Henry met at the army induction center and within an hour they were fast friends. But their friendship was short-lived, even for an hour. Wally passed his physical, but Henry was deferred because of an old back ailment.

"I sure hate to go," said Wally mournfully. "Who's gonna look after my beautiful, sexy, lonely wife?"

"What's her address?" asked Henry.

Everybody's Happy

When Caroline reported for work as usual one Monday morning, her employer was surprised—to put it mildly. "I thought you were getting married over the weekend and that you were going away on your honeymoon."

"I did get married," Caroline explained. "We was plannin' a honeymoon at Niagara Falls but my sister never been there so I let her go in my place. An' you know what? My hubby such a gentleman he never once objected!"

Proof Positive

A particularly no'count guy who shunned all efforts at honest toil, went to see his brother hoping to scrounge another loan—money he never repaid.

"I'm gonna tell you somethin' for your own good," said the brother. "I'm not givin' you another dime. Why don't you get a job? Hard work never killed anybody."

"Now you know better'n that," was the reproachful answer. "I lost three wives from nothin' else!"

Blame the Fatties

Randy and Andy took an instant dislike to each other the moment they met. Randy, a six-footer, was long, lean and lanky, and he weighed 140 pounds in his socks. Andy, who was short, fat and squatty, weighed 225 pounds.

"From the looks of you, there musta been a famine," grinned Andy to the skinny fellow.

"An' from the looks of you," snapped Randy, "you're the guy who caused it."

Super-Boss!

"I am sorry to announce dat dis here meetin' uv de Gran' an' Glorious Lodge will be pos'poned fer a couple o' weeks," said the speaker.

"How come?" asked one of the lodge members.

" 'Cause we got nobody to lead the meetin'," explained the speaker. "The All-Powerful, Invincible, Mos' Supreme, Unconquerable Potentate done got his head busted by his wife.

Innocents a-broad

My folks raised me up so strict, I was fourteen years old before I found out that a girl isn't just a soft boy.

CORN FRITTERS

Like his poor white counterpart, the Black farmer's indispensable crop was corn. Although he did not enjoy the convenience of buying canned corn, fritters were always a favorite—at breakfast, dinner or supper.

1 cup canned corn	2 tsp. baking powder
¾ cup flour	1 tsp. sugar
½ tsp. salt	dash nutmeg
2 tbs. butter	1 egg

Sift dry ingredients. Add corn and egg; then melted butter. Mix well. Drop in deep hot fat with teaspoon. Fry 8 to 10 minutes until brown. Serves 6.

Corn Fritters—Country Style

1 can creamed corn	1 tbs. baking powder
4 egg yolks	dash salt
1 cup flour	1 tsp. sugar

Mix corn and egg yolks. Add salt and sugar. Blend with flour and baking powder. Drop each fritter into deep hot fat with tablespoon. Fry until brown, about 3 minutes. Turn, if necessary. Drain on brown paper. Serve hot. Serves 6 to 8, allowing 2 fritters per person.

Fresh Voice in the Night

Rrriiinnng!

"Salvation Army. Can I help you?"

"You sure can, baby. I hear the Salvation Army saves girls. That right?"

"Yes, it is."

"Then how about savin' one for me, Saturday night?"

Fragrant Frankie

"Where you been these pas' four days?" demanded the irate wife as her husband, Frankie, wearily entered the house.

"In jail," Frankie moaned.

"What you done?"

"Nothin', b'lieve me. The man come up to me an' ax do I have a job. I say, "No."

He say, "You live 'roun' here?"

I say, "No."

He say, "You onder arres'!"

I say, "Whuffo?"

He say, "Fo' fragrancy."

I say, "You cain' do this to me! I's a respeckable citizen."

He say, "Move!"

So I moved.

"So he arres' you for fragrancy, huh?" echoed the wife, whose education was somewhat better than Frankie's. "Well, he sure didn't make no mistake!"

Jack Johnson, Prophet*

The story is probably apochryphal, but merits re-telling as another of the legends which surround Jack Johnson, the first black heavyweight champion.**

---

* Jack Johnson (1878-1946), acclaimed by *Ring* magazine as "the greatest fighter of them all," was born in Galveston, Texas, the son of a school janitor. As a boy he was so undersized he was nicknamed "Li'l Arthur," a name which stuck with him throughout his career. After fighting for nine years, losing three of some 100 bouts, he won the heavyweight crown from Tommy Burns in Australia. In 1919, the former champion, Jim Jeffries, in response to widespread clamor for a "Great White Hope," came out of retirement to recapture the title. They fought in Reno, Nevada, on July 4th of that same year, and Johnson knocked out Jeffries in the 14th round. He was defeated by Jess Willard in 1915, in Havana, Cuba. Johnson earned the enmity of the racists of that day because he had married a white woman. He died in an automobile crash in North Carolina.

** Although Jack Johnson was the first black man to win the heavyweight boxing championship, there were a number of black fighters who fought for the title in their weight divisions prior to Johnson. The first American contender for a world championship (black or white) was Tom Molineaux, a Virginia slave, who fought the English title-holder, Tom Crib, in 1810.

Johnson, the challenger, and Tommy Burns, the reigning champ, were about to start the title bout in Sydney, Australia—the bout which was to make Johnson the new champion. As they met in the center of the ring for the referee's instructions, Burns surveyed his opponent coolly and remarked, "Boy, I'm gonna whip you good. I was *born* with boxing gloves on."

Johnson's mouth spread in a wide grin. "I have news for you, white man. You're about to die the same way!"

Walter at the Altar

A couple of fellows were discussing old Walt as they sipped beer at the corner tavern.

"I hear tell Walt has been married eight times, an' he's a hunnerd an' ten years old," commented the younger man.

"I ain't surprised," said the other. "That many wives would age anybody!"

Joe Louis, Doctor of Slumber

Joe Louis was at the peak of his boxing fame when a fresh young fellow applied at the training camp for a job as sparring partner.

"When I hit somebody he sure knows it," boasted the confident young man.

Joe Louis made no answer for a few moments, and when he spoke his voice was soft and meaningful: "When *I* hit someone," he replied, "he don't know *nothin'* for a whole hour!"*

Revolving Door Rentals

This Harlem cat was visiting down around Houston, and his cousin was bragging on the new buildings in his city.

"I don't think they're so big," said the New Yorker who was used to real skyscrapers.

---

* Joe Louis held the heavyweight championship longer than anyone else (11 years, eight months, seven days), and defended it more often than any other heavyweight champion. His 25 title fights were more than the combined total of the eight champions who preceded him. Born in a sharecropper's shack in Chambers County, Alabama, in 1914, Louis moved to Detroit as a small boy where he became an amateur boxer, winning 50 out of 59 bouts, 43 by knockouts. He turned professional in 1934, and a year later knocked out former champion Primo Carnera who was staging a comeback. The fight earned Louis the nickname, "The Brown Bomber." It is believed by most experts that if Jack Johnson and Joe Louis could have fought against each other while at the peak of their abilities, Louis would have defeated the earlier champion. No other fighter, with the possible exception of Muhammad Ali (Cassius Clay), possessed the skill, speed and power of Joe Louis.

"It ain't the size," said the Texas cousin. "It's how fast we put up our buildings. We start construction on Monday, and by Friday the tenants are moving in."

"Hmmmph!" snorted the Harlemite, "that's nothin'. Where I come from they start putting up a building in the morning, and come evening the new tenants are out on the street for non-payment of rent."

Modern Plumbing

Jim had left his little farming community outside of Bowie, Maryland, several years earlier. Now he was returning in style, with a thirty-foot house trailer, elegantly furnished.

He parked the magnificent trailer behind his parents' shack but it wasn't long before every farmer and his family in the vicinity were gathered at the place, exclaiming at this marvel of the modern age.

"Haven't they ever seen a house trailer before?" asked the son.

"It isn't that," explained the youth's father. "They're saying it's the fanciest, wing-dingest, swing-daddy outhouse in the whole world!"

Vengeance Is Mine, Sayeth the Truck Driver

The driver of a big truck-trailer rig was in a highway restaurant quietly minding his own business and eating his dinner when two Hell's Angels cyclists swaggered in, took empty seats on both sides of him, and embarked on a campaign of intimidation.

"Hey, black boy, look over there!" When the truck driver turned his head to see what the other was pointing at, the cyclist grabbed his plate and transferred the food to his own plate.

It was now the other punk's turn. "Hey, Mr. Spade, you don't want your coffee, do you?" He reached out and confiscated the coffee, taking the man's apple pie as well.

The trucker remained silent, never uttering a sound of protest. He rose from his seat at the counter, paid his check for the uneaten meal and then left, the derisive laughter of the two white ruffians ringing in his ears.

Inside the cafe, the cyclists exchanged quips about the silent victim. "That guy isn't much of a man," observed the first cyclist. The other nodded assent. "Yeah, he didn't make a move to get back at us. I thought those black guys are supposed to be militant."

"He's not much of a driver, either," interjected the waiter behind the counter. He pointed to the window. "Look at that, will you? He just ran that great big truck over those two cycles out front!"

PART FIVE

BAYONETS, BULLETS AND BLACKS*

Introduction

The black man may well take pride in the military achievements of his people—a documented history which goes back into the dim mists of time to the Pharaohs. It is important to note that the Nubians and Ethiopians of the day, and for centuries later, were a highly civilized people boasting universities and academies where mathematics and the military sciences were taught. Indeed, without an elite, well-educated officer corps these great military strategists could not have existed, let alone conquer mighty Egypt.

Six thousand years ago, Egypt was united under a single monarch, the Pharaoh. As the power of the state increased through the centuries, the powerful nation exacted tribute from neighboring countries, either by conquest or the threat of military invasion. The Nubians, however, were not the timid people envisioned by the Egyptians. They descended upon the "master race" and by 2000 B.C. their influence in affairs of state grew to such magnitude that a Nubian, Ra Nahesi, finally sat on the throne of the Pharaohs.

Piankhi, the King of Nubia, conquered Egypt in 721-720 B.C. A military strategist of remarkable acumen, he decided that he would end the tribute of gold and slaves which his nation had been forced to pay to Egypt for the past 1,800 years. Sailing down the Nile at the head of an armada ostensibly laden with tribute, but filled with warriors and weapons, he attacked and defeated one town after another until he reached the fortress city of Memphis, at that time the capital of Egypt and the stronghold of that nation's military power. Expecting the black King to attack their western wall, the Egyptians concentrated their forces at that point to repel the coming attack. Piankhi, instead, deployed his fleet and gained control of the harbor, scaled the eastern wall which, as he had suspected, was less strongly defended, and was soon the master of the city and all Egypt. King Osorkin III surrendered and the tribute-laden ships were reversed—this time from Egypt to Nubia. "To the victor belongs the spoils" was an accepted consequence of war, understood by all.

From those ancient days to modern times the black man has proved his merit in the various military establishments of the world. In pre-Colombian Spain as well as in the expeditions of the *conquistadores* he proved his mettle time and time again, not only as a faceless soldier but as a leader. In Russia,

---

* The anecdotes in this section refer to the Civil War and to World War I. For stories relating to World War II, Korea and Vietnam, see *Military Maneuvers*, Book Seven, of this volume.

Abram Hannibal (1697-1782), captured in Africa at the age of eight, became the favorite of Peter the Great. Permitted to join the French army, he attained the rank of commander. Upon returning to Russia he became commandant of the city of Reval where, as a youth, he had been an obscure slave. Married to a German girl, Abram Hannibal was the grandfather of Alexander Pushkin, Russia's greatest poet. Nor can we overlook Menelik II (1844-1913), founder of modern Ethiopia. For more than 2000 years, Ethiopia, alone among all other African countries, maintained a record of continuous independence, with the exception of the Italian occupation of 1935-1940. As late as the 19th century, Ethiopia constituted a collection of tribes rather than a unified nation. It was Menelik (born Sahala Mariem) who welded a semblance of unity among the tribal leaders, but he is also acclaimed as the military strategist who startled the world by defeating the Italian invaders (October, 1896), thus putting other would-be colonialists on notice that his nation was not just another apple on the imperialist tree, ripe for the plucking.

In America, Negroes have been an integral part of military history from its very inception. Serving first under the Spanish and then French flags, they fought under the British colors and served with valor and distinction in the Continental army and navy of the thirteen colonies. Since then, Negroes have participated in every war in which this country has been engaged.

The War of Independence: Some 5,000 blacks served in the Revolutionary War. All were in integrated units until ten months after the Battles of Lexington and Concord, in 1775, when a policy of exclusion developed in Georgia and South Carolina. Nevertheless, they fought in all of the major battles of the war, including those of Brandywine, Yorktown, Monmouth, White Plains, Stillwater, Bennington, Saratoga, Trenton, Rhode Island, Savannah and others.

First to fall in the War of Independance was the Negro patriot, Crispus Attucks, believed by many historians to have been the same man who was advertised as a runaway slave from Framingham, Massachusetts, in 1750. Little is known of his life, other than that he was a seaman and laborer. In an account of his burial, the *Boston Gazette and Country* described him as a "stranger, being six feet two inches in height, and a mulatto." At approximately nine o'clock, on the night of March 5, 1770, Attucks and some 50 patriots converged on the British garrison on King Street, where they were met with a volley of musket fire. Crispus Attucks, standing defiantly in the front rank and most easily distinguishable because of his color, fell dead— the first man, black or white, to die for the concept of freedom which his own people were not to share until the end of the Civil War, a century later. Thus, the Boston Massacre, as the skirmish was called, not only commemorates the beginning of open hostilities between the colonists and England, but honors the black man, Crispus Attucks, the first American symbol of resistance to tyranny.

The War of 1812: Upon the advent of the War of 1812, peacetime militia

PANCAKES

You haven't tasted the real thing until you've sampled great-Grandmother's pancakes. "Modern" doesn't always mean "best"—as this recipe from the rural South of yesteryear indicates.

Old-Fashioned Pancakes

2 eggs, beaten
2 tbs. melted fat or butter
2 cups milk
2 tsp. sugar

2 cups flour
2 tsp. baking powder
1 tsp. salt

Beat eggs well. Add milk, fat and dry ingredients which have been sifted. Serves 6.

(For variety, and for that country-style hoecake flavor and texture, add ¼ cup corn meal instead of flour, and ¼ cup more milk.)

Sour Milk Pancakes

2 cups flour
½ tsp. salt
1¼ tsp. baking powder
     dash nutmeg
2 eggs

2 tbs. butter
2 tbs. sugar
2 cups sour milk
     pinch of soda

Mix and sift dry ingredients. Add milk and eggs beaten together with melted butter. Beat well. Grease a hot griddle or skillet with butter. Pour on a very thin layer of batter. Make each cake about 5 inches in diameter. Brown on each side. Spread each pancake with jam or jelly, or sprinkle with powdered sugar. Roll while hot. Pancakes may also be rolled plain and served with syrup.

enlistments were restricted to "able-bodied white males" by an Act of Congress. In some states, however (e.g. Georgia, North Carolina and Louisiana), "certain free men of color" were accepted in the state militia. Despite the exclusions, they nevertheless acquitted themselves nobly; particularly the two battalions of black soldiers who served under General Andrew Jackson when he defeated the British in the decisive Battle of New Orleans.

Many Negroes also saw naval service during the War of 1812, on the high seas and especially in the Great Lakes region where they played an important and heroic role in the Battles of Lake Erie and Lake Champlain (as well as other naval engagements) which were factors bearing on the successful conclusion of the war.

On December 18, 1814, General Jackson issued a proclamation to Negro troops following the Battle of New Orleans in which he lauded "the men of color":

> "Soldiers!
>
> . . . You surpassed my hopes. I have found in you that noble enthusiasm which impels to great deeds."

On February 18, 1820, the Adjutant and Inspector General's Office of the United States Army expressed its "thanks" to the black Americans for their military contributions by issuing the following order:

> *"No Negro or Mulatto will be received as a recruit of the Army."*

The Civil War: At the outbreak of the War between the States, President Abraham Lincoln and his military advisors were confident that the armies of the secessionist states would be forced to surrender within a few months. This confidence quickly evaporated with the disastrous defeat of the Union forces in the Battle of Bull Run. Until then, Lincoln had sought to woo the border states to the Union cause by refraining from arming Negroes. Now, however, it became apparent that the South would not crumble with the first onslaught and that a protracted conflict could be expected. Fifty thousand slaves were enlisted for "volunteer labor" and assigned to the Quartermaster Department of the Union Army.

In less than a year after Bull Run, in May, 1862, the First South Carolina Regiment was organized by Major General David Hunter. A month later, the *Corps d'Afrique*, comprising the 1st, 2nd and 3rd Native Guards, was brought into action. These were the first Negro *combat* troops of the war. By January 1, 1863, the date of the Emancipation Proclamation, the exclusion of Negroes as combat troops came to an end. Frederick Douglass, who had been urging Lincoln to free the slaves and arm them for combat, did yeoman service in the recruitment of Negroes for the Union armies, among them his own sons.

Of the 186,000 blacks who served during the war, some 29,000 saw action in the Union Navy—roughly 25% of the Navy's personnel. They were aboard the *Kearsage* when she defeated the *Alabama*, the *Monitor* in its engagement with the *Merrimac*, and Farragut's flagship in the Battle of Mobile Bay.

The contribution of the Negroes to the preservation of the Union is self evident: They fought in 201 battles, produced 16 Congressional Medal of Honor recipients, and earned the praise of every commanding officer under whom they served. At the close of the war, more than 36,000 black soldiers had sacrificed their lives for the right of their people to stand as equals among men.

The Indian Wars (1870-1890): The USCT (United States Colored Troops), during the Indian Wars, comprised only two regiments of cavalry (the 9th and the 10th) and two of infantry (the 24th and the 25th). These regiments were assigned to isolated posts in hostile Indian territory covering Texas, New Mexico, Colorado, Arizona and Mexico. The Apache, Sioux and other Indian tribes whom they met in combat referred to the black fighters as "Buffalo Soldiers," and under that nomenclature they earned a well-merited place in history. The 9th U.S. Cavalry produced 12 Congressional Medal of Honor winners; the 24th Infantry, two.

The Spanish-American War: As with their white fellow citizens, a patriotic fervor seized American Negroes and sixteen full regiments of black volunteers were raised during the Spanish-American War. Of these, four regular Negro regiments distinguished themselves in the Battle of San Juan Hill, together with Teddy Roosevelt's "Rough Riders"—a fact appearing in all too few text books. Particularly notable, in addition, was the key Battle of Santiago and the Battle of El Caney, in which the 10th Cavalry made its famous charge. It was his all-Negro 10th Cavalry—Troops H, M, and G—which produced five Congressional Medal of Honor winners.

World War I: Of the 370,000 Negroes who participated in World War I, about 135,000 were assigned to the 92nd and 93rd combat divisions. Regiments within the 92nd, after initial training in the United States, were sent to France where they served as all-Negro units in the French army. Members of the four infantry regiments of the 93rd, however, were deployed as individuals in fully integrated units in the French command. Most of these black soldiers, for the first time in their lives, finally knew the meaning of equality, being regarded by their comrades-in-arms as *men* rather than as *black* men.

The "Brothers" proved to be valiant fighters. The first Americans to be decorated in France for bravery, Henry Johnson and Needham Roberts, both Negroes, received the celebrated *Croix de Guerre*. Of the all-black regiments, two of the units themselves were awarded the coveted medal by the government of France for courage above and beyond the call of duty. One of them, the illustrious 369th, was the first American regiment of either race to reach the Rhine River, opening the floodgates which led to the collapse of Germany's military capacity and to the Armistice.

World War II: The involvement of Negroes in World War II began in the very first hours of the conflict. On December 7, 1941, the Japanese struck at Pearl Harbor in wave after wave of devastating aerial attacks aimed at American naval installations. In the holocaust that ensued, Dorie Miller of Waco, Texas, a messman aboard the *U.S.S. Arizona,* distinguished himself by manning a machinegun and bringing down four enemy planes. For his act of heroism he was awarded the Navy Cross. Miller was killed in action in the South Pacific in December, 1943, at the age of 24. A number of other Negroes were also cited for heroism, including Leonard Roy Harmon, of the *U.S.S. San Francisco,* and William Pinckney, of the *U.S.S. Enterprise,* both of whom were awarded the Navy Cross, and Elbert H. Oliver of the *U.S.S. Intrepid,* who received the Silver Star.

A number of "firsts" occurred during the war. On June 18, 1942, Bernard W. Robinson was made an ensign in the Navy, becoming the first Negro to win a commission in this branch of the service. In 1943, the 99th Pursuit Squadron—the first Negro flying unit—flew its first combat mission in the Mediterranean theater. In Italy, an all-Negro squadron of the 332nd Fighter Group attached to the 15th Air Force was commanded by a Negro captain, Andrew O. Tanner. This was the group which was later placed under the command of Col. Benjamin O. Davis, Jr., son of the highest-ranking Negro in the European theater, Brigadier General Benjamin O. Davis, Sr. In 1945, Davis, Jr.—later a general in his own right—was given command of Godman Field in Kentucky. On March 8, 1945, Phyllis Mae Dailey was sworn into the Navy Nurse Corps in New York City, to become the first Negro nurse to serve in that branch of the service.

All told, more than a million blacks were inducted into the armed forces during the war years. These troops were assigned to posts in such countries as Italy, France, England, Wales, Scotland, Germany, Algeria, Morocco, Liberia, Holland, Egypt, Belgium and Luxembourg. The 92nd Division, one of the first units to be sent overseas, received 542 Bronze Stars, 82 Silver Stars, 12 Legion of Merit awards, two Distinguished Service crosses, and one Distinguished Service medal—a thrilling record indeed!

Korean War (1950-1953): On July 26, 1948, Executive Order 9981 was issued by President Harry Truman ending segregation in the Armed Forces. Troop integration progressed to a point where, during the Korean conflict, only a few scattered units could be identified as racially segregated. There remained, however, the 24th Infantry, an all-Negro regiment which had been part of the Regular Army for over 80 years. Upon the outbreak of the war, the 24th was flown to the combat area from its base in Japan and, only three weeks after the North Korean army invaded South Korea, met the enemy in battle. The victory won by the fighting 24th Infantry at the railhead city of Yech'on represented the first for the United Nations forces in Korea.

Two Congressional Medal of Honor recipients were named, both New Yorkers; Pfc William Thompson, Company M, and Sergeant Cornelius Charlton, Company C, 24th Infantry. Thompson, it should be noted, was the first Negro to be awarded the CMH since the Spanish-American War. He was killed on August 6, 1950, after fighting off an entire enemy regiment singlehanded. Charlton was the second black soldier to win the CMH in Korea. He lost his life on June 2, 1951, while leading a platoon attack on a ridge held by the North Koreans.

Despite President Truman's Executive Order, mistreatment and discrimination of Negro troops continued. Supreme Court Justice Thurgood Marshall, then representing the NAACP, investigated the court-martial procedures of one case which involved the sentencing of 39 black soldiers. As a result, most were released or given less severe sentences.

Vietnam: At this writing (1971), the role of the Negro in Vietnam has yet to be evaluated and chronicled. Although the unpopular war has been marked with controversy since its inception, by black and white citizens alike, its social consequences for the Negro has assumed a degree of significance far surpassing any previous military experience. Equal opportunity in the armed forces, the abolition of all racial restrictions, and the rulings against segregated non-military facilities in the areas surrounding the military bases have been largely successful because of the firm posture taken by civil rights groups and militant black soldiers themselves. Among the questions which future historians will have to answer is the reason for the inordinate percentage of Negroes who have been killed or wounded, in relation to their numbers. Indeed, as long ago as 1965, Defense Department statistics placed the percentage of Negro casualties among enlisted men at 22.1% of the total.

Among the first true heroes of the Vietnam War was Pfc Milton L. Olive III, Company B, 503rd Infantry, 173rd Airborne Brigade. On October 22, 1965, Olive, who had not yet reached his 19th birthday, met his death when he saved the lives of his fellow soldiers by throwing himself upon a grenade and absorbing the shock of the explosion with his body. The Congressional Medal of Honor was awarded posthumously to the young soldier's parents by President Lyndon B. Johnson at the White House, April 21, 1966.

The year 1971 was memorable for black officers of star and flag rank in the armed services, with three Army colonels promoted in May to brigadier general and a naval officer appointed to the rank of admiral.

Selected for elevation to brigadier general were:

Oliver W. Dillard, of Margaret, Alabama, a senior province adviser in Vietnam. General Dillard, awarded the Silver and Bronze Star medals for bravery, has a background in foreign affairs for which he holds a master's degree from George Washington University;

James F. Hamlet, of Alliance, Ohio, commander of the 1st Cavalry Division's 11th Aviation Group in Vietnam. General Hamlet is a decorated infantry officer who was first commissioned in 1944 and is now an expert in helicopter warfare;

Roscoe C. Cartwright, of Kansas City, Missouri, assistant chief of staff for force development. General Cartwright holds degrees in social science and business administration from San Francisco State College and the University of Missouri. An artillery officer, he also served in various administrative posts before his current assignment to the Pentagon.

The announcement of the three promotions was made by the only Negro general in the Air Force, Daniel (Chappie) James, now on active duty. General James serves as deputy assistant secretary of defense for public affairs. The nominations were immediately approved by President Richard M. Nixon and forwarded to the United States Senate for routine confirmation.

Since the Army broke the color line in 1940 with the promotion of the late Benjamin O. Davis, giving him the distinction of being the first black general in U.S. military history, only one other black army officer has pinned on general's stripes—Major General Frederic Dawson, who is still on active duty. Davis' son, Benjamin O. Davis Jr., retired in 1970 as an Air Force lieutenant general.

In April, 1971, Samuel L. Gravely Jr., became the first black admiral in the history of the Navy. At this writing, the Marine Corps remains the only branch of the armed forces without Negro general officers, the highest ranking blacks listed as four lieutenant colonels.

This introduction to the black man in the military establishment, from the ancient Nubians of 2000 B.C. to the gallant young men in Vietnam, has little in common with the droll anecdotes which follow. The editor confesses, without a scintilla of shame, that he has recounted the jokes and stories for the sole purpose of arousing an interest in the reader to explore the inspiring history of a people who have always fought gallantly for the principles which they held dear. If this is too obvious a device to lure the reader into further, serious study, let us hope that it is, at least, an entertaining one.

1   1   1

Perspective

During the height of the Battle of Richmond, a Negro in the Union army shot another black soldier in the Confederate ranks.*

A Confederate officer who witnessed the shooting turned to a fellow officer and snarled, "Did you see what that nigger did to our colored boy?"

Every Man for Himself

One of the few pleasant aftermaths of General Ulysses S. Grant's march on Richmond was that his army left many freed men, women and children in its wake. Nor was it always physical contact with the Union troops that forced the slave owners to free their captives. More often they simply fled

---

* The Confederate states did not assign blacks for combat duty. It was feared that armed Negroes might attempt an insurrection against the white establishment of the South—a fear that was quite possibly justified.

before the advancing army. General Grant was not especially known for his leniency toward last-minute holdouts among the plantation owners.

Two ex-slaves, on one such abandoned plantation, were discussing their immediate future.

"I'm gonna git me a gun an' j'ine up wid de Union ahmy," said the older man.

"I'm gonna git me a gun too," said the other, "an' I'm gonna j'ine de Union ahmy—paht time."

"Paht time! You crazy?"

"Not zackly. I studied on it all night, an' when I woked up dis mawnin' I said to myse'f, 'Now looka heah, boy—you go git yo'se'f a gun, j'ine de Union ahmy—an' do a little rabbit huntin' on de side.' "

Let's You and Him Fight

Samuel Hart, who was later to distinguish himself in the famed 54th Massachusetts Negro Regiment during the Civil War, recalled in his memoirs that he was not so militant in his early youth. He was about fourteen years old when he and his family escaped from slavery in Maryland. His rescuing angel was Harriet Tubman, who guided the family to Auburn, New York, in the year 1855.*

Upon reaching safety, young Samuel found himself to be the center of interest among persons who were curious to know "if slavery was all that bad." At a recruiting center in Auburn, a number of young officers were discussing the role of the black man in the conflict between the states. One of them turned to Mr. Hart. "Is it true that the Negroes in the south are doing nothing to help the Union cause?"

Samuel Hart considered the plight of the slave and replied, "Does the turkey arm himself at Thanksgiving?"

"But," persisted the junior officer, "what is the Negro doing about the war in the North? Surely he knows what all the fighting is about."

"My dear friend," replied Mr. Hart, "as an ex-slave, permit me to intro-

---

* Often called the greatest "conductor" on the Underground Railway, Harriet Ross Tubman was born into slavery in Maryland, about 1820. She escaped at the age of 25, even though her husband had threatened to report her to the master. She returned to the South at least nineteen times to lead others to freedom. Rewards totalling $40,000 were offered for her capture, but she was never arrested, nor did she ever lose one of her 300 or more charges in transit along the one-way Underground Railway from South to North. Like Frederick Douglass, she was forced to flee to Canada for a short time (Douglass was suspected of being a collaborator with John Brown), but returned at the outbreak of the Civil War, serving as nurse, soldier, spy, and scout for the Union army. She died in poverty, in Auburn, N. Y. in 1913. As a postscript, she did not receive a pension until more than thirty years after the close of the Civil War—the sum of $20 per month. Yet, with that small stipend, she helped found a refuge for the aged and needy, later to be called The Harriet Tubman Home, in Auburn.

duce you to the black man's philosophy. You have undoubtedly seen two dogs fighting over a bone.

"Yes, many times."

"Then tell me," concluded Hart, "have you ever seen the bone participate in any of the fighting?"

Home Is Where the Heart Is

The chaplain was giving the new soldiers a pep talk. "Remember this," he said. "If, unfortunately, you should get killed, your home will be in Heaven."

"Maybe so," muttered one of the men, "but right now I ain't homesick."

Dangerous Furloughs

The new recruit telephoned his mother with some good news. "Mom," he said excitedly, "I'm coming home on a furlough."

"That's fine, but don't go taking no furlough," replied the anxious mother. "Do like the other boys do and take a train."

Freddie the Fugitive

Freddie was in the sack, dreaming of the time he would be out of the army, when he was awakened and told that the Chaplain wanted to see him —on the double! Within minutes he was in that gentleman's office.

"I have a letter here from your wife," the chaplain began, eyeing the soldier sternly. "She claims you did not list her as a dependent and she is in need of money. Young man, did you desert your wife?"

"Sir, I ain't no deserter," explained Freddie. "If you knew my wife you'd say I was sort of a refugee!"

It All Depends

An army officer was busily engaged in helping new recruits complete their many questionnaires. "Do you have any dependents?" he asked a young rookie.

"No, none," answered the youth.

The officer re-examined the fellow's insurance application. "But it says here you are married."

"Yes sir, I have a wife," the new soldier acknowledged, "but that ain't sayin' she's dependable!"

Piece Work

"Next!" called the officer at the Army Induction Center as the long line of waiting youths moved forward.

The officer regarded the boy in front of him and sighed. Slight of build, obviously near-sighted and, equally apparent, a gentle soul, he was hardly what the officer would have sought for dangerous duty. "No doubt you would like a commission," he said, in an attempt at levity.

The boy shook his head. "No suh, I don't want no commission," he answered. "I'd rather work for reg'lar wages like my pa."

What's in a Name

A long, lanky country boy stood before the recruiting sergeant, waiting for his army papers to be processed. The first question asked was his name. "What are you called?" growled the sergeant.

"Byminishils," said the boy promptly.

The sergeant lifted his pen and glanced up from the desk. "What was that again?"

"Byminishils."

"You mean that's your name?"

"No, it ain't," answered the youth. "You didn't ax my name. You axed whut I am called," he explained, now speaking very carefully, "an' I done tol' you—I'm called by my 'nitials!"

PART SIX

GAMBLING, DRINKING, VICE
AND VERSA

Addressing the Undressed

A thoroughly inebriated young man was reeling down the street, wearing one sandal. A kind old lady approached him. "Lose a shoe?" she asked sympathetically.

"No ma'am," replied the drunk. "I found one."

Sin, Skin and Gin

Joe, the barber, kept reasonably sober during the week, but weekends were something else.

One Monday morning the local preacher came to Joe's emporium for a shave. With a shaky hand, and smelling like a brewery truck, the barber proceeded to shave the servant of the Lord. Halfway through his labors, he happened to nick the preacher's chin.

"You see?" chided the preacher. "That's what happens when a man drinks too much."

"That's a fack," agreed Joe pleasantly. "Drinkin' do make the skin tender, don't it?"

Heavenly Silence

Jesse, middle-aged but as active as in his youth, was being scolded by the deacon of his church. "You oughtta be ashamed of yourself, drinkin' an' fightin' an' carousin' aroun' in public like that. The least you could do is set a good example for the children."

"I don't set no bad example for the kids," protested Jesse in his own defense. "I do all my hell-raisin' at night, when they're sleepin'."

The deacon shook his head sadly. "Oh Jesse, you know that the Lord sees all—day or night."

"Maybe so," Jesse retorted, "but you gotta admit, the Lord don't never *talk!*"

Gamblin' Man

Randolph Page Dexter, the richest white man in Virginia, was a lavish tipper. For years he regularly visited his favorite restaurant where he was always served by one waiter—faithful, quiet, efficient William—just like in the Uncle Tom books.

One evening, as Mr. Dexter seated himself at the table, he was handed a menu by another waiter.

"Where is William?" asked the wealthy diner.

"He's here, suh, but he ain't gonna wait on you no more," said the new man. "I won you in a crap game."

Seth's Breath

"Seth," reproached the youth's grandfather, "how you gonna explain that smell of alcohol an' tobacco on your breath when St. Peter meets you at the heavenly gates?"

"To tell the truth, Grandpa," replied Seth amiably, "I wasn't expecting to take my breath with me."

Julius Gets Juiced

The defendant stood before the bar of justice, weaving, and somewhat steadied by the firm grasp of a supporting bailiff. The judge glowered down at the miscreant.

"Julius," said the magistrate, "you've been brought to this court for excessive drinking."

"Tha's jes' fine, your honor," said Julius thickly. "When do I start?"

Intoxication Test

One thing the white guys learned in the Vietnam War—don't even try to drink with the black soldiers.

A mixed platoon of GI's were polishing off a couple of fifths of joy juice when one of the white fellas slumped to the barracks floor. The others eyed the prostrate figure owlishly. "Maybe we oughtta pick 'im up an' put him to bed," suggested a white boy.

"Hell," snorted one of the black soldiers, "he ain't drunk. I just saw his pinkie move."

Booze Blues

"I feel fine today, but I'll make up for it tomorrow!"

The Bottle and the Snake

It was the fifth time that the defendant had stood before the very same judge on charges of public intoxication.

"Your honor," said the alcoholic, "I give you my word that this will never happen again. This is the first time in my life that I have ever said I would take the pledge, and I mean it!"

"When did you arrive at this decision to reform?" asked the judge.

"Yesterday," replied the ex-drinker. "I spent all morning on my front lawn trying to kill the garden hose."

Deserter

"The last time I swore off drinking," sighed Dan Sping, "four bartenders sued me for non-support."

Jeff and the Juggled Jug of Joy Juice

A wealthy but miserly landowner not only amassed a fortune by cheating his sharecroppers unmercifully, but enjoyed a prosperous sideline as a distiller of illegal corn liquor. But he would never give his tenant farmers a taste, and when they bought the whiskey he charged them twice the price that he did the white people.

One day he heard that the revenue agents had been alerted to his bootlegging activities, so he decided to hide the evidence until after the Federal agents had departed. He called Jeff, one of his trusted field hands.

"Jeff, it looks like some busybody told the government about my still. I want you to bury this sour mash until the Feds leave."

Dutifully, Jeff hoisted the full ten-gallon jug to his shoulders and set off for a far corner of the property. He returned a few minutes later.

"What the hell are you doing back here?" stormed the landowner.

"I done buried the cawn liquor like you tol' me," said Jeff, his face a picture of innocence. "Now, what you want me to do with this here empty jug?"

Friendly Persuasion

The man was a compulsive kleptomaniac whose thefts had landed him in countless jails. He just couldn't resist the impulse to steal—usually items of little value for which he had no need. As a last resort he consulted a psychiatrist. For two years the doctor labored over him, prying into his mind and bringing to light his most intimate secrets. At last he announced that the patient was cured.

"Doctor, I don't know how to thank you," said the grateful ex-crook.

"Well, there's one way you can express your appreciation, if you like," said the psychiatrist. "If you should ever suffer a relapse, would you mind picking me up a toaster?"

Doing It the Hard Way

It was midnight and the store was just about to close when a guy walked in, brandishing a two-by-four.

"This is a stick-up," he snarled. "Hand over the cash or I'll knock you cold."

The clerk hastily reached for the cash register. "Here, take the money," he cried, "and for chrissake go buy yourself a gun. You're gonna kill somebody with that damn board!"

Passing the Time of Day

Two cronies were discussing their respective neighborhoods.

"Where I come from, on Chicago's South Side, when someone asks 'What time is it?' you first thank him for asking, *then* you tell him the time."

"That's nothing," retorted the other. "I just moved into a neighborhood in New York that's so tough, *nobody* asks you for the time. They just take your watch!"

Prove It!

"Mr. Johnson," intoned the Judge, "the indictment charges you with stealing a car from the plaintiff. How do you plead—guilty or innocent?"

"Your honor," answered Mr. Johnson, his voice steady, "isn't that what you have to prove in the trial?"

Payment Guaranteed

Timidly, the stranger entered the attorney's office and asked for legal advice. "Before I start, I gotta tell you I'm broke—flat busted," he said, his face downcast. Suddenly he was struck with a bright idea. "If you defend me in court I can pay you with a blue an' white 1971 Ford Mustang."

The lawyer nodded. "Very well, I'll accept that. What are you charged with?"

The client smiled and then purred, "I'm charged with stealin' a blue an' white 1971 Ford Mustang."

PART SEVEN

THE THOMPSON STREET
POKER CLUB*

"Thou shalt lie down with kings"—Thanatopsis
"I would give all my fame for a pot"—Henry I
"Now might I do it pat"—Hamlet
"I cannot draw"—Lear
"Straight let us seek"—King John
"O for the touch of a vanished hand"—Tennyson

Two Jacks and a Pistol

The Thompson Street Poker Club was in session and a substantial jackpot had been opened. There were evidently big hands out, for the bets and excitement ran high.

---

* Mitchell and Miller, Inc., 1884. Edited and revised by Dan Spring, 1971, for Jonathan David, Publishers, New York.

JOHN HENRY BEEF STEW

At the close of the nineteenth century, this West Virginia recipe was named in honor of John Henry, the "steel-drivin' man" of the period.

(May also be made with lamb or veal)

2 lbs chuck or brisket beef
½ tsp. garlic salt
1 tsp. salt
4 cups boiling water
1 med. onion, chopped
1 tsp. lemon juice
6 carrots
½ tsp. curry powder
¼ cup flour

1 tsp. Worcestershire sauce
several whole cloves
2 bay leaves
dash nutmeg
8 to 10 small onions
6 to 8 small potatoes
½ tsp. pepper
1 tsp. sugar

Sprinkle meat with flour and seasonings. Brown on all sides in a small amount of fat. Add boiling water, lemon juice, curry powder, Worcestershire sauce, chopped onion, cloves and other spices. Simmer 2 hours. Add whole onions, carrots and potatoes. Cook 20 minutes longer. Serve piping hot. Serves 5.

"Looka heah, Gus Johnson, whuffo you rise dat pot?" demanded Mr. Tooter Williams.

"Nevah you min'! You call, ef you ain't 'fraid! dat's all!" retorted Gus.

"I won't call! I rise you back," said Mr. Williams, his vertebrae ascending. Gus was undaunted. "I rise you ag'in."

And so they went at each other until chips, money and collateral were gone. Mr. Williams concluded to call. "What you got, dat you do all dat risin' on? I ax you, what you got?"

Gus laid down his hand: Ace, king, queen, jack, and ten of clubs. "Is dat good?" he inquired with a slow smile as he sized up the pot.

"No, dat's not good," said Mr. Williams, reaching behind him.

"What you got den?" asked Gus.

Mr. Williams hexed him with his best evil-eye. "I got two jacks an' a gun."

"Dat's good!" said Gus.

Smith Is Not to Be Bluffed

Mr. Tooter Williams astonished the Thompson Street Poker Club Saturday night by raising Gus Johnson sixty-five cents when that gentleman opened the last jackpot of the evening. Mr. Johnson showed up two small pairs and precipitately fell out, but the Rev. Mr. Thankful Smith stood the raise and drew four cards. Mr. Williams stood pat. After the draw, Mr. Smith skinned his cards, breathed deeply and bet a postage stamp and a battered cent. Mr. Williams promptly raised him a dollar and forty cents. Mr. Smith hesitated, but finally drew forth his wallet. "Okay, what you got dat you gittin' so brash?"

"You fin' out ef you bet dat dollah fo'ty—jes' you see," retorted Mr. Williams.

"You done rise me wunst too often," snapped the Rev. Smith, putting his money into the pot. "Now, what you got?"

Mr. Wlliams was obviously disconcerted. "I—I jes' got a small king full," he confessed, his voice faltering.

"Dat's good," sighed the Rev. Smith, disappointed.

"But I ain't got it," said Mr. Williams, skinning his cards for the third time.

"Man, quit jivin' me. What *has* you got?"

"I—I ain't got nothin'."

"Well, *dat's good!*"

Rev. Smith's Trouble with the Bank

Owing to the unfortunate fact that the chips loaned to the Thompson Street Poker Club by Mr. Rube Jackson had been garnisheed by Mr. Gus Johnson (see Rule 147, which provides for payment of I.O.U.'s), the members present last Saturday evening were compelled to play with beans—a limited quantity of which had been thoughtfully secured by the Rev. Mr. Thankful Smith while passing a produce store in the late afternoon.

The cards ran well, and as Mr. Smith himself was responsible for the bank, the betting was unusually brisk. Mr. Smith was never in better luck, nor Mr. Tooter Williams in worse. Notwithstanding the heavy losses of the latter gentleman, however, his supply of beans seemed never to run short, and after several hours of play the banker's suspicions were aroused.

"Lemme jes' cash up an' see how de bank stan's," said the preacher-turned-banker, after an unusually prodigal burst of beans from Mr. Williams had startled the players.

Mr. Gus Johnson passed in ninety-six beans and got his money.

Professor Brick had thirty-nine and a half, but consented, after some haggling, to call it plain thirty-nine.

Mr. Rube Jackson had seventy-two beans, but owed the bank seventy-five. He settled the difference with coin.

All accounts had now been squared away except that of Mr. Williams. The Rev. Mr. Smith emptied the beans into his hat, put the pack into his pocket, and made away with the stuffed wallet. Every eye was fixed on Mr. Williams.

But Mr. Williams was far from cowed. "Looka heah," he demanded of the banker, "whar's de cash fo' dese beans?"

By way of reply, Mr. Smith emptied the bank upon the table and requested the Committee of the Whole to count it. The return was nine hundred and seventy-two beans.

The room was deadly quiet as Mr. Smith, his manner and voice accusing, said, "I only had fo' hunnerd an' sixty beans tuh start; I winned all de jackers an' most of de stray tussels, an' yet I's a dollah fo'ty-two out. Dis bank's solvent ez long's de bettin's squar', but de debbil hisse'f cain't cash ag'in de man what's got a umbreller-case full o' beans dribblin' from his sleeve. No suh! Dis bank am 'spended!"

The Club adjourned.

One Black, Two Whites—Two Blacks, One White...

There was no poker game on Saturday evening. Mr. Gus Johnson was engaged to sing a revival in Hoboken. Professor Brick wrote a note to the effect that his coal man had prevented his recuperation sufficiently on the cash system; and Mr. Rube Jackson, who had promised to call upon Elder Boss Jones, of Florida, and steer him against the game, failed to put in an appearance.

The Rev. Thankful Smith was relating the experiences of the previous meeting when, with the saddened air of a man who has lost his grip on his reputation, Mr. Tooter Williams and the odor of a Bowery cigar entered together.

"What de mattah, Toot?" asked Mr. Smith with the easy familiarity of a man in luck. You look 'spondent."

"I done los' dat sixty-fo' dollahs I winned on de hoss race," Mr. Williams explained, his face clouded in gloom.

"Hoccum you los' all dat money?"

"Bettin'. An' I done los' it bettin' ag'in black men, too. Dat's what make de remorse bite."

The deepest interest having been aroused, Mr. Williams proceeded to enlighten the several members who had shown up that night. "I was standin' in a do' on Seventh Avn'ya an' up comes a white man in a plug hat; sezee, 'Why *heel-o* Mistah Robinson, how is you?' "

"Bunko!" remarked Mr. Smith with the air of one who has had experience.

"Dat's what *I* thought," said Mr. Williams; "a con man. I was gonna tell him my name ain't Robinson, but I kep' shet. So I say to him, 'How is *you?*' "

" 'I's a stranger yar, Mistuh Robinson,' sezee, 'an' I mus' say I nevuh did see so many black folks togiddah ez dey is on Seventh Avn'ya. Dey's mo' blacks dan white pussons.' 'Oh no,' sez I, 'dey's mo' white dan black pussons.' 'I'll bet you two to one dey isn't,' sezee. 'All right,' sez I. So off he goes an' comes back wid a frien' who weighed 'bout two hunnerd, an' had a bad eye."

Mr. Williams sighed, blew his nose, and continued. "Den sezee, 'Now we will bofe put up a hunnerd dollahs wif dis genelman an' stan' yar in de do'. Ev'y white man passes, he'll give you two dollahs, an' ev'y black man passes he'll give *me* a dollah.' "

"Sho'!" said Mr. Smith who, like the other members, was fascinated by the story.

"Well, fus' dey comes along two white men, an' de man wif de bad eye say dat was fo' dollahs to my credit. Den along comes six white men an' he say dat's twelve dollahs mo' f' me. Den along comes a black man an' I lose a dollah. Den fo' mo' white men, an' I win eight. Den fo' white men mo', den one black, den two blacks, den seven whites, an' de man wif de bad eye he say I was fo'ty two dollahs ahead."

"De soffes' deal I evah heah," said Mr. Smith, whose eyes were glistening over Mr. Williams' winnings.

"Den along comes fo' white men," said Mr. Williams, "an' de man wif a bad eye he say dat was eight dollahs mo', an' *den*. . . ." Here Mr. Williams paused, as if his recollection had overpowered him.

"An' den. . . ?" echoed everybody, wildly excited.

"Why, den," said Mr. Williams desperately, "dey comes around' de cornah. . . ."

"De cops," gasped Mr. Smith.

"No," Mr. Williams said, tears in his eyes. "A black funer'l!"

The Scraped Trey

Mr. Tooter Williams was late at the meeting of the Thompson Street Poker Club, Saturday evening, but as he had a new "pigeon"—Elder Boss Dickerson—in tow, the secretary remitted the usual fine. It was confidentially learned that the Elder had just received $17.50 on an extensive calsomining contract, and was probably good for as much more. It had already been secretly remarked by older members that whenever the Club played with an old pack, Mr. Williams' luck was invariably steadier and more brilliant, and as Mr. Williams had already played with the deck of cards now upon the table, the game promised to be one of extraordinary interest. Also, Mr. Rube Jackson had consented, for a small percentage, not to play but to sit in a sociable way behind the Elder's chair.

Having been introduced to the Rev. Mr. Thankful Smith, Mr. Gus Johnson, and Professor Brick, the Elder divested himself of his coat, produced a corpulent wallet, purchased $1.79 worth of blues and reds, and opened the game with an expression of determination and a thumping blind which made the nervous Mr. Johnson's jaw hang open. Seven hands were played, and as Mr. Jackson, who sat behind the Elder, had evidently forgotten the code of signals to the extent that he winked with his right eye when he should have winked with his left, Mr. Williams was already out ninety-seven cents, and was correspondingly furious.

At last, however, Mr. Jackson was made aware of his error by a searching kick delivered beneath the table, and a new deck, which had been thoughtfully placed on ice by the Rev. Mr. Smith before the company assembled, was produced. It was Mr. Johnson's deal, and the Elder's blind.

Everybody came in.

The Elder raised the blind sixty-five cents.

The decisive moment had come.

"I rise dat rise a dollah," said the Rev. Thankful Smith, with the calmness of one who expects to fill a royal flush.

"I sees you dat, an' I lif' you a dollah mo' " ventured Mr. Williams.

"I calls," said the Elder.

Mr. Smith also called, and the three proceeded to draw cards. Mr. Williams wanted two cards, the Rev. Mr. Smith guessed he'd take one, and the Elder concluded to stand pat.

Mr. Smith led out with a two-dollar stack. Mr. Williams slowly pulled out a bulging wallet, fixed a belligerent glare apparently on Mr. Smith, banged the wallet heavily on the middle of the table, and said, impressively, "I goes you dat two, an' six dollahs rise."

"I rise you six," said the Elder, but without putting up chips.

The Rev. Smith dropped out. Mr. Williams pointed to the wallet and said, "I goes you six mo'."

The Elder raised one foot and placed it neatly on top of Mr. Williams' wallet. "I rise dat ten," he said.

"Whar's de money?" inquired Mr. Williams with a polite smile.

"Whar's *yo'* money?" retorted the Elder, just as sweetly.

Mr. Williams pointed to the wallet underneath the Elder's heel.

"Dat's all right, den," said the Elder. "I's got jes' ez much leather on dis yar table ez you."

"What you mean by dat?" demanded Mr. Williams.

"Put up or shet!" said the Elder.

Mr. Williams drove his knife through the cards, pinning them to the table, and called out the Rev. Mr. Smith for a consultation in the next room. The Elder thoughtfully whistled a tune, drew a pen-knife from his pocket and seemed to be trying its edge on the surface of his bottom card. Mr. Jackson watched Mr. Williams' hand to see that nothing got away, and Mr. Johnson kept his eye on the pack.

Mr. Williams returned triumphantly and counted out thirty dollars which he had evidently borrowed from Mr. Smith. "I calls," he said.

The Elder put up his pen-knife, shook $29 out of his wallet, made up a dollar more with a mutilated coin, some pennies and a postage stamp. "What you got?" he said tersely.

"Fo' kings," said Mr. Williams with a deadly gleam in his eye.

"Not good," said the Elder.

"Wha-wha-*whaaat?*"

"Fo' aces." With this, the Elder showed four aces, swept the pot into his hat, and left the room. The five sat dazed.

"I done guv him three aces an' two treys, sho'," said Mr. Johnson.

"I put dat han' up myse'f," asserted Mr. Smith, bewildered.

"I seed bofe dem treys in his han'," observed Mr. Jackson.

Mr. Williams said nothing but silently examined the Elder's hand. His voice was hoarse when he finally spoke. "Did he have a razor?"

"No, but he had a little knife," said Mr. Jackson. "He play wid it de whole time you was outen de room."

Mr. Williams rose with a withering look and put on his coat.

"What's de mattah, Toot?" asked Mr. Smith. "How you splain it?"

Mr. Williams pointed to the ace of diamonds, lately in the Elder's hand. "Give any crook de trey o' diamonds an' a sharp knife an' three aces, an' what kin fo' kings do? Dat cheatin' rascal played me outen thutty dollahs on a scraped trey."

Mr. Williams stalked out of the room, muttering, "Dat's what makes me 'spise pokah!"

Dat's Gamblin'!

At the regular meeting of the Thompson Street Poker Club, on Saturday evening, owing to the fact that both his eyes had that morning accidentally collided with the knuckles of the Rev. Mr. Thankful Smith after a slight financial misunderstanding, and that for two hours he had lost every jackpot he had opened, Mr. Tooter Williams presented an aspect of mounting gloom. Mr. Gus Johnson was one dollar and forty-nine cents ahead, having an unusually steady two-pair streak; Mr. Rube Jackson had sixty-nine cents' worth of velvet before him; Professor Brick was a few coppers and a postage stamp on the right side; and Mr. Williams, who was banking, was the only loser. Since it was his deal, three kings wandered into his hand and might have proved effectual but for the sad fact that everybody noticed the expression of his eye and fled. A jackpot was then in order, and after it had climbed to aces the players braced up and knew that the event of the evening had come. At that moment the door opened and the Rev. Mr. Smith entered, took his seat behind Mr. Jackson's chair, and glared a renewal of the morning's hostilities at Mr. Williams. That gentleman haughtily refused to notice it, however, but opened the pot with a burst of chips which scared Mr. Johnson half to death. Professor Brick came in.

"Rise dat," said the Rev. Mr. Smith to Mr. Jackson. Then he whispered audibly, "Dem three nines'll win dat pot, sho'."

Mr. Jackson elevated the bet as directed by the man behind him, but with an idea of what the good Reverend had in mind. Mr. Williams was delighted at this apparent slip of the tongue, for he had three jacks. He then returned the raise.

"Rise him ag'in," commanded the Rev. Mr. Smith, and then whispered as before: "Don' leggo dem nines."

Back came Mr. Williams, and then the Rev. Mr. Smith counseled Mr. Jackson to "jes' call, an' see what dem nines'll ketch in draw."

Mr. Jackson wanted two cards and caught a pair of treys. Mr. Williams held up a king and drew one card which, after elaborately combing his hand, he discovered to be another king. The battle was then resumed.

"I'll back dem nines for all I's wuff," said Mr. Smith, slipping his wallet into Mr. Jackson's hand. And so they went at each other until even Mr. Williams' new collar button was up, and he was forced to call. "What you got, black man?"

"What you got yo'se'f?" retorted Mr. Jackson.

"A jack-full—*dat's* what *I* got!"

"Sho'm down," said Mr. Smith, his manner cool and collected.

Mr. Williams proudly skinned out three jacks and a pair of kings, and inquired, rather superciliously, "Is dat good?"

"We's loaded fo' b'ar ovah yar," said Mr. Smith evasively.

"What?" exclaimed the astonished Mr. Williams. As dealer, he was certain he had not given Mr. Jackson a fourth nine. His voice was shaky as he said, "All right, sho'p dem nines!"

Mr. Smith showed them up. Without a reply he spread out Mr. Jackson's hand. It consisted mainly of queens, with a flavor of treys to give it strength. He then gathered in the pot and, with Mr. Jackson, quitted the room.

Mr. Williams sat in deep thought. After a little while he said, "I like de game fer fun—jes' to pass away de time. But *dat*"—here Mr. Williams waved a hand towards the debris of the recent encounter with the air of one asserting a lofty moral—"dat's *gamblin'!*"

Dar's No Suckahs in Hoboken

For three weeks, until last Saturday, The Thompson Street Poker Club had no session. This was partly due to the fact that the proprietor of the building, a sordid lout, had closed the room and kicked Mr. Gus Johnson, the treasurer, downstairs, on learning that owing to some inexplicable phenomenon not understood by the Club, the kitty had not yielded enough to pay for the kerosene in the lamps, much less the rent.

As a regular rake on two pairs and upward had been made for a month, this delinquency amazed the Club. Various scientific theories were advanced, among them one involving a search of Mr. Johnson's private pocket, but investigation had shown them to be false. An inspection of the table-drawer was then made. It was shown that a knot-hole existed in the bottom thereof, large enough to admit the insertion of two fingers or the abstraction of three dollars, which was the amount of the missing kitty. It was also demonstrated that the knot-hole had been in perihelion, so to speak, with Mr. Tooter Williams. Therefore, while it was clear that the money was hopelessly gone, it was impossible to account for its absence by any other theory than that offered by Mr. Williams himself that "de mice done smell dat las' week welch rabbit offen Mr. Johnson's fingahs on de bills an' run off wid it." This explantation was received in lieu of a better one. The Rev. Mr. Thankful Smith paid the rent and assumed charge of the kitty until he should be reimbursed; Mr. Johnson magnanimously forgave the gentleman who had kicked him downstairs, and Mr. Tooter Williams expressed his belief in Mr. Johnson's integrity as treasurer, and all was again in harmony.

Mr. Cyrus Whiffles, for a moderate percentage, had volunteered to steer his brother-in-law against the game, and, to use a technical expression, rook him for all he was worth. The gentleman in question, Mr. Highland Dilsey, was a Hoboken barber with a steady income, a total ignorance of draw poker, a childlike confidence, and other advantages of mind and person which impressed Mr. Williams favorably.

The Rev. Mr. Smith instructed the neophyte in those fundamental principles known as "coming in," "straddling," "rising," and "sweetenin' de jacker," and by tacit consent he was allowed to win some small successive pots and thus got himself into a glorious humor. Then Mr. Williams winked at Mr. Gus Johnson, and that gentleman dealt.

Mr. Williams had straddled the blind and the Rev. Mr. Smith straddled him. All came in and drew three cards apiece, except the stranger, Mr. Dilsey, who wanted only one. Mr. Williams bet a dollar. Mr. Smith raised him two.

Professor Brick called, as did also Mr. Whiffles. All eyes were upon Mr. Dilsey, and the silence was so profound that Mr. Johnson could hear his hair grow.

"Does you jes'—jes' call, Mistah Dilsey?" asked Mr. Williams with a lovely smile, "or does you rise it?"

Mr. Dilsey passed his cards in review, hesitated, and asked, "Kin I rise it?"

"Sartinly," replied Mr. Williams who had a great deal of benevolence and also three kings. "Rise it all you want."

Thus encouraged, Mr. Dilsey raised the pot six dollars. Everybody breathed hard with suppressed excitement, and Mr. Johnson's eyes might have served for a hat rack. Mr. Williams raised back and Mr. Smith raised him. The others, according to previous agreement, fled.

Mr. Dilsey called. "What you got to beat two p'ar?"

"Is sev'ral fat smilin' kings any good?" asked Mr. Williams kindly.

"Sho'm up," said Mr. Dilsey.

Mr. Williams unfolded his private collection of royalty, and Mr. Smith exhibited a panorama of spades which reflected with great credit upon Mr. Johnson's dealing.

"I's sorry, Mistah Dilsey," observed Mr. Williams.

"Dat's de way wif cyards," remarked the Rev. Mr. Smith, sententiously. "Gamblin's onsartin."

Mr. Dilsey spoke not, but began to count up the pot.

"Wha-what you doin' wif de spondles?" asked Mr. Williams.

"Leggo my pot!" commanded Mr. Smith.

Mr. Dilsey coolly rolled up the bills and inserted them in an abyss under his vest, and swept the coppers and Mr. Whiffle's plated watch-chain into his pocket. "Look here," he said in a tone which made Mr. Johnson feel like a refrigerator, "I's from Hoboken, an' I cut men's ha'r an' shave deir faces fo' a livin'. When a Hoboken barbah comes ter Thompson Street he kerries his perfession wif him, an' right now I's got a pocket full er de implements of my craf'. You heah me?"

All signified by silence that they heard. Then Mr. Dilsey laid down three jacks and a pair of sixes, and calmly jammed Mr. Whiffles' hat down over his eyes and departed.

The Club sat stricken for three minutes. Then the door slowly opened again and Mr. Dilsey's sepulchural voice floated to them. He then vanished, but his words still rang in their ears:

"Dar's no suckah's in Hoboken!"

The Seven Cents

A special meeting of the Thompson Street Poker Club was held last Saturday evening for the purpose of discussing the ways and means of aiding the Bartholdi Pedestal Fund. Mr. Tooter Williams, who had not entirely recovered from an acute attack of something-or-other, contracted on New Year's Eve, was found to be too unparliamentary and uproarious to occupy the Chair, so that power was conferred upon the Rev. Thankful Smith who, though evidently convalescing from the same malady, was drowsy but dignified, and banked as usual.

Mr. Rube Jackson opened the question and the jackpot by remarking that he had seen a photograph of the statue and thought that its complexion should strongly recommend it to the zeal of the black people.

Mr. Gus Johnson passed out with the comment that he "never did have no luck on jackers nohow," and wanted to hear the Bartholdi matter more fully discussed before venturing an opinion.

Mr. Cyrus Whiffles came in without a statement at all.

Mr. Tooter Williams woke up and said he would open the pot for a dollar and a half. Mr. Rube Jackson, who saw there was trouble coming, quickly but mildly assured him it had already been opened for thirty-five cents.

Then said Mr. Williams in a voice of war, "I rise dat two dollahs, 'n I'll knock de tar outen anybody who don' rassle."

This definite proposition had the effect of scaring the wits out of Mr. Jackson, and of recalling the Rev. Mr. Smith from the temporary state of coma into which he had lapsed. He drowsily ran over his hand, inquired who had opened the pot, and on being informed of Mr. Williams' belligerent burst of chips, electrified all present by drawing forth the honorable wallet and slapping it on the table with great violence. He then said to Mr. Williams:

"Look hyar, Toot; what you doin'?"

"I jes'—well—I jes' rised de pot," faltered Mr. Williams, who had not forgotten past experiences with that wallet.

"You *rised* it, did yer?" asked Mr. Smith, his voice oozing sarcasm. "You rised it?" Here he opened the wallet and shook out a roll of bills. "I see dat rise 'n I swole dat pot ten—twenny—no, fo'ty dollahs!" He leaned back and smiled reassuringly on Mr. Jackson who had begun to breathe again.

Mr. Williams ran over his hand once again. It somehow did not seem to be as large as before. "I—I 'sidered dis pot was fer—fer de fun'."

"Fun? What fun?" asked Mr. Smith.

"De pedestal fun'."

"Dat's why you swole de jacker?"

"Y-yes."

"Well, den, fer de sake ob de pedestal fun', I jes' swole it fo'ty dollahs."

Mr. Williams respiration was labored for a few minutes, during which time he ran his hand over again. "I's a patriot," he said, "an' I'll do anyfing in de cause."

"Den you call dat rise?"

Mr. Williams threw up his hand. The Rev. Mr. Smith raked in the jack, counted it over twice, and said:

"De gross proceeds of dis entertainment am five dollahs 'n seventy-two cents. Five from thutteen, nine, carry one; six 'n fo' is nine—dat leaves jes' seven cents profit fer de fun'. Brothah Jackson will take charge ob de seven cents," he concluded, passing that sum over in coppers.

"But whar—whar's de res' ob de money goin'?" inquired Mr. Williams.

"De res' ob de money," said Mr. Smith evenly, "is 'sorbed by de 'spences ob de entertainment. Brothah Jackson will now pass aroun' de aces."

Wharjer Git Dem Jacks?

Mr. Tooter Williams had a bad eye and several kings when the Rev. Mr. Thankful Smith opened the first jackpot at the regular meeting of the Thompson Street Poker Club Saturday night. Mr. Gus Johnson saw that a powerful brew of mischief was at hand and prudently laid down two pair, while Mr. Cyrus Whiffles, who had a severe cold, a pair of eights, and very little horse sense, came in.

"I rise dat two dollahs," said Mr. Williams.

"You's gittin' too brash," remarked the Rev. Mr. Smith testily. "Ef you finks you's de Vandybilk er dis pahty, jes' stack em' up. I rise you six dollahs."

Mr. Williams considered for a moment, during which time he thoughtfully examined the cards which, with great foresight, he had previously pinned to the leg of the table. "I calls," he said at length. "Gimme two cyards."

Mr. Whiffles fled.

The Rev. Mr. Smith dealt Mr. Williams two cards and conscientiously helped himself to the last ten-spot remaining in the pack. He then banged the honored wallet on the table. "'Leven dollahs," he said.

"I calls you," said Mr. Williams, secretly unpinning the hidden hand from the table leg and counting the money.

The Rev. Mr. Smith swept the pot into his pocket.

"Whadjer doin'?" gasped Mr. Williams, aghast at these unparliamentary proceedings.

"Fo' tens," said the Rev. Mr. Smith, showing down that remarkable hand. "How many freckles you got on yo' han'?"

"Sho'm up," said the reverend gentleman.

Mr. Williams unfolded four jacks. They were all there.

"Wharjer git 'em?" was the next point in the Rev. Smith's cathechism.

"Outen de pack, er course," said Mr. Williams, breathing hard.

The Rev. Mr. Smith, who had made it a point to refrain from dealing face cards of any kind to his opponent, reached over and wove his fingers firmly through the roots of Mr. Williams' hair. Then he thrashed around the room with him for a few turbulent minutes before he sat down upon him. Mr. Williams was breathing more heavily than he had prior to the unwanted exercise.

"Wharjer git dem jacks?"

"Outen de pack," again responded Mr. Williams, making a feeble effort to get up.

The Rev. Mr. Smith butted his head nineteen times against the floor with great rapidity and violence, and again inquired, "Wharja git 'em?"

"Outen de pack. Leggo my ha'r!"

"Whar-jer-git-dem-jacks?" grated the Rev. Mr. Smith, emphasizing each word with a double butt.

"Outen de—de—bug!" said Mr. Williams at last. "Lemme up."

The Rev. Mr. Smith unloaded himself from Mr. Williams' abdomen, arose, crossed the room, and took possession of the extra cards pinned to the table. "Dis whadjer call de 'bug?' "

"Dat's it."

"Toot," began the Rev. Mr. Smith as he donned his overcoat, "by the prowishuns ob rule sixty fo', you am suspended till de nex' meetin', an' don' you wuck de bug no mo'. Mistah Cyrus Whiffles an' Gus Johnson will now come down ter de s'loon an' rassle wif a sassenger an' some beer."

The Club then adjourned and Mr. Williams, still breathing heavily, stooped down and picked up the Reverend's wallet from where it had fallen during the scuffle. He extracted a suitable amount to recompense him for his troubles and was not at all surprised to see, therein, four jacks.

Trod Sof'ly, Brothahs

Mr. Tooter Williams opened the first jackpot with a little hesitation and four white chips, Saturday evening at the Club. Deacon Trotline Anguish, who had strayed in under the chaperonage of Mr. Cyrus Whiffles, and who apparently had jacks-up and a very superficial knowledge of Mr. Williams, came in. Mr. Rube Jackson felt a strong temptation to put a plaster on the back of the wall-eyed king he had caught, hold him up with deuces and try and pull something, but the studied indifference with which Mr. Williams gazed into space made him lay down his hand and wish he were dead. Mr. Cyrus Whiffles borrowed a blue chip from the Deacon and came in. Then all eyes naturally centered on the Rev. Mr. Thankful Smith who, in addition to a barricade of chips which made Mr. Whiffles' mouth water, had a four flush and a cheerfulness of demeanor which boded no good.

"Ez my frien' Toot's done open dat jacker," he began sweetly, "I rises it." So saying, he put up such a stack of blue chips that Mr. Whiffles nearly fainted.

"What you go an' do dat fo', Brothah Thankful?" scolded the Deacon. "Dat's not de sperrit ob de Gospel."

"Whar you fin' draw-pokah in de Gospel?" Mr. Smith retorted, sarcasm lending an edge to his humor. "Does you fink de Possles 'n de 'Vangelis's writ de Scriptah aftah rasslin' wid a two-cyard draw ag'in a flush? No, Brothah Anguish. Le's ten' ter business. Dis ain't no pra'r meetin'—'ceptin' Brothah Williams seems ter be on de anxious seat."

"*Who's* on de anxious seat?" Mr. Williams demanded heatedly. "You jes' come on; I rises you fo' dollahs."

The Deacon sadly ran over his hand. "De Gospel, Brothah Thankful; 'membah de Gospel."

"Cut dat out!" snapped the Rev. Mr. Smith. "Is you goin' ter pray or poke?"

"I's gonna poke," promised the Deacon. "I's also gonna see yo' rise." He shoved up another stack—"An' I's gonna rise it jes' a leetle, 'cordin' ter de sperrit ob de Good Book." Here he shoved up six dollars.

Mr. Whiffles fled.

Mr. Jackson was breathing still, but that was all.

The Rev. Mr. Smith glared defiance. "I rise you back."

"I rise you," said Mr. Williams.

"An' I rise Toot," said the Deacon.

The Rev. Mr. Smith was aghast. He was dealing, and knew by intuition that he would catch his fifth club, but there was a serenity on the other side of the table which affrighted him. ""I jes'—jes' calls," he said.

"I calls," echoed Mr. Williams.

"Help de genelman," said the Deacon with the benevolence which invariably accompanies a pat hand.

Mr. Williams broke his two pair and drew to his jacks.

The Rev. Mr. Smith got his club.

"Six dollahs," said the Deacon, after Mr. Williams had timidly ventured one chip.

"I calls," said the Rev. Mr. Smith sullenly.

"I rise dat six mo'," said Mr. Williams.

"I rise you six," said the deacon.

"I calls," gasped Mr. Smith, shoving up his last chip and his snuff box.

"Six mo'," said Mr. Williams.

"Six mo'," said the Deacon.

Mr. Smith shucked off his overcoat and added to it his spectacles. "I calls," he said, as though speaking from the tomb.

"Six mo'," said Mr. Williams.

"Six mo'," said the Deacon.

"I—I ain't got nothin' mo'," stammered the Rev. Mr. Smith.

"How 'bout dem new boots?" suggested the Deacon.

"Shove up dat watch," said Mr. Williams.

"An' dat gol'-headed cane," urged Mr. Jackson, who, of course, had no business to speak and was accordingly suppressed.

The Rev. Mr. Smith hesitated. Then he sighed and threw up his hand. To his great astonishment, Mr. Williams did the same. The elder softly hummed a gospel tune, tried the focal length of Mr. Smith's eyeglasses, took possession of Mr. Smith's overcoat, thoughtfully inserted Mr. Smith's watch-chain in his vest pocket, collared the bank, counted it, and then, with a cheerful smile at Mr. Williams, left the room. The latter gentleman departed a few moments later.

The silence for several minutes was sepulchural. Mr. Jackson's voice was the first to be heard. "I's 'fraid. . . ."

"You's 'fraid ob what?" asked the Rev. Mr. Smith savagely.

"Dat Toots played you fo' a suckah."

"Whaaat!"

"Dat Deacon Anguish, dat pious hypocrip, he's Toot's fus' cousin. He's Toot's pa's nevvy," explained Mr. Jackson.

A light broke upon the Rev. Mr. Smith. "Dey was risin' an' risin' ter—

ter knock de tar outen *me?*" he asked in a voice which froze Mr. Whiffles' marrow.

"Zackly!" Mr. Jackson confirmed, making sure the table was well between them.

Mr. Smith was about to inquire why they hadn't enlightened him earlier when he might have done something about it, but he shrugged and, instead, turned over Mr. Tooter Williams' hand. It contained two jacks. He examined the Deacon's. It held just three hearts, a spade and a club. He then re-examined his own flush. It was still perfect.

"Breth'n," he said with the calmness of despair, "go out sof'ly an' lemme alone. I's been a-prayin' an' a-rasslin' wid Satan now gwine on thutty-fo' y'ar, an' dis am de fus' time I done evah got roped in by de combination er Gospel an' draw. Go out sof'ly, breth'n. I want ter rassle wif de dictionary an' de angel ob wrath awhile, an' den git de mos' feasible words an' club I kin fin' ter spress my feelin's ter Brothah Toot an' Brothah Anguish. . . .

"Trod sof'ly, genelmen—trod out sof'ly!"

They trod, wondering what kind of flowers would be most suitable for Mr. T. and Deacon A.

PART EIGHT

THE WORKADAY WORLD

His Own Boss

Back around the turn of the century there used to be a brass cannon—a relic of the War of 1812—on display in Courthouse Square, in the picturesque town of Williamsburg, Virginia.

Oldtimers will recall that the ancient cannon gleamed and glistened as brightly as on the day it was manufactured, and the reason for that shiny lustre was old man Sam, a former slave, who had polished it faithfully every day for the past twenty-five years. One morning, bright and early, he made his way to the Mayor's office. "Suh," he began, "I got a business proposition to 'scuss wid you."

"Sure," said the mayor agreeably. "What do you have in mind?"

"Well, I bin savin' my money evah since I stahted polishin' dat brass cannon on Co'thouse Squa'h twenny-five yeahs ago, an' now I wanna buy it."

"You want to buy that cannon!" echoed the mayor incredulously. "What in Heaven's name for?"

Old Sam drew himself up, his manner proud and dignified. "I 'cided to go intuh business fo' myse'f."

Grassroots Capitalism

Millicent was a good cook and housekeeper—the best that Mrs. Pompadour Astorbilt ever had. But Millicent had one failing—she sometimes arrived too late in the morning to prepare breakfast for the family.

"Millicent," complained Mrs. Astorbilt one day when the girl had again arrived late, "this has got to stop. From now on, every time you get here too late to fix breakfast I'm going to deduct fifty cents from your wages."

For a few days Millicent arrived on time, but on the next Friday she attended a wing-ding party and didn't get home and to bed until four in the morning. Consequently, she failed to hear the alarm clock, overslept, and when she awoke it was past ten. Hurriedly, she dressed and raced over to to her place of employment.

"You're three hours late!" Mrs. Astorbilt wailed. "Millicent, how could you! I had to fix breakfast for everybody myself."

"What you so upset about?" retorted Millicent indignantly. "Ain't I payin' you for it?"

How Cheap Can You Get?

It was Sally's second day on the job as cook for the fashionable Williamson family. The white folks liked this quiet, very efficient young lady, but she had one fault that annoyed them. Sally made the worst coffee—strong as lye and so thick it poured like syrup.

"Sally, I want to talk to you about the coffee," said Mrs. Williamson. "Are you sure you are measuring it right?"

"Of course," replied Sally. "One heaping teaspoon for each cup."

"Yes, that's correct," said her employer. "But do you measure the water carefully "

"Measure the water!" exclaimed Millie, outraged. "Looka here, ma'am; cheap as water is, if I got to measure it, I quit!"

Fractured Fractions

A wealthy patron of the Krazy Kopper Klub marveled at the speed and dexterity with which Slingin' Sam, the bartender, mixed all drinks. The customer approached the bar.

"Sam," he said, "I'm having a party at my place this Saturday night. I'll pay you well to tend bar. How about it?"

"Sure," said the bartender cheerfully.

That Saturday night, over a hundred guests were in attendance, but as the party progressed the host saw, to his dismay, that the people were stacked up three and four deep around the bar. Never had he seen such a slow bartender.

"Sam," he asked, drawing him aside, "what's wrong?"

"Nothin's really wrong," explained Sam. "I know I ain't mixin' the drinks fast like I do at the club, but the trouble with these high-class folks, they all wants a jiggle an' a *half!*"

Us Professors

Joseph Lewis, janitor for some thirty years at Chicago University, and affectionately known to all as Uncle Joe, was feeling the pinch of rising prices. Determined to ask for a raise, he made straightaway for the office of Smedley Hufnagel, the university's Superintendent of Buildings.

"Mr. Hufniggle. . . ."

"Hufnagel," the superintendent corrected for the hundredth time.

"Well, Mr. Hugniffle, I need mo' money. My fambly got to have warmer clo's, the lan'lawd he boos'ed my rent, an' we just can't make ends meet on my sal'ry."

Mr. Hufnagel shook his head sympathetically. "I understand your predicament, Uncle Joe, but I don't see how we can pay you any more, considering what you do here at the university."

Uncle Joe stared in open-mouthed amazement. "Now just a minute!" he cried when he could again find his voice. "You know as well as me that I do mo' work aroun' here than any other member of the faculty!"

Pore Pay

George worked in a filling station on the outskirts of Montgomery. One day a shiny new car with New York license plates pulled into the station and asked the owner for directions to Mobile, while George industriously washed the windshield.

The tourist was given a map and, without so much as a ten cents tip, he waved in a friendly manner, said "Right on!" and then drove away.

"Right on, my foot!" grumbled George. "What bank he think I'm gonna cash that in? These here 'right ons' and the boll weevil gonna ruin us black folks yet, financially speakin'."

Value of Education

"A man needs a good education if he ever expects to amount to anything," commented old Dan, in a reminiscent mood. "I remember the time I was offered a job as doorman at the Tropic Paradise Club. A mighty good job it was too—paid more than a hundred a week without counting tips."

Uncle Dan's nephew smiled and nodded his head. "I know that club," he said. "It has all that semi-tropical decor, and even the shrubbery outside comes from the Equatorial jungles. And I really dig the costumes the employees wear—tropical helmets and Bermuda shorts."

"That's just what I was about to mention," said Uncle Dan. "This white lady who owns the place, she asked me if I'd have any objection to wearing Bermuda shorts, and when I told her I didn't mind, she asked to see my ankles. So I hitched up my pants cuffs. Then she said, 'Let me see your knees.' So I lifted up my pants legs and she got a good look at my knees."

"Finally she said, 'I think you'll do very well for the job. Now, please show me your testimonials.'"

"Like I said," concluded Uncle Dan, "if only I had a better education I'd have got that job."

Basic Arithmetic

The folks tell about the time, down Tallahassee way, the mayor of the city learned that two plus two equals four only when you have a second two to add to the first two.

The mayor was walking across Courthouse Square when he noticed old Amos whitewashing a fence. But what struck him as odd was the worn-out brush Amos was using.

"Amos, why don't you use a brush with more bristles in it?" asked his honor. "You could get twice as much work done."

"Reckon I could," said the oldtimer after some thought, "but I ain't got twice as much work to do."

Brains and Brawn

Jack Simpson was glad to have the job, hard though the work was. He soon found out, however, why so many of the other men would quit their jobs soon after being signed on: The foreman was a cruel taskmaster, always pushing the men to turn out more work, even beyond their normal physical strength.

After a few days, Jack decided to straighten the man out and tell him where it's at. "Boss," he said, "you know my name?"

"Sure! Don't worry, you're on the payroll."

"I'm not worried about the payroll, Boss," said Jack quietly. "I just wanted to be certain you know my name is Simpson—not Samson!"

Hold That Tiger!

Times were tough enough for the whites, so you can imagine the situation that most blacks found themselves in during the Depression.

Back in 1931, Johnny's brother came home one evening with what he thought was some pleasant news. "I got you a job right next door to where I work," he announced. "It's at the Lucky Tiger Laundry."

"Man, you gotta be kiddin'!" moaned Johnny, backing off. "That's no job for me. I ain't proud, an' I ain't lazy, but with all the rotten luck I been havin' lately, I ain't washin' no lucky tigers for no-o-o-body!"

Born Leader

This kid got him a summer job pickin' fruit down in the Valley, an' he had a real Simon Legree-type of a boss. That white man don't get offen the kid's back for a minute, an' when lunchtime come, he tells the little guy to keep right on workin' while he goes off to eat.

When he gets back he sees the boy layin' on the grass in the shade of a big ol' tree, an' there pickin' fruit is another kid.

So the boss say, "What you doin', layin' under that tree when you s'pose to be workin'?"

The kid say, "I done hire that other boy to do the work."

"You *hire* him! How much you payin' that boy?"

"A dollar an' a quarter a hour."

"You crazy or somethin'?" say the white man. "You losin' twenty-five cents on the deal. I only payin' you a dollar a hour."

"I know," say the kid, "but it's worth a quarter jes' to be a slave-driver for once."

Watch Those Bachelor Apartments

Two sisters, both of them domestic workers, were discussing their employers.

"It's getting so I can't stand that woman I work for another day," complained the older, homely sister. "She's always diggin' at me about something or other. Seems like all I ever say is 'yes ma'am, yes ma'am, yes ma'am.' "

"I know what you mean," sighed the younger, pretty sister. "But what I keep saying is no *sir*, no *sir*, no *sir!*"

Too Cool

During World War II the shipyards gave many blacks their first chance at well-paying jobs. Some men escaped the draft by becoming "essential workers" and were "frozen" in their jobs at the risk of being conscripted into military service. Most, however, were frozen as essential workers, the draft notwithstanding, because they were or became skilled in their tasks. But—and for the black man there was usually a "but"—the old expression "last to be hired, first to be fired" was still a force to be reckoned with.

Toward the end of the war, when it was obvious to all that The Third Reich was in its death throes, dismissal notices were handed out among the workers at the Fairfield shipyard in Baltimore. As might be expected, many of them were black. Two of those who had been fired were discussing the dismissals over a beer.

"I didn't expect to be fired," said the first man. "I thought we was froze on this job."

"We was," affirmed the second man with a sigh, "but we been defrosted."

Git-Got Grammar

Mary, who had never missed a day in her ten years as a cook for the Johnson family, was unable to come to work for a few days because of an attack of rheumatism.

On the following Monday, she reported as usual for her daily chores. Mrs. Johnson was sympathetic. "I do hope you are all better now," she said gently.

Mary shrugged. "Doctah say this heah roomatiz gits wuss ez time goes by."

"Now Mary," protested the lady of the house, "you mustn't say 'git.' The proper pronunciation is 'get' or 'got.' "

"Miz Johnsing," replied Mary stiffly, "it don't make no diffunce how you say it. When roomatiz *gits* ya it *got* ya!"

The Great Train Clobbery

Two brothers were employed as Pullman porters. Mac worked for the Southern Pacific, and Moe worked for the Santa Fe. One Sunday, over a drink, they were discussing the merits of their respective railroads, each stoutly defending his company.

"I know one thing for sure—my South'n Pacific hauled twice as many passengers as your li'l Santa Fe done," boasted Mac.

Moe bristled with loyal indignation. "Man, you just plain can't count! My Santa Fe *killed* more people than you hauled!"

Longest Railroad

It was Roy's first day on his new job with the Chicago, Buffalo and Quebec Railroad. At quitting time, the foreman complimented him on his good work and handed him an application for company insurance, retirement benefits, and so forth. "Bring it back tomorrow, all filled out," said the foreman.

At home, Roy was laboriously filling out the questionnaire when his wife leaned over for a look. "What's that C-B-Q mean?" she asked.

Roy tried hard to remember, but the names eluded him. Then he snapped his fingers in recollection. "I remember now," he said. The 'C' for Chicago, the 'B' for Buffalo, an' the 'Q' for—hmmm—oh yes—the 'Q' stan's for Quba."

Coincidence

Harvey was honored to be appointed as head porter on the Presidential Special. Richard M. Nixon, the nation's Chief Executive, members of the Cabinet, and all nine Supreme Court Justices were Harvey's responsibilities on the overnight train from Washington, D. C. to Boston.

Throughout the night, listening contentedly to the clickety-clack of steel wheels on the tracks, Harvey kept himself busy shining shoes until they glistened. At five in the morning, with everyone's shoes polished to a brilliant luster and set in place, he began the breakfast preparations.

An hour later, as the train was pulling into the Boston station, a worried Secret Service man entered the kitchen. "Harvey," he said in a low, ominous voice, "President Nixon wants to see you—on the double!"

Wondering what could be wrong, Harvey entered the Presidential car. "You sent for me, Mr. President?"

The Chief Executive fixed him with a cold eye. "Harvey, you picked up my shoes last night and shined them?"

"Yes sir."

"And did you notice the color of those shoes?"

"Certainly, sir. They was black."

"Then why," snapped President Nixon, "do I now have one black and one brown shoe?"

Harvey stared at the offending shoes, his mouth agape in surprise. "Mr. President, this sure is a coincidence," he finally managed to gasp. "It's the second time that's happened this here very morning!"

Bert Williams—Fish Merchant*

As the 19th century faded into history and the new dawn of the 20th spread its inchoate light upon a world that was hardly aware of the epochal years ahead, the master entertainer of them all, Bert Williams, was evoking gusty laughter from an entire nation.

Among his favorites was the story of his experience as a fish peddler when he was a small boy. Williams lived on the bank of a creek, running at the foot of a mountain whose summit was, as he would impishly grin, "seven

---

* Bert Williams (1876-1922) is considered by many to be the greatest Negro vaudeville performer in the history of the American stage. Born in the Bahamas, Williams moved to New York and then to California where he studied engineering. In 1895 he teamed with George Walker to form a highly successful vaudeville team. Five years later they opened in New York in *The Sons of Ham* and were acclaimed for the characterizations that became their stock-in-trade: Walker as a dandy, and Williams in blackface. Walker and Williams produced and starred in several musical comedies until Walker's death in 1909. Thereafter Williams was a featured single for ten years in a few versions of the Ziegfeld Follies. His most famous songs were *Woodman Spare That Tree; O, Death, Where Is Thy Sting?* and *Nobody,* his own composition and trademark. He died of pneumonia at the age of 46.

thousand feet high." Every morning, he would catch a string of fish in the brook and start up the mountainside where the white people lived.

"One mornin', bright 'n early, I starts up the mountain with my string of fish an' I comes to the fus' house, but they didn't want no fish," Williams would explain. "So I go on up higher to the secon' house, but they don't want no fresh fish nuther, an' I keep on climbin' higher 'n higher up that mountain, but none of the white folks wants fresh fish that mornin'. I continues till I reach the top, seven thousan' feet high, an' there I see a ole white man standin' at the do' of his little house.

"I walks over to him an' I say, 'Mister, you want some fresh fish?' He says to me, he says, 'No, I don't want no fish today.'

"Well, there's nothin' left for me to do but climb down that seven thousan' feet mountain, an' when I'm most down to the bottom I hear a rumblin', an' when I look up I see a big lan'slide comin' down, an' pretty soon it hits me, an' down I go with tons of rocks 'n stones 'n dirt 'n tree-branches 'n whatall. At the foot of the mountain, by the creek, I digs myse'f out an' looks up to see if the whole mountain done come down with me, but what do I see but that ole white man, standin' on the plum top, an' beckonin' to me to come on back. So I says to myse'f, 'Praise the Lawd, that white man done went an' changed his mind.'

"So I clum' back up that seven thousan' feet mountain, all the way to the top an' I walks over to him with my string of fish.

"He don't say nothin' for a minute, an' then he says to me. . . .

" 'An' I won't be needin' any fish tomorrer neither!' "

7

THE NEW BREED

BOOK SEVEN

The New Breed

INTRODUCTION

It has been said that history is the lengthened shadow of a man. If so, then the wedding of history and folklore brings human substance to that shadow. Granted, there are many who will assert that America's black citizens cast their most meaningful shadow only since the mid-1950's, but that is to deny the evidence of continuity and precedent in their long struggle for justice. The perceptive reader will grasp the reality of past accomplishments and their influence on today's activities; that the structure of modern black society could not have attained its present level if those who came before had not evolved the blueprints and constructed the foundations upon which that structure rests.

It has also been proclaimed that the attitudes and ambitions of contemporary blacks are more forthright, and wider in scope than those of their ancestors. This editor does not think so. For unyielding forthrightness of expression we hearken back to the year 1852 when, in Rochester, New York, Frederick Douglass delivered his scathing *What to the Slave Is the Fourth of July?* oration—"your celebration a sham; your boasted liberty an unholy license; your national greatness, swelling vanity; . . ."* As to the ambitions,

---

* Excerpts from the Independence Day speech of 1852, *What to the Slave Is the Fourth of July?*, by Frederick Douglass, who has often been called the father of the protest movement:

"I am not included within the pale of this glorious anniversary. Your high independence only reveals the immeasurable distance between us. The blessings in which you this day rejoice are not enjoyed in common. The rich inheri-

we cannot equate the goals of yesteryear with those of today; the overriding issue, prior to emancipation, was freedom—now it is equality in all areas of our social, political and economic life. It may well be that the so-called "new breed" is a misnomer, when we consider that every generation has produced its own "new breed" whose aspirations were unique and relative to the times.

---

tance of justice, liberty, prosperity and independence, bequeathed by your fathers, is shared by you, not by me. The sunlight that brought life and healing to you, has brought stripes and death to me. This Fourth of July is yours, not mine. You may rejoice. I must mourn.

"To drag a man in fetters into the grand illuminated temple of liberty, and call upon him to join you in joyous anthems was inhuman mockery and sacrilegious irony. . . . For the moment it is enough to affirm the equal manhood of the Negro race. Is it not astonishing that, while we are plowing, planting and reaping, using all kinds of mechanical tools, erecting houses, constructing bridges, building ships, working in metals of brass, iron, silver and gold; that while we are reading, writing and ciphering, acting as clerks, merchants and secretaries, having among us lawyers, doctors, ministers, poets, authors, editors, orators and teachers; that while we are living in families as husbands, wives and children, and, above all, confessing and worshiping the Christian's God, and looking hopefully for life and immortality beyond the grave—we are called upon to prove that we are men? . . .

"Oh! Had I the ability, and could I reach the nation's ear, I would today pour out a fiery stream of biting ridicule, blasting reproach, withering sarcasm, and stern rebuke. For it is not light that is needed, but fire. It is not the gentle shower but thunder. We need the storm, the whirlwind, and the earthquake.

"The feeling of the nation must be quickened; the conscience of the nation must be roused; the propriety of the nation must be startled; the hypocrisy of the nation must be exposed; and its crimes against God must be proclaimed and denounced.

"What to the American slave is the Fourth of July? I answer: a day that reveals to him more than all the other days in the year the gross injustice and cruelty to which he is the constant victim.

"To him, your celebration is a sham; your boasted liberty an unholy license; your national greatness, a swelling vanity; your sounds of rejoicing are empty and heartless; your denunciation of tyrants, brass-fronted impudence; your shouts of liberty and equality, hollow mockery.

"Your prayers and hymns, your sermons and thanksgivings, with all your religious parade and solemnity, are to him mere bombast, fraud, deception, impiety, and hypocrisy—a thin veil to cover up crimes that would disgrace a nation of savages."

TABLE NO. 1

CHRONOLOGY OF SLAVE CONSPIRACIES AND RACE RIOTS
1663-1966

Year	Place	Event
1663	Gloucester, Virginia	First major conspiracy between Negro slaves and white indentured servants against their masters, betrayed by a house servant.
1712	New York City, New York	Slave revolt leads to the execution of 21 blacks, six suicides, and the death of nine whites.
1739	Stono, S. Carolina	Cato leads slave revolt resulting in the death of 30 whites. The blacks lost many more but a few managed to escape.
1741	New York City, New York	Alleged "conspiracy to burn the City of New York and murder its inhabitants" (according to the indictment) results in 33 executions. Thirteen blacks burned at the stake, 16 hanged, along with four whites.
1800	Richmond, Virginia	Under the leadership of Gabriel Prosser, some 1,000 slaves and several whites conspire to free all slaves in Richmond by a concerted attack on the city. Plan betrayed by two slaves. Prosser and 15 followers caught and hanged.
1811	New Orleans Louisiana	Charles Deslandes leads a slave revolt in two parishes about 35 miles from New Orleans. Uprisings suppressed by U.S. troops.
1822	Charleston, So. Carolina	House slave betrays Denmark Vesey, leader of a far-reaching conspiracy involving thousands. Four whites and 131 blacks arrested; 37 hanged, including Vesey and five sub-leaders.
1831	Southampton County, Virginia	Nat Turner leads the greatest slave revolt in American history, with more than 60 whites killed and the entire South thrown into a panic. Turner is captured on October 30 and hanged in Jerusalem (Virginia) 12 days later.
1839	Montauk, Long Island	Aboard the slave ship *Amistad*, African captive Cinque leads a revolt against the ship's officers and crew, killing Captain Ferrer. Sailing the vessel from Cuban waters to Montauk, young Cinque and his fellow captives are defended before the Supreme Court by former President John Quincy Adams and awarded their freedom.
1841	Hampton, Virginia	Aboard the slave ship *Creole*, African captives attack and overpower the officers and crew. The slaves sail the ship to the Bahamas where they are granted their freedom.

Year	Place	Event
1859	Harpers Ferry, W. Virginia	John Brown, white abolitionist, and 18 followers (13 whites, five blacks) attack Harpers Ferry. Two blacks killed, two captured, one escapes. Brown later hanged at Charles Town, W. Va.
1863	New York City, New York	Whites destroy The Negro Orphan Asylum on Fifth Avenue; 1,000 blacks killed in the "Draft Riots," among the bloodiest in U.S. history. Estimated property damage: $1.5 million.
1878	Grant Parish Louisiana	Ten years after the race riots in New Orleans, Opelousas and St. Bernard Parish, the Colfax Massacre in Grant Parish results in the murders of more than 600 blacks by shooting, hanging, burning and clubbing.
1898	Wilmington, N. Carolina	Eight blacks slain in race riot.
1900	New Orleans, Louisiana	Thirty Negro homes burned, several blacks injured in race riot. One Negro school damaged.
1906	Brownsville, Texas	Black soldiers of the 25th Regiment attack Brownsville as a result of racial slurs, killing one white and injuring two others. President Theodore Roosevelt musters three companies out of the 25th Regiment.
1906	Atlanta, Georgia	Martial law is declared after race riots in which 10 blacks and two whites are killed and 70 persons injured.
1917	E. St. Louis, Illinois	Martial law declared in the aftermath of race riots, with estimates on numbers of blacks killed ranging from 40 to 200.
1917	Houston, Texas	Black soldiers of the 24th Infantry Regiment involved in race riot. Two blacks, 17 whites killed. Thirteen members of the regiment hanged in what has since been termed a mass lynching.
1918	Chester, Pennsylvania	Five dead in race riot.
1919		(Known as "The Red Summer" of 1919.)
	Longview, Texas	Race riots in Longview and Gregg County.
	Washington, D. C.	Six dead and 150 injured in race riots.
	Chicago, Illinois	Bloody race riot suppressed by Federal troops. Fifteen whites and 23 blacks killed; 537 injured.
	Elaine, Arkansas	Five whites, 25 to 50 blacks killed in rioting throughout Phillips County, but centered in Elaine.
1921	Tulsa, Oklahoma	Citywide race riot results in death of 21 whites and 60 blacks.

Year	Place	Event
1942	Detroit, Michigan	Race riot at the Sojourner Truth Home, builds resentment among blacks resulting in riots of 1943 in which 34 persons died in Detroit. In the same year, two died in Beaumont, Texas, riots, and several injured in Harlem riots.
1946	Columbia, Tennessee	Two killed and 10 injured in race riot.
	Athens, Alabama	Fifty to 100 blacks injured in race riot.
1960	Chattanooga, Tennessee	Sit-in demonstrations result in race riot.
	Biloxi, Mississippi	Wade-in demonstration by blacks at a beach leads to race riot.
	Jacksonville, Florida	Ten days of sit-ins erupt into race riot.
1964	Harlem, New York City, New York	Riots in protest of oppression and slum conditions lead to one dead and 144 injured.
	Rochester, New York	Riots result in four dead and 350 injured.
	New Jersey	Riots in Jersey City, Paterson, and Elizabeth cause injuries to more than 125 persons.
	Chicago, Illinois	Race riots end with more than 340 persons injured.
	Philadelphia, Pennsylvania	Numerous demonstrations and lack of response by city authorities lead to general riot.
1965	Watts, Los Angeles California	The arrest of a black youth and his alleged mistreatment on charges of being drunk while driving, a charge denied by the victim and his witnesses, result in a six-day rampage, from August 11 to 16, of looting, burning and rioting, plunging Watts into a state of virtual anarchy. Thousands of National Guardsmen are called up to quell the angry rioters. Thirty-five are dead, 883 injured, another 3,598 arrested. Fire damage: $1.7 million; property damage: $46 million. Ultimate financial loss, in the 150-block area, reaches staggering total of $200 million. To quell the riot, the authorities call in 12,634 Guardsmen, 1,430 city police, 1,017 county sheriff's deputies and 68 state highway patrolmen.

The last "long, hot summer" occurred in 1968, the year Dr. Martin Luther King and Senator Robert F. Kennedy were murdered. Dr. King's assassination angered blacks into a riot in Washington, D.C. Throughout the nation 86 persons died and 4,767 were injured in hundreds of civil disturbances. In 1967, the count was 87 dead and 2,446 injured. A final tally on property damage was never taken, but the best estimate runs over one billion dollars.

Contemporary Negroes, especially (and regrettably) the younger, more militant blacks, are too often inclined to dismiss as poppycock the mention of an activist attitude among the slaves, freed men and, later, the emancipated Negroes of the Reconstruction and following periods. But were they the faceless, spineless, cringing anonymities that they are sometimes represented to be; or were they a valiant people who awaited only the opportunity to throw off their chains and shackles at a time when the very law of the land was a mighty fist raised against them? How many of us, today, would have the courage to defy such an all-powerful, closed society where arrest often meant automatic conviction? Yet, there were many who did just that!

Table No. 1, *Chronology of Slave Conspiracies and Race Riots,* begins with the Gloucester Conspiracy of 1663, but it is important to note that Negro resistance to the system of slavery was recorded in various other areas of the Western Hemisphere, and at much earlier dates. In the 1550's, for example, there were frequent outbreaks of violence in Cartagena (Colombia). During the 17th century similar upheavals occurred in Bahia and Rio de Janeiro, Brazil. The historical evidence is indisputable: In the New World alone, the black man has shed his blood and sacrificed his life for more than 400 years so that his children might breathe the air of freedom.

The first European nation to abolish slavery in the Western Hemisphere was France, in 1794. The French proclamation provided for the theoretical, if not actual, emancipation of all slaves in the French West Indies. The distinction of having been the first nation in the New World to do away with slavery belongs to Haiti (1804). Slavery was abolished in England in 1772, and the British slave trade halted in 1807. Parliament, however, waited until 1833 before it passed an act eliminating slavery (after payment of compensation to slaveowners) in all British overseas possessions—including Canada, the mainland colonies in Central and South America, and the island colonies in the Caribbean. But it was not until five years later, in 1838, that the measure was fully enforced. On the Spanish and Portuguese mainland, the abolition of slavery was linked with the independence movements of various subject territories. Slaves were freed in the United Provinces of Central America in 1824; in Mexico, 1828; in Latin America, to all intent and purpose, by 1855; in Cuba, 1886; and in Brazil, 1888.

The first "slaves" in what was to become the United States of America consisted of Europeans, mostly of English, Scot-Irish and German ancestry, who emigrated to these shores as indentured servants, and Negroes from the African continent. The Europeans comprised two classes: those who bound themselves over to a master for a number of years in payment for their voluntary passage to the New World, and those who had been deported from their native lands as paupers or debtors, to enter forced servitude for a period of (usually) seven years before becoming eligible for freedom. Others were children who were kidnapped, shipped to the colonies and sold into service.

The 20 Negroes who arrived at Jamestown, Virginia, in 1619, were not "slaves" in the strictest sense of the word. Like the Europeans, they were indentured for a definite number of years and upon completion of their time, some were assigned land of their own while others chose to become members of the "free working class." The Negro's right to choose his own destiny, however, ended in the 1640's when he was no longer regarded as a "servant"—indentured or otherwise—and his status changed from "servant" to "chattel slave"—one who remained an item of property for the duration of his life.

The greatest concentration of blacks occurred in those areas of the agrarian South where the economy was based primarily on the production of cotton, indigo, tobacco and rice. The invention of the cotton gin and the growth of foreign textile markets resulted in an increased demand for cheap labor and also helped to institutionalize the idea of lifetime servitude. With the passage of time, white indentured servants disappeared from the colonial labor market, leaving slavery as a social phenomenon based solely on color. The growth and geographical division of slavery in the American colonies may be determined in the following table:

	1630	1640	1650	1660	1670	1680	1690	1700
North	10	427	880	1,162	1,125	1,895	3,340	5,206
South	50	170	720	1,758	3,410	5,076	13,389	22,611
Total	60	597	1,600	2,920	4,535	6,971	16,729	27,817

	1710	1720	1730	1740	1750	1760	1770	1780
North	8,303	14,091	17,323	23,958	30,222	40,033	48,460	56,796
South	36,563	54,748	73,698	126,066	206,198	285,773	411,362	518,624
Total	44,866	68,839	91,021	150,024	236,420	325,806	459,822	575,420

The year 1763 represents a significant date in the history of the slave inasmuch as it inaugurated an era during which anti-slavery sentiment began to gain a foothold in America, and to achieve widespread prominence in the public domain. In 1773, Reverend Isaac Skillman made the radical assertion that slaves should rebel against their masters. Thomas Jefferson, in his early draft of the Declaration of Independence, included a violent denunciation of slavery, a clause which was later eliminated by others. It would not be amiss to point out that Jefferson, who was a staunch supporter of complete and immediate freedom for the slaves in whatever part of America they might reside, took a far more forthright stand initially than did Abraham Lincoln, who assumed the presidency believing that slavery was evil, but arguing nonetheless, that the federal government had no right to prohibit slavery in the South. Said Lincoln: "If I could save the Union without freeing any slave, I would do it; if I could save it by freeing all the slaves, I would do it; and if I could save it by freeing some and leaving others alone, I would also do that. What I do about slavery and the colored race, I do because it helps save the Union. . . ."

But, despite his earlier reservations, there is no denying to Lincoln his title, *The Great Emancipator*. In September, 1862, the President issued a preliminary Emancipation Proclamation, holding out to slaveowners the possibility of compensation, and continuing to suggest to freedmen the prospect of voluntary colonization in Africa. (It simply did not occur to Lincoln that the freedmen were as thoroughly American as he, and that after some 200 years of national absence from the Dark Continent, they would be as hopelessly lost in the jungle-surrounded villages of Africa as any other American, whatever his race.) On January 1, 1863, a further proclamation declared that all slaves living in the *seceded states* of the Confederacy were to be "thenceforward and forever free." It conferred legal, though not actual, emancipation on three-fourths of the slave population, yet made no provisions for some 800,000 Negroes living outside the South who remained technically enslaved. Constitutional emancipation did not come for all slaves until 1865 with the passage of the 13th Amendment—the single, all-embracing legislative enactment which brought the United States a step closer to its motto: *Land of the Free*.

Slavery was not merely an evil; it was an historic fact of enormous consequence. Emancipation salved the white man's conscience but it did not solve the black man's problems. No provision was made for the former slave's economic rehabilitation, nor was any program inaugurated for his education, as we shall see in the following paragraph. Now, more than a century later, the nation has yet to come to grips with the historic effects of slavery. When one considers the oppressive conditions under which the slaves existed—in what, for them, was tantamount to a police state—one can only marvel at the desperate courage which led some of them to armed revolt against the system. Nor were those who later fought the Jim Crow laws any less courageous than their fathers and grandfathers, when brutal beatings and summary lynchings were invoked for the most trivial of reasons. Yes, they too constituted a "new breed" who earned a niche in history, and around whom an appreciative and loving people have woven a whole new category of folklore.

But there were other facets of the Negro character which still scintillate along the corridors of time. These traits included artistic skills in the fields of literature, painting and sculpture, as well as his creative abilities in the areas of science and invention. Some, but all too few, have been memorialized in folk song and story; not alone for their genius but because they were able to overcome obstacles of formidable dimensions. In 1870, more than 80% of the blacks in this country were illiterate and, even by the year 1920, more than one-third of the Negro population over 10 years of age had never been to school. It is against this background of systematic educational deprivation that the achievements of the Negro inventor and scientist can be seen in their sharpest perspective.

The Constitution of the United States, Section 8, provides that "The Congress shall have Power . . . To promote the Progress of Science and useful Arts, by securing for limited Times to Authors and Inventors the exclusive Right to their respective Writings and Discoveries." This categorical edict, which gave rise to our copyright and patent laws, is perfectly clear. For the Negro inventor and scientist, however, the Constitutional safeguard afforded little protection. Prior to the Civil War, for example, slaves were unable to secure patents, and consequently no record exists of the countless black inventors whose work was expropriated by their masters. The loss was not only monetary; they were robbed of their due intellectual credit and stripped of their identities as sentient human beings. Free Negroes, too, often suffered because of racial prejudice, as will be noted in the case of Garret A. Morgan, inventor of the inhalator.

Lack of formal schooling, the many legal and illegal obstacles, and his isolation from the centers of research and industry, all combined to exclude the Negro from the fields of science and invention. Yet, despite these awesome barriers, many forged ahead and obtained patents for their discoveries and creations. Some are widely in use today: There is the familiar potato chip, invented by the Saratoga chef, Hyram S. Thomas; ice cream, invented in 1832 by Augustus Jackson, a Philadelphia confectioner; the common mop-holder, created by Thomas W. Stewart, and the player piano invented by J. H. Dickinson. These, and many others, will be found in Table No. 2, *Inventions by Negroes—1870-1900.* The schedule is only indicative, of course. Many thousands of inventions, as we have noted, were lost to whites who affixed their own names to the patent applications. Nevertheless, even the *verifiable* inventions, also in the thousands, represent a remarkable Negro achievement, individually and collectively, when one considers the overwhelming odds that confronted them.

TABLE NO. 2

Inventions by Negroes
1870-1900

Inventor	Invention	Date	Patent
Allen, C. W.	Self-Levelling Table	Nov 1, 1898	613,436
Allen, J. B.	Clothes Line Support	Dec 10, 1895	551,105
Ashbourne, A. P.	Process for Preparing Coconut for Domestic Use	June 1, 1875	163,962
Bailes, William	Ladder Scaffold-Support	Aug 5, 1879	218,154
Bailey, L. C.	Combined Truss and Bandage	Sept 25, 1883	285,545
Bailey, L. C.	Folding Bed	July 18, 1899	629,286
Beard, A. J.	Rotary Engine	July 5, 1892	478,271
Beard, A. J.	Car-Coupler	Nov 23, 1897	594,059
Becket, G. E.	Letter Box	Oct 4, 1892	483,525
Bell, L.	Locomotive Smoke Stack	May 23, 1871	115,153
Benjamin, M. E. (Miss)	Gong and Signal Chairs for Hotels	July 17, 1888,	497,747
Binga, M. W.	Street Sprinkling Apparatus	July 22, 1879	217,843
Blackburn, A. B.	Railway Signal	Jan 10, 1888	376,362
Blackburn, A. B.	Spring Seat for Chairs	Apr 3, 1888	380,420
Blair, Henry	Corn Planter	Oct 24, 1834	—
Blair, Henry	Cotton Planter	Aug 31, 1836	—
Blue, L.	Corn Shelling Device	May 20, 1884	298,937
Boone, Sarah	Ironing Board	Apr 26, 1892	473,653
Bowman, H. A.	Flag-Making Equipment	Feb 23, 1892	469,395
Brooks, C. B.	Street-Sweepers	Mar 17, 1896	556,711
Brown, Henry	Receptacle for Storing and Preserving Papers	Nov 2, 1886	352,036
Brown, L. F.	Bridle Bit	Oct 25, 1892	484,994
Brown, O. E.	Horseshoe	Aug 23, 1892	481,271
Brown and Latimer	Water Closets for Railway Cars	Feb 10, 1874	147,363
Burr, J. A.	Lawn Mower	May 9, 1899	624,749
Burr, W. F.	Switching Device for Railways	Oct 31, 1899	636,197
Butler, R. A.	Train Alarm	Jun 15, 1897	584,540
Butts, J. W.	Luggage Carrier	Oct 10, 1899	634,611
Byrd, T. J.	Apparatus for Detaching Horses from Carriages	Mar 19, 1872	124,790
Carrington, T. A.	Cooking Range	July 25, 1876	180,323
Carter, W. C.	Umbrella Stand	Aug 4, 1885	323,397
Certain, J. M.	Parcel Carrier for Bicycles	Dec 26, 1899	639,708
Cherry, M. A.	Velocipede	May 8, 1888	382,351
Cherry, M. A.	Street Car Fender	Jan 1, 1895	531,908
Church, T. S.	Carpet Beating Machine	July 29, 1884	302,237
Cook, G.	Automatic Fishing Device	May 30, 1899	625,829
Coolidge, J. S.	Harness Attachment	Nov 13, 1888	392,908
Cooper, A. R.	Shoemaker's Jack	Aug 22, 1899	631,519
Cralle, A. L.	Ice-Cream Mold	Feb 2, 1897	576,395
Creamer, H.	Steam Feed Water Trap (Six more patents granted)	Mar 17, 1895	313,854
Cosgrove, W. F.	Automatic Stop Plug for Gas Oil Pipes	Mar 17, 1885	313,993
Darkins, J. T.	Ventilation Valve	Feb 19, 1895	534,322

Inventor	Invention	Date	Patent
Davis, W. D.	Riding Saddles	Oct 6, 1896	568,939
Davis, W. R., Jr.	Library Table	Sept 24, 1878	208,378
Dickinson, J. H.	Pianola (in Detroit, Mich.)	— 1899	—
Dorticus, C. J.	Device for Applying Dye to Shoe Soles and Heels	Mar 19, 1895	535,820
Dorticus, C. J.	Equipment for Embossing Photos	Apr 16, 1895	537,442
Dorticus, C. J.	Photographic Print Wash	Apr 23, 1895	537,968
Downing, P. B.	Electric Switch for Railroads	Jun 17, 1890	430,118
Elkins, T.	Refrigerating Apparatus	Nov 4, 1879	221,222
Evans, J. H.	Convertible Settees	Oct 5, 1897	591,095
Falkner, H.	Ventilated Shoe	Apr 29, 1890	426,495
Ferrell, F. J.	Steam Trap	Feb 11, 1890	420,993
	(Ferrel patented 8 valves between 1890 and 1893)		
Fisher, D. A.	Joiners' Clamp	Apr 20, 1875	162,281
Fisher, D. A.	Furniture Castor	Mar 14, 1876	174,794
Goode, Sarah E.	Folding Cabinet Bed	July 14, 1885	322,177
Grant, G. F.	Golf-Tee	Dec 12, 1899	638,920
Gray, R. H.	Baling Press	Aug 28, 1894	525,203
Gregory, J.	Motor	Aug 26, 1887	361,937
Gunn, S. W.	Boot or Shoe Cutter	Jan 16, 1900	641,642
Hammonds, J. F.	Apparatus for Holding Yarn Skeins	Dec 15, 1896	572,985
Harding, F. H.	Extension Banquet Table	Nov 22, 1898	614,468
Hawkins, J.	Gridiron	Mar 26, 1845	3,973
Headen, M.	Foot Power Hammer	Oct 5, 1886	350,363
Hearness, R.	Sealing Attachment for Bottles	Feb 15, 1898	598,929
Hilyer, A. F.	Water Evaporator Attachment for Hot Air Registers	Aug 26, 1890	435,095
Hunter, J. H.	Portable Weighing Scales	Nov 3, 1896	570,553
Hyde, R. N.	Composition for Cleaning and Preserving Carpets	Nov 6, 1888	392,205
Jackson, B. F.	Heating Apparatus	Mar 1, 1898	599,985
Jackson, B. F.	Gas Burner	Apr 4, 1899	622,482
Jackson, W. H.	Railway Switch	Mar 9, 1897	578,641
Jackson, W. H.	Automatic Locking Switch	Aug 23, 1898	609,436
Johnson, D.	Grass Receivers for Lawn Mowers	June 10, 1890	429,629
Johnson, I. R.	Bicycle Frame	Oct 10, 1899	634,823
Johnson, W.	Velocipede	June 20, 1899	627,335
Johnson, W. H.	Overcoming Dead Centers	Feb 4, 1896	554,223
Johnson, W.	Egg Beater	Feb 5, 1884	292,821
Jones and Long	Caps for Bottles	Sept 13, 1898	610,715
Joyce, J. A.	Ore Bucket	Apr 26, 1898	603,143
Latimer, L. H.	Manufacturing Carbons	June 17, 1882	252,386
Latimer, L. H.	Apparatus for Cooling and Disinfecting	Jan 12, 1886	334,078
Lavslette, W. A.	Printing Press Variation	Sept 17, 1878	208,208
Lee, H.	Animal Trap	Feb 12, 1867	61,941
Lee, J.	Bread Crumbing Machine	June 4, 1895	540,553
Leslie, F. W.	Envelope Seal	Sept 21, 1897	590,325
Lewis, A. L.	Window Cleaner	Sept 27, 1892	483,359
Lewis, E. R.	Spring Gun	May 3, 1887	362,096
Linden, H.	Piano Truck	Sept 8, 1891	459,365

Inventor	Invention	Date	Patent
Love, J. L.	Pencil Sharpener	Nov 23, 1897	594,114
Marshall, T. J.	Fire Extinguisher Variation	May 26, 1872	125,063
Marshall, W.	Grain Binder	May 11, 1886	341,599
Martin, W. A.	Lock	July 23, 1889	407,738
Matzeliger, J. E.	Nailing Machine	Feb 25, 1896	421,954
Matzeliger, J. E.	Lasting Machine	Sept 22, 1891	459,899
McCoy, E.	Lubricator for Steam Engines	July 2, 1872	129,843
	(McCoy patented 26 other inventions for lubricators, lawn sprinklers, ironing tables, and drip cups.)		
McCree, D.	Portable Fire Escape	Nov 11, 1890	440,322
Miles, A.	Elevator	Oct 11, 1887	371,207
Mitchell, J. M.	Cheek Row Planter	Jan 16, 1900	641,462
Murray, G. W.	Cotton Chopper	June 5, 1894	520,888
	(Murray patented 5 other inventions involving fertilizer distributors, planters and reapers.)		
Newson, S.	Oil Heater or Cooker	May 22, 1894	520,188
Nichols and Latimer	Electric Lamp Variation	Sept 13, 1881	247,097
Nickerson, W. J.	Mandolin and Guitar Attachment for Pianos	June 27, 1899	627,739
O'Connor and Turner	Alarm for Boilers	Aug 25, 1896	566,612
Outlaw, J. W.	Horseshoes	Nov. 15, 1898	614,273
Phelps, W. H.	Apparatus for Washing Vehicles	Mar 23, 1897	579,242
Pickering, J. F.	Air Ship	Feb 20, 1900	643,975
Pickett, H.	Scaffold	June 30, 1874	152,511
Purdy and Sagwar	Folding Chair	June 11, 1889	405,117
Purvis, W.	Fountain Pen	Jan 7, 1890	419,065
	(Purvis was granted additional patents for his Bag Fastener, Hand Stamp, Electric Railway Improvement, Electric Railway Switch, Magnetic Railway Car Balancing Device, and 10 patents between 1884 and 1894 for his bag machines.)		
Queen. W.	Guard for Ship's Companion Ways and Hatches	Aug 18, 1891	458,131
Ray, L. P.	Dust Pan	Aug 3, 1897	587,607
Reed, J. W.	Dough Kneader and Roller	Sept 23, 1884	305,474
Reynolds, H. H.	Safety Gate for Bridges	Oct 7, 1890	437,937
Reynolds, R. R.	Non-Refillable Bottle	May 2, 1899	624,092
Rhodes, J. B.	Water Closets	Dec 19, 1899	639,290
Richardson, A. C	Churn	Feb 17, 1891	446,470
	(Richardson was also awarded patents for his Casket Lowering Device, Insect Killer, and Bottle.)		

Inventor	Invention	Date	Patent
Richardson, W. H.	Cotton Chopper	June 1, 1886	343,140
Richardson, W. H.	Child's Carriage	June 18, 1889	405,559
Rickman, A. L.	Overshoe	Feb 8, 1898	598,816
Robinson, E. R.	Electric Railway Trolley	Sept 19, 1893	505,370
Robinson, J. H.	Life Saving Guards for Locomotives	Mar 14, 1899	621,143
Robinson, J.	Dinner Pail	Feb 1, 1887	356,852
Sampson, G. T.	Clothes Drier	June 7, 1892	476,416
Scottron, S. R.	Curtain Rod	Aug 30, 1892	481,720
Smith, J. W.	Lawn Sprinkler	May 4, 1897	581,785
Smith, P. D.	Potato Digger	Jan 21, 1891	445,206
Spears, H.	Portable Shield for Infantry	Dec 27, 1870	110,599
Standard, J.	Oil Stove	Oct 25, 1889	413,689
Standard, J.	Refrigerator	July 14, 1891	455,891
Stewart and Johnson	Metal Bending Machine	Dec 27, 1887	375,512
Stewart, E. W.	Punching Machine	May 3, 1887	362,190
Stewart, T. W.	Mop	June 13, 1893	499,402
Sutton, E. H.	Cotton Cultivator	Apr 7, 1874	149,543
Sweeting, J. A.	Device for Rolling Cigarettes	Nov 30, 1897	594,501
Taylor, B. H.	Rotary Engine	Apr 23, 1878	202,888
Thomas, S. E.	Waste Trap *(Thomas was also granted patents for his Casting, Pipe Connections and Water Trap for basins, etc.)*	Oct 16, 1883	286,746
Toliver, George	Propeller for Vessels	Apr 28, 1891	451,086
Tregoning and Latimer	Globe Supporter for Electric Lamps	Mar 21, 1882	255,212
Walker, Peter	Machine for Cleaning Seed Cotton	Feb 16, 1897	577,153
Washington, Wade	Corn Husking Machine	Aug 14, 1883	283,173
Watts, J. R.	Bracket for Miner's Lamp	Mar 7, 1893	493,137
White, J. T.	Lemon Squeezer	Dec 8, 1896	572,849
Winn, Frank	Direct Acting Steam Engine	Dec 4, 1888	394,047
Winters, J. R.	Fire Escape Ladder	May 7, 1878	203,517
Woods, G. T.*	Steam Boiler Furnace	June 3, 1884	299,894

*Between 1884 and 1899, G. T. Woods patented 22 of his inventions, as follows: Steam Boiler Furnace, 1884; Telephone Transmitter, 1884; Apparatus for Transmission of Messages by Electricity, 1885; Relay Instrument, 1887; Polarized Relay, 1887; Electro-Magnetic Brake Apparatus, 1887; Railway Telegraphy, 1887; Induction Telegraph System, 1887; Overhead Conducting System for Electric Railway, 1888. Electro-Motive Railway System, 1888; Tunnel Construction for Electric Railway, 1888; Galvanic Battery, 1888; Railway Telegraphy Improvement, 1888; Automatic Safety Cut-Out for Electric Circuits, 1889; Electric Railway System, 1891; Electric Railway Supply System, 1893; Electric Railway Conduit, 1893; System of Electrical Distribution, 1896; Amusement Apparatus, 1899.

Outstanding Inventors and Scientists

Let us review the accomplishments of a few of the more outstanding black inventors and scientists:

BENJAMIN BANNEKER (1731-1806)—*Inventor, mathematician, gazeteer*. Banneker was born in Ellicott, Maryland, November 9, 1731, of a free mother and a slave father who purchased his own freedom. The boy, who was considered free, was thus able to join an integrated private school in the eighth grade. His genius for mechanical inventiveness led him to construct the first clock to be made in America, one so accurate—although made of wood—that it kept perfect time and struck each hour unfailingly for more than 20 years. His aptitude in mathematics and astronomy enabled him to predict the solar eclipse of 1789. He published *Benjamin Banneker's Almanac* for over ten years, the first scientific publication written by an American Negro. Banneker is mainly remembered for his service as a surveyor on the six-man team which helped lay out the blueprints for what was to become the city of Washington, D.C. When the chairman of the committee, Major L'Enfant, abruptly resigned and returned to France, taking all the plans with him, Banneker reproduced them in their entirety, *from memory!*

ANDREW J. BEARD—*Inventor*. Beard's invention of the car coupler, an automatic device called the "Jenny Coupler," secured two railroad cars by merely bumping them together. Prior to his invention, hundreds of men lost their hands and arms in accidents during the manual coupling of cars which called for them to drop a metal pin into place as two cars crashed together. Frequently, the man would be crushed to death during this split-second operation. In 1897, Beard received $50,000 for his invention which has since prevented the death or maiming of countless numbers of railroad men.

HENRY BLAIR—*Inventor*. The prominence of corn as a leading grain crop in the United States and elsewhere received its initial impetus because of Blair's invention of a corn-planting machine for which he was granted a patent on October 14, 1834. Patent Office records describe him as "a colored man"—the only instance of racial identification in those early files. Since slaves were prohibited from obtaining patents, Blair was evidently a freedman, and is probably the first Negro inventor to receive a U.S. patent. In 1836, Blair also patented a machine for the planting of cotton.

GEORGE WASHINGTON CARVER (1864?-1943)—*Agricultural chemist*. Born a slave in Diamond, Missouri, Dr. Carver was only an infant when he and his mother were kidnapped by slave raiders. His mother was sold and shipped to another state, but the boy was ransomed by his master in exchange for a horse. Largely on his own in his early teens, he managed to acquire a high school education and, after becoming the first Negro student at Simpson College in Indianola, Iowa, he then attended Iowa State

College where, in 1894, he earned a degree in agricultural science while working as the school janitor. Two years later, he received his master's degree from the same school and became the first Negro to serve on its faculty. Booker T. Washington offered him a post at Tuskegee Institute and in 1896 he became director of Tuskegee's department of agricultural research. He retained this post for the rest of his life, his work winning him international acclaim. It may be said that Dr. Carver's research led to the liberation of the South from its dependence on a single crop: cotton. His efforts to improve the economy in the cotton states included the teaching of soil improvement as well as the diversification of crops. He is best known, however, for the hundreds of products he evolved from the peanut, the sweet potato and the soybean, thus stimulating the culture of those crops. He also discovered many new products derived from cotton waste, and successfully extracted blue, purple and red pigments from local clay. Dr. Carver, who contributed his life savings to a foundation for research at Tuskegee Institute, did not patent his many discoveries. "God gave them to me," he said. 'How can I sell them to someone else?" He is buried alongside his old friend and colleague, Booker T. Washington. Carver's epitaph reads, "He could have added fortune to fame, but caring for neither, he found happiness and honor in being helpful to the world." In 1953, his birthplace was designated a national monument.

CHARLES DREW (1904-1950)—*Medical researcher.* Dr. Drew, sometimes called "The father of the blood bank," developed the technique for separating and preserving blood, and won world renown for his advanced research in the vital field of blood plasma, which helped save untold lives in World War II, Korea and Vietnam. Born in Washington, D. C., on June 3, 1904, Dr. Drew graduated from Amherst College in Massachusetts, where he received the Messman Trophy for having brought the most honor to the school during his four-year stay there. After receiving his medical degree from McGill University in 1933, Drew returned to Washington, D. C., where he taught pathology at Howard University. In 1940, while taking his Doctor of Science degree at Columbia University, he wrote a dissertation on "banked blood," which led the British government to assign him to establish the first blood bank in England. During World War II, he was appointed director of the American Red Cross blood donor project and later served as chief surgeon of Freedmen's Hospital in Washington, D. C. He was killed in an automobile accident on April 1, 1950.

WILLIAM A. HINTON (1883-1959)—*Medical scientist.* A world authority on venereal disease, Dr. Hinton developed what is now known as the "Hinton Test," a reliable method for the detection of syphilis. A native of Chicago, Dr. Hinton graduated from Harvard at the age of 22 and, seven years later, in 1912, completed his studies at Harvard Medical School. After serving in the pathological laboratory at Massachusetts General Hospital for three years, he was engaged in laboratory practice at the Boston Dispensary and at the Massachusetts Department of Public Health for an additional eight years. Dr. Hinton then became an assistant lecturer in preventive medicine and hygiene at the Harvard University Medical School, and in 1949 he became the first Negro to be granted a professorship there.

PERCY JULIAN—*Chemist*. Born in Montgomery, Alabama, in 1898, Dr. Julian's research has resulted in relief from pain for millions of persons afflicted with arthritis. He graduated (Phi Beta Kappa) from De Pauw University in Greencastle, Indiana, where he had lived in the attic of a fraternity house and worked as a waiter. After teaching at Fisk and Howard universities for several years, he attended Harvard and continued his formal education at the University of Vienna. Later forming his own company, Julian Laboratories, he perfected a method of extracting sterols from soybean oil which lowered the cost of the sterols to less than 20 cents a gram, enabling millions of arthritis sufferers to obtain relief from cortisone, a sterol derivative, at a price they could afford. Dr. Julian attained additional fame when, in 1935, he successfully synthesized physostigmine, the drug which is used today in the treatment of glaucoma.

LEWIS HOWARD LATIMER (1848-1928)—*Inventor, draftsman, engineer*. Three important "firsts" are among Latimer's bequests to posterity. (1) He made the patent drawings for the first telephone as a consultant to Alexander Graham Bell. (2) In 1881 he invented and patented the first incandescent electric light bulb with a carbon filament. (3) He wrote the first textbook on the lighting system used by the Edison Company. Born in Chelsea, Massachusetts, Latimer enlisted in the Union Navy at the age of 15, and began the study of drafting upon completion of his naval service. A self-educated man, he became an engineer for the Edison Company and supervised the installation of electric lights in New York, Philadelphia, Montreal and London. He also served as chief draftsman for the General Electric and Westinghouse Companies. Latimer died at the age of 80 in 1928.

JAN MATZELIGER (1852-1889)—*Inventor*. The shoe-lasting machine invented by Jan Matzeliger, a Negro from Dutch Guiana, not only revolutionized the shoe industry but also made Lynn, Massachusetts the "shoe capital of the world." Born in Paramaribo, on September 15, 1852, Matzeliger found employment in the government machine works at the age of 10. Eight years later, he emigrated to the United States, settling first in Philadelphia, where he worked in a shoe factory and learned the trade. He then left for New England, settling permanently in Lynn. The Industrial Revolution then in progress in this country had by this time resulted in the invention of a number of machines to cut, sew and tack shoes, but none had been perfected to last a shoe. Matzeliger lost little time in designing and patenting just such a device, one which he refined over the years to such a point that it was able to adjust a shoe, arrange the leather over the sole, drive in the nails, and deliver the finished product—all in one minute's time. Matzeliger's patent was bought by Sydney W. Winslow who founded the United Shoe Machine Company, a multi-million dollar concern. The continued success of this business brought about a 50% reduction in the price of shoes across the nation, doubled wages, and improved the working conditions for millions of people dependent on the shoe industry for their livelihood. Matzeliger was only 37 when he died in the summer of 1889, long before he had the chance to benefit financially from the enormous profits derived from his invention.

ELIJAH McCOY (1844-1928?)—*Inventor*. McCoy, who patented hundreds of inventions dealing with the lubrication of moving machinery, is best known for his design of the "drip-cup," a tiny container filled with oil whose flow to the essential moving parts of heavy-duty machinery was regulated by a "stopcock." The drip-cup was a key device in perfecting the overall lubrication system used in large industry today. McCoy was born in Canada but moved to Ypsilanti, Michigan after the Civil War and, over the next 40 years, procured some 57 patents for devices to streamline his automatic lubrication process. He is believed to have died in 1928.

GARRETT A. MORGAN (1877-1963)—*Inventor*. During World War I the lives of thousands of soldiers were saved because of the gas mask, but few, if any, of them, knew that the gas mask was a modified version of the "gas inhalator," invented by a black man, Garrett A. Morgan. Morgan's inhalator first proved its worth when a devastating tunnel explosion occurred in the Cleveland Waterworks, trapping seven men 200 feet below the surface of Lake Erie. Several white men attempted, unsuccessfully, to rescue the doomed crew, and at this time Morgan, his brother, and two other volunteers—all wearing inhalators—descended into the smoke and gas-filled tunnel and saved those who were still alive from asphyxiation. One might reasonably expect that Morgan would have immediately acquired great wealth, and indeed he was deluged with orders from fire companies and others throughout the nation, but as soon as they learned of Morgan's race many of the orders were cancelled. In the South, Morgan found it necessary to employ a white man to demonstrate the inhalator. His first invention, an improvement on the sewing machine, brought him a mere $150. By the year 1923, however, his reputation was so firmly established because of the gas inhalator, he was able to command a price of $40,000 from the General Electric Company for his invention of the automatic stop-sign. Morgan, who was born in Paris, Kentucky, died at the age of 86, in Cleveland.

DANIEL HALE WILLIAMS (1856-1931)—*Surgeon, civil rights leader*. As a medical scientist and pioneer in open heart surgery, Dr. Williams has few peers. His early life was anything but auspicious. His father died when young Williams was only 11, and his mother deserted him after first apprenticing him to a cobbler. He worked as a roustabout on a lake steamer for awhile and then, to finance his education, he became a barber, graduating from the Chicago Medical College in 1883. Dr. Williams practiced medicine from his office on Chicago's South Side at a time when that city prohibited black doctors from using the facilities of its hospitals. Operations of the most serious nature were often performed on kitchen tables in the crowded tenements in the Negro neighborhoods. Dr. Williams stopped that sort of racial nonsense by founding Provident Hospital which welcomed all races. It was here, at Provident, that Dr. Williams performed the open heart surgery that has since saved the lives of thousands of patients. On July 10, 1893, a young man was admitted to the emergency ward with a knife wound in an artery, the merest fraction of an inch from the heart. With six staff surgeons as aides, Dr. Williams made an incision in the patient's chest and operated successfully on the artery. The rest is medical history. After a lifetime devoted to his two main interests—the NAACP and the construction of hospitals and training schools for Negro doctors and nurses—Dr. Williams died in 1931 at the age of 75.

GRANVILLE T. WOODS (1856-1910)—*Inventor*. (For a partial list of Woods' inventious, see Table No. 2.) Granville T. Woods was born in Columbus, Ohio, on April 2, 1856, where he attended school until he was ten. Even then his mechanical aptitude was apparent. His first job was in a machine shop where he learned the fundamentals of mechanics, and at the age of 16 he was employed by a railroad, following with another job in a steel rolling mill in 1874, when he was 18 years old. In 1878, after studying mechanical engineering at college, Woods became an engineer aboard the British steamer, *Ironsides*, and two years later, when he was 22, he was handling a steam locomotive on the D & S Railroad. His most advanced invention was the Synchronous Multiplex Railway Telegraph, which he patented in 1887. This device was designed "for the purpose of averting accidents by keeping each train informed of the whereabouts of the one immediately ahead or following it, in communicating with stations from moving trains, and in promoting general social and commercial intercourse." The system is still in use everywhere. Woods' inventiveness enabled him to obtain some 50 patents, ranging in diversification from amusement devices to an incubator, the prototype of modern machines which are capable of hatching 50,000 eggs at a time. Woods died in New York City on January 30, 1910, at the early age of 54.

✓   ✓   ✓

An obvious question now arises: In view of yesteryear's great statesmen, educators, scientists, inventors, and those in the creative arts, what, then, is the difference between the old and the new breed? The answer, it seems to this editor, is that the slave fought for his physical freedom and the freedmen struggled to maintain it; but today's black man has planted his feet in the soil of that hard-won freedom and made his stand for justice—to separate whiteness of the law from rightness of the law. True, almost every forward step has been met with a scowl and a growl by many white diehards, but also with a sigh of resignation. For the most part, the black man has ascended from his former state of rural naiveté to a plateau of urban sophistication, and one which has brought with it the concomitant awareness of his real potential.

"I have a dream," proclaimed Martin Luther King, Jr., on August 28, 1963. The occasion was the March on Washington, the largest single protest demonstration in the history of the United States. More than 200,000 citizens of all races converged on Washington, D. C. to stage a non-violent civil rights protest, appropriately enough, on the steps of the Lincoln Memorial. Among the principal speakers were: James Farmer, head of the Congress for Racial Equality (CORE); Roy Wilkins, executive secretary of the National Association for the Advancement of Colored People (NAACP); A. Philip Randolph, the venerable "elder statesman" of the movement, and generally recognized as the chief architect of the march; and John Lewis, president of the Student Nonviolent Coordinating Committee (SNCC).

But of all the speeches delivered on that sultry summer's day, the most compelling oration was made by the Rev. Martin Luther King, of the Southern Christian Leadership Conference, whose every word articulated the hopes and aspirations of his people. Among the most moving lines of Dr. King's speech were the following:

"I say to you today, my friends, that in spite of the difficulties and frustrations of the moment, I still have a dream. It is a dream deeply rooted in the American dream.

"I have a dream that one day this nation will rise up and live out the true meaning of its creed: 'We hold these truths to be self-evident; that all men are created equal.'

"I have a dream that one day, on the red hills of Georgia, the sons of former slaves and the sons of former slaveowners will be able to sit down together at the table of brotherhood.

"I have a dream that one day even the state of Mississippi, a desert state sweltering with the heat of injustice and oppression, will be transformed into an oasis of freedom and justice.

"I have a dream that my four little children will one day live in a nation where they will not be judged by the color of their skin but by the content of their character.

"I have a dream today.

"I have a dream that one day the state of Alabama, whose governor's lips are presently dripping with the words of interposition and nullification, will be transformed into a situation where little black boys and black girls will be able to join hands with little white boys and white girls and walk together as sisters and brothers.

"I have a dream today.

"I have a dream that one day every valley shall be exalted, every hill and mountain shall be made low, the rough places will be made plains, and the crooked places will be made straight, and the glory of the Lord shall be revealed, and all flesh shall see it together."

There is a beacon aglow on the horizon, giving light and warmth to a renaissance of spiritual faith and a rare nostalgia for the folkways of the past—an innate yearning for that simpler, less complicated way of life our fathers knew, but which our intellect tells us can never and must never be revived. The "new breed" has turned its face to the future: toward that great day in the morning when a people's struggle for dignity and equality will have flowered into fulfillment. Yet, we can pause for a few idyllic moments in our forward march and reflect upon those who preceded us—the obscure and the famous—seeing them not only in their fallibilities, idiosyncracies and predilections, but in their demonstrated strengths as well.

Crispus Attuks! Frederick Douglass! Harriet Tubman! George Washington Carver! Dorie Miller! Langston Hughes! W. E. B. DuBois! Whitney M. Young! Martin Luther King! Sing out their praises! They have joined a host of others who braved the storm and who now walk together in that eternal Glory Line.

In rhyme, in song, and in story we honor them!

A Note on Humor*

Humor is laughing at what you haven't got when you ought to have it. Of course, you laugh by proxy. You're really laughing at the other guy's lacks, not your own. That's what makes it funny—the fact that you don't know you are laughing at yourself. Humor is when the joke is on you but hits the other fellow first—because it boomerangs. Humor is what you wish in your secret heart were not funny, but it is, and you must laugh. Humor is your own unconscious therapy.

What does this book mean? Simply that humor can be like a dropped brick or the roar of Niagara Falls. Humor maintains its distance while at the same time keeping you company so long as you are capable of meeting it halfway. Humor does not force itself on you (in fact, cannot) because it has none of the qualities of a bad joke, none of the vulgarity of the wisecrack, or the pushiness of the gag. Humor is a forgotten "Good morning" remembered tomorrow, a lent dime returned in needy time, a gesture from across the room better than a handshake, a friend who looks like a stranger but isn't because you realize you have known him all your life. Humor is your own smile surprising you in the mirror. But, like the child Onyx, in one of the anecdotes in this book, its name is derived from the fact that the arrival is so "*on-ex*pected." Like a welcome summer rain, humor may suddenly cleanse and cool the earth, the air, and you.

LANGSTON HUGHES

---

* *The Book of Negro Folklore*, by Langston Hughes, copyright 1966, Dodd, Mead & Company, New York. Reprinted by permission.

PART ONE

TELL IT ON THE MOUNTAIN

Old Man Cassius*

(Time: One hundred and fifty years from today)

Child: Daddy, Daddy, why are the flags flying today?

Daddy: It's a national holiday, son. Today is Cassius Clay's birthday.

Child: Oh, Cassius Clay. Is he the man who chopped down the cherry tree?

Daddy: Why, no. He is the man who chopped down Sonny Liston.

Child: Oh, Mommy, how long ago did he do that?

Mommy: Over one hundred and fifty years ago.

Child: Wow, gosh, he must have been a great man.

Daddy: What do you mean, must have been? He still is. Just think, he's one hundred and seventy-five years old today. The oldest living ex-president.

Mommy: And outside there is going to be a parade in his honor.

Child: A parade! What's in a parade?

Daddy: Just Cassius, son. Why don't you go outside and see it. Say, this child didn't brush his teeth.

Mommy: I know, but you can't expect him to brush after every meal.

Daddy: Cassius Clay does. Cassius is being interviewed on television. I think I'll turn on the wall.

Interviewer: Tell the audience, Mr. Clay, how does it feel to be one hundred and seventy-five today?

Cassius: This is my happiest birthday. The day of my greatest joy, for this morning my wife presented me with a bouncing baby boy.

Interviewer: Marvelous! What are you going to call him?

Cassius: I am naming him after me, just like the other ninety-three.

Interviewer: Sir, looking back, what is the greatest honor you've ever received?

Cassius: I've been honored everywhere. I am the world's greatest honor receiver. I am the only man with honorary degrees from Southern Methodist, Notre Dame, and Yeshiva.

Interviewer: You must be very grateful.

Cassius: Yes, I'm grateful. And because this nation has been so kind to the Lip from Louisville, I didn't forget my country when I made out my will:

> To this nation I've made my bequest,
> So spread the word North and South.

Some folks leave their brains to science,
But when I go I am leaving my mouth.
It's the greatest!

by *Muhammad Ali*
(*Cassius Clay*)

Clearing the Color Bar*

Isn't this the most fascinating country in the world? Where else would I have to ride on the back of the bus, have a choice of going to the worst schools, eating in the worst restaurants, living in the worst neighborhoods—and average $5,000 a week just talking about it?

I was thinking of taking a bus tour of Alabama, only my Blue Cross has expired. . . . Then, again—better *it* than *me!*

You remember Brotherhood Week? The only week in the year when you wanna take a Negro to lunch you gotta ask for a number? I've already got nine invitations to lunch, twelve to dinner, thirty-six cocktail parties—then come midnight I turn to the lunch counter again. . . . Then, again, you can't turn any of them down, you know. 'Cause hell hath no fury like a Liberal scorned! If you're on a diet come Brotherhood Week, forget it!

The international situation raises some interesting problems. Like, if Orval Faubus is driving through one of our neighborhoods when they drop the bomb, would he go into a colored shelter? And if he did, should we let him in? "Orval, stop pounding on that door! Don't you know it's three o'clock in the morning?"

Some people have a wonderful way of looking at things. Like the ones who hire us to baby-sit—so they can go to a Ku Klux Klan meeting.

Let's see now. They've broken the four-minute mile, the sixteen-foot pole vault—how 'bout clearing the color bar next?

You gotta say this for the white race—its self-confidence knows no bounds. Who else could go to a small island in the South Pacific where there's no poverty, no crime, no unemployment, no war, and no worry—and call it a "primitive society?"

I was planning to write much more, but prudence dictates we end it here. Governor Faubus may ask for equal space.

DICK GREGORY**

---

* From *Dick Gregory: The Back of the Bus*, edited by Bob Orben. Copyright © 1962 by Dick Gregory Enterprises, Inc. Reprinted by permission of E. P. Dutton & Co., Inc.

** Dick Gregory, born in St. Louis, in 1932, is credited with introducing to the general public the satirical, unabashed racial humor which other nationally known black comedians have since adopted. It was his original intention to escape from the poverty of his ghetto surroundings through his athletic abilities, having won the Missouri State mile championship in 1951 and again in 1952 while in high school. He attended Southern Illinois University on a

CORN MEAL GRIDDLE CAKES

Hoecake, with collard greens, ham, and yams, make a grand meal, as captured so intimately in the poem "Hoecake an' Hominy," on page 294.

Corn Meal Griddle Cakes—Farmer's Style

¾ cup corn meal	1 tsp. soda
1 or 2 eggs	½ cup hot water
¾ cup flour	1 tsp. sugar
½ tsp. sugar	1½ cups sour milk

Scald meal with hot water. Add flour and salt. Beat eggs well. Add to corn meal. Put soda in milk and add to corn meal mixture. Beat well. Bake on hot griddle as pancakes. (Sweet milk may be used by omitting soda and adding 1 teaspoon baking powder.)

Intellectual Dialogue*

The lady looked at me severely; I glanced away. I had addressed the little audience at some length on the disenfranchisement of my people in society, politics and industry, and had studiously avoided the while her cold, green eye. I finished and shook weary hands, while she lay in wait. I knew what was coming and I braced my soul.

"Do you know where I can get a good colored cook?" she asked.

W. E. B. DuBois**

On the Road***

Getting a night's sleep was a continual drag. We were playing big towns and little towns, proms and fairs. A six-hundred-mile jump overnight was standard. When we got to put up at a hotel, it was usually four cats to a

track scholarship, but left in 1955 (in his second year) to join the army, where he launched his career as a comedian in Special Services shows. On January 13, 1961, he substituted at Chicago's Playboy Club for an ailing comedian and was received with such enthusiasm by the white audience who had never before been confronted with his type of visceral humor, that he was held over and then booked into the nation's foremost nightclubs. Gregory has suffered great financial loss in his struggle for civil rights in behalf of the poor and oppressed, black and white. A man of high standards and ethics, he is also a man of courage. He was shot while attempting to quiet the Watts rioters in 1965, and on June 11, 1965, he was arrested while leading a CORE demonstration in protest against the slow pace of school integration. In 1968, Gregory was an independent candidate for the presidency of the United States.

* Published here with the permission of Mrs. W. E. B. DuBois, and may not otherwise be reproduced.

** William Edward Burghardt DuBois, critic, editor, scholar, author and civil rights leader, was born in Great Barrington, Massachusetts, on February 23, 1868. Among the most prominent and influential Negro leaders of the 20th century, DuBois received a bachelor's degree from Fisk University, and a second bachelor's as well as a Ph.D. from Harvard. He was, for a time, professor of Latin and Greek at Wilberforce and the University of Pennsylvania, and also served as a professor of economics and history at Atlanta University. One of the founders of the NAACP in 1909, he served that organization as director of publications and editor of *Crises* magazine until 1934. In 1944 he became head of the NAACP's special research department, a post he held until 1948. Dr. DuBois emigrated to Africa in 1961 and became editor-in-chief of the *Encyclopedia Africana*, an enormous publishing venture which had been planned by Kwame Nkrumah, since then deposed as president of Ghana. DuBois' lifetime position was that it was vitally necessary for the Negro to cultivate his own aesthetic and cultural values even as he made strides toward social emancipation. In this he was opposed by Booker T. Washington, who felt that the Negro should concentrate on technical and mechanical skills. DuBois joined the Communist Party at the age of 93, and died two years later, in 1961.

*** Excerpts from *Lady Sings the Blues*, by Billie Holiday. Copyright © 1956 by Eleanora Fagan and William F. Dufty. Reprinted by permission of Doubleday & Co., Inc.

room. We might finish at Scranton, Pennsylvania, at two in the morning, grab something to eat, and make Cleveland, Ohio, by noon the next day. The boys in the band had worked out a deal for getting two night's sleep for one night's rent. We'd drive all night, hit a town in the morning, register and turn in early, and sleep until time to go to work. When the job was through, we'd sleep the rest of the night, clear out in the morning, and hit the road. This would work every other day and save loot. On the $125 a week I made, that was still very important.

This would have been fine except that I had to double up with another vocalist. I don't think she liked Negroes much, and especially not me. She didn't want to sleep in the same room with me. She only did because she had to. Artie Shaw had asked me to help her to phrase her lyrics; this made her jealous. Then once I made the mistake of telling somebody we got along fine, and to prove it I mentioned how she let me help her phrase. This made her sore. It was true, there were some places where the management wouldn't let me appear, and I'd have to sit in the bus while she did numbers that were arranged for me. She was always happy when she could sing and I couldn't.

I'll never forget the night we were booked at this fancy boys' school in New England. She was real happy because she was sure I was going to have to sit in the bus all night again because I was too black and sexy for those young boys. But when the time came to open, the head man of the school came out and explained that it wasn't me; they just didn't want any female singers at all. So the two of us had to sit in the bus together all night and listen to the band playing our songs.

Did I razz her! "You see, honey," I said, "you're so fine and grand. You may be white, but you're no better than me. They won't have either of us here because we're both women."

BILLIE HOLIDAY*

---

* Billie ("Lady Day") Holiday belongs to the great blues tradition dominated by Ma Rainey and Bessie Smith. It was tenor saxophonist Lester ("Prez") Young who dubbed Miss Holiday "Lady Day" and it was she who, in turn, nicknamed Young "President," later shortened to "Prez," while both were with Count Basie. While still a young girl she moved from her hometown of Baltimore to New York City and, at the age of 14, began her singing career in Harlem night spots. Her first recordings were made with Benny Goodman in 1933, and for the next six years she established her reputation with a series of records made while she was a vocalist with Teddy Wilson, Count Basie, Artie Shaw and several other all-star bands. Although Billie Holiday has often been compared with Bessie Smith, her style and material were really far removed from those of the older singer. In fact, there is no earlier jazz artist who is known to have had a direct influence on Miss Holiday. What she shared with Bessie Smith and other blues singers was an ability to project a universal sense of loneliness—that feature which is thought to be at the core of true blues artistry. Miss Holiday died in New York, in 1959, after having overcome an addiction to drugs and alcohol. Her greatest triumphs, "Strange Fruit" and "God Bless the Child," depicted the harsh realities of Southern lynchings and the personal alienation she had experienced because of them.

PIE CRUST

This recipe may be used for any of the pies described on pages 436, 443, and 445.

2 cups *sifted* flour	⅔ cup shortening
1 tsp. salt	½ tsp. sugar
1 tsp. vinegar	pinch, baking powder
cold water	

Sift flour, sugar, salt and baking powder. Add shortening. Cut in with fork or use pastry blender. Pour the vinegar and water into the flour mixture, a few drops at a time, mixing with a fork until it will hold together. Chill. Roll out as quickly as possible. Makes a double crust for one 9-inch pie or 2 pie shells.

VIEW FROM THE DISTAFF SIDE*
by Sandra Haggerty

Racial Santa-gration
or
The Problems of an Integrated Staff

"Hold it down," soothed Santa Red Cloud. "You guys are going to wake up the world."

"Oh brother!" groaned Santa Cleotis as he nervously ran his hand over his black beard.

Santa Chin and Santa Montoya wore looks of dismay.

"Don't panic," said Santa Claus. "Let's check those addresses again."

"To get down to the nitty-gritty, we done goofed," said Santa Cleotis.

His breath coming out in a whistle, Santa Claus shook his head negatively as he looked at the long list. "Not in Klan territory!"

Santa Cleotis shook his head in the affirmative.

Another groan from Santa Claus. "And the whitest and richest county in the state of California!"

Further down the list. "Don't tell me," said Santa Claus, "that *Cleotis* covered Alcatraz."

A sigh of exasperation came from Santa Red Cloud.

"Well," began Santa Montoya, "maybe people will understand. After all, this *is* our first year as syndicated Santas."

"Let's recapitulate," began scholarly Santa Chin. "What happened?"

"Yeah, what *did* happen?" asked Santa Cleotis.

"In previous years," said Santa Red Cloud, "we've always stayed at the North Pole on Christmas Eve while Claus made the rounds."

"Si," agreed Santa Montoya. "Most people don't even know we're part of the whole Santa operation."

"And last year," Santa Chin went on, "because of the extreme work load on Claus, the four of us went out briefly, but only to the homes of our own people."

"Even then we were finished long before Claus could make all his stops," added Santa Red Cloud.

Santa Claus agreed woefully. "That's why we divide the work load into five equal parts this year."

"Team work!" chimed in Santa Cleotis.

"We finished much earlier this year. Didn't miss a single home." Santa Chin tried to sound encouraging.

"We should have made a racial notation for each house. You know, the

* *Racial Santa-gration; Hardships of Symbolizing Your Status; Getajob! Oompa, Oompa; A Rose by Any Other Name*, by Sandra Haggerty. Copyright 1969, 1970, Los Angeles Times Syndicate.

RHUBARB PIE

The most frequent complaint about baking rhubarb pie is that "it never turns out just right." This one, adapted from an old "Aunt Dicy" recipe (see "Aunt Dicy Tales,") is about as foolproof as a recipe can be. For pie crust, use recipe on page 434.

3 cups rhubarb	1¼ cups sugar
2 tbs. flour	1 tsp. butter
2 beaten eggs	¼ tsp. nutmeg
dash salt	

Peel rhubarb and cut into small pieces. Add spices. Line pie pan with plain pastry. Mix flour, salt, sugar, eggs and butter. Add to rhubarb and pour into crust. Cover with top crust. Cover with top crust. Press edges together and trim. Bake in a quick oven 15 minutes. Reduce heat to 350°. Bake 30 minutes. Makes one 9-inch pie.

way they do on the corner of some application forms. Then we wouldn't have to worry about who got what." Santa Cleotis sank back in his chair.

"Well, what are we going to do?" asked Santa Montoya.

"It's too late to go back and switch the gifts around," said Santa Chin.

"Yeah, some of the children are getting up already," agreed Santa Red Cloud.

Santa Claus groaned. "After all these years, too. This is probably my last, all because I succumbed to the pressure to integrate the staff."

"Integrate!" objected Santa Montoya. "We've been here all along!"

"Pressure!" added Santa Cleotis. "Who was helping whom?"

"I know," smiled Santa Claus, "but integration is the nation's Number One cause of confusion—just thought I'd use it, too. Can't seem to come up with anything else."

"Excuses," interjected Santa Chin, "will get us nowhere. I suggest we start writing to the employment agencies."

"How!" agreed Santa Red Cloud.

Three days after Christmas the Pole was deluged with mail. This was highly unusual because the greatest volume of mail was always received *before* Christmas. The Clauses were leery of this after-the-fact mail and called a staff meeting. It's easier to sustain any kind of a blow in a group, something like mob action and reaction. Anyway, the mail was read:

Dear Santa:

My name is Susie, and I love this little black doll you brought me. I had never seen a black doll before. I named her Shatsie, and she has tea with my white dolls.

Dear Santa:

I live in Chinatown and have always gotten Oriental dolls at Christmas time. This year you gave me a Mexican doll with a red shawl around her shoulders. She is beautiful.

Dear Santa:

My name is Maria. We usually go to Mexico for Christmas to visit my grandmother. This year we stayed home and I'm glad we did because I love the tiny Oriental doll you left under the tree for me.

And a letter signed "A Group of Parents":

Dear Santa:

Regarding this year's Christmas, thank you for having the courage to do what many of us parents had not the "grit" to do. We will all hold hands, yet.

Stroking his kinky beard, Santa Cleotis shrugged his shoulders. "Man, I *told* you guys about team work!"

Hardships of Symbolizing
Your Status

It used to be that nothing rankled whites and impressed blacks more than seeing a shiny Cadillac parked in front of a tenement building or a broken-down house. Today, even though Cadillacs are still much in evidence, a new status symbol has emerged in the black community—the color TV set.

In and of itself, a color television is not that big a thing. And one would assume that owning such a set, even the most expensive model, would be a lot cheaper than driving a Cadillac. But is it?

Let's examine what's involved in housing a color TV, especially in the black community. First of all, you purchase the set—on credit. So, from the "git-go," add three years worth of carrying charges to Cost X. Next, you buy special insurance against theft and for the repair and tuning of the set. Then, of course, you must purchase a special antenna to make your living color live. Add prices to Cost X.

About that antenna. Not only is it expensive, it is also as good as a multicolor flag waving on the roof, signaling to the neighborhood burglars that your home is now equipped with the hottest item on the black market—the color TV.

About that burglar. People in the black community, where the crime rate is highest, have learned to live with this saboteur of status basking. It's almost like having a gopher in your yard. You can't catch him, but you know he's there.

So it becomes a match of wits. The *real* status in having a color TV is not getting it, but the challenge involved in keeping it.

After locking doors and windows, the next step is to purchase a watchdog. A cur was sufficient for sounding the alarm when someone was trying to heist your black-and-white set. But really, a color set is Class with a capital C, so only a registered purebred will do. Add another $150 to Cost X. And everyone knows you don't feed a purebred scraps off the table. Add a few years' worth of expensive dog food to Cost X.

Now, fully insured, with antenna and dog properly positioned, you can sit back and be mesmerized by the make-believe world of living color. You can glance out the window, past your VW (or the like) to your neighbor's Cadillac and think how smart you are to "live within your means" with the new "reasonable" status symbol.

Getajob!—Oompa, Oompa...

My Man once more scans the application form that he has carefully filled out. Handing it to the syrupy-sweet receptionist, he then sits back to wait for his interview.

The final words of last night's argument with his wife echo in his mind. "Getajob! A real job." Huh, same thing his mama used to tell him. "Getajob! A real job."

He laughs silently to himself. Add a drumbeat to that "getajob" and he would have a best-seller on the top 10 record chart. *Getajob, oompa, oompa—a real job, oompa, oompa—geta. . . .*

"Mr. Jones? Right this way." The interviewer has a butch haircut. My Man wonders if he has cut (ah, pain) his natural down far enough. (Second verse: Cut your hair, oompa, oompa.)

"Have a seat," says Mr. Crewcut as he looks over My Man's application.

"Is this your real name?" My Man is surprised and somewhat amused at the seriousness of the interviewer's tone.

"Jones," he nods affirmatively. "Cleotis P. Jones." (Mundane question number one. Oh well, maybe Cleotis P. Jones is an unlikely name.)

"Let's see now. Oh, you did graduate from high school." Mr. Crewcut smiles approvingly.

"That's right," says My Man. (*Went to school, oompa, oompa.*)

"But why have you worked only as a laborer?"

Why, indeed, thinks My Man. (*Feed your kids, oompa, oompa.*)

Mr. Crewcut goes on: "What kind of work were you doing when you weren't employed as a laborer?"

"Well, for a while I was a fighter—a boxer."

"I was referring to a *real* job." Mr. C. gestures uncertainly.

Just what his wife had said, a real job—an establishment-endorsed job, a starvation-salary job. (*Oompa, oompa, oom-pa-pa.*)

"Surely you've done some other things," Mr. C. goes on. "Even though we're prepared to train the person for this job, this particular position requires selling ability. It requires a personable type of fellow. Someone able to meet the public."

My Man takes a chance. He matter-of-factly begins to run down his non-real job experience (experience he did not put down on the application): Pop bottle returner, age 4; hanger collector and re-seller, age 5; shopping-cart hustler, age 6; dog walker, age 7; lawn mower and junk cleaner-upper, age 8; shoeshine boy, age 9; paper boy, age 10; dishwasher, age 11; car washer, age 12; janitor, age 13.

Mr. C. listens politely.

My Man has blown it already, so he carries on. "And before I went to jail I ran the numbers, sold weed and was the distribution manager of a very efficient auto-theft club."

"Any chance of your going back to jail?" asks Mr. C. calmly.

"None," says My Man with authority. "Wherever my thing is, it's not behind bars."

Two hours later My Man's wife greets him at the door. "I'm sorry about last night," she begins.

He grins at her. "I got a job."

She doesn't smile. "But you hate carrying hod. And I hate it when you're doing something you hate."

He kisses her. "You're now looking at XYZ Co. Inc.'s newest salesman!"

She still hesitates. "What are you gonna sell?"

"Not weed or 'hots,' baby! But good old bona fide legal goods—for pay."

A dimple creases the side of her face. "You got a job!"

(*Gotta-oom-job-pa!*)

That Changing Name of the Game

"Things are changing" is a very popular statement today. And, indeed, things have changed to some degree. But more than things, names have changed.

For a variety of technological, social and screwball reasons, many professions, industries and people have changed their names. Suffice it to say that "image" is very important in USA, 1970's.

Remember when there were porters? Then they became janitors. Today they are sanitation specialists. Garbage men used to be garbage men—now they are refuse-removal specialists. Cooks (who still cook) are called food specialists, dieticians and gourmets. The undertaker is now a mortician and dead bodies are now the deceased or loved ones. (Could it be the word "body" now smacks of pornography?)

The social sciences have updated their titles also. Employment agencies are now departments of human resources. People "on the state" are welfare recipients and the poor are underprivileged and/or deprived. Old folks' homes are now Rest Estates and Guest Homes. Our elderly are now Senior Citizens.

Crazy folk are now the mentally disturbed. This change was a "must" since so many Americans fit into the "nut" category (more of 'em out than in).

Roads have gone from streets to highways, to freeways and airways.

Today the boss is called the employer, but he's still the boss-man. The employees are staff, but, as with the bees, they're still the workers. Farmers are agricultural engineers and livestock specialists. Free time is now leisure time (or organized free time) overseen by a degree'd recreational specialist. Auto exhaust is air pollution, and "too many kids" is people pollution. The city is now an urban center, and junior colleges are becoming community colleges. Draft dodgers are now military dissenters, and conscientious objectors, in some camps, are called traitors.

Riots are being nice-ified and referred to as social unrest and social disturbances, especially now that whites as well as blacks are involved in them.

And we black folks have really gone through some image changes. We started out as blacks (ironically) and we have come from nigger to colored, to Negro and currently back to black.

We used to call the white man Mr. Charlie. Then, after a few meals of corn mush, we got cocky and called him Charles. After learning to read, we shortened it to Chuck. Today, he's the Man.

Yes, things have changed—at least the names of things. And all to make Cleotis L. Public comfortable with SOS (same old stuff).

IS BROTHERHOOD COLORED?

Simple Writes Dr. Butts*

Scene: Harlem, U.S.A. Night—One Cold February Day

Dear Dr. Butts:

I seen last week in the colored papers where you have writ an article for the *New York Times* magazine part section of the paper in which you say that in spite of all America is still the greatest country in the world for the Negro race, and democracy is the greatest kind of government for all, but it would be better if all deliberate speed picked up a little bit. America is great, you say, *but,* you continue, it would be better if the Mississippi pattern was not patented in so many other parts of the South also, and you *but* this and *but* that and *but* the other fourteen pages more. Once you get started writing, all the latter part of your article is hanging on to your *but.*

You start off talking about how great American democracy is, then you *but* it all over the place. In fact, the *but* end of your seesaw is so far down on the ground I do not believe the other end can ever pull it up. So me myself, I would not write no article for no *New York Times* if I had put in so many *buts.* I reckon maybe you come by it naturally, though, that being your name, dear Dr. Butts.

I hear tell you are a race leader, but I do not know who you lead because I have not heard tell of you before and I have not laid eyes on you in all this shuffle about integration. *But* if you are leading me, make me know it, because I do not read the *New New York Times* very often, less I happen to pick up a copy blowing around in the subway, so I did not know you were my leader. *But* since you are my leader, lead on, and see if I will follow behind your *but*—because there is more behind that *but* than there is in front of it.

Dr. Butts, I am glad to read that you writ an article in the *New York*

---

* Reprinted by permission of Harold Ober Associates, Inc. Copyright © 1958 by Langston Hughes.

Times, but also sometimes I wish you would write one in the colored papers and let me know how to get out from behind all these *buts* that are staring me in the face. I know America is a great country *but*—and it is that *but* that has been keeping me where I is all these years. I can't get over it, I I can't get under it, and I can't get around it, so what am I supposed to do? If you are leading me, lemme see. Because we have too many colored leaders now that nobody knows until they get from the white papers to the colored papers and from the colored papers to me who has never seen hair nor hide of you. Dear Dr. Butts, are you hiding from me—and leading me, too?

From the way you write, a man would think my race problem was made out of nothing but *buts.* *But* this, *but* that, and, yes, there is Jim Crow in Georgia *but*—America admits they bomb folks in Alabama—*but* Hitler gassed the Jews. Mississippi is bad—*but* Russia is worse. Harlem slums are awful—*but* compared to the slums in India, Lenox Avenue is Paradise.

Dear Dr. Butts, Hitler is dead. I don't live in Russia. India is across the Pacific Ocean. And I do not hope to see Paradise no time soon. I am nowhere near some of them foreign countries you are talking about being so bad. I am here! And you know as well as I do, Mississippi is hell. There ain't no *but* in the world can make it out different. They tell me when Nazis gas you, you die slow. But when they put a bomb under you like in Birmingham, you don't have time to say your prayers. I don't know nothing about India, but I been in Washington, D. C. If you think there ain't slums there, just take your *but* up Seventh Street late some night, and see if you still got it by the time you get to Howard University.

I should not have to be telling you these things. You are colored just like me. To put a *but* after all this Jim Crow fly-papering around our feet is just like telling a hungry man, *"But* Mr. Rockefeller has got plenty to eat."* It's just like telling a joker with no overcoat in the wintertime, *"But* you will be hot next summer."* The fellow is liable to haul off and say, "I am hot now!" And bop you over your head.

Are you in your right mind, dear Dr. Butts? Or are you just writing? Do you really think a new day is dawning? Do you really think the Civil Rights Bill has civilized anything? Do you honest-to-God think Christians are having a change of heart? I can see you now taking your pen in hand to write, *"But* just last week the Southern Denominations of Hell-Fired Salvation resolved to work toward Brotherhood."* In fact, that is what you already writ. Do you think Brotherhood means colored to them southerners?

Do you reckon they will recognize you for a brother, Dr. Butts, since you done had your picture taken in the Grand Ballroom of the Waldorf-Astoria shaking hands at some kind of meeting with five hundred white big shots and five Negroes, all five of them Negro leaders, so it said underneath the picture? I did not know any of them Negro leaders by sight, neither by name, but since it says in the white papers that they are leaders, I reckon they are. Anyhow, I take my pen in hand to write you this letter to ask you to make yourself clear to me. When you answer me, do not write no

PUMPKIN PIE

"Punkins" have always been part of soul food lore. Granddaddy, on page 29, tells us they are inferior to sweet potatoes. One of the funniest pre-Civil War stories, "Alphie Hatches a Donkey" (page 54), depicts little Alphie attempting to hatch a baby donkey from a pumpkin. But, sweet potatoes and donkeys to the contrary, the pumpkin makes a truly delicious pie.

⅔ cup brown sugar
½ tsp. salt
1 tsp. cinnamon
½ tsp. ginger
½ tsp. cloves

2 eggs
1½ cups milk
½ cup pancake or maple syrup
1½ cups canned pumpkin
1 tsp. lemon juice

Mix sugar and spices, add eggs, beat slightly. Add remaining ingredients. Blend well. Pour in 9-inch pie pan lined with unbaked pastry. Bake in hot oven 1 hour or until a silver knife comes out clean.

"so-and-so *but*—"; I will not take *but* for an answer. Negroes have been looking at democracy's *but* too long. What we want to know is how to get rid of that *but*.

Do you dig me, dear Dr. Butts?

Sincerely very truly
Jesse B. Semple

LANGSTON HUGHES*
(1902-1967)

Faith and Experience**

When it is dark enough you can see the stars. I shall never forget the first time I took a night flight in one of our powerful jets. As that mighty plane lifted up into the heavens, I looked out of my window and saw great spurts of flame pouring out from the sides of the plane. I became a little concerned. The stewardess, noticing this, came over to explain to me that those flames emanated from jet planes at all times when they took off in flight. She told me that they were there when the planes took off in the daytime. The point was, you couldn't see them unless it was dark enough. Now I want you to know that the fears which had come to me at the sight of those flames didn't indicate that I have no faith in God in the air. It's just that I have more experience with Him on the ground.

REV. MARTIN LUTHER KING

---

* Langston Hughes, renowned as the "Negro poet laureate of the 20th century," was born in Joplin, Missouri, on February 1, 1902. At the age of 14 he moved to Cleveland where he attended Central High School. After spending a year in Mexico he attended Columbia University in New York and then roamed the world as a seaman. He won the Witter Byner Prize for undergraduate poetry while attending Lincoln University, later his alma mater (1928). In 1930 he received the Harmon Award and, five years later, he journeyed to the Soviet Union and Spain under a Guggenheim Fellowship. In addition to his poetry, his other works include: *Not Without Laughter* (1930), *The Big Sea* (his autobiography) 1940, *The Book of Negro Folklore* (with Arna Bontemps) 1958, and *The Book of Negro Humor* (1966). Hughes was also an accomplished song lyricist, librettist and newspaper columnist. As a columnist he created the famous character, Jesse B. Simple, around whom he produced the musical comedy, *Simply Heavenly*. Langston Hughes died in 1967.

** From a sermon delivered by the late Dr. Martin Luther King, at Ebenezer Baptist Church, Atlanta, Georgia.

SWEET POTATO PIE

The numerous references in this book, referring to sweet potato pie, pertain mostly to the southern style of baking. However, the northern style, which requires a little more preparation, is just as mouth-watering. Try both recipes for very pleasant variety. For pie crust, use recipe on page 434.

Sweet Potato Pie—Northern Style

¼ cup butter
3 eggs
1½ cups mashed sweet potatoes
½ cup white sugar
1 tsp. nutmeg

2 tbs. lemon juice
⅓ cup milk
½ tsp. salt
1 tsp. vanilla
1 tsp. cinnamon

Beat eggs and sugar. Add melted butter and spices. Blend with potatoes and lemon juice. Pour into unbaked pie shell and bake in hot oven 10 minutes. Reduce heat. Continue to bake 40 minutes longer. Serve plain or with cream.

Sweet Potato Pie—Southern Style

1½ lbs. sweet potatoes, or
2 large ones
2 cups sugar
¼ lb. butter

2 tsp. vanilla
1 tsp. cinnamon
½ tsp. nutmeg
4 slightly beaten eggs

Boil sweet potatoes in jackets until tender. Drain. Remove skin and mash with butter. Combine sugar, vanilla, cinnamon, nutmeg and eggs. Beat for 5 minutes. Bake in moderate oven (350°) 45 minutes, or until knife inserted in center comes out clean. Makes one 9-inch pie.

PART TWO

CALL ME MISTER

The "Boy" Who Was a Man!

Ray was an auto mechanic and a good one, too. But work was scarce for skilled black labor in Biloxi, so he decided to try his luck up north. He went to the railroad station to buy a ticket to Chicago, but was immediately ordered out and told to use the "Colored Entrance" and wait for his train in the separate waiting room.

When he finally boarded the train, he was approached by the conductor, who growled, "Where ya goin' boy?"

"Chicago, sir," answered Ray.

"Show me yer ticket, boy!"

"Certainly, sir. Here it is."

The conductor was about to turn away when Ray asked, "Excuse me, sir, but how long will it be before we are in Illinois?"

"Soon, boy," snapped the conductor. "And don't you leave this nigger car, you hear, boy?"

A little while later, Ray again asked, "Are we in Illinois yet?"

"No. I keep tellin' you, we'll be there soon, boy."

Twice more he asked the same question, and upon the third time, the conductor rasped, "Yes, we are now in Illinois. What about it, boy?"

"This about it," answered Ray in a voice as cold as ice: "You call me 'boy' just one more time and I'm gonna set you loose from your teeth!"

Time and Place

A young soldier, in uniform, was seated in the front of a Birmingham bus, in the days when the white folks of that city had not yet gotten straightened out about civil rights. At the next stop a white man boarded the vehicle, paid his fare, and approached the ebony soldier. "I'll take that seat," he said imperiously. "You move to the back where you belong."

The soldier didn't budge. "I have a question for you," he said, his voice low and even. "If we were on the battlefield, would you still want me to move to the back while *you* stayed up front?"

Insurance

It happened on the third night of the Watts riot, when conditions were at their worst. A squad car full of police gave chase after a speeding car in the flaming center of the city. The driver was ordered to pull over to the curb where, with pistols drawn, the officers ordered him out of the car for a search.

"I'm neutral," he protested. "You can't do this to me."

"The hell we can't!" growled an officer in the time-honored manner of standard police courtesy. In a few moments they found a revolver in the man's pocket.

"All right, buddy; what are you doing with this gun if you're so neutral?"

"That gun," said the driver, "is for just in case somebody doesn't believe me!"

Billy Bad-Mouths a Banker

Billy Williams was unemployed and desperate for funds to feed his family and pay the rent on his shabby Harlem flat. So he went to the Last National Bank of New York for a loan.

"Do you have any collateral, Billy?" asked the banker, eyeing the tattered man with suspicion.

"No," was the reply. "If I had collateral I wouldn't be here."

"Sorry, Billy," said the oily banker in his offensively avuncular manner. "We can't lend you any money."

Dejected, the man returned to the streets, but he was a determined fellow, and soon he found a low-paying job as a janitor in a real estate office. He quickly picked up the fundamentals of the business and before long he opened his own real estate office. All went well and he prospered. Within a few years he owned several apartment houses and profitable industrial sites.

One day he went to the bank to make a loan—the same bank that had turned him down when he was poor. He spoke to the same banker. "I want to borrow a hundred thousand dollars," he said quietly, thrusting his business card under the banker's nose.

The banker nodded. "Of course, Billy. . . ."

"The name is Bill Williams," he snapped. "*Mister* Williams!"

The banker's face paled. "Of—of c-c-course, Mister Williams," he stammered. "Just sign your name to this form. We'll take care of all the rest."

"I'll do nothing of the sort," retorted Mister Williams haughtily. "I don't sign my name to anything—I *dictate* it!"

Inflation

A wealthy but tight-fisted business tycoon checked into the Mayflower Hotel in Washington, D. C. and loudly demanded "a colored boy" to carry his luggage to his suite. The "boy," a student working his way through Howard University, brought the bags to the man's rooms as requested and opened the windows, as bellhops usually do, while waiting for the expected tip. He turned as the man asked, "Boy, have you got change for a dollar?"

The student looked at the bill and then met the other's eyes. "Sir," he replied smoothly, "in this hotel a dollar *is* change!"

Those White Kinfolks

Mr. Robert Carter, a retired school teacher down South, was working in his little vegetable garden one Sunday. It was a hot, August day and Mr. Carter grew very thirsty. "A nice, cold Coke would sure hit the spot," he said to himself. So, still wearing his old gardening clothes, he strolled to the new drugstore and was approached by the clerk, one that the ex-school teacher had never seen before.

"What would you like, Uncle?" asked the counterman.

Now if there was one thing that irked Mr. Carter the most, it was being addressed as "Uncle"—or for that matter as "boy." Nor did he like the female members of his race to be addressed as "Auntie." He regarded the clerk for a moment and then answered, "Would you mind, first, telling me what *you* would like?"

"Wh-what *I* would like?" stammered the surprised clerk. "I don't understand."

"It's all very simple," explained Mr. Carter. "You called me 'Uncle.' Now, whenever I meet one of my many nephews they always ask me for something or other. So I repeat: What would *you* like?"

Slim Slams a Snippy Southerner

Slim Robinson was one of the wealthiest farmer-landowners in his part of Connecticut, with upward of 40,000 acres under cultivation and another 5,000 lying fallow for next season's crop. Slim was a good-natured fellow of sixty or so, but a shrewd man, nevertheless. One *has* to be twice as smart as a white man to achieve that kind of wealth, and Slim knew his worth.

One day he donned some old clothes and set out on a tour of inspection, noting where further drainage was necessary, new grading needed, and all the while casting an expert eye on the condition of the soil and the growth rate of his crops. Soon he came upon a grader that was refinishing a gravel road on his vast proprty. He walked over to the operator. "You're making the left bank too steep," he said.

The young operator, newly arrived from the South, and on his first job in a northern state, gave the old man a quick scrutiny. "Uncle, this heah's the way the town ordered the road to be graded, an' that's the way it's gonna get done."

"Wrong on both counts," snapped Mr. Robinson. "I am not related to you, so don't call me Uncle. As to the town, I have news for you—you're *talking* to the town right now!"

United We Stand

A militant young guy made a private investigation of the books at the local library and was incensed to find more than fifty books which included the word "nigger" in their pages. He strode over to the librarian's desk and voiced his strong disapproval. "And what's more," he concluded ominously, "if those books are not off the shelves by tomorrow my people will picket this place."

"Why don't you colored people stop griping and bellyaching?" retorted the librarian. "There are hundreds and hundreds of books about whites that use the words 'bastards'—so what's the difference?"

"I'll tell you the difference right off," snapped the young militant. "You white bastards aren't organized!"

No Ma'm, Damn-Ya Ma'm

All her life, Eunice, a domestic worker, had heard of the almost "unbelievable freedom" enjoyed by black people in New York. The day came when she could no longer stand the South, so she bought a bus ticket and soon found herself in New York City.

When she found a place to live, she checked the job opportunities in the Sunday papers and before long she was being interviewed by a prospective employer—a Mrs. Schuyler van Throckmorton, of Park Avenue.

"Do you have any local experience?" asked Mrs. van Throckmorton.

"I jes' got heah," explained Eunice. "All my speriences bin in Sippi."

"Where?"

"Sippi."

"Oh, you mean *Missis*sippi," corrected the lady, smiling in a condescending manner.

"No, I mean zackly whut I say—*Sippi!*" Eunice repeated. "When I lef' dat place I done swo' I'd nevuh say Missus ag'in—to nobody!"

Fastest Cuss on the Bus

It was mid-December, 1955, in Montgomery, and the historic bus boycott was in its second successful week.* Emotions were running high among

---

* The 382-day Montgomery, Alabama, bus boycott started on December 1, 1955, to dramatize the racial discrimination practised by the Cleveland Avenue bus line in downtown Montgomery which forced Negroes to occupy seats in the rear, thus reserving seats in the front for whites. The late Louis Lomax, among other writers, educators and historians, traces the entire current Negro revolt to the moment Mrs. Rosa Parks, an obscure seamstress, defied the Jim Crow ordinance and refused to surrender her seat to a white passenger and move to the back of the bus. Her arrest was the "last straw" to the outraged Negro community, and within 24 hours, the decision was made to boycott the public conveyances and keep 17,000 blacks from giving financial support to their oppressors. The task of organizing the boycott fell to Martin Luther King, Jr., then an unheralded 27-year-old clergyman with little experience in the techniques of mass protest. Dr. King organized the Montgomery Improvement Association (MIA), a church oriented agency, as a focal point for all

blacks as well as whites, with both races reported to be buying guns and ammunition in the event of a "show-down." But there was a voice of reason that rose like a clarion call for common sense—the voice of the apostle of non-violence, the Rev. Martin Luther King, Jr.

"Victory will prevail only if we conduct the boycott in a peaceful manner," Dr. King warned his brethren. "I urge you to throw your guns in the trash can."

"Very well," said one of his followers, "I'll do as you say and throw my gun in the trash can, but believe me, Reverend, anybody comes around messin' with me, I'm gonna be back with the trash in a flash!"

He Won the Case

The judge glared down at the young student who was charged with creating a disturbance at his university by clamoring for a black studies department.

"Where is your legal counsel?" asked his honor. "You are entitled to a court-appointed lawyer if you cannot afford to retain one."

"I am representing myself," said the student.

"Have you studied law?"

"No, your honor, but I read a lot."

"Very well, how do you plead?"

"I plead *nollo contendere.*"

Taken aback by the "no contest" plea from this mere college kid, the judge asked, "Are you sure you know the meaning of *nollo contendere?*"

"Certainly," replied the young man. "It means I'm not guilty but how the hell am I gonna prove it?"

Maintaining Good Race Relations

She was young, she was curvacious, she was bronze and she was beautiful. And she was standing on the sidewalk outside the Greyhound Bus terminal in Washington, D. C.

A blonde, blue-eyed guy—the kind with narrow shoulders and a wide Cadillac—approached her in his luxurious car and pulled over to the curb. "Hi, baby, want a lift?" he called out. "I'm going all the way to California."

The young beauty was well acquainted with these white Lochinvars with a yearning for dark meat. She flashed her teeth in a wide smile. "How sweet of you, Paleface," she crooned. "Don't forget to bring me back an orange."

---

those in support of the boycott, a show of unity which enraged local authorities who sued immediately to have the boycott declared illegal. After arrests and stalemates, the U.S. Supreme Court, on December 13, 1956, ruled that Alabama's segregated seating laws were unconstitutional. It was this boycott that established Martin Luther King as a great Negro leader.

Apropos Apt Advertising

It is rumored that a bail bondsman in Los Angeles has stopped giving the usual business card, as is traditional. Now he hands out pocket combs. One side is imprinted with his name and address. On the other appears the advertising slogan: "Keep the fuzz out of your hair."

Militant Missives

Pity the poor correspondence-school principals. They're getting so nervous reading about school riots and campus disorders they're afraid to open their mail.

Vanity, Vanity—All Am Vanity

For more than a year, a young militant appeared on numerous television panels where he was interviewed by nationally known personalities. And almost daily his picture would be in a newspaper or magazine. He finally became so blown up with his own importance that he carried a card in his wallet reading:

I am a leader of my people.
In case of accident, call a reporter

Bye-Bye!

From Howard University comes this tidbit about the campus militant who was voted by his classmates as being the one "most likely to secede."

Black Power

"My son joined the Black Panthers," sighed the peace-loving old man. "I can't say I go along with everything they do, but at least they are making the whites act more courteously to our people. Only the other morning, I was in an elevator and a banker turned to the black operator and said, "I'd like to get to the fifth floor—if it isn't out of your way."

Pardon My Progress

At an NAACP banquet, a prominent member was discussing his home town and his reason for entering politics.

"The Mississippi town where I was born," he began, his eyes twinkling, "had a sheriff with an unlisted telephone number. So did the fire department.

We had only one doctor—a heart specialist whose office was seven flights up.

"I decided to get into politics so that I could more effectively campaign for a black man on the United States Supreme Court. If that happened, it was my hope we could shorten its name to The Supremes!"

Forester Hypo's a Hippie*

Elnathan Forester, the only black merchant in his area of Watts, not only demands but commands the respect of the younger generation.

A young man, sporting a do-rag on his head, and barefooted, entered the store as Mr. Forester was sorting some cartons. "Hey man, gimme an empty box!" ordered the youth.

The white-haired old storekeeper regarded him solemnly for a few moments and then, his voice quiet, he replied, "Hey Man quit this place two hours ago. He couldn't stand the freaks in the neighborhood. There's just me here, and I'm *Sir!*"

The youth came out of his slouch as if he'd received an electric shock, stood erect, and said with military smartness, "Yes *sir!*"

Then, as a dozen customers gaped in astonishment, the teenager continued, "Sir, would you permit me to take an empty carton home with me, if you please?"

Old Mr. Forester said he thought it could be arranged.

"I appreciate this," the young man concluded. "May I express my apologies for my thoughtless remark?"

Perhaps the youngster was being derisive, perhaps not. But ever since, old Mr. Forester has been addressed in a respectful manner by the neighborhood toughs.

Jumping to Conclusions

A Southern racist and a Northern "liberal," both white, decided to share expenses and go on an African safari together. They were after big game—lions and tigers and such.

Loaded down with high-powered rifles, they were stalking through the Congolese jungle, about twenty or thirty feet apart, when the northerner heard the crack of a rifle. He rushed over to where his hunting partner was smiling proudly.

"What did you shoot?" asked the guy from the North.

"I just shot a black panther," said the Southerner proudly.

"What?" exclaimed the other, horrified. "Without even a trial?"

---

* From the late Matt Weinstock's column in the *Los Angeles Times*, July 24, 1969. Copyright, *The Los Angeles Times*.

He Was There When They Scandalized His Name

A patrol car was cruising the area when the two policemen in the car spotted a man beating another man with a two-by-four. They pulled over to the curb, jumped out and collared the attacker.

"All right," said one of the officers when the two participants had been separated and quieted down, "what was this fighting all about?"

"He called me a black bastard," snarled the smaller man.

"Well, that wasn't nice, but you didn't have to nearly kill him with a two-by-four," argued the policeman.

"Oh yeah? What would you do, man, if he called *you* a black bastard?"

The white policeman tried hard to suppress a smile. "He would hardly call me that."

"Maybe not," replied the other insistently, "but supposin' he called you the kind of bastard you are!"

Too True!

Have you heard about the young architect who visited Harlem for the first time?

He took one look at the tenements and muttered "Early Caveman!"

Great Leap Forward

Dick Gregory was ruminating on the fact that, as yet, we do not have any Negro astronauts.

"Just think," he said, "if we get a black astronaut we'll be the first race of people in history to go directly from the back of the bus to the moon."

Cosby's Cautious Comment

"God is trying to solve the race relations problem without making it look like a miracle."

BILL COSBY
(NBC-TV: April 4, 1970)

Passing

. . . well, at least my *teeth* are white!"

Tell It Like It Is, Judge!

Supreme Court Justice Thurgood Marshall* was addressing a large assembly in commemoration of Emancipation Day. Toward the end of his speech, he observed:

"The United States has been called the melting pot of the world. But it seems to me that the colored man either missed getting into the pot or he got melted down."

To Whom It May Concern

Don't call a black man "boy" unless he's under ten years of age.

Goin' Down the Road Feelin' Sad

If you ever been to Crawdad Junction then you know that place next to the swamp where the four roads cross, one t'other. There's one road headin' south, another goin' north, and the other two pointin' east and west.

One time, my pa was passin' by where the roads all meet, and a big shiny Cad'lac druv up and come to a stop alongside him. The rich cracker what's drivin' the car leans outen the window and yells, "Hey, you, boy!—Where this road go?"

My pa, him bein' seventy year old, don't 'preciate bein' called 'boy,' but all he say is "I don't know."

The white man ask, "Then where this other road go?"

Pa, he say "I don't know."

"How about this here road?"

"I don't know that either."

The white man gets all red in the face and hollers, "Boy, don't you know nothin'?"

And pa say, "I know one thing—I ain't lost!"

---

* Thurgood Marshall was born in Baltimore, in 1908. He received a B.A. degree from Lincoln University as a pre-medical student and was then admitted to the Howard University Law School, where he graduated in 1933 at the top of his class. After private practice in Baltimore he joined the National Association for the Advancement of Colored People, and, in 1938, he became head of that organization's legal staff. In 1958 he was named director-counsel of NAACP's Legal Defense and Education Fund. He played a vital role in the now historic 1954 Supreme Court decision on school desegregation in addition to many other important cases in his distinguished career. In July, 1961, he was appointed a judge of the U.S. Court of Appeals, and in July, 1965 he became Solicitor General. Thurgood Marshall was elevated to the United States Supreme Court in 1967, the first Negro to attain that position in American history.

CORN BREAD

A soul food dinner without home-made corn bread is unthinkable. These old recipes represent the best variety of corn bread which was "ash-cake pone," baked in, or over, wood ashes. It is celebrated in the poem, "De Old 'oman An' Me," pages 305-306.

Corn Bread—Alabama Style

2 cups white cornmeal	2 tsp. baking powder
2 eggs	2 tbs. drippings or shortening
1 tbs. sugar	2½ cups milk or buttermilk
1 tsp. salt	

Put cornmeal, sugar, salt and baking powder into mixing bowl. Add eggs and milk. Melt drippings or shortening in baking pan in oven. Stir into batter. Pour batter into pan and bake 20-25 minutes at 450°.

Corn Bread with Salt

Follow corn bread recipe. Dice one cup salt pork, and brown in oven. Use drippings in batter, pour batter over salt pork in baking pan. Bake 25-30 minutes at 450°.

Misplaced Railroad

A Federal official was out in a rural section of Louisiana, snooping around on some government business or other, asking the same interminable questions of the black folks that they have been asking for years. Without prior notice, he received a telegram requesting that he return to Washington, D. C. immediately.

He packed his luggage and asked the desk clerk in the dilapidated little house that passed for a hotel, "How do I get to the railroad depot?"

"The train don't stop here," he was informed. "Our porter will drive you to the next town, though."

The government man expected a pick-up truck, or at least an old car, but the porter showed up with a mule-drawn wagon. As they bumped along the dusty, rutted road, the official became increasingly irritated with the primitive service. After an hour or so of the turtle-paced journey, the government man exploded. "No wonder you people can't get anywhere," he fumed. "Didn't you ever think of building the depot closer to town?"

The porter nodded. "We thought of it some," he agreed, "but then we 'cided to build it 'longside the railroad!"

The Linguist

This Harlem cat was on his way to California in his beat-up old jalopy. Crossing New Mexico, he came to a little border town and, feeling hungry, he stopped and went into a small cafe for a sandwich and coffee. He sat down at the counter and waited to be served. Finally, the counterman came over and said, "Beat it! We don't serve Nigras here."

"I ain't a Negro," said the guy. "I'm Mexican."

"Yeah?" said the waiter, reaching under the counter for a .38 Special. "Let's hear you say somethin' in Spanish."

This Harlem cat, he got off the seat, walked to the door, and said, *"Adios!"*

Junior's One-Day Illness

After the Watts riot, many parents of ghetto schoolchildren threatened to keep their offspring out of school for one day, as a form of protest, unless certain conditions were improved. The white principal of one all-black school warned that such absence would not be tolerated unless a good reason was provided.

One irate father sent this note to school:

Dear Sir:
     Please excuse my son, John, for his absence from school yesterday. He had to remain home because of illness. . . . He was sick of segregation!

Seek and Ye Shall Find

Two cooks were needed at the university's cafeteria. The first to get a job was one of the students, a highly intelligent girl who was working her way through college. The other was a near-illiterate who had dropped out of school in the fourth grade.

Their first day on the job, the uneducated girl asked crossly, "Where my pie-pan at?"

Replied the college student, "Right there in back of your personal pronoun!"

Color Scheme

George, who was rather light-complexioned, was having an argument with Bob. "Man, you're black as midnight," taunted George.

"Maybe so," Bob replied coolly, "but I'd rather be black as midnight than green with envy!"

Ghost Town

One does not need a university degree to enunciate the taut retort—the classic put-down. Consider the case of Joshua, a country lad who visited the "big city" of Charlottesville for the first time.

Josh had applied for a job as handyman on the University of Virginia grounds, and on his way into the main building he stopped to watch a construction crew. They had excavated a large hole to accommodate the foundation for a new annex. The foreman on the job was in a talkative mood, though it scarcely improved his manners.

"A mighty big hole, eh, boy?"

"Yes, it sure is."

"You a student here, boy?"

"No, I never did get to high school."

"Well, boy, you know what a hole is, don't you?"

Josh, whose temperature rose three degrees every time the man uttered the word "boy," muttered "Yeah, I know what a hole is. What you gonna do with it?"

The foreman grinned. "We're gonna bury every sonofabitch in Charlottesville in this hole—that's what we're gonna do, boy."

Josh reflected on this information for awhile and then asked, "Who you gonna get to cover y'all up?"

Greater Pay Hath No Man

Ambassador Carl T. Rowan,* it is said, delights in telling of an encounter during his first weeks in Washington, D. C. Apocryphal or not, the amusing "put down" merits repeating.

It seems that Rowan was mowing his lawn one afternoon in the fashionable section of the District where he had just moved. A neighbor watched him for awhile and then sauntered over. "I'd like to get my grass cut, too," he began. "How much are they paying you for mowing this lawn?"

Ambassador Rowan looked around, as though to divulge a great secret. "Confidentially, I don't get paid at all," he said. "The lady of the house just lets me sleep with her!"

The Diplomat

The manager of the Dixie Hotel called the bell boy to his office. "You remember that society lady in room 314? She checked out this morning and asked me to give you this five dollar tip. She said you were the politest man she had ever seen. What happened?"

"It wasn't just politeness," explained the boy. "Yesterday, when I thought she was out, I opened her bathroom door and there she was in the tub."

"My God! What did you do?"

"I just said 'Excuse me, sir,' and went out. That 'excuse me' was courtesy," he concluded, "and the 'sir' was tact."

Parable of the Goose and the Fox

Josie arrived home in tears. "I not only lost the case but they fined me fifty dollars," she sobbed. "And I was innocent, too!"

Her aged grandfather, who happened to be visiting, asked what had happened.

"I was driving along Peachtree Street and obeying all the traffic rules, when suddenly this white man drove right into my car—from behind. There were even witnesses who said it was his fault," she wept. "But when my trial came up they found *me* guilty! I don't understand it."

---

* Carl T. Rowan, outstanding journalist and author, served as Ambassador to Finland in 1963, and in the following year as Director of the United States Information Agency (USIA), resigning from that post in 1965 to continue his career in journalism. Born in Ravenscroft, Tennessee, August 11, 1925, Rowan, at the age of 19, became one of the first 15 Negroes to be commissioned by the U.S. Navy during World War II. Following the war, he acquired his B.A. from Oberlin College, in Ohio, and later earned an M.A. in journalism from the University of Minnesota. Rowan's first book, *South of Freedom*, was partly autobiographical. His second and third books, *The Pitiful and the Proud* (1956), and *Go South in Sorrow* (1957), both won critical acclaim, as did his biography of Jackie Robinson, the famous baseball star, *Wait Till Next Year* (1960). Mr. Rowan is now a newspaper columnist, syndicated throughout the United States.

"Hush your crying, honey," said her grandfather. "Dry your eyes and listen, while I tell you a story:

"Many years ago a fat goose was paddling across a lake with nothing more on its mind than getting to the other side. But, hiding in the woods on the other shore, watching and waiting for her, was a fox. The moment the goose reached dry land, the fox jumped out of the bushes and grabbed her.

" 'This is my lake, and these are my woods,' said the fox. 'You are guilty of trespassing, so as punishment, I am going to eat you up.'

"But the goose demanded her civil rights. 'This lake and these woods belong to everybody,' she protested. 'They're just as much mine as yours. I demand a trial by jury.'

"The fox agreed, and they went to the nearest court. But when the case came up for a hearing, Sister Goose saw that the judge was a fox, that her own court-appointed lawyer was a fox, and that every member of the jury was a fox.

"There's no need to tell you the details of the trial: Sister Goose was convicted and all the foxes shared in eating her flesh."

Josie's grandfather put his arm around her shoulder. "Honey, don't you ever forget this," he said, his voice gentle but grim: "When the judge, the lawyers and the jury are all foxes, only a goose would expect anything else than to be eaten!"

RSVP

"Listen to this, grandma," exclaimed the young man as his eye fell on a newspaper story. "The Reverend Martin Luther King has been invited to the White House for lunch."

"Who done the invitin'?" asked the grandmother.

"Lyndon Johnson, the President of the United States of America, that's who!"

"I ain't so sure the President really likes our people," said the grandmother after thinking it over. "Ef he was to ax me, I'd say 'Thankee, suh, but I ain't hongry!' "

Remembered Quote

"One nice thing about silence—it can't be repeated."

MALCOLM X*

---

* The fiery, controversial Malcolm X was born Malcolm Little in Omaha, May 19, 1925, the son of a Baptist preacher. As a boy his parents took him to Lansing, Michigan, where his father was run over and killed by a streetcar and his mother committed to a mental institution. Leaving school after the eighth grade, he made his way to New York, working for a time as a waiter at Smalls Paradise, in Harlem. He soon became part of the seamy underworld life of the ghetto, selling marijuana and himself turning to cocaine addiction. In 1946 he was sentenced to a 10-year prison term for burglary. While in prison he became acquainted with the Black Muslim sect and was converted

Wrath of God

Father Divine, founder of the Peace Mission cult, has been quoted many times as saying, "I do not claim to be God, but I produce God and shake the earth with it." Nevertheless, his followers worshipped him as God incarnate on earth, nor did he make any serious attempts to dissuade them from that belief.

It may never be known exactly what Father Divine thought of himself, or whether he was sincere or enjoying a private joke with reference to his trial in Long Island, New York. He had been arrested in Sayville, charged with being a "public nuisance," and sentenced to a six-month term in jail. Ironically, however, four days after the trial, the judge in his case died of a heart attack.

Said Father Divine: "I hated to do it!"

PART THREE

MILITARY MANEUVERS

Confidence Supreme

Frankly speaking, Dan wasn't the best educated man in the world, but none can deny that he knew how to use what brains he had.

The day he was inducted into the army, a recruiting sergeant confronted him with a long list of questions.

"Name?" asked the sergeant.

Dan told him.

"Age?"

Dan told him that, too.

"Race?"

Dan's mouth spread in a wide smile, his chocolate-brown face crinkled with amusement.

---

to its point of view. Unlike the sect's founder, Elijah Muhammad, Malcolm X sought wide publicity and made a number of inflammatory statements before predominantly white audiences. When in 1963, he characterized the Kennedy assassination as "chickens coming home to roost," he was suspended from the Black Muslims by Elijah Muhammad, whereupon he formed his own protest group, the Organization of Afro-American Unity. He was shot to death in 1965, in what observers saw as a vendetta murder by Black Muslim "enforcers," a claim which Elijah Muhammad publicly denied. Malcolm X was buried as Al Hajj Malik al-Shabazz, the name he assumed after his pilgrimage to Mecca in 1964.

The sergeant also smiled and checked off the proper box. "Now for the last question," he said. "Who do you want your remains sent to?"

Dan studied the question for a few moments and then said, "Nobody. I expect I'll bring them home myself!"

Force of Habit

Poor Willie was the most hen-pecked man in all Vernon Parish—perhaps in the whole state of Louisiana. His wife, a domineering, complaining, quick-tempered woman, nagged him unmercifully with a tongue that could clip a hedge.

The day finally came when he was able to get away from her—he was conscripted into the army. His first day on the drill grounds was a nightmare. The sergeant screamed his orders, shouted at the recruits in his squad in a way that even surpassed Willie's wife.

"Forward! Left! Right! Halt! About face! Mark time! March!"—the drill sergeant's words came spitting out like machine-gun bullets.

Willie, confused at all these rapid-fire orders, turned the wrong way and kept marching after the order halt. "Hey, you stupid jerk!" bellowed the sergeant. "Can't you obey simple orders?"

"Yes, darlin'," mumbled Willie.

Sweet Sympathy

It was his very first day in the army and the recruit was unlucky enough to draw down KP. He was clumsily washing pots and pans when the company commander strode into the mess hall on a tour of inspection.

"How long have you been in the army?" asked the officer, after watching the youth perform his tasks in such an awkward manner.

"This here's my first day, man," replied the young fellow, who had not the faintest notion of an officer's insignia. "How long you been in?"

The astonished officer was unable to speak for a few moments. Realizing, however, that the boy could hardly be aware of his rank, he smiled and replied, "Thirty-two years."

"Chris'amighty!" exclaimed the recruit. "Man, if I was you I'da gone over the hill long ago!"

Playing It Safe

"Chaplain, kin I borry a Ol' Tes'amint what the Jews use fer a Bible?" asked the GI.

"Now see here," protested the chaplain; "last week you borrowed a Catholic Bible, and only the other day you asked for the Protestant Scriptures. I happen to know you are a Baptist. What in the world do you want with all those different versions?"

"I heer'd we're goin' to Vietnam," explained the young soldier, "and I ain't takin' no chances."

Parley Vous...

There was much talk about the imminence of D-Day, when the Allies were expected to invade the continent of Europe and clobber Hitler's armies.

Jack was sure he'd be stationed in France, so he decided to learn a little of the French language. He listened attentively while in a restaurant and heard the patron order a meal from the haughty waiter. Now it was his turn.

"Suh," he began grandly, waving the menu, "I'll start off with one o' those demi tassies—an' you kin bring me a cupacawfee on the side."

Be It Ever So Humble

It was Christmas Eve in the Middle East, and two GI's, stationed in Bethlehem, were reminiscing about past Yule seasons.

"At least we're in Bethlehem, where Christ was born," commented one soldier.

"Personally," replied the other, "I wish for Christ sake I was back in Newark, where I was born!"

If It Moves, Salute It!

A brand new soldier, fresh out of Chicago's southside, was on his way over to the PX one evening when he encountered a young lieutenant, fresh out of West Point, and a stickler for rules and regulations.

The Chicago boy smiled pleasantly. "How you this mawnin'?"

The outraged lieutenant stopped him abruptly and gave him a tongue-lashing. "And what's more," he concluded, "you will henceforth obey all military commands, observe all the courtesies due an officer of the United States Army and—don't you *ever* forget this!—you will salute!"

"Fevensake, man!" muttered the recruit. "If I knowed you was gonna take on like this I wouldn'ta spoke to you a-tall!"

Color Charley Black

The black GI's who landed in France during World War II were pleasantly surprised with the courteous, friendly treatment accorded them by the French people. For many, this was the first time they had ever been looked upon as equals, without a shred of hypocrisy by the whites.

But a few segregation-minded officers at the Pentagon took a dim view of this attitude. To put an end to such fraternizing, one of the racist officers drafted a letter in which it was cautiously stated that blacks were "different" than whites and should be treated accordingly.

Upon receipt of the letter, it was turned over to a high-ranking French officer for reply.

"Gentlemen," he wrote, "I am forced to agree with your evaluation. The black Americans are indeed different than we had expected, but your white men are absolutely impossible!"

Hero Worship—Army Style

This was the first day in the army for heavyweight boxing champion Joe Louis. A young 2nd lieutenant approached the champ with a thick sheaf of papers. "Just sign these and you can get your uniform," he said cheerfully.

Joe nodded, sat down at the table, and proceeded to affix his signature to each and every sheet, as ordered. A half hour later, when he had completed the task, the white lieutenant returned, gathered up the papers and, to the other's surprise, murmured a distinct "thank you."

"Tell me something, sir," inquired Joe, "how come you needed all those signatures when every one of the papers was the same?"

The officer smiled. "To tell the truth," he answered, "the original, the duplicate and the triplicate are strictly official. The other fifty are autographs!"

Meet the New Permanent K.P.

Wally was the only black soldier in his outfit and the other fellows, although they liked him, took every opportunity to play practical jokes on the poor guy. But Wally learned fast. He could dish it out as well as take it, and his sharp wit earned him the respect of the rest of the men.

One evening, Gen. Robert Christ, of the 1st Division, decided to make a surprise inspection. He approached the gate and was halted by good ol' Wally. "Who goes there?" he called, as per regulations.

"General Christ," answered the officer.

"Oh, yeah?" cried Wally, thoroughly alert to the many practical jokes he had endured. "Advance and give the Sermon on the Mount."

Playing for Keeps

Jimmy became discouraged with army life within two hours after he was sworn in. He had just filled out the application for his $10,000 life insurance policy when he asked the chaplain, "Sir, why did I have to complete these death benefit papers in triplicate?"

Replied the chaplain: "One for the Father, one for the Son and one for the Holy Ghost!"

Moment of Truth

The unpopular Vietnam war was at its height and countless thousands of reluctant young men were being drafted into the military service.

"I already got my 'greetings,' " said one youth mournfully. "Guess we'll all be in it before the year is over."

"Well, I ain't shooting it out with no Congs," declared another of the young men. "The minute them bullets start flyin', I'm takin' off."

"You can't do that," said the first lad. "You can be court-martialed for cowardice."

"I got news for you," retorted the prospective draftee. "I'd rather have people say 'Yonder he goes' instead of 'Here he lies!' "

The More Firma the Less Terra

The only close-up view of an airplane Jack had ever seen was in the movies or on television. They just don't have landing fields in the vicinity of Drexel Boulevard, in Chicago. So, understandably enough, he was somewhat apprehensive when Uncle Sam inducted him into the Air Force.

"Sir," he protested to the officer in charge, "I ain't no pilot. I don't even *like* them airplanes!"

"Have you ever been up in a plane?" asked the officer.

"Hel-l-l no!"

"Then you're hardly in a position to judge. I'm sending you up for a ride with our most experienced pilot instructor. Report to me when you come back down."

A half hour later, visibly shaken, Jack returned to complete his interview.

"I hope you enjoyed your first plane ride," said the officer amiably.

"Well, as long as you mention it," Jack grumbled, "I didn't 'specially care for either one of them."

"Either one? What are you talking about? You only had one ride."

"You ain't counting the way I do," said Jack. "I had two—my first and my last!"

A Time for Everything

When Jerry returned home after two years in Vietnam, his old buddies gathered around to hear about his exploits. But one friend recalled Jerry's determination to stay out of the war. "You said you would never fight," he reminded the war hero. "How come you got all them medals on your chest?"

"It all started when I got that draft notice," explained Jerry. "I told the draft board 'I ain't mad at no Viet Congs and I ain't gonna fight.' So they sent two big MP's after me and they dragged me to boot camp.

"At boot camp, I told the drill sergeant, 'I ain't mad at no Viet Congs and I ain't gonna fight.' But they whupped my tail in line and three months later they put me on a ship.

"I told the ship's captain, 'I ain't mad at no Viet Congs and I ain't gonna fight,' but that ship just kept sailing along until we got to Vietnam. I got assigned to a squad and we set out for a rice paddy in enemy territory.

"I told my corporal, 'I ain't mad at no Viet Congs and I ain't gonna fight.'

"Then the Viet Congs started the bullets flying. I ducked and yelled out, "Ya sons-a-bitches, who the hell ya think ya shootin' at?' "

Surface Opinion

This farm boy from someplace deep in the heart of Texas had never been more than ten miles from his home. One day he was drafted and, after boot training, was shipped off to Vietnam.

The ship was in the middle of the Pacific Ocean, and as far as the eye could see there was nothing but water—vast, rolling, mysterious—from horizon to horizon.

"Man, I never did see so much water in my life," said the farm boy to his buddy.

"This is nothing," said the other, a wise guy from the big city, "You're just looking at the top of it!"

Discipline

"Don't you pay no mind to all them stories about democracy in the army," said the newly-released soldier. "The army ain't changed a speck. You still do exactly what you're told. When they say 'eyes right!' they expect to hear 'em *click!*"

GI Debut

"Ain't no doubt I'm in the army now," moaned the draftee. "I was sworn in and cussed out all in one hour!"

Swivel Rights

Tired, homesick, and longing for a friendly voice, a Georgia boy was walking his lonely post, doing sentry duty in a jungle outpost in the Far East.

It was past three in the morning when he heard the sound of an approaching truck. Alert, every nerve quivering, he held his rifle at the ready and waited. Soon the truck loomed out of the mist and came to a halt in front of him where he was clearly outlined in the glare of the truck's headlights.

"Who goes there?" called the sentry, expecting, of course, to hear the proper password.

"Get the hell out of the road, nigger," came a snarling voice from the truck, "or I'll run right over your black hide!"

"Pass on through," called the sentry. "I ain't heard them familiar words since I left Georgia to fight for democracy!"

Butterfingers!

"General, one drop of this germ warfare fluid can wipe ten billion people off the face of the earth in just . . . OOOPS!"

PART FOUR

LET MY PEOPLE GO VOTE

The Littlest Brother

Jonas, who lived in a small community in the deep south, left home to vote—for the first time in his life. But when he returned, a few hours later, his wife at once noticed his grim expression. "What happened?" she cried.

"I never did get to vote," he said. "I was met by a delegation of Klansmen. I'm afraid, honey, they'll be here tonight. We'll have to leave—right now!"

Frightened, the wife immediately began to pack, while her husband went to the railroad depot to purchase tickets to the North. During his absence, the wife crammed all their belongings into boxes and suitcases until only one suitcase was left. She gathered up a few items of clothing and opened the suitcase—and jumped back with a scream. Inside was a huge black rat.

The wife grabbed a broom to defend herself.

"Please, lady, don't git scairt!" pleaded the rat, sitting up on its haunches. "I'm jes' tryin' to get outen this damn place myse'f!"

BISCUITS

Hot biscuits, with gobs of melted butter and honey—now *that's* soul food! The Carolinas get the credit for these Colonial-times recipes.

Beaten Biscuits—Old-Fashioned Style

2 cups flour	½ cup shortening
½ tsp. salt	⅓ cup milk

Measure and sift dry ingredients into mixing bowl. Measure shortening, then milk. Cut shortening into flour as in biscuit making. Add milk gradually. Mix thoroughly, making a stiff dough. Flour board or block. Put dough on board and knead for about 5 minutes. Beat dough with smooth wooden stick for 20 minutes—about 1,000 strokes. Beat dough until flat. Fold and continue beating hard as possible. Roll dough to ⅓-inch thickness. Fold and roll ½-inch thickness. Cut the dough with biscuit cutter. Prick each biscuit with fork three or four times. Place on oiled baking sheet ½ inch apart. Bake at 375°, 25 minutes or until light brown. Serve hot or cold. Yield: 24 biscuits.

Southern Yeast Biscuits

5 to 6 cups flour	2 tsp. salt
¼ cup shortening	1 tbs. sugar
1 yeast cake	2 cups milk
¼ cup warm water	1 egg
2 tbs. melted butter	

Scald milk, add shortening and sugar. Cool. Dissolve yeast in warm water and stir into milk. Stir in 2 cups flour and egg. Blend well. Set aside to rise in a warm place. When double its bulk, place dough on bread board and knead in the rest of flour until smooth and elastic. Roll dough out to half-inch thickness. Cut with biscuit cutter. Dip each biscuit in a bit of melted butter. Place on a cookie sheet, about one inch apart, to rise. When doubled in bulk, bake in a hot oven, 400°, 20-25 minutes.

Democracy in the Polling Place

Al, a recent college graduate, applied to vote in Mississippi.
"What you want, boy?" snapped the white (naturally) registrar.
"I want to vote."
"Oh, you do, eh? You had any schoolin'?"
"I'm a college graduate."
"One o' them kind, eh? Well, you gotta take a lit'racy tes'."
"I'm ready."

The clerk shuffled some papers and, without looking up, asked, "Tell me, what are all the amendments to the Constitution?"

Without hesitation, Al named them—*all!*

The registrar looked up—for the first time. "Hmmm. Well, tell me, boy; who were the wives of the first twenty Vice Presidents of the United States, and what were their favorite breakfast foods?"

Al named them, and elaborated on their breakfast preferences.

The registrar's face was fiery red with suppressed fury. "All right, here's your last question," he snarled. "Tell me, if you're so damned smart, what's going to happen to you if you ain't out of this democratic polling place in ten seconds flat?"

Generation Gap

The white folks in and around Delta, Alabama, were mighty worried now that the Federal Government was enforcing the law of the land. No longer could they foist white supremist politicians upon the black citizens. In self-defense, the local Democratic Party nominated a man who suddenly claimed to be a "moderate" toward Negroes—whatever that means.

The "moderate" politician, a man named Walker, decided to visit the black section of town to garner their votes, without which he could not win the election. The first man he ran into was none other than a former employee. "Hello, Uncle Joe," he greeted the elderly man with a fine show of friendship, though he carefully refrained from holding out his hand for the customary political handshake, "I hope you're gonna vote for me."

"I sure am," said Joe.

"Fine! I always knew you had good sense—for a Nigra. And how about that son of yours: He gonna vote for me, too?"

The old man shook his head. "No, I don't think so," he replied. "My son can read."

They Just Dropped in for Tea

A Federal judge in Mississippi was hearing a case in which certain whites were charged with intimidating a Negro.

"You say that ten members of the Ku Klux Klan visited your home on the night of November 3rd?"

"Yes, your honor."

"Did they state the purpose of their visit?"

"They urged me to stay away from the voting booths on Election Day."

"Is that all?" asked the judge. "I would hardly call that intimidation."

"I don't know what to call it, either, your honor," said the plaintiff, "but it did make me wonder why it took ten men to do the urging."

Don't Quo Your Status

The minister faced his congregation, his manner grave. "My subject, this Sunday, is the contemporary socio-economic status of the disenfranchised, impoverished black recipients of less than their rightful due under the constitutional guarantees afforded Americans of Caucasian heritage."

"What's he sayin'?" whispered Mrs. Wilcox to her husband.

"He say," whispered back the husband, "he's gonna talk about the mess we's in."

Call Me by My Rightful Name

In 1970, a Federal judge in Florida ruled that the busing of black children to white schools was mandatory. Governor Claude Kirk, of that state, lost his battle to prevent school integration, and among the first to present himself at a lily-white school was an eight-year-old black boy from an impoverished rural section.

The first day in class, the white teacher, a dyed-in-the-wool Dixiecrat, asked the youngster his name. "Mister Tibbs," replied the boy.

The shocked teacher asked him to repeat. "Mister Tibbs," said the boy again. Several times more she urged him to give his first name but was always met with the same answer. In desperation, she finally sent for the boy's mother and explained her problem.

"There ain't no problem a-tall," said the mother slowly. "When he was borned I knowed he'd be called 'boy' or some other name, long as he lived in the South—but never 'Mister.' So I done somethin' 'bout it. I *christened* him Mister—that's his name an' that's whut y'alls are gonna call him— *Mister* Tibbs!"

Maddox Visits a Negro School

Georgia's Governor Lester Maddox, he of the infamous Pickrick axe-handles for beating black people, decided to show the nation how liberal-minded he was by visiting a rural schoolhouse, all of whose pupils were Negroes.

The flustered young teacher introduced him to the fifth grade students.

"Boys and girls, this is the Honorable Lester Maddox, the governor of our state."

Maddox arranged his features in the semblance of a benign smile and said, "Children, Ahm gonna ast ya a few questions. Now don' yawl be ascairt, jes' 'cause Ah'm a white man. Ah want ya ter speak right out an' tell me—your frien'—whut's on your mind."

"Oh Lord," the teacher prayed silently but fervently, "let him pick on some of our brighter pupils."

And the Lord took his eye off the sparrow for a moment and said "OK."

Governor Maddox pointed to one of the boys. "You there, what's your name?"

The youngster rose from his seat. "My name, sir, is James Barton."

Maddox beamed. "How 'bout that! You talk jes' like white folks—like me!"

James thought it more prudent to keep his big mouth shut. He simply nodded.

But the governor's eyes suddenly grew hard. "Don' you shake your head at me, boy!" he snapped. "Jes' say 'yassuh' or 'nosuh.'"

"Yazzuh," said the boy dutifully.

"That's much better. Now, tell me somethin', boy. Hoccum you ain't talkin' like your mammy an' pappy learned ya? You tryin' ter sound white, boy?"

"Nosuh, massa, guv'nuh. Ah ain't speakin' nothin' seppin whut Ah wuz l'arned."

Maddox smiled again. "That's much better. "A nigra is much better off talkin' like he's s'posed ta."

Master James Barton had about all he could take. "That depends on the environmental, social, economic and spiritual factors involved," he began, enunciating carefully. "Dialect is a matter of local custom, its usage differing from region to region in accordance with changing mores, among other reasons. My parents are both teachers and they articulate the English language in a manner that would scarcely be understood by the less privileged Caucasians of this state. On the other hand, your own articulation of the same language would be fairly comprehensible to the uneducated Afro-Americans of the great and glorious state of Georgia."

"Wh-what was that you said?" gasped the astounded, uncomprehending governor.

"I say, Boss, you is absolutely correck."

High in the heavens there was a faint rumbling of thunder—soft, rolling and far away, but which sounded mighty like a chuckle.

Grammar Lesson

It was during the Great Depression when Howard Blye, a white youth, joined the Civilian Conservation Corps in New York City and, after processing at Fort Dix, New Jersey, was sent to Leesville, Louisiana.

There were few recreational facilities at the CCC camp, so Howard began to visit the town during the evening hours. Soon, he became involved in a teaching program conducted by local Negroes—among the very first voter registration classes for blacks in the entire state.

A few evenings after the white Northerner had started teaching his class, he was approached by the sheriff. "What's your name?" asked the officer, his voice steely.

"Howard Blye, sir," responded the white lad.

The sheriff eyed him narrowly. "What are you—some kind of nigger lover?"

Howard considered the question for a moment or two before he answered. "*Ne*gro lover!" he corrected.*

Witness for the State

It was a time of racial crises in the sovereign state of Mississippi. Headlines throughout the nation proclaimed the unwillingness of the state to accommodate blacks in the schools, in housing, employment, voting and the rest of the oppressive tactics so familiar to Americans everywhere.

To counter all this adverse publicity, the governor decided to embark on a course of favorable public relations. He called the legislature into emergency session and they agreed upon a plan to utilize the facilities of all three television networks—CBS, NBC and ABC. It was further agreed that they would have a black man open the program by praising the state of Mississippi and denouncing all detractors as liars. There remained only one problem: Where would they find such a man? After being rejected by every Negro to whom they broached the subject, the governor remembered his gardener, an old man who was the very essence of the stereotyped Uncle Tom. He sent for him at once.

"Amos, I'll give you fifty dollars if you will tell the people of the United States—indeed, the whole world—how wonderful it is for a nig—er—I mean a *Nee*gro—to live in this blessed state. Tell them how free you are, what fine schools you people have, all the good jobs and things you enjoy here."

"How I gonna do that, boss?" asked Amos, his eyes wide.

"On television. Just think, Amos, you'll be a big TV star and everybody will respect you. In fact, you can take my word for it, we'll all *love* you!"

"Sho', boss, I'd like that fine. I'll do it!"

So the great day came. Representatives of the world press were there; television cameras were everywhere; huge spotlights flooded the area, illuminating the scores of high state officials who were attending the gala occasion. All over the nation, and in fifty foreign countries, vast numbers of people tuned in their TV sets. Millions of others switched on their radios. From

---

* The incident occurred in Leesville, Louisiana, in April, 1934. The officer referred to in the story was Sheriff Word; the discussion witnessed by writer Dan Sping.

the White House to Buckingham Palace, from the Vatican to the Kremlin, the planet Earth was as one, waiting for this humble black man who was about to denounce his own people as a pack of liars and agitators, and to glorify the state of Mississippi.

Amos sidled up to the center of the stage and nervously eyed the twenty-five TV cameras stationed around him. The governor made a short introduction and then announced, ". . . and now, ladies and gentlemen, I am proud to present to you the one honest Nigra in Mississippi—the one man whose word is gospel. He will now tell you the truth about our grand state. I now present to you the one and only UNCLE AMOS'"

Amos cleared his throat and approached the microphones with a copy of the well-rehearsed speech in his trembling hands. He leaned forward, the better to be heard, and, with perspiration stippling his forehead, he yelled—

"Hel-l-l-p!"

Eternal Fraternals

Many of us have heard of the NAAWP—the National Association for the Advancement of White People—a racist organization that flourished briefly in the southeastern states in the late fifties and early sixties.

Now the bigots have dreamed up a new one: SPONGE—the Society for the Prevention of Negroes Getting Everything.

Barefaced Bear Farce

We can't swear to the truth of this report, but it seems that the head keeper at the Bronx Zoo crossed a polar bear with a brown bear and got a threatening letter from the Ku Klux Klan.

Militancy Can Go Too Far

Nancy was not only an active militant for civil rights but an ardent feminist as well. When she wasn't demonstrating for the betterment of the black community she was off somewhere attending a women's liberation protest.

Her husband had been listening to this mixture of complaints for an hour when he suddenly interrupted. "Honey, stop your fussin'." he said. "I have it all figured out. If you really want equal rights for our people and for women too, then how about demanding that ladies be bussed to barrooms?"

Non-Violence Supreme

The doting mother, an ardent activist, tried to hide her disappointment in her sixteen-year-old son. "My boy is at that in-between age," she apologized. "He can't make up his mind whether to go out and march or go upstairs and lie down."

Revolutionary Repartee

In 1969, two organizations, The Black Students Union (BSU) and the Students for a Democratic Society (SDS), were whooping it up on campuses throughout the country. This bit of doggerel insures that we will not forget that chaotic year.

> Said the BSU to the SDS,
> "The world is in a terrible mess."
> "It'll get worse before we're through,"
> Said the SDS to the BSU.

Ah, Cru-wel Fate!

"Seems like this here George Wallace wants to take over the world," remarked one student.

"Good!" snapped the other student who had just been reading the day's depressing headlines. "They deserve each other!"

Honky-Panky at the Polls

A grizzled, illiterate white man, his toothless gums showing through his tobacco-stained whiskers, slouched into a Georgia polling place and looked about helplessly.

A well-groomed Negro, a Hampton graduate, handed him a political leaflet. "I hope, sir, you will vote this ticket," he said politely.

The cracker glanced at the printed slip momentarily and then shrugged. "I cain't read," he muttered. "What's it say?"

The other was flabbergasted. "If you can't read, then how will you be able to tell what's on the ballot?"

The man looked at him, his face a complete blank. "What's a ballot?"

"Look," suggested the Negro, "why not vote for our candidate? I'll show you how."

"What's your candy-date stan' fer?"

"He is in favor of equal voting rights for all people—white and colored."

"What?" cried the cracker, his voice rising in outrage. "Why, you know as well as me, nigras ain't ready fer the vote!"

Points of View

A young member of the Black Panther movement, a confirmed atheist, was discussing the voter registration drive with his father, a venerable preacher of the gospel.

"I sometimes think that if God himself were to come down to earth in human form, and He was a black man," said the preacher sadly, "He wouldn't be allowed to vote in Mississippi."

"Pop, with all due respect to you," snorted the atheist son, "if there really was a God, there wouldn't *be* a Mississippi!"

Turn-About

Quitchakiddin' Department: Sammy Davis Jr. is now raising colored cotton on his plantation. He's got white folks picking it.

PART FIVE

LIFE IN THE BIG CITY

Slow and Easy, Friend!

Although the Harlem Globetrotters and innumerable Negro school-teams had long since demonstrated that the black man could excel in basketball, it was not until comparatively recent days that they were given the opportunity to make their mark in this sport.

One youth, a young man who stood seven feet tall in his socks, impressed the basketball coach of Columbia University with his latent ability. The youth had the height, he moved well, and he enjoyed the attributes of strength, stamina and determination. But there was one drawback: The young man originated from a rural area where educational opportunities were minimal—he was not what you might call a scholar.

However, the coach needed him on the university team, so he proceeded to teach him the fundamentals of the game. "Now this," began the coach, holding up a basketball, "is the ball you will be playing with. That's *ball*, b-a-l. . . ."

"Hold on there, coach," protested the youth. "Not so fast!"

Fair Warning

Mrs. Wilkerson lived in one of those dilapidated, ancient tenement houses in Harlem which had long since been abandoned by the absentee slumlord. The building was in such disrepair that the improvements would cost more than the house was worth—the taxes alone were higher than the rents would provide to a landlord.

One day a welfare worker called on Mrs. Wilkerson. "My goodness, what a run-down apartment," she exclaimed. "Why don't you ask the owner to fix up the place?"

"I don't know the owner," confessed the lady.

"Who do you pay your rent to?"

"I don't pay no rent. I ain't paid nothin' for three-four years."

"Well," observed the welfare worker, "you really can't complain about that."

"I sure can," retorted Mrs. Wilkerson. "If somebody don't start paintin' an' fixin' up this apartment right soon I'm gonna move out!"

Courtesy

"College is really doing wonders for my son," bragged the proud mother. "Only the other day he bought a raincoat and sent a thank-you note to Inspector 15."

Insulted

Nellie, a farm girl, had never before been to the big city. Now she was married and walking excitedly down Beale Street while her proud bridegroom pointed out all the new and wonderful sights. On their way they passed a drugstore with a big display sign in the window announcing, SPECIAL SALE ON AGFA FILM.

"What's that AGFA?" Nellie asked, puzzled.

Her hubby, too vain to admit that he did not know, replied, "toilet paper."

"Well," said the country girl, "if it's on sale I better go in and buy some."

In a minute or two she came rushing out of the store, her face contorted with outrage, her eyes blazing with indignation. "I been insulted," she wailed.

"What in the world happened?"

"I asked the man for a roll of AGVA," wept the bride, "and he said 'How big is your Brownie?' "

Razorless Society

A young cub reporter for *The Amsterdam News* had been out all day on his very first assignment. Now he was back at the office, boasting to the editor about his exclusive "scoop."

"I took a survey to disprove the silly notion that all blacks carry a razor as a weapon," he said enthusiastically.

"You did, eh?" growled the tough old editor. "What did you find out?"

"Sir, my survey showed that not a single one had ever seen a straight razor, let alone carry one. Most used a safety razor and the rest used electric razors."

"Where did you take this survey?"

"In the suburbs—among black doctors, judges, professors, preachers. . . ."

Wheels of Fortune

It's easy to spot the middle-class affluent guy nowadays. He has *two* cars jacked up in his front yard.

Homespun Banker

A workingman, judging by his faded coveralls, approached the teller's window at the bank and presented a withdrawal slip for three dollars.

"Sorry," said the teller curtly, "but the minimum amount you can withdraw is five dollars."

The man's face broke out in a friendly smile. "Okay, I'll take the five."

A few minutes later he was back at the window. "Suh," he said sweetly, "I wanna deposit two dollars."

Saga of the Teenaged Hot-Rodder

"So your son got himself a racing car," said the neighbor. "I didn't know he could drive that well."

"For a kid of sixteen he's pretty good," commented the father. "You should see the way that boy handles a souped-up car. His eyes narrow against the hammering heat of the ground as he strains against the bite of the seat belt and harness. His body tenses at the angry growl of the highly-tuned engine; he grips the wheel as the tortured tires scream their protest; he turns to the left; he turns to the right; his eyes are now pinpoints of glittering diamonds as he gives it that last ounce of gas . . . and then he pulls out of the garage!"

Advice to the Ladies

If you have a boy-friend who has everything, there's only one meaningful thing you can give him for his birthday—encouragement!

Caucasian Blues

Will, a white man, and his friend, Gil, who was black, worked for the same company. One day, during lunchtime, Will began a long series of complaints.

"My wife gave me hell again this morning and didn't fix my breakfast," he said mournfully. "My daughter is running around with some punk kid who won't work or go to school. My car is about to break down and I can't afford a new one. Not only that, but with another baby on the way we need a bigger house and I haven't got a dime saved to buy a larger place. I tell you, Gil," he concluded, his white face bitter, "you don't know the meaning of tough luck."

Gil looked at his friend sharply for a moment, and then drawled, "Man, where you been all your life?"

The Pre-"Natural" Look

"I'll be a little late this evening, mother," announced the loving daughter. "I'm going to the beauty parlor to get a permanent straight."

Easy Pregnancy

Mrs. White was expecting her first child and, being in her eighth month and having gained thirty pounds, she waddled like a duck.

"Oh Lord," she sighed as she and her neighbor, Mrs. Brown, were having tea, "my feet sure are killing me. They're all swole up."

"What you should do is quit wearing them high-heeled shoes," advised Mrs. Brown, who had birthed six and was trying hard for a seventh. "Get yourself a pair of oxfords—the kind that girl scouts and waitresses wear."

Mrs. White was more than willing to try anything, so next morning she purchased a pair of sandals. When Mrs. Brown next came to call, the young mother-to-be smiled with relief. "I sure do thank you for the advice," she said. "Believe me, I'll never get into a fix like this again without some low-heeled shoes."

Double Indemnity

Mary decided to fix a great big mess of neckbones, but she didn't have a pot big enough to cook them in. Amos, her husband, remembered that their neighbor, Mrs. Willoughby, had just what they needed—a large, 12-quart pan. He went to her house, next door, and politely asked if she could lend the big pan to them. "Certainly," she said.

A week later, Mrs. Willoughby knocked on their door and Amos answered the summons. "Amos," she said, "may I have my pot back? I'll need it for a big roast I'm planning for tonight."

"Sure," replied Amos. "Now lemme see, where did I put that thing?" He scratched his head in thought and then, after a minute, he beamed. "Oh yes, I remember now. It's either in the basement or under Mary's side of the bed."

Keeping Up with Whitey

Frank and Elizabeth moved into a suburban community, keenly aware that, as the only black couple in the area, they would have to set a good example so that other blacks could follow.

First thing they noticed was a sign on their neighbor's front lawn— "Keep Off the Grass." Not to be outdone, Frank, who fancied himself as something of a literary man, posted this sign on his own lawn:
REFRAIN FROM AMBULATING ON THE GREENSWARD

Hysterical Historics

Future historians will learn one thing from this Encyclopedia that they can learn nowhere else: Ex-Governor Lester Maddox of Georgia refused to watch *color* TV—and he loved every variety of cookies . . . except *brownies!*

Weathering the Weather

At the height of World War II, Ben had journeyed all the way from Alabama to work in a defense plant near the city of Utica, New York. The winter was bitter cold, but the pay was good.

During the lunch break one day, Ben and a co-worker grew nostalgic about their respective home towns. "I sure will be glad to get back home to Birmin'ham when this job is finished," said Ben.

"Well, I can't say as I blame you," said the co-worker. "A man has to be born up here to stand this cold weather."

"What?" gasped Ben in astonishment. "You mean to say folks live here when there ain't no war?"

Unfinished Symphony

This cat was driving down Amsterdam Avenue in his brand new Caddy. When he stopped for a red light he found that his fancy car wouldn't start

up again after the light turned green. He flagged down the very next motorist
—a woman—and asked for a push to get his car moving.

"I have an automatic transmission," he explained, "so you'll have to get
up a speed of thirty-five miles an hour to get me started real good."

"Okay," said the lady. "Thutty-five miles a houah."

So this Cadillac cat climbed back into his car and then waited and
waited. He was wondering what had happened to her when he caught sight
of her in the rear view mirror. . . .

There she came, engine going full blast, barreling down on him at thirty-
five miles an hour!

Entirely Welcome

"I'll never visit a nudist camp again," sniffed the girl. "The first thing
that was said to me when I went to one yesterday was 'Glad to see you-all!' "

King's English

Daisy King, a lifelong resident of Possum Swamp, Louisiana, a community of sixty-odd hardy souls who eked out a sparse existence on the
fringe of the bayous, received a letter from her older sister that a good job
was awaiting her in the mystical, faraway City of New York.

Miss King packed her belongings in a shoe-box and entrained for the
fabulous land of Gotham. Her sister, she learned, had found her a job as a
hat-check girl in a top nightclub. The only requirement was that the girl
must speak impeccable English.

Daisy, understandably enough, had her misgivings about her qualifica-
tions. "Ah cain't even *onderstan'* dese heah white folks," she complained.

"Don't you worry a-tall," her sister comforted. "You ain't hardly got no
south'n accent."

Her first night on the job, two gentlemen got their hats and hat-checks
mixed up.

"Heah now," said Daisy, "don't you gen'lmens go frettin' 'bout dem
hat-checks. I membuhs who's gittin' an' who's got." She handed one hat to
the tall patron. Then she turned to the shorter man, smiled, and crooned,
"An this un's yallzun's."

Fear of a Fading Fannie

Lulu Saunders, sepia model whose lovely figure has graced countless
magazine covers, tells of the most frightening experience of her life. "I
thought my career as a model was over," she said. "I was driving down
Lenox Avenue when I stopped for a light. Just then another driver pulled
up alongside my car, stuck his head out of the window, and yelled, "Lady,
your left rear's most flat!"

Drama on a Lonely Corner

It was a dark, starless night. Not a soul could be seen anywhere, yet a sense of foreboding hung over the area like an evil shroud. On a corner, waiting for a bus, an elderly white man glanced about nervously, imagining sinister figures lurking in every shadow.

Suddenly, as though he had sprung out of the very asphalt, a black man appeared. The old, white man almost fainted.

"Don't be frightened," said the stranger as the white man was about to take to his heels, "I'm scared too!"

Fresh!

She: I'm looking for a furnished house to replace my small flat.
He: Your small flat *what?*

Inflation Hits Home

The woman was a study in indecision as she surveyed the valuables spread out so temptingly in the showcase before her. She clutched a respectable roll of bills in her fist and nervously eyed the haughty salesman who would not even condescend to advise her on the comparative values.

Finally, in an act of sheer grit and determination, she made up her mind. "Very well," she said, unfolding the large roll of bills, "I'll have a pound of ground round, two lambchops and a small steak."

Urban Renewal Plea

"I don't rightly know why nobody ever mentions it," grumbled a resident of the black community, "but what we need here are some new hotels. The owners of the biggest hotel in our area are so stingy they're stealing towels from the guests!"

Color Blind

In Winston Salem, a rabid segregationist whose racist rantings were known to the entire city, was driving down the main thoroughfare when he noticed a woman standing on the corner, waiting for a bus. True southern gentleman that he was, he gallantly offered her a lift.

At the first traffic light he slowed down and said, "Madam, would you mind telling me whether that light is red or green? I'm color blind."

"Yessuh," was the prompt reply. "You sho' is!"

Nehemiah Obediah Hezekiah Smith

The pleasant-looking little man in his work clothes applied to the Department of Motor Vehicles for a driver's license.

"What is your name?" asked the clerk.

"Nehemiah Obediah Hezekiah Smith," the man replied, "but jes' do like I do an' write a *X*."

Grammarian

Bessie Lomax, of Schenectady, New York, tells of the time her mother forgot her own admonitions to her children to speak correctly. "Slurring your words and using southern dialect is only a matter of laziness," she would scold.

One Sunday morning, Bessie's mother telephoned the local newspaper office to complain that the paper had not been delivered that day. Apparently the circulation manager began to infuriate the lady with his excuses and alibis. Finally, after several minutes of impatient listening, while her anger mounted, she burst forth with, "Now see here, sir! I fully understand your problems, but just answer this one question: Is you is or is you ain't gonna deliver my paper?"

What Was That Again?

Jake, newly arrived in the city from a little country village, found a job and a place to live. He liked the high-sounding address of his residence, 1000 Garner, Rear Court.

Next morning he applied to the personnel office before starting on his new job. "Where do you live?" he was asked.

Jake inflated his chest proudly and told him—"Garnerear Court."

I's Right!—Eyes Right!

"Did you enjoy the social?" asked Linda's husband when she returned home from the neighborhood affair.

"Well, that cousin of yours was there. I swear to goodness, she was wearing a miniskirt and she had on a see-through blouse that was cut so low you could see her liver, front and back. Wasn't anything you couldn't see if she leaned right. And *talk!* As my grandfather used to say, 'that gal sho' do beat her gums.'"

"But, Linda, I didn't ask you about my cousin," he protested. "How was the program?"

"That's what I'm talking about," said the wife. "When your cousin comes to a social, she *is* the program!"

The Great Coming Out Party

Mrs. Verily Vandersniffle was one of those upper-crust members of society who haughtily reminded one and all that she was a high-class Negro, not a common black person like, for example, her new maid, Wilma.

On this occasion she rang for Wilma and explained that the delivery man would soon arrive with a large shipment of flowers and she would require the girl to help with the floral arrangements.

"You throwin' a party or somethin'?" asked Wilma.

"In a way," explained Mrs. Vandersniffle in her usual haughty manner. "Tomorrow my daughter makes her debut in high society. We're celebrating her coming out."

"Comin' out!" echoed the maid. "What she been in for?"

Motto for the Affluent

Now that her husband's auto repair shop was prospering and they had enough money to do the things they had always dreamed about, Sarah moved to an upper-class integrated neighborhood, bought some brand new French antiques and, as a finishing touch to show her good breeding, an attractive sign reading ICI ON PARLE FRANÇAIS.

Sarah and her hubby were quite proud of their new home and the lovely furnishings, so they had a housewarming and invited their fancy neighbors to the affair.

The assembled guests were admiring the furniture and antiques when one of them noticed the sign. "I didn't know you speak French," said the neighbor.

"I don't," said Sarah. "Only English."

The guest pointed to the sign. "But it says French is spoken here."

"Why, the nerve of that salesman!" gasped Sarah. "He told me it meant God Bless Our Humble Home!"

Marguerite's Black Pride

Marguerite belonged to the affluent society, and though her complexion was ebony black, she had acquired all the prejudices and airs of her white peers.

One day she decided to buy a new fur coat. At one of the most exclusive salons in all New York the saleslady tried desperately to please her, but Marguerite could find nothing to her taste. However, after trying on several coats of mink, sable, ermine and beaver, she finally found one that suited her. The saleslady breathed a sigh of relief. "It looks stunning on you," she said—her customary analysis.

Marguerite surveyed herself in the full-length mirror, turning this way and that. "Well," she said, her chocolate face in a half-smile, "I must say it's nice, but"—she hesitated uncertainly—"don't you think it makes me look too Jewish?"

Money Isn't Everything

The ladies at the social club were boasting about the alimony they were receiving from their former husbands. Everyone in the group had revealed the exact amount except Gwendolyn. Now all eyes were upon her. "Gwennie," said one of the women, asking the question outright, "did you get any alimony when you divorced Jim?"

"No, not a penny," confessed Gwendolyn, "but he did give me a wonderful letter of recommendation."

Time-Drag

Southerner: You ever been to Mississippi?
Northerner: Yeah, I spent a whole week there one day.

Cooperation

This was the daughter's first day home from college and she was determined to bring some culture to her parents. At the moment, they were having breakfast.

The father turned to his wife. "You got any mo' bacon?"

"How many slices you already had?"

"I think I et seven."

The daughter was horrified to hear her own father say *et*. "Oh Daddy," she scolded, "you must say *ate!*"

"Awright, baby darlin'," he replied, smiling agreeably, "I done et *eight!*"

Over the Back Fence

First Gossip: How about those Barr's? She won't tell her age and he won't act his.

Second Gossip: No wonder they're called the Hershey Bar's. She's plain and he's nuts!

The Gourmet

Cynthia Wilkerson had never been inside a white school before, let alone attend one. Now she was enrolled at a predominantly white university and she was determined to show that she was just as ladylike as any Caucasian on the campus.

Her first opportunity to display her refinement occurred at noon when she entered the school cafeteria. She got a tray and moved slowly and sedately down the line in front of the steam table, selecting choice tidbits. However, she was hungry and wanted something more substantial, so she pointed to one of the displays and asked, "What is that?"

"Tongue," replied the counter girl. "Try some. It's really good."

"Oh, mercy me, I could *never* eat something that came out of an animal's mouth," said Miss Wilkerson, wrinkling her nose delicately. "Just give me some scrambled eggs."

Census Nonsense

It was census-taking time and the enumerator was ushered into a small store that had been converted to living quarters. The occupant opened a can of beer, took a long drink, and said, "Ask me anything."

"Well, first of all," began the census-taker, "what kind of work do you do?"

"I own a hand laundry," said the man in a big-business voice.

The enumerator regarded the shabby place and then looked at the man with mounting suspicion. "Where?" he asked.

"Right there," said the laundry executive as his wife came in.

Nearer My Todd to Thee

"I think we can approve this loan," said the bank clerk. "Just one question: You say your brother, Todd, is your closest relative? You seem rather young to have no parents. Are you an orphan?"

"No sir, I got a father, mother, and four sisters," explained the young man, "but they all live way over on the other side of town. My brother, Todd, is my closest relative—he lives right next door."

Manners

"You haven't arrived, socially," wrote Dan Sping, "until you've learned which fingers to use to whistle for the waiter."

PART SIX

RESTAURANT RUMBLES

Vanilla and Chocolate

The Ambassador to the United States from Tanzania was arriving to take up his official residence in the nation's capital. However, having heard so much of the Mardi Gras in New Orleans, he decided to land there first. During the festivities he was served a "Washington sundae." It consisted of two huge scoops of vanilla ice cream, topped with whipped cream, sprinkled with chopped pecans, and further embellished with a red cherry and choice of three syrups. It tasted perfectly delicious.

As soon as he arrived in Washington, D. C., the Ambassador ordered another "Washington sundae," but when it was served he looked at it with dismay.

"This isn't a 'Washington sundae,'" he complained. "It's supposed to have vanilla, not chocolate, ice cream."

"Sir," replied the waiter courteously, noticing his foreign accent, "there are two well-known Washingtons in this country's history. There's George —that's the southern sundae—and there's the northern style—Booker T."

Integration at the College Level

The president of Hampton Institute and the white professor of a northern university were traveling to New York where they were to give a series of lectures. It was approaching high noon and they decided to stop for lunch. They parked their car in front of a restaurant in Alexandria, Virginia, and the professor went inside to clear the way for his black companion.

"I'd like to have lunch here with my friend who is waiting outside in the car," explained the educator.

"Bring him on in," said the manager.

"Well, you see, he's a Negro, but let me assure you that he is a college president and. . . ."

The manager interrupted with a wave of his hand. "That's okay," he said airily. "I got nothing against college presidents."

Crooks Have to Eat, Too

George entered the busy cafeteria, filled his tray at the counter, hung up his hat and coat, and then sat down to enjoy his meal.

Within a few minutes, however, his peaceful attitude turned to deep anger. He called the manager and pointed to the sign up on the wall: WATCH YOUR HAT AND COAT.

The manager shrugged. "The sign means what it says. If you had watched, no one could have stolen your things."

"That ain't it at all," protested George. "What I'm burned up about is just the opposite—while I was watching my hat and coat someone stole my steak."

The Man Who Came to Dinner

Thanks to the sit-in demonstrators, all restaurants in Alabama were legally enjoined to cease barring any person from equal service because of color. But there are a hundred subtleties which owners, managers and waiters use to discourage black patronage. Sometimes it takes old-fashioned sass plus staunch determination to overcome such obstacles, as this vignette illustrates.

It was only three days after desegregation in public eating places had been ordered by a Federal court when a self-possessed man entered a formerly restricted restaurant in Mobile. He waited patiently for some minutes but was studiously ignored by the waiters who managed to seat the white patrons who entered the fancy establishment.

It became obvious that forthright action was in order. He walked to the center table, glistening with polished silver, and located right in front of the dais where every diner in the place had a perfect view of the dark-skinned stranger.

The headwaiter scurried over. "Sorry, but you can't sit here," he said, his voice almost strangling.

"Why not?" asked the man coolly.

"This table is reserved."

"Indeed! For whom?"

The waiter became even more flustered. "Why, it's reserved for a—for—well—for an important gentleman," he finally managed to stammer.

"That's good," said the patron as he scanned the menu. "You're talking to him."

To Each His Own

Newspapers everywhere headlined the news that no restaurant henceforth could refuse to serve black patrons nor to discriminate in any way. Thus emboldened, a Negro entered a hitherto all-white restaurant and seated himself at a table.

"I'll have some chitlins and black-eyed peas," he told the waiter.

"I'm sorry, but we haven't any," replied the waiter.

"Then bring me some hominy grits and gravy."

"Never heard of it.

"Forget it! Just bring me some cornbread and molasses on the side, and a cup of coffee."

"Well," apologized the waiter, "I can bring you the coffee but we don't have any cornbread—and no molasses, either."

"F'r chrissake!" exploded the outraged diner as he rose to leave. "It'll be another hundred years before this place is ready for integration!"

Ham What Am

He was a big, burly truck-driver and he found himself with an idle hour in the city while his truck was being loaded for return to his home town. Feeling hungry he went into a drugstore and seated himself at the lunch counter and ordered a ham sandwich.

After a short wait the countergirl brought his order—two slices of bread cut into dainty quarters. Looking as though he could eat twenty of such morsels, he lifted a piece of bread and solemnly inspected the pale bit of tomato, the wilted shred of lettuce and, picking up the ham between thumb and forefinger, he held it aloft and regarded it at eye-level. Sure enough, he could see the light through it.

"Miss," he called the waitress, "did you make this sandwich?"

"Yes sir, I did."

"And did you slice this ham?"

"Yes, why?"

"I just thought you'd like to know," he said smoothly, "you damn near missed it!"

Just Call Me Lightning

"Don't always go blamin' the white man for sassin' us blacks," observed Horatio, the hometown philosopher. "Our own people can get pretty arrogant too—'specially the upper-class Negroes. Reminds me of the time this here college professor at the university in our town come into the Paradise Cafe and ordered a full course meal.

"Sam, the waiter, brings him coffee first, like he was asked, and the professor complains about the slow service. Then Sam brings the soup, and the college guy grumbles about it takin' so long. All through dinner, from the meat to the dessert, that professor just natchly wore Sam out with his complainin'. Finally, he asks for another cup of coffee. But when Sam brings it, the professor blows his stack. 'You are the slowest waiter I ever did see,' he hollers. 'How come my coffee so cold?'

"Sam, he's madder'n a mule on a rainy mornin', and he says, 'Mister, I run so fas' the coffee done cooled off in the draft!'"

Quick Thinking

"Sam, the waiter at the Paradise Cafe, is really somethin' else!" continued Horatio, the hometown philosopher. "He ain't *never* lost for the right words. I rec'lect the time these two ladies come in and the first one says, 'I'll have coffee and scrambled aigs and toas'.'"

"Old Sam, he nods and turns to the other lady and she says, 'I'll have the same but eliminate the toas'.'

"Well, Sam he looks at her like he gonna ask what the hell she talkin' about, but then he smiles and says, 'Sorry, lady, but the handle on the 'liminator got busted this mornin'!' "

One Negro on Rye, Please!

There are many versions of this delightful story, but comedian Dick Gregory is generally credited as the originator.

A black man happened to be in a strange neighborhood, and as it happened to be lunch time, he entered a fancy restaurant and seated himself at one of the tables. He was studying the menu when a waiter approached. "I'm sorry," he said haughtily, "but we don't serve Negroes here."

"Don't let that bother you, my good man," said the patron just as haughtily, "I don't *eat* Negroes!"

No Discrimination

A southern bigot found it necessary to visit Chicago on business. While there, he decided to seek a little entertainment so he hailed a cab and told the taxi-driver to take him to the best nightclub in town.

In a few minutes he found himself at the Chez Paree, and he was just about to order a highball when who should walk in but Sidney Poitier with a party of friends. "Never mind the drink," snapped the bigot, rising to quit the place. "I don't mingle with niggers."

Another cab took him to a North Michigan Avenue hotspot. He was beginning to relax when in walked Pearl Bailey, her white husband, drummer Louis Belson, and a racially mixed group of friends. Again the southerner left, muttering "I don't care to mingle with niggers."

At the next place, he found Sammy Davis Jr.; at the next, Dick Gregory; following that, Harry Belafonte. In several other clubs he found that blacks as well as whites were not only mingling but enjoying themselves immensely. He decided to try one more place. Calling another taxi, he said to the driver, "Take me to a club that only allows whites." The driver shrugged and drove him to a club where he very well knew there was no discrimination—but a fare was a fare!

The man got out of the cab and went inside, but just to make sure, he asked the hat-check girl, "Does this place allow niggers?"

"Sure!" answered the girl brightly. "Step right in!"

A Question of Semantics

Man walks into a restaurant and asks for a menu.

"Sorry," says the waiter, "but we don't serve Negroes here."

"What!" yells the man. "You mean to say you practice discrimination?"

"Of course not," explains the waiter. "It's just that this place ain't integrated."

How Now, Slightly-Browned Cow!

Waiter: Did you enjoy your steak, sir?

Diner: Frankly, no! I don't mind a rare steak occasionally, but I've seen cows hurt worse than this and get well.

Word to the Wise

He had not even had a chance to taste his morning coffee before his wife began her usual argument. In disgust, he rose from the table, slammed the door behind him and went to a little restaurant on the corner where, at least, he could have his breakfast in peace.

"Good morning, brother," said the smiling, pretty waitress. "What would you like this lovely morning?"

The poor guy glowed with pleasure at the sight of this friendly face and the sound of her sweet voice. "I'll have two eggs, toast and coffee," he said—and as an afterthought—"and a few kind words."

"All right, honey, I'll bring the eggs," said the agreeable waitress, "and the kind words are 'don't eat 'em!'"

PART SEVEN

THERE'S NO BIZ LIKE SHOW BIZ— FORTUNATELY!

The Boob Tube

"I really don't think we should criticize the fact that so few black people have been employed on television," observed the late Dorothy Dandridge. "After all, the whites made TV what it is today . . . *lousy!*"

Congo Bongo Cools
Cleveland Cats

Two Cleveland musicians, now serving with the Army Air Force in the African campaign, were flying over the Congo region when their plane developed engine trouble and they were forced to bail out.

Deep in the impenetrable jungle, they were trying to figure how they could get back to civilization when suddenly they heard the ominous sound of native drums.

"Man, I don't like the sound of that drummin'," said the first musician nervously.

"Can't say I like it, either," responded the second cat, "but maybe he ain't their regular drummer."

Lions Ain't Vegetarians

The casting director at Paramount Studios, in Hollywood, sent out a hurry call for a dozen black actors to appear in an African safari motion picture. Among those who appeared for the roles was a likely-looking actor to play the part of the assistant to the Great White Hunter.

"See that lion in the cage?" asked the film director. "Well, your role calls for you to walk up to that lion, grab him by the mane, and spit in his eye."

"Who, me?" exclaimed the actor. "Man, you gotta be kiddin'!"

"That's what the script calls for," argued the director. "You needn't fear that lion. I admit he looks ferocious, but he's gentle as a lamb. Why, he was raised on milk."

"So was I," retorted the actor, backing off, "but I sure eat meat now!"

No Black Keys on
All-White Pianos

Many of the old-time theatrical agents were not usually known for their intelligence or higher learning. A case in point is the off-Broadway agent who was at his desk one day when the telephone rang.

"Yeah? Joe speakin'."

"Can you use a singer?" asked a lady's voice. She sounded cultured, and he noticed a slight Southern accent.

"Maybe. How are you on the blues?"

"Well, I do some blues singing, but mostly the better pop tunes. I also sing classical—I'm a coloratura."

He snapped to alert attention. "A *what?*"

"A coloratura."

"Sorry," said the agent, "but I only book whites."

Home on the Gas Range

The newly-organized Beverly Hills Branch of the NAACP* sent a representative to the Motion Picture Producers Association in Hollywood to demand that more Negroes be employed in films.

"Very well, we'll think about it," said the executive producer in charge, repeating himself for the twentieth time in as many months.

"You don't have to think about it," said the NAACP representative curtly. "It is our understanding that you are about to make a cowboys and Indians picture—a ten-million-dollar film about the winning of the West."

"Yes, that's true enough," admitted the producer reluctantly, "but on the other hand, tell me, whoever heard of a picture with cowboys and Negroes?"**

Pardon My Accent

At the height of radio's popularity, long before the advent of television, one of the most listened-to shows on the air was called "The Shadow." Almost everyone could (and did) quote the closing line, always recited in mellifluous though eerie tones.

It so happened that the regular announcer became ill and a replacement was needed at once. They found one—a black man whose voice was beautifully modulated and just right for the signature line.

That very evening, the new announcer strode to the microphone, closed his eyes and, in that rich, baritone voice, delivered the crucial line:

"Who knows what evil lurks in the minds of men? . . . *De Shadow* do!"

P-p-prejudice

A representative of the Beverly Hills branch of the NAACP wanted to make sure that black actors were being given an equal chance in a new picture about to be filmed, so he went to the studio's casting office to keep the Man straight.

Pretty soon a young actor from the Watts Student Theater came in for

---

* The Beverly Hills branch of the National Association for the Advancement of Colored People differs from other branches in that it is primarily concerned with widening employment opportunities, technical as well as creative, in the motion picture and television industries. Its efforts are directed, additionally, to the improvement of the "black image" in the entertainment field. Although only a few years old, this branch has successfully pioneered many of the advances made within the film and television industries in the Hollywood area.

** There is no valid reason why a "Negroes and Indians" motion picture should not be produced. During the Indian Wars the "Buffalo Soldiers," as the black troops were called, produced 14 Congressional Medal of Honor winners fighting the Apache, Sioux and other hostile tribes. See page 375.

an audition. He entered the casting director's office but in a minute or two he came out, his face showing bitter disappointment.

"How come you didn't get the acting job?" asked the NAACP agent.

"I-I-I'll t-tell you why," said the young student angrily. It's b-b-because I'm c-c-c-colored!"

Zany Time Zones

Godfrey Cambridge said it first many years ago:

"West Coast singers and comics prefer to work in the East because they get paid three hours earlier."

Diahann Disputes a Dilemma

Diahann Carroll, the lovely singer and actress, and the first black woman to star in a dramatic network series of her own, gave this rebuttal to those who complained that her TV show, *Julia,* was not a real reflection of Negro life:

"Okay, name me one television show that's a real reflection of *white* life!"

Envy

Hollywood and Vine gossips are saying that Sidney Poitier is so rich he just bought his dog a boy.

A Man of His Word

The country girl was really stage-struck, so she left her little village and arrived in Hollywood. But it wasn't long before disillusionment set in.

"There I was, at my first party in filmland, with all those important white stars. Then this producer came over, handed me a glass of champagne and whispered in my ear, 'Baby, how'd you like to go to a small, intimate spot?'

" 'Sure,' I said.

"So he took me to a closet!"

Double Feature

"I was absolutely captivated by Romeo and Juliet last night at a drive-in theatre," said the beauteous Lena Horne. "They were sitting in a car next to mine."

Front Page Story

Edie Jamison, at one time the highest-paid sepia model in New York, tells of the time her publicity agent telephoned her with a "terrific, fabulous, stupendous, magnificent" idea for a page-one photo in the newspapers.

"All right, I'm willing," agreed Edie, though with some reservations, being quite accustomed to his superlatives.

"Did you read where the battleship *Missouri*—the famous 'Mighty Mo' —arrives in port tomorrow? Well, I want you to get down there to the dock so I can get a picture of you and the boat."

"What! Me and that big ship? I don't get it," said Edie.

"Can't you just see the caption under that picture?" he cried, his voice rising in excitement: *"Edie Meetie Mighty Mo!"*

Cotton-Pickin' Problem

There's the story about Sammy Davis Jr. exclaiming to his mother: "Mama, on Passover you're picking cotton?"

Complexion Woes

Godfrey Cambridge was in his dressing room at the Hollywood studio where he was starring in the motion picture *The Night the Sun Came Out*. In the film, Cambridge portrayed a Caucasian, and quite naturally, his make-up consumed several hours each day.

"If I knew being white was that much trouble I would never have taken the role," he quipped. "And another thing, it's the first time in my life I ever walked into a drugstore and almost bought a tube of suntan cream."*

Close Observer

"Have you ever stopped to think," queried Dan Sping, "that the soul singers who get richest are those who sing about poverty?"

---

* Godfrey Cambridge, star of the stage, feature films and television, was born in New York City, but attended grammar school in Nova Scotia where his grandparents lived. He graduated from Flushing High School, in New York, and attended Hofstra College, after which formal education he began his studies in dramatic acting. Cambridge made his Broadway debut in *Nature's Way*, and was featured in *Purlie Victorious*, in both the stage and screen versions. His off-Broadway successes include *Lost in the Stars, Take a Giant Step* and *The Detective Story*. As a comedian, he has won fame on many variety shows on CBS, NBC and ABC television stations, and he has performed dramatically on a number of TV series. In 1965, he starred in the stock version of *A Funny Thing Happened on the Way to the Forum*. Godfrey Cambridge won the Obie award for the 1960-61 season's most distinguished performance in *The Blacks*. Today, his material is presented in the style of the "new breed" of Negro comedians, drawn from contemporary racial situations.

Instinct

It is no secret that Errol Garner, among the greatest contemporary jazz pianists, cannot read a note of music.

He had just finished a recital at New York's Carnegie Hall one evening, when a woman rushed up to him and gushed, "Oh, Mr. Garner, how can anyone play so divinely without knowing how to read music?"

Garner smiled. "The same way a beaver knows how to build a dam without going to engineering school."

Banjo Banter

A famous musician arrived in Augusta, Georgia. The mayor, remembering that elections were not far off, thought it might be a good idea to appear congenial. So he went to the club where the musician was playing, and between shows he was ushered into the performer's dressing room.

"I hear you were born with a banjo on your knee," said the mayor, in what he thought was a very funny approach.

The entertainer regarded him coldly for a moment and then nodded. "Yes, I was. But when I was five years old my parents had it surgically removed!"

PART EIGHT

MAD MOMENTS IN MEDICINE

Instant Cavities

Dr. Benton had only recently graduated from the School of Dentistry and it was with much pride that he hung out his shingle. "Now," he thought, "I'll be able to do something constructive for my people." He was well aware that the only other dentist in that part of the ghetto was a white man who had amassed a fortune, and that he made his money by cheating the poor blacks, many of whom had just recently arrived from various southern rural areas.

The young dentist had only been in practice for a mere two weeks when an aged man entered his office. "Ah wants two teeth filled with real gol'," he said.

Dr. Benton made a careful and thorough examination. "You don't need a filling," he said at length. "Your teeth are perfectly sound."

A few days later Dr. Benton met the oldtimer on the street. "How do you feel?" he asked.

"Jes' fine," replied the other. "I went to the white dentis' an' he filled them two teeth for me."

"That's strange," said Dr. Benton. "I couldn't find any cavities when I examined you."

"He couldn't either," was the cheerful reply—"leastwise not till he drilled for a spell."

Can't Blame Her

The girl was rushed to the maternity ward at the local hospital; and just in time, too, as her labor pains had long since started. Quickly she was placed on a bed and surrounded by a white-robed doctor, two student interns and an anaesthetist also robed in white, and several nurses in their snowy white gowns. All, of course, wore surgical masks over their faces.

As the anaesthetic gradually wore off, the young lady, who had just arrived in the north from Alabama, slowly opened her eyes, took one look at the masked, white-clad figures, raised herself from the pillow, and shrieked, "Get these damn Ku Kluxers out of here!"

The Patient Patient's Friend

Jim learned that his friend, Bill, had suffered an attack of dysentery and was now a patient at the local hospital. He went to pay his buddy a call, but learned that visiting hours were over.

"How's he doing?" Jim asked the nurse in charge.

"Pretty well," answered the girl. "Right now he's convalescing."

"Well, if that's all," said Jim, "I'll just sit here and wait till he's through."

Too Anxious

The husband hovered over his wife's sick-bed while the doctor felt her waning pulse.

"Ain't there no hope for her a-tall?" the husband asked.

"That depends," answered the doctor. "What are you hoping for?"

Diabolical Diagnosis

Melissy, age 16, noticed that her ankles were beginning to swell, her stomach was growing perceptibly rounder, and for some unknown reason, she suffered from morning sickness. Her mother, suspicions aroused, ordered her to consult a physician.

SCRAPPLE

This South Carolina scrapple recipe has been typical since long before Emancipation. Modern black chefs who specialize in soul food, often add some lean beef to the pork. As Langston Hughes once declared, "If you haven't had a slice or two of fried scrapple for breakfast on a cold and gray morning, you haven't lived, brother; you haven't lived!"

South Carolina Style

1 lb. pork   2/3 cup cornmeal
4 cups water   1 large onion
1 tsp. salt   2 to 3 tsp. ground sage

Cook meat, covered, in boiling salted water, keep at simmering until meats falls from bones. Remove meat from broth. Cut or grind into small pieces. Strain broth into top of a double boiler. Add cornmeal, and cook over direct heat for five minutes, stirring constantly to prevent lumping. Add meat, chopped onions, and seasoning. Cook over boiling water for one hour. Pack into mold or small loafpans. Serve cold, or slice and pan fry with or without batter.

"What that doctor say?" the older woman asked when her daughter returned home.

"I didn't rightly understand," the girl replied. "He say I'm sufferin' from acute indiscretion."

Night Call

"Hello, that you, Dr. Jackleg?"

"Yeah. Who's this?"

"Mrs. Brimstone. Please come quick. I'm hurtin' all over."

"You still owe me for the last visit."

"But I got money this time. Eight half-dollars, nine quarters, fifteen dimes and thirty-two nickels."

"Lemme hear 'em jingle!"

Cancer Fighter

Dan Sping claims there's a doctor who invented the world's first non-cancer cigarette lighter. Instead of lighting it coughs.

Medical Note

Just in case you don't know the statistics, ninety-five per cent of all cases of female cancer of the breast are caused by men who smoke excessively.

Advice to the Loveworn

A female representative of the U.S. Department of Health, Education and Welfare, was sent to the deep south to help alleviate some of the problems among the impoverished, uneducated residents. Upon her arrival she was shocked to learn that there was not a doctor, a registered nurse or the simplest medical facilities in the area. Quickly she assembled a group of the ladies who lived in the rural village.

"Tell me," she began, "do any of you know what to do when you find a girl pregnant?"

No one answered, so she repeated the question. This time, a very old woman raised her hand.

"Very well," said the government lady briskly. "You are probably the midwife here. Just what do you do?"

"Soon's I see a gal whut's pregnan'," instructed the ancient woman, "I allus say, 'Listen, gal, you go right out an' fin' dat man whut's 'sponsible *an' git ma'ied!*'"

That's Life

For the past year, Lawrence had not had a day off at the Columbia University School of Medicine where he was in his last semester. Soon he would be a full-fledged doctor. But unless he took a few days off to relax he felt that he would have a breakdown. So, to get a little rest and also to visit his family at the same time, he flew down to Georgia and made his way to the little town where he was born. His family, of course, was overjoyed to see him, quite naturally proud of their doctor-son.

After dinner, they chatted about the one thing that concerned them all, the career Lawrence had chosen. He informed that he planned to specialize in obstetrics—explaining to them that he meant maternity cases.

Lawrence's father was not impressed. "I seed some of them incubators," he said, "where they hatches out babies like they was chickens. They keep them li'l babies in storage till they're paid for."

The young doctor grinned. "Well, at least babies don't die like they used to when they were delivered by midwives."

"You mean grannies?" barked the old man. "Lemme tell you somethin', young felluh, them grannies didn't go to college but they sho' knew about bornin' babies. A granny borned you. A granny borned me an' yo' mama. An' look at us—we all lived!"

Lawrence glanced around the humble cottage, his father's work-worn hands and poor clothes, his mother's weary face—old before her time. His voice was soft and infinitely tender as he replied:

"You call this *living?*"

PART NINE

THE LAW IS A ASS!

You bless us, please Sah, even if we's
doin' wrong tonight,
'Cause then we'll need the blessin' more'n
ef we's doin' right;
And let the blessin' stay with us until
we come to die
And go to keep our Christmas with
*them sheriffs in the sky.**

---

* *Christmas Night in the Quarters* (1917). "Blessing the Dance."

Swear-word or Prayer-word?

For half an hour the defendant attempted to convince the judge that he was an innocent man and that he had been wrongfully accused, arrested and imprisoned without bail.

The judge, however, was unimpressed. "This court finds you guilty," he said.

As the bailiff was leading the prisoner away the judge heard him mutter an obscene, irreverent phrase. "Just a moment, bailiff," called the judge. "Bring that man back here."

"Don't you know I can add to your sentence by finding you in contempt of court?" barked the judge. "You can't get away with insulting me!"

"Yo' honuh, I didn't insult you or the court," maintained the prisoner stoutly. "All I said was 'God am de judge, God am de judge!'"

That's Right—You're Wrong!

"It is the opinion of the court," intoned the Alabama judge, "that this innocent Negro is guilty as charged!"

Thinkin' Ain't Knowin'!

The new district attorney of Jiveass Junction, Georgia, was questioning Franklin who had been summoned to court as a witness in a murder trial.

"Now if I understood you correctly," said the D.A., "you testified that you observed the defendant running from the building shortly after the crime was committed."

"No *suh!* I didn't say that nowise. I said I *think* it was him."

"You think!" exclaimed the exasperated prosecutor. "If you *think* something then you *know* it, don't you?"

"Not zackly, suh," replied Franklin. "Las' year when you was a private lawyer you defen'ed me fo' a traffic vi'lation, an' you say you gonna git me off free. Well, I *think* you is but I *knows* you ain't!"

Dat Ham Am Sam's Damn Ham

Sam, the defendant, stood before the bar of justice, trembling beneath the judge's steely gaze. "Did you or did you not appropriate to yourself a Smithfield ham without rendering due recompense to the plaintiff?"

"I don't rightly know what all that means," replied Sam, puzzled.

"Then let's put it this way: Where were you at eleven o'clock last night?"

"In the barn."

"What? You have a perfectly good house but you sleep in the barn?"

"No suh," replied Sam dejectedly, "I was hidin' that Smithfield ham."

CORN CHOWDER

Great-grandma didn't "saute" onions—she *fried* them "golden brown." She creamed her own corn. And paper towels had yet to be invented. But she would be the first to admit, were she here today, that Black folks' soul cookin' has indeed improved. This Arkansas recipe would have pleased great-great-grandma greatly.

½ pound bacon, cut into 1-inch pieces
2 small onions, sliced
1 tbs. all-purpose flour
1 cup water
2 cups finely diced raw potatoes

½ cup chopped celery
2 bay leaves
2 one-pound cans cream-style corn
1 cup milk
1 tsp. salt
¼ tsp. white pepper

Fry bacon until crisp, drain on paper towels, and set aside. Reserve ¼ cup bacon drippings and place in a kettle. Saute onions in bacon drippings for about five minutes. Blend in flour and mix to a smooth paste. Gradually add the water and stir until smooth. Add the potatoes, celery, and bay leaves. Cover and cook over low heat for about 15 minutes or until potatoes are done. Stir occasionally. Blend in corn, milk, seasonings, and bacon. Heat for 15 minutes. Serve hot. Yield: 5 to 6 servings.

Nothing Is Impossible

He was named *After John* because his birth followed that of his brother John. But he was known to all as Aft.

Aft was a married man, but sometimes he had a roving eye for the ladies—especially after a visit to the local tavern. It came as no surprise, therefore, when he was summoned to court on paternity charges—involving not one, but *two* women.

The judge examined the indictment with care. Finally he looked at Aft and nodded. "You say you are innocent and I'm inclined to agree with you. The charges state that you spent the night with Alice; that you arrived at ten o'clock in the evening and stayed with her until seven the next morning. However, it also states that you spent the night with Ruth, and on the same date and during the very same hours. It further appears that Alice and Ruth live ten miles apart. I therefore declare the case dismissed on the grounds of insufficient evidence. You couldn't possibly be with both women at the same time."

Aft started to leave, and the judge added, "I hope that you are now going home to your neglected wife."

"Yes, your honor," replied Aft, "but first I'm gonna stop off at my twin brother's house."

Drama in a Courtroom

SCENE: *A courtroom in Biloxi, Mississippi*

Judge: Well now, let's get started with this case. Have you retained a lawyer to defend you?

Defendant: No, yo' honah.

Judge: Haven't you even tried to get an attorney to represent you?

Defendant: Yes, suh. Ah went out an' 'sulted one, an' he tol' me to jes' come in an' th'ow mahse'f on de igno'ance of de co't!"

Heads I Win, Tails You Lose

Grandpa was a contented resident of Detroit, and he repeatedly vowed that he would never return to his native town of Alexandria, Louisiana—not even for a visit.

One day he received an invitation from his grandson in Alexandria, to attend the young man's wedding. "I ain't goin'," he said to his friend. "The courts don't never give justice to a black man in that city."

"What do you care about the courts?" asked his buddy.

"Well, I ain't never told you this, but the Alexandria police got a warrant out for my arrest. A traffic vi'lation. I didn't go to court because I was innocent, and besides, I was leavin' the state anyway."

"Then get a lawyer to defend you," suggested the friend.

"*What!*" cried Grandpa. "Me pay a fine and a lawyer both?"

English as She Is Spoke

Jeff was a product of Baltimore's ghetto, a school dropout at thirteen, and unable to find work because of his youth. Naturally, his attitudes and companions were not exactly refined.

One day, as Jeff was shooting dice with several other boys on a street corner he was caught red-handed by the cops. He soon found himself in Juvenile Court.

"Are you the defendant accused of participating in a game of chance?" demanded the judge, glaring down at the youngster.

Jeff, who understood none of this legal jargon, answered sullenly, "No, I ain't. I'm the onlies' one in the crap game what was ketched!"

Experience Is the Best Teacher

A young lawyer, recently graduated from Howard University and newly admitted to the bar, was determined to specialize in civil rights cases. An idealistic fellow, he looked forward to aiding his people in their march toward equality.

Setting up shop in Arkansas, he quickly found out all about justice—southern style—and lost his first case. Frustrated, he appealed to a higher court, but this time his presentation was far more detailed. He cited precedent after precedent, case after case, pointing out many instances where the defendant had been acquitted in similar circumstances.

"Just a moment," interrupted the weary judge after listening for an hour, "you can rest assured that I understand the basics of equality under the law, and you can also be sure that this court is familiar with the elementary concept of justice."

"Your honor," the young lawyer sighed, "that was the mistake I made in the lower court."

Miracle Worker

Joshua was being tried in court on charges of operating an illegal still.

"Are you the biblical Joshua who made the sun stand still?" grinned the judge, his voice heavy with sarcasm.

"No suh," answered the defendant. "I's de Joshua what made de moonshine."

Confusion in the Courtroom

It has only been in recent years that the state of Virginia relaxed and then voided many of its repressive laws aimed specifically at black people.

In Albemarle County, a Negro was hailed into court on some trumped-up charge or other, the purpose of which was to keep him from voting. The defendant, an illiterate but shrewd old man, was on the witness stand, listening carefully to the legalistic nonsense but saying little.

A question was asked and the Negro startled the court by announcing that he did not understand the question. Therefore, he maintained, he would need a lawyer to represent him—and he could not afford to retain one. There being no lawyers in the county who would dare defend a black man so that he might go to the polls and vote, the prosecuting attorney, the judge, and a bevy of legal advisors entered into heated debate as to just how they would handle this perplexing case. After arguments and objections that lasted for an hour or more, they agreed on a plan. Once again the prosecutor asked, "Did you or did you not attempt to vote? That is a simple question. Do you understand it?"

"No suh," replied the oldtimer promptly. "I's es' as igno'nt of de law as you is."

Do She or Don't She?

Margie was being tried on a charge of shoplifting. Appearing in her behalf, as a character witness, was her best friend, Mona.

"Now please tell the court, in your own words: how long have you known Margie?"

"All my life, yo' honuh an' them's my own wuhds, like you said."

"Very well," replied the judge, hiding a smile. "What can you tell us about her veracity?"

Mona hung her head in embarrassment. In a low voice, she answered, "I wouldn' rightly know 'bout nothin' that pussonal, yo' honuh. Some say she do, some say she don't!"

Unbeatable Odds

In the 1920's a man could be sentenced to a year, and sometimes several years, on a Georgia chain gang for minor offenses. These cruel imprisonments were applied against blacks, of course, and seldom against whites.

One day, an inoffensive old codger was arrested and brought to trial because he had failed to step off the sidewalk and into the gutter when a white man passed. In vain, the oldtimer attempted to explain that he had been deep in thought and simply had not seen the white pedestrian.

In court, the prosecutor read the indictment: "The State of Georgia against Amos Wilkins. . . ." On and on the prosecuting attorney read off the charges while the judge dozed, knowing full well what the sentence would be.

When the lawyer had finished, old Amos said, "Please, mistuh lawyuh, would you min' readin' the first paht ag'in? I didn't heah it good."

Obligingly, the prosecutor started over: "The State of Georgia against Amos Wilkins. . . ."

"Hol' it right there!" interrupted Amos, to the complete astonishment of the court. "Effen the whole state of Jawja is ag'in me I might as well give up widout no mo' fussin'!"

Legal Reward

Andy was accused of stealing a man's wallet. However, he was a glib talker and the judge, after due consideration, decided that the evidence was insufficient to convict the defendant. "You are acquitted," ruled his honor.

"I *what?*" asked Andy, hearing the unfamiliar word.

"Acquitted," repeated the judge. "You can go home."

"Y-you mean," Andy stammered, "I get to keep the wallet?"

Disappearing Act

Judge: You say you had nothing to do with the crime?

Defendant: Not a thing, your honor.

Judge: It is the court's understanding that you were at the scene of the crime. What were you doing when the police and the robbers started shooting at each other.

Defendant: I was busy organizin' my feet!

Levels of Excellence

The man on the witness stand, in his sincere attempt to explain the situation, was using words and phrases seldom heard by whites, but quite familiar to most black people.

". . . an' so, that's how come this jackleg preacher. . . ."

"Now just a moment," interrupted the lawyer, obviously irritated. "I wish you'd speak understandable English. What's a jackleg preacher?"

"Well," explained the witness, "a jackleg preacher is diffrent from a first class preacher like you is diffrent from a first class lawyer."

Night Sight

Lawyer: Now let's get this straight. You say it was a very dark night; yet you maintain that you saw the car accident 500 yards off. Just how far do you think you can see on a dark night?

Witness: A million miles, I s'pose. How far is it to the moon?

Circumstantial Evidence

Judge: Camus Porter, you are charged with assault and battery, and of mutilating the plaintiff by biting off a piece of his ear. How do you plead?

Camus Porter: Innocent, your honor. There were four of us in that poker game and we all got into the fight. It could've been any of us that bit off his ear.

Judge: No, it couldn't. The injured man saw you spit it out!

Objective Witness

Judge: Tell the court, please, just how the fight started.

Witness: It started with each of us calling the other what he really was.

The Smile of Guile

The judge glared down at the far-from-contrite defendant. "John Wesley Adams, did you or did you not beat up the plaintiff, Miss LaVerne Camp, without reason?"

"I had reason," muttered Mr. Adams.

"You are entitled to state your case, Mr. Adams. Why did you hit Miss Camp?"

"She promised to marry me if I got her some new store-boughten teeth, your honor. But when I got 'em for her, and reminded her 'bout marryin' me, she jes' stand there grinnin' at me. And that's when I whopped her, suh! How would *you* like someone grinnin' at you with your own teeth?"

PART TEN

GIVE ME THAT NEW TIME RELIGION

It Pays to Advertise

The revival meeting was at its height and the Spirit had seized many of the shouting, singing, praying congregants.

Sister Grace raised her hands to the heavens and chanted, "Hallelujah! Glory, Glory, Glory!" Overwhelmed with religious fervor, she shouted, "Last night I was in the arms of the devil! Tonight I am in the arms of the Lord!"

Deacon Jones, who had been casting covetous eyes upon Sister Grace, sidled up to her and crooned, "Hey baby, what you doin' *tomorrow* night?"

Why Waste Your Breath?

"Brother Biggs," said the preacher sternly, "you said you were turning over a new leaf when you joined this church. Why didn't you come down to the mourner's bench today and confess your sins and talk to the Lord?"

"Because," explained the unrepentent Brother Biggs, "the Lord ain't settin' on the Gran' Jury!"

Equal Treatment Under God

A church member who had found summer employment in another city returned to his home town after three months of absence. To his consternation, he found that one of the rowdiest men in the church had been appointed a deacon.

"I don't understand it," said the good Christian. "You drink too much, you gamble, you cuss, and you're always fighting. How did you ever become a deacon?"

"Because us minority groups have their rights too," he growled. "The rough element in the church got organized and demanded recognition!"

Heavenly Caution

A minister who had pastored in the deep south ever since his ordination was called to a much larger church in New York. He was delighted with his new ministry; he loved the congregation and was thrilled with being a part of the Big City. But as time passed he grew homesick for his little southern town with its easy ways, its down-home cooking, its familiar sights and sounds, and above all, his family and lifelong friends.

The day finally arrived when he could no longer put off the decision—whether to remain in New York or return to his beloved little town in the south. He knew he would be passing up a fine career, so he called on the Lord to help him make up his mind.

"Please, dear Lord," he prayed, "tell me what to do. Shall I stay here or return to my people in the south?"

And the Lord answered, "Go where your heart is, my son."

The minister could scarcely retain his joy. "I need you to sustain me, Lord. Will you go south with me?"

"All right," answered the Lord, "but only as far as Baltimo'!"

Tired Christian

The young mother went into the bedroom and shook her sleeping son. "Sunday morning," she announced cheerily. "Time to get up."

"Aw, Ma, lemme sleep a li'l more," protested the drowsy boy. "I believe in God, I love Jesus, I renounce the devil an' all his works—but I don't wanna go to Sunday School this mornin'!"

Let's Bus on up to God's Heaven

The preacher was at his eloquent best as he described the splendors that awaited the penitent sinners who were admitted to Paradise.

"Yes, my friends," he concluded, "we're going to heaven in a great big chariot of fire—all of us, lifted up into the arms of Jesus. And when He sees that great big golden chariot he's gonna spread his lovin' arms and welcome all of us."

Just then the preacher spotted an old reprobate who hadn't set foot inside a church for the last twenty years. "And that goes for you too, brother!" shouted the preacher, joyful at the prospect of saving another soul. "You're comin' aboard that fiery chariot the same as everybody else. You may be last but you sure ain't least!"

The oldster got up and made for the exit. "Don't bother waitin' for me," he called over his shoulder. "I ain't ridin' in the back of *no*body's chariot!"

You Get What You Pay For

The Rev. Adam Clayton Powell was reading the announcements for the week. "Next Saturday, at Morningside Park, the Abyssinian Baptist Church will hold its annual Strawberry Festival. However, because of the poor collection these past few weeks," he concluded, "stewed prunes will be served!"

Biblical Students

Gil and Gabe, two brothers, had never been to church in their lives. One day, however, Gabe got religion, joined the Glory to J.C. Church, and, like a reformed alcoholic who constantly importunes his former drinking companions to mend their ways, he set about trying to convert Gil to a Christian life.

"Gil, if you would just live by the Good Book you'd find a whole new world opening up for you," admonished Gabe.

"How long you been a Christian?" asked his brother sarcastically.

"Three weeks."

"Hell, man, what do you know about the Good Book? In three weeks you ain't got past the first couple pages. Bet you a dollar you don't even know the Lord's Prayer."

"Oh yeah? Well, I'll take that bet," retorted Gabe. "Now I lay me down to sleep, I pray. . . ."

"Never mind, never mind!" snapped Gil, interrupting his brother. "Here's your dollar. I really didn't think you knew it!"

Lyin' Lou from Kalamazoo

Brother Louis, known to all as Lying Lou from Kalamazoo, decided to turn over a new leaf. Never again, he vowed, would he ever tell another falsehood. To prove his earnestness, he requested that he be baptized.

It was a bitter cold day in December when Lou waded into the icy water of the baptizing stream, accompanied by the minister and deacon. The deacon reached forward, pinched Lou's nostrils together and then ducked him two feet below the surface of the river. When he drew the penitent up again his lips were blue and his teeth were chattering.

"Was the water cold?" asked the preacher.

"No," said Lou, shivering and shaking.

"Duck 'im again, Deacon," snapped the minister. "The rascal's still lyin'!"

Why the Lord Made Negroes
As They Are

Sanford finished reading the evening papers and sighed with dejection. Everywhere, it seemed, his brothers and sisters were being denied the rights granted to all Americans under the United States Constitution. It was growing dark, but so despondent was he that he did not bother to turn on the lights. "Oh Lord," he groaned, "how long are You going to let our people suffer like this?"

All at once an eerie glow rose from the darkness, growing brighter and brighter. And from the depths of that strange glow there came a majestic Voice: "My son, be not downcast, for I am with you."

For a moment, Sanford was too terrified to utter a sound, but he quickly conquered his fear. "If—if You are who I think You are, I have a few complaints."

"Give me not a hard time, my son; I have enough troubles of my own."

"Well, how about answering a few questions?"

"Go ahead and ask, my son. I'm not a mind-reader, you know."

"First, what's the idea of giving me a head of kinky wool instead of straight hair like a certain other race I could mention?"

"The reason for that, my son, was to prevent ancient tribal enemies from grasping you by the hair when in combat. Your short kinky hair is also cooler in the hot African sun. It also enables you to steal through the jungles without getting your hair caught in bushes. Seems to me, young man, you would have thought that one out by yourself."

Sanford shrugged, and then asked, "Well, how about my skin? I would have been satisfied with plain old white. Did you have to go messin' around with fancy colors?"

"It was for your own good, my son," came the Voice from within the glowing light. "You had to hunt for a living and a white skin would have made you too conspicuous in the African jungles. You would starve to death with a white skin, or a tiger would see you a mile off and eat you up. Also, the pigmentation filters out the injurious rays of the African sun."

"Couldn't you at least have given me nice blue eyes?"

"No, my son. Brown eyes are sharper than blue eyes. You needed the better vision to see the animals in the forest and to spot your enemies from a distance. Besides, blue eyes would clash with your color scheme."

"You think of everything, don't you?"

"I try," said the Voice, modestly.

"Then tell me this," Sanford demanded. "If I need kinky hair to protect me from tribal enemies; and a black skin to get around in the jungles without being noticed and to keep out the African sun rays; and brown eyes to spot jungle enemies—what am I doing here in the middle of Cleveland?"

Ouch!

The preacher was highly insulted. It seems that one of his church members, Aaron, had asked him to pray for his ailing kidney.

"I don't know why you should feel insulted," Aaron complained in self-defense. "Only last week you asked us to pray for the loose livers."

Suspense Story

She was an upstanding Christian lady and it had taken her years to persuade her ever-lovin' hubby to attend church with her. Now, in the front row, she proudly sat beside her husband to whom every word and action in the church was completely strange.

The preacher had chosen for his text, the life of Christ. As he described the Savior's ministry, His miracles and the growing conspiracy against Him, the new convert leaned forward in rapt attention. His wife put her lips to his ear and was about to say something when he hissed—

"Shhh—don't tell me the ending!"

Irresistible

Maude, who had not seen her sister Mary since she moved to New York thirty years earlier, was now visiting her at her Harlem apartment.

They had just returned from services at the Abyssinian Baptist Church and Maude was perplexed about something that had occurred.

"Mary," said the sister, "didn't you tell me you joined that church many years ago?"

"Uh-huh."

"Then how come you go up to the altar and join up again?" asked Maude.

"I can't help myself," said Mary. "Everytime that good-looking Rev. Adam Clayton Powell asks me to do something I do it. Why, I been joining that church regular every week for the last twenty years!"

Ah, For One Last Sweet Kiss

For some months, the congregation of the Rose of Sharon Baptist Church had been without a spiritual leader. Discord and discontent were so rampant that the two previous ministers had quit in disgust, while the last one was brusquely fired. It began to seem that the pastorate would never be occupied. But finally, a minister from a distant city agreed to fill the pulpit—a man who had no idea he was about to affiliate with the ornriest, grumblin'est, fightin'est, meanest, discombobulated congregation to be found anywhere in Atlanta, state of Georgia, in these United States of America, planet Earth.

As might be expected, the congregants soon began to bicker with the new pastor and before long they had completely turned against him too, as they had against all the others. Within a few short weeks they demanded his resignation—again as they had demanded of all the former, hapless ministers.

The good preacher, a mild-mannered man, offered no resistance, nor did he bother to answer the many accusations hurled at him. On the Sunday when he delivered his last sermon he made no mention of his imminent departure, nor of the unjust charges and taunts to which he had been subjected. Instead, he alluded to the Sermon on the Mount, spoke of brotherly love, and called on the blessings of the Lord for his flock. Meekly, he ended the services without a hint of rancor.

But as the recessional was played and he was about to walk down the center aisle of the packed church and out the door forever, he made one last announcement:

"Brothers and Sisters," he said, "in a minute or two I shall go down the aisle for the last time. As I pass you, I beg of you to take note of the little sprig of mistletoe fastened to my coattail!"

"Our Father . . ."

Two recently ordained ministers were having lunch and reminiscing about their boyhood days.

"When I was a kid," said one, smiling, "I never knew my name wasn't Honey Chile until my mother registered me for school."

The other preacher laughed. "When I was a youngster," he said, continuing the same theme, "I always thought God's name was Howard."

"Whatever gave you that notion?"

"I got it from the Lord's Prayer: 'Our Father who art in Heaven, Howard be Thy name. . . .' "

Morgan, the Mighty Master of Mixed Metaphors

Preacher Andrew Morgan was a man of limited education but he had a remarkably retentive mind and sound native intelligence. His desire for perfection was almost an obsession, so he went to New York for a month-long study of the oratorical style used by the big-city preachers. He listened attentively to their sermons and after four weeks was convinced he could now preach as well as they.

The first Sunday after his return to his little town, he began his carefully prepared sermon by extolling the glory of the Baptist Church, picturing it as a ship "sailing proudly on through battle and storm, past dangerous shoals and shores." He then went on to say:

"After all this stormy voyage, the majesty of the Church still floats in triumphant glory. And now, my brethren, why does it float? I'll tell you why it floats: Because it is founded upon *a rock!*"

What's the Hurry?

A young minister, fresh out of theology school, was preaching his first sermon. A fundamentalist, his oration was full of fire and brimstone, warning of the horrors of hell and the delights of heaven. Finally, amidst the fervent shouting of his flock, the youthful preacher asked for a show of hands.

"All those who want to go to heaven, raise your hand."

All except one old man in the back row raised their hands.

The preacher glared at him for a moment and then, his voice dripping sarcasm, he called out, "Everyone who wants to go to hell, raise your hand."

The little old man remained perfectly still. Not a single motion did he make.

"What's the matter with you?" cried the exasperated young firebrand. "Make up your mind—do you want to go to heaven or hell?"

"What's the big rush, Sonny?" asked the oldtimer mildly. "I like it right here where I'm at."

The preacher's voice grew harsh. "Just remember this," he choked. "We must all go, sooner or later."

"Go?" the old man repeated. "When my time comes, the Lord will have to come and *get* me—I ain't *going* no place!"

Lesson in Humility

The late Rev. Rollo W. Handy, of Grace Afro-American Church in Washington, D. C., was fond of relating the circumstances of his first sermon as a young man.

Rev. Handy had just graduated from the seminary when he was called to replace the retiring minister of Grace Afro-American. As soon as the older minister had finished with his introduction, the younger preacher bounded to the podium, took a lion-like stance at the lectern, and at once launched into his text with all the zeal of a biblical prophet. He denounced the worshippers of the golden calf in thunderous tones, his bombast and multi-syllabled rhetoric conjuring up all the agonies of eternal damnation for the non-believers, the doubters, the backsliders. But the congregation was unmoved. No response could he evoke, no matter how he flailed his arms and exhorted for repentance.

Less sure of himself now, the newly ordained preacher continued in a somewhat subdued voice, entreating, bullying, cajoling, pleading for the sinners to confess their transgressions and beg the Savior's forgiveness. Once again his oratory rose to lyrical heights, but not a sound was heard from the usually responsive congregants, nor did they step forward in droves as he had anticipated. Dejected and thoroughly discouraged, he brought his sermon to an abrupt end, his self-confidence utterly shattered. Humbly, he left the platform.

Sinking wearily into a seat beside the old, retiring minister, he sighed, "Tell me, Reverend, why did I get such a poor reception? What did I do that was wrong?"

The wise old preacher placed a hand on the younger man's shoulder and, his manner exceedingly kind, replied, "Son, if you had gone up on that platform the same way you got off, you would have got off the same way you got on!"

Changing Economy

The preacher finished counting the morning's contributions and turned to his deacon. "I declare," he sighed, "when I look at my well-dressed congregation I wonder where all the poor people are. But when I take up the collection I wonder where all the rich folks went."

Speaking of Tongues . . .

In a little village in Virginia, a young man called on his preacher to tell him his secret ambition. "I want to be a preacher like you," he said. "But I want a real big church in the city."

"It's a mighty fine calling," said the old man. "But to be a big city preacher you'll have to study."

"Oh, I'll be glad to study."

"And you'll have to learn how to speak in unknown tongues," he continued—"Hebrew, Latin, Greek. . . ."

Gonna Walk All Over God's Heaven

Down around Port Gibson, Mississippi, there used to be a small, ramshackle church called Salvation in Christ. It wasn't much to look at but it won a place in the hearts of the black people for miles around before it was torn down some forty years ago to make way for a larger house of worship. All of that affection (and pride, too) stemmed from one incident. This is the way the oldtimers tell it:

Rev. Gaines was in the midst of a financial drive to raise money for building the newer, larger church, but he knew that it would take a great many years before the poor people in the black community could contribute the necessary amount to begin construction. So he applied to the white Southern Baptist Church of Port Gibson for help. He pleaded with their minister to come preach in the colored church and to bring some of his wealthy parishioners with him, hoping they would help with substantial donations.

The white minister agreed, and the following week, he appeared at little Salvation in Christ church to preach, bringing with him several of his congregants. But his sermon astounded the black folks. He spoke of "rendering unto Caesar that which is Caesar's," stressing the importance of "doing God's will by acknowledging the superiority of the white race—because Jesus was white." Finally, he closed his sermon by admonishing that God had planned an orderly universe. "Heaven, too, is segregated," he claimed. "When black people get to heaven they must forget about walking the streets of gold without restriction."

At the conclusion of the surprising sermon, Rev. Gaines returned to the pulpit and gazed out at his people, all of whom sat in stony silence. Then he turned to the white preacher who was sitting with his wealthy friends, apart from the blacks, and it was at this point that he won a kind of spiritual and moral immortality. Disregarding the financial consequences, he said, "Brethern an' sistern, we-all have jes' heerd that us black folks ain' gonna walk the golden streets of heaven like the white folks. Well, all I gotta say is this: We gonna walk anyplace we damn please!"

Explained in Full

The bishop was visiting a small town church in his diocese. "What is the financial condition of your church?" he asked the preacher.

"Let's put it this way," the preacher answered slowly: "We've never had to stop in the middle of a collection to go empty the plate."

Southern Comfort

The preacher and the deacon had an intense dislike for each other, but they retained an outward semblance of peace to preserve the unity of the church. Nevertheless, they seldom missed an opportunity to get in a sly dig at each other—when they felt they could do so and still appear innocent.

One Sunday, the preacher, a rabid prohibitionist, was delivering a sermon on the evils of drink. "I say unto you," he thundered, "if I was President of the United States I'd pour every drop of liquor into the Potomac River. If I was Governor of Mississippi I'd dump all whiskey, wine and gin into the Mississippi River. If I was Governor of Ohio I'd empty every bottle of alcoholic beverage into the Ohio River." With this final pronouncement, he raised his arms. "And now, Deacon Jones will lead us in song."

The quick-thinking deacon saw his chance. Opening his hymnal, he called out, "Page 126, everybody! Sing it loud and clear: *Shall We Gather at the River!*"

End of the Road

Alabama's George Wallace finally died and found himself at the entrance of Paradise. He knocked loudly on the Pearly Gate for admission.

"Who dat knockin' at de do'?" called St. Peter from within.

Wallace paled. "Never mind," he muttered as he turned to leave. "Forget it!"

Immersion, Integrated Style

Luther opened his eyes and, to his utter amazement, found he had sprouted wings. Higher and higher he flew, past the Big Dipper, around the Little Dipper, flying higher and higher into the limitless vastness of space. Soon he observed a golden castle a few miles off. Doing a couple of Immelman loops and fancy turns to test his new wings further, he landed plum at the Pearly Gate. He knocked loudly.

A venerable-looking black man opened the door. "All right, come in an' stop makin' sech a racket," he grumbled.

"Who are you?" asked Luther.

"Call me Pete."

"*Saint* Peter?"

"Yeah, if you dig titles."

Luther could scarcely restrain his surprise. "I didn't know St. Peter was a black man."

"I ain't orange or polka-dotted. Now you jes' sign this here register an' I'll take you over to the Riverside Drive Apartments."

"You mean with the white folks?"

"No, this place is segregated," St. Peter explained. "We keep the whites over on the other side of Paradise where we don't have to mess with 'em. We gotta keep 'em in their place. First thing you know they'll be wantin' to marry our women an' go to school with our kids."

"But that's terrible!" cried Luther. "Even Alabama is integrating. Why, back home in Birmingham, I even joined a white church. I went right down to the river to get baptized and a white preacher and two white deacons immersed me."

"Then what happened?" asked St. Peter.

Luther scratched his head in perplexity. "C-come to think about it," he stammered, "that's the last thing I remember."

Earthy Humor

She: How come you to buy a burial plot an' you so young?
He: It was dirt cheap.

Limited Forgiveness

Linus was walking down the street and minding his own business when suddenly an old enemy leaped from the darkness and stabbed him in the chest. A preacher was summoned to the hospital to help guide the man to the heavenly kingdom.

"Linus," pleaded the minister, "won't you please forgive your enemy for the great wrong he committed?"

The critically wounded man lifted his head and, his voice weak, replied, "All right, Reverend. If I'm dyin', then I forgive him for stabbin' me, an' I hope the Lord makes his soul white as snow. But if I ain't dyin' an' I get well, I'm gonna beat the livin' hell outen that bastid!"

Dying by Inches

An old man died peacefully in his sleep. His grandson, who had been quite fond of the oldtimer, went to the local newspaper. "How much is an announcement in the obituary column?" he asked.

"Three dollars an inch," said the advertising manager.

"*Three dollars an inch?*" gasped the young fellow. "Man, you don't know what you're saying! My grandfather was six-feet-four!"

The Skeptic

Cynical Sid, the Harlem Kid, attended the funeral of a neighbor. As he was sauntering through the cemetery after the services, he came upon a headstone with the epitaph *Not Dead—Just Sleeping*.

Sid contemplated the inscription for several moments and then walked on, muttering, "That cat ain't foolin' nobody but hisself!"

PART ELEVEN

THE MINI MOD SQUAD

Following are excerpts from compositions written by fourth grade pupils of the Los Angeles County School District during Negro Week, 1970. The subject: "What Civil Rights Means to Me."

Civil Rites is when you have to go to the bathrom white peeple say oky doky.

DOROTHY YOUNG

Civil Rights means white people get to ride in the back of the bus.

ROBERT DICKENSON

I dont like civil rights because my farther spanks me when Im bad.

JAMES CROWDER

Civvil Rits is very hard to spell.

RAY WALTERS

When I get big I am going to marry a wite boy then he cant insullt me becuase of my color or I will hit him.

IMOGENE WILLIS

I like Civil Rights because now black people can get a good edducation even if I dont like school much myself.

VINCENT SHIELDS

I like civil rites because if I don't the black panthers will beat me up.

SANDRA CHRISTIAN

I like civil rights but I like Christmas better.

RICHARD BANKS

Index*

Adams, John Quincy, 411
Aesop, 4, 5, 6
Ali, Muhammad, 369, 431
Allen, C. W., 418
Allen, J. B., 418
Allen, Richard, 160, 161
American Negro Songs and Spirituals, 226
The American Songbag, 233
Armstrong, Louis, 228
The Arrest of the Two-year-old, 78
Asbury, Francis, 76
Ashbourne, A. P., 418
Atlanta Constitution, 7, 51
Attucks, Crispus, xii, 372, 428
"Aunt Dicy Tales," 70, 75, 76
Aunt Hagar's Blues, 227

Babcock, W. H., 333
Babrius, 5
Bachelor's Lament, 338
Bailes, William, 418
Bailey, L. C., 418
Balboa, 3
The Ballad of the Boll Weevil, 258
"Ballads Surviving in the United States," 230
Banneker, Benjamin, 422
Barb-ree Allin, 230, 232
The Barn Is Burning, 150
Basie, Count, 433
Battle of Little Rock, 286

Beale Street Blues, 227
Beard, Andrew J., 418, 422
Becket, G. E., 418
Bell, Alexander Graham, 424
Bell, L., 418
Benjamin Banneker's Almanac, 422
Benjamin, M. E. (Miss), 418
Bennington (battle), 372
Bethune, Dr. Mary McLeod, xiii
The Big Sea, 444
Bile Dem Cabbage Down, 264
Binga, M. W., 418
Bishop, Lawrence, 212
Bishop's Book of Humor, 212
Blackburn, A. B., 418
Blair, Henry, 418, 422
Bloodstoppers and Bearwalkers, 143
Blue, L., 418
The Boll Weevil, 258
Bontemps, Arna, 5, 9, 444
The Book of Negro Folklore, 5, 428, 444
The Book of Negro Humor, 444
The Book of Negro Wit and Humor, 143
Boone, Sarah, 418
Boston Gazette and Country, 372
Boston Massacre, 372
Both Were Proud, 78
Bowman, H. A., 418
Boyd, Catherine G., 91
Brandywine (battle), 372

---

* This index has been confined to people, events, and titles of works mentioned in the introductions, elucidations, and notes contained in this volume.